T0212502

Lecture Notes in Computer Science 9977

Commenced Publication in 1973
Founding and Former Series Editors:
Gerhard Goos, Juris Hartmanis, and Jan van Leeuwen

Editorial Board

David Hutchison
Lancaster University, Lancaster, UK
Takeo Kanade
Carnegie Mellon University, Pittsburgh, PA, USA
Josef Kittler
University of Surrey, Guildford, UK
Jon M. Kleinberg
Cornell University, Ithaca, NY, USA
Friedemann Mattern
ETH Zurich, Zurich, Switzerland
John C. Mitchell
Stanford University, Stanford, CA, USA
Moni Naor
Weizmann Institute of Science, Rehovot, Israel
C. Pandu Rangan
Indian Institute of Technology, Madras, India
Bernhard Steffen
TU Dortmund University, Dortmund, Germany
Demetri Terzopoulos
University of California, Los Angeles, CA, USA
Doug Tygar
University of California, Berkeley, CA, USA
Gerhard Weikum
Max Planck Institute for Informatics, Saarbrücken, Germany

Kwok-Yan Lam · Chi-Hung Chi
Sihan Qing (Eds.)

Information and Communications Security

18th International Conference, ICICS 2016
Singapore, Singapore, November 29 – December 2, 2016
Proceedings

 Springer

Editors
Kwok-Yan Lam
Nanyang Technological University
Singapore
Singapore

Sihan Qing
Peking University
Beijing
China

Chi-Hung Chi
CSIRO
Hobart, TAS
Australia

ISSN 0302-9743   ISSN 1611-3349   (electronic)
Lecture Notes in Computer Science
ISBN 978-3-319-50010-2   ISBN 978-3-319-50011-9   (eBook)
DOI 10.1007/978-3-319-50011-9

Library of Congress Control Number: 2016959174

LNCS Sublibrary: SL4 – Security and Cryptology

© Springer International Publishing AG 2016
This work is subject to copyright. All rights are reserved by the Publisher, whether the whole or part of the material is concerned, specifically the rights of translation, reprinting, reuse of illustrations, recitation, broadcasting, reproduction on microfilms or in any other physical way, and transmission or information storage and retrieval, electronic adaptation, computer software, or by similar or dissimilar methodology now known or hereafter developed.
The use of general descriptive names, registered names, trademarks, service marks, etc. in this publication does not imply, even in the absence of a specific statement, that such names are exempt from the relevant protective laws and regulations and therefore free for general use.
The publisher, the authors and the editors are safe to assume that the advice and information in this book are believed to be true and accurate at the date of publication. Neither the publisher nor the authors or the editors give a warranty, express or implied, with respect to the material contained herein or for any errors or omissions that may have been made.

Printed on acid-free paper

This Springer imprint is published by Springer Nature
The registered company is Springer International Publishing AG
The registered company address is: Gewerbestrasse 11, 6330 Cham, Switzerland

Preface

This volume contains the proceedings of the 18th International Conference on Information and Communications Security (ICICS) that took place in Singapore, from November 29 to December 2, 2016. ICICS is a key annual event for researchers and practitioners in information, systems, communication, and cyberspace security. Since 1997, ICICS has brought together leading computer science researchers, IT decision makers, systems architects, solution designers, practitioners, and regulators to discuss security challenges, models, and solutions from the perspectives of academia, industry, and government. ICICS focuses not only on the frontier science challenges in security and privacy research, but also on the applicability and impacts of security solutions in real-life environments.

This year ICICS received 60 submissions from 15 countries all over the world, including USA, Austria, Germany, UK, Greece, France, Switzerland, Italy, Estonia, South Africa, Russia, China (including Hong Kong), India, Singapore, and Australia. Out of these, 20 high-quality research papers were accepted as full papers after a thorough review process by the Program Committee (PC) for originality, novelty, rigor, and relevance. In addition, the authors of 16 short papers that were accepted presented their on-going work in information and communications security. The conference program was complemented by an invited talk and two feature keynote speakers (one by Mr. Anthony Bargar, who served in the United States Department of Defense and Intelligence Community, and another by Prof. Dongyan Xu, who is a Professor of Computer Science and Interim Director of CERIAS, Purdue University).

We would like to express our gratitude to everyone who helped make ICICS 2016 a success: the conference Organizing Committee for providing an excellent environment for the conference, and the Program Committee members for their conscientious and diligent work to ensure the high quality of the conference scientific program. Finally, and most importantly, we want to thank all the authors for their high-quality submissions.

We hope that you will find the conference and the papers in the proceedings interesting and inspiring.

November 2016

Kwok-Yan Lam
Chi-Hung Chi

Organization

Honorary Chair

Thambipillai Srikanthan   Nanyang Technological University, Singapore

General Co-chairs

Wee Keong Ng   Nanyang Technological University, Singapore
Sihan Qing   Peking University, China

Program Co-chairs

Kwok Yan Lam   Nanyang Technological University, Singapore
Chi-Hung Chi   CSIRO, Australia

Publicity Chair

Alvin Tiu   Nanyang Technological University, Singapore

Local Chair

Adams Kong   Nanyang Technological University, Singapore

Web Master

Ho Thanh Nghia   Nanyang Technological University, Singapore

Program Committee

Man Ho Au	Hong Kong Polytechnic University, Hong Kong, SAR China
Alex Biryukov	University of Luxembourg, Luxembourg
Zhenfu Cao	East China Normal University, China
Chin-Chen Chang	Feng Chia University, Taiwan
Zhong Chen	Peking University, China
Sherman S.M. Chow	Chinese University of Hong Kong, Hong Kong, SAR China
Chen Ding	Ryerson University, Canada
Dieter Gollmann	Hamburg University of Technology, Germany
Jian Guo	Nanyang Technological University, Singapore
Rene Rydhof Hansen	Aalborg University, Demark

Hsu-Chun Hsiao	National Taiwan University, Taiwan
Patrick Hung	University of Ontario Institute of Technology, Canada
Meng Chow Kang	CISCO, Singapore
Tiffany Hyun-Jin Kim	Carnegie Mellon University, USA
Kwangjo Kim	KAIST, Korea
Marina Krotofil	Hamburg University of Technology, Germany
Tieyan Li	Huawei, Singapore
Paul Liu	Social Mind Analytics (Research and Technology) Limited, Hong Kong, SAR China
Di Ma	University of Michigan-Dearborn, USA
Sjouke Mauw	University of Luxembourg, Luxembourg
Chris Mitchel	Royal Holloway, University of London, UK
Wee Keong Ng	Nanyang Technological University, Singapore
Raphael C.-W. Phan	Loughborough University, UK
Josef Pieprzyk	Queensland University of Technology, Australia
Joachim Posegga	University of Passau, Germany
Christian W. Probst	Technical University of Denmark, Demark
Sihan Qing	Peking University, China
Kouichi Sakurai	Kyushu University, Japan
Pierangela Samarati	Università degli Studi di Milano, Italy
Sebastian Schinzel Münster	University of Applied Sciences, Germany
Willy Susilo	University of Wollongong, Australia
Wen-Guey Tzeng	National Chiao Tung University, Taiwan
Huaxiong Wang	Nanyang Technological University, Singapore
Andreas Wespi	IBM Zurich Research Laboratory, Switzerland
Raymond Wong	University of New South Wales, Australia
Chan Yeob Yeun Khalifa	University of Science, Technology and Research, United Arab Emirates
Yu Yu	Shanghai Jiao Tong, University China
Fangguo Zhang	Sun Yat-sen University, China
Yunwei Zhao	Nanyang Technological University, Singapore
Wei Zhao	CSIRO, Australia
Wen Tao Zhu	Institute of Information Engineering, Chinese Academy of Sciences, China

Contents

Attack Behavior Analytics

Authentication and Authorization

Engineering Issues of Cryptographic and Security Systems

Privacy Protection

Risk Evaluation and Security

Key Management and Language-Based Security

Network Security

IoT Security

ECDSA on Things: IoT Integrity Protection in Practise

Johannes Bauer[1], Ralf C. Staudemeyer[1(✉)], Henrich C. Pöhls[1],
and Alexandros Fragkiadakis[2]

[1] Institute of IT-Security and Security Law (ISL),
University of Passau, 94032 Passau, Germany
{rcs,hp}@sec.uni-passau.de
[2] Institute of Computer Science, Foundation for Research and Technology-Hellas,
Heraklion, Crete, Greece
alfrag@ics.forth.gr

Abstract. This paper documents some experiences and lessons learned during the development of an IoT security application for the EU-funded project RERUM. The application provides sensor data with end-to-end integrity protection through elliptic curve digital signatures (ECDSA). Here, our focus is on the cost in terms of hardware, runtime and power-consumption in a real-world trials scenario. We show that providing signed sensor data has little impact on the overall power consumption. We present the experiences that we made with different ECDSA implementations. Hardware accelerated signing can further reduce the costs in terms of runtime, however, the differences were not significant. The relevant aspect in terms of hardware is memory: experiences made with MSP430 and ARM Cortex M3 based hardware platforms revealed that the limiting factor is RAM capacity. Our experiences made during the trials show that problems typical for low-power and lossy networks can be addressed by the chosen network stack of CoAP, UDP, 6LoWPAN and 802.15.4; while still being lightweight enough to drive the application on the constrained devices investigated.

1 Introduction

The Internet-of-Things will generate a plethora of communication messages, that are stored, forwarded and used by higher applications to make decisions. To provide adequate protection in case of a cyber attack, strong security mechanisms must be in place and enabled at an early stage. Here we focus on integrity protection and strong authentication through digital signatures. We aim to push security mechanisms towards the edge of the IoT, ideally running on 'things' itself, i.e. on constrained devices. In this paper, we share the lessons learned within the European and national research projects we participated in[1]. The RERUM framework [1] allows to build IoT applications while considering security and privacy mechanisms early in their design phase.

---

[1] EU-funded project RERUM ict-rerum.eu (last accessed 03 Oct 2016).
   BMBF-funded project FORSEC bayforsec.de (last accessed 03 Oct 2016).

© Springer International Publishing AG 2016
K.-Y. Lam et al. (Eds.): ICICS 2016, LNCS 9977, pp. 3–17, 2016.
DOI: 10.1007/978-3-319-50011-9_1

Attacks we address and mitigate concern the manipulation of IoT data in transit and the spoofing of an authorised message origin. Digital signature's offering of strong origin authentication primarily protects against attackers inserting messages. Inserted messages can have unwanted consequences, like sending an 'open window' command or falsifying a 'lock door' command. Integrity protection paired with the knowledge of the sensor-data source, allows us to make better decisions on the reputation of data based on its authenticated origin.

All in all integrity alone would help against malicious tampering and could be achieved by symmetric MACs, but only with digital signatures we also reach strong authentication of the data's or command's source. By this the IoT's last mile is not any more the weakest link, but the attacker must now be able to compromise back-ends and control systems, which we already have good defence mechanisms for. Thus, showing that we can put ECDSA on things in practice proves that another important information security goal [2] for protection in depth against cyber attacks in the IoT is possible.

2   Background Information

In the EU-funded project RERUM we developed a framework which enables IoT applications to consider security and privacy mechanisms early in their design phase. One of the goals of RERUM is to provide end-to-end integrity protection down to the wireless sensor network. Part of this framework is an application that runs on constrained devices and provides ECDSA signed sensor data using standard IoT protocols. This paper presents the experiences and lessons learned during development and testing of the signing application. We described early results that present the overhead of signatures in terms of runtime, memory, energy consumption and communication in [3], with energy overhead being the focus. Here we discuss the practical impact of signatures by showing how long the sensor device used in the trials can actually work running on battery. This paper extends previous findings by adding new measurements we did using a hardware accelerated ECDSA implementation. We also examine the impact of problems like an unreliable network connection, a typical aspect of low-power and lossy networks, and complement a number of considerations done previously [1,3,4].

2.1   Hardware Platform

For the proof-of-concept implementation of ECDSA integrity protection, we initially used the Z1 platform[2] [5]. It is based on a MSP430 16bit RISC CPU with 8 KB RAM, approximately 60 KB (usable) flash memory, and the CC2420, a 2.4 GHz IEEE 802.15.4 [6–8] compliant RF transceiver.

Later we switched hardware platform to a Zolertia RE-Mote[3] [9]. The RE-Mote incorporates the CC2538 Cortex-M3 SOC from Texas Instruments with

---

[2] zolertia.io/product/hardware/z1-platform (last accessed 02 Oct 2016).

[3] zolertia.io/product/hardware/re-mote (last accessed 02 Oct 2016).

32 MHz, 512 KB flash and 32 KB RAM[4] [10]. The CC2538 contains a hardware crypto engine that accelerates cryptographic operations like SHA2, AES and ECC. The RE-Mote did run Contiki[5] [11], a lightweight operating system designed with Internet-of-Things, and the restrictions and needs of constrained devices in mind. We used the RE-Mote hardware platform during all trials and all measurements, and explanations in this paper are based on it, unless explicitly stated otherwise.

2.2   JSS and Signed CoAP Message

JSON Sensor Signatures (JSS) is a valid JSON format that contains additional meta-data about the embedded signature and the algorithm applied. It is an encoding scheme that transports the digital signature and its meta data alongside the JSON data [4]. This enables to keep the plain information accessible to all involved processes that can handle JSON. By this the signature can remain attached for end-to-end protection as long as JSON data can be stored. This is the case for a number of IoT storage backends, like Couchbase or MongoDB.

In IoT terminology the device will expose its sensed data as resources. Here, following IoT-A[6] and RERUM terminology [12], the device's resources can be accessed via a RESTful interface [13] and return data in the JSON format. The resources can be requested in two representations: unsigned with the Constrained Application Protocol (CoAP) content-format `application/json` and signed with a newly introduced content-format `application/jss`.

```
{
    "jss.protected":
    {
        "alg": "ES192"
    },
    "amb_temp": 20965,
    "measurement_id": 21,
    "jss.signature": "le4uz7vWD_z•••WL"
}
```

Fig. 1. Sample JSS message. Omitted characters are indicated with dots (•••). Whitespace is added for better readability. The framed message parts are the JSS related additions. Note that unsigned messages contain only the sensor value itself.

While `application/jss` is no official standard mime-type, this design decision was made to maintain backwards compatibility to clients that aren't capable of handling signatures. The sample JSS message depicted in Fig. 1 shows its internal structure: a header section (`jss.protected`) describing the ECC-based signature scheme [14], a field `measurement_id`, and the signature itself,

---

[4] ti.com/product/cc2538 (last accessed 02 Oct 2016).
[5] contiki-os.org (last accessed 02 Oct 2016).
[6] iot-a.eu/public/terminology (last accessed 02 Oct 2016).

encoded in BASE64URL [15] (`jss.signature`). The payload itself was hashed with SHA-256 [16] and then signed with `secp192r1` (indicated by `ES192`[7]).

We build the signature itself following the steps we suggested in [4]:

1. clean JSON keys that are part of payload (i.e. not part of signature metadata; clean = remove non-alphanumerical characters)
2. sort key-value pairs of previous step alphanumerically
3. encode measurement_id in BASE64URL
4. encode payload in BASE64URL
5. concatenate encoded measurement_id and payload with dot character ('.')
6. build SHA-256 hash of concatenated string
7. sign hash generated
8. encode signature in BASE64URL

For verifying a received JSS message, the first six steps are performed to generate the hash. Then the received BASE64URL encoded signature is decoded and fed together with the hash and public key to the verification function.

The JSS field `measurement_id` was introduced for signed JSS messages to protect against replay attacks. In replay attacks a potential attacker could sniff packets and replay them later. The client has no means to distinguish between the valid messages and the replayed ones, as the replayed packets do contain valid signatures.

The measurement_id gets incremented after each measurement (here every 30 s). These are used for generating the signature and a client can use them to detect previous measurements. Of course, this protects against replay attacks only, if the measurement_ids are not repeating.

For reducing the overhead, we use a 32bit unsigned integer for storing the measurement_id, allowing for $2^{32} = 4,294,967,295$ messages with different measurement_ids. We consider this as safe, as with a typical sensing interval of 30 s, it would take more than 4.000 thousand years for one measurement_id to repeat. Furthermore, possible restarts or crashes of the sensing device due to updates, power issues, battery changes that lead to resetting of the measurement_id counter to zero have to be considered. To circumvent this, the measurement_id should additionally be stored on a non-volatile memory, like the internal flash.

3   ECDSA Signatures Implementation

For the proof-of-concept implementation, we used a reference implementation from NIST[8] together with the p160 curve on the Zolertia Z1. It revealed, that the Z1s capabilities are too restricted to provide security on an adequate level ($\geq$192bit curve size [17]): while runtime performance proved fine, the RAM and flash memory sizes were too limited [4]. Our Performance and overhead measurements [3] revealed MicroECC [18] to be a well suited ECDSA implementation.

---

[7] RFC7518 [14] actually does not provide an identifier for SHA-256 hashing in combination with `secp192r1` signing. However, it does for SHA-256 hashing in combination with P-256 signing (`ES256`). Therefore we use `ES192` analogue to this convention.

[8] github.com/nist-emntg/ecc-light-certificate (last accessed 02 Oct 2016).

3.1 Implementation Details

The RERUM sensing application consists of multiple parts:

1. Implementation of sensing routines for several internal and external sensors (e.g. ambient temperature, humidity, noise, and various analogue sensors).
2. ECDSA signature generation with MicroECC.
3. Encoding and formatting of sensed value with JSS.
4. Exposing resources, i.e. signed sensor data through a standards compliant RESTful CoAP interface.

MicroECC was adapted to the needs of our use case as follows: To generate SHA-256 hashes, we used the CC2538's hardware acceleration engine. The CC2538 random number generator delivers the nonce[9] required for the signing process. We configured MicroECC to use the optional in-line assembly optimisations (here referred as ASM fast). In order to encode the signatures, we extended a BASE64 implementation to support BASE64URL compliant encoding.

Contiki ships with various integrated applications like the IPv6 network stack and application layer protocols. This simplified the implementation of signatures significantly, since it allowed increasing the focus on signature generation and encoding rather than on the network stack. That's why all network related libraries were taken directly from Contiki like CoAP, the REST implementation, and the lower layer implementations as well (like UDP, IPv6, and 6LoW-PAN). Contiki's CoAP implementation was extended by a monitor concept that encapsulated the resource representation, exchange and signature generation and allows to easily add new sensors without rewriting network specific operations.

This approach permitted us to reduce code complexity and maintainability, and as well simplified the integration of different external sensors.

3.2 Hardware Acceleration

We compared different ECC signature libraries in terms of runtime overhead, firmware size and energy consumption on the RE-Mote hardware [3]. Among those examined libraries is MicroECC [18], a library implementing the standard NIST curves secp160r1, secp192r1, secp224r1, secp256k1 and secp256r1[10]. MicroECC is a platform-independent ECC implementation written in C that was especially designed with constrained devices in mind. It has a small code footprint, does not require dynamic memory allocation, and runs on 8-, 32-, and 64bit CPUs. To increase performance, MicroECC can be optionally configured to use in-line assembler for the AVR, ARM, and Thumb platforms in two modes with speed vs. code size optimisations: ASM small (little code size overhead) and ASM fast (optimised on speed, but with more code size overhead). Since measurements showed acceptable performance of MicroECC, we selected its ECDSA library for further development.

---

[9] nonce: arbitrary number only used once.
[10] github.com/kmackay/micro-ecc (last accessed 02 Oct 2016).

We presented the MicroECC runtime overhead in relation to the different ECC curves and assembly optimisations [3]. This paper extends those results by new measurements that contemplate the impact of hardware acceleration.

In this section, we present the runtime of a single hashing and signing step with the different implementations. To avoid any influences that could distort the results, i.e. hardware interrupts, the firmware images flashed on the RE-Motes contain only the necessary parts to perform the measured operations; the Contiki network stack was disabled.

For encoding the signatures, we improved a plain C implementation of the BASE64 encoding scheme in order to support BASE64URL compliant encoding. The message buffer that gets signed depends only on the signature size, i.e. the size of the ECC curve. The runtime overhead of BASE64URL encoding either for secp192r1 (signature with 48bytes) or secp256r1 (signatures with 64bytes) is negligible with both less than 1 ms. Thus we did not further examine this step, since it has little impact on the signing process.

The RE-Mote's CC2538 features a hardware encryption engine that is capable of accelerating the generation of SHA2 hashes. The RERUM application already uses this feature for hashing the message payload prior getting signed; where the message that gets hashed is between 30 and 50 characters long (depends on the measurement_id and resource identifier).

Table 1. Runtime overhead of SHA256: 39bytes refers to a typical JSS payload (here: amb_temp for ambient temperature resource); the 1024bytes where randomly chosen.

Size [byte]	Un-accelerated [ms]	Accelerated [ms]
39	0.669	0.059
1024	5.834	0.471

The results are shown in Table 1: Hashing 39bytes, a typical payload length within the RERUM application, has an negligible overhead of less than 1 ms. However, the values of hardware accelerated hashing compared to the un-accelerated ones indicate a speed-up by a factor of approximately eleven. We verified the factor in another measurement by randomly chosen 1024bytes buffers to exclude any inaccuracies that could come from the timer at such small intervals. These measurements show a similar difference: while the plain C implementation needs ~5 ms for hashing, the accelerated one does not even need half a millisecond leading to a performance boost by a factor of approximately twelve.

Besides the hardware acceleration for SHA2 hashes, the RE-Mote's CC2538 features also a ECC hardware acceleration engine. Fortunately Contiki contains a ECC implementation (secp192r1 and secp256r1) that utilizes hardware acceleration since October 2015. Table 2 shows the results: the measurements for un-accelerated, ASM small and ASM fast signing with MicroECC were taken from [3] and extended by the results from the hardware accelerated implementation. While the in-line assembly optimisations ASM small reduces the runtime for signing about a quarter and ASM fast even more than a half, hardware acceleration reduces the runtime about almost three-quarters. Surprisingly, for the verification MicroECC with ASM fast beats the hardware accelerated implementation. Currently, we can't explain this behaviour.

Table 2. Runtime for signing and verifying with secp256r1 curves; un-accelerated, ASM small and ASM fast refer to MicroECC measurements we presented in [3].

Configuration	Un-accelerated	ASM small	ASM fast	Accelerated
secp256r1 sign [ms]	1177	855	537	341
secp256r1 sign [%]	100	72.6	45.6	29
secp256r1 verify [ms]	1320	957	595	697
secp256r1 verify [%]	100	72.5	45	52.8

We note that the hardware accelerated implementation leaves it up to the user of this library to choose the random nonce used for signing. It is important to be aware of the fact that using the same nonce more than once [19] or relying on a bad random number generator [20] offers attackers the possibility to extract the private key used for signing. MicroECC instead keeps care of choosing and processing this random number correctly and furthermore considers possible side channel attacks [21].

Table 3. Signing and verifying runtimes for TweetNaCl Ed25519 implementation.

Configuration	Un-accelerated [ms]
Ed25519 sign	3332.9
Ed25519 verify	6646.9

To compare the results of Table 2, we used the Ed25519 curve implementation of the TweetNaCl [22] library[11]. This implementation is quite compact[12], but not optimised for speed. Signing and verifying takes with roughly 3.3 and 6.6 s (see Table 3) significantly longer than with the secp256r1 curve implementations described previously.

Unfortunately, like MicroECC's secp256r1, Ed25519's RAM requirements are too high in order to fit in the RERUM application. Even with further optimisations, we did not succeed to use TweetNaCl's Ed25519 curve alongside with the CoAP interface, the sensor library, and the other routines required.

3.3 Challenges Overcome

The runtime overhead of generating signatures is smaller than expected, however, a lot of signing operations within a short period can reduce the availability and

---

[11] tweetnacl.cr.yp.to.
[12] TweetNaCl fits into 100 Twitter Tweets.

responsiveness for clients issuing requests. This increases also the danger for easy Denial-of-Service attacks for attackers flooding one sensing RE-Mote with too many requests. For this reason we decided not to sense and sign new sensor values for every incoming request. Instead, sensing and signing takes place once within a configurable interval down to five seconds.

The RE-Mote made it possible to implement the use-case, unlike the Z1 which was too constrained. However also the RE-Mote's RAM size was limiting: Signing with `secp256r1` together with the described network stack and the JSS format caused stack overflows during runtime. Attempts to circumvent this by increasing the stack was not helping.

Therefore we decided to use `secp192r1`. It has 80 minimum bits of security [23] and is still considered as an adequate security level with an equivalent symmetric key size of 96bits [17]. Also the RAM limits the number of resources that can get provided with signatures to approximately five. The reason is that for each signed resource we pre-allocate memory for the buffers to store the last signed value in order to be able to respond to queries quickly. In practice this restriction is mitigated as we implemented the application in such a way that is easy to configure signing on a per-resource basis during build time. This fulfils the different needs for different use-cases and sensors while the code can be still developed centrally from one consistent code base.

4   Trial Scenario

Our trial scenario was placed in Heraklion, Greece: RE-Motes together with attached sensors were installed. They measured and provided resources like ambient temperature and ambient humidity.

4.1   Network Architecture and Components

For the trials, we used a 3-tier network architecture, as shown in Fig. 2, consisting of a RERUM device, RERUM gateway, and RERUM middleware. RERUM devices are our wireless RE-Motes that we use for sensing the environment. Each RE-Mote carries several sensors that collect data like ambient temperature and humidity, noise, light, etc. Each distinct type of sensory data is made available through a CoAP resource.

The RERUM gateway has several roles. First, it interconnects the devices through an 802.15.4 wireless sensor network by initiating the RPL [24] routing protocol. Second, it also provides the interconnection between the sensor network and the outside world. Third, it keeps a list of the registered sensors and performs several housekeeping operations (device resetting, etc.). Furthermore, we note that it is possible to verify signatures on the gateway. However, additional functionality triggered by the verification result of the gateway is of separate interest, and further discussed by us in [25, 26].

The RERUM middleware comprises the backend, where the sensory data is stored. Authorised end-used applications can request sensory data through

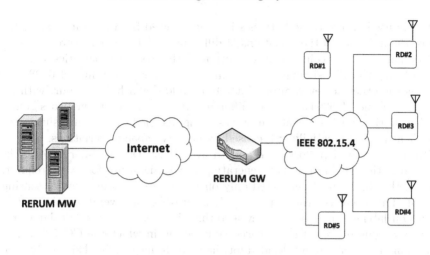

Fig. 2. Network topology used for the trials

the middleware. For every distinct client request, the middleware communicates with the gateway using an appropriate protocol over HTTP. Next, the gateway translates this request to a CoAP one, and transmits the corresponding sensory data back to the middleware. We note, that the communication between the middleware and the gateway is performed through a secure VPN connection.

The trials were performed in a wireless sensor network with one RERUM gateway and eleven RERUM devices. All components were installed in a building owned by the Heraklion municipality. The RERUM devices were sensing, signing and transmitting new values every 30 s.

4.2   Battery Runtime and Energy Consumption

To get a practical comparison of signed sensing in a real world environment, we installed a test setup of two RE-Motes with coin cells and AAA batteries. Those RE-Motes sensed the ambient temperature and provided it throughout the CoAP interface. The firmware images deployed were exact the same. The only difference was, that one device had signing enabled. The signed messages were provided in JSS format. For signing, we used MicroECC with enabled in-line assembly optimisations and `secp192r1` curve. The CoAP client requested the resources once in a 30 s interval. It was running on a standard PC connected via a border router to the sensing devices.

First tests with standard 3V CR2430 coin cells revealed that coin cells are not well suited to drive the RE-Motes: both ran for a maximum of roughly three and a half hours before shutting down. There was no notable difference in runtime of the device signing messages and the one emitting just plain messages. Slight differences were most probably caused by variations of the coin cells capacities.

To increase runtime and reveal real runtime differences, we decided to switch to standard AAA/LR03 batteries with a voltage of 1.5 V. For each of the RE-

Motes we used two of those batteries in series, picked from the same batch (to reduce the influence of the variations of different battery manufacturers).

Compared to the coin cell, the runtime with two AAA batteries was significantly higher. The signing device achieved an average runtime of 6228 min, whereas the other achieved approximately an additional half an hour, with an average runtime of 6264 min. The difference in runtime between two signing-enabled runtime measurements and two signing-disabled runtime measurements was 2% at most; potentially still caused by battery capacity variations.

To increase total performance and to avoid easy Denial-of-Service attacks on sensing, the RE-Mote is not generating a new signature for every request. Instead, the signature is generated only once within the (configurable) sensing interval. This decreases the impact of signatures for the overall runtime effectively. Our lab measurements [3], revealed that the energy overhead of signatures basically originates from the increased time period in which the CC2538 is not in sleep mode. Therefore we decided for the trials to measure and sign only once in every 30 s for each resource. The experiments show that signing with such a low frequency does have little to no measurable impact on the overall battery runtime in a real-world scenario.

5   Experimental Validation

The investigated logs cover a period of two days of measurements resulting in roughly 2.800 messages each for the resources ambient temperature and ambient humidity; both in signed JSS format and as well plain, unsigned, JSON. The signatures were all verified as valid, which indicates that the network error correction mechanisms described were working successfully and no message was manipulated. To rule out implementation errors, we tampered signatures manually by introducing single bit errors, which immediately caused the verifier to correctly recognize them as manipulated.

The RE-Mote is using the 6LoWPAN adaption layer over 802.15.4 for sending the JSS messages. Since the MTU is only 127bytes before packets get fragmented, JSS messages with typical length of about 160bytes and more do not fit into a single 6LoWPAN packet. While RFC7252 [27] states that a "CoAP message [...] SHOULD fit within a single IP packet" in order to avoid fragmentation on the IP layer, no strict requirements considering message size for constrained networks are given. This problem gets addressed by the CoRE Working Group: "Block-wise transfers in CoAP" [28]. This draft extends CoAP "with a pair of 'Block' options, for transferring multiple blocks of information from a resource representation in multiple request-response pairs".

The block options exist for both, requests (option Block1, e.g. POST and PUT) and responses (option Block2, e.g. responses for GET requests), but for the use-case of the RERUM application, only the Block2 option for (JSS) responses is relevant. The block sizes can be chosen by the client and must be of the power-of-two, ranging from $2^4 = 16$ to $2^{10} = 1024$bytes. The RERUM application supports only sizes up-to 64bytes, since greater block sizes would again lead to fragmentation on the 6LoWPAN/802.14.5 layers. The block sizes used during development and the trials is indeed 64bytes, since lower values would increase the number of messages exchanged and thus the overall transmission overhead.

A sample interaction between a client requesting a resource (e.g. ambient-temperature) on a RE-Mote is depicted in Fig. 3. This sample resource is requested as a signed JSS representation and has total length of 164bytes. Block-wise transfer means that these JSS messages get divided into three blocks of $64 + 64 + 36$bytes (the last block contains the remainder and is typically smaller than the block size). The client specifies the desired block sizes and sends the request to the RE-Mote, which answers with the first block of the requested resource. Furthermore, the RE-Mote specifies the number of this block in the sequence and if there are more blocks available for this resource. The client subsequently requests the following blocks until it receives the last one. The RE-Mote itself acts completely stateless and does neither need to do flow control nor maintain any session information.

The RERUM application is deployed on constrained devices in low-power and lossy networks [29]. Unreliable communication channels and high packet loss are some of the challenges of those constrained networks. Since the RE-Mote itself is a constrained device with limited memory and CPU performance, the overhead of lost packets and transmission errors, and their impact are important to consider. Here we examined the transmission overhead in case of lost packets and transmission errors.

The sensing RE-Mote is exposing the resources through the RESTful CoAP interface. A normal personal computer with installed Firefox and the Firefox CoAP add-on Copper [30][13] is acting as a client. If the client issues a CoAP GET request, this request gets passed to the network interface 'tun0' that is created

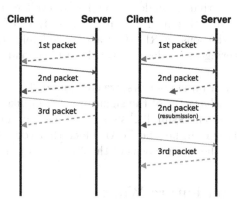

Fig. 3. A client is requesting a CoAP resource represented as a JSS message in three CoAP blocks. The left side shows a communication without errors. To the right the 2nd CoAP block gets lost and the client requests re-submission prior requesting the 3rd block. Note that requests are represented as straight lines and responses as dashed.

---

[13] people.inf.ethz.ch/mkovatsc/copper.php (accessed 23 Aug 2016).

by Contiki's `tunslip` script[14]. This network tunnel is forwarding the IP packets to the border router via the serial interface [31]. A second RE-Mote is acting as the border router, flashed with the border router firmware image provided by the Contiki project. The border router is responsible for translating between 6LoWPAN packets from the wireless sensor network and the other, 'normal' IPv6 packets. Once it receives packets through the serial line, it converts and sends them to the wireless sensor network (which consists in our setup of one sensor host only).

In the focus of this setup are packets that were coming from the sensing RE-Mote; we did not manipulate packets from the client to the RE-Mote. We altered the border router source code to simulate different network behaviours. We implemented a feature to configure a drop frequency n, that triggers the border router to drop every n-th packet coming from the sensing RE-Mote. This allows to effectively simulate an unreliable communication link, where packets get lost during transmission with a configurable 'unreliability'.

The second feature triggers bit errors such as flipping bits: a 'flip_signature_bit' parameter m can be configured to flip single bits of every m-th JSS signature transmitted. We examined the network traffic that goes through the `tunslip` tunnel on the client machine with Wireshark[15].

The sample GET interaction depicted in Fig. 3 shows that the client is requesting the individual CoAP blocks one by one. Each request is marked as 'confirmable' and the client only succeeds if it has received an acknowledgement ('ACK') for its request. To minimise the messages exchanged, the sensing RE-Mote piggy-packs the acknowledgements onto the responses. If a packet loss occurs and the client doesn't receive the second CoAP block, the client waits for the two seconds timeout and requests this block again. After successfully receiving the missing block, the client proceeds with requesting the last block. This interaction shows, that a single packet loss doesn't cause the whole JSS message to be retransmitted, but only that part, i.e. the CoAP block, that got lost. In this scenario, the sensing RE-Mote acts completely stateless and is not involved in the recovering of the lost packet, it just responds to the additional request.

Now to simulate transmission errors, we configured the border router to flip the last bit of the first character of the signature. Again, like in the scenario of the packet loss, the UDP checksum [32] signals to the client a transmission error and only the UDP datagram, i.e. the CoAP block that contained this bit error is retransmitted, while the other blocks of the JSS message are unaffected.

6   Conclusion and Future Work

In this paper, we presented the practical impact of using integrity protected communication through elliptic curve based signatures performed in a real-world

---

[14] github.com/contiki-os/contiki/blob/master/tools/tunslip6.c.
[15] wireshark.org.

IoT trial scenario. We proved that integrity protection on constrained devices is possible now, however with some restrictions.

We showed that the Zolertia Z1 with the MSP430 chip was too constrained to build a secure IoT application [4]. We did not succeed to build a sensing application that incorporates a standard IoT operating system like Contiki, a standards compliant CoAP and REST interface in combination with ECC signatures on an adequate security level (more or equal than 192bit curve size) on a chip with only 8 KB RAM and around 60 KB flash memory.

However we showed that the resources provided by the Zolertia RE-Mote using a CC2538 chip with a ARM Cortex-M3 32bit chip, 32 KB RAM and 512 KB flash are sufficient [3]. The lab results proved to be sufficiently stable using a 192bit curve size to go into trials.

In Lab testing we analysed several existing elliptic signature implementations and libraries [3,4]. In terms of runtime and power consumptions MicroECC provided the best results and was therefore selected. Our new results show that this turned out to be a good choice. MicroECC is in active development, easy to use and performs well in terms of runtime and code footprint overhead.

Switching to the RE-Mote and the measurements, however, proofed that it is possible to build a IoT application that provides integrity protection through digital signatures and communicates with modern, standard-compliant protocols. However, we did not tackle the key-distribution problem which needs to be considered when building IoT applications with end-to-end security.

Besides the results from the trial scenario, additional runtime overhead measurements were done. These extend the comparison of different ECC libraries presented in [3] by an implementation that utilises the hardware crypto engine capabilities of the CC2538 chip significant. Our results reveal that the hardware accelerated implementation is performing better in terms of runtime, than the already well performing MicroECC library. However, besides the runtime other aspects like the problem of side channel attacks that MicroECC addresses have to be considered in depth in future work.

This paper also extends the theoretical communication overhead considerations done in [3], by practical aspects that influence the number of messages exchanged in low-power and lossy networks, such as packet loss and transmission errors. Our results show that CoAP and UDP offer robust and reliable communication, while still being lightweight. Transmission errors are treated in such a way that also constrained devices, like the RE-Mote platform can handle them with little overhead.

It is worth noting that our JSS message format used is not optimal for exchanging messages in terms of size. Therefore we expect that one can reduce the communication overhead further by improving the formatting of the message and the embedded signature. Another option is to limit signatures to average values as we suggest in [25,26].

Acknowledgements. J. Bauer, R.C. Staudemeyer, H.C. Pöhls, and A. Fragkiadakis were supported by the European Unions 7th Framework Programme (FP7) under grant agreement $n°609094$ (RERUM). H.C. Pöhls and R.C. Staudemeyer were also supported by the European Unions Horizon 2020 Programme under grant agreement $n°644962$ (PRISMACLOUD). Additionally J. Bauer and H.C. Pöhls were supported by the Bavarian State Ministry of Education, Science and the Arts as part of the FORSEC research association.

References

1. Pöhls, H.C., Angelakis, V., Suppan, S., Fischer, K., Oikonomou, G., Tragos, E.Z., Diaz Rodriguez, R., Mouroutis, T.: RERUM: building a reliable IoT upon privacy- and security-enabled smart objects. In: Wireless Communications and Networking Conference Workshop on IoT Communications and Technologies (WCNC 2014), pp. 122–127 (2014)
2. Staudemeyer, R.C., Pöhls, H.C., Watson, B.W.: Security & privacy for the internet-of-things communication in the SmartCity. In: Angelakis, V., Tragos, E., Pöhls, H.C., Kapovits, A., Bassi, A. (eds.) Designing, Developing, Facilitating Smart Cities: Urban Design to IoT Solutions, 30 p. Springer, Heidelberg (2016)
3. Mössinger, M., Petschkuhn, B., Bauer, J., Staudemeyer, R.C., Wojcik, M., Pöhls, H.C.: Towards quantifying the cost of a secure IoT: overhead and energy consumption of ECC signatures on an ARM-based device. In: Proceedings of the 5th Workshop on the Internet of Things Smart Objects and Services (IoTSoS 2016), 6 p. (2016)
4. Pöhls, H.C.: JSON sensor signatures (JSS): end-to-end integrity protection from constrained device to IoT application. In: Proceedings of the Workshop on Extending Seamlessly to the Internet of Things (esIoT 2015), pp. 306–312 (2015)
5. Zolertia, "Z1 datasheet," 20 p. (2010)
6. Montenegro, G., Kushalnagar, N., Hui, J., Culler, D.: RFC4944 – transmission of IPv6 packets over IEEE 802.15.4 networks. Requests for Comments (2007)
7. IEEE Standards Association, Part 15.4g: Low-Rate Wireless Personal Area Networks (LR-WPANs) Amendment 3: Physical Layer (PHY) specifications for low-data-rate, wireless, smart metering utility networks. IEEE (2012)
8. Olsson, J.: "6LoWPAN demystified," Texas Instruments, 13 p. (2014)
9. Zolertia, "RE-Mote datasheet," 2 p. (2015)
10. Texas Instruments, "CC2538 datasheet," 32 p. (2015)
11. Dunkels, A., Grönvall, B., Voigt, T.: Contiki – a lightweight and flexible operating system for tiny networked sensors. In: 29th Annual IEEE International Conference on Local Computer Networks (LCN 2004), pp. 455–462 (2004)
12. Angelakis, V., Cuellar, J., Fischer, K., Fowler, S., Gessner, J., Gundlegård, D., Helgesson, D., Konios, G., Lioumpas, A., Lunggren, M., Mardiak, M., Moldovan, G., Mouroutis, T., Nechifor, S., Oikonomou, G., Pöhls, H.C., Ruiz, D., Siris, V., Suppan, S., Stamatakis, G., Stylianou, Y., Traganitis, A., Tragos, E.Z.: The RERUM system architecture (RERUM Deliverable D2.3). Technical report (2014)
13. Fielding, R.T.: Architectural styles and the design of network-based software architectures. Ph.D. dissertation, Department of Information and Computer Science (2000)
14. Jones, M.: RFC7518 – JSON Web Algorithms (JWA). Technical report, Requests for Comments, Internet Engineering Task Force (2015)
15. Josefsson, S.: RFC4648 – The Base16, Base32, and Base64 data encodings. Technical report, Requests for Comments, Network Working Group (2006)
16. Dang, Q.H.: Secure hash standard. National Institute of Standards and Technology, Gaithersburg, MD, Technical report, August 2015

17. European Network of Excellence in Cryptology II: ECRYPT II Yearly Report on Algorithms and Keysizes (2011–2012). Katholieke Universiteit Leuven, Technical report (2012)
18. MacKay, K.: micro-ecc. http://kmackay.ca/micro-ecc/
19. fail0verflow (bushing, marcan, segher, sven), "Console Hacking 2010 - PS3 Epic Fail (slides)," 27th Chaos Communications Congress (27C3) (2010). http://events.ccc. de/congress/2010/Fahrplan/attachments/1780_27c3_console_hacking_2010.pdf
20. Klyubin, A.: Some SecureRandom Thoughts (2013). http://android-developers. blogspot.de/2013/08/some-securerandom-thoughts.html
21. Brumley, B.B., Tuveri, N.: Remote timing attacks are still practical. In: Atluri, V., Diaz, C. (eds.) ESORICS 2011. LNCS, vol. 6879, pp. 355–371. Springer, Heidelberg (2011). doi:10.1007/978-3-642-23822-2_20
22. Bernstein, D.J., Gastel, B., Janssen, W., Lange, T., Schwabe, P., Smetsers, S.: TweetNaCl: a crypto library in 100 tweets. In: Aranha, D.F., Menezes, A. (eds.) LATINCRYPT 2014. LNCS, vol. 8895, pp. 64–83. Springer, Heidelberg (2015). doi:10.1007/978-3-319-16295-9_4
23. Turner, S., Brown, D., Yiu, K., Housley, R., Polk, T.: RFC5480 - elliptic curve cryptography subject public key information. Technical report, Requests for Comments, Network Working Group (2009)
24. Brandt, A., Hui, J., Kelsey, R., Levis, P., Pister, K., Struik, R., Alexander, R.: RFC6550 – RPL: IPv6 routing protocol for low-power and lossy networks. Technical report, Requests for Comments, Internet Engineering Task Force (2012)
25. López, D.R., Cuellar, J., Staudemeyer, R.C., Charalampidis, P., Fragkiadakis, A., Kasinathan, P., Pöhls, H.C., Suppan, S., Tragos, E., Weber, R.: Modelling the trustworthiness of the IoT (RERUM Deliverable D3.3), Technical report (2016)
26. Tragos, E.Z., Bernabe, J.B., Staudemeyer, R.C., Luis, J., Ramos, H., Fragkiadakis, A., Skarmeta, A., Nati, M., Gluhak, A.: Trusted IoT in the complex landscape of governance, security, privacy, availability and safety. In: Digitising the Industry – Internet of Things Connecting the Physical, Digital and Virtual Worlds. River Publishers Series in Communications, pp. 210–239 (2016)
27. Shelby, Z., Hartke, K., Bormann, C.: RFC7252 – The Constrained Application Protocol (CoAP). Technical report, Requests for Comments, Internet Engineering Task Force (2014)
28. Bormann, C., Shelby, Z.: Block-wise transfers in CoAP. Working Draft, IETF, Internet-Draft (2016)
29. Shelby, Z., Hartke, K., Bormann, C.: RFC7228 – terminology for constrained-node networks. Technical report, Requests for Comments, Internet Engineering Task Force (2014)
30. Kovatsch, M.: Demo abstract: human-CoAP interaction with Copper. In: International Conference on Distributed Computing in Sensor Systems and Workshops (DCOSS 2011), pp. 1–2, Barcelona, Spain (2011)
31. Romkey, J.: RFC1055 – Nonstandard for transmission of IP datagrams over serial lines: SLIP. Technical report, Requests for Comments, Network Working Group (1988)
32. Postel, J.: RFC768 – User Datagram Protocol. Technical report, Requests for Comments, Internet Engineering Task Force (1980)

Identity in the Internet-of-Things (IoT): New Challenges and Opportunities

Kwok-Yan Lam[1(✉)] and Chi-Hung Chi[2]

[1] School of Computer Science and Engineering,
Nanyang Technological University, Singapore, Singapore
kwokyan.lam@ntu.edu.sg
[2] Data61, CSIRO, Geraldton, Australia
chihungchi@gmail.com

Abstract. From digitization to datafication, Internet-of-Things (IoT) plays an important role as enabler in the value creation process from big data. As is expected, security has naturally become one main concern in the IoT deployment. Due to the unique features and requirements of IoT, including limited compute resources, power, bandwidth and massive number of deployed IoT objects, and its loosely coupled networked architecture, new strategies and techniques are needed to provide feasible and practical solutions to IoT security. While substantial research efforts have been focusing on the lightweight communication protocols and cryptography/compression engines, one fundamental science question being asked is on the notion of "Identity in the Internet-of-Things" (or IDoT). In this paper, we would like to first explore the concept of IDoT and analyze why it is so unique as compared to the concept of "Identity of Users" (IDoU) in traditional networks and systems. Then we will survey on attribute-based, multi-factor authentication as an important approach to put this IDoT concept into practice. We will conclude this paper with open research issues in this direction.

1 Introduction

The Internet-of-Things (IoT) [1] has already become the most important platform to support digital intelligence for smart nations. Gartner predicts that within the next five years, there will be more than 25 billion objects deployed in every part of our daily lives and business. While this can be viewed as opportunities, it also raises a big concern about cybersecurity [2–4]. For example, hackers might use portable RFID readers to read other people's credit cards on public transports illegally using paypass since there is no verification on the identity of the reader's owner. Another example is that hackers can easily sniff the IoT network to get hold of the IMEI (International Mobile Equipment Identity) number of sensors and use it to pollute the IoT database through flooding it with "poisoned" data messages.

Compared to security in traditional systems, network, and data security, security in IoT is a new challenge because of its unique features and requirements. First, many IoT objects are small and have only limited CPU and battery power. As a result, strong encryption schemes are often found to be non-practical. Instead, lightweight cryptography [5–8] and protocols such as MQTT (MQ Telemetry Transport) and CoAP

© Springer International Publishing AG 2016
K.-Y. Lam et al. (Eds.): ICICS 2016, LNCS 9977, pp. 18–26, 2016.
DOI: 10.1007/978-3-319-50011-9_2

(MQ Telemetry Transport) [9–11] are being investigated for IoT deployment. Second, security protection software such as those from anti-virus (AV) companies is not applicable to IOT objects because of their physical limitations. Wide variety of IoT objects from different vendors and standard groups, together with their different firmware and embedded OS further make the support of AV on every object difficult. Network security for IoT is also another challenge due to different new transport protocols of IoT objects and also the exponential increase in network traffic for cost-effective security analysis. Finally, IoT needs both encryption key management and identity management. Scalability issue comes when millions of objects are involved in the IoT network.

To address the security issues in IoT, while research efforts are still on-going in lightweight protocols, cryptography engines, and protocol stacks, researchers start to go back to the more fundamental question of what is "Identity" in the Internet-of-Things. It is hoped that this "Identity" concept can serve as the solid foundation on which cost-effective IoT security solutions can be inspired, built and put in practice.

The rest of the paper is as follows. In Sect. 2, the notion of "Identity" in the IoT is discussed. In Sect. 3, one important research topic in IoT security, attribute-based authentication, will be used to illustrate how the concept of "Identity" in the IoT can be supported. Finally, the paper will conclude in Sect. 4.

2   Concept of Identity in the Internet-of-Things (IDoT)

Under IoT, one of the root problems, in the context of cybersecurity assurance, is the lack of a rigorous notion of "Identity" in the Internet-of-Things (IDoT).

In traditional systems and networks, multi-factor authentication is often used to define and recognize the "Identity" of a user (IDoU). Typically, three categories of information are involved. They are knowledge (something they know), procession (something they have), and inherence (something they are) [12]. Good examples of these three categories are password (know), USB token or smart card (have), and finger or other biometric identifier (are) respectively. Furthermore, two or more factors might be used together to strengthen the authentication process. For Internet banking, a user is usually required to use a hardware USB token (have) and also to input his/her own password in order to verify the identity.

However, for IoT security, multi-factor authentication approach is much more complex and challenging. This is due to the new difficulties and challenges in defining and composing identity for IoT objects. In the next two sub-sections, we will first analyze different information categories that can possibly serve as identifiers to composite identity for IoT objects. Then we will discuss additional complication issues when managing these information in the IoT network.

2.1   Information Categories for Identity in the IoT

Leveraging the ideas from "Identity" of a user (IDoU) from traditional systems and network, the information stack for "Identity" in the IoT (IDoT) is shown in Fig. 1. In this information stack, there are four categories: inheritance, association, knowledge, and context.

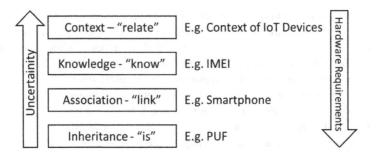

Fig. 1. Information stack for identity in the IoT (IDoT)

The first information category in the stack is the "inheritance". Just like the biometrics identifiers (such as fingerprints and retina) of human, researchers are exploring similar type of information that are inherited from the IoT object hardware. The result is the PUF (physical unclonable function) [13], which is defined as a physical entity that is embodied in a physical structure and is easy to evaluate, but hard to predict even for an attacker with physical access, or practically impossible to duplicate even given the exact manufacturing process that produced it. Very often, it depends on the uniqueness of their physical microstructure and manufacturing process. A typical example is the Silicon PUF that is embedded into an integrated circuit [14]. When the PUF is queried with a challenge or physical stimulus, it will return an unpredictable (but repeatable) response that depends on both stimulus and the unique object-specific physical characteristics of the object containing the PUF.

This "inheritance" information categories is very attractive to aid the definition and construction of IDoT. However, as expected, it is not as flexible as other information categories because it depends on the chip/hardware manufacturers. Furthermore, since PUF can be very noisy, precautions will be needed to ensure that the expected requirements for the function can be achieved. Currently, it is only used in applications with high security requirements.

The second information category in the stack is the "association". Unlike the "procession" information category for IDoU, it is not easy for an IoT object to process something external such as hardware token. However, under some specific situations or for some specific IoT objects such as personal wearables, it is common for the IoT objects to be associated (or linked) to a given personal gateway such as smartphone so that data will only be sent to the data cloud store through the predefined smartphone.

The third information category in the stack is the "knowledge". Similar to the second information category, the kind and amount of information that the IoT object can know is limited when compared to the case of IDoU. One typical example of this information type is the IMEI (International Mobile Equipment Identity) of the mobile phone [15]. But changing IMEI of a mobile phone is not as trivial as changing the password, in particular when the owner of a given IoT network wants to change the IMEI of all the IoT objects that he/she deploys. Recently, one new research direction that people are investigating under this information category is to use the historical sensed data that a given IoT object has captured to define/construct its dynamic "Identity". However, this is still in the early stage of research.

The last information category in the stack is the "context". Unlike in the situation of IDoU where this information category is not used so often, this category attracts a lot of attention in IoT security. Normally, IoT sensors are deployed in groups that are related to each other (e.g. all body sensors belonging to the same person being monitored). By studying the monitored behavior profile of different members within the same group and comparing it against the expected behavior profile, certain aspects of IDoT can be derived. Note that unlike the first three categories that come from the same IoT object, this information category is likely to derive from multiple inter-related IoT objects. The precision and quality of information in this category is relative lower than the other three information categories. More details of this approach will be given at the end of Sect. 3.

2.2   Complication and Challenges

From the last section, it is clear that using the proposed information stack to define IDoT is indeed a new challenge, as compared to that for IDoU. Due to the limited information availability in the middle categories (i.e. "association" and "knowledge"), together with the inflexibility of the category "inheritance" and the imprecision of the category "context", risk based authentication [16] using multi-factors would definitely be the preferred option. And the category "context" will likely be the information target for IDoT researchers to explore. On top of the challenges to use multi-factors from the proposed information stack to define and construct IDoT, there are at least two additional issues in IoT that further complicates the management of IDoT.

The first issue is related to the ownership and user identity relationship of an IoT object. At any time t, every IoT object should have an owner, but might have one or more users. The relationship among the IoT object, owner, and users might also change with respect to time in its lifecycle. For example, a weight scale such as those from Withings can support more than one person. And the ownership of the scale might change from the manufacturer to a retirement home. Furthermore, each IoT object might capture one or more data sources (e.g. Apple iWatch has multiple sensors). All these complicate the IDoT for authentication and other subsequent processes, including authorization and governance, in particular when the upper information categories such as "context" are used to define IDoT.

The second issue is related to the management of identifies and namespace of IoT objects. On the Internet, each resource has an URI (Uniform Resource Identifier). There is also DNS (Domain Name System) that maps URI to its current resource IP address; and this DNS is managed by the organization Internet Assigned Numbers Authority (IANA) [17]. With this namespace and identifier mapping framework, the dynamics of identifiers such as IP address of an URI can be hidden and communication between URIs becomes much easier. However, in the IoT space, due to the wide variety of already existing mapping solutions from different manufacturers, defining this kind of unified identity framework will not be easy, at least not in the near future. Obviously, this will have negative impacts on IDoT when the information category "context" is used. It also affects the practicability of edge computing on IoT security [18].

3   Attribute-Based Authentication

In the last section, we see that the notion of Identity in the Internet-of-Things (IDoT) is likely to be built from multi-factors, each one of which can be considered as an attribute (or identifier) of a given IoT object. Survey on IoT security shows that there are substantial existing related work on attribute-based authentication. In this section, we would like to give an overview on what has been done on this subject. It is hoped that this overview can give inspirations on how IDoT can move forward.

In the past few years, attribute-based authentication schemes that make use of attributes of objects as part of their identifier is getting lots of attention. It is viewed as one promising way to address the identity issue in IoT because of at least three reasons. First, there are lots of semantically rich attributes associated to both the objects and the context where the objects are in. Second, the attribute values might be continuously being updated, making them to be unique as part of the identifier. Third, data owners can enforce fine-grained access policies based on the nature of data. All these make the hackers difficult to counterfeit the attribute-based digital identity.

However, designing an effective and efficient attribute-based authentication scheme is hard, given that most of current schemes are still static attribute-based, with high algorithmic complexity in communication and computation. To support IDoT, the direction should target on the design of efficient lightweight, attribute-based active authentication schemes to support the robust notion of "identity" within the Internet-of-Things with its attribute-based credential container covering not only static attributes of objects, but also dynamic behaviour attributes (e.g. those with values dependent on time) of objects and attributes of the context (e.g. location) that the object is inside.

3.1   Overview of Existing Attribute-Based Authentication Schemes

Attribute-based encryption (ABE) is defined as a type of public-key encryption in which the secret key of a user and the ciphertext are dependent upon attributes. In such a system, the decryption of a ciphertext is possible only if the set of attributes of the user key matches the attributes of the ciphertext [19]. It was firstly proposed by Sahai and Waters [20]. Later, the concept of attribute-based signature (ABS) was introduced [21], and the idea of using a credential bundle to hold the attributes of a user was proposed [22]. Most ABS adopt bilinear pairings in their schemes and this makes them complicated and less practical. In [23], Anada et al. proposed an ABS scheme without pairings in the random-oracle model. There are two main types of ABE. The first one is key-policy based [24] and the second one is ciphertext-policy based [25]. Other variants, including multi-authority ABE [26, 27] and fully decentralized ABE [28, 29], are also available.

In the design of attribute-based encryption or signature, the following properties should to be ensured:

- Zero knowledge proofs – Signer and verifier might not have prior knowledge of each other.
- Unforgeability – It should be hard to forge signatures and/or proof of possession of attributes.
- Multi-show unlinkability – Given two signatures, it is hard to know whether the signer is the same.
- Selective disclosure – Selection of attributes should only be done to those necessary for completing a transaction.
- Collusion resistance – Multiple parties cannot collude and combine all their attributes to produce a valid signature if any one party could not do it individually.
- Threshold attribute-based authentication – The verification ensures that the signer has a threshold number of at least t attributes in common with the verification attribute set.

3.2   Attribute-Based Authentication Schemes for IDoT

In the context of IoT, attribute-based authentication scheme faces both new opportunities and challenges. In addition to the intrinsic attributes of an IoT object, new types of attributes are now available to be used potentially in authentication. These include the behaviour attribute data (either as a single value or as a data sequence) of the IoT object and the attributes of the context where the object is in (e.g. location). In particular, the behaviour attribute data is interesting to be explored because under typical IoT context, both the IoT object (e.g. sensor or tracker) and the receiver (e.g. cloud store) will have access to the same sequence of monitored data, which might make DUKPT (derived unique key per transaction) management possible.

Managing both static and dynamic attributes in attribute-based authentication schemes effectively and efficiently is a real challenge. In theory, there could be more attributes than any given scheme can accommodate. Current attribute-based authentication schemes are already facing the complexity and performance challenges, in both communication and computation. With the possible expansion of the attribute set, how to select a good subset of attributes for the scheme is not trivial, given that the decision might also be influenced by the dynamic characteristics of the behaviour attribute data. Revocation of attributes is also expected to be more frequent due to the potential continuous updating of attributes. How to design an effective and efficient attribute-based authentication scheme to support both static and dynamic attributes and how to construct and maintain the attribute tree to support fast revocation are some of the open questions for research.

One important deployment scenario of IoT objects such as trackers worth mentioning here is the continuous monitoring of certain behaviour aspect of the IoT object such as location. With the continuous uploading of the monitored data stream from the device to the backend (cloud) server, both sides can access the same sequence pattern of temporal data. Thus, it might be possible to use some kind of multidimensional data stream summarization techniques to map the data stream into an important attribute to be included in the scheme. Note that the choice of the summarization technique and the selection of attributes will be influenced by the expected dynamic pattern of its data stream. And the timestamp can be used to address the out-of-order issue of the data stream.

3.3 Context-Aware Approach to IDoT and Authentication

In the past few years, there are increasing research efforts on using situational information for IDoT authentication [30, 31]. The assumption behind this approach is that there is often expected profile on the context in which the IoT object is in [32] and on how the object should behave [33, 34]. For example, the IP address of a given IoT object should be in some predefined range; the geolocation of the object should be within a certain area; and the temperature sensor should report the body temperature of an elderly person. If the monitored behavior data profile is close to the expected norm, authentication can be granted (or at least serving as a positive assist). On the other hand, if the derivation between the monitored and the expected ones exceeds certain threshold, explicit authentication using other means might be triggered. Currently, most of these work are based on the authentication using group key agreement protocol [35].

Despite its potentials, there are a number of open research issues for this approach. Compared to the other three information categories ("inheritance", "association", and "knowledge"), the context information is relatively imprecise and is subject to noise. So, what will be its weight in the authentication process? Selection of attributes and setting of the threshold cut-off for the attribute norm value are also tricky because they are both application and requirements specific. More importantly, what is the science ground of making this decision? As a result, this approach serves more as an assist rather than the absolute mean to do authentication. Another piece of related work is to use neighbors to serve as notaries in the authentication scheme [36]. While this idea is able to improve the strength of the authentication scheme, the incurred cost will be an important concern for large scale IoT network.

4 Conclusion

Internet-of-Things (IoT) has generally been agreed to the foundation for digital economy; and cybersecurity is always a big concern when mission critical applications are built on top of IoT. In this paper, we argue that one root problem for IoT security is the lack of the rigorous notion of "Identity" in the Internet-of-Things (IDoT). To solve the identity problem, we propose a new information stack to describe IDoT. Different from the "Identity" of a user, this new information stack puts a strong emphasis on situational information, which is expected to be imprecise and noisy. With the expectation of using multi-factor authentication in IoT security, we survey on attribute-based authentication and analyze the pros and cons of current techniques to support IDoT. It is hoped that by granting this deep understanding, IDoT can be addressed in a more systematic and effective way.

References

1. Palattella, M.R., Accettura, N., Vilajosana, X., Watteyne, T., Grieco, L.A., Boggia, G., Dohler, M.: Standardized protocol stack for the internet of (important) things. IEEE Commun. Surv. Tutorials **15**(3), 1389–1406 (2013)
2. Granjal, J., Monteiro, E., Silva, J.S.: Security for the internet of things: a survey of existing protocols and open research issues. IEEE Commun. Surv. Tutorials **17**(3), 1294–1312 (2015)
3. Zhao, K., Ge, L.: A survey on the internet of things security. In: Proceedings of Ninth IEEE International Conference on Computational Intelligence and Security (2013)
4. Sathish Kumar, J., Patel, D.R.: A survey on internet of things: security and privacy issues. Int. J. Comput. Appl. **90**(11), 20–26 (2014)
5. McKay, K.A., Bassham, L., Turan, M.S., Mouha, N.: NISTIR 8114: Draft Report on Lightweight Cryptography. Technical Report, National Institute of Standards and Technology, U.S. Department of Commerce, August 2016
6. Bogdanov, A., Knezevic, M., Leander, G., Toz, D., Varc, K., Verbauwhede, I.: SPONGENT: the design space of lightweight cryptographic hashing. IEEE Trans. Comput. **62**(10), 2014–2053 (2013)
7. Eisenbarth, T., Kumar, S.: A survey of lightweight-cryptography implementations. IEEE Des. Test Comput. **24**(6), 522–533 (2007)
8. Mouha, N.: The design space of lightweight cryptography. IACRA Cryptology ePrint Archive (2015) http://eprint.iacr.org/2015/303.pdf
9. Jaffey, T.: MQTT and CoAP, IoT Protocols. Eclipse Newsletter. http://www.eclipse.org/community/eclipse_newsletter/2014/february/article2.php
10. IBM, Eurotech. MQ Telemetry Transport (MQTT) V3.1 Protocol Specification (2010). http://public.dhe.ibm.com/software/dw/webservices/ws-mqtt/mqtt-v3r1.html
11. Shelby, Z., Hartke, K., Bormann, C.: Constrained Application Protocol (CoAP). Draft-IETF-Core-CoAP-18, June 20 (2013)
12. Wikipedia. Multi-factor Authentication. https://en.wikipedia.org/wiki/Multi-factor_authentication
13. Maes, R., Verbauwhede, I.: Physically unclonable functions: a study on the state of the art and future research directions. In: Sadeghi, A.-R., Naccache, D. (eds.): Towards Hardware-Intrinsic Security, pp. 3–37. Springer, Heidelberg (2010). Wikipedia. Physical unclonable function
14. Katzenbeisser, S., Kocabaş, Ü., Rožić, V., Sadeghi, A.-R., Verbauwhede, I., Wachsmann, C.: PUFs: myth, fact or busted? a security evaluation of physically unclonable functions (PUFs) cast in silicon. In: Prouff, E., Schaumont, P. (eds.) CHES 2012. LNCS, vol. 7428, pp. 283–301. Springer, Heidelberg (2012). doi:10.1007/978-3-642-33027-8_17
15. Wikipedia. International Mobile Station Equipment Identity. https://en.wikipedia.org/wiki/International_Mobile_Station_Equipment_Identity
16. Williamson, G.: Enhanced authentication in online banking. J. Econ. Crime Manage. **4**(2), 18–19 (2006)
17. Internet Assigned Numbers Authority (IANA). http://www.iana.org/
18. Shi, W., Cao, J., Zhang, Q., Li, Y., Xu, L.: Edge computing: vision and challenges. IEEE Internet of Things J. **3**(5) (2016)
19. Wikipedia. Attribute-based Encryption. https://en.wikipedia.org/wiki/Attribute-based_encryption
20. Sahai, A., Waters, B.: Fuzzy identity-based encryption. In: Cramer, R. (ed.) EUROCRYPT 2005. LNCS, vol. 3494, pp. 457–473. Springer, Heidelberg (2005). doi:10.1007/11426639_27

21. Guo, S.Q., Zeng, Y.P.: Attribute-based signature scheme. In: Proceedings of IEEE International Conference on Information Security and Assurance (2008)
22. Maji, H.K., Prabhakaran, M., Rosulek, M.: Attribute-based signatures. In: Kiayias, A. (ed.) CT-RSA 2011. LNCS, vol. 6558, pp. 376–392. Springer, Heidelberg (2011). doi:10.1007/978-3-642-19074-2_24
23. Anada, H., Arita, S., Sakurai, K.: Attribute-based signatures without pairings via the fiat-shamir paradigm. In: Proceedings of the 2nd ACM Workshop on ASIA Public-Key Cryptography (2014)
24. Goyal, V., Pandey, O., Sahai, A., Waters, B.: Attribute-based encryption for fine-grained access control of encrypted data. In: Proceedings of the 13th ACM Conference on Computer and Communications Security (2006)
25. Bethencourt, J., Sahai, A. Waters, B.: Ciphertext-policy attribute-based encryption. In: Proceedings of IEEE Symposium on Security and Privacy (2007)
26. Chase, M.: Multi-authority attribute based encryption. In: Vadhan, S.P. (ed.) TCC 2007. LNCS, vol. 4392, pp. 515–534. Springer, Heidelberg (2007). doi:10.1007/978-3-540-70936-7_28
27. Chase, M., Chow, S.S.M.: Improving privacy and security in multi-authority attribute-based encryption. In: Proceedings of 16th ACM Conference on Computer and Communications Security (2009)
28. Lewko, A., Waters, B.: Decentralizing attribute-based encryption. In: Paterson, K.G. (ed.) EUROCRYPT 2011. LNCS, vol. 6632, pp. 568–588. Springer, Heidelberg (2011). doi:10.1007/978-3-642-20465-4_31
29. Okamoto, T., Takashima, K.: Efficient attribute-based signatures for non-monotone predicates in the standard model. In: Catalano, D., Fazio, N., Gennaro, R., Nicolosi, A. (eds.) PKC 2011. LNCS, vol. 6571, pp. 35–52. Springer, Heidelberg (2011). doi:10.1007/978-3-642-19379-8_3
30. Wang, H., Lymberopoulos, D., Liu, J.: Sensor-based user authentication. In: Abdelzaher, T., Pereira, N., Tovar, E. (eds.) EWSN 2015. LNCS, vol. 8965, pp. 168–185. Springer, Heidelberg (2015). doi:10.1007/978-3-319-15582-1_11
31. Shrestha, B., Saxena, N., Truong, H.T.T., Asokan, N.: Drone to the rescue: relay-resilient authentication using ambient multi-sensing. In: Christin, N., Safavi-Naini, R. (eds.) FC 2014. LNCS, vol. 8437, pp. 349–364. Springer, Heidelberg (2014). doi:10.1007/978-3-662-45472-5_23
32. Hayaski, E., Das, S., Amini, S., Hong, J., Oakley, I.: "Casa" Context-Aware Scalable Authentication. In: Proceedings of the 9th Symposium on usable Privacy and Security (2013)
33. Kayacik, G., Just, M., Baillie, L., Aspinall, D., Micallef, N.: Data driven authentication: on the effectiveness of user behaviour modelling with mobile device sensors. In: Proceedings of the Workshop on Mobile Security Technologies (MOST) (2014)
34. Shi, E., Niu, Y., Jakobsso, M., Chow, R.: Implicit authentication through learning user behavior. In: Proceedings of the 13th International Conference on Information Security (2011)
35. Singh, K., Muthukkumarasamy, V.: Using physiological signals for authentication in a group key agreement protocol. In: Proceedings of 2011 IEEE Conference on Computer Communications Workshops (INFOCOM WKSHPS) (2011)
36. Gehani, A., Chandra, S: PAST: probabilistic authentication of sensor timestamps. In: Proceedings of 22nd Annual Computer Security Applications Conference (ACSAC 2006) (2006)

A Lightweight Method for Accelerating Discovery of Taint-Style Vulnerabilities in Embedded Systems

Yaowen Zheng[1,2,3], Kai Cheng[1,2,3], Zhi Li[1,2(✉)], Shiran Pan[2,3], Hongsong Zhu[1,2,3], and Limin Sun[1,2,3]

[1] Beijing Key Laboratory of IOT Information Security Technology, Beijing, China
[2] Institute of Information Engineering, Chinese Academy of Sciences, Beijing, China
{zhengyaowen,chengkai,lizhi,panshiran,zhuhongsong,sunlimin}@iie.ac.cn
[3] University of Chinese Academy of Sciences, Beijing, China

Abstract. Nowadays, embedded systems have been widely deployed in numerous applications. Firmwares in embedded systems are typically custom-built to provide a set of very specialized functionalities. They are prone to taint-style vulnerability with a high probability, but traditional whole-program analysis has low efficiency in discovering the vulnerability. In this paper, we propose a two-stage mechanism to accelerate discovery of taint-style vulnerabilities in embedded firmware: first recognizing protocol parsers that are prone to taint-style vulnerabilities from firmware, and then constructing program dependence graph for security-sensitive sinks to analyze their input source. We conduct a real-world experiment to verify the mechanism. The result indicates that the mechanism can help find taint-style vulnerabilities in less time compared with whole-program analysis.

Keywords: Taint-style vulnerability · Embedded security · Protocol parser · Binary analysis · Reverse engineering

1 Introduction

Nowadays, embedded systems have been widely deployed in numerous applications. For example, routers and web cameras are normally used in home and office environment, and programmable logic controllers (PLC) are widely employed in industrial plants. If the security of such embedded systems are compromised, there might be serious consequences. For example, people's private information could be leaked to public or primary production process could be affected. Firmware of embedded systems is typically custom-built to provide a set of very specialized functionalities. Due to the resource-constrained nature of embedded systems, usually, firmware developers are more concerned about implementing the functionality and maximizing system performance; security concerns are often treated as afterthoughts and thus they are often treated inadequately. As a result, embedded system firmware is prone to vulnerabilities. Among various kinds of vulnerabilities, taint-style vulnerability refers to the case where

© Springer International Publishing AG 2016
K.-Y. Lam et al. (Eds.): ICICS 2016, LNCS 9977, pp. 27–36, 2016.
DOI: 10.1007/978-3-319-50011-9_3

data propagates from an attacker-controlled input source to a security-sensitive sink without undergoing proper sanitization which could cause program crash or execute unauthorized operation [20]. Since embedded devices have frequent interaction with outside world through various user-input interfaces, undoubtedly, embedded systems are prone to taint-style vulnerabilities with a higher probability. In fact, taint-style vulnerabilities of embedded systems are reported frequently in various vulnerability reporting sources, including the Common Vulnerabilities and Exposures (CVE) [2], exploit-db [6] in recent years. With the increasing amount of embedded devices, the inability to quickly discover taint-style vulnerabilities will result in more serious security breaches in the future.

Taint-style vulnerability discovery technologies such as fuzz testing [14], symbolic execution [18], tainting analysis [16] could be applied to embedded systems. However, such traditional technologies suffer from low efficiency when analyzing firmware of embedded systems. First, source codes and design documents are often proprietary and thus only binary firmware image might be available, so that static analysis is time-consuming due to lack of semantic information. Then, as peripherals of different embedded devices have profound discrepancy, the unified dynamic simulation analysis is extremely difficult. In addition, firmware comparison technologies aimed at quickly finding homologous vulnerabilities in different devices have been studied. But they still suffer from large temporal and spatial overhead and low accuracy.

According to our study, current taint-style vulnerability discovery has a significant defect. Due to little understanding of code function, most approaches treat all codes equally and waste a lot of time on unimportant codes which have nothing to do with users input. To accelerate discovery of taint-style vulnerability, we investigate function modules that are more prone to this kind of vulnerability. Protocol parsers are function modules that handle protocol interaction and they are first lines of programs dealing with users input. They consume external input and either build an internal data structure for use, or orchestrate the execution of the proper functionality based on the input values. We assume that in firmware of embedded devices, once taint-style vulnerabilities exist, they are generally concentrated in protocol parsers. Therefore, we take two steps to accelerate discovery process. First, we construct a classifier using a set of features to recognize protocol parsers. Then, we derive program dependence graph (PDG) to analyze the input source of security-sensitive sinks. It help quickly extract insecure sinks where a static data flow path from attacker-controlled input source exists. The mechanism is lightweight as no time-consuming technology such as symbolic execution is employed. Finally, average time cost of insecure sinks finding is evaluated to prove efficiency of our work.

To summarize, our contributions include the following:

- We have proposed a two-stage mechanism to accelerate discovery of taint-style vulnerability in embedded devices.
- We have conducted a real-world experiment on firmwares of two cameras and reduced time cost of insecure sink finding by 81.4 and 44.2 percent.

The rest of the paper is structured as follows. We propose a two-stage mechanism to accelerate discovery of taint-style vulnerabilities in Sect. 2. Then we present experiment details about the classifier for protocol parsers and compare our work with whole-program analysis to illustrate the effectiveness of the proposed method in Sect. 3. Related work is presented in Sect. 4. Finally, conclusions are summarized in Sect. 5.

2   Two-Stage Mechanism

In the two-stage mechanism, we first recognize protocol parsers from firmware to narrow down the analysis scope of security-sensitive sinks, and then analyze input source of sinks based on PDG to help extract insecure cases. Insecure sinks refer to cases where a static data flow path from attacker-controlled input source exists. They need be further checked about data sanitization to finish the discovery of taint-style vulnerability. The mechanism is committed to quickly find insecure sinks in the former stage, which accelerate the discovery of taint-style vulnerabilities.

2.1   Protocol Parsers Recognition

Firmware is a software that provides control, monitoring and data manipulation of embedded systems. It is normally constitute of operating system, file system and user programs. To find out protocol parsers from firmware, we first extract the main service program from firmware. Then, we select a set of discriminative features. Finally, we use support vector machine (SVM) model to construct a classifier for parser recognition.

Firmware Pre-processing. In the pre-processing phase, we obtain the firmware of embedded system by downloading it from the official website. As it is compressed using standard compression algorithm and the file system adopt cramfs, jffs, yaffs these common formats, we use Binwalk [1] and firmware-mod-kit [4] to automatically extract binary programs from the firmware. Then, we manually find out the main service program that contain most of functional services. In general, the main service program is always running on online device and has various protocol keywords in it. It could be simply located with manual analysis.

Features. After finding out the main service program, we select a group of representative features from the respective of assembly form to represent functions. All features are shown in Table 1. In the following, we introduce the motivation why we choose these features.

First, the protocol parser should have features related to service. Since it has complex processing logic, the number of blocks is larger than other function modules. The protocol parser is usually called by various components, so it owns more parent functions. Similarly, the protocol parser implements its functionality by calling other modules, so it also owns more child functions. In addition, the protocol parser normally executes different functionality depending on received network data, thus the number of child functions appearing in paths of switch branches is also important in recognizing the protocol parser. In Table 1, *blocks*, *inedges*, *outedges*, *switch_call* are used to represent above features.

Then, the protocol parser should have control structure features. As the protocol parser normally deal with external input, it would execute in different path depending on the received network data. Moreover, the process may run in cycles constantly. So a parser need contain switch statements or successive if-else statements, and it should have a parent function that calls it in a while structure. From the perspective of assembly form, the parser function should has a block that owns more than three branches or successive blocks all of which have side branches. Meanwhile, the parser function should be surrounded by a loop structure. In Table 1, *switch* and *loop* are relevant features.

Finally, the protocol parser should have features related to protocol processing. As the protocol parser normally deals with protocol communication, it follows the protocol specification and resolves particular characters and strings. For example, the HTTP protocol parser need compare the front part of header with GET and POST strings to determine the request method. Similarly, newline and return character would appear in the protocol parser as it is used to split protocol fields. Thus the occurrence frequency of const strings and string manipulation functions can reflect the likelihood of being a parser for a function. As shown in Table 1, *cmp_banner*, *strcmp* and *strstr* are features that represent the number of const strings, occurrence frequency of strcmp and strstr function calls. Besides, *cmp_spec* is to represent occurrence frequency of CMP instruction with ASCII code of character as the second argument.

Table 1. List of features

Features	Explanation
switch	Number of switch branches
loop	Equal 1 when surrounding loop structure exists otherwize 0
cmp_spec	Character comparison times
cmp_banner	String comparision times
strcmp	Frequency of strcmp occurrence
strstr	Frequency of strstr occurrence
switch_call	Number of functions invoked in switch branches
blocks	Number of blocks in functions
inedges	Number of parent functions
outedges	Number of child functions

SVM Learning. After extracting features, we use SVM learning to construct the classifier which can recognize parsers. First, we combine all features to construct a feature vector and normalize them to represent each function. Though observation, the feature value is either an integer value that is greater than zero or a boolean variable. As the distribution of feature values is not uniform and has a long tail, the Min-Max scaling transformation is not suitable. We take logarithmic transformation to normalize all feature values.

$$\overline{x_f} = \log_{10} x_f \tag{1}$$

where x_f represents the feature f's value for a given function. $\overline{x_f}$ represents the feature f's value after normalization. Then, we select Standard Support Vector Machine (C-SVM) with linear kernel to train our classifier based on normalized samples. The result of classifier training is presented in Sect. 3.

2.2 Analysis of Security-Sensitive Sinks

After recognizing protocol parsers from firmware, we first design a selection mechanism for security-sensitive sinks. Then, we construct PDG to identify related input source and extract insecure sinks.

Selection of Security-Sensitive Sinks. The security-sensitive sink refers to the common library function which could be affected by malicious external input if the verification of input data is not strict. Since both buffer overflow and command injection belong to taint-style vulnerability, we list their related vulnerable functions as sinks in Table 2.

To accelerate the discovery of the vulnerability, we only analyse sinks in the parser function and its child functions. If a child function is deeper from the parser function, the probability of suffering from vulnerability for the sink is lower as external data usually does not spread too deep. Thus, we limit the scope of our analysis to the parser function itself and its child functions within three layers.

Table 2. Security-sensitive sinks

Category	Functions
Buffer overflow vulnerability	strcpy sprintf strcat memcpy gets fgets getws sscanf strncpy memmove
Command injection vulnerability	system exec execv execl

Program Dependence Graph. PDG is firstly constructed to guarantee precise backtracking to source for sinks. It is an intermediate program representation that makes explicit both the data and control dependence for each operation in a program [13]. Three kinds of directed edges are contained in PDG, and we describe

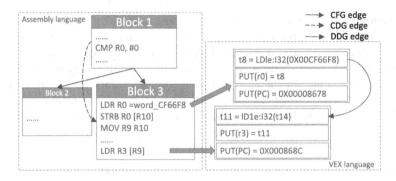

Fig. 1. PDG diagram

them in detail using a diagram of binary sample shown in Fig. 1. First, control flow edge [10] represents the transition between program blocks. Second, control dependance edge [12] refers the relationship that execution result of one specific statement affects execution of the other statement. In Fig. 1, one of control dependence analysis is that execution result of comparison instruction in Block 1 determines execution of all instructions in Block 3. In addition, data dependence edge [13] represents the production and consumption of data in program. Instructions in assembly form are transformed to VEX intermediate language and data dependence is analyzed by construction and inferring of def-use chain [21]. In Fig. 1, one of data dependence analysis is that R0 in first instruction of Block 3 and R3 in last instruction of Block 3 points to the same address. Source of any instruction's argument could be deduced iteratively in this way.

Since most external inputs are located in parser functions, we then construct PDG from the entry point of identified parser functions to all child functions within three layers. Based on PDG, we can identify the input source of sinks. If the type of input source is string constant or from read-only data segments like *.rodata*, we take it as insecure sinks. Finally, it need be deeply analyzed to confirm the existence of vulnerability and the analysis does not belong to the work of this paper.

3   Evaluation

In this section, we first describe the implementation details, then present training result of the classifier. Next, we evaluate the performance of parsers recognition on real-world embedded devices. Finally, the performance of our mechanism is compared with whole-program analysis.

3.1   Implementation

We implement the two-stage mechanism on a server. It is Ubuntu 14.04.2 LTS(GNU/Linux 3.13.0-48-generic x86 64) with Intel Xeon(R) E5-2687W v3 CPU and 125.8 GiB of memory. In the first stage, the main service program is loaded in The Interactive Disassembler (IDA) [9] which can disassemble the program from binary to assembly form and recover its control flow graph. Since features are unrelated to instruction set architecture and the disassembler code is sufficient for analysis, we write python scripts using programming API supported by IDA to extract feature values. Then we use open source tool scikit-learn [7] to train classifier based on SVM learning. In the second stage, we modify the code of tool Angr [21] to support PDG and analyze the input source of security-sensitive sinks which help quickly find out insecure cases. Finally, We conduct the experiment on firmwares of Hikvision and TVT brand camera. Hikvision [5] and TVT [8] are famous camera manufacturers and their cameras are wildly deployed in numerous applications. We select DS-2CD6223F model for Hikvision camera and TD-9436T model for TVT camera. The main programs from two cameras firmwares are centaurus (13.2 MB) and ipcamera (14.4 MB). The performance of the classifier and two-stage mechanism are evaluated on them.

3.2   Cross Validation for Classifier

In the learning phase of classifier, We label 63 parsers from several firmwares as positive samples, and choose 300 negative samples at random. We divide samples into training set and validation set, respectively are S1 and S2. The experiment starts to take 10 features as candidates and construct an initial classifier on S1. Then the classifier is tested on S2, and the feature with lowest weight would be discarded. The rest of features are kept training, and the result indicates that when candidate features are reduced to specified 5 features, the recognition accuracy rate is the best. The best features combination are *switch*, *com_spec com_banner*, *strcmp* and *strstr*. The corresponding weights are 0.93, 1.76, 0.61, 1.88 and 1.71.

Unimportant features are *loop*, *inedge*, *switch_call*, *blocks* and *outedge* sorted by unimportance. The *loop* feature cannot be easily extracted since the broken chain of function calls from IDA perspective. So it appears to be unimportant in recognition of parser functions. Conversely, other features are indeed unimportant for parser recognition. Through our experiment, we find features like *cmp_spec*, *strcmp* and *strstr* may be more significant.

3.3   Performance of Classifier

To evaluate performance of the classifier, we manually label parser functions and normal functions in centaurus and ipcamera. The classifier is applied to them and the parser recognition accuracy is shown in Table 3. The mechanism tolerates imprecision of parsers recognition to a certain extent as it is an intermediate step to accelerate the speed of finding code locations where probability of the taint-style vulnerability existence is high.

3.4   Performance of Two-Stage Mechanism

In whole-program analysis, functional modules are treated equally without discrimination so that the entire security-sensitive sinks are analysed in spite that

Table 3. Recognition accuracy of classifier

Program	Identified parsers	Correct num	Accuracy
centaurus	93	79	84.9%
ipcamera	97	83	85.6%
Total	190	162	85.3%

many of these are free of vulnerability. In our two-stage mechanism, only sinks inside parser functions are analysed which greatly reduce the time cost. To prove the efficiency, we get the number of function analyzed, sinks analyzed and insecure sinks within them for specified sink types in different methods and calculate time cost of each insecure sink discovery.

Table 4. Analysis of two camera firmwares

	ipcamera		centaurus	
	Global analysis	Our method	Global analysis	Our method
Analysis time	2950.8s	252.6s	3007.1s	321.4s
Function num	16053	1174	7232	853
Total (insecure/all)	623/2094	288/655	287/4528	54/427
strcpy (insecure/all)	116/180	22/34	36/92	8/13
memcpy (insecure/all)	352/1328	221/451	141/2347	29/287
strncpy (insecure/all)	20/252	6/73	11/1638	4/39
sscanf (insecure/all)	4/29	4/22	8/67	5/52
sprintf (insecure/all)	120/288	34/73	63/318	7/30
Time per insecure sink	4.74 s	0.88 s	10.48 s	5.85 s

The evaluation result on ipcamera and centaurus program is shown in Table 4. It shows that to ipcamera and centaurus, average time cost of each insecure sink discovery by our method are 0.88 s and 5.85 s. And the corresponding time cost by whole-program analysis are 4.74 s and 10.48 s. By comparison, our mechanism reduce the time cost of insecure sink discovery by 81.4 and 44.2 percent. Therefore, our method has an advantage over accelerating discovery of the taint-style vulnerability in embedded systems.

4 Related Work

4.1 Static Analysis

Yamaguichi et al. [19,20] propose to design code property graph representation and path traversal patterns for various vulnerability types. Unfortunately, code property graph is depended on source code, hence it cannot be applied directly on embedded binary programs. Angr [21] extracts control flow, control dependence, data dependence graph and discovers vulnerabilities by using backward slicing and symbolic execution technologies. However, accurate analysis still suffers from low efficiency. PIE [11] finds parsers by extracting features and using machine learning. However, only structure features are selected which affects accuracy of protocol parsers recognition and vulnerability analysis work is rare.

4.2 Dynamic Analysis

Dynamic approaches like fuzz testing have been proposed to discover vulnerability more precisely. Codenomicon Defensics [3], a mature network protocol fuzzing product, supports many species of industrial protocols. However, code coverage for testing is usually low and vulnerabilities in uncommon paths are not found. As a remedy, some dynamic analysis tool like Driller [17] is proposed to combine fuzz testing with symbolic execution to guide analysis into specified code areas. Unfortunately, it requires simulation of programs which is difficult to implement in embedded systems. In the aspect of dynamic simulation, Avatar framework [22] is proposed to dynamically analyze embedded systems by orchestrating the execution of an emulator together with the real hardware. Decaf [15] is proposed to support virtual machine based, multi-target, whole-system dynamic binary analysis. However, both frameworks have not been used to directly analyze vulnerabilities.

5 Conclusion

In this paper, we propose a lightweight method to accelerate discovery of taint-style vulnerabilities in embedded systems. Instead of analyzing entire security-sensitive sinks, we focus on protocol parsers which are more prone to taint-style vulnerabilities. We firstly use machine learning technologies to construct a classifier that can recognize parser functions accurately. Then, we derive PDG to identify input source of sinks that can help extract insecure cases quickly. We demonstrate effectiveness of our work by comparing it with whole-program analysis. Our work can effectively help analysts spend less time on insignificant codes and find taint-style vulnerabilities in time. In the future, we need improve protocol parsers recognition model and extend our work to cover more vulnerability types.

Acknowledgments. This work was supported in part by the National Key Research and Development Program (Grant No. 2016YFB0800202), the National Defense Basic Research Program of China (Grant No. JCKY2016602B001), the "Strategic Priority Research Program" of the Chinese Academy of Sciences (Grant No. XDA06040100), and the National Defense Science and Technology Innovation Fund, CAS (Grant No. CXJJ-16M118).

References

1. Binwalk — firmware analysis tool. http://binwalk.org/
2. Cve - common vulnerabilities and exposures (cve). http://www.wooyun.org/
3. Defensics - fuzzing - fuzz testing - black box testing - negative testing — code-nomicon. http://www.codenomicon.com/products/defensics/
4. Firmware-mod-kit - google code. https://code.google.com/archive/p/firmware-mod-kit/
5. Hikvision usa. http://www.hikvision.com/
6. Offensive security exploit database archive. https://www.exploit-db.com/
7. scikit-learn: machine learning in python. http://scikit-learn.org/
8. Shenzhen tvt digital technology co., ltd. http://www.tvt.net.cn/
9. Welcome to hex-rays!. https://www.hex-rays.com/index.shtml
10. Allen, F.E.: Control flow analysis. In: ACM Sigplan Notices, vol. 5, pp. 1–19. ACM (1970)
11. Cojocar, L., Zaddach, J., Verdult, R., Bos, H., Francillon, A., Balzarotti, D.: Pie: parser identification in embedded systems. In: Proceedings of the 31st Annual Computer Security Applications Conference, pp. 251–260. ACM (2015)
12. Cytron, R., Ferrante, J., Rosen, B.K., Wegman, M.N., Zadeck, F.K.: Efficiently computing static single assignment form and the control dependence graph. ACM Trans. Program. Lang. Syst. (TOPLAS) 13(4), 451–490 (1991)
13. Ferrante, J., Ottenstein, K.J., Warren, J.D.: The program dependence graph and its use in optimization. ACM Trans. Program. Lang. Syst. (TOPLAS) 9(3), 319–349 (1987)
14. Godefroid, P., Levin, M.Y., Molnar, D.A., et al.: Automated whitebox fuzz testing. In: NDSS, vol. 8, pp. 151–166 (2008)
15. Henderson, A., Prakash, A., Yan, L.K., Hu, X., Wang, X., Zhou, R., Yin, H.: Make it work, make it right, make it fast: building a platform-neutral whole-system dynamic binary analysis platform. In: Proceedings of the 2014 International Symposium on Software Testing and Analysis, pp. 248–258. ACM (2014)
16. Newsome, J., Song, D.: Dynamic taint analysis for automatic detection, analysis, and signature generation of exploits on commodity software (2005)
17. Stephens, N., Grosen, J., Salls, C., Dutcher, A., Wang, R., Corbetta, J., Shoshitaishvili, Y., Kruegel, C., Vigna, G.: Driller: augmenting fuzzing through selective symbolic execution. In: Proceedings of the Network and Distributed System Security Symposium (2016)
18. Wang, T., Wei, T., Lin, Z., Zou, W.: Intscope: automatically detecting integer overflow vulnerability in x86 binary using symbolic execution. In: NDSS. Citeseer (2009)
19. Yamaguchi, F., Golde, N., Arp, D., Rieck, K.: Modeling and discovering vulnerabilities with code property graphs. In: 2014 IEEE Symposium on Security and Privacy, pp. 590–604. IEEE (2014)
20. Yamaguchi, F., Maier, A., Gascon, H., Rieck, K.: Automatic inference of search patterns for taint-style vulnerabilities. In: 2015 IEEE Symposium on Security and Privacy, pp. 797–812. IEEE (2015)
21. Shoshitaishvili, Y., Ruoyu Wang, C., Salls, C., Stephens, N., Polino, M., Dutcher, A.: (state of) the art of war: offensive techniques in binary analysis (2016)
22. Zaddach, J., Bruno, L., Francillon, A., Balzarotti, D.: Avatar: a framework to support dynamic security analysis of embedded systems' firmwares. In: NDSS (2014)

Cloud Security

A Self-adaptive Hopping Approach of Moving Target Defense to thwart Scanning Attacks

Duohe Ma[1], Cheng Lei[1,2,3]($\boxtimes$), Liming Wang[1], Hongqi Zhang[2,3], Zhen Xu[1], and Meng Li[4]

[1] State Key Laboratory of Information Security,
Institute of Information Engineering of CAS, Beijing, China
{maduohe,wangliming,xuzhen}@iie.ac.cn, leicheng12150@126.com
[2] China National Digital Switching System Engineering
and Technological Research Center, Zhengzhou, Henan, China
zhq37922@126.com
[3] Henan Key Laboratory of Information Security, Zhengzhou, Henan, China
[4] Department of Computer Science,
Hong Kong Baptist University, Hong Kong, China
mli@comp.hkbu.edu.hk

Abstract. End-point hopping is one of important moving target defense (MTD) mechanisms to kill the attacker's reconnaissance. This method involves periodically changing the network configuration in use by communicating end points. Since without the awareness of attack strategies, existing end-point hopping mechanisms is blind which leads the network defense to low security effectiveness and high overhead. In this paper we propose a novel MTD approach named self-adaptive end-point hopping, which is based on adversary strategy awareness and implemented by Software Defined Networking (SDN) technique. It can greatly counterpoise the defense benefit of end-point hopping and service quality of network system. Directed at the blindness problem of hopping mechanism in the course of defense, hopping trigger based on adversary strategy awareness is proposed for guiding the choice of hopping mode by discriminating the scanning attack strategy, which enhances targeted defense. Aimed at the low availability problem caused by limited network resource and high hopping overhead, satisfiability modulo theories and are used to formally describe the constraints of hopping, so as to ensure the low-overhead of hopping. Theoretical and experimental analysis shows the ability to thwart scanning attacks in a relatively reasonable hopping cost.

Keywords: Moving target defense · Software defined networking · Self-adaptive hopping · Scanning attack strategy

1 Introduction

In current network environment, the static nature of network configuration makes it easy for attackers to detect the target system and find only a single exploitable bug to successfully implement intrusion. Specifically, static and

© Springer International Publishing AG 2016
K.-Y. Lam et al. (Eds.): ICICS 2016, LNCS 9977, pp. 39–53, 2016.
DOI: 10.1007/978-3-319-50011-9_4

fixed IP address allows network scanners to aggregate information in order to construct an accurate and persistent maps of the network. The unvarying nature of this network topology enables adversaries to collaboratively share and reuse their collected reconnaissance information in order to launch a larger attack. In the security battle, time is on the attackers side. Attackers have time to study targeted network to determine potential vulnerabilities and choose the time of attack to cause maximal impact. Once attackers attack and breach a system, they can maintain illegal access privileges for extended periods of time without being detected.

In the opposite, it is difficult for the defender to block all the vulnerabilities and filter all attacks in the case of IT system becoming increasingly complex. Although heavily secured perimeter firewalls and intrusion detection systems are deployed to protect the network from outside attackers, in practice they are not effective for Zero-day attack and Advanced Persistent Threats (APT), and can be avoided by skilled attackers. Without awareness of private information of the opponent, the defender may use static protection mechanisms and spend substantial effort to protect an asset which may not be the target of the attacker.

Moving target defense (MTD) has been proposed to change the game by wresting the advantage from the attacker because it eliminates the availability of constant or slowly-changing vulnerability windows that allow attackers to lie in wait and conduct useful experiments on persistent vulnerabilities [1]. Its purpose is to provide a dynamic, non-deterministic and non-sustained runtime environment [2]. Network MTD (NMTD) breaks the dependency requirements of the attack chains to the deterministic and consistency of network environment by multi-level dynamical changes [4]. As one of the hot spots of NMTD, end-point hopping is one of the effective mechanisms [5,6] to mitigate network attacks.

Although lots of hopping methods have been proposed [7–11,13], existing mechanisms lack the ability to adapt to different reconnaissance strategies, which leads the network defense to blindness. To summarize, there are two major problems in existing end-point hopping researches. First, the benefits from hopping defense decrease due to the inadequate dynamic of network hopping, caused by self-learning insufficiency in reconnaissance attack strategy, leading to the blindness of hopping mechanism selection. Second, due to the limited network resources and high overhead, the availability of hopping mechanism is poor.

To address the above problems, Network Moving Target Defense based on Self-adaptive End-point Hopping Technique (SEHT) is proposed. The key contributions of this paper can be shown in the following aspects:

(1) Directed to the lack of self-adaptive to scanning attack of existing hopping mechanism, hopping trigger based on adversary strategy awareness is designed. It uses hypothesis tests to analyze scanning attack strategy, and guides the choice of hopping strategy, which enhances the defense benefit.
(2) Aimed at limited network resources and high hopping overhead, end-point hopping based on satisfiability modulo theories is proposed. It uses satisfiability modulo theories (SMT) [18] to formally describe the constraints of hopping, so as to ensure the low-overhead of hopping, which increase the availability of hopping mechanism.

2 Background and Related Works

2.1 Category of Network Scanning Attacks

Network scanning is a kind of network reconnaissance technique by means of sending probe packets to selected end-point space range [19]. With different scanning technique constantly springs up, network scanning attack improves its efficiency based on the network structural characteristics and knowledge gained [20]. Accordingly, scanning attack strategy can be classified into three types: blind scanning, half-blind scanning and follow-up scanning:

(1) *Blind scanning strategy:* It is used when an attacker has to scan the entire active end-point. Since the structure of existing network information system has the characteristic of certainty and the static, attackers adopt blind scanning strategy so as to improve its efficiency by evenly scanning without repetition [21].

(2) *Half-blind scanning strategy:* It is used when an attacker knows the node distribution of the selected range of end-point information to scan. Half-blind scanning strategy is adopted so as to achieve higher success rate by unevenly scanning with repetition [22].

(3) *Follow-up scanning strategy:* It is directed at network systems implementing NMTD mechanisms When knowing the node distribution and the use of mutation mechanism, attackers try to obtain the mutation pattern of end-points by spatial compression and scanning frequency change. Based on it, follow-up scanning strategy is adopted so as to follow the hopping of specific end-point by uneven scanning with changeable frequency [23].

The reason to discriminate scanning attack strategy is that network scanning is used as a precondition technique the initial phase of attacks, which plays an important role in network attacks [3,4]. Therefore, this paper discriminates scanning strategy by analyzing behavior characteristic of different scanning strategies, which achieves self-adaptive end-point hopping.

2.2 Research Works About MTD Hopping

In traditional network architecture, Atighetchi *et al.* [7] proposed a hopping mechanism using false IP and port information to confuse scanning attack during net-flow exchange. Lee and Thing [8] proposed a random port hopping mechanism, which calculates next hopping end-point information to evade scanning attack by using pseudo-random function or shared secret key, but the method is vulnerable to network delay interference. MT6D [9] uses large IPv6 address space property to implement end-point information hopping so as to increase the unpredictability. Hari and Dohi [10] introduced a discrete Markov chain based on RPH so as to improve the success rate among communication parties. Lin et al. [11] proposed a novel synchronization method by additionally opening the corresponding end-point information of the previous and the after hopping period. HOPERAA algorithm was designed in [12], eliminating the influence of linear clock drift on hopping synchronization. The drawback of these methods is hard to implement on network.

Software defined networking (SDN) [13] with the feature of logic control plane being separate from data transfer plane has brought a new solution of effective collaborative management in distributed routing. For that, end-point hopping based on SDN can change hopping period and hopping rules dynamically. NASR [14] prevents connection requests not within the service period by using address transition of packet header and the update of flow table based on DHCP update. SDNA [15] confuses scanning attackers by virtual hopping, which deploys a hypervisor node in each subnet to ensure hopping consistency. OF-RHM [16] proposed virtual end-point mapping mechanism based on Openflow [13]. It converts real IP to virtual IP so as to implement end-point hopping. However, since OF-RHM only implements space hopping, attackers can improve success rate of scanning attack by changing scanning frequency. To address this problem, Jafarian et al. [17] proposed ST-RHM hopping mechanism, which can resist cooperative scanning attack effectively by using temporal-spatial mixed hopping based on SDN. Because of the double hopping in spatial and temporal hopping, it leads to the increase of overhead and the loss of service.

In the rest of this paper, we will give the detail of Self-adaptive End-point Hopping Technique (SEHT) to solve these problems mentioned above. The main notions used in this paper are given below (Table 1).

Table 1. The main notions used in this paper

Character	Description
$SEHT$	Self-adaptive End-point Hopping Technique
SMT	Satisfiability modulo theories
BHR	Base hopping range
$LTHR$	Low-frequency temporal hopping range
$HTHR$	High-frequency temporal hopping range
T_{BHR}	The hopping period of base hopping
T_{LTHR}	The hopping period of low-frequency hopping
T_{HTHR}	The hopping period of high-frequency hopping
T_{EHP}	The hopping period of end-point
hEI	Hopping end-point information, as $<IP, Port>$
m_B, m_L, m_H	The number of hEI range in different layer
N_{fail}	The number of failed requested packet
w_i^{EI}	Weighted value
$C(hR_i)$	The maximum router capacity
C_{j_1,j_2}, b_i^k	Boolean variable
δ_i, B_f	The setting threshold value

3   The Mechanism of Self-adaptive End-Point Hopping

End-point hopping is shown in Fig. 1, it tricks, evades and prevents scanning attack by changing network configuration, such as IP address and port, and status dynamically. Therefore, it increases the usage difficulty of vulnerabilities and backdoors so as to ensure the security of targeted systems. Existing end-point hopping mechanisms mainly adopt random hopping strategy [14,16].

As is shown in solid part in Fig. 1, hopping configuration manager is used to configure end-point hopping on the basis of security objectives. After that, hopping implementation engine is used to implement end-point hopping. However, since random hopping is lack of offensive and defensive situational awareness, the effectiveness and availability of end-point hopping is limited.

Self-adaptive end-point hopping adds analysis engine and hopping trigger engine based on random hopping. Analysis engine is used to perceive and analyze network system security status. According to it, different hopping strategies are triggered in hopping trigger engine which based on adversary strategy awareness, and end-point hopping constraints are generated consequently.

3.1   Adversary Strategy Awareness and Hopping Trigger Engine

According to the behavior characteristics of different network scanning strategies, SEHT adopts Sibson entropy [24] to obtain the distribution of failed requested packets so as to discriminate scanning strategy. Only failed request packets are chosen because successful requests contain both normal packets of

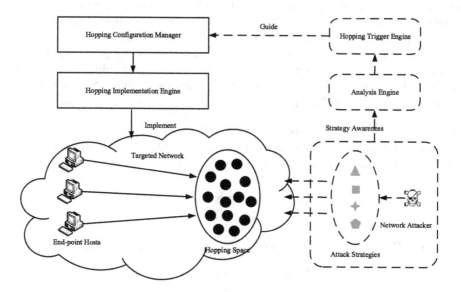

Fig. 1. Traditional hopping V.S self-adaptive of hopping.

legitimate users and the successful probe packets of attackers, but there is only one valid hEI for each end-point in every hopping period.

It has high accuracy and good stability in different anomalous awareness application scenarios [25].

Suppose the total number of failed request packets in the tth mutation period is N_{fail}. The number of failed request packets in the ith divided hEI space is denoted as N_{fail}^i. Equation (1) is used to calculate the probability distribution of the source and the destination address of failed requests in one mutation period denoted as $P_i^{Src}(\pi)$ and $P_i^{Dst}(\pi)$ respectively, with $j \in \{Src, Dst\}$, $\pi \in \{hEI\}$. Based on it, follow-up scanning strategy is discriminated after analyzing source address probability distribution of probe packets in adjacent T_{LTHR}. Besides, blind scanning strategy is then discriminated after analyzing destination address probability distribution of probe packets in each T_{EHP}.

Equation (2) indicates the Sibson entropy of the source address probability distribution of the failed request packets in the two consecutive T_{LTHR} of the ith end-point, in which $D_i(p,q) = \sum_{\pi \in \Pi_i} p(\pi) \cdot \log \frac{p(\pi)}{q(\pi)}$, and $\overline{P^{Src}} = \frac{1}{2}[P_{t-1}^{Src}(\pi) + P_t^{Src}(\pi)]$. In order to prevent the interference of network jitter, Sibson entropy is calculated in two consecutive T_{LTHR} instead of it in two consecutive T_{EHP} of the ith end-point. Based on Eq. (2), whether the scanning is follow-up strategy or not can be discriminated by comparing the Sibson entropy with the setting threshold.

Chauvenet criterion, shown as Eq. (3), is used to eliminate the abnormal high-frequency temporal mutation space. If blind scanning strategy is used, attackers are to scan the entire end-point space. The average number of scanned times of every end-point is $N_{fail}/m_B m_L$ in the ideal condition. However, because attackers might not always complete the scan of the whole end-point space within one T_{EHP}, the Sibson entropy directly calculated based on the distribution of failed probe packets of destination address and that of $N_{fail}/m_B m_L$ in one T_{EHP} will be larger. Therefore, the destination address probability distribution of the failed probe packets in the tth T_{EHP} and its modified Sibson entropy are calculated by using Eq. (4), where $D(p,q) = \sum_{\pi \in \Pi} p(\pi) \cdot \log \frac{p(\pi)}{q(\pi)}$, and $\overline{P_t^{Dst}} = \frac{1}{2}(P_t^{Dst}(\pi) + \frac{n_{fail}}{m_B' m_L'})$. By comparing with the setting threshold, whether blind scanning strategy is adopted or not can be determined. If not adopted, attackers will use half-blind reconnaissance strategy.

$$P_i^j(\pi) = \pi_k \cdot \left(\sum_{k=1}^{N_{fail}} \pi_k \right)^{-1} \tag{1}$$

$$D_S(P_{t-1}^{Src}(\pi), P_t^{Src}(\pi)) = \frac{1}{2}\{D_i[P_{t-1}^{Src}(\pi), \overline{P^{Src}}] + D_i[P_t^{Src}(\pi), \overline{P^{Src}}]\} \tag{2}$$

$$\frac{N_{fail}^i - N_{fail}/m_B m_L}{(m_B m_L)^2/12} < -\xi \tag{3}$$

$$D_S(P_t^{Dst}(\pi), \frac{N_{fail}}{m_B' m_L'}) = \frac{1}{2}\{D[P_t^{Dst}(\pi), \overline{P_t^{Dst}}] + D[\frac{N_{fail}}{m_B' m_L'}, \overline{P_t^{Dst}}]\} \tag{4}$$

In order to improve the unpredictability of end-point mutation, SEHT select different hopping strategy according to the discrimination of scanning attack strategy. Consequently, hEI space is generated. The scanning attack strategies can be calculated as following. If there is $\sqrt{D_S(P_{t-1}^{Src}(\pi), P_t^{Src}(\pi))} \leq \delta_1$, follow-up scanning strategy is implemented by attackers. And when $\sqrt{D_S(P_t^{Dst}(\pi), \frac{N_{fail}}{M'})} \leq \delta_2$, blind scanning strategy is implemented by attackers. Otherwise, when $\sqrt{D_S(P_t^{Dst}(\pi), \frac{N_{fail}}{M'})} > \delta_2$ and $\sqrt{D_S(P_{t-1}^{Src}(\pi), P_t^{Src}(\pi))} > \delta_1$ establishes, half-blind scanning strategy is implemented by attackers.

Furthermore, if attackers use mixed scanning strategies, based on the self-learning of scanning strategies, SEHT implements corresponding hopping strategy according to the priority of follow-up scanning, half-blind scanning and blind scanning for efficient defense.

3.2   End-Point Hopping Based on SMT

In order to achieve the manageability and low overhead in the process of hopping implementation, SMT solver is used to obtain the required hEI set, which meets the security and performance constraints in end-point hopping.

Define Boolean variable $b_T^v(k)$ indicates whether hopping switch v forwards the kth net-flow in T_{EHP} or not. If hopping switch v forwards the kth net-flow in T_{EHP}, there is $b_T^v(k) = 1$. Otherwise, there is $b_T^v(k) = 0$. The details of SEHT constraints are shown as follows

(1) Capacity constraint: This constraint is used to select hopping routers that can carry the maximum net-flow table size so as to prevent packet loss caused by data overflow [26].

   Equation (5) indicates the exponential function of marginal cost, where $\sigma = 2n$ is a tuning parameter [27]. $1 - \frac{C_v(k)}{C_v}$ indicates the utilization ratio of the forwarding table of v when the forwarding table of the kth net-flow is added. Equation (6) indicates the accumulated cost of added net-flow table should under the maximum net-flow table size C_{max}^v that hopping routers can carry.

   Equation (7) reduces route overhead by using route aggregation and adjacent allocation principles in routing update, which prevents the explosion of flow table size. $D_{j_1,j_2}^k = B_{j_1}^k \wedge B_{j_2}^k \wedge C_{j_1,j_2}$ means the assigned end-point information j_1 and j_2 in consecutive T_{EHP} to the same subnet are continuous, in which $B_j^k = \bigvee_{h^i \in s^k} b_j^i$ represents there is at least one end-point node h^i in subnet s_k assigned to hopping space j. Besides, Φ is the lower bound of the number of end-point information in each hopping space.

$$c_v(k) = C_v(\sigma^{1 - \frac{C_v(k)}{C_v}} - 1) \tag{5}$$

$$\forall hR_i, \quad C_{max}^v - \sum_{i=1}^{k} b_T^v(i) \cdot c_v(i) \geq C_{th}^v, \quad b_T^v(i) = 1 \tag{6}$$

$$\sum_k \sum_{j_1} \sum_{j_1 \neq j_2} B_{j_1}^k \wedge B_{j_2}^k \wedge C_{j_1,j_2} \geq \Phi \tag{7}$$

(2) Hopping space selection constraint: This constraint ensures the unpredictability of SEHT by limiting repetition rate in hEI selection. Equation (8) ensures that every end-point node can be assigned hEI. Equation (9) sets repetition rate threshold δ_3 so as to ensure the repetition of selected hEI not exceed the threshold. Furthermore, Eq. (10) requires that the assigned hEI in the last hopping period won't be assigned in the following hopping period. This constraint ensures every node can be assigned required hEI, and improves the unpredictability of hopping.

$$\sum_{1<j\leq M} b_i^j \geq 1 \tag{8}$$

$$\sum b_i^j \geq \frac{N_{LTHR}^i - 1}{2\delta_3 n_{HTHR}} \tag{9}$$

$$\forall hEI \in Fb_i^j = 0 \tag{10}$$

(3) Reachability constraint: This constraint means all net-flows in forwarding routers are reachable to destination end-point nodes. Equation (11) represents that the in-degree and out-degree of each router in the forwarding path is equal. Equation (12) means each router in the forwarding path is physically adjacent to its last hopping router and next hopping router, in which $\chi(hR_i)$ is routing set eliminating source and destination routers in the forwarding path. However, forwarding net-flows from one router to its next physical adjacent router is not enough to guarantee the reachability of net-flow. Equation (13) requires the distance from the next hopping router to destination router is not larger than the distance from the current hopping router to destination router, in which d_k^{i-Dst} represents the distance from router i to destination router.

$$\text{If} \quad b_T^k = 1, k \in [1, n], \quad \sum_{i \in I} b_T^v(i) = \sum_{o \in O} b_T^v(o) \tag{11}$$

$$\text{If} \quad b_i^k = 1, \forall hR_j \in \chi(hR_i), \quad \sum b_j^k = 2 \tag{12}$$

$$\text{If} \quad \forall hR_j \in \{hR | next\text{-}hop \text{ of } hR_i\}, \quad d_k^{j-Dst} \leq d_k^{i-Dst} \tag{13}$$

(4) Forwarding path delay constraint: This constraint prevents service performance decrease due to the excessive transmission delay. Since net-flow transmission delay is positively correlated with the number of routing nodes [28], Eq. (14) indicates that the maximum length of forwarding path cannot exceed the threshold $L_{\max}$.

$$\sum b_i^k \leq L_{\max} \quad i \in \{Src, hR_1, ..., Dst\} \tag{14}$$

4 Implementation of SEHT Based on SDN

As is shown in Fig. 2, SEHT uses hopping switch (HS), randomization controller (RC) and the trusted hopping components (THC) of end-point nodes to implement network hopping collaboratively. RC divides $\{hEI\}$ to BHR according to the number of subnet and its scale. HS divides BHR to LTHR according to the number of end-points and their importance. THC selects hEI according to hopping strategy by using shared parameters with HS.

RC mainly consists with hopping trigger, hopping decision engine, and SMT solver of hopping space module. The function of hopping trigger module is to analyze scanning strategy based on hypothesis tests, according to the illegal connection packets reported by HS. Hopping decision engine is to select different hopping strategies according to scanning strategies. While SMT solver is to obtain the required end-point information set according to hopping constraints and global view of SDN. After that, RC updates LTHR to HS.

THC of end-point nodes is used to negotiate mutation with THC in other end-points, and implementing virtual mapping from EI to hEI. THC in SEHT is based on a universal virtual-network kernel driver TAP. In order to be transparent to users' applications, network hopping needs to operate Ethernet frames using TAP under Linux.

In order to ensure the hopping efficiency of SEHT and the stability of network sessions, end-points will store two hEI the first time. One is considered as the active hopping end-point information. The other will be utilized at the next

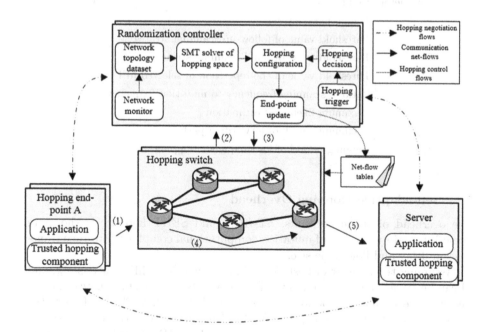

Fig. 2. SEHT Structure based on SDN.

hopping period, which is pre-calculated so as to notice other communicating THCs to be prepared to hopping when T_{EHP} is expired. At the same times, since there are still ongoing sessions in the network during end-point hopping, Change Time To Live (CTTL) is set so that expired hEI is retained to receive packets of existing sessions.

Since the flow tables need to update because of end-point and routing mutation during network communications, it is necessary to prevent the inconsistency of flow table update and packet loss. Directed to this problem, SEHT adopts *delete in sequential order, and add in reverse* update policy.

5   Experiments and Analysis

In order to verify the feasibility and effectiveness of SEHT, we use Mininet to build simulation network topology and adopt Erdos-Renyi model for random network topology generation. We choose OpenVSwitch (OVS) supporting Openflow protocol as HS, and OpenDaylight as RC. SEHT is deployed on OpenDaylight and OVS. Besides, Z3 SMT solver is used to solve the constraints. Linux CentOS 6.5 is used in Web Server and FTP Server. Windows7 is used in client. Besides, hEI is composed of Class B IP address pool and 2^{16} size port pool. The configuration of SEHT is shown in Table 2.

Table 2. Initial parameters of SEHT configuration

Parameter	Signification	Value
σ	Tuning parameter	5
δ_1	Threshold value of follow-up scanning strategy	0.05
δ_2	Threshold value of blind scanning strategy	0.075
δ_3	Threshold value of the repetition of selected hEI	0.005
γ	Ratio of scanning frequency to mutation frequency	0.4
λ	Maximum likelihood estimation	0.02
$L_{\max}$	Maximum length of forwarding path	32
T_{LTHR}	Hopping period of low-frequency hopping	50 s

5.1   Self-adaptive Hopping Overhead

The overhead of static networks, ST-RHM and SEHT hopping is shown in Table 3. It mainly consists of mutation computational complexity, average transmission delay and flow table size.

Assuming the number of host nodes in a subnet is n_t, hEI space is n_m, and EI can be aggregated is n_a. The size of net-flow table size in static network is n_t. Because in each hopping period, hEI is selected from all available hEI set, the size of net-flow table is $1 + n_m m_H$. While with capacity constraints, the size of net-flow table is $1 + m_H n_m / n_a$. Compared with ST-RHM, SEHT can effectively reduce the size of net-flow table.

Table 3. End-point hopping overhead

Hopping mechanism	Computational complex	Average transmission delay	Net-flow table size
Static network	$O(1)$	$t \times L_s$	n_l
OF-RHM	$O(\gamma n_h)$	$t \times L_s$	$1 + n_m/n_s$
ST-RHM	$O((\gamma n_h)^2)$	$t \times L_s$	$1 + n_m m_H$
SEHT	$O((\gamma n_h)^2)$	$t \times L_s$	$1 + m_H n_m/n_a$

5.2 Defend Scanning Attacks Analysis

Suppose there are n_l active end-point nodes in the network, the end-point information space is m, scanning width of attacker is $1/T_{SCN}$, and the scanning frequency is $n_s = w \cdot t/T_{SCN}$. The number of the end-point information scanned by the attack is $n_s = w \cdot t/T_{SCN}$, $n_s \leq m$. The ratio of scanning frequency to mutation frequency is $r = T_{EHP}/T_{SCN}$.

(1) The Capability of Resist Blind Scanning Attack. Since the blind scanning strategy is used to enhance the scanning rate. The success rate of scanning x active end-point nodes by attackers in static network, which can be supposed as $T_{EMP} = \infty$, obeys hypergeometric distribution expressed as $P_b(x) = (C_{n_l}^x \cdot C_{m-n_l}^{n_s-x})/C_m^{n_s}$.

Hence, the success rate of attackers in static network is $P_{hb}^{static}(x > 0) = 1 - aC_{\varphi m - n_l'}^{n_s/a}/\varphi C_{\varphi m}^{n_s/a}$. In OF-RHM [16], ST-RHM [17], and SEHT network, the probability of successfully scanning x active nodes during one mutation period obeys Bernoulli distribution. The success rate of attackers using blind scanning strategy is $P_b(x > 0) = 1 - [1 - rwn_l/(mn_l + mrw)]^{n_s}$. Particularly when $r = 1$, the scanning attack frequency is the same as the hopping frequency, the probability that an attacker successfully launching blind scanning is $P_b^{static}(x > 0) = 1 - C_{m-n_l}^{n_s}/C_m^{n_s}$. Compared with static network, it can be concluded that OF-RHM, ST-RHM, and SEHT can effectively resist blind scanning strategy, which is consistent with the conclusion in [29].

(2) The Capability of Resist Follow-Up Scanning Attack. When attackers use follow-up scanning strategy, there will be $r \geq 1$ in active scanning. Suppose attackers can repeat scanning b times in one T_{EMP}. The success rate of attackers in OF-RHM is $P_{fu}(x > 0) = 1 - [1 - bn_l'/(n_l' + \varphi mb)]^{n_s}$, which is consistent with the analysis in [11]. The success rate of attacker in ST-RHM is $P_{fu}(x > 0) = 1 - [1 - (bn_l' - n_\gamma)/(n_l' + \varphi mb)]^{n_s}$. Since SEHT deploys hopping period stretch policy, the hopping rate will lead to $r \leq 1$ after the follow-up scanning strategy is learnt by SEHT. As a result, the success rate of attackers in SEHT is $P_{fu}(x > 0) = 1 - [1 - (rn_l' - n_\gamma)/(n_l' + \varphi m)]^{n_s}$. Analysis shows that compared with ST-RHM, SEHT can effectively defend the follow-up scanning by combining spatial hopping with hopping period stretch policy.

(3) The Capability of Resist Half-Blind Scanning Attack. Since half-blind scanning strategy is used to actively scan specific range of end-point information which is physically adjacent to scanning source, it can be assumed that attacker can repeat scanning a times, and the scanning range is φm, $\varphi \in (0, 1)$, where there are n'_l active end-point nodes. Since OF-RHM adopts random hopping, the success rate of attackers using half-blind scanning strategy in OF-RHM is $P_{hb}(x > 0) = 1 - a[1 - wrn'_l/(\varphi mn'_l + \varphi mwr)]^{n_s}$. As for ST-RHM, it uses deceiving hopping. It can be assumed that there are n_γ hEI invalid at the end of each hopping period. The success rate of attackers using half-blind scanning strategy in ST-RHM is $P_{hb}(x > 0) = 1 - a[1 - (wrn'_l - \varphi mn_\gamma)/(\varphi mn'_l + \varphi mwr)]^{n_s}$. Since SEHT deploys random mutation based on weighted value, σ hEI will be selected for the next hopping period in each T_{EHP}. The success rate of half-blind hopping strategy in SEHT is $P_{hb}(x > 0) = 1 - a[1 - \sigma wrn'_l/(\varphi mn'_l + \varphi mwr)]^{n_s}$.

(4) The Capability to Resist Mixed Scanning Attack. In practical environments, the attacker often filtered EI through blind scanning. On this basis, half-blind or follow-up scanning is used in specific EI range. The success rate of mixed scanning attack is shown in Fig. 3(d). Since in static network, the success

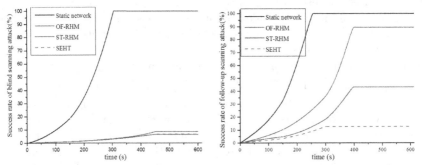

(a) Success rate of blind scanning attack strategy.   (b) Success rate of follow-up scanning attack strategy.

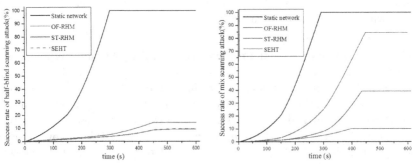

(c) Success rate of half-blind scanning attack strategy.   (d) Success rate of mixed scanning attack strategy.

Fig. 3. SEHT Assessments to defend scanning attacks.

rate of attacker increases dramatically when the strategy changes from blind scanning attack to half-blind scanning attack. Since SEHT introduces hopping period stretch policy after discriminate follow-up scanning, it can effectively reduce about 29% scanning attack compared with ST-RHM and can reduce about 75% scanning attack compared with OF-RHM.

6 Conclusion

Without the awareness of attack strategies, existing end-point hopping mechanisms have two major problems. First, the hopping mechanism selection is blindness. Second, high hopping overhead leads the defense system to bad availability. To address these challenges, a novel MTD approach named Self-adaptive End-point Hopping Technique (SEHT) is proposed, which is based on adversary strategy awareness and implemented by Software Defined Networking (SDN). The advantages of this mechanism are represented by two aspects. Hopping trigger based on adversary strategy awareness is proposed for guiding the choice of hopping mode by discriminating the scanning attack strategy. And to ensure the low-overhead of hopping, satisfiability modulo theories and are used to formally describe the constraints of hopping. Theoretical analysis and simulation experiments show that SEHT can resist almost 90% scanning attack even in mixed scanning strategy with low-overhead hopping.

Acknowledgments. This paper is supported by the National Basic Research Program of 973 Program of China (2011CB311801); the National High-Tech Research and Development Plan of China (863 Program) (2012AA012704, 2015AA016106); the Strategic Priority Research Program of the Chinese Academy of Sciences, Grants No. XDA06010701, XDA06010306. Zhengzhou Science and Technology Talents (131PLKRC644).

References

1. Cybersecurity   Game-Change   Research   Development   Recommendations.   NITRD   CSIA   IWG   (2010).   http://www.nitrd.gov/pubs/CSIA-IWG-Cybersecurity-GameChange-RD-Recommendations-20100513.pdf
2. Jajodia, S., Ghosh, A.K., Swarup, V., et al.: Moving Target Defense: Creating Asymmetric Uncertainty for Cyber Threats. Springer Science & Business Media, New York (2011)
3. Kewley, D., Fink, R., Lowry, J., et al.: Dynamic approaches to thwart adversary intelligence gathering. In: Proceedings of DARPA Information Survivability Conference & Exposition II, DISCEX 2001, vol. 1, pp. 176–185. IEEE (2001)
4. Lei, C., Ma, D., Zhang, H.: Moving target network defense effectiveness evaluation based on change-point detection. Math. Probl. Eng. **2016**, 1–11 (2016). Article ID 6391502
5. Xu, J., Guo, P., Zhao, M., et al.: Comparing different moving target defense techniques. In: Proceedings of the 2014 ACM SIGSAC Conference on Computer and Communications Security, Scottsdale, Arizona, pp. 97–107 (2014)

6. Al-Shaer, E.: Toward network configuration randomization for moving target defense. In: Jajodia, S., Ghosh, A.K., Swarup, V., Wang, C., Sean Wang, X. (eds.) Moving Target Defense, pp. 153–159. Springer, New York (2011)

7. Atighetchi, M., Pal, P., Webber, F., et al.: Adaptive use of network-centric mechanisms in cyber-defense. In: Sixth IEEE International Symposium on Object-Oriented Real-Time Distributed Computing, pp. 183–192. IEEE (2003)

8. Lee, H.C.J., Thing, V.L.L.: Port hopping for resilient networks. In: 2004 IEEE 60th Vehicular Technology Conference, VTC 2004-Fall, vol. 5, pp. 3291–3295. IEEE (2004)

9. Dunlop, M., Groat, S., Urbanski, W., et al.: MT6D: a moving target IPv6 defense. In: Military Communications Conference, 2011-Milcom, pp. 1321–1326. IEEE (2011)

10. Hari, K., Dohi, T.: Dependability modeling and analysis of random port hopping. In: 2012 9th International Conference on Ubiquitous Intelligence & Computing and 9th International Conference on Autonomic & Trusted Computing (UIC/ATC), pp. 586–593. IEEE (2012)

11. Lin, K., Jia, C.F., Shi, L.Y.: Improvement of distributed timestamp synchronization. J. Commun. **33**(10), 110–116 (2012)

12. Malathi, P.: Mitigating distributed denial of service attacks in multiparty applications in the presence of clock drifts. In: 2013 Fourth International Conference on Computing, Communications and Networking Technologies (ICCCNT), pp. 1–6. IEEE (2013)

13. Kirkpatrick, K.: Software-defined networking. Commun. ACM **56**(9), 16–19 (2013)

14. Antonatos, S., Akritidis, P., Markatos, E.P., et al.: Defending against hitlist worms using network address space randomization. Comput. Netw. **51**(12), 3471–3490 (2007)

15. Yackoski, J., Xie, P., Bullen, H., et al.: A self-shielding dynamic network architecture. In: Military Communications Conference, 2011-MILCOM, pp. 1381–1386. IEEE (2011)

16. Jafarian, J.H., Al-Shaer, E., Duan, Q.: Openflow random host mutation: transparent moving target defense using software defined networking. In: Proceedings of the First Workshop on Hot Topics in Software Defined Networks, pp. 127–132. ACM (2012)

17. Jafarian, J.H.H., Al-Shaer, E., Duan, Q.: Spatio-temporal address mutation for proactive cyber agility against sophisticated attackers. In: Proceedings of the First ACM Workshop on Moving Target Defense, pp. 69–78. ACM (2014)

18. Bjner, N., De Moura, L.: Z310: applications, enablers, challenges and directions. In: Sixth International Workshop on Constraints in Formal Verification (2009)

19. Ma, L.B., Li, X., Zhang, L.: On modeling and deploying an effective scan monitoring system. J. Softw. **20**(4), 845–857 (2009)

20. Ma, D., Xu, Z., Lin, D.: Defending blind DDoS attack on SDN based on moving target defense. In: Tian, J., Jing, J., Srivatsa, M. (eds.) SecureComm 2014. LNICSSITE, vol. 152, pp. 463–480. Springer, Heidelberg (2015). doi:10.1007/978-3-319-23829-6_32

21. Wang, Y., Wen, S., Xiang, Y., et al.: Modeling the propagation of worms in networks: a survey. IEEE Commun. Surv. Tutor. **16**(2), 942–960 (2014)

22. Badishi, G., Herzberg, A., Keidar, I.: Keeping denial-of-service attackers in the dark. IEEE Trans. Dependable Secur. Comput. **4**(3), 191–204 (2007)

23. Zhao, C.L., Jia, C.F., Weng, C., et al.: Research on adaptive strategies for end-hopping system. J. Commun. **32**(11A), 7–57 (2013)

24. Sibson, R.: Information radius. Zeitschrift f Wahrscheinlichkeitstheorie und ver-wandte Gebiete **14**(2), 149–160 (1969)

25. Yu, S., Thapngam, T., Liu, J., et al.: Discriminating DDoS flows from flash crowds using information distance. In: Third International Conference on Network and System Security, NSS 2009, pp. 351–356. IEEE (2009)

26. Kar, K., Kodialam, M., Lakshman, T.V., Tassiulas, L.: Routing for network capac-ity maximization in energy-constrained ad hoc networks. In: Proceedings of INFO-COM (2003)

27. Huang, M., Liang, W., Xu, Z., et al.: Dynamic routing for network throughput maximization in software-defined networks. In: IEEE INFOCOM The 35th Annual IEEE International Conference on Computer Communications, pp. 978–986. IEEE (2016)

28. Peng, B., Kemp, A.H., Boussakta, S.: QoS routing with bandwidth and hop-count consideration: a performance perspective. J. Commun. **1**(2), 1–11 (2006)

29. Carroll, T.E., Crouse, M., Fulp, E.W., et al.: Analysis of network address shuffling as a moving target defense. 2014 IEEE International Conference on Communica-tions (ICC), pp. 701–706. IEEE (2014)

Research on Security Algorithm of Virtual Machine Live Migration for KVM Virtualization System

Wei Fan[1], Zhujun Zhang[1(✉)], Tingting Wang[1], Bo Hu[1],
Sihan Qing[1,2,3], and Degang Sun[1]

[1] Institute of Information Engineering,
Chinese Academy of Sciences, Beijing, China
{fanwei,zhangzhujun,wangtingting9071,
hubo,qsihan,sundegang}@iie.ac.cn
[2] Institute of Software, Chinese Academy of Sciences, Beijing, China
[3] School of Software and Microelectronics, Peking University, Beijing, China

Abstract. Live migration of virtual machine is the process of moving VMs from one physical server to another server keeping services running in VMs, and facilitates load balancing, energy saving, hardware dependent, remote migration and so on. This novel technology brings a huge convenience, and also presents new security challenges that the security concern is the major factor effecting this technology widely adopted in IT industry. Live migration exposes VM's data as plaintext to the network as a result of vulnerabilities in the migration protocol. The traditional protection way is using the SSL protocol, but that consume too much time and not as safe as it used to be, few users adopt this way. So we design a security algorithm based original migration algorithm making up for the lack of security. In this paper, firstly, we analyze and verify security threats to live migration. Secondly, through the analysis on the live migration mechanism, the bottom driver, and the source code of KVM virtualization system, we design a security algorithm for live migration to meet the security needs of different users. Thirdly, the new security algorithm which we innovatively add three functions to the original algorithm to ensure migration data to remain confidential and unmodified during the transmission. The security algorithm make up the security vulnerabilities of original migration mechanism and take less time than the SSL. Finally, a series of experiments validate the algorithm that could solve the balance of the security and performance in live migration process.

Keywords: Live migration · Security threats · Security algorithm · KVM virtualization system

1 Introduction

Cloud computing is increasingly assuming a prominent and leading role in businesses for the purpose of operational efficiency and cost reduction. As the foundations of cloud computing, virtualization allows many OS instances to run concurrently on a single physical machine with high performance, providing better use of physical

© Springer International Publishing AG 2016
K.-Y. Lam et al. (Eds.): ICICS 2016, LNCS 9977, pp. 54–70, 2016.
DOI: 10.1007/978-3-319-50011-9_5

resources and isolating individual OS instances [1]. It has attracted considerable interest in recent years, particularity from the data center and cluster computing communities [2]. It consolidates many physical servers into a single physical server saving the hardware resources, physical space, power consumption, air conditioning capacity and man power to manage the servers [3, 4]. VM (Virtual machine) migration means to move a VM from one host to another. The migration of virtual machine is divided into two types, Static Migration and Live Migration.

Static Migration is the process of virtual machine in shutdown or suspended state from one physical server to another physical server.

Live Migration is the transition of a running VM from one physical server to another without halting the VM. Provided the service uninterruptedly is a key requirement to many applications, live migration is usually used to achieve load balancing, energy efficiency, and easy hardware maintenances. In spite of the numerous benefits, users remain anxious about migration security and data protection over time [5]. There are many security problems in live migration process, one of which is that the VM data as plaintext could be sniffed easily during the migration [6, 7]. Because of security concerns, banking, government and national defense hesitate to make use of live migration. The generally way to solve this problem is using the SSL protocol, in addition to that takes too much time and is not as safe as it used to be, then users seldom adopt this way. So how to ensure data security of VM during live migration is the main topic of this paper.

We innovatively propose a security algorithm to guarantee the security of live migration for the KVM (Kernel-based Virtual Machine) virtualization platform. It has following four characteristics:

(1) It is designed based on KVM source code, instead of using cryptographic protocols to provide communication security over network, promoting the development of secure live migration mechanism.
(2) It narrows the encoded data range, only encoding users' sensitive data, reducing the consumption in secure live migration process.
(3) It is implemented by three functions, the special highlight is that the security function using different encoding algorithms to meet the security and performance requirements for different users.
(4) It is satisfactory to security and performance.

The rest of this paper is organized as follows. Section 2 introduces the related work. Section 3 presents the security algorithm in detail. Section 4 verifies the security algorithm from security and performance. Section 5 concludes our work.

2 Related Work

2.1 Security Threats in Live Migration

Most of the virtualization technologies now support live migration, such as Xen, KVM, VMware's VMotion. Unfortunately, they all have vulnerabilities in live migration process. There are approaches from both academia and industry that cover insecure live migration from different perceptions. Jon Oberheide et al. [8] in 2008 analyzed live migration threats from three layers, VMM (Virtual Machine Monitor) control layer, data layer and migration module layer. For example, an attacker could gain access to the transmission channel using techniques such as ARP/DHCP poisoning, DNS poisoning and IP/route hijaking to perform passive or active attacks. He designed the Xensploit tool which could automatically or manually to manipulate data in the Man-in-the-middle attack during a live VM migration process. This tool tampered with system's memory data of migrated VM, verifying that these attack strategies could be exploited in the XEN and VMware virtualization platform. Ms. Yamuna Devi. L researched on security in VM live migration and implemented live migration experiments in the KVM virtualization platform [9], which was also easy for attackers to hijack the live migrate process or hypervisor where these migrations occur. But there is no concrete implementation process to confirm this conclusion. Fan Wei [10] in 2014 ever captured memory data on live migration further proves the existence of security threats only in XEN and VMware Virtualization platform. As a kind of special information assets in the computer system, VM in security problems of live migration could be summarized as the following three aspects:

- Insecure communication channel

One of the VM migration protocol vulnerabilities is that migration data is plaintext over the network. If attacker was monitoring transmission channel, migration data would be accessed or even modified. By listening to the network between the source and the target server, the attacker could get the user's application data, user's password and other sensitive information [11]. Attackers also could modify the VM memory to specific data making the virtual machine under their control [12].

- Lack of access control strategies

An inappropriate access control strategy allows an unauthorized user to initiate, migrate and terminate a virtual machine. The attacker could initiate large numbers of outgoing migrations onto a legitimate virtualized host server [13], consuming server resources, decreasing its performance and even causing denial of service. Attackers also could transfer a VM with malware, Trojan horses or malicious code, to attack target server or other VMs on the target server. Attackers also could cause VMs to migrate from one server to another affecting the normal operation of VM or transfer a VM to an unauthentic host [14, 15].

- Vulnerabilities in virtualization software

There are vulnerabilities as stack, heap and integer overflows in the virtualization platform as common software [16–18]. Such vulnerabilities provide attackers the opportunity to inject malicious code breaking confidentiality, integrity and availability of other VM's code or data. Once the attacker successfully gains access to hypervisor through exploiting vulnerabilities, then the attacker will take control of the migration of VM.

2.2 Simulation Attack Experiments

• The attacker model

We assume a realistic attacker model where an attacker not only has access to network data but could also modify or inject messages into the network. We also assume that he is computationally bounded and hence, brute force attacks on cryptographic schemes are difficult. We still assume that the attacker does not have physical access to platforms between which the migration occurs.

• Attack Principle

The VM data must be transferred through network, and as this paper mentioned before, the transmission channel is insecurely, the migration functionality exposes the entire machine state of VM to device module which listens to the incoming live migration requests from remote platforms. So we assume that attackers could monitor the transmission channel to get sensitive data and modify the transmitted data. This way is not only easy to implement but also the attacker frequently used, so we set port mirroring on the switch which is the bridge of the two connected host to eavesdrop on sensitive data of VM, simulating attack process and verifying the threat of leaking sensitive information during live migration process.

• Experimental Design

The experiment is designed as Fig. 1, the same CPU type hosts both running QEMU-KVM released 1.5.3. Guest 1, Guest 2 and Guest 3 are the VM. Host1 and Host2 both are the Lenovo K4450 with Intel(R) Core i7 CPU and 8G RAM. The switch is H3C S1526. Because storage migration requires a lot of time, we migrate Guest 2 based on NFS shared storage. Only memory data and CPU status need to be transferred from the host1 to the host2. We use the software to sniff the whole transport channel.

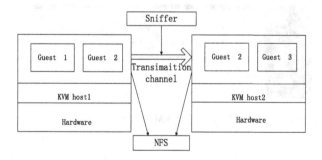

Fig. 1. Experimental structure.

• Results and Analysis

Scenario 1: Start a virtual machine configured for Linux OS, log into the system with the ordinary user "iie", and switch the user of the system with the "root" user, the password is "centospassword". Then migrating this VM to another host. Figure 2 shows the state of VM before migration. Figure 3 shows the analysis of the captured data packets.

Figures 2 and 3 show that the Linux root user's password is quite dangerous on the condition of VM being migrated, which means that attackers could get the root password of the Linux system during the live migration as well as the general user's password. Attackers could use password to do illegal things causing more serious security risks.

Scenario 2: Open the Notepad software of Windows OS, input some characters and numbers, and save the file and start migrating.

Fig. 2. The VM state no. 1

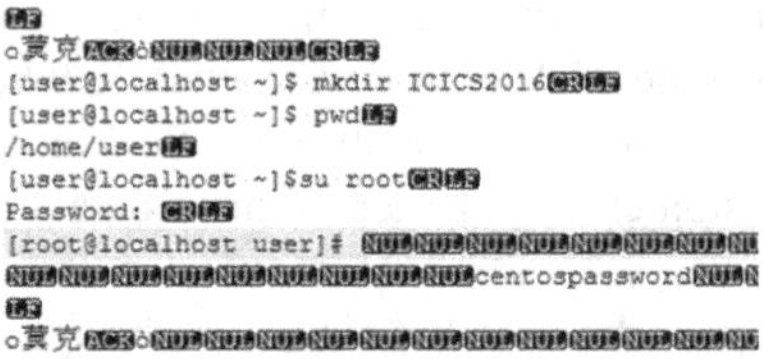

Fig. 3. The analysis of the captured data packets no. 1.

From Figs. 4 and 5, we could see that attackers could get all the data being used by applications of VM during the live migration.

The analyses imply that the vulnerability of live migration do exist which attackers could get sensitive data of VM during live migration process whatever the OS of VM.

Fig. 4. The VM state no. 2.

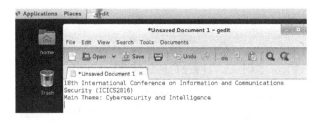

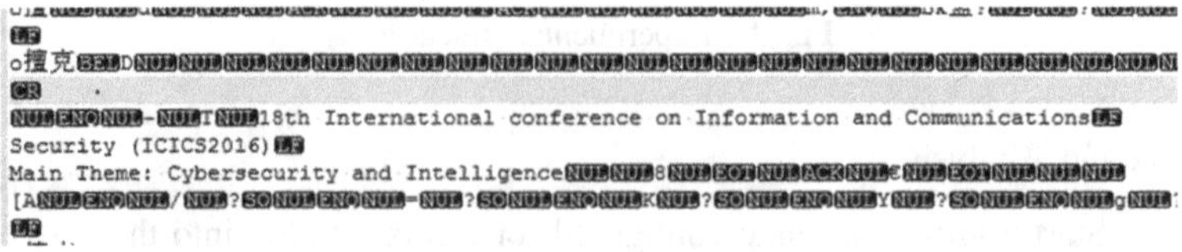

Fig. 5. The analysis of the captured data packets no. 2.

3 Proposed the Security Algorithm

The SSL protocol is adopted to protect VM data security during live migration process. But this way requires a lot of time and not applied to high service requirements conditions. Besides, many vulnerabilities in SSL have been found [19], which means that it is no longer secure as before. In order to improve the security of migration mechanism, and achieve the balance of performance and security, we extraordinarily present a security algorithm based on the source code.

We analyze codes and algorithm about live migration for QEMU-KVM released 1.5.3., which could be summarized as follows:

Stage 0: Pre-migration. There is an active VM on source physical host A. The source informs destination B to start reserving resources.

Stage 1: Iterative Pre-copy. During the first iteration, all pages are set dirty and transferred from A to B. Subsequent iterations only copy those pages dirtied during the previous transfer phase.

Stage 2: Stop-and-Copy. In this phase, CPU state and any remaining inconsistent memory pages are then transferred. At the end of this stage there is a consistent suspended copy of the VM at both A and B. The VM related network is redirected to target B through unsolicited ARP reply adverting.

3.1 Security Algorithms Design

- Performance improvement

The measurement of virtual machine migration efficiency is generally from the following several aspects:

(1) Total time: the time required of VM migrating from the source host to the destination host and resuming it.
(2) Service downtime: VM on the source host or on the destination host is out of service in the migration process. During this time VM on the source host has to stop the service, while VM on the destination host has not been restored.
(3) The impact on the performance of services: contains the performance of the VM application, and the performance of other services (or other VMs) on the host server during the migration process.

The most fundamental factor influencing migration efficiency is the amount of data to be transmitted. The SSL protocol is the only existing way for migration protection that all the VM data must be encrypted, which greatly increases the migration time.

Memory data is the most important part of transferred data. In order to resist the threat of insecure communication channel and reduce time cost, we only choose to protect VMs' sensitive memory data. The memory of Linux operating system includes kernel space and user space, while the memory of windows operating system includes user space and system space. It can be distinguishing from each other by the characteristic of memory. The contents of kernel memory are always the same system information in different VM. However, privacy data currently being processed by the user is within the user memory space, so we especially focus on the confidentiality of the user space data and the integrity of the system space data, reducing the time cost in secure live migration, ensuring the security of the private data at the same time.

Hypervisor, also known as VMM, manages the several virtual machines placed on a single hardware [20], could access all physical devices on the server. It is responsible for creating the virtual environment on which the guest virtual machines operate. It supervises the guest systems and makes sure resources are allocated to the guests as necessary [21]. All guest software (including the guest OS) runs in user mode; only the VMM runs in the most privileged level (kernel mode) [22]. Due to the particularity of its role, it is not only the favorite attack target, but also the important part that security professionals adopt a lot of defensive measures to protect. If this part was not secure, the security of VMs or other service could not be guaranteed. In another word, VMM could be considered the most secure part of virtual system. All the VM relevant data must go through VMM during the VM migration. If encryption is done at the VMM level, there would be less overhead, less downtime [23]. So the design of security algorithms is based on the secure VMM that security professionals have guaranteed its security from other aspects. The monitoring function is designed to monitor the memory data needing to be protected, then call the security function to encode.

- Security improvement

This part is the most important part of the security algorithm. In order to prevent attackers from illegally getting plaintext of VM and modifying on purpose, we present security algorithm applied in source host and destination host from confidentiality and integrity:

- **Algorithm principle**

In order to allow the attacker not to get sensitive data, and ensure the speed of the migration, we design an encoding algorithms for VM user space and also adopt timestamp mechanism to avoid reply attack.

The RC4 algorithm is a typical stream cipher based on nonlinear transform of array, applied on the SSL protocol to protect Internet information flow. It is based on Key-scheduling algorithm (KSA) and Pseudo-random generation algorithm (PRGA). The secret key length is within 1–256 bytes, then the possibility of the secret key is $256 + 256^2 + 256^3 + \ldots 256^{256} \approx 256^{256}$ kind's possibilities more than 10^{600}. Its simplicity and speed make it more suitable for live migration. However, the fatal weakness of RC4, which is that secret key being used for a long time, may cause attackers frequency analysis and crack, so we propose this new algorithm combined with the RC4 using different seed secret keys in each iteration of live migration. Assuming that each VM migration needs n times memory iterations, this algorithm makes the source data have 2^{2048n} conversion forms. As Fig. 6 shows the migration iteration timeline, Round n is the nth of migration iteration, State 1 is the memory state of Round n, Round n + 1 is the (n + 1)th of migration iteration, State 2 is the memory state of Round n + 1, ③page and ④page are the new dirty pages during Round nth iteration. At this moment, this algorithm checks whether ③page and ④page belong to user's space. If any pages belong to user's space, secret key function we designed will generate seed key to encode these pages with RC4 as Fig. 7 shows. So are the other iterations. The Key in Fig. 7 is the seed secret key generated in each iterations by secret key function. This algorithm make use of IV (Initialization Vector) and Key generated Stream by PRNG (Pseudo Random Noise Generation). Using multiple keys in each migration destroys the law of encoded data, and makes the attacker analyze and crack more difficult. Moreover it narrows down the field of data need to be encoded, making it is remarkable that this algorithm reaches a high level of security and takes shorter time than using SSL.

The encryption process can be concluded in three steps as follows:

a. Calculating the checksum: set message as M, CRC (Cyclical Redundancy Check) checksum for M as C (M), get the plaintext P = <M, C (M)>;
b. Data encryption: set the initial vector as v, key as k, the key sequence as RC4 (v, k), get cipher text C = P $\oplus$ RC4 (v, k);
c. Data transmission: in the end, the IV and cipher text transmitted through net. Figure 8 shows the specific encryption process.

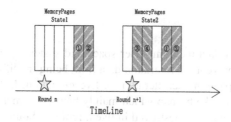

Fig. 6. The migration iteration TimeLine.

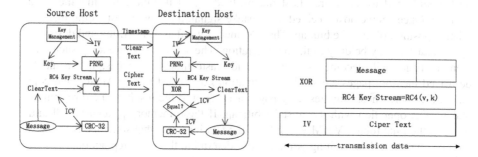

Fig. 7. The entire algorithm implementation process.   **Fig. 8.** The specific encryption process.

The decryption process can be concluded in two steps as follows:

a. The decryption process is the reverse of encryption process. The receiver generates key according to the received Timestamp. Then, the receiver could generate the same key sequence RC4(v,k). The cipher text make XOR operation with RC4(v,k) getting the plaintext.

b. Integrity checking. Decomposing P into <M, C>, recalculate the checksum C (M)' compared with the received C(M). Only are they equal to each other, this data frame can be regarded as effective, therefore ensure the integrity of the data frame.

- **Confidentiality**

To ensure the receiver to generate the same seed secret key, the secret key function in source host generates random numbers and public key according to the current time firstly. Random numbers are used as the seed secret key for encoding and public key is used for encoding the hash value. Then source host sends this time as Timestamp to the destination host, if the time is acceptable, the destination host would generate random numbers and public key based on the received time, because of the same secret key generation mechanism, destination host could generate same random numbers and public key for decoding. Similarly, for the next iteration, source host and destination host generates the same secret key according to their current time. Therefore, live migration uses different key in each iteration ensuring VM data to have higher confidentiality.

- **Integrity**

To prevent the VM data including user space and system space from being modified, we add CRC to prevent the migration data from being modified. The dirty bitmap is used to mark dirty page in each iteration of live migration. In the integrity mechanism, we present the mistake bitmap which mainly be used to mark the memory pages that the attacker has changed or destroyed in live migration. Source host calculates data hash value, uses public key to encode, and the destination host uses public key to decode the hash value confirming data integrity, if data had been modified, destination host would send to the source host the mistake signal including the modified data position. Once source host received the mistake signal, the source host would mark on relative position of mistake bitmap. The VM memory, often be rewriting and destroyed by the attacker may be dirty in the next iteration. The source host resending such dirty memory pages will become meaningless and waste time, so we design that all the destroyed memory pages are send to destination host at last round. At stop-and-copy phase, the source host migrates dirty pages according to the result of the dirty bitmap making OR operation with the mistake bitmap. If these memory pages are still tampered in the final round, VMM will inform the administrator that someone is trying to modify migration data, waiting administrator determine the next step action.

3.2   Main Algorithm Functions

This secure algorithm is mainly implemented through adding three functions to the traditional migration mechanism, called monitor function, secret key function and security function.

- Monitor Function

This function mainly narrows the range of VM data needed to encode or decode by monitoring the transmitted data. In source host, this function calculate the VM data including user space and system space, and monitor the data belonging to the user space. Once the data belong to the user space, it calls the security function. In destination host, this function monitors the received VM data whether have been encoded. When the data has been encoded, it calls the security function.

- Secret Key Function

This function mainly generates seed keys and public keys in each iteration. Time is one of the influencing factors for generating the seed secret key. The seed secret key is the core for encode and decode. In source host, security function uses seed secret keys for encoding VM data and its hash value. In destination host, security function uses this seed secret for decoding VM data and its hash value.

- Security Function

This function mainly uses optimized RC4 for encoding or decoding. In source host, this function encodes the calculated hash value and VM data, then sends encoded data and timestamp to destination. In destination host, this function compares the time of timestamp with current time and judges whether the received time belongs to the acceptable range. If time was illegal, destination host would stop migration process and send attacked signals. If time was legal, destination host would decode received data of user space and calculate all the received data hash value. If hash values were different, destination host would skip this memory page and send mistake signal, if hash values were same, destination host would put these data in right place.

3.3   Specific Algorithm Process

Although the security algorithm is based on the original algorithm, its process is more or less different from the original algorithm. Specific process is shown in Fig. 9.

The algorithm process at source host is summarized as follows:

(1) After the source host establishes connection with destination, initials mistake bitmap and other migration related parameters.
(2) Secret key function generates the seed secret key, and saves this time as timestamp.
(3) Monitor function monitors VM memory data. If this memory page was sensitive, call the security function, if not, its contents would be copied to the QEMU file waiting to be sent.
(4) Security function calculates the hash values of memory data, and encodes sensitive data and its hash value using the seed secret key. Then the encoded data will be copied to QEMU file waiting to be sent.
(5) If source host received the mistake signal during live migration process, source host would make marks on the mistake bitmap in the corresponding position. In the last stage, source host transmits dirty memory pages according to the result of

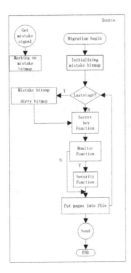
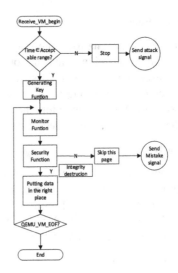

Fig. 9. Algorithm process at source.   **Fig. 10.** Algorithm process at destination

dirty bitmap making OR operation with mistake bitmap. If the last round migration data continued being destroyed, source host would stop migration, report that someone is trying to destroy this migration.

The algorithm process at destination host is shown in Fig. 10. The destination does the opposite operation to the source host. When destination host finds the page modified, host will skip this page and send mistake signal to source host. If the received time was unacceptable, host would stop this migration and report to the VM user.

3.4   Expectation

The security algorithm of this paper mainly improve the traditional migration mechanism from two aspects, one is the protection object, and the other one is the protection algorithm.

• Time complexity

Traditional protection method encrypts all of the VM data in transport layer or network layer to prevent attackers from eavesdropping or modifying, and this security algorithm narrows the range of data needing to be protected, reducing the time of security migration in the same time. Table 1 summarizes the parameters and notations used throughout this paper. Assume the migrating algorithm proceeds in n (n <= N) rounds. Let v_i (0 <= i <= n) denote the data volume transmitted at each pre-copying round, and t_i (0 <= i <= n) denote the elapsed time at each round. The data transmitted in round i is calculated in Eq. (1).

Table 1. Parameters for VM live migration modeling.

Symbol	Description
M	Size of VM memory image
M_u	Size of VM users' memory image
r	Network transmission rate during migration
d	Memory dirtying rate during migration
V_{thd}	Threshold of the remaining dirty memory that should be transferred during the stop-and-copy phase
N	The pre-defined maximum number of rounds for iterative pre-copying in migration algorithm
t_t	The time of generating Timestamp
t_k	The time of generating secret key
k_1	The factor of encryption speed of the new security algorithm

$$v_i = \begin{cases} M, & if\ i = 0; \\ d \cdot t_{i-1}, & otherwise. \end{cases} \tag{1}$$

The elapsed time at round i is calculated in Eq. (2).

$$t_i = \begin{cases} \frac{M}{r}, & if\ i = 0; \\ \frac{d \cdot t_{i-1}}{r}, & otherwise. \end{cases} \tag{2}$$

To evaluate the convergence rate of VM migration algorithm

We calculate the total number of rounds by the inequality $v_n < V_{thd}$. It is the condition to terminate the iterative pre-copying and to start the stop-and-copy phase. Furthermore, it should not be larger than the pre-defined parameter N. As a result, the number of pre-copying iterations becomes:

$$n = \min\left\{ \left\lceil \log \frac{V_{thd}}{M} \middle/ \log \frac{d}{r} \right\rceil |N \right\}. \tag{3}$$

For a given VM, M and V_{thd} (determined by migration algorithms) can be viewed as constants. Consequently, the iterative pre-copying would converge faster if d/r was smaller. Then define d/r as the convergence coefficient of VM live migration.

The data of the new security algorithm in round i is calculated in Eq. (4). M_u is smaller than M. The elapsed time of the new security algorithm at round i is calculated in Eq. (5).

$$v_i = \begin{cases} M_u, & if\ i = 0; \\ d \cdot t_{i-1}, & otherwise. \end{cases} \tag{4}$$

$$t_i = \begin{cases} \frac{M_u}{r} + t_t, & if\ i = 0; \\ k_1 \cdot \frac{d \cdot t_{i-1}}{r} + t_k, & otherwise. \end{cases} \tag{5}$$

- Anti-attack capability

  The new security algorithm could resist security attack types as follows:

  - Anti-Replay Attacks: Time is one of the influencing factors for generating the seed secret key. Once the received timestamp was illegal, destination host would refuse to accept the VM data leading attacker to fail.
  - Anti-Eavesdrop: The insecure and unprotected transmission channel is the result from vulnerabilities of migration protocol. The migration protocol does not encrypt the data as it travels over the network, susceptible to Eavesdrop attack. This security algorithm makes attackers could not get plaintext of VM data, and uses a number of different keys leading to attackers harder to frequency analysis and crack.
  - Anti-modification: This security algorithm adds the integrity verification to the process of migration. Destination host checks the integrity of received data. If integrity was destroyed, destination host would notify the source host to send again, therefore modified data is useless.

The new security algorithm is designed based on KVM source code. In spite of this algorithm implemented based on RC4, it should be noted that the new algorithm use a number of different keys in every migration and never let keys exposure in the network. Hence it is impossible to crack unless the attacker knows the seed secret key generation mechanism. Besides it narrows down the field of data need to be encode, and add timestamp and integrity verification, ensuring the security of migrating data, meanwhile, guaranteeing the efficiency of migration. The security algorithm is a part of migration module in VMM layer which any users couldn't get into, thus ensuring the algorithm is secure. It only encodes user space data reducing the consumption of the secure live migration process. So the security algorithm guarantee the security of migrating VM and the acceptable migration time.

The focus of this article is the protection of vulnerabilities in live migration mechanism, which is based on the version of the VMM has owned the official security certification. Therefore, we put the monitoring module and security module on the VMM layer to ensure the security of the algorithm itself. The security problems of the VMM layer also is our research direction in the future.

4 Implementation and Evaluations

In order to evaluate the security algorithm, we verify it from perspective of functionality and performance by applying it to the KVM virtualization platform.

4.1 Function Verification

We have made a lot of experiments to test the security of VM data. One of them is that the user enters any characters through the Gedit editor in the Linux system, then migrates VM from the source host to the destination host.

The attacker could get the encoded data during normal migration, but attackers could not find the sensitive information when migrated VM protected by applying the new security algorithm. Due to the limited essay space, we don't show the results of these experiments one by one. As the new algorithm encodes the sensitive data, the sensitive data is messy code in transmit channel. The attacker is hard to distinguish the meaningful messy code from the messy code. The new algorithm fully achieves the expected security features.

4.2   Performance Verification

Migrations have executed a lot of times for evaluation purpose under the condition of the same load state. Performance evaluation is divided into three categories which are live migration without change (Normal), live migration with security algorithm based on improved RC4 (The new algorithm) and live migration with SSL implementation. As mentioned above, the measurement of virtual machine migration efficiency is generally from several aspects, total time, downtime and the impact on the performance of other services. So we make a comparison from three aspects, total time, downtime and peak CPU usage.

When migrating with the new security algorithm, it costs more time than normal migration, and less time than live migration with SSL implementation.

The usage of the new security algorithm makes downtime longer than normal, but its downtime is shorter than the way using the SSL protocol at the same time.

The higher CPU usage, the greater impact on other services' (or other VMs) performance on the host server. How much CPU overhead occurs is observed by measuring the peak CPU usage (%) during the live migration. In this experiment, the peak CPU usage is measured using the top command because it provides an ongoing look at the activities of processor in real time which is suitable as to measure and calculate the peak CPU usage during the migration. The peak CPU usage of the source host machine is calculated during the migration process. It is understood that security needs performance penalty. Live migration with SSL implementation requires the greatest CPU resource. By contrast, the new security algorithm is more acceptable.

Based on the results, SSL implementation probably meets the requirement for the secure live migration of virtual machines to some extent, consuming more CPU usage and longer migration time. We also test the traditional RC4 for migration encryption. RC4 takes less time than the new protection way. However, for the widespread of RC4, its cracked difficulty is far less than the theoretical value. Live migration based on the new security algorithm makes the balance of security and performance come true. It only takes very little time but increase index cracked difficulty than RC4.

4.3   Contrast and Summary

- Performance

The traditional protection way SSL have a significant impact on the total migration time [24]. The new security algorithm of this article is implemented by three functions and not brings as much burden as SSL to living migration. Compared to SSL, the security algorithm only encodes user space data, making migration more efficient. The new algorithm could guarantee the integrity and confidentiality of data which are based on the original migration mechanism.

- Security mechanism

SSL sessions consist of two phases, the SSL Handshaking Protocol and the Record Protocol, and the client and server agree on various parameters used to establish the connection's security. One of the SSL protocol weaknesses is that the selected encryption algorithm and key are transport through network in plain text. The attacker could modify encryption algorithm to weak one at this time. Leading to transported encrypted packets may be cracked easily. OpenSSL is an open source project that provides a robust, commercial-grade, and full-featured toolkit for the Transport Layer Security (TLS) and Secure Sockets Layer (SSL) protocols. Lately, the vulnerabilities (CVE-2016-0701) were released by OpenSSL official. In OpenSSL1.0.2, due to the program didn't correctly generate the prime number for the Diffie-Hellman protocol, remote attacker could use the vulnerability to obtain the encryption key and sensitive information. Besides, because the SSL protocol is widely adopted, more and more holes are discovered, its security level is no longer as high as the past. As stated earlier, the security algorithm is based on the migration algorithm, so source host firstly needs to transmit timestamp to destination host to notice of the secret key in this migration, the destination host timestamp verification mechanism could ensure the legitimacy of this migration preventing illegal tampering with the secret key or implementing replay attacks. Thus in this sense, the new security algorithm has higher security than SSL.

5 Conclusion

In this paper, we innovatively propose a security algorithm, using different seed secret keys in each iteration and checking the modified migration data at last round iteration, to strengthen the protection of user space data, and making up for the vulnerabilities in live migration protocol of KVM virtualization. The simulation experimental results demonstrate that the proposed algorithm ensures the confidentiality and integrity of migrated VM's data and cost less time than SSL implementation. In the future, we plan to develop a compression function to reduce the migration time in the security algorithm. Furthermore, we also intend to implement our approach to different versions of KVM virtualization systems to generalize findings and refinement of the work.

Acknowledgment. This work was supported by the National Natural Science Foundation of China (Grant No. 61502486; 61170282).

References

1. Barham, P., Dragovic, B., Fraser, K., Hand, S., Harris, T., Ho, A., Neugebauer, R., Pratt, I., Warfield, A.: Xen and the art of virtualization. In: Proceedings of the Nineteenth ACM Symposium on Operating Systems Principles (SOSP19), pp. 164–177. ACM Press (2003)
2. Clark, C., Fraser, K., Hand, S., Hansen, J.G., Jul, E., Limpach, C., Pratt, I., Warfield, A.: Live migration of virtual machines. In: Proceedings of NSDI, pp. 273–286. USENIX Association, Berkely (2005)
3. Padala, P., Zhu, X., Wang, Z., et al.: Performance evaluation of virtualization technologies for server consolidation. Virtualiz. VMware ESX Serv. 9, 161–196 (2007)
4. Murugesan, S.: Harnessing green IT: principles and practices. In: Proceeding of IT Professional, vol. 10, pp. 24–33. IEEE Computer Society (2008)
5. Djenna, A., Batouche, M.: Security problems in cloud infrastructure. In: The 2014 International Symposium on Networks, Computers and Communications, pp. 1–6. IEEE (2014)
6. Ristenpart, T., Tromer, E., Shacham, H., et al.: Hey, you, get off of my cloud: exploring information leakage in third-party compute clouds. In: CCS Conference, pp. 199–212 (2009)
7. Fan, W., Kong, B., Zhang, Z.J., Wang, T.T., Zhang, J., Huang, W.Q.: Security protection model on live migration for KVM virtualization. J. Softw. 27(6), 1402–1416 (2016). (in Chinese)
8. Oberheide, J., Cooke, E., Jahanian, F.: Empirical exploitation of live migration of virtual machines. In: Black Hat DC Briefings, Westin Washington DC City Center (2008)
9. Yamunadevi, L., Aruna, P., Sudha, D.D., et al.: Security in virtual machine live migration for KVM. In: 2011 International Conference on Process Automation, Control and Computing (PACC), pp. 1–6. IEEE (2011)
10. Fan, W., Huang, W.Q., Jiang, F., Liu, C., Lv, B., Wang, R.R.: Research on security of memory leakage in live migration based virtualization. In: Twenty-Fourth National Conference on Information Security (IS 2014), vol. 09, pp. 12–17 (2014)
11. Dawoud, W., Takouna, I., Meinel, C.: Infrastructure as a service security: challenges and solutions. In: The 7th International Conference on Informatics and Systems (INFOS), pp. 1–8 (2010)
12. Anala, M.R., Shetty, J., Shobha, G.: A framework for secure live migration of virtual machines. In: 2013 International Conference on IEEE Advances in Computing, Communications and Informatics (ICACCI), pp. 243–248 (2013)
13. Aiash, M., Mapp, G., Gemikonakli, O.: Secure live virtual machines migration: issues and solutions. In: 2014 28th International Conference on Advanced Information Networking and Applications Workshops (WAINA), pp. 160–165. IEEE Computer Society (2014)
14. Garfinkel, T., Rosenblum, M.: When virtual is harder than real: security challenges in virtual machine based computing environments. In: Workshop on Hot Topics in Operating Systems (2005)
15. Sun, D., Zhang, J., Fan, W., et al.: SPLM: security protection of live virtual machine migration in cloud computing. In: Proceedings of the 4th ACM International Workshop on Security in Cloud Computing, pp. 2–9. ACM (2016)
16. Ballani, H., Francis, P., Zhang, X.: A study of prefix hijacking and interception in the internet. ACM SIGCOMM Comput. Commun. Rev. 37(4), 265–276 (2007)
17. Zargar, S.T., Joshi, J., Tipper, D.: A survey of defense mechanisms against distributed denial of service (DDoS) flooding attacks. IEEE Commun. Surv. Tutor. 15(4), 2046–2069 (2013)
18. Cowan, C., Wagle, F., Pu, C., et al.: Buffer overflows: attacks and defenses for the vulnerability of the decade. In: Information Survivability Conference and Exposition (2000)

19. Wang, J., Yang, Y., Chen, L., Yang, G., Chen, Z., Wen, L.: A combination of timing attack and statistical method to reduce computational complexities of SSL/TLSside-channel attacks. In: 2015 11th International Conference on Computational Intelligence and Security (CIS) (2015)
20. Awasthi, A., Gupta, R.: Multiple hypervisor based open stack cloud and VM migration. In: 2016 6th International Conference - Cloud System and Big Data Engineering (Confluence), Noida, pp. 130–134 (2016)
21. Graziano, C.D.: A performance analysis of Xen and KVM hypervisors for hosting the Xen Worlds Project. Graduate Theses and Dissertations, Paper 12215 (2011)
22. King, S.T., Chen, P.M.: SubVirt: implementing malware with virtual machines. In: IEEE Symposium on Security & Privacy, pp. 314–327. IEEE (2006)
23. Ravi, P., Shah, P.H.: Security in live virtual machine migration. Wichita State Univ. 5(5), 31 (2011)
24. Hu, Y., et al.: Performance analysis of encryption in securing the live migration of virtual machines. In: 2015 IEEE 8th International Conference on Cloud Computing, New York City, NY, pp. 613–620 (2015)

Towards Efficient Re-encryption for Secure Client-Side Deduplication in Public Clouds

Lei Lei[1,2,3], Quanwei Cai[1,2], Bo Chen[4,5(✉)], and Jingqiang Lin[1,2,3]

[1] Institute of Information Engineering, Chinese Academy of Sciences, Beijing, China
{leilei,qwcai,linjq}@is.ac.cn
[2] Data Assurance and Communication Security Research Center,
Chinese Academy of Sciences, Beijing, China
[3] University of Chinese Academy of Sciences, Beijing, China
[4] Department of Computer Science, University of Memphis, Memphis, TN, USA
bchen2@memphis.edu
[5] Center for Information Assurance, University of Memphis, Memphis, TN, USA

Abstract. By only storing a unique copy of duplicated data possessed by different users, data deduplication can significantly reduce storage cost, and is thus used extensively in cloud storage. When combining with confidentiality, deduplication will become problematic as encryption performed by different users may differentiate identical data. MLE (Message-Locked Encryption) is thus utilized to derive the same encryption key for the identical data. As keys may be leaked and users may be revoked, re-encrypting the outsourced data is of paramount importance to ensure continuous confidentiality. This problem is unfortunately not well addressed in deduplication-based encrypted cloud storage.

In this paper, we design SEDER, a SEcure client-side Deduplication system for cloud storage enabling Efficient Re-encryption. A salient advantage of SEDER is that it allows data owners to efficiently re-encrypt the data to ensure continuous data confidentiality for cloud storage using client-side deduplication, by smartly leveraging all-or-nothing transform, proofs of ownership as well as delegated re-encryption. Experimental evaluation validates the efficiency of SEDER.

Keywords: Secure deduplication · Client-side deduplication · Re-encryption · Cloud storage

1 Introduction

Cloud storage services are widely deployed nowadays. Popular services include Amazon S3 [1], Apple iCloud [5] and Microsoft Azure [6]. By using cloud services, data owners pay for the storage they use, eliminating the expensive cost of maintaining dedicated infrastructures.

As more and more users turn to clouds for storage, the amount of data stored in the clouds grows rapidly. Conventionally, the clouds simply store what have been sent by the users. This unfortunately will lead to significant waste of storage space, as different users may upload identical data. A promising remediation

© Springer International Publishing AG 2016
K.-Y. Lam et al. (Eds.): ICICS 2016, LNCS 9977, pp. 71–84, 2016.
DOI: 10.1007/978-3-319-50011-9_6

is to perform data deduplication, in which the clouds only store a unique copy of duplicated data from different users to reduce the unnecessary waste of storage space. For example, recent research from Microsoft [34] showed that deduplication can achieve 50% and 90–95% storage savings in the standard file systems and backup systems, respectively. Almost all the existing popular file hosting services like Dropbox [4] and Box [2] perform data deduplication.

There are two popular data deduplicaiton mechanisms: server-side deduplication and client-side deduplication. The main difference between them lies in the location of deduplication. In server-side deduplication, servers transparently perform deduplication on the data outsourced by the clients. In client-side deduplication, however, the servers and the clients cooperate to perform deduplication. Compared to the server-side deduplication, the client-side deduplication has a significant benefit that the clients do not need to upload the data which have already stored by the servers, significantly reducing bandwidth consumption. Therefore, the client-side deduplication has been used extensively in the public file hosting services [2,4].

Encryption is necessary to protect confidentiality of sensitive data. However, it creates a severe obstacle for deduplicaiton, as identical plain-texts may be encrypted into different cipher-texts by different users using different keys. Message-Locked Encryption (MLE) [13] is a cryptographic primitive which can resolve the aforementioned issue. MLE can derive encryption keys from messages being encrypted, such that different users are able to generate the same key for the identical data. Existing MLE schemes include CE [23], DupLESS [12], Duan Scheme [24], and LAP scheme [33].

To ensure continuous data confidentiality for encrypted cloud storage, re-encryption seems unavoidable, due to the potential key exposure [3,8] or user revocation [39,41]. Compared to conventional encrypted cloud storage, re-encryption in deduplication-based cloud storage is much more challenging, as it needs to be performed in such a manner that deduplication should not be disturbed. Li et al. proposed REED [32] to address the re-encryption problem for deduplication-based storage systems by smartly transforming the encrypted data such that they can be efficiently re-encrypted when revoking keys/users. REED however is specifically designed for *server-side deduplication*, which is not immediately applicable to the more beneficial *client-side deduplication*.

To design a secure client-side deduplication system which supports efficient re-encryption, we face several challenges: (1) To conform to the notion of storage outsourcing, we usually outsource both the data and the management of data [16, 19], such that once the data have been outsourced, the client will be involved as little as possible. It is thus challenging to allow re-encryption with least client intervention. (2) Different from server-side deduplication, in which the client will always upload the data being outsourced, in client-side deduplication, the client will not upload the data when he/she convinces the cloud server that he/she possesses the data which have already been stored in the cloud, and the keys for decrypting these data will be disclosed to such clients after re-encryption. To ensure continuous confidentiality, we need a technique which can allow the cloud server to differentiate valid or invalid clients by efficiently verifying the possession of the file in the clients without being able to learn the plaintext of the file. (3) Considering the data stored in clouds are usually large in size, re-encrypting them may be prohibitively expensive. An efficient re-encryption approach is usually challenging.

In this paper, we propose SEDER, the first secure client-side deduplication system for cloud storage supporting efficient re-encryption. Our key insights are threefold: First, we leverage proofs of ownership (PoWs), by which we can ensure that after re-encryption, the new key is only disclosed to valid users who can prove they are the owners of the data. Second, we leverage all-or-nothing transform, by which it is possible to re-encrypt a file by only re-encrypting a small portion of it. Third, by observing that the existing proxy re-encryption can not be used in SEDER directly, we re-design a delegated re-encryption scheme, by which we can freely delegate the re-encryption to the cloud server without disclosing the plaintext data. This is advantageous as the client can be released from the burden of re-encryption and remains lightweight.

Comparison. Although both SEDER and REED [32] aim to address the re-encryption problem, they are different in multiple aspects: (1) REED resolves the re-encryption problem for server-side deduplication. However, SEDER resolves this problem for client-side deduplication, which has a more complicate design and hence a larger attack surface; (2) REED has very expensive computation/communication overhead for uploading files, as the client always needs to perform the expensive all-or-nothing transform and upload the file. In SEDER however, the amortized computation/communication overhead for uploading files is significantly reduced, as the clients do not need to perform the expensive all-or-nothing transform and upload the file if it exists in the cloud server; (3) In REED, the client is heavily involved in the re-encryption process which imposes significant burden on the client and contradicts with the notion of storage outsourcing. In SEDER however, the re-encryption is delegated to the cloud server who has rich computation resources, such that the client can always remain lightweight.

Contributions. We summarize our contributions in the following:

- We initiate the research of designing efficient re-encryption schemes for secure client-side deduplication in cloud storage.
- We design a delegated re-encryption scheme which can be used to delegate re-encryption to the untrusted third party. In addition, we design SEDER by smartly leveraging all-or-nothing transform (AONT), proofs of ownership (PoWs), and delegated re-encryption (DRE).
- We evaluate the performance of SEDER. Experimental results validate the efficiency of SEDER.

2   System and Adversarial Model

System Model. We consider two entities: (1) *Cloud server* (CS). CS provides storage services and wants to perform client-side deduplication to reduce both storage and bandwidth cost; (2) *Cloud users* (U). The users outsource their data to the cloud. To maintain confidentiality of their outsourced data, they will encrypt the data before outsourcing them. Note that when the cloud user tries to upload a file that has been stored in the cloud server, CS will append this cloud user to the owner list of the corresponding file without requiring uploading the file again.

Adversarial Model. We consider an honest-but-curious cloud server [39,41]. CS will honestly store the encrypted data uploaded by the users, perform data deduplication, and respond the requests from the users. Moreover, CS will not disclose the data to any parties who fail to prove ownership of the data. However, it is curious and attempts to infer information about the encrypted users' data. In addition, there is a malicious entity (ME) who has obtained the key materials and tries to have access to the sensitive data.

Assumptions. We assume the MLE used in SEDER is secure[1]. All the communication channels among the CS and U are protected by SSL/TLS, so that any eavesdroppers cannot infer the messages being transmitted. Each entity (CS and U) has an asymmetric key pair, and the private key is well protected. We also assume that CS and ME will not collude with each other.

3   Building Blocks

Message-Locked Encryption (MLE). MLE [13] is a cryptographic primitive which can derive encryption keys from messages being encrypted. In MLE scheme, different users are able to generate the same key for the identical data. Existing MLE schemes include CE [23], DupLESS [12], Duan Scheme [24], and LAP scheme [33]. MLE uses symmetric encryption to encrypt a message with its MLE key.

All-or-Nothing Transform (AONT). AONT [35] is an unkeyed, invertible and randomized transformation. No one can succeed to perform the inverse transformation without knowing the entire output of the AONT. Specifically, given message m of s-blocks: $m = m_1 || \ldots || m_s$ where $||$ denotes block concatenation, AONT transforms m into message m' of t-blocks: $m' = m'_1 || \ldots || m'_t$ where $t \geq s + 1$, and satisfies the following properties:

- Given m, $m' \leftarrow \mathsf{AONT}(m)$ can be computed efficiently. That is, the complexity of $\mathsf{AONT}(m)$ is polynomial to the length of m.
- Given m', $m \leftarrow \mathsf{AONT}^{-1}(m')$ can be computed efficiently.
- Without knowing the entire m' (i.e., if one block is missing), the probability of recovering m is negligibly small.

In this paper, we instantiate AONTwith the package transform [35], which takes input an s-block message m and outputs an $(s + 1)$-block message m'.

---

[1] The MLE has been well investigated in the literature, and we believe a secure MLE can be found and directly applied here.

Proofs of Ownership (PoWs). PoWs [26] is a cryptographic protocol that allows the cloud server (as a verifier) to efficiently and securely validate that the data owner (as a prover), who wants to upload the data file that has been already stored in the server, really possesses that data file. Here the efficiency means that the communication is far less than the bandwidth of uploading the data file, and the security means that the data owner cannot cheat the server in non-negligible probability even if he/she possesses a large portion of the file and its metadata (e.g., hash value).

- witness ← PoWs.Init(f): Given a data file f, the verifier first preprocesses it and obtains some auxiliary data witness for the verification purpose:
  - The verifier uses an α-erasure-code EC to encode the data file f, where α denotes the erasure recovery capability.
  - The verifier computes the Merkle tree $MT_{H,b}(f)$ of the data file f, where H is a hash function used in computing Merkle tree and b is the size of a Merkle-tree leaf. The root value of Merkle-tree $r_{MT}(f)$ will be witness.
- challenge ← PoWs.Challenge: When a prover declares that he/she owns a file f, the verifier chooses randomly x leaf indexes $l_1, l_2, ..., l_x$ and sends challenge $= (l_1, l_2, ..., l_x)$ to the prover, where ϵ is the soundness bound and x is the minimum integer satisfying $(1 - \alpha)^x < \epsilon$.
- prof ← PoWs.Prove($challenge, f$): The prover builds the Merkle tree on top of data file f and returns the proof prof which consists of the sibling-paths of $l_1, l_2, ..., l_x$.
- $\{0, 1\}$ ← PoWs.Verify(witness, challenge, prof): The verifier returns 1 if all the sibling-paths are valid with the Merkle tree root, and 0 otherwise.

4   SEDER

In this section, we first present a delegated re-encryption scheme (DRE) which allows to delegate re-encryption to an untrusted third party, and then elaborate the design of SEDER by leveraging DRE and other building blocks (Sect. 3).

4.1   Delegated Re-encryption

Proxy re-encryption (PRE) [14,27] allows a proxy to convert the ciphertext, which can only be decrypted by the delegator, into another ciphertext that can be decrypted by the delegatee, without leaking the plaintext to the proxy. Proxy re-encryption has been well studied and many promising features have been proposed, such as uni-direction, key privacy and no-interaction key generation. However, proxy re-encryption cannot be used here, because it cannot support unlimited hops. Based on the scheme [11] which only supports single hop, we re-design a delegable re-encryption scheme supporting unlimited hops (DRE). The detail of DRE is as follows:

- DRE.SetUp(1^ℓ): G is a multiplicative cyclic group of prime order q (q is an ℓ-bit system parameter, and ℓ is large enough). g is chosen from G at random and is known to all the parties.

- DRE.KeyGen(U_i): Given user U_i, this algorithm generates the public key $pk_i = \{g^{a_i}\}$ and $sk_i = \{a_i\}$, where a_i is chosen at random from $\mathbb{Z}_q$.
- DRE.Enc(pk_i, m): Message m is encrypted into $c_i = (c_{i_1}, c_{i_2}) = ((g^{a_i})^{k_i}, mg^{k_i})$, where k_i is chosen at random from $\mathbb{Z}_q$.
- DRE.ReKeyGen(sk_i, pk_j, c_{i_1}): Given user U_i's private key sk_i, user U_j's public key pk_j (note that by running PRE.KeyGen(U_j), U_j generates public key $pk_j = \{g^{a_j}\}$ and $sk_j = \{a_j\}$, where a_j is chosen at random from $\mathbb{Z}_q$) and c_{i_1}, the re-encryption key $rk_{i \to j}$ can be generated: $rk_{i \to j} = (rk_{i \to j_1}, rk_{i \to j_2}) = ((g^{a_j})^{k_j}, \frac{g^{k_j}}{(c_{i_1})^{1/a_i}})$, where k_j is randomly selected from $\mathbb{Z}_q$.
- DRE.ReEnc($rk_{i \to j}, c_i$): Given the re-encryption key $rk_{i \to j} = (rk_{i \to j_1}, rk_{i \to j_2})$, the proxy can re-encrypt the ciphertext $c_i = (c_{i_1}, c_{i_2})$ to c_j by computing: $c_j = (c_{j_1}, c_{j_2}) = (rk_{i \to j_1}, c_{i_2} rk_{i \to j_2})$.
- DRE.Dec(sk_j, c_j): Given the ciphertext $c_j = (c_{j_1}, c_{j_2})$, the user U_j decrypts it using $sk_j = \{a_j\}$ by computing: $m = \frac{c_{j_2}}{(c_{j_1})^{1/a_j}}$.

4.2   Design Rational of SEDER

SEDER contains several key designs: First, we use AONT and DRE together to support efficient re-encryption of the outsourced file. Specifically, given a file, we apply MLE, obtaining the MLE ciphertext. MLE ensures that the same ciphertext will be generated from different users if the file content is the same. Then AONT is applied to MLE ciphertext, generating a set of data blocks. Note that without fetching all the data blocks, the MLE ciphertext cannot be recovered thanks to the interesting property of AONT. In this way, to re-encrypt a data file, the data owner only needs to re-encrypt one data block, rather than all the data blocks. In addition, by leveraging DRE, we can delegate the re-encryption process to the untrusted cloud server, without leaking the plaintext of the file. This is advantageous as we can eliminate the burden on the client who is supposed to be kept lightweight.

Second, to ensure only the valid data owners are able to decrypt the data being re-encrypted, we perform the following: (1) We leverage proofs of ownership (PoWs) to distinguish valid and invalid data owners. A valid data owner for a file should be able to prove his/her ownership as he/she possesses the file. When a data owner passes the verification, the cloud server will add him/her to the owner list of the file. (2) The cloud user who re-encrypts the file will compute new assisting information that is required to decode the file being re-encrypted. The new assisting information will only be disclosed to the valid data owners. The malicious entity, even though have obtained the secret key, will not be able to pass the PoWs verification, and thus cannot obtain the new assisting information which is required to decode the re-encrypted file.

4.3   Design Details of SEDER

Let λ and β be the security parameter. Let π_{DRE} be a delegated re-encryption scheme, such that $\pi_{DRE} = (\pi_{DRE}.SetUp, \pi_{DRE}.KeyGen, \pi_{DRE}.Enc, \pi_{DRE}.ReKeyGen,$

$\pi_{DRE}.ReEnc$, $\pi_{DRE}.Dec$). π_{sym} is a symmetric encryption scheme such that $\pi_{sym} = (\pi_{sym}.KeyGen, \pi_{sym}.Enc, \pi_{sym}.Dec)$, and π_{asym} is an asymmetric encryption scheme such that $\pi_{asym} = (\pi_{asym}.KeyGen, \pi_{asym}.Enc, \pi_{asym}.Dec)$. Let H_1 be a cryptographic hash funciton: $H_1 : \{0,1\}^* \rightarrow \{0,1\}^\lambda$. In the following, we describe the design details of SEDER, which contains six phases: SetUp, PreUpload, Upload, Update, Download and Delete.

SetUp: This is to bootstrap the system parameters, and initialize cryptographic parameters for cloud users and cloud server. The system runs $\pi_{DRE}.SetUp(1^\beta)$ to initialize the system parameters. In addition,

- Cloud user U_i: He/She runs the key generation algorithm of asymmetric encryption scheme to generate the public/private key: $(\pi_{asym}.pk_{U_i}, \pi_{asym}.sk_{U_i}) \leftarrow \pi_{asym}.KeyGen(1^\beta)$.
- Cloud server: It runs the key generation algorithm of asymmetric encryption scheme to generate the public/private key: $(\pi_{asym}.pk_{CS}, \pi_{asym}.sk_{CS}) \leftarrow \pi_{asym}.KeyGen(1^\beta)$.

PreUpload: The PreUpload phase is run by the cloud user U_i before U_i uploads file f to the cloud. U_i uses MLE [12,13,23,24] to obtain the file key k_f for file f. MLE can ensure that different users are able to generate the same key for the same file content.

Upload: The Upload phase is run by U_i to upload file f. Note that U_i has obtained the file key k_f during the PreUpload phase. U_i encrypts f by running $ct = \pi_{sym}.Enc(k_f, f)$. U_i then computes a tag for f: $Tag_f = H_1(ct)$, and sends Tag_f to cloud server CS. CS proceeds as follows:

Case 1: Tag_f does not exist in the cloud server: In this case, the cloud user conducts the following operations and uploads the corresponding file to the cloud:

- Given ct, U_i runs PoWs.Init(ct) to generate the witness.
- Assume that the encrypted file ct consists of s blocks: $ct = ct_1||ct_2||... ct_s$. U_i first applies all-or-nothing transform on ct, generating $s+1$ blocks, such that $ct' \leftarrow AONT(ct)$ where $ct' = ct'_1||ct'_2||...||ct'_s||ct'_{s+1}$.
- U_i generates a pair of public/private key by applying $(\pi_{PRE}.pk_i, \pi_{PRE}.sk_i) \leftarrow \pi_{PRE}.KeyGen(U_i)$.
- U_i randomly selects a data block ct'_z from $ct'_1, \ldots, ct'_{s+1}$. Then U_i applies the delegated re-encryption scheme π_{PRE} to encrypt ct'_z into c, such that $c = (c_1, c_2) = \pi_{DRE}.Enc(\pi_{DRE}.pk_i, ct'_z)$. Therefore, the final ciphertext to be uploaded is: $ct_{Upload} = ct'_1||\cdots||ct'_{z-1}||c||ct'_{z+1}||\cdots||ct'_{s+1}$.
- Using file key k_f, U_i encrypts $\pi_{DRE}.sk_i$ using $\pi_{sym}.Enc$ such that $ct^*_{sym} = \pi_{sym}.Enc(k_f, \pi_{DRE}.sk_i)$.
- Using the cloud server's public key $\pi_{asym}.pk_{CS}$, U_i encrypts ct^*_{sym} such that $ct_{asym} = \pi_{asym}.Enc(pk_{CS}, ct^*_{sym})$.
- U_i uploads ct_{Upload}, witness, and ct_{asym}.

– After receiving the aforementioned information, CS organizes them in the format $< \mathsf{Tag}_f, \mathsf{ct}_{\mathsf{Upload}}, \mathsf{witness}, \mathsf{ct}_{\mathsf{asym}}, \text{user list } ul_{\mathsf{ct}_{\mathsf{Upload}}} >$. By decrypting $\mathsf{ct}_{\mathsf{asym}}$ using $\mathsf{sk}_{\mathsf{CS}}$, CS obtains the assisting information $\mathsf{ct}^*_{\mathsf{sym}}$, which will be distributed to valid cloud users in the following manner: encrypt $\mathsf{ct}^*_{\mathsf{sym}}$ using each user's public key and send the corresponding ciphertext to that user.

Case 2: Tag_f exists in the cloud server: To further confirm that U_i really possesses f, CS and U_i proceed as follows:

– CS runs PoWs.Challenge to generate a challenge which is sent to U_i.
– U_i computes a proof prof by running PoWs.Prove(challenge, ct).
– CS further runs PoWs.Verify(witness, challenge, prof). If the output is 1, CS appends u_i to the user list $ul_{\mathsf{ct}_{\mathsf{Upload}}}$ and sends the assisting information of file f to U_i. Otherwise, CS terminates.

<u>Update</u>: When a data owner finds his file key is compromised, he needs to re-encrypt the corresponding file and makes sure that other data owners of the file can decrypt the latest ciphertext of the file. Thanks to AONT we only need to re-encrypt the encrypted block c rather than the entire outsourced file. Note that $c = (c_1, c_2)$, and c_1 is also sent to cloud users when CS distributes the assisting information $\mathsf{ct}^*_{\mathsf{sym}}$. The Upload phase is performed between cloud user U_j (who is on the user list of file f) and CS. The phase proceeds as:

– U_j runs DRE.KeyGen(U_j) to generate a pair of public/private key, namely $(\mathsf{DRE.pk}_j, \mathsf{DRE.sk}_j) \leftarrow \mathsf{DRE.KeyGen}(\mathsf{U}_j)$.
– U_j decrypts $\mathsf{ct}^*_{\mathsf{sym}}$ using k_f, obtaining $\mathsf{DRE.sk}_i$.
– Using $\mathsf{DRE.sk}_i, c_1$ and $\mathsf{DRE.pk}_j$, U_j generates the delegable re-encryption key $rk_{i\rightarrow j} \leftarrow \mathsf{DRE.ReKeyGen}(\mathsf{DRE.sk}_i, \mathsf{DRE.pk}_j, c_1)$.
– Using k_f, U_j encrypts $\pi_{\mathsf{DRE}}.\mathsf{sk}_j$: $\mathsf{ct}^{\#}_{\mathsf{sym}} = \pi_{\mathsf{sym}}.\mathsf{Enc}(k_f, \pi_{\mathsf{DRE}}.\mathsf{sk}_j)$.
– Using $\pi_{\mathsf{asym}}.\mathsf{pk}_{\mathsf{CS}}$, U_j encrypts $\mathsf{ct}^{\#}_{\mathsf{sym}}$: $\mathsf{ct}'_{\mathsf{asym}} = \pi_{\mathsf{asym}}.\mathsf{Enc}(\mathsf{pk}_{\mathsf{CS}}, \mathsf{ct}^{\#}_{\mathsf{sym}})$.
– U_j sends $\mathsf{ct}'_{\mathsf{asym}}$ and $rk_{i\rightarrow j}$ to CS.
– CS runs $c' \leftarrow \pi_{\mathsf{DRE}}.\mathsf{ReEnc}(rk_{i\rightarrow j}, c)$ and replaces c with c'. In addition, CS replaces $\mathsf{ct}_{\mathsf{asym}}$ with $\mathsf{ct}'_{\mathsf{asym}}$, decrypts $\mathsf{ct}'_{\mathsf{asym}}$ obtaining $\mathsf{ct}^{\#}_{\mathsf{sym}}$, and distributes $\mathsf{ct}^{\#}_{\mathsf{sym}}$ to the users on the user list $ul_{\mathsf{ct}_{\mathsf{Upload}}}$.

<u>Download</u>: If user U_i wants to download $\mathsf{ct}_{\mathsf{Upload}}$ from the cloud server, U_i will send a download request $(Tag_f, download)$ to CS. When CS receives the request, CS returns $\mathsf{ct}_{\mathsf{Upload}}$ to the requestor. U_i uses the file key and the assisting information to decode $\mathsf{ct}_{\mathsf{Upload}}$.

<u>Delete</u>: When CS receives a delete request $(Tag_f, delete)$ from user U_i, CS will delete U_i from $ul_{\mathsf{ct}_{\mathsf{Upload}}}$. If $ul_{\mathsf{ct}_{\mathsf{Upload}}}$ turns empty, CS will delete $\mathsf{ct}_{\mathsf{Upload}}$.

5   Security Analysis and Discussion

5.1   Security Analysis

Correctness and Security of DRE. When receiving the ciphertext c_j, U_j can successfully decrypt it as follows:

$$\frac{c_{j_2}}{(c_{j_1})^{1/a_j}} = \frac{c_{i_2} rk_{i \to j_2}}{(rk_{i \to j_1})^{1/a_j}} = \frac{c_{i_2}\left(\frac{g^{k_j}}{(c_{i_1})^{1/a_i}}\right)}{((g^{a_j})^{k_j})^{1/a_j}} = \frac{mg^{k_i}\left(\frac{g^{k_j}}{((g^{a_i})^{k_i})^{1/a_i}}\right)}{g^{k_j}} = \frac{mg^{k_j}}{g^{k_j}} = m.$$

In addition, by knowing g, user U_i's public key g^{a_i} and user U_j's public key g^{a_j}, the proxy cannot learn anything about plaintext m by observing: (1) $c_i = (c_{i_1}, c_{i_2}) = ((g^{a_i})^{k_i}, mg^{k_i})$; and (2) $rk_{i \to j} = (rk_{i \to j_1}, rk_{i \to j_2}) = ((g^{a_j})^{k_j}, \frac{g^{k_j}}{(c_{i_1})^{1/a_i}}) = ((g^{a_j})^{k_j}, \frac{g^{k_j}}{g^{k_i}})$, due to the hardness of discrete logarithm problem.

Data Confidentiality. In the following, we show that cloud server CS and the malicious entity ME are not able to learn the plaintext of the encrypted data.

CS possesses the following information: Tag_f, $\mathsf{ct_{Upload}}$, $\mathsf{ct^*_{sym}}$, $\mathsf{ct^\#_{sym}}$ and witness. Based on $\mathsf{ct_{Upload}}$, CS is not able to obtain ct, as it is not able to decrypt block c or c' (security of AONT). By knowing Tag_f, CS may try to learn ct which is computationally impossible. Even if CS can learn something about ct, without knowing the file key k_f, CS still cannot learn anything about the plaintext of the file. Also, as witness is computed from ct, it cannot help to learn the plaintext of the file. The users who really possess a file can prove their ownership of the corresponding file to CS. This ensures that only valid data owners can obtain the latest assisting information from CS and hence are able to recover the original file from $\mathsf{ct_{Upload}}$.

ME is not able to prove to CS the ownership of f, and is thus not able to obtain the new assisting information from CS. Upon having access to $\mathsf{ct_{Upload}}$, ME cannot use the old assisting information to decrypt the re-encrypted block c, and is thus not able to decode $\mathsf{ct_{Upload}}$ to obtain ct (security of AONT). Therefore, even if he/she can have access to the file key k_f, he/she is not able to obtain f.

5.2   Discussion

Zero-Day Attack. SEDER is vulnerable to the zero-day attack, in which the key is leaked and the re-encryption has not been performed. During this period, the adversary can have access to the original file using the obtained key materials. This seems to be unavoidable and we currently do not have a good solution for mitigating such a strong attack.

Supporting User Revocation. Considering the scenario that each data owner has a few users, and the data owner wants to revoke a certain user, which requires re-encrypting the outsourced file. SEDER can be simply adapted to this scenario, but may face an additional attack: the malicious user can store the decrypted version of block c, and is always able to decode $\mathsf{ct_{Upload}}$, even though he/she is not able to obtain the new assisting information. This attack can be mitigated by re-encrypting a randomly chosen block during each re-encryption process.

The Nature of the Storage Being Supported by SEDER. Currently, SEDER only supports archival storage [10,15,20,22]. We will extend SEDER to support dynamic storage (i.e., supporting dynamic operations like insert, delete, modify, and append [17,18,25,39]) in our future work.

6   Experimental Evaluation

We evaluated the overhead of each operation in SEDER. We used OpenSSLv1.0.0e [7] for data encryption/decryption and large number modular operations. The symmetric and asymmetric encryption/decryption function are instantiated by AES-128 and RSA-1024 respectively. Throughout the experiment, the client and the server both ran on local workstations with Intel i7-2600 (3.4 GHz) CPU and 10 GB RAM.

The PreUpload phase just uses existing MLE schemes. Therefore, we only focus on the performance overhead in Upload, Download and Update phases.

6.1   Performance Evaluation

Communication. SEDER only introduces the following extra communication between the user and cloud server: the ciphertext (i.e., 512 bits) for encrypting one block of the transformation encrypted data, verification information (i.e., 256 bits) and the assisting information (i.e., 256 bytes) in Upload phase; the delegable re-encryption public key (i.e., 512 bits) and the assisting information (i.e., 256 bytes) in Update phase.

Computation. We evaluated the processing time for uploading, downloading and re-encrypting data with size varying from 100 MB to 2 GB. Results are averaged over 100 runs.

The computation overhead is shown in Fig. 1(a). In SEDER, the user has to perform AONT which consists multiple AES encryption (determined by the size of the data) and XOR operations on the regular encrypted data. We observed that the computation overhead increases with the size of the processed data and is slightly larger than the regular data encryption in regular MLEs, as we store the intermediate data in the disk to reduce the needed memory in the users.

In Upload phase, when a cloud user (User 1) has accomplished the above operation, it has to perform the asymmetric encryption on one block of the transformation encrypted data. The user has to generate the asymmetric key pair, encrypt one block of the transformation encrypted data with the corresponding public key, and encrypt the corresponding private key using the file key and the public key of the cloud server in order. From Fig. 1(b), we observed that the processing overhead (denoted as $User1BlEncrypt$) is the same for different sizes of the data, and is less than 0.5 ms, which is rather small. The cloud

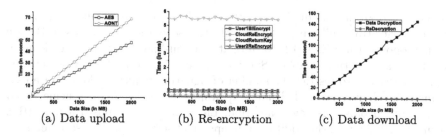

(a) Data upload   (b) Re-encryption   (c) Data download

Fig. 1. SEDER performance

server processes the ciphertext of ct^*_{sym} and returns the re-encrypted ct^*_{sym} to the user (denoted as $CloudReturnKey$ in Fig. 1(b)).

When a user (User 2) wants to update the key, he/she requires the cloud server corporately to perform the re-encryption. The user generates delegable re-encryption key $rk_{i \to j}$ and encrypts $\pi_{\mathsf{DRE}}.\mathsf{sk}_j$ with the MLE key and cloud public key in order(denoted as $User2ReEncrypt$), and requires the cloud to complete the re-encryption (denoted as $CloudReEncrypt$). We observed that the performance overhead for re-encryption is independent of the size of data, and is very small (less than 6 ms) compared to the time for encryption data (more than 2,000 ms for 100 MB data).

To download the data, the user needs to decrypt the re-encrypted block (denoted as $ReDecryption$ in Fig. 1(c)) when one or more re-encryption is executed. Then, the user performs the inverse transformation of AONT and decrypts the plain data finally ($DataDecryption$). From Fig. 1(c), we observed that the performance overhead caused by re-encryption is the same (less than 6 ms) for different sizes of data, which is negligible compared to the cost of data decryption (more than 7,000 ms for 100 MB data). The processing time for data decryption increases with the size of data, and is almost equal to the time for data encryption and AONT transformation, which is reasonable. Compared with the basic MLE schemes, SEDER spent about double time processing the outsourced file, which is acceptable, as it is one time only. And also, the users can achieve highly efficient re-encryption in the Update phase.

7   Related Work

Bellare et al. [13] formalized a new cryptographic primitive "MLE" (Message-Locked Encryption) to derive encryption/decryption key from the message being encrypted/decrypted. This new primitive can facilitate performing deduplication over data encrypted by different users.

Douceur et al. [23] proposed convergent encryption (CE), the first MLE scheme in which the key used to encrypt a file is the hash value of the file, so that the same file possessed by different users can be encrypted by the same key. CE has been used in a few systems [21, 28, 30, 31, 36, 37, 40]. CE however, is vulnerable to an off-line dictionary attack as file data are usually from a predictable space [13]. Following CE, several MLE schemes were proposed. Bellare et al. proposed DupLESS [12] to mitigate the off-line dictionary attack using per-client rate limiting strategy. Specifically, they introduced a key server during key derivation to restrict the number of signature requests allowed for a user during a fixed time interval. Duan [24] proposed another MLE scheme based on distributed oblivious key generation. Liu et al. [33] proposed a new MLE scheme by eliminating the additional independent servers. In their scheme, users use PAKE to exchange the file encryption key with the help of cloud servers. In order to prevent online dictionary attack, their scheme realizes a per-file rate limiting strategy (every user limits under the number of key agreement he/she takes part in).

REED [32] aimed at addressing the key revocation problem for secure server-side deduplication in cloud storage. In order to efficiently replace old keys and re-encrypt the data, REED introduced two special all-or-nothing transforms derived from CAONT (CANOT is a special case of all-or-nothing transforms in which the key used for AONT is the hash of message). ClearBox [9] is a transparent deduplication scheme, in which storage service providers can attest to users the number of owners of a file transparently, so that users can share the fee of storing the same file. Li et al. [29] proposed $SecCloud^+$ to achieve data integrity and deduplication simultaneously. Tang et al. [38] performed data deduplicaiton on CP-ABE.

8   Conclusion

In this paper, we propose SEDER to address the re-encryption problem for secure client-side deduplication in cloud storage. Security analysis and experimental results show that our design brings in acceptable overhead in various phases while being able to ensure continuous confidentiality for encrypted cloud storage based on client-side deduplication.

Acknowledgments. This work was supported by National Program on Key Basic Research Project of China (973) (2014CB340603). The authors would like to thank the valuable discussion from Qingji Zheng. Bo Chen would also like to thank the support from Center for Information Assurance at the University of Memphis.

References

1. Amazon simple storage service. http://aws.amazon.com/cn/s3/
2. Box. https://www.box.com/
3. Debian security advisory. https://www.debian.org/security/2008/dsa-1571
4. Dropbox. https://www.dropbox.com/
5. Icloud. https://www.icloud.com/
6. Microsoft azure. http://www.windowsazure.cn/?fb=002
7. Openssl. https://www.openssl.org/

8. These are not the certs youre looking for. http://dankaminsky.com/2011/08/31/notnotar/
9. Armknecht, F., Bohli, J.M., Karame, G.O., Youssef, F.: Transparent data deduplication in the cloud. In: The ACM SIGSAC Conference, pp. 886–900 (2015)
10. Ateniese, G., Burns, R., Curtmola, R., Herring, J., Kissner, L., Peterson, Z., Song, D.: Provable data possession at untrusted stores. In: Proceedings of the 14th ACM Conference on Computer and Communications Security, pp. 598–609. ACM (2007)
11. Ateniese, G., Fu, K., Green, M., Hohenberger, S.: Improved proxy re-encryption schemes with applications to secure distributed storage. ACM Trans. Inf. Syst. Secur. 9(1), 1–30 (2006)
12. Bellare, M., Keelveedhi, S., Ristenpart, T.: DupLESS: server-aided encryption for deduplicated storage. In: USENIX Conference on Security, pp. 179–194 (2013)
13. Bellare, M., Keelveedhi, S., Ristenpart, T.: Message-locked encryption and secure deduplication. In: Johansson, T., Nguyen, P.Q. (eds.) EUROCRYPT 2013. LNCS, vol. 7881, pp. 296–312. Springer, Heidelberg (2013). doi:10.1007/978-3-642-38348-9_18
14. Blaze, M., Bleumer, G., Strauss, M.: Divertible protocols and atomic proxy cryptography. In: Nyberg, K. (ed.) EUROCRYPT 1998. LNCS, vol. 1403, pp. 127–144. Springer, Heidelberg (1998). doi:10.1007/BFb0054122
15. Bowers, K.D., Juels, A., Oprea, A.: Hail: a high-availability and integrity layer for cloud storage. In: Proceedings of the 16th ACM Conference on Computer and Communications Security, pp. 187–198. ACM (2009)
16. Chen, B., Ammula, A.K., Curtmola, R.: Towards server-side repair for erasure coding-based distributed storage systems. In: Proceedings of the 5th ACM Conference on Data and Application Security and Privacy, pp. 281–288. ACM (2015)
17. Chen, B., Curtmola, R.: Robust dynamic provable data possession. In: 2012 32nd International Conference on Distributed Computing Systems Workshops, pp. 515–525. IEEE (2012)
18. Chen, B., Curtmola, R.: Robust dynamic remote data checking for public clouds. In: Proceedings of the 2012 ACM Conference on Computer and Communications Security, pp. 1043–1045. ACM (2012)
19. Chen, B., Curtmola, R.: Towards self-repairing replication-based storage systems using untrusted clouds. In: Proceedings of the Third ACM Conference on Data and Application Security and Privacy, pp. 377–388. ACM (2013)
20. Chen, B., Curtmola, R., Ateniese, G., Burns, R.: Remote data checking for network coding-based distributed storage systems. In: Proceedings of the 2010 ACM Workshop on Cloud Computing Security Workshop, pp. 31–42. ACM (2010)
21. Cox, L.P., Murray, C.D., Noble, B.D.: Pastiche: making backup cheap and easy. ACM SIGOPS Oper. Syst. Rev. 36(SI), 285–298 (2002)
22. Curtmola, R., Khan, O., Burns, R., Ateniese, G.: MR-PDP: multiple-replica provable data possession. In: The 28th International Conference on Distributed Computing Systems, ICDCS 2008, pp. 411–420. IEEE (2008)
23. Douceur, J.R., Adya, A., Bolosky, W.J., Dan, S., Theimer, M.: Reclaiming space from duplicate files in a serverless distributed file system. In: International Conference on Distributed Computing Systems, pp. 617–624 (2002)
24. Duan, Y.: Distributed key generation for encrypted deduplication: achieving the strongest privacy. In: CCSW, pp. 57–68 (2014)
25. Erway, C.C., Küpçü, A., Papamanthou, C., Tamassia, R.: Dynamic provable data possession. ACM Trans. Inf. Syst. Secur. (TISSEC) 17(4), 15 (2015)

26. Halevi, S., Harnik, D., Pinkas, B., Shulman-Peleg, A.: Proofs of ownership in remote storage systems. In: ACM Conference on Computer and Communications Security, pp. 491–500. ACM (2011)

27. Ivan, A.A., Dodis, Y.: Proxy cryptography revisited. In: Network and Distributed System Security Symposium, NDSS 2003 (2003)

28. Killijian, M.O., Powell, D., Es, L.: A survey of cooperative backup mechanisms. Ubiquitous Computing (2006)

29. Li, J., Li, J., Xie, D., Cai, Z.: Secure auditing and deduplicating data in cloud. IEEE Trans. Comput. **1**, 1 (2016)

30. Li, J., Chen, X., Li, M., Li, J., Lee, P.P.C., Lou, W.: Secure deduplication with efficient and reliable convergent key management. IEEE Trans. Parallel Distrib. Syst. **25**(6), 1615–1625 (2014)

31. Li, J., Li, Y.K., Chen, X., Lee, P.P.C., Lou, W.: A hybrid cloud approach for secure authorized deduplication. IEEE Trans. Parallel Distrib. Syst. **26**(5), 1206–1216 (2015)

32. Li, J., Qin, C., Lee, P.P.C., Li, J.: Rekeying for encrypted deduplication storage. In: IEEE/IFIP International Conference on Dependable Systems and Networks (2016)

33. Liu, J., Asokan, N., Pinkas, B.: Secure deduplication of encrypted data without additional independent servers. In: Proceedings of the 22nd ACM SIGSAC Conference on Computer and Communications Security, pp. 874–885 (2015)

34. Meyer, D.T., Bolosky, W.J.: A study of practical deduplication. ACM Trans. Storage **7**(4), 1 (2012)

35. Rivest, R.L.: All-or-nothing encryption and the package transform. In: Biham, E. (ed.) FSE 1997. LNCS, vol. 1267, pp. 210–218. Springer, Heidelberg (1997). doi:10.1007/BFb0052348

36. Stanek, J., Sorniotti, A., Androulaki, E., Kencl, L.: A secure data deduplication scheme for cloud storage. In: Christin, N., Safavi-Naini, R. (eds.) FC 2014. LNCS, vol. 8437, pp. 99–118. Springer, Heidelberg (2014). doi:10.1007/978-3-662-45472-5_8

37. Storer, M.W., Greenan, K., Long, D.D.E., Miller, E.L.: Secure data deduplication. In: ACM Workshop on Storage Security and Survivability, pp. 1–10 (2008)

38. Tang, H., Cui, Y., Guan, C., Wu, J., Weng, J., Ren, K.: Enabling ciphertext deduplication for secure cloud storage and access control. In: ACM on Asia Conference on Computer and Communications Security (2016)

39. Wang, Q., Wang, C., Li, J., Ren, K., Lou, W.: Enabling public verifiability and data dynamics for storage security in cloud computing. In: Backes, M., Ning, P. (eds.) ESORICS 2009. LNCS, vol. 5789, pp. 355–370. Springer, Heidelberg (2009). doi:10.1007/978-3-642-04444-1_22

40. Xu, J., Chang, E.C., Zhou, J.: Weak leakage-resilient client-side deduplication of encrypted data in cloud storage. In: ACM SIGSAC Symposium on Information, Computer and Communications Security, pp. 195–206 (2013)

41. Yu, S., Wang, C., Ren, K., Wenjing, L.: Achieving secure, scalable, and fine-grained data access control in cloud computing. In: INFOCOM 2010, pp. 1–9. IEEE (2010)

Applied Cryptography

The Security of Individual Bit for XTR

Kewei Lv[✉], Si-wei Ren, and Wenjie Qin

Institute of Information Engineering
Data Assurance and Communication Security Research Center,
Chinese Academy of Sciences, Beijing 100093, People's Republic of China
kwlu@ucas.ac.cn

Abstract. We consider bit security of public key cryptosystem XTR, presented by Lenstra and Verheul in 2000. Using the list-decoding method, we prove finding one of its pre-image of XTR if single bit of its plaintext is predicted with a non-negligible advantage. That is, every single bit of plaintext of XTR is a hardcore predicate if XTR is one-way.

Keywords: List-decoding · XTR · One-way function · Hardcore predicate

1 Introduction

One-way functions (OWFs) are functions that are easy-to-evaluate but hard-to-invert. It has numerous cryptographic applications. However, its definition does not say much about the security of a particular predicate over its pre-image. For instance, how about the most significant bit of the pre-image of one-way function? If one can guess this bit with a non-negligible advantage beyond 1/2, one might be able to obtain (partial) secret information that is hidden by this one-way function. So to prove that some bit is hard to be predicted is of primary interest. The kind of bit is called hard-core predicate of one-way function and we also say it is hard.

There are three main methods to study a hardcore predicate in our view: The first one is the traditional reduction technique, which is based on the multiplicative or additive homomorphism property of some one-way functions. Specifically, if there exists an oracle with a non-negligible advantage to predict one bit of the pre-image from ciphertext, then one could construct other ciphertexts and invoke the oracle to predict the bit of pre-images of the fresh ciphertexts. Thus we could transform the advantage of oracle into the probability of correctly inverting one-way function. This method only applies to some one-way functions with homomorphism property, such as DL, RSA, Rabin, ECL, Paillier, etc., [1,3,7,8,21], and that $O(\log n)$ bits are simultaneous hard [1,3,22]. All the subsequent works make efforts to prove the simultaneous or individual security of $O(n)$ bits for these candidate one-way functions (see [5,17]). The second method is hidden number problem (HNP) method. If we are given an oracle to predict partial

This work is partially supported by NSF of China No. 61272039.

© Springer International Publishing AG 2016
K.-Y. Lam et al. (Eds.): ICICS 2016, LNCS 9977, pp. 87–98, 2016.
DOI: 10.1007/978-3-319-50011-9_7

relevant information about the secret called hidden number, then we try to find out the hidden number. In this method, we choose a series of samples uniformly and randomly to query oracle. The oracle answers partial information about the hidden number. Then we use these samples and answers of oracle to construct a lattice. Using the lattice reduction algorithm and bounds of exponential sums, we could recover the hidden number in probabilistic polynomial time. This method is uniform but it only shows us there exists a hardcore predicate in a section of a bit string (see [2,14,19,20] and therein). [11] proved that for every one-way function there is a predicate that is hard to be predicated, given the value of any one-way function. The techniques they used indeed is a application of sub-linear time list-decoding Hadamard code. Following this idea, Akavia et al. [4] proposed the third method, a uniform elegant method called list-decoding method, to prove that a predicate is hard-to-compute for some one-way functions, which avoids the cumbersome bit manipulations in 2003. Using it, bit security can be studied for entire classes of functions. The method relies on the construction of a code that encodes the pre-images of one-way function we try to invert. That is, given a one-way function $f : X \to Y$ and a predicate $P(x)$ for $x \in X$, we construct a code C^P that associates $x \in X$ with a codeword C_x^P. If we could have access to a corrupted codeword w (which we can get by an oracle on predicting the bit), there is a PPT algorithm that computes a list of all $x \in X$ such that C_x^P is close to w (usually using Hamming distance). So we can find exact x by exhausting the list, which show the predicate P is hard-to-compute for one-way function f. This method has a strong point, that is, since code C^P associates $x \in X$ with a codeword C_x^P and each codeword is bijective to one pre-image x, the final list must contain all x corresponding to codeword close to w whether or not f is an injective function. The method can be used widely to study bit security of one-way functions, such as RSA, Rabin, EXP, ECDL and so on (see [4,5,10], etc.). [14,15] studied bit security of LUC function (see [6]) over RSA modulo and over an extension field of degree 2 respectively.

As a generalization of LUC to an extension field of degree 6, XTR is presented in [16], which takes advantage of traces to calculate and represent powers of elements of a subgroup of a finite field. Its idea is to gain a secure cryptosystem basing on discrete logarithms problem in $\mathbb{F}_{p^6}$ while the messages exchanged and actual computation are performed over $\mathbb{F}_{p^2}$. It contributes to substantially savings both in computational and communication cost without compromising security when being applied in cryptographic protocols. It has been proved that the security of XTR is computationally equivalent to solving discrete logarithms in $\mathbb{F}_{p^6}$ (see [9,16]). In this paper, we study the bit security of XTR. We use list-decoding method based on list-decoding via discrete Fourier transforms and construct the XTR multiplication code as [15]. We show, if given a probabilistic polynomial time (PPT) algorithm with a non-negligible advantage to predict the k-th bit of pre-image x accessing a noisy codeword that can be list-decoded, we could recover its pre-image of XTR by constructing proper access algorithm with witness, which results in inverting XTR.

Related Works: The first hardcore predicate was found by Blum and Micali [8] for the discrete logarithm problem (DL) over a prime field $\mathbb{F}_p$. Subsequently, the question of finding hardcore predicates of one-way functions was studied extensively. For example, [12] showed that every bit of RSA plaintext is hard-to-compute. Similarly, for exponent function modulo a Blum composite, [13] showed that all the bits are hard-to-compute. By changing representation of the bits, [18] showed that almost all of the bits in the DL function modulo a prime are hard-to-compute. A similar result but independent of the bit representation was proven in [12]. Each proof of these results need cumbersome bit manipulations and algebraic techniques, which only applies to a specific one-way function and have to be significantly modified to be used on another OWF (or even most cannot be used at all). Thus, finding generic method to study hardcore predicates that apply to most general collections of one-way functions is highly desirable.

[4] presented a uniform elegant method to prove that a predicate is hard-to-compute for some one-way functions. This method avoids the cumbersome bit manipulations. Using it, bit security can be studied for entire classes of functions. The method relies on the construction of a code that encodes the pre-images of one-way function we try to invert and can be used to study bit security RSA, Rabin, EXP and ECDL. Indeed, security of the $O(\log n)$ least and most significant bits of these functions are proved, where n is the size of pre-image of one-way function. [17] proved the security of all bits in RSA, Rabin and Paillier function for RSA moduli using a specific analysis of the Fourier coefficients that maps an element of $\mathbb{Z}_N$ to the value of the k-th bit of its corresponding representative in $[0, N-1]$. Bit security of the argument for one-way function based on elliptic curve also is proved using this method in [3]. [10] defined a very natural variation of Diffie-Hellman problem over $\mathbb{F}_{p^2}$ and proved the unpredictability of every single bit of one of the coordinates of the secret DH value is hardcore.

Our Works: It is believed that breaking XTR is computationally equivalent to solving discrete logarithms in $\mathbb{F}_{p^6}$. Using hidden number problem method and tool of lattice, [14] proved that the $\log^{1/2} p$ most significant bits of Diffie-Hellman type variation of XTR are secure, but specific hardcore predicates could not be shown. Furthermore, [14] showed that XTR is not a injective function, so it could not be studied as that of LUC. So far, bit security of XTR should be more studied. Here, we study the bit security of XTR using the list-decoding method, and show the k-th bit of x of XTR is a hardcore predicate. But, using list-decoding method and properties of XTR, we could invert XTR.

Given a PPT algorithm with a non-negligible advantage to predict the k-th bit of x, we first construct a new multiplication code (XTRMC) such that it is list-decodable and accessible. Then we use discrete Fourier transforms on abelian groups to study its Fourier concentration and recoverability, and, based on the learning algorithm of [4], prove that XTRMC is list-decodable and accessible. Finally, we give an inverting algorithm to find pre-image of XTR, which results in inverting XTR. Although XTR is not an injective function, that is, for one value of XTR, there exists three pre-images x, xp^2 and xp^4, we can construct an access algorithm with witness using Theorem 1 such that its output values contain a witness $S_j(Tr(g^x)) = (Tr(g^{(j-1)x}), Tr(g^{jx}), Tr(g^{(j+1)x}))$. For any $j' \neq j$, $S_j(Tr(g^x)) \neq S_{j'}(Tr(g^x))$ by Sect. 3.2, which assure that access algorithm can not bring another pre-image into list. Thus, each j is bijective to unique accessed value. By learning algorithm, a list of characters is output, which contains heavy characters of corrupted codeword with a high probability. So Inversing algorithm can use recovery algorithm to find a list containing pre-image x such that x is uniquely determined.

Notations: Let $\mathbb{N}$ be the set of natural number and $\mathbb{R}$ be the set of real number. Given an element $x \in \mathbb{F}_q$, define $[x]$ as the representative of the class of x in $[0, q-1]$ and $abs_q(x) = min\{[x], q - [x]\}$. Let A be a set, then $x \in_R A$ denotes that x is chosen randomly, uniformly and independently in A.

2   Organization

The paper is organized as follows: Sect. 3 gives some preliminaries. In Sect. 3, we introduce some basic notions, XTR cryptosystem and properties of discrete Fourier transforms on abelian groups and also present the learning algorithm due to Akavia et al. In Sect. 4, we present our main theorem. In Sect. 5, we summarize our contribution and some extensions are discussed.

3   Preliminaries

3.1   Basic Concepts

Definition 1. *A function* $\nu : \mathbb{N} \to \mathbb{R}$ *is called negligible if for every constant* $c \in \mathbb{R}$ *and* $c > 0$, *there exists a* $k_0 \in \mathbb{N}$ *such that* $|\nu(k)| < k^{-c}$ *for all* $k > k_0$. *A function* $\rho : \mathbb{N} \to \mathbb{R}$ *is non-negligible if there exists a constant* $c \in \mathbb{R}$, $c > 0$ *and a* $k_0 \in \mathbb{N}$ *such that* $|\rho(k)| > k^{-c}$ *for infinite number of* $k > k_0$.

Definition 2. *A function* $f : X \to Y$ *is called one-way if it satisfies that:* *(1) Given* $x \in X$, *one can compute* $f(x)$ *in polynomial time in* $\log |X|$; *(2) For every probabilistic polynomial time in* $\log |X|$ *algorithm* $\mathcal{A}$, *there exists a negligible function* $\nu_{\mathcal{A}}$ *such that* $Pr[f(z) = y : y = f(x), z = \mathcal{A}(y)] < \nu_{\mathcal{A}}(\log |X|)$, *where the probability is taken over random coin tossing of* $\mathcal{A}$ *and choice of* $x \in X$ *uniform and random. That is, for every PPT in* $\log |X|$ *algorithm* $\mathcal{A}$, *its advantage of inverting* f *is negligible.*

Definition 3. *A Boolean function* $P : D \to \{\pm 1\}$ *is called a predicate for a function* f *if both share a common domain. In order to do with biased predicates, let* $maj_P = \underset{b \in \{\pm 1\}}{max} \underset{x \in_R D}{Pr}[P(x) = b]$ *and* $minor_P = \underset{b \in \{\pm 1\}}{min} \underset{x \in_R D}{Pr}[P(x) = b]$. *Obviously,* $maj_P = 1 - minor_P$.

Definition 4. *We say an PPT algorithm $\mathcal{B}$ efficiently predicts predicate P for f if there exists a non-negligible function ρ, s.t. $\Pr[\mathcal{B}(f(x)) = P(x)] \geqslant maj_P + \rho(\log |D|)$, where the probability is taken over random coin tossing of $\mathcal{B}$ and choices of $x \in D$. We say predicate P is hardcore for a one-way function f if it could not be predicted efficiently.*

3.2 XTR

Let $F(c, X) = X^3 - cX^2 + c^pX - 1 \in \mathbb{F}_{p^2}[X]$ be an irreducible polynomial for prime p, then the roots of $F(c, X)$ take the form h, h^{p^2}, h^{p^4} for some $h \in \mathbb{F}_{p^6}$ of order dividing $p^2 - p + 1$ and larger than 3. For $n \in \mathbb{Z}$, we set $c_1 = c$, $c_n = h^n + h^{np^2} + h^{np^4}$. Thus $c_n = Tr(h^n)$, where the trace $Tr(h^n)$ over $\mathbb{F}_{p^2}$ is $\mathbb{F}_{p^2}$-linear, and $c_{-n} = c_p^n$. For any $g \in \mathbb{F}_{p^6}$ which have order q for a prime $q > 3$ and $q|p^2 - p + 1$, its minimal polynomial is $F(Tr(g), X)$. Furthermore, $Tr(g^n) \in \mathbb{F}_{p^2}$ and $F(Tr(g^n), g^n) = 0$ for all n. It is shown that, for such g, the trace value fully specifies g's minimal polynomial, and thus its conjugates, which gives the fundamental idea of XTR. As shown in [16], if $p \equiv 2 \mod 3$, then c_n can be computed efficiently given $c = c_1$ using a recurrence relation, and c_{n-1} and c_{n+1} are obtained at no extra cost as a side result. It is almost three times faster than computing g^n from g using traditional exponentiation methods. Thus, in XTR we replace powers of g by their traces, thereby saving a factor of three both in storage and in computing time. Note that an actual representation of g is not required, and that it suffices to have its trace $Tr(g)$.

Given $Tr(g)$ and the order of g, the subgroup $\langle g \rangle$ generated by g (unknown) is called the XTR group, and function $f : \mathbb{F}_q^* \to \mathbb{F}_{p^2}$ with $f(x) = Tr(g^x)$ is called XTR one-way function. XTR parameters consists of primes p and q as the prior, where $p \equiv 3 \mod 4$, and the trace $Tr(g)$ of a generator of the XTR group. The primes p and q of appropriate sizes can be found using either of the two methods given in [16]. To find a proper $Tr(g)$, it suffices to find $c \in \mathbb{F}_{p^2} \backslash \mathbb{F}_p$ such that $F(c, X) \in \mathbb{F}_{p^2}[X]$ is irreducible, and $c_{(p^2-p+1)/q} = 3$, and set $Tr(g) = c_{(p^2-p+1)/q}$. Since the probability that $c_{(p^2-p+1)/q} \not\equiv 3$ if $F(c, X)$ is irreducible is only $1/q$, usually the irreducible $F(c, X)$ works.

Theorem 1 [14]. *Let $S_n(c) = (c_{n-1}, c_n, c_{n+1})$. Given the sum of c of the roots of $F(c, X)$, there exists an algorithm computing the sum c_n of the n-th powers of the roots which takes $8 \log n$ multiplications in $\mathbb{F}_p$.*

3.3 Fourier Transforms

Let G be a finite abelian group and $C(G)$ be the space of all complex valued functions $f : G \to \mathbb{R}$. For any $f, g \in C(G)$, their inner product is defined as $\langle f, g \rangle = \frac{1}{|G|} \sum_{x \in G} f(x)\overline{g(x)}$. The ℓ_2-norm of function f is $\|f\|_2 = \sqrt{\langle f, f \rangle}$. A character of G is a homomorphism $\chi : G \to \mathbb{R}$ satisfying $\chi(x + y) = \chi(x)\chi(y)$ for all $x, y \in G$. The set of all characters of G forms a group $\hat{G}$ called character group. Elements of $\hat{G}$ form a normal orthogonal base of $C(G)$ (i.e. Fourier basis).

Then a function $f \in C(G)$ can be described by its Fourier expansion $f(x) = \sum_{x \in G} \langle f, \chi \rangle \chi$. So its Fourier transform $\hat{f} : \hat{G} \to \mathbb{R}$ is defined by $\hat{f}(\chi) = \langle f, \chi \rangle$. The coefficients $\hat{f}(\chi)$ in the Fourier basis $\{\chi\}_{x \in \hat{G}}$ are called Fourier coefficients of f. We can approximate a function $f \in C(G)$ using subsets $\Gamma \subset \hat{G}$ of characters via its restriction $f_\Gamma = \sum_{x \in \Gamma} \hat{f}(\chi) \chi$. When $G = \mathbb{Z}/n\mathbb{Z}$, characters of G are defined by $\chi(\alpha) = \omega_n^{\alpha x}$ for $\alpha \in \mathbb{Z}_n$ and $\omega_n = e^{\frac{-2\pi i}{n}}$. Weight of a Fourier coefficient $\hat{f}(\chi)$ is $\|\hat{f}(\chi)\|_2^2$. So we define heavy characters of a function f.

Definition 5 (Heavy character). *Given a function $f : G \to \mathbb{R}$ and a threshold τ, $Heavy_\tau(f)$ denotes a set of characters for which weight of the corresponding Fourier coefficient of f is at least τ. That is, $Heavy_\tau(f) = \{x \in \hat{G} \| \|\hat{f}(\chi)\|^2 \geqslant \tau\}$.*

Definition 6 (Fourier Concentration). *We say a function $f : \mathbb{Z}_N \to \mathbb{R}$ is Fourier concentrated if, for every $\epsilon > 0$, there exists a set Γ consisting of $poly(\log N/\epsilon)$ characters, so that $\|f - f_\Gamma\|_2^2 = \sum_{\alpha \notin \Gamma} \|\hat{f}(\alpha)\|^2 \leqslant \epsilon$. For simplicity, f is called to be ϵ-concentrated on set Γ.*

The heavy character of f is any character for which the projection of f on it has a large norm. So, given $\tau > 0$ and f, we set $Heavy_\tau(f) = \{\chi_\alpha \| \|\hat{f}(\alpha)\|^2 \geqslant \tau\}$.

3.4 Code and List-Decoding Method

To encode elements of $\mathbb{Z}_N$, we will only consider codewords of length N. Thus, a binary code is a subset $C \subset \{\pm 1\}^N$, and each of codeword C_x is a function $C_x : \mathbb{Z}_N \to \{\pm 1\}$ expressed as $(C_x(0), C_x(1), \cdots, C_x(N-1))$.

Definition 7 (Hamming distance). *The normalized Hamming distance between two functions $g, h : \mathbb{Z}_N \to \{\pm 1\}$ is $\Delta(g, h) = \Pr_{x \in \mathbb{Z}_N}[g(x) \neq f(x)]$.*

Definition 8 (List-decodable code). *A code $C = \{C_x : \mathbb{Z}_N \to \{\pm 1\}\}$ is list-decodable if there exists a PPT algorithm which, given access to a corrupted codeword w and on input a threshold δ, ϵ, and 1^N, returns a list $L \supseteq \{x | \Delta(w, C_x) < minor_{C_x} - \epsilon\}$ with a probability $1 - \delta$.*

Definition 9 (Concentration). *We say a code C is concentrated if each of its codewords $C_x \in C$ is Fourier Concentrated.*

Definition 10 (Accessibility). *For each $n \in \mathbb{N}$, assume $I_n \subseteq \{0,1\}^n$ be a countable set and $I = (I_n)_{n \in \mathbb{N}}$. Let $P = (P_i)_{i \in I}$ be a collection of predicates and $\mathcal{F} = \{f_i | D_i \to \{\pm 1\}^*\}_{i \in I}$ be a family of one-way functions. We say that P is accessible with respect to $\mathcal{F}$ if there exists a PPT access algorithm $\mathcal{A}$ such that for all $i \in I_n$, C^{P_i} is accessible to f_i, namely*

1. *Code access: $\forall x, j \in D_i$, $\mathcal{A}(i, f_i(x), j)$ returns $f_i(x')$ such that $C_x^{P_i}(j) = P_i(x')$;*
2. *Well spread: For uniformly distributed $C_x^{P_i} \in C^{P_i}$ and $j \in D_i$, the distribution of x' satisfying $f_i(x') = \mathcal{A}(i, f_i(x), j)$ is statistically close to uniform distribution on D_i;*

3. *Bias preserving: For a non-negligible fraction of codeword $C_x^{P_i}$, $|Pr[C_x^{P_i}(j) = 1|j \in D_i] - Pr[P_i(z) = 1|z \in D_i]| \leqslant \nu(n)$, where ν is a negligible function.*

Now we give a sufficient conditions that a code is list-decodable and its detailed explanation can be found in [4].

Theorem 2 (List-decoding method). *Let $C = \{C_x|C_x : \mathbb{Z}_N \to \{\pm 1\}\}$ be a concentrated and recoverable code, then C is list-decodable.*

3.5   The Learning Algorithm

[4] extends the algorithm of learning heavy Fourier coefficients of a function $f : \{0,1\}^k \to \{0,1\}$ to the function $f : \mathbb{Z}_N^k \to \mathbb{R}$. Specifically, they devise an efficient search procedure to find fewer relevant characters.

Theorem 3 [4]. *There is an algorithm $\mathcal{A}$ that, given query access to $g : \mathbb{Z}_N \to \{\pm 1\}$, $\tau > 0$ and $\delta \in (0,1)$, outputs a list L of $O(1/\tau)$ characters (each can be encoded in $\log N$ bits), that contains $Heavy_\tau(g)$ with a probability at least $1 - \delta$; and its running time is $\tilde{O}(\log N) \cdot \ln^2(1/\delta)/\tau^{5.5}$.*

Remark. $\tilde{O}(\cdot)$ indicates that terms of complexity which is a polynomial in $\log(1/\tau)$, $\log N$ or $\ln\ln(1/\delta)$ have been omitted. The theorem implies that if we could access a function defined on an abelian group, then it is computationally feasible to obtain a list of all the Fourier coefficients. It is helpful for us to construct the recovering algorithm for XTRMC (see Subsect. 4.1).

4   Main Theorem

Throughout, we set bits values to be $\{\pm 1\}$ instead of $\{0,1\}$. That is, we take values $(-1)^b$ for $b \in \{0,1\}$. For $\mathbb{F}_p$, let $P : \mathbb{F}_p \to \{\pm 1\}$ be the predicate defined by $P(x) = B_i(x)$, where $B_i(x)$ denotes the i-th bit of an element x. We show it is a hardcore predicate for XTR one-way function $f : \mathbb{F}_q^* \to \mathbb{F}_{p^2}$ with $f(x) = Tr(g^x)$.

Definition 11. *Let p, q be two primes selected by XTR cryptosystem, $g \in \mathbb{F}_{p^6}$ have order q dividing $p^2 - p + 1$ and larger than 3. We say that $\mathcal{A}$ has a advantage $\rho \in (0,1)$ of predicting the predicate P of the argument of XTR one-way function $f : \mathbb{F}_q^* \to \mathbb{F}_{p^2}$ with $f(x) = Tr(g^x)$ if $|\Pr[\mathcal{A}(f(x), z) = P(x)] - maj_P| > \rho$. The probability is taken over $x \in F_q^*$ chosen uniformly and randomly, and random coins z of $\mathcal{A}$. When ρ is a non-negligible function, let $1/\rho = poly(\log q)$.*

We state the main theorem:

Theorem 4. *Let $\rho \in (0,1)$ be a non-negligible function, both p and q be primes as above. Let $f : \mathbb{F}_q^* \to \mathbb{F}_{p^2}$ with $f(x) = Tr(g^x)$ be a XTR one-way function. If there exists an algorithm $\mathcal{A}$ to predict P with a non-negligible advantage ρ in time $poly(\log q)$, where $\rho(\log q) > 0$. Then there exists an algorithm INV that inverts $f(x)$ in time $poly(\log |q|, 1/\rho)$ for at least $\frac{\rho}{2}|\mathbb{F}_q^*|$ of x.*

4.1   Proof of Main Theorem

Before we prove the main theorem, we first construct multiplication code of XTR function (XTRMC).

Definition 12 (XTRMC). *Let p, q, g and $B_i(x)$ be defined as above. We define multiplication code $C^P = \{C_x^P : \mathbb{F}_q^* \to \{\pm 1\}\}_{x \in \mathbb{F}_q^*}$, where $C_x^P(j) = P(j \cdot x \mod q)$, x is the argument of XTR one-way function f. We denote the code $C = C^P = \{C_x^P\}$.*

Lemma 1. *Let $P : \mathbb{F}_q^* \to \{\pm 1\}$ be a predicate and C^P be accessible to f. If there exists a PPT algorithm $\mathcal{A}_k$ that predicts P from f with advantage ρ', then there exists a set S and $|S| \geqslant \frac{\rho'}{2}|C^P|$ such that $\forall C_x^P \in S$, given $f(x)$, we have query access to a corrupted codeword w_x satisfying $\Delta(w_x, C_x^P) \leqslant minor_{C_x^P} - \rho(k)$, where ρ is a non-negligible function and $k = \log q$.*

Proof. Since C^P is accessible with regard to f, there exists an access algorithm $\mathcal{D}$ satisfying $\mathcal{D}(f(x), j) = f(x')$. Let $w_x(j) = \mathcal{A}_k(\mathcal{D}(f(x), j))$ and set $\alpha_{x,j} \in \mathbb{F}_q^*$ such that $f(\alpha_{x,j}) = \mathcal{D}(f(x), j)$. By the construction of $\mathcal{D}$, there is only j here. Since the code is well spread and $\mathcal{A}_k$ has an advantage $\rho'(k)$ to predict P, $Pr[\mathcal{A}_k(f(\alpha_{x,j})) = P(\alpha_{x,j})] \geqslant maj_P + \rho'(k)$, where the probability is taken over random coin tosses of $\mathcal{A}_k$ and random choice of $C_x^P \in C^P$ and $j \in \mathbb{F}_q^*$.

Let S be a set satisfying $Pr[\mathcal{A}_k(f(\alpha_{x,j})) = P(\alpha_{x,j})] \geqslant maj_P + \frac{\rho'(k)}{2}$ for all $C_x^P \in S$. Then $|S| \geqslant \frac{\rho'(k)}{2}|C^P|$, s.t. $\forall C_x^P \in S$, $Pr[\mathcal{A}_k(f(\alpha_{x,j})) = P(\alpha_{x,j})] \geqslant maj_P + \frac{\rho'(k)}{2}$. Note that the code is bias preserving, $|maj_{C_x^P} - maj_P| \leqslant \nu'(k)$, where ν' is a negligible function. So $\mathcal{A}_k$ has a non-negligible function $\rho(k) = \frac{\rho'(k)}{2} - \nu'(k)$ s.t. $\forall C_x^P \in S$, $Pr[\mathcal{A}_k(f(\alpha_{x,j})) = P(\alpha_{x,j})] \geqslant maj_P + \rho(k)$. Namely, $\forall C_x^P \in S$, $\Delta(w_x, C_x^P) \leqslant minor_{C_x^P} - \rho(k)$. This completes the proof.

Fourier Concentration of XTRMC. In order to bound the size of the fourier coefficients $\hat{P}(\alpha)$ and sieve the heavy ones, we could use the method of [17] to obtain a careful analysis of function $P(x)$ and find out the concentrated set of XTRMC accurately.

Let $q = r2^{i+1} \pm m$ for $m \in (0, 2^i)$. For $\alpha \in [-\frac{q-1}{2}, \frac{q-1}{2}]$ and function $g(x) = \frac{P(x+2^i)+P(x)}{2}$, its Fourier transform coefficient is $\hat{g}(\alpha) = \frac{w_q^{2^i \alpha} + 1}{2} \hat{P}(\alpha)$, where $w_p = e^{\frac{2\pi i}{q}}$. For both $x \in [(r-1)2^{i+1} + 2^i - m, (r-1)2^{i+1} + 2^i - 1]$ and $x \in [2^{i+1}r, 2^{i+1}r + m - 1]$, we compute $\hat{g}(\alpha)$ respectively and obtain in both cases $|\hat{P}(\alpha)|^2 = \frac{1}{q^2} \cdot \frac{\sin^2(\frac{m\alpha}{q})}{\sin^2(\frac{\alpha}{q})\sin^2(\frac{2^i\alpha}{q})}$. So $|\hat{P}(\alpha)|^2 \leqslant \frac{1}{\pi^2(1-\pi^2/12)^2} \cdot \frac{abs_q^2(m\alpha)}{abs_q^2(\alpha)abs_q^2(2^i\alpha - q/2)}$.

To be asymptotic $|\hat{P}(\alpha)|^2$ closer, we set $2^i\alpha = \frac{q-1}{2} + \delta_\alpha + q\lambda_\alpha$ such that $\delta_\alpha = 2^i\alpha - \frac{q-1}{2} \mod q$ and $\lambda_\alpha \in [0, 2^{i-1} - 1]$ for $\alpha \in [0, \frac{q-1}{2}]$; and $\delta_\alpha = 2^i\alpha + \frac{q-1}{2} \mod q$ and $\lambda_\alpha \in [0, 2^{i-1} - 1]$ for $\alpha \in [-\frac{q-1}{2}, 0]$, where λ_α is integer.

Proposition 1. *For all $\alpha \in F_p^*$, we have $abs_q(\alpha) = (2\lambda_\alpha + 1) \pm \mu_\alpha$, where λ_α is define as above and $\mu_\alpha \in [0, r]$ is a integer. Furthermore, $|\hat{P}(\alpha)|^2 < O(\frac{1}{\lambda_\alpha^2 \mu_\alpha^2})$.*

Proof. $\forall \alpha \in F_q^*$, $abs_q(\alpha) = k_r r \pm \mu_r$, where $\mu_r \in [-r/2, r/2]$. If $k_r = 2k+1$, then $abs_q(\alpha) = (2k+1)r \pm \mu_r$. So we can set $\lambda_\alpha = k$ and $\mu_\alpha = \mu_r$. Else, if $k_r = 2k$, then $abs_q(\alpha) = (2k+1)r - (r - \mu_r)$ for $\mu_r > 0$ and $abs_q(\alpha) = (2k-1)r + r - \mu_r = (2(k+1) - 1)r - (r - \mu_r)$ for $\mu_r < 0$. So λ_α and μ_α can be set. Furthermore, since $abs_q^2(\alpha)abs_q^2(2^i\alpha - \frac{q-1}{2}) \geqslant \lambda_\alpha^2 \cdot \mu_\alpha^2 \cdot r^2 \cdot 2^{2i+2} \cdot 1/4$, $|\hat{P}(\alpha)|^2 < O(\frac{1}{\lambda_\alpha^2 \mu_\alpha^2})$.

Lemma 2. *Let P be a predicate defined as above. Then P is τ-concentrated on* $\Gamma = \{\chi_\alpha | \lambda_\alpha < O(1/\tau), \mu_\alpha < O(1/\tau)\}$.

Proof. The proof is almost identical to Theorem 7 in [17], we present it here for completeness. At first, we give an injective map

$$\pi : \left[-\tfrac{q-1}{2}, \tfrac{q-1}{2}\right] \to [0, 2^{i-1} - 1] \times [0, r] \times \{\pm 1\} \times \{\pm 1\}$$
$$\alpha \quad \to \quad (\lambda_\alpha, \quad \mu_\alpha, \quad s_\alpha, \quad s_\delta)$$

where $s_\delta = sgn(\delta)$, $s_\alpha = sgn(\alpha)$ for sign function $sgn(\cdot)$.

All characters of Z_N consists of $\Gamma \cup \Gamma_0 \cup \Gamma_1 \cup \Gamma_2 \cup \Gamma_3 \cup \Gamma_4$, where $\Gamma = \{\chi_\alpha | \lambda_\alpha \leqslant O(1/\tau), \mu_\alpha \leqslant O(1/\tau)\}$, $\Gamma_0 = \{\chi_\alpha | \lambda_\alpha = 0, \mu_\alpha \geqslant O(1/\tau)\}$, $\Gamma_1 = \{\chi_\alpha | \lambda_\alpha \geqslant O(1/\tau), \mu_\alpha = 0\}$, $\Gamma_2 = \{\chi_\alpha | \lambda_\alpha \geqslant 1, 1 \leqslant \mu_\alpha \leqslant O(1/\tau)\}$, $\Gamma_3 = \{\chi_\alpha | \mu_\alpha \geqslant 1, 1 \leqslant \lambda_\alpha \leqslant O(1/\tau)\}$, $\Gamma_4 = \{\chi_\alpha | \lambda_\alpha \geqslant O(1/\tau), \mu_\alpha \geqslant O(1/\tau)\}$. We bound the sum of $|\hat{P}(\alpha)|^2$:

$$\sum_{\chi_\alpha \in \Gamma_0} |\hat{P}(\alpha)|^2 \leqslant O(m^2) \sum_{\chi_\alpha \in \Gamma_0} \frac{1}{abs_N^2(2^i\alpha - \frac{N-1}{2})} < O(m^2) \sum_{\chi_\alpha \in \Gamma_0} \frac{1}{(2^i\mu_\alpha)^2} < O(\tau),$$

$$\sum_{\chi_\alpha \in \Gamma_1} |\hat{P}(\alpha)|^2 \leqslant O(r^2) \sum_{\chi_\alpha \in \Gamma_1} \frac{1}{abs_N^2(\alpha)} < O(r^2) \sum_{\chi_\alpha \in \Gamma_1} \frac{1}{\lambda_\alpha^2} < O(\tau) \qquad \text{and}$$

$$\sum_{\chi_\alpha \in \Gamma_2} |\hat{P}(\alpha)|^2 + \sum_{\chi_\alpha \in \Gamma_3} |\hat{P}(\alpha)|^2 + \sum_{\chi_\alpha \in \Gamma_4} |\hat{P}(\alpha)|^2$$
$$\leqslant \sum_{1 \leqslant \mu_\alpha \leqslant k} \frac{1}{\mu_\alpha^2} \left(\sum_{\lambda_\alpha > k} \frac{1}{\lambda_\alpha^2} \right) + \sum_{1 \leqslant \lambda_\alpha \leqslant k} \frac{1}{\lambda_\alpha^2} \left(\sum_{\mu_\alpha > k} \frac{1}{\mu_\alpha^2} \right) + \sum_{\mu_\alpha \geqslant k} \frac{1}{\mu_\alpha^2} \left(\sum_{\lambda_\alpha > k} \frac{1}{\lambda_\alpha^2} \right) \leqslant O(\tau)$$

So the predicate is τ-concentrated on $\Gamma = \{\chi_\alpha | \lambda_\alpha < O(1/\tau), \mu_\alpha < O(1/\tau)\}$.

Recoverability of XTRMC. We have proved C^P is τ-concentrated on Γ. To prove C^P is list-decodable, we need C^P is recoverable. Namely, there exists a PPT recovery algorithm on input a character χ_β and a threshold parameter τ to output a list L containing $x \in F_q^*$ such that $\chi_\beta \in Heavy_\tau(C_x^P)$.

Lemma 3. *For any prime q, C^P is recoverable.*

Proof. By Lemma 2, C^P is τ-concentrated in $\Gamma' = \{\chi_\beta | \beta = \alpha \cdot x \mod q, \chi_\alpha \in \Gamma\}$, where $\Gamma = \{\chi_\alpha | \lambda_\alpha < O(1/\tau), \mu_\alpha < O(1/\tau)\}$. The recovery algorithm (Table 1) will output a list containing $x \in F_q^*$ such that $\chi_\beta \in Heavy_\tau(C_x^P)$.

As C^P is τ-concentrated in Γ', $\chi_\beta \in Heavy_\tau(C_x^P)$ implies $\chi_\beta \in \Gamma'$ and thus $\beta = \alpha \cdot x \mod q$ for $\lambda_\alpha < O(1/\tau)$ and $\mu_\alpha < O(1/\tau)$. The algorithm outputs list $L = \{x | x = \beta/\alpha \mod q, \chi_\alpha \in \Gamma\}$ containing all x such that $\chi_\beta \in Heavy_\tau(C_x^P)$. Since we can choose parameter $1/\tau \in poly(\log q)$, the length of list and running time of the recovery algorithm will be in $poly(\log q/\tau)$.

Combining Lemmas 2 and 3, we prove C^P is list-decodable for any q.

Table 1. The recovery algorithm

Input: A character χ_β, a threshold parameter τ with $1/\tau \in poly(\log q)$.
Output: A list L containing $x \in F_q^*$ such that $\chi_\beta \in Heavy_\tau(C_x^P)$.

1. $L = \emptyset$, $L_\alpha = \emptyset$.
2. Calculate $\Gamma = \{\chi_\alpha | \lambda_\alpha < O(1/\tau), \mu_\alpha < O(1/\tau)\}$.
3. For $\chi_\alpha \in \Gamma$ do.
4. $x = \beta/\alpha \mod q$.
5. $L_\alpha = \{x\}$.
6. $L = L \cup L_\alpha$.
7. End for.
8. Return L.

Accessibility w.r. to XTR. Assuming discrete logarithm problem in $\mathbb{F}_{p^6}$ is intractable, we have XTR collection of one-way functions

$$\text{XTR} = \{\text{XTR}_{(p,q,g)}(x) = Tr(g^x)\}_{(p,q,g)\in I},$$

where $I = \{(p,q,g)|$ Both p,q are primes, $g \in \mathbb{F}_{p^6}$ of order q s.t $q|p^2 - p + 1\}$.

Lemma 4. *The code $C^P = \{C_x^P\}_{x\in\mathbb{F}_q^*}$ is accessible to XTR one-way function.*

Proof. We construct the access algorithm $\mathcal{D}$:

On input p, q, g, j and $XTR_{p,q,g}(x)$ For $j \in \mathbb{F}_q^*$, we can use Theorem 1 to compute $S_j(Tr(g^x)) = (Tr(g^{(j-1)x}), Tr(g^{jx}), Tr(g^{(j+1)x})) \in \mathbb{F}_{p^2}^3$ and return $Tr(g^{jx})$. Output $Tr(g^{jx})$ and $S_j(Tr(g^x))$ as its witness.

Fixed $x \in \mathbb{F}_q^*$ and j, for any $j' \in \{1, p^2, p^4\}$, both $Tr(g^{xj'}) = XTR_{p,q,g}(x') = Tr(g^{jx})$ and $S_j(Tr(g^x)) = S_{j'}(Tr(g^x))$ should hold. Since $S_j(Tr(g^x)) \neq S_{j'}(Tr(g^x))$ for $j \neq j'$, the other two choices is discarded. So the distribution of x' on $\mathbb{F}_q^*$ is close to uniform, and the code is well-spread and bias-preserving.

Continuing to Prove Theorem 4. Since C^P is list-decodable and there exists a non-negligible codewords w_x which is accessible, by Theorem 2, the predicate P is a hardcore for the XTR one-way function. Indeed, if there exists an oracle $\mathcal{A}$ which has a non-negligible advantage to predict $P(x) = B_i(x)$, then we could construct a PPT algorithm INV (see Table 2) which returns a list with a high probability containing at least one pre-image of XTR. Using $\mathcal{A}$, we can have access to C^P and there are at least $\frac{\rho}{2}|\mathbb{F}_q^*|$ of x by Lemma 1. Since the learning algorithm in step 3 runs in time $\tilde{O}(\log q) \cdot \ln^2(1/\delta)/\tau^{5.5}$ and the recovery algorithm in step 4 runs in time $poly(\log q/\tau)$, the INV algorithm runs in time $poly(\log q, 1/\rho)$. This completes the proof of Theorem 4.

Table 2. XTR OWF inverse algorithm

Input: A query access to XTR function $f : \mathbb{F}_q^* \to \mathbb{F}_{p^2}$ with $f(x) = Tr(g^x)$ and its witness $S_{j_0}(Tr(g^x))$ for some $j_0 > 1$, where both p, q are primes, g is of order q s.t $q|p^2 - p + 1$; an oracle $\mathcal{A}$ has a non-negligible advantage to predict $P(x)$ given $y = f(x)$.
Output: $z \in \mathbb{F}_q^*$ such that $f(z) = y$.

1. Choose τ such that $1/\tau \in poly(\log q)$, $\delta \in (0,1)$. Let $L = \emptyset$ initially.
2. Use the oracle $\mathcal{A}$ to obtain a corrupted codeword w_x.
3. Invoke the learning algorithm(theorem 3) with δ and τ. Output all the heavy coefficients of the w_x, i.e., $\Gamma = \{\beta | \chi_\beta \in Heavy_\tau(w_x)\}$.
4. For $\chi_\beta \in Heavy_\tau(w_x)$, run recovery algorithm(Table 1) and return all x such that $\chi_\beta \in Heavy_\tau(C_x)$ and set $L_\beta = \{x | \chi_\beta \in Heavy_\tau(C_x)\}$. Let $L = L \cup L_\beta$.
5. End for.
6. For $z \in L$.
7.   Compare $f(z)$ with y and $S_{j_0}(Tr(g^z)) = S_{j_0}(Tr(g^x))$. If they all are equal, then return z.
8. End for.
9. Exit and failed.

---

5   Remark and Conclusion

In [14], DH-type XTR was only studied by HNP, but it is much rougher than list-decoding method. In this paper, we study the bit security of the XTR one-way function by the list-decoding method. Although XTR is not injective, using XTR inverse algorithm (Table 2), the pre-image z can be found such that $f(z) = y$. Indeed, the access algorithm we constructed have an output with a witness. It is the witness that assures that pre-images are bijective to codewords such that exact pre-image could be found when it is list-decoded correctly. Thus we prove that the individual bit is hardcore for XTR one-way function, which is also considered as a supplement to the work of the Akavia et al. For bit security of XTR variation of Diffie-Hellman problem, this method is also applied.

References

1. Alexi, W., Chor, B., Goldreich, O., Schnorr, C.P.: RSA and Rabin functions: certain parts are as hard as the whole. SIAM J. Comput. **17**(2), 194–209 (1988)
2. Boneh, D., Venkatesan, R.: Hardness of computing the most significant bits of secret keys in Diffie-Hellman and related schemes. In: Koblitz, N. (ed.) CRYPTO 1996. LNCS, vol. 1109, pp. 129–142. Springer, Heidelberg (1996). doi:10.1007/3-540-68697-5_11
3. Duc, A., Jetchev, D.: Hardness of computing individual bits for one-way functions on elliptic curves. In: Safavi-Naini, R., Canetti, R. (eds.) CRYPTO 2012. LNCS, vol. 7417, pp. 832–849. Springer, Heidelberg (2012). doi:10.1007/978-3-642-32009-5_48
4. Akavia, A., Goldwasser, S., Safra, S.: Proving hard-core predicates using list decoding. In: FOCS, vol. 3, pp. 146–156, October 2003

5. Akavia, A., Goldwasser, S., Vaikuntanathan, V.: Simultaneous hardcore bits and cryptography against memory attacks. In: Reingold, O. (ed.) TCC 2009. LNCS, vol. 5444, pp. 474–495. Springer, Heidelberg (2009). doi:10.1007/978-3-642-00457-5_28

6. Bleichenbacher, D., Bosma, W., Lenstra, A.K.: Some remarks on Lucas-based cryptosystems. In: Coppersmith, D. (ed.) CRYPTO 1995. LNCS, vol. 963, pp. 386–396. Springer, Heidelberg (1995). doi:10.1007/3-540-44750-4_31

7. Blum, L., Blum, M., Shub, M.: A simple secure pseudo-random number generator. SIAM J. Comput. **15**(2), 364–383 (1986)

8. Blum, M., Micali, S.: How to generate cryptographically strong sequences of pseudorandom bits. SIAM J. Comput. **13**(4), 850–864 (1984)

9. Brouwer, A.E., Pellikaan, R., Verheul, E.R.: Doing more with fewer bits. In: Lam, K.-Y., Okamoto, E., Xing, C. (eds.) ASIACRYPT 1999. LNCS, vol. 1716, pp. 321–332. Springer, Heidelberg (1999). doi:10.1007/978-3-540-48000-6_26

10. Fazio, N., Gennaro, R., Perera, I.M., Skeith lll, W.E.: Hard-core predicates for a Diffie-Hellman problem over finite fields. In: Canetti, R., Garay, J.A. (eds.) CRYPTO 2013. LNCS, vol. 8043, pp. 148–165. Springer, Heidelberg (2013). doi:10.1007/978-3-642-40084-1_9

11. Goldreich, O., Levin, L.A.: A hard-core predicate for all one-way functions. In: Proceedings of the 21st STOC, pp. 25–32 (1989)

12. Hastad, J., Naslund, M.: The security of individual RSA bits. In: Proceedings of 39th FOCS, pp. 510–519 (1998)

13. Håstad, J., Schrift, A.W., Shamir, A.: The discrete logarithm modulo a composite hides O(n) bits. J. Comput. Syst. Sci. **47**(3), 376–404 (1993)

14. Li, W.-C.W., Näslund, M., Shparlinski, I.E.: Hidden number problem with the trace and bit security of XTR and LUC. In: Yung, M. (ed.) CRYPTO 2002. LNCS, vol. 2442, pp. 433–448. Springer, Heidelberg (2002). doi:10.1007/3-540-45708-9_28

15. Lv, K., Ren, S.: Bit security for Lucas-based one-way function. In Proceedings of 2014 Ninth Asia Joint Conference on Information Security, pp. 111–118. IEEE (2014)

16. Lenstra, A.K., Verheul, E.R.: The XTR public key system. In: Bellare, M. (ed.) CRYPTO 2000. LNCS, vol. 1880, pp. 1–19. Springer, Heidelberg (2000). doi:10.1007/3-540-44598-6_1

17. Morillo, P., Ràfols, C.: The security of all bits using list decoding. In: Jarecki, S., Tsudik, G. (eds.) PKC 2009. LNCS, vol. 5443, pp. 15–33. Springer, Heidelberg (2009). doi:10.1007/978-3-642-00468-1_2

18. Schnorr, C.P.: Security of almost all discrete log bits. Electr. Colloq. Comput. Complex. Univ. Trier **TR98-033**, 1–13 (1998)

19. Shparlinski, I.E.: Playing "hide-and-seek" in finite fields: the hidden number problem and its applications. In: Proceedings of 7th Spanish Meeting on Cryptology and Information Security, vol. 1, pp. 49–72 (2002)

20. Su, D., Wang, K., Lv, K.: The bit security of two variants of Paillier trapdoor function. Chin. J. Comput. **33**(6), 1050–1059 (2010)

21. Su, D., Lv, K.: Paillier's trapdoor function hides $\Theta(n)$ bits. Sci. China Inf. Sci. **54**(9), 1827–1836 (2011)

22. Vazirani, U.V., Vazirani, V.V.: Efficient and secure pseudo-random number generation (extended abstract). In: Blakley, G.R., Chaum, D. (eds.) CRYPTO 1984. LNCS, vol. 196, pp. 193–202. Springer, Heidelberg (1985). doi:10.1007/3-540-39568-7_17

On the Robustness of Learning Parity with Noise

Nan Yao[1], Yu Yu[1,3($\boxtimes$)], Xiangxue Li[2,3,4($\boxtimes$)], and Dawu Gu[1]

[1] Department of Computer Science and Engineering,
Shanghai Jiao Tong University, Shanghai, China
yyuu@sjtu.edu.cn
[2] Department of Computer Science and Technology,
East China Normal University, Shanghai, China
xxli@cs.ecnu.edu.cn
[3] Westone Cryptologic Research Center, Beijing, China
[4] National Engineering Laboratory for Wireless Security, XUPT, Xi'an, China

Abstract. The Learning Parity with Noise (LPN) problem is well understood in learning theory and cryptography and has been found quite useful in constructing various lightweight cryptographic primitives. There exists non-trivial evidence that the problem is robust on high-entropy secrets (and even given hard-to-invert leakages), and the justified results by Dodis, Kalai and Lovett (STOC 2009) were established under non-standard hard learning assumptions. The recent progress by Suttichaya and Bhattarakosol (Information Processing Letters, Volume 113, Issues 14–16) claimed that LPN remains provably secure (reducible from the LPN assumption itself) as long as the secret is sampled from any linear min-entropy source, and thereby resolves the long-standing open problem. In the paper, we point out that their proof is flawed and their understanding about LPN is erroneous. We further offer a remedy with some slight adaption to the setting of Suttichaya and Bhattarakosol.

Keywords: Learning Parity with Noise · High-entropy secrets · Provable security · Leftover Hash Lemma

1 Introduction

LEARNING PARITY WITH NOISE. The computational version of learning parity with noise (LPN) assumption with parameters $n \in \mathbb{N}$ (length of secret), $q \in \mathbb{N}$ (number of queries) and $0 < \mu < 1/2$ (noise rate) postulates that it is computationally infeasible to recover the n-bit secret $s \in \mathbb{Z}_2^n$ given $(a \cdot s \oplus e, a)$, where a is a random $q \times n$ matrix, e follows Ber_μ^n, Ber_μ denotes the Bernoulli distribution with parameter μ (i.e., $\Pr[\text{Ber}_\mu = 1] = \mu$ and $\Pr[\text{Ber}_\mu = 0] = 1 - \mu$), '·' denotes matrix vector multiplication over GF(2) and '$\oplus$' denotes bitwise XOR. The decisional version of LPN simply assumes that $a \cdot s \oplus e$ is pseudorandom (i.e., computationally indistinguishable from uniform randomness) given a. While seemingly stronger, the decisional version is known to be polynomially equivalent to its computational counterpart [4,8,21].

© Springer International Publishing AG 2016
K.-Y. Lam et al. (Eds.): ICICS 2016, LNCS 9977, pp. 99–106, 2016.
DOI: 10.1007/978-3-319-50011-9_8

HARDNESS OF LPN. The computational LPN problem represents a well-known NP-complete problem "decoding random linear codes" [6] and thus its worst-case hardness is well understood. LPN was also extensively studied in learning theory, and it was shown in [15] that an efficient algorithm for LPN would allow to learn several important function classes such as 2-DNF formulas, juntas, and any function with a sparse Fourier spectrum. Under a constant noise rate (i.e., $\mu = \Theta(1)$), the best known LPN solvers [9,25] require time and query complexity both $2^{O(n/\log n)}$. The time complexity goes up to $2^{O(n/\log\log n)}$ when restricted to $q = \mathsf{poly}(n)$ queries [26], or even $2^{O(n)}$ given only $q = O(n)$ queries [28]. Under low noise rate $\mu = n^{-c}$ ($0 < c < 1$), the security of LPN is less well understood: on the one hand, for $q = n + O(1)$ we can already do an efficient distinguishing attack with advantage $2^{-O(n^{1-c})}$ that matches the statistical indistinguishability (from uniform randomness) of the LPN samples ; on the other hand, for (even super-)polynomial q the best known attacks [5,7,10,24,31] are not asymptotically better, i.e., still at the order of $2^{\Theta(n^{1-c})}$. We mention that LPN does not succumb to known quantum algorithms, which makes it a promising candidate for "post-quantum cryptography". Furthermore, LPN also enjoys simplicity and is more suited for weak-power devices (e.g., RFID tags) than other quantum-secure candidates such as LWE [30].

LPN-BASED CRYPTOGRAPHIC APPLICATIONS. LPN was used as a basis for building lightweight authentication schemes against passive [18] and even active adversaries [20,21] (see [1] for a more complete literature). Recently, Kiltz et al. [23] and Dodis et al. [13] constructed randomized MACs based on the hardness of LPN, which implies a two-round authentication scheme with man-in-the-middle security. Lyubashevsky and Masny [27] gave an efficient three-round authentication scheme whose security can be based on LPN or weak pseudorandom functions (PRFs). Applebaum et al. [3] showed how to constructed a linear-stretch pseudorandom generator (PRG) from LPN. We mention other not-so-relevant applications such as public-key encryption schemes [2,14,22], oblivious transfer [11], commitment schemes and zero-knowledge proofs [19], and refer to a recent survey [29] on the current state-of-the-art about LPN.

THE ERROR IN [32] AND OUR CONTRIBUTIONS. In the standard LPN, the secret vector is assumed to be generated uniformly at random and kept confidential. However, for the version where the secret vector is sampled from some arbitrary distribution with sufficient amount of min-entropy, its hardness is still unclear. In the paper [32], the authors claimed a positive answer on the open question. More specifically, they show that if the l-bit secret is of min-entropy $k = \Omega(l)$, then the LPN problem (on such a weak secret) is hard as long as the standard one is (on uniform secrets). Unfortunately, we find that the claim in [32] is flawed. Loosely speaking, the main idea of [32, Theorem 4] is the following: denote by $\mathcal{D}$ a distribution over $\mathbb{Z}_2^l$ with min-entropy $k = \Omega(l)$ and let $n = k - 2\log(1/\epsilon)$ for some ϵ negligible in the security parameter[1], sample $B \xleftarrow{\$} \mathbb{Z}_2^{m \times n}$, $C \xleftarrow{\$} \mathbb{Z}_2^{n \times l}$,

---

[1] The security argument in [32] is quite informal: it defines a number of parameters without specifying which one is the main security parameter. We assume WLOG that the security parameter is l (the length of the secret).

$E \leftarrow \mathsf{Ber}_\alpha^{m \times n}$, $F \xleftarrow{\$} \mathbb{Z}_2^{n \times l}$ and $e \leftarrow \mathsf{Ber}_\beta^m$, and let $A = BC \oplus EF$. The authors of [32] argue that $As \oplus e$ is computationally indistinguishable from uniform even conditioned on A and that A is statistically close to uniform. Quantitatively, the standard $\mathsf{LPN}_{n,\frac{1}{2}-\frac{(1-\alpha)^n}{2}}$ assumption implies $\mathsf{LPN}_{\frac{1}{2}-(\frac{1}{2}-\beta)(1-\alpha)^n}^{\mathcal{D}}$. We stress that the proofs are incorrect for at least the following reasons:

1. For a reasonable assumption, the noise rate should be bounded away from uniform at least polynomially, i.e., $(1-\alpha)^n/2 \geq 1/\mathsf{poly}(l)$. Otherwise, the hardness assumption is trivial and useless as it does not imply any efficient (polynomial-time computable) cryptographic applications.
2. $A = BC \oplus EF$ is not statistically close to uniform. BC is sampled from a random subspace of dimension $n < k \leq l$ and thus far from being uniform over $\mathbb{Z}_2^{m \times l}$ (recall that $m \gg l$). Every entry of matrix EF is distributed to $\mathsf{Ber}_{1/2-(1-\alpha)^n/2}$ for $(1-\alpha)^n/2 \geq 1/\mathsf{poly}(l)$ (see item 1 above). Therefore, the XOR sum of BC and EF never amplifies to statistically uniform randomness.
3. There are a few flawed intermediate statements. For example, the authors prove that every entry of EF is distributed according to $\mathsf{Ber}_{1/2-(1-\alpha)^n/2}$ and then conclude that EF follows $\mathsf{Ber}_{1/2-(1-\alpha)^n/2}^{m \times l}$, which is not true since there's no guarantee that the entries of EF are all independent.

We fix the flaw using the "sampling from random subspace" technique [16,33].

2   Preliminaries

NOTATIONS AND DEFINITIONS. We use $[n]$ to denote set $\{1, \ldots, n\}$. We use capital letters (e.g., X, Y) for random variables and distributions, standard letters (e.g., x, y) for values, and calligraphic letters (e.g. $\mathcal{X}$, $\mathcal{E}$) for sets and events. The support of a random variable X, denoted by $\mathsf{Supp}(X)$, refers to the set of values on which X takes with non-zero probability, i.e., $\{x : \Pr[X = x] > 0\}$. For set $\mathcal{S}$ and binary string s, $|\mathcal{S}|$ denotes the cardinality of $\mathcal{S}$ and $|s|$ refers to the Hamming weight of s. We use Ber_μ to denote the Bernoulli distribution with parameter μ, i.e., $\Pr[\mathsf{Ber}_\mu = 1] = \mu$, $\Pr[\mathsf{Ber}_\mu = 0] = 1 - \mu$, while Ber_μ^q denotes the concatenation of q independent copies of Ber_μ. For $n \in \mathbb{N}$, U_n denotes the uniform distribution over $\mathbb{Z}_2^n$ and independent of any other random variables in consideration, and $f(U_n)$ denotes the distribution induced by applying function f to U_n. $X \sim D$ denotes that random variable X follows distribution D. We use $s \leftarrow S$ to denote sampling an element s according to distribution S, and let $s \xleftarrow{\$} \mathcal{S}$ denote sampling s uniformly from set $\mathcal{S}$.

ENTROPY DEFINITIONS. For a random variable X and any $x \in \mathsf{Supp}(X)$, the sample-entropy of x with respect to X is defined as

$$\mathbf{H}_X(x) \stackrel{\mathsf{def}}{=} \log(1/\Pr[X = x])$$

from which we define the Shannon entropy and min-entropy of X respectively, i.e.,

$$\mathbf{H}_1(X) \stackrel{\mathsf{def}}{=} \mathbb{E}_{x \leftarrow X}[\, \mathbf{H}_X(x) \,], \quad \mathbf{H}_\infty(X) \stackrel{\mathsf{def}}{=} \min_{x \in \mathsf{Supp}(X)} \mathbf{H}_X(x).$$

INDISTINGUISHABILITY AND STATISTICAL DISTANCE. We define the (t,ε)-*computational distance* between random variables X and Y, denoted by $X \underset{(t,\varepsilon)}{\sim} Y$, if for every probabilistic distinguisher D of running time t it holds that

$$| \Pr[D(X) = 1] - \Pr[D(Y) = 1] | \leq \varepsilon.$$

The *statistical distance* between X and Y, denoted by $\mathsf{SD}(X,Y)$, is defined by

$$\mathsf{SD}(X,Y) \overset{\text{def}}{=} \frac{1}{2} \sum_x |\Pr[X = x] - \Pr[Y = x]| \, .$$

Computational/statistical indistinguishability is defined with respect to distribution ensembles (indexed by a security parameter). For example, $X \overset{\text{def}}{=} \{X_n\}_{n \in \mathbb{N}}$ and $Y \overset{\text{def}}{=} \{Y_n\}_{n \in \mathbb{N}}$ are computationally indistinguishable, denoted by $X \overset{c}{\sim} Y$, if for every $t = \mathsf{poly}(n)$ there exists $\varepsilon = \mathsf{negl}(n)$ such that $X \underset{(t,\varepsilon)}{\sim} Y$, and they are statistically indistinguishable, denoted by $X \overset{s}{\sim} Y$, if $\mathsf{SD}(X,Y) = \mathsf{negl}(n)$.

SIMPLIFYING NOTATIONS. To simplify the presentation, we use the following simplified notations. Throughout, n is the security parameter and most other parameters are functions of n, and we often omit n when clear from the context. For example, $q = q(n) \in \mathbb{N}$, $t = t(n) > 0$, $\epsilon = \epsilon(n) \in (0,1)$, and $m = m(n) = \mathsf{poly}(n)$, where poly refers to some polynomial.

We will use the decisional version of the LPN assumption which is known to be polynomially equivalent to the computational counterpart.

Definition 1 (LPN). *The **decisional** $\mathsf{LPN}_{\mu,n}$ problem (with secret length n and noise rate $0 < \mu < 1/2$) is hard if for every $q = \mathsf{poly}(n)$ we have*

$$(A, \ A{\cdot}X{\oplus}E) \overset{c}{\sim} (A, U_q) \tag{1}$$

*where $q \times n$ matrix $A \sim U_{qn}$, $X \sim U_n$ and $E \sim \mathsf{Ber}_\mu^q$. The **computational** $\mathsf{LPN}_{\mu,n}$ problem is hard if for every $q = \mathsf{poly}(n)$ and every PPT algorithm D we have*

$$\Pr[\, D(A, \ A{\cdot}X{\oplus}E) = X \,] \ = \ \mathsf{negl}(n),$$

where $A \sim U_{qn}$, $X \sim U_n$ and $E \sim \mathsf{Ber}_\mu^q$.

Lemma 1 (Leftover Hash Lemma [17]). *Let $(X, Z) \in \mathcal{X} \times \mathcal{Z}$ be any joint random variable with $\mathbf{H}_\infty(X|Z) \geq k$, and let $\mathcal{H} = \{h_b : \mathcal{X} \to \mathbb{Z}_2^l, b \in \mathbb{Z}_2^s\}$ be a family of universal hash functions, i.e., for any $x_1 \neq x_2 \in \mathcal{X}$, $\Pr_{b \xleftarrow{\$} \mathbb{Z}_2^s}[h_b(x_1) = h_b(x_2)] \leq 2^{-l}$. Then, it holds that*

$$\mathsf{SD}\left((Z, B, h_B(X)) \, , \, (Z, B, U_l) \right) \ \leq \ 2^{l-k},$$

where $B \sim U_s$.

3   Correcting the Errors

3.1   The Main Contribution of [32]

In the standard LPN, the secret is assumed to be generated uniformly at random and kept confidential. However, it remains open whether or not the hardness of the LPN can still hold when secret is not uniform but sampled from any distribution of linear entropy (in the secret length). The recent work [32] claims a positive answer on the open question. More specifically, the authors show that the standard $\mathrm{LPN}_{n,\frac{1}{2}-\frac{(1-\alpha)^n}{2}}$ assumption implies $\mathrm{LPN}^{\mathcal{D}}_{\frac{1}{2}-(\frac{1}{2}-\beta)(1-\alpha)^n}$ for any $\mathcal{D}$ of min-entropy $k = \Omega(l)$ and $n = k - 2\log(1/\epsilon)$.

3.2   How the Proof Goes Astray

The statement in [32, Theorem 4] does not hold. We recall that the setting of [32]: let $\mathcal{D}$ be any distribution over $\mathbb{Z}_2^l$ with min-entropy $k = \Omega(l)$ and let $n = k - 2\log(1/\epsilon)$ for some negligible ϵ, sample $B \xleftarrow{\$} \mathbb{Z}_2^{m \times n}$, $C \xleftarrow{\$} \mathbb{Z}_2^{n \times l}$, $E \leftarrow \mathrm{Ber}_\alpha^{m \times n}$, $F \xleftarrow{\$} \mathbb{Z}_2^{n \times l}$ and $e \leftarrow \mathrm{Ber}_\beta^m$, and let $A = BC \oplus EF$. As we pointed out in Sect. 1, there are a few flaws in their proof. First, the noise rate $1/2 - (1-\alpha)^n/2$ is too strong to make any meaningful statements. Second, the matrix A is far from statistically uniform and there's not even any evidence that it could be pseudorandom. Third, the claim that EF follows $\mathrm{Ber}_{1/2-(1-\alpha)^n/2}^{m \times l}$ is not justified since they only show that each entry of EF follows $\mathrm{Ber}_{1/2-(1-\alpha)^n/2}$. It remains to show that entries of EF are all independent, which is less likely to be proven. Notice that here machinery such as two-source extraction does not help as the extracted bits are biased.

3.3   The Remedy

Now we give an easy remedy using the techniques from [16,33]. Let $\mathcal{D} \in \mathbb{Z}_2^l$ be any distribution with min-entropy $k = \Omega(l)$, $n = k - \omega(\log l)$, let $B \xleftarrow{\$} \mathbb{Z}_2^{m \times n}$, $C \xleftarrow{\$} \mathbb{Z}_2^{n \times l}$, $A = BC$ and $e \leftarrow \mathrm{Ber}_\alpha^m$, According to Leftover Hash Lemma, we have

$$(C, C \cdot s) \overset{s}{\sim} (C, U_n),$$

which in turn implies

$$(BC, (BC) \cdot s \oplus e) \overset{s}{\sim} (BC, B \cdot U_n \oplus e).$$

Note that the standard $\mathrm{LPN}_{n,\alpha}$ implies

$$(B, B \cdot U_n \oplus e) \overset{c}{\sim} (B, U_m).$$

It follows that

$$(BC, (BC) \cdot s \oplus e) \overset{c}{\sim} (BC, U_m)$$

and therefore completes the proof. This also simplifies the proof in [32] by eliminating the need for matrices E and F. Notice that we require that A is sampled from a random subspace of dimension n, instead of a uniform distribution.

4   Remarks on the Applications

In [32], the authors apply their result to the probabilistic CPA symmetric-key encryption scheme in [12], where the secret key is sampled from an arbitrary distribution with sufficient min-entropy. However, the noise rate $\frac{1}{2} - \frac{(1-\alpha)^n}{2}$ is either statistically close to uniform (and thus infeasible to build any efficient applications), or it does not yield the desired conclusion due to flawed proofs.

Acknowledgments. The work was supported by the National Natural Science Foundation of China Grant (Nos. 61472249, 61572192, 61572149, 61571191), and International Science & Technology Cooperation & Exchange Projects of Shaanxi Province (2016KW-038).

References

1. Related work on LPN-based authentication schemes. http://www.ecrypt.eu.org/lightweight/index.php/HB
2. Alekhnovich, M.: More on average case vs approximation complexity. In: 44th Annual Symposium on Foundations of Computer Science, pp. 298–307. IEEE, Cambridge, October 2003
3. Applebaum, B., Cash, D., Peikert, C., Sahai, A.: Fast cryptographic primitives and circular-secure encryption based on hard learning problems. In: Halevi, S. (ed.) CRYPTO 2009. LNCS, vol. 5677, pp. 595–618. Springer, Heidelberg (2009). doi:10.1007/978-3-642-03356-8_35
4. Applebaum, B., Ishai, Y., Kushilevitz, E.: Cryptography with constant input locality. In: Menezes, A. (ed.) CRYPTO 2007. LNCS, vol. 4622, pp. 92–110. Springer, Heidelberg (2007). doi:10.1007/978-3-540-74143-5_6. Full version: http://www.eng.tau.ac.il/ bennyap/pubs/input-locality-full-revised-1.pdf
5. Becker, A., Joux, A., May, A., Meurer, A.: Decoding random binary linear codes in $2^{n/20}$: how $1 + 1 = 0$ improves information set decoding. In: Pointcheval, D., Johansson, T. (eds.) EUROCRYPT 2012. LNCS, vol. 7237, pp. 520–536. Springer, Heidelberg (2012). doi:10.1007/978-3-642-29011-4_31
6. Berlekamp, E., McEliece, R.J., van Tilborg, H.: On the inherent intractability of certain coding problems. IEEE Trans. Inf. Theory **24**(3), 384–386 (1978)
7. Bernstein, D.J., Lange, T., Peters, C.: Smaller decoding exponents: Ball-Collision decoding. In: Rogaway, P. (ed.) CRYPTO 2011. LNCS, vol. 6841, pp. 743–760. Springer, Heidelberg (2011). doi:10.1007/978-3-642-22792-9_42
8. Blum, A., Furst, M., Kearns, M., Lipton, R.J.: Cryptographic primitives based on hard learning problems. In: Stinson, D.R. (ed.) CRYPTO 1993. LNCS, vol. 773, pp. 278–291. Springer, Heidelberg (1994). doi:10.1007/3-540-48329-2_24
9. Blum, A., Kalai, A., Wasserman, H.: Noise-tolerant learning, the parity problem, and the statistical query model. J. ACM **50**(4), 506–519 (2003)
10. Canteaut, A., Chabaud, F.: A new algorithm for finding minimum-weight words in a linear code: application to mceliece's cryptosystem and to narrow-sense BCH codes of length 511. IEEE Trans. Inf. Theory **44**(1), 367–378 (1998)
11. David, B., Dowsley, R., Nascimento, A.C.A.: Universally composable oblivious transfer based on a variant of LPN. In: Gritzalis, D., Kiayias, A., Askoxylakis, I. (eds.) CANS 2014. LNCS, vol. 8813, pp. 143–158. Springer, Heidelberg (2014). doi:10.1007/978-3-319-12280-9_10

12. Dodis, Y., Kalai, Y.T., Lovett, S.: On cryptography with auxiliary input. In: ACM Symposium on Theory of Computing, pp. 621–630 (2009)
13. Dodis, Y., Kiltz, E., Pietrzak, K., Wichs, D.: Message authentication, revisited. In: Pointcheval, D., Johansson, T. (eds.) EUROCRYPT 2012. LNCS, vol. 7237, pp. 355–374. Springer, Heidelberg (2012). doi:10.1007/978-3-642-29011-4_22
14. Döttling, N., Müller-Quade, J., Nascimento, A.C.A.: IND-CCA secure cryptography based on a variant of the LPN problem. In: Wang, X., Sako, K. (eds.) ASIACRYPT 2012. LNCS, vol. 7658, pp. 485–503. Springer, Heidelberg (2012). doi:10.1007/978-3-642-34961-4_30
15. Feldman, V., Gopalan, P., Khot, S., Ponnuswami, A.K.: New results for learning noisy parities and halfspaces. In: 47th Symposium on Foundations of Computer Science, pp. 563–574. IEEE, Berkeley, 21–24 October 2006
16. Goldwasser, S., Kalai, Y., Peikert, C., Vaikuntanathan, V.: Robustness of the learning with errors assumption. In: Innovations in Theoretical Computer Science, ITCS 2010, pp. 230–240. Tsinghua University Press (2010)
17. Håstad, J., Impagliazzo, R., Levin, L., Luby, M.: Construction of pseudorandom generator from any one-way function. SIAM J. Comput. **28**(4), 1364–1396 (1999)
18. Hopper, N.J., Blum, M.: Secure human identification protocols. In: Boyd, C. (ed.) ASIACRYPT 2001. LNCS, vol. 2248, pp. 52–66. Springer, Heidelberg (2001). doi:10.1007/3-540-45682-1_4
19. Jain, A., Krenn, S., Pietrzak, K., Tentes, A.: Commitments and efficient zero-knowledge proofs from learning parity with noise. In: Wang, X., Sako, K. (eds.) ASIACRYPT 2012. LNCS, vol. 7658, pp. 663–680. Springer, Heidelberg (2012). doi:10.1007/978-3-642-34961-4_40
20. Juels, A., Weis, S.A.: Authenticating pervasive devices with human protocols. In: Shoup, V. (ed.) CRYPTO 2005. LNCS, vol. 3621, pp. 293–308. Springer, Heidelberg (2005). doi:10.1007/11535218_18
21. Katz, J., Shin, J.S.: Parallel and concurrent security of the HB and HB$^+$ protocols. In: Vaudenay, S. (ed.) EUROCRYPT 2006. LNCS, vol. 4004, pp. 73–87. Springer, Heidelberg (2006). doi:10.1007/11761679_6
22. Kiltz, E., Masny, D., Pietrzak, K.: Simple chosen-ciphertext security from low-noise LPN. In: Krawczyk, H. (ed.) PKC 2014. LNCS, vol. 8383, pp. 1–18. Springer, Heidelberg (2014). doi:10.1007/978-3-642-54631-0_1
23. Kiltz, E., Pietrzak, K., Cash, D., Jain, A., Venturi, D.: Efficient authentication from hard learning problems. In: Paterson, K.G. (ed.) EUROCRYPT 2011. LNCS, vol. 6632, pp. 7–26. Springer, Heidelberg (2011). doi:10.1007/978-3-642-20465-4_3
24. Kirchner, P.: Improved generalized birthday attack. Cryptology ePrint Archive, report 2011/377 (2011). http://eprint.iacr.org/2011/377
25. Levieil, É., Fouque, P.-A.: An improved LPN algorithm. In: Prisco, R., Yung, M. (eds.) SCN 2006. LNCS, vol. 4116, pp. 348–359. Springer, Heidelberg (2006). doi:10.1007/11832072_24
26. Lyubashevsky, V.: The parity problem in the presence of noise, decoding random linear codes, and the subset sum problem. In: Chekuri, C., Jansen, K., Rolim, J.D.P., Trevisan, L. (eds.) APPROX/RANDOM -2005. LNCS, vol. 3624, pp. 378–389. Springer, Heidelberg (2005). doi:10.1007/11538462_32
27. Lyubashevsky, V., Masny, D.: Man-in-the-middle secure authentication schemes from LPN and weak PRFs. In: Canetti, R., Garay, J.A. (eds.) CRYPTO 2013. LNCS, vol. 8043, pp. 308–325. Springer, Heidelberg (2013). doi:10.1007/978-3-642-40084-1_18

28. May, A., Meurer, A., Thomae, E.: Decoding random linear codes in $\tilde{\mathcal{O}}(2^{0.054n})$. In: Lee, D.H., Wang, X. (eds.) ASIACRYPT 2011. LNCS, vol. 7073, pp. 107–124. Springer, Heidelberg (2011). doi:10.1007/978-3-642-25385-0_6

29. Pietrzak, K.: Cryptography from learning parity with noise. In: Bieliková, M., Friedrich, G., Gottlob, G., Katzenbeisser, S., Turán, G. (eds.) SOFSEM 2012. LNCS, vol. 7147, pp. 99–114. Springer, Heidelberg (2012). doi:10.1007/978-3-642-27660-6_9

30. Regev, O.: On lattices, learning with errors, random linear codes, and cryptography. In: Gabow, H.N., Fagin, R. (eds.) STOC, pp. 84–93. ACM (2005)

31. Stern, J.: A method for finding codewords of small weight. In: Cohen, G., Wolfmann, J. (eds.) Coding Theory 1988. LNCS, vol. 388, pp. 106–113. Springer, Heidelberg (1989). doi:10.1007/BFb0019850

32. Suttichaya, V., Bhattarakosol, P.: Solving the learning parity with noises open question. Inf. Process. Lett. **113**(14–16), 562–566 (2013)

33. Yu, Y., Zhang, J.: Cryptography with auxiliary input and trapdoor from constant-noise LPN. In: Robshaw, M., Katz, J. (eds.) CRYPTO 2016. LNCS, vol. 9814, pp. 214–243. Springer, Heidelberg (2016). doi:10.1007/978-3-662-53018-4_9

The Linear Complexity and 2-Error Linear Complexity Distribution of 2^n-Periodic Binary Sequences with Fixed Hamming Weight

Wenlun Pan[1,2], Zhenzhen Bao[3(✉)], Dongdai Lin[1], and Feng Liu[1,2]

[1] State Key Laboratory of Information Security,
Institute of Information Engineering,
Chinese Academy of Sciences, Beijing 100093, China
wylbpwl@gmail.com, {ddlin,liufeng}@iie.ac.cn
[2] University of Chinese Academy of Sciences, Beijing 100049, China
[3] Shanghai Jiao Tong University, Shanghai 200240, China
baozhenzhen10@gmail.com

Abstract. The linear complexity and k-error linear complexity of sequences are important measures of the strength of key-streams generated by stream ciphers. Based on the characters of the set of sequences with given linear complexity, people get the characterization of 2^n-binary sequences with given k-error linear complexity for small k recently. In this paper, we put forward this study to get the distribution of linear complexity and k-error linear complexity of 2^n-periodic binary sequences with fixed Hamming weight. First, we give the counting function of the number of 2^n-periodic binary sequences with given linear complexity and fixed Hamming weight. Provide an asymptotic evaluation of this counting function when n gets large. Then we take a step further to study the distribution of 2^n-periodic binary sequences with given 2-error linear complexity and fixed Hamming weight. Through an asymptotic analysis, we provide an estimate on the number of 2^n-periodic binary sequences with given 2-error linear complexity and fixed Hamming weight.

Keywords: Sequence · Linear complexity · k-error linear complexity · Counting function · Hamming weight · Asymptotic analysis

1 Introduction

The linear complexity of an N-periodic sequence is defined by the length of the shortest linear feedback shift register (LFSR) that can generate the sequence. By Berlekamp-Massey algorithm [7], we only need the first $2L$ elements of the sequence to recover the whole sequence, where L is the linear complexity of the sequence. For this reason, a secure key stream must has high linear complexity. But this is not sufficient. If altering a few elements in the sequence can result in greatly decrease its linear complexity, then the sequence is not cryptographically strong. This observation gives rise to the study of the stability of sequence [1] and develops to the concept of k-error linear complexity [11] which is defined

© Springer International Publishing AG 2016
K.-Y. Lam et al. (Eds.): ICICS 2016, LNCS 9977, pp. 107–123, 2016.
DOI: 10.1007/978-3-319-50011-9_9

as the minimum linear complexity of the sequence altering not more than k elements from the original sequence. A cryptographically strong sequence must both have larger linear complexity and k-error linear complexity.

Let $S = (s_0 s_1 \cdots s_{N-1})^\infty$ be an N-periodic sequence with the terms in finite field $\mathbb{F}_2$. And we denote S^N the set of all N-periodic binary sequences. For a given sequence $S \in S^N$, we denote the support set of S by $supp(S)$, which is the positions of nonzero elements in S, that is, $supp(S) = \{i : s_i \neq 0, 0 \leq i < N\}$. For $i, j \in supp(S)$, we define the distance between i and j as $d(i,j) = 2^t$ where $|i - j| = 2^t b$ and $2 \nmid b$. Let $w_H(S)$ denote the Hamming weight of sequence S which is the number of nonzero elements of S in one period.

The linear complexity of S, denoted by $LC(S)$, is given by [1]

$$LC(S) = N - \deg(\gcd(x^N - 1, S(x))) \tag{1}$$

where $S(x) = s_0 + s_1 x + s_2 x^2 + \ldots + s_{N-1} x^{N-1}$ and is called the corresponding polynomial to S. According to Eq. (1), we can get the following two lemmas:

Lemma 1 [8]. *Let S be a 2^n-periodic binary sequence. Then $LC(S) = 2^n$ if and only if the Hamming weight of the sequence S is odd.*

Lemma 2 [8]. *Let S and S' be two 2^n-periodic binary sequences. Then we have $LC(S + S') = \max\{LC(S), LC(S')\}$ if $LC(S) \neq LC(S')$, and $LC(S + S') < LC(S)$ for otherwise.*

In this paper, we focus on 2^n-periodic binary sequences. Based on the observation $x^{2^n} - 1 = (x - 1)^{2^n}$, we have

$$\gcd(x^{2^n} - 1, S(x)) = \gcd((x - 1)^{2^n}, S_L(x) + x^{2^{n-1}} S_R(x))$$
$$= \gcd((x - 1)^{2^n}, (S_L(x) + S_R(x)) + (x + 1)^{2^{n-1}} S_R(x)),$$

and according to Eq. (1), we get

$$LC(S) = \begin{cases} 2^{n-1} + LC(S_L + S_R) & \text{if } S_L \neq S_R, \\ LC(S_L) & \text{otherwise,} \end{cases} \tag{2}$$

where S_L, S_R are the left and right half part of the sequence S respectively and $S_L(x) = s_0 + s_1 x + \cdots + s_{2^{n-1}-1} x^{2^{n-1}-1}$, $S_R(x) = s_{2^{n-1}} + s_{2^{n-1}+1} x + \cdots + s_{2^n-1} x^{2^{n-1}-1}$. And the summation of two sequences $S = (s_0 s_1 \cdots s_{N-1})$, $S' = (s'_0 s'_1 \cdots s'_{N-1})$ is defined as $S + S' = (u_0 u_1 \cdots u_{N-1})$ where $u_i = s_i + s'_i$ for $0 \leq i < N$.

Iterating Eq. (2) on the length of sequence, one can immediately get the linear complexity of the 2^n-periodic binary sequence (note that, for sequence of length 1, $LC((1)) = 1$ and $LC((0)) = 0$). This iteration algorithm is known as Games-Chan Algorithm developed in [3].

For $0 \leq k \leq N$, the k-error linear complexity of S, denoted by $LC_k(S)$, is definable by

$$LC_k(S) = \min_{w_H(E) \leq k, \ E \in S^N} LC(S + E), \tag{3}$$

where E is called the error sequences.

For a given sequence $S \in S^N$, denote $merr(S) = \min\{k : LC_k(S) < LC(S)\}$, which is called the first descend point of linear complexity of S. Kurosawa et al. in [6] derived a formula for the exact value of $merr(S)$.

Lemma 3 [6]. *Let S be a nonzero 2^n-periodic binary sequence, then the first descend point of S is*

$$merr(S) = 2^{w_H(2^n - LC(S))}. \tag{4}$$

The counting function of a sequence complexity measure depicts the distribution of the sequences with given complexity. It is useful to determine the expected value and variance of a given complexity measure of a family of sequences. Besides, the exact number of available good sequences with high complexity measure value in a family of sequences can be known. Rueppel [10] determined the counting function of linear complexity for 2^n-periodic binary sequences as follows:

Lemma 4 [10]. *Let $N(L)$ and $A(L)$ respectively denote the number of and the set of 2^n-periodic binary sequences with given linear complexity L, where $0 \leq L \leq 2^n$. Then*

$$N(0) = 1, \qquad A(0) = \{(00 \cdots 0)\}, \text{ and}$$
$$N(L) = 2^{L-1}, \quad A(L) = \{S \in S^{2^n} : S(x) = (1-x)^{2^n - L} a(x), \ a(1) \neq 0\} \text{ for } 1 \leq L \leq 2^n.$$

Let $A_k(L)$ and $N_k(L)$ denote the set of and the number of 2^n-periodic binary sequences with k-error linear complexity L, $A^w(L)$ and $N^w(L)$ denote the set of and the number of 2^n-periodic binary sequences with Hamming weight w and linear complexity L, and $A_k^w(L)$ and $N_k^w(L)$ denote the set of and the number of 2^n-periodic binary sequences with Hamming weight w and k-error linear complexity L respectively, which can be formally defined as

$$A_k(L) = \{S \in S^{2^n} : LC_k(S) = L\} \quad \text{and} \quad N_k(L) = |A_k(L)|,$$

$$A^w(L) = \{S \in S^{2^n} : LC(S) = L \text{ and } w_H(S) = w\} \quad \text{and} \quad N^w(L) = |A^w(L)|,$$

$$A_k^w(L) = \{S \in S^{2^n} : LC_k(S) = L \text{ and } w_H(S) = w\} \quad \text{and} \quad N_k^w(L) = |A_k^w(L)|.$$

By Lemma 4, one can get fully knowledge of the distribution of 2^n-periodic binary sequences with given linear complexity. Based on the characters of $A(L)$ and using algebraic, combinatorial or decomposing method [2,5,9,13], people get the counting function $N_k(L)$ for small k. However, under the current state of art, distribution of 2^n-periodic binary sequences with given linear complexity when fixed Hamming weight remains unclear. In this paper we first provide a solution to this interesting problem. And then get the distribution of 2-error linear complexity with fixed Hamming weight which is a more difficult question to answer. In other words, we study the counting function for the number of balanced 2^n-periodic binary sequences with given values of complexity measure. As a contribution, we provide asymptotic evaluations as well as the explicit formulas of the counting functions.

2   The Characterization of $\mathcal{A}^w(L)$

In this section we discuss the linear complexity distribution of 2^n-periodic binary sequences with fixed Hamming weight.

2.1   Counting Functions for $\mathcal{N}^w(L)$

Let us first review the Games-Chan Algorithm. For a 2^n-periodic binary sequence S, one can use Eq. (2) recurrently on the length of sequence to get the linear complexity of S. Now to counting the sequences, we reverse this process, namely, we use a short sequence to construct the long. In this reversed process, we make the linear complexity of the constructed sequence equal to L step by step. Simultaneously, we restrict the Hamming weight of constructed sequences to w to get the number of sequences which meet the requirements. We begin with a simple case that is less general than what can actually be said.

Lemma 5. *Let $\mathcal{N}^w(L)$ be the number of 2^n-periodic binary sequences with Hamming weight w and linear complexity L, then one have*

$$
\mathcal{N}^w(2^r + 1) = \begin{cases} 2^{2^r} & \text{if } w = 2^{n-1}, \\ 0 & \text{otherwise,} \end{cases}
\tag{5}
$$

$$
\mathcal{N}^w(2^{r_1} + 2^{r_2} + 1) = \begin{cases} 2^{2^{r_2} + 2^{r_1} - 1} \binom{2^{r_1}-1}{m} & \text{if } w = 2^{n-2} + m \cdot 2^{n-r_1} \text{ and } 0 \le m \le 2^{r_1}-1, \\ 0 & \text{otherwise,} \end{cases}
\tag{6}
$$

where $0 \le r < n$ and $0 \le r_2 < r_1 < n$.

Proof. Let $S = (s_0 s_1 \cdots s_{N-1})$ be binary sequence of linear complexity $2^r + 1$ and length N with $N = 2^{r+1}$. According to Eq. (2), we have $S_L \ne S_R$ and $LC(S_L + S_R) = 1$ and then we get $s_i + s_{i+N/2} = 1$ for $0 \le i < N/2$ where S_L and S_R denote the left and right half part of S respectively. Therefore, the number of 2^{r+1}-periodic binary sequences of linear complexity $2^r + 1$ is 2^{2^r} and we denote the set of all those sequence by $\mathcal{A}$.

For any sequence S in $\mathcal{A}$, we can construct a sequence S_1 of length 2^{r+2} preserving linear complexity by connecting two S, i.e. $S_1 = S||S$. In the same way, we can construct a serial sequences S_i, $1 < i \le n - i$, preserving the linear complexity where the length of S_i is 2^{r+i+1}. As a result, we can construct 2^{2^r} sequences of periodic 2^n and linear complexity $2^r + 1$. From Games-Chan Algorithm we can know that there does not exist sequences of linear complexity $2^r + 1$ except for those constructed above. Thus, the number of 2^n-periodic binary sequences of linear complexity $2^r + 1$ is 2^{2^r} and the Hamming weight of the sequence must be $(2^r)^{n-r-1} = 2^{n-1}$.

Similarly, there are $2^{2^{r_2}}$ binary sequences of length 2^{r_2+1} having linear complexity $2^{r_2}+1$. We can extend those sequences to sequences of length 2^{r_1} using the same method. It is clear that the Hamming weight of those extended sequences are 2^{r_1-1} and we denote the set of those sequences by $\mathcal{A}_1$.

For any sequence S in $\mathcal{A}_1$, suppose the support set of S is $supp(S) = \{i_1, i_2, \cdots, i_{N_1}\}$ where $N_1 = 2^{r_1-1}$ and $0 \le i_1 < i_2 < \cdots < i_{N_1} < 2^{r_1}$. Denote $U_s = \{0, 1, \cdots, 2^{r_1} - 1\}$ and $U_r' = U_r - supp(S)$. Choose m points $j_1, j_2, \cdots, j_m$ from the set U_r' where $0 \le m \le 2^{r_1-1}$ and construct a sequence $S_1 = (s_0 s_1 \cdots s_{N_2})$ where $N_2 = 2^{r_1+1}$ and $s_{i_u} + s_{i_u+2^{r_1}} = 1$, $s_{j_v} + s_{j_v+2^{r_1}} = 2$ for $1 \le u \le N_1$, $1 \le v \le m$ and $s_t = 0$ for $t \notin \{i_1, \cdots, i_{N_1}, i_1 + 2^{r_1}, \cdots, i_{N_1} + 2^{r_1}, j_1, \cdots, j_m, j_1 + 2^{r_1}, \cdots, j_m + 2^{r_1}\}$. It can be confirmed that the linear complexity of S_1 is $2^{r_1} + 2^{r_2} + 1$ and the Hamming weight of S_1 is $2^{r_1-1} + 2m$. We use the same method to extend the length of S_1 to 2^n preserving the linear complexity. And the Hamming weight of constructed sequences are $(2^{r_1-1} + 2m) \cdot 2^{n-r_1-1} = 2^{n-2} + m \cdot 2^{n-r_1}$. Because for each sequence S we can construct $2^{2^{r_1-1}} \cdot \binom{2^{r_1-1}}{m}$ different sequences S_1, then we can construct $2^{2^{r_2}} \cdot 2^{2^{r_1-1}} \cdot \binom{2^{r_1-1}}{m}$ different sequences with Hamming weight $2^{n-2} + m \cdot 2^{n-r_1}$ and linear complexity $2^{r_1} + 2^{r_2} + 1$. Consequently, we get the counting function for $\mathcal{N}^w(2^{r_1} + 2^{r_2} + 1)$ as shown above. $\square$

This argument readily extends to general cases in which binary representation of L involves an arbitrary number of ones.

Theorem 1. *Let $\mathcal{N}^w(L)$ be the number of 2^n-periodic binary sequences with Hamming weight w and linear complexity L. Then when $L = 2^{r_1} + 2^{r_2} + \cdots + 2^{r_t} + 1$ and w is even, we have*

$$\mathcal{N}^w(L) = \sum_{\sum_{j=1}^{t-1} m_j \cdot 2^{n-r_j-j+1} = w - 2^{n-t}, \, m_j \ge 0} 2^{2^{r_t}} \prod_{j=1}^{t-1} 2^{u_j} \cdot \binom{2^{r_j} - u_j}{m_j} \quad (7)$$

where $0 \le r_t < r_{t-1} < \cdots < r_1 < n$, $2 \le t < n$ and $u_{t-1} = 2^{r_{t-1}-1}$, $u_j = (2m_{j+1} + u_{j+1}) \cdot 2^{r_j - r_{j+1} - 1}$ for $1 \le j < t - 1$.

Proof. The proof of Lemma 5 applies verbatim here.

First we construct $2^{2^{r_t}}$ sequences of length 2^{r_t+1} and linear complexity $2^{r_t} + 1$, and at the same time all those sequences have Hamming weight 2^{r_t}. Denote the set of those sequences by $\mathcal{A}_t$. For any sequence S_t in $\mathcal{A}_t$, we extend the length of it to $2^{r_{t-1}}$ in the same way as we did in the previous proof, and denote the extended sequence by S_t'. It is apparent that the Hamming weight of S_t' is $2^{r_{t-1}-1}$.

Suppose the support set of S_t' is $supp(S_t') = \{i_1, i_2, \cdots, i_{N_{t-1}}\}$ where $N_{t-1} = 2^{r_{t-1}-1}$. Denote $U_{t-1} = \{0, 1, \cdots, 2^{r_{t-1}} - 1\}$ and $U_{t-1}' = U_{t-1} - supp(S_t')$. By choosing m_{t-1} points $j_1, j_2, \cdots, j_{m_{t-1}}$ from U_{t-1}', we can construct a sequence $S_{t-1} = (s_0 s_1 \cdots s_{N_{t-1}})$ where $N_{t-1} = 2^{r_{t-1}+1}$ and $s_{i_u} + s_{i_u+2^{r_{t-1}}} = 1$, $s_{j_v} + s_{j_v+2^{r_{t-1}}} = 2$ for $1 \le u \le N_{t-1}$, $1 \le v \le m_{t-1}$ and $s_k = 0$ for $k \notin \{i_1, \cdots, i_{N_{t-1}}, i_1+2^{r_1}, \cdots, i_{N_{t-1}}+2^{r_{t-1}}, j_1, \cdots, j_{m_{t-1}}, j_1+2^{r_{t-1}}, \cdots, j_{m_{t-1}} + 2^{r_{t-1}}\}$. We can confirm that the constructed sequence has linear complexity $2^{r_{t-1}} + 2^{r_t} + 1$ and Hamming weight $2^{r_{t-1}-1} + 2 \cdot m_{t-1}$. For each S_t' we can construct $2^{2^{r_{t-1}-1}} \binom{2^{r_{t-1}-1}}{m_{t-1}}$ different S_{t-1} of linear complexity $2^{r_{t-1}} + 2^{r_t} + 1$ and the same Hamming weight by choosing different m_{t-1} points from the set U'_{t-1}. Denote the set of those constructed sequences by $\mathcal{A}_{t-1,m_{t-1}}$.

For any sequence S_{t-1} in $\mathcal{A}_{t-1,m_{t-1}}$, we extend the length of it to $2^{r_{t-2}}$ and preserving the linear complexity at the same time, which results in a sequence S'_{t-1}. It can be verified that Hamming weight of S'_{t-1} is $u_{t-2} = (2^{r_{t-1}-1} + 2m_{t-1}) \cdot 2^{r_{t-2}-r_{t-1}-1}$.

Suppose the support set of S'_{t-1} is $supp(S'_{t-1}) = \{i_1, i_2, \cdots, i_{u_{t-2}}\}$. Denote $U_{t-2} = \{0, 1, \cdots, 2^{r_{t-2}} - 1\}$ and $U'_{t-2} = U_{t-2} - supp(S'_{t-1})$. In the same vein, by choosing m_{t-2} points $j_1, j_2, \cdots, j_{m_{t-2}}$ from the set U'_{t-2}, we can construct a sequence $S_{t-2} = (s_0 s_1 \cdots s_{2^{r_{t-2}+1}})$ where $s_{i_u} + s_{i_u+2^{r_{t-2}}} = 1$, $s_{j_v} + s_{j_v+2^{r_{t-2}}} = 2$ and $s_k = 0$ for $1 \le u \le u_{t-2}$, $1 \le v \le m_{t-2}$ and $k \notin \{i_1, \cdots, i_{u_{t-2}}, i_1 + 2^{r_{t-2}}, \cdots, i_{u_{t-2}}+2^{r_{t-2}}, \cdots, j_1, \cdots, j_{m_{t-2}}, j_1+2^{r_{t-2}}, \cdots, j_{m_{t-2}}+2^{r_{t-2}}\}$. For each S'_{t-1} we can construct $2^{u_{t-2}} \cdot \binom{2^{r_{t-2}}-u_{t-2}}{m_{t-2}}$ different S_{t-2} of linear complexity $2^{r_{t-2}} + 2^{r_{t-1}} + 2^{r_t} + 1$ and Hamming weight $u_{t-2} + 2m_{t-2}$ by choosing different m_{t-2} points from U'_{t-2}. Denote the set of those constructed sequences by $\mathcal{A}_{t-2,m_{t-2}}$.

For each sequence S_{t-2} in $\mathcal{A}_{t-2,m_{t-2}}$, we extend it length to $2^{r_{t-3}}$ and preserving its linear complexity, which results in a sequence S'_{t-2}.

Proceeding in precisely the same manner as the previous process by recurrence, we can eventually extend the length of a sequence S_t in $\mathcal{A}_t$ to 2^n and make the final constructed sequence have linear complexity $2^{r_1} + 2^{r_2} + \cdots + 2^{r_t} + 1$ step by step. For each S_t in $\mathcal{A}_t$ we can get the set $\mathcal{A}_{t-1,m_{t-1}}$ by adding m_{t-1} points to S'_t and similarly for each sequence S_{t-1} in $\mathcal{A}_{t-1,m_{t-1}}$ we can get the set $\mathcal{A}_{t-2,m_{t-2}}$ by adding m_{t-2} points to S'_{t-1}. In this way, we can construct $2^{2^{r_t}} \cdot \prod_{j=t-1}^{1} 2^{u_j} \binom{2^{r_j}-u_j}{m_j}$ sequences of linear complexity L and Hamming weight $(u_1 + 2m_1) \cdot 2^{n-r_1-1}$ where $u_{t-1} = 2^{r_{t-1}-1}$ and $u_j = (u_{j+1} + 2m_{j+1}) \cdot 2^{r_j-r_{j+1}-1}$ for $1 \le j < t - 1$.

As a result, for given linear complexity L and Hamming weight w, the number of sequences of linear complexity L and Hamming weight w is the summation of $2^{2^{r_t}} \cdot \prod_{j=t-1}^{1} 2^{u_j} \binom{2^{r_j}-u_j}{m_j}$ for all $m_1, m_2, \cdots, m_{t-1}$ such that $w = (u_1 + 2m_1) \cdot 2^{n-r_1-1} = \sum_{i=1}^{t-1} m_i \cdot 2^{n-r_i-i+1} + 2^{n-t}$ and from here, we achieve Eq. (7). $\qquad \square$

Furthermore, we observe that when $r_t = 0$ the linear complexity $L = 2^{r_1} + 2^{r_2} + \cdots 2^{r_t} + 1$ has the form $L = 2^{r_1} + 2^{r_2} + \cdots 2^{r_{t'}+1}$ where $0 \le r_t < r_{t-1} < \cdots < r_1 < n$, $t < n$, and $r_{t'-1} - r_{t'} > 1$, $r_j - r_{j+1} = 1$ for $t' < j \le t$. In this case, we can use a similar method to construct sequences with linear complexity L and length 2^n from sequences with linear complexity $2^{r_{t'}}$ and length $2^{r_{t'}}$.

Corollary 1. *Let $\mathcal{N}^w(L)$ be the number of 2^n-periodic binary sequences with Hamming weight w and linear complexity L. When $L = 2^{r_1} + 2^{r_2} + \cdots + 2^{r_t}$, we have*

$$\mathcal{N}^w(L) = \sum_{\substack{m=1, m \text{ is odd} \\ \sum_{j=1}^{t-1} m_j \cdot 2^{n-r_j-j+1} = w-m\cdot 2^{n-r_t-t+1}}}^{2^{r_t}} \sum \binom{2^{r_t}}{m} \cdot \prod_{j=1}^{t-1} 2^{u_{m,j}} \cdot \binom{2^{r_j} - u_{m,j}}{m_j}$$

$$(8)$$

where $0 < r_t < r_{t-1} < \cdots < r_1 < n$, $2 \le t < n$ *and* $u_{m,t-1} = m \cdot 2^{r_{t-1}-r_t}$, $u_{m,j} = (2m_{j+1} + u_{j+1}) \cdot 2^{r_j-r_{j+1}-1}$ *for* $1 \le j < t-1$.

Proof. This corollary can be derived from Eq. (7) by exchanging the order of summations. We can also give a constructive proof similar to the one used for Theorem 1 and get the equation directly. Firstly, the number of sequences with length 2^{r_t}, linear complexity 2^{r_t} and Hamming weight m is $\binom{2^{r_t}}{m}$ where m must be odd. And denote the set of those sequences by $\mathcal{A}_{m,t}$. For sequence S_t in $\mathcal{A}_{m,t}$ we can extend the length to 2^n and make the linear complexity to be L using a similar method to the one in the proof for Theorem 1 step by step. And we can get the number of 2^n-periodic binary sequences with linear complexity L and Hamming weight $w = (u_{m,1} + 2m_1) \cdot 2^{n-r_1-1}$ which is $\binom{2^{r_t}}{m} \sum_{u_{m,1}+2m_1=w} \prod_{i=1}^{t-1} 2^{u_{m,i}} \binom{2^{r_i}-u_{m,i}}{m_i}$ where $u_{m,t-1} = m \cdot 2^{r_{t-1}-r_t}$ and $u_{m,i} = (u_{m,i+1} + 2m_{i+1}) \cdot 2^{r_i-r_{i+1}-1}$ for $1 \le i < t-1$. Then by enumerating all possible value of m and we can get Eq. (8). $\qquad\square$

Because $w = \sum_{i=1}^{t-1} m_i \cdot 2^{n-r_i-i+1} + 2^{n-t}$ and $2^{n-r_1} \le 2^{n-r_j-j+1}$ for $1 < j \le t-1$, thus $2^{n-r_1}|w$. Combine with the fact that w is in range from 2^{n-t} to $2^n - 1$, we have

Corollary 2. *Let S be a 2^n-periodic binary sequence, if the linear complexity of S is $L = 2^{r_1} + 2^{r_2} + \cdots + 2^{r_t} + 1$, where $0 \le r_t < r_{t-1} < \cdots < r_1 < n$ and $t < n$, then the Hamming weight of S only can be $2^{n-1} + l \cdot 2^{n-r_1}$ and $2^{r_1-t} - 2^{r_1-1} \le l \le 2^{r_1-1} - 2^{r_1-t}$.*

To get the exact value of $\mathcal{N}^w(L)$, we need to get all solutions of equation $\sum_{j=1}^{t-1} m_j \cdot 2^{n-r_j-j+1} = 2^{n-1} - 2^{n-t}$. This may turns out to be impossible to solve when n is large. Thus, the result for $\mathcal{N}^w(L)$ in this subsection is perhaps not too useful for grasping the number of the sequence when n gets large, so that asymptotic analysis is called for.

To this end, we make asymptotic analysis of $\mathcal{N}^w(L)$, provide lower bound and upper bound of its value in the following subsection.

2.2 Asymptotic Analysis for $\mathcal{N}^w(L)$

Suppose $L = 2^{r_1} + 2^{r_2} + \cdots + 2^{r_t} + 1$ with $0 \le r_t < r_{t-1} < \cdots < r_1 < n$ in the sequel.

Let us begin with a simple case in which $t = 3$, and $w = 2^{n-1}$. According to Eq. (7), when $L = 2^{r_1} + 2^{r_2} + 2^{r_3} + 1$, $0 \le r_3 < r_2 < r_1 < n$ and $w = 2^{n-1}$, we have

$$\mathcal{N}^w(L) = 2^{2^{r_3}+2^{r_2-1}+2^{r_1-2}} \cdot \sum_{m=0}^{2^{r_2}-1} 2^{m \cdot 2^{r_1-r_2}} \binom{2^{r_2}-1}{m} \binom{3 \cdot 2^{r_1-2} - m \cdot 2^{r_1-r_2}}{3 \cdot 2^{r_1-3} - m \cdot 2^{r_1-r_2-1}}.$$

$$(9)$$

The following lemma provides an asymptotic estimate for this case.

Lemma 6. *Let $\mathcal{N}^w(L)$ be the number of 2^n-periodic binary sequences with Hamming weight w and linear complexity L. Then when $L = 2^{r_1} + 2^{r_2} + 2^{r_3} + 1$ where $0 \leq r_3 < r_2 < r_1 < n$ and $w = 2^{n-1}$, we have*

$$
\mathcal{N}^w(L) \geq 2^{2^{r_3} + 2^{r_2 - 1} + 2^{r_1} - 0.5 r_1 - 0.9107} (1 + 2^{\frac{0.7213}{3 \cdot 2^{r_2 - 2}}})^{2^{r_2 - 1}},
$$
$$
\mathcal{N}^w(L) \leq 2^{2^{r_3} + 2^{r_2 - 1} + 2^{r_1} - 0.5 r_1 - 0.9107} (1 + 2^{\frac{1.1887}{3 \cdot 2^{r_2 - 2}}})^{2^{r_2 - 1}}. \tag{10}
$$

Proof. From Stirling's formula

$$
n! = \sqrt{2\pi n}(\frac{n}{e})^n e^{\frac{\theta_n}{12n}}, \quad 0 < \theta_n < 1, \tag{11}
$$

it implies that

$$
\binom{2n}{n} = \frac{(2n)!}{n!n!} = \frac{\sqrt{2\pi \cdot 2n}(\frac{2n}{e})^{2n} e^{\frac{\theta_{2n}}{24n}}}{(\sqrt{2\pi n}(\frac{n}{e})^n e^{\frac{\theta_n}{12n}})^2} = 2^{2n - 0.5 \log n - 0.5 \log \pi + \frac{\theta}{3n}} = 2^{2n - 0.5 \log n - 0.8257 + \frac{\theta}{3n}}, \tag{12}
$$

where $-0.7214 < \theta < 0.1084$.

Accordingly, the logarithmic transformation of the number of combinations $\binom{3 \cdot 2^{r_1 - 2} - m \cdot 2^{r_1 - r_2}}{3 \cdot 2^{r_1 - 3} - m \cdot 2^{r_1 - r_2 - 1}}$ yields:

$$
\log \left(\frac{3 \cdot 2^{r_1 - 2} - m \cdot 2^{r_1 - r_2}}{3 \cdot 2^{r_1 - 3} - m \cdot 2^{r_1 - r_2 - 1}} \right)
$$
$$
= 3 \cdot 2^{r_1 - 2} - m \cdot 2^{r_1 - r_2} - 0.5 \log(3 \cdot 2^{r_1 - 2} - m \cdot 2^{r_1 - r_2}) - 0.3257 + \varepsilon
$$
$$
= 3 \cdot 2^{r_1 - 2} - m \cdot 2^{r_1 - r_2} - 0.5 r_1 + \frac{\log e}{2} \frac{m}{3 \cdot 2^{r_2 - 2}} (1 + \sum_{i=2}^{\infty} \frac{1}{i} (\frac{m}{3 \cdot 2^{r_2 - 2}})^{i-1}) - 0.9107 + \varepsilon
$$

where $\varepsilon = \frac{\theta}{3(3 \cdot 2^{r_1 - 2} - m \cdot 2^{r_1 - r_2})}$ and $-0.7214 < \theta < 0.1084$.

By observing that $0 \leq \frac{m}{3 \cdot 2^{r_2 - 2}} \leq \frac{2}{3}$, and $\frac{\theta}{9 \cdot 2^{r_1 - 2}} < \varepsilon < \frac{\theta}{3 \cdot 2^{r_1 - 2}}$, we have

$$
\log \left(\frac{3 \cdot 2^{r_1 - 2} - m \cdot 2^{r_1 - r_2}}{3 \cdot 2^{r_1 - 3} - m \cdot 2^{r_1 - r_2 - 1}} \right) \geq 3 \cdot 2^{r_1 - 2} - 0.5 r_1 + (\frac{0.7213}{3 \cdot 2^{r_2 - 2}} - 2^{r_1 - r_2}) \cdot m - 0.9107,
$$
$$
\log \left(\frac{3 \cdot 2^{r_1 - 2} - m \cdot 2^{r_1 - r_2}}{3 \cdot 2^{r_1 - 3} - m \cdot 2^{r_1 - r_2 - 1}} \right) \leq 3 \cdot 2^{r_1 - 2} - 0.5 r_1 + (\frac{1.1887}{3 \cdot 2^{r_2 - 2}} - 2^{r_1 - r_2}) \cdot m - 0.9107.
$$

Altogether, the asymptotic evaluation of $\mathcal{N}^w(L)$ is well summarized by Lemma 6. □

By completing a similar yet much harder analytic task, we next provide the asymptotic form of $\mathcal{N}^w(L)$ for more general case.

Theorem 2. *Let $\mathcal{N}^w(L)$ be the number of 2^n-periodic binary sequences with Hamming weight w and linear complexity L. Then when $L = 2^{r_1} + 2^{r_2} + \cdots + 2^{r_t} + 1$ with $0 \leq r_t < r_{t-1} < \cdots < r_1 < n$, $3 < t < n$ and $w = 2^{n-1}$, we have*

$$
\mathcal{N}^w(L) \geq 2^{2^{r_t} + 2^{r_1} - 0.5 r_1 - 0.3257 + \frac{0.7213}{2^{t-1}}} \prod_{j=2}^{t-1} b_j^{2^{r_j}} (\frac{2}{b_j})^{2^{r_j - t + j}}
$$
$$
\mathcal{N}^w(L) \leq 2^{2^{r_t} + 2^{r_1} - 0.5 r_1 - 0.3257 + \frac{1.2203}{2^{t-1}}} \prod_{j=2}^{t-1} a_j^{2^{r_j}} (\frac{2}{a_j})^{2^{r_j - t + j}} \tag{13}
$$

where $a_1 = 2^{1-\frac{1.2203}{2^{r_1}}}$, $b_1 = 2^{1-\frac{0.7213}{2^{r_1}}}$ and $a_j = 1 + \prod_{i=1}^{j-1}(\frac{2}{a_i})^{2^{r_i-r_j+i-j+1}}$, $b_j = 1 + \prod_{i=1}^{j-1}(\frac{2}{b_i})^{2^{r_i-r_j+i-j+1}}$ for $1 < j < t$.

Proof. Recall that $u_{t-1} = 2^{r_t-1}-1$ and $u_j = (2m_{j+1} + u_{j+1}) \cdot 2^{r_j-r_{j+1}-1}$ for $1 \le j < t-1$, there follows:

$$u_1 = (u_2 + 2m_2) \cdot 2^{r_1-r_2-1}$$

$$= \cdots$$

$$= \sum_{j=2}^{t-1} m_j \cdot 2^{r_1-r_j-j+2} + u_{t-1} \cdot 2^{r_1-r_{t-1}-t+2}$$

$$= \sum_{j=2}^{t-1} m_j \cdot 2^{r_1-r_j-j+2} + 2^{r_1-t+1}.$$

Compared with $\sum_{j=1}^{t-1} m_j \cdot 2^{n-r_j-j+1} = 2^{n-1} - 2^{n-t}$, we get

$$m_1 = 2^{r_1-1} - u_1/2.$$

It is evident that the value of u_1 can take the maximum only when all m_j take the maximum value $2^{r_j} - u_j$. Let $m_j = 2^{r_j} - u_j$ for $1 \le j \le t-1$, then

$$u_j = (2m_{j+1} + u_{j+1}) \cdot 2^{r_j-r_{j+1}-1}$$
$$= (2(2^{r_{j+1}} - u_{j+1}) + u_{j+1}) \cdot 2^{r_j-r_{j+1}-1}$$
$$= 2^{r_j} - u_{j+1} \cdot 2^{r_j-r_{j+1}-1},$$

thus

$$u_j \cdot 2^{-r_j} = 1 - \frac{1}{2}u_{j+1} \cdot 2^{-r_{j+1}}.$$

Then by recursive substitutions, we obtain

$$u_1 \cdot 2^{-r_1} = 1 - \frac{1}{2}u_2 \cdot 2^{-r_2} = \cdots = \sum_{j=0}^{t-3}(-\frac{1}{2})^j + (-\frac{1}{2})^{t-2}u_{t-1} \cdot 2^{-r_{t-1}} = \frac{2}{3}(1-(-2)^{-t})$$

which provides the maximum value of u_1:

$$\max\{u_1\} = \frac{1}{3}(1-(-2)^{-t}) \cdot 2^{r_1+1}.$$

Obviously, $u_1 \ge 2^{r_1-t+1}$, and consequently we have

$$\frac{1}{2^{t-1}} \le \frac{u_1}{2^{r_1}} \le \frac{2}{3}(1-(-2)^{-t}). \tag{14}$$

Again, utilizing Stirling's formula, we obtain

$$\log\binom{2^{r_1}-u_1}{m_1} = 2^{r_1} - u_1 - 0.5\log(2^{r_1}-u_1) - 0.3257 + \varepsilon$$

$$= 2^{r_1} - 0.5r_1 - u_1 + \frac{0.7213u_1}{2^{r_1}}(1+\sum_{i=2}^{\infty}\frac{1}{i}(\frac{u_1}{2^{r_1}})^{i-1}) - 0.3257 + \varepsilon$$

where $\varepsilon = \frac{\theta}{3(2^{r_1}-u_1)}$ and $-0.7214 < \theta < 0.1084$.

We only consider the cases in which $t > 3$ and r_1 is large, say $r_1 > 12$. In these cases, $0 \leq \frac{u_1}{2^{r_1}} \leq \frac{11}{16}$ and $\varepsilon < 0.0001$. Thus

$$
\begin{aligned}
\log\left(\frac{2^{r_1} - u_1}{m_1}\right) &\geq 2^{r_1} - 0.5r_1 + (\frac{0.7213}{2^{r_1}} - 1)u_1 - 0.3257, \\
\log\left(\frac{2^{r_1} - u_1}{m_1}\right) &\leq 2^{r_1} - 0.5r_1 + (\frac{1.2203}{2^{r_1}} - 1)u_1 - 0.3257.
\end{aligned}
\tag{15}
$$

From here, we are ready to evaluate the upper bound of $\mathcal{N}^w(L)$. The derivations are as follows:

$$
\mathcal{N}^w(L) = \sum_{\sum_{j=1}^{t-1} m_j \cdot 2^{n-r_j-j+1} = 2^{n-1}-2^{n-t}} 2^{2^{r_t}} \prod_{j=1}^{t-1} 2^{u_j} \cdot \binom{2^{r_j} - u_j}{m_j}
$$

$$
= 2^{\sum_{j=1}^{t} 2^{r_j-t+j}} \sum_{m_{t-1}=0}^{2^{r_{t-1}}-u_{t-1}} \cdots \sum_{m_2=0}^{2^{r_2}-u_2} \binom{2^{r_1} - u_1}{m_1}
$$

$$
\cdot \prod_{j=2}^{t-1} (2^{\sum_{k=1}^{j-1} 2^{r_j-k-r_j-k+1}})^{m_j} \binom{2^{r_j} - u_j}{m_j}
$$

$$
\leq 2^{\sum_{j=2}^{t} 2^{r_j-t+j}+2^{r_1}-0.5r_1-0.3257+\frac{1.2203}{2^{t-1}}} \sum_{m_{t-1}=0}^{2^{r_{t-1}}-u_{t-1}}
$$

$$
\cdots \sum_{m_2=0}^{2^{r_2}-u_2} a_1^{-(\sum_{i=2}^{t-1} m_i 2^{r_1-r_i-i+2})} \cdot \prod_{j=2}^{t-1} (2^{\sum_{k=1}^{j-1} 2^{r_j-k-r_j-k+1}})^{m_j} \binom{2^{r_j} - u_j}{m_j}
$$

$$
= 2^{\sum_{j=2}^{t} 2^{r_j-t+j}+2^{r_1}-0.5r_1-0.3257+\frac{1.2203}{2^{t-1}}} \sum_{m_{t-1}=0}^{2^{r_{t-1}}-u_{t-1}}
$$

$$
\cdots \sum_{m_3=0}^{2^{r_3}-u_3} a_1^{-(\sum_{i=3}^{t-1} m_i 2^{r_1-r_i-i+2})} a_2^{2^{r_2}-u_2} \cdot \prod_{j=3}^{t-1} (2^{\sum_{k=1}^{j-1} 2^{r_j-k-r_j-k+1}})^{m_j}
$$

$$
\binom{2^{r_j} - u_j}{m_j}
$$

$$
= 2^{\sum_{j=2}^{t} 2^{r_j-t+j}+2^{r_1}-0.5r_1-0.3257+\frac{1.2203}{2^{t-1}}} a_2^{2^{r_2}-2^{r_2-t+2}} \sum_{m_{t-1}=0}^{2^{r_{t-1}}-u_{t-1}} \cdots \sum_{m_3=0}^{2^{r_3}-u_3}
$$

$$
a_1^{-(\sum_{i=3}^{t-1} m_i 2^{r_1-r_i-i+2})} a_2^{-(\sum_{i=3}^{t-1} m_i 2^{r_2-r_i-i+3})} \cdot \prod_{j=3}^{t-1} (2^{\sum_{k=1}^{j-1} 2^{r_j-k-r_j-k+1}})^{m_j}
$$

$$
\binom{2^{r_j} - u_j}{m_j}
$$

$$
= \cdots \cdots
$$

$$
= 2^{2^{r_t}+2^{r_1}-0.5r_1-0.3257+\frac{1.2203}{2^{t-1}}} \prod_{j=2}^{t-1} a_j^{2^{r_j}} (\frac{2}{a_j})^{2^{r_j-t+j}}.
$$

Estimate of the lower bound can be obtained via a similar derivation, and we finally achieve that

$$\mathcal{N}^w(L) \geq 2^{2^{r_t}+2^{r_1}-0.5r_1-0.3257+\frac{0.7213}{2^{t-1}}} \prod_{j=2}^{t-1} b_j^{2^{r_j}} (\frac{2}{b_j})^{2^{r_j-t+j}}$$

where $a_1 = 2^{1-\frac{1.2203}{2^{r_1}}}$, $b_1 = 2^{1-\frac{0.7213}{2^{r_1}}}$ and $a_j = 1 + \prod_{i=1}^{j-1}(\frac{2}{a_i})^{2^{r_i-r_j+i-j+1}}$, $b_j = 1 + \prod_{i=1}^{j-1}(\frac{2}{b_i})^{2^{r_i-r_j+i-j+1}}$ for $1 < j < t$.   □

Denote the upper and lower bounds of $\mathcal{N}^w(L)$ by $\text{Upper}(\mathcal{N}^w(L))$ and $\text{Lower}(\mathcal{N}^w(L))$ respectively. Then we find

$$\frac{\text{Upper}(\mathcal{N}^w(L))}{\text{Lower}(\mathcal{N}^w(L))} \leq \frac{\binom{2^{r_1}-u_1}{m_1}_{max}}{\binom{2^{r_1}-u_1}{m_1}_{min}} = 2^{(1.2203-0.7213)u_1/2^{r_1}} \leq 2^{0.4990 \cdot \frac{11}{16}} = 1.2684.$$

This implies that the upper and lower bounds of $\mathcal{N}^w(L)$ are larger and smaller than $\mathcal{N}^w(L)$ at most 26.84% and $1 - 1/1.2684 = 21.16\%$ respectively.

We next turn our attention to the cases in which w takes other values.

According to Corollary 2, it is effortless to see that the Hamming weight of sequence of linear complexity $L = 2^{r_1} + 2^{r_2} + \cdots 2^{r_t} + 1$ must be $w = 2^{n-1} + l \cdot 2^{n-r_1}$. This leads to $m_1 = \frac{w}{2^{n-r_1}} - \frac{u_1}{2} = \frac{1}{2}(2^{r_1} - u_1) + l$. For small l we can easily transform the binomial coefficient $\binom{2^{r_1}-u_1}{m_1}$ to $\binom{2^{r_1}-u_1}{\frac{1}{2}(2^{r_1}-u_1)}$. For instance, when $l = \pm 1$, we get $m_1 = \frac{1}{2}(2^{r_1} - u_1) \pm 1$ and $\binom{2^{r_1}-u_1}{m_1} = \frac{2^{r_1}-u_1}{2^{r_1}-u_1+2}\binom{2^{r_1}-u_1}{\frac{1}{2}(2^{r_1}-u_1)}$. Utilizing Eq. (14), we get

$$\binom{2^{r_1}-u_1}{m_1} \geq \frac{(1-(-2)^{1-t}) \cdot 2^{r_1}}{(1-(-2)^{1-t}) \cdot 2^{r_1} + 6}\binom{2^{r_1}-u_1}{\frac{1}{2}(2^{r_1}-u_1)},$$

$$\binom{2^{r_1}-u_1}{m_1} \leq \frac{(1-2^{1-t}) \cdot 2^{r_1}}{(1-2^{1-t}) \cdot 2^{r_1} + 2}\binom{2^{r_1}-u_1}{\frac{1}{2}(2^{r_1}-u_1)}.$$

Adopting a calculation analogous the one used for deriving Theorem 2, we can get the bounds of $\mathcal{N}^w(L)$ for the cases in which $w = 2^{n-1} \pm 2^{n-t}$ as follows.

Corollary 3. *Let $\mathcal{N}^w(L)$ be the number of 2^n-periodic binary sequences with Hamming weight w and linear complexity L. Then when $L = 2^{r_1}+2^{r_2}+\cdots+2^{r_t}+1$ with $0 \leq r_t < r_{t-1} < \cdots < r_1 < n$, $3 < t < n$ and $w = 2^{n-1} \pm 2^{n-r_1}$, we have*

$$\mathcal{N}^w(L) \leq \frac{(1-2^{1-t}) \cdot 2^{r_1}}{(1-2^{1-t}) \cdot 2^{r_1} + 2} \cdot 2^{2^{r_t}+2^{r_1}-0.5r_1-0.3257+\frac{1.2203}{2^{t-1}}} \prod_{j=2}^{t-1} a_j^{2^{r_j}} (\frac{2}{a_j})^{2^{r_j-t+j}},$$

$$\mathcal{N}^w(L) \geq \frac{(1-(-2)^{1-t}) \cdot 2^{r_1}}{(1-(-2)^{1-t}) \cdot 2^{r_1} + 6} \cdot 2^{2^{r_t}+2^{r_1}-0.5r_1-0.3257+\frac{0.7213}{2^{t-1}}} \prod_{j=2}^{t-1} b_j^{2^{r_j}} (\frac{2}{b_j})^{2^{r_j-t+j}},$$

$$(16)$$

where $a_1 = 2^{1-\frac{1.2203}{2^{r_1}}}$, $b_1 = 2^{1-\frac{0.7213}{2^{r_1}}}$ and $a_j = 1 + \prod_{i=1}^{j-1}(\frac{2}{a_i})^{2^{r_i-r_j+i-j+1}}$, $b_j = 1 + \prod_{i=1}^{j-1}(\frac{2}{b_i})^{2^{r_i-r_j+i-j+1}}$ for $1 < j < t$.

From here, the counting problem for the number of 2^n-periodic binary sequences of given linear complexity and with fixed Hamming weight is solved.

3   The Characterization of $\mathcal{A}_2^w(L)$

In this section, we turn our attention to the counting problem for the number of 2^n-periodic binary sequences of 2-error linear complexity and with fixed Hamming weight.

Let $\mathcal{A}_2'(L)$ denote the set of 2^n-periodic binary sequences of 2-error linear complexity L and linear complexity smaller than 2^n, and let $\mathcal{N}_2'(L)$ denote the size of set $\mathcal{A}_2'(L)$, which can be formally defined as

$$\mathcal{A}_2'(L) = \{S \in S^{2^n} : LC_2(S) = L \text{ and } LC(S) < 2^n\} \quad \text{and} \quad \mathcal{N}_2'(L) = |\mathcal{A}_2'(L)|. \tag{17}$$

Let us first briefly introduce how to get $\mathcal{N}_2'(L)$. It is clear that, if there is a sequence S with 2-error linear complexity L then there must be another sequence S' of linear complexity L which satisfy that the Hamming distance between S and S' being no more than 2. According to Lemma 1, which states that the linear complexity of sequences with odd Hamming weight are 2^n, we get

$$\mathcal{A}_2'(L) \subseteq \mathcal{A}(L) \bigcup \mathcal{A}(L) + \mathbf{E}_2 \tag{18}$$

where $\mathbf{E}_2 = \{E \in S^{2^n} : w_H(E) = 2\}$.

From Lemma 4, it is apparent that for any sequence S in $\mathcal{A}(L)$, the corresponding polynomial of S satisfies that $S(x) = (x-1)^{2^n-L}a(x)$ and $a(1) \neq 0$. Combined with Eq. (1): $LC(S) = N - \deg(\gcd(x^N - 1, S(x)))$, we can easily verify the following two lemmas.

Lemma 7 [4]. *Let $\mathcal{A}(L)$ be the set of 2^n-periodic binary sequences of linear complexity L and E, E' be two error sequences, then we have*

$$\mathcal{A}(L) + E = \mathcal{A}(L) + E' \text{ or } (\mathcal{A}(L) + E) \bigcap (\mathcal{A}(L) + E') = \emptyset. \tag{19}$$

Lemma 8. *Let E, E' be two error sequences in $\mathbf{E}$, then $\mathcal{A}(L) + E = \mathcal{A}(L) + E'$ if and only if there exist two sequences S, S' in $\mathcal{A}(L)$ such that $S + E = S' + E'$.*

Next, we devote to characterize the set $\mathcal{A}_2'(L)$ and evaluate its size $\mathcal{N}_2'(L)$ based on the properties provided in the above two lemmas. This problem has already received a treatment in [5,12], here we provide a more concise formula and proof.

Lemma 9. *Let $\mathcal{A}_2'(L)$ and $\mathcal{N}_2'(L)$ denote the set of and the number of 2^n-periodic binary sequences with 2-error linear complexity L and linear complexity less than 2^n respectively, then we have*

- if $L = 2^n - 2^r$, $0 \leq r < n$, then $\mathcal{A}'_2(L) = \emptyset$ and $\mathcal{N}'_2(L) = 0$.
- if $L = 2^n - (2^{r_1} + 2^{r_2})$, $0 \leq r_2 < r_1 < n$, then

$$\mathcal{A}'_2(L) = \mathcal{A}(L) \bigcup (\mathcal{A}(L) + \mathbf{E}) \quad \text{and}$$
$$\mathcal{N}'_2(L) = (1 + 2^{r_1}(2^{r_1+1} - 3 \cdot 2^{r_1-r_2-1} - 1)) \cdot 2^{L-1} \tag{20}$$

where $\mathbf{E} = \{\{i, j\} : \ 0 \leq i < j < 2^{r_1+1}, 2^{r_2} < d(i, j) < 2^{r_1}$ and $i + j < 2^{r_1+1}$ or $0 < d(i, j) < 2^{r_2}\}$.

- if $L = 2^n - (2^{r_1} + 2^{r_2} + x)$, $0 < r_2 < r_1 < n$ and $0 < x < 2^{r_2}$ then

$$\mathcal{A}'_2(L) = \mathcal{A}(L) \bigcup (\mathcal{A}(L) + \mathbf{E}) \quad \text{and}$$
$$\mathcal{N}'_2(L) = (1 + 2^{r_1}(2^{r_1+1} - 2^{r_1-r_2-1} + 2^{r_2-r_1+1} - 1)) \cdot 2^{L-1} \tag{21}$$

where $\mathbf{E} = \{\{i, j\} : \ 0 \leq i < j < 2^{r_1+1}, d(i, j) = 2^{r_1}$ and $0 \leq i < 2^{r_2+1}$ or $2^{r_2} < d(i, j) < 2^{r_1}$ and $i + j < 2^{r_1+1}$ or $0 < d(i, j) \leq 2^{r_2}\}$.

Proof. According to Lemma 7, to get the size of $\mathcal{A}'_2(L)$, it is sufficient to get the maximum subset of error sequences set $\mathbf{E}_0 \bigcup \mathbf{E}_2$ in which for any pair of error sequences E, E' it satisfies that $\mathcal{A}(L) + E \subseteq \mathcal{A}'_2(L)$ and $(\mathcal{A}(L) + E) \bigcap (\mathcal{A}(L) + E') = \emptyset$. Next, we proceed the proof case by case.

- Case 1. $L = 2^n - 2^r$, $0 \leq r < n$. In this case, it can be observed that $merr(S) = 2$ for any sequence S in $\mathcal{A}(L)$, which follows $\mathcal{A}(L) \bigcap \mathcal{A}'_2(L) = \emptyset$. Suppose the support set of error sequence E in $\mathbf{E}_2$ is $supp(E) = \{i, j\}$. For each E in $\mathbf{E}_2$, we can construct an error sequence E' of which the support set is $supp(E') = \{i, j'\}$ and $d(j, j') = 2^r$. Then we have $LC(E + E') = 2^n - 2^r = L$, that is to say $LC_2(S + E) \leq LC(S + E + E') < L$. Therefore we have $(\mathcal{A}(L) + \mathbf{E}_2) \bigcap \mathcal{A}'_2(L) = \emptyset$. As a result, we have $\mathcal{A}'_2(L) = \emptyset$ and $\mathcal{N}'_2(L) = 0$.
- Case 2. $L = 2^n - (2^{r_1} + 2^{r_2})$, $0 \leq r_2 < r_1 < n$. In this case, one can observe that $merr(S) = 4$, which follows $\mathcal{A}(L) \subseteq \mathcal{A}'_2(L)$. For any error sequence E in $\mathbf{E}_2$, suppose the support set of E is $supp(E) = \{i, j\}$. If $d(i, j) > 2^{r_1}$, for any sequence S in $\mathcal{A}(L)$ we have $LC(S + E) = L$ that is to say $S + E \in \mathcal{A}(L)$. According to Lemma 8, we have $\mathcal{A}(L) + E = \mathcal{A}(L)$. If $d(i, j) = 2^{r_1}$ then we can construct an error sequence E' of which the support set is $supp(E') = \{i', j'\}$ such that $d(i, i') = d(j, j') = 2^{r_2}$. Then $LC(E + E') = L$ and $LC_2(S + E) \leq LC(S + E + E') < L$, thus we have $(\mathcal{A}(L) + E) \bigcap \mathcal{A}'_2(L) = \emptyset$. Similarly, when $d(i, j) = 2^{r_2}$, we also have $(\mathcal{A}(L) + E) \bigcap \mathcal{A}'_2(L) = \emptyset$. Suppose $2^{r_2} < d(i, j) < 2^{r_1}$ or $0 < d(i, j) < 2^{r_2}$. We construct an error sequence E' of which the support set is $supp(E') \doteq \{i', j'\}$ where $i' = i \mod 2^{r_1+1}$ and $j' = j \mod 2^{r_1+1}$. Then we have $(E + E')(x) = x^i + x^j + x^{i'} + x^{j'} = (x+1)^{2^{r_1+1}} b(x)$ or 0 and $(S + E + E')(x) = (x+1)^{2^{r_1}+2^{r_2}_2} a(x) + (x+1)^{2^{r_1+1}} b(x) = (x+1)^{2^n-L}((x+1)^t b'(x) + a(x))$ or equal to $S(x)$ itself where $b(x) \neq 0$ and $t > 0$. Thus $S' = S + E + E' \in \mathcal{A}(L)$ and $S + E = S + E'$. According to Lemma 8, we have $\mathcal{A}(L) + E = \mathcal{A}(L) + E'$. Therefore we only need to consider those error sequences in $\mathbf{E}_2$ with support set $\{i, j\}$ where $0 < i < j < 2^{r_1+1}$ and $2^{r_2} < d(i, j) < 2^{r_1}$ or $0 < d(i, j) < 2^{r_2}$. If $2^{r_2} < d(i, j) < 2^{r_1}$, we construct error

sequence E' with support set $supp(E') = \{i', j'\}$ where $|i' - i| = |j' - j| = 2^{r_1}$. Similarly we have $S' = S + E + E' \in \mathcal{A}(L)$ and thus $\mathcal{A}(L) + E = \mathcal{A}(L) + E'$. Consequently, there are half of those error sequences in the set $\{\{i,j\} : 0 \leq i < j < 2^{r_1+1}, 2^{r_2} < d(i,j) < 2^{r_1}\}$ satisfying the requirements and we can choose this half part of the set which denoted by $SubE_1 = \{\{i,j\} : 0 \leq i < j < 2^{r_1+1}, 2^{r_2} < d(i,j) < 2^{r_1} \text{ and } i+j < 2^{r_1+1}\}$. Denote $SubE_2 = \{\{i,j\} : 0 \leq i < j < 2^{r_1+1}, 0 < d(i,j) < 2^{r_2}\}$. It is easy to verify that for any error sequences E and E' in $SubE_1 \bigcup SubE_2$ they satisfy that $(\mathcal{A}(L) + E')\bigcap(\mathcal{A}(L) + E') = \emptyset$ and $\mathcal{A}(L) + E \subseteq \mathcal{A}'_2(L)$. By combinatorial theory, we can state that the size of $SubE_1$ and $SubE_2$ are $\binom{2^{r_2+1}}{1}\binom{2^{r_1-r_2-1}}{2} \cdot 2^2/2 = 2^{r_1}(2^{r_1-r_2-1} - 1)$ and $\binom{2^{r_2}}{2}\binom{2^{r_1-r_2+1}}{1}^2 = 2^{2r_1-r_2+1}(2^{r_2}-1)$ respectively. As a consequence, we obtain that

$$\mathcal{A}'_2(L) = \mathcal{A}(L)\bigcup(\mathcal{A}(L) + \mathbf{E}) \quad \text{and} \quad \mathcal{N}'_2(L) = (1 + 2^{r_1}(2^{r_1+1} - 3 \cdot 2^{r_1-r_2-1} - 1)) \cdot 2^{L-1}$$

where $\mathbf{E} = \{\{i,j\} : 0 \leq i < j < 2^{r_1+1}, 2^{r_2} < d(i,j) < 2^{r_1} \text{ and } i + j < 2^{r_1+1} \text{ or } 0 < d(i,j) < 2^{r_2}\}$.

- Case 3. $L = 2^n - (2^{r_1} + 2^{r_2} + x)$ where $0 < r_2 < r_1 < n$ and $0 < x < 2^{r_2}$. Similar to the analysis for Case 2, we can get $\mathcal{A}(L) \subseteq \mathcal{A}'_2(L)$ and only need to consider those error sequences in $\mathbf{E}_2$ with support set $\{i,j\}$ which satisfy that $0 \leq i < j < 2^{r_1+1}$. If $d(i,j) = 2^{r_1}$, we construct an error sequence E' with support set $supp(E') = \{i', j'\}$ where $i' = i \mod 2^{r_2+1}$ and $j' = j \mod 2^{r_2+1}$. It can be verified that $S' = S + E + E' \in \mathcal{A}(L)$ and then $\mathcal{A}(L) + E = \mathcal{A}(L) + E'$. Thus, for the error sequences set $\mathbf{E} = \{\{i,j\} : 0 \leq i < j < 2^{r_1+1} \text{ and } d(i,j) = 2^{r_1}\}$ we only need to consider its subset $SubE_3 = \{\{i,j\} : 0 \leq i < 2^{r_2+1} \text{ and } j = i+2^{r_1}\}$. Denote $SubE_4 = \{\{i,j\} : 0 \leq i < j < 2^{r_1+1} \text{ and } d(i,j) = 2^{r_2}\}$. Similar to the analysis for Case 2, it can be verify that for any error sequences E and E' in $SubE_1 \bigcup SubE_2 \bigcup SubE_3 \bigcup SubE_4$ they satisfy that $(\mathcal{A}(L) + E')\bigcap(\mathcal{A}(L) + E') = \emptyset$ and $\mathcal{A}(L)+E \subseteq \mathcal{A}'_2(L)$, where $SubE_1$ and $SubE_2$ are mentioned in the analysis for Case 2. By combinatorial theory, we can state that the size of $\mathbf{E}_3$ and $\mathbf{E}_4$ are 2^{r_2+1} and $\binom{2^{r_2}}{1}\binom{2^{r_1-r_2}}{1}^2 = 2^{2r_1-r_2}$ respectively. As a consequence, we obtain that

$$\mathcal{A}'_2(L) = \mathcal{A}(L)\bigcup(\mathcal{A}(L) + \mathbf{E}) \quad \text{and}$$
$$\mathcal{N}''_2(L) = (1 + 2^{r_1}(2^{r_1+1} - 2^{r_1-r_2-1} + 2^{r_2-r_1+1} - 1)) \cdot 2^{L-1}$$

where $\mathbf{E} = \{\{i,j\} : 0 \leq i < j < 2^{r_1+1}, d(i,j) = 2^{r_1} \text{ and } 0 \leq i < 2^{r_2+1} \text{ or } 2^{r_2} < d(i,j) < 2^{r_1} \text{ and } i + j < 2^{r_1+1} \text{ or } 0 < d(i,j) \leq 2^{r_2}\}$. $\square$

From Corollary 2, we can know that the Hamming weight w of sequence S in $\mathcal{A}(L)$ satisfy that $2^{n-r_1}|w$ where $L = 2^{r_1} + 2^{r_2} + \cdots + 2^{r_t} + 1$, $t < n$ and $0 \leq r_t < r_{t-1} < \cdots < r_1 < n$ (Notice that, in Lemmas 9 and 10, we used a different expression form of L, which is actually determined by the binary representation of $n - L$). Thus, when $r_1 \neq n - 1$, the Hamming weight of S in $\mathcal{A}(L)$ can be 2^{n-1} but must not be $2^{n-1} \pm 2$. Now, let us first consider a simple case: $r_1 \neq n - 1$ and $w = 2^{n-1}$ and try to get the value of $\mathcal{A}_2^w(L)$ based on the properties of $\mathcal{A}_2'(L)$.

Lemma 10. *Let* $\mathcal{N}_2^w(L)$ *be the number of* 2^n-*periodic binary sequences with 2-error linear complexity* L *and Hamming weight* w, *then we have*

- *if* $L = 2^n - 2^t$, $0 \leq t < n$, *then* $\mathcal{N}_2^w(L) = 0$.
- *if* $L = 2^{n-1} - 2^t$, $0 \leq t < n - 1$ *and* $w = 2^{n-1}$, *then*

$$(2^{2n-2} - 3 \cdot 2^{2n-t-3} + 1)\mathcal{N}^w(L) \leq \mathcal{N}_2^w(L) \leq (2^{2n-2} + 1)\mathcal{N}^w(L).$$

- *if* $L = 2^{n-1} - 2^t - x$, $0 \leq t < n - 1$, $0 < x < 2^t$ *and* $w = 2^{n-1}$, *then*

$$(2^{2n-2} - 2^{2n-t-3} + 2^{t+1} + 1)\mathcal{N}^w(L) \leq \mathcal{N}_2^w(L) \leq (2^{2n-2} + 1)\mathcal{N}^w(L).$$

Proof. It is obvious that $\mathcal{A}_2^w(L) = \emptyset$, and $\mathcal{N}_2^w(L) = 0$ when $L = 2^n - 2^t$ and $0 \leq t < n$. According to Corollary 2, the Hamming weight of sequences in $\mathcal{A}(L)$ can not be $2^{n-1} \pm 2$, then $\mathcal{A}_2^w(L) \subseteq \mathcal{A}^w(L) \bigcup (\mathcal{A}^w(L) + \mathbf{E})$ based on Eq. (20) where $\mathbf{E}$ is defined in Eq. (20). Then the main problem of getting $\mathcal{A}^w(L)$ is how to eliminate those sequences with Hamming weight $w \pm 2$ or preserving the Hamming weight when adding an sequence E to S where $E \in \mathbf{E}$ and $S \in \mathcal{A}$. For any sequence S in $\mathcal{A}^w(L)$, there are at most $\binom{w}{1}\binom{2^n - w}{1} = 2^{2n-2}$ possibilities when we adding a sequence E in $\mathbf{E}$ to it and preserving the Hamming weight of S. And it is clear that there are at most $\binom{w}{2} = \binom{2^{n-1}}{2}$ and $\binom{2^n - w}{2} = \binom{2^{n-1}}{2}$ possibilities when we adding a sequence E in $\mathbf{E}$ to S and changing the Hamming weight of S to $w - 2$ and $w + 2$ respectively. Therefore there are at most $2^{2n-2}\mathcal{N}^w(L)$ and at least $(|\mathbf{E}| - 2\binom{2^{n-1}}{2})\mathcal{N}^w(L)$ sequences with Hamming weight w in the set $\mathcal{A}^w(L) + \mathbf{E}$. Thus we get

$$(2^{2n-2} - 3 \cdot 2^{2n-t-3} + 1)\mathcal{N}^w(L) \leq \mathcal{N}_2^w(L) \leq (2^{2n-2} + 1)\mathcal{N}^w(L).$$

if $L = 2^{n-1} - 2^t - x$, $0 \leq t < n - 1$, $0 < x < 2^t$ follows an analysis analogous the one used for the previous case and we thus omit it here.   □

Let $L = 2^n - (2^{r_1} + 2^{r_2} + \cdots 2^{r_t})$ and $w = 2^{n-1}$ where $0 \leq r_t < r_{t-1} < \cdots < r_1 < n$, when $r_1 < n - 1$, according to $\mathcal{A}_2(L) \subseteq \mathcal{A}(L) \bigcup (\mathcal{A}(L) + \mathbf{E}_2)$ we have

$$\mathcal{A}_2^w(L) \subseteq \mathcal{A}^w(L) \bigcup (\mathcal{A}^w(L) + \mathbf{E}_2) \bigcup (\mathcal{A}^{w-2}(L) + \mathbf{E}_2) \bigcup (\mathcal{A}^{w+2}(L) + \mathbf{E}_2). \quad (22)$$

A similar analysis to the one in Lemma 10 provides the following theorem.

Theorem 3. *Let* $\mathcal{N}_2^w(L)$ *denote the number of* 2^n-*periodic binary sequences with 2-error linear complexity* L *and Hamming weight* w, *then we have*

- *if* $L = 2^n - 2^r$, $0 \leq r < n$, *then* $\mathcal{N}_2^w(L) = 0$.
- *if* $L = 2^n - (2^{r_1} + 2^{r_2})$, $0 \leq r_2 < r_1 < n$ *and* $w = 2^{n-1}$, *then*

$$\mathcal{N}_2^w(L) \geq (2^{2r_1} - 3 \cdot 2^{2r_1 - r_2 - 1} + 1)\mathcal{N}^w(L) +$$
$$(2^{2r_1} - 3 \cdot 2^{2r_1 - r_2 - 1} - 4)(\mathcal{N}^{w+2}(L) + \mathcal{N}^{w-2}(L)),$$
$$\mathcal{N}_2^w(L) \leq (2^{2r_1} + 1)\mathcal{N}^w(L) + (2^{2r_1} - 4)(\mathcal{N}^{w+2}(L) + \mathcal{N}^{w-2}(L)).$$

– if $L = 2^n - (2^{r_1} + 2^{r_2} + x)$, $0 < r_2 < r_1 < n$, $0 < x < 2^{r_2}$ and $w = 2^{n-1}$, then

$$\mathcal{N}_2^w(L) \geq (2^{2r_1} - 2^{2r_1 - r_2 - 1} + 2^{r_2 + 1} + 1)\mathcal{N}^w(L) +$$
$$(2^{2r_1} - 2^{2r_1 - r_2 - 1} + 2^{r_2 + 1} - 4)(\mathcal{N}^{w+2}(L) + \mathcal{N}^{w-2}(L))$$
$$\mathcal{N}_2^w(L) \leq (2^{r_1} + 1)\mathcal{N}^w(L) + (2^{2r_1} - 4)(\mathcal{N}^{w+2}(L) + \mathcal{N}^{w-2}(L)).$$

Based on the above theorem and combining the bounds of $\mathcal{N}^w(L)$, $\mathcal{N}^{w\pm2}(L)$ provided in inequalities (13) and (16), we can get the bounds of $\mathcal{N}_2^w(L)$.

4   Conclusions

In this paper, we devote to get the distribution of linear complexity and k-error linear complexity of 2^n-periodic binary sequences with fixed Hamming weight. First, we use short sequence to construct special longer sequence in a manner similar to the reversed process of the Games-Chan algorithm. And we get the explicit formula of the number of sequences with given linear complexity L and Hamming weight w. Besides, we provide an asymptotic evaluation of this counting function when n gets large. Particularly, we analyze the bounds of counting function of the number of balance sequences with given linear complexity. And extend those bounds to the case of some special Hamming weight. Secondly, we characterize the 2-error linear complexity of 2^n-periodic binary sequences using a simple method. And then based on those characters we get the bounds of the number of 2^n-periodic balance binary sequence with fixed 2-error linear complexity. By further analyzing the bounds of the number of sequences with given Hamming weight, using our method can get the bounds of the counting functions of the k-error linear complexity of 2^n-periodic binary sequences with special Hamming weight and for some large k. Along this line of study, one can get evaluations on the number of sequences of other period or/and of other values of complexity measures and with fixed Hamming weight.

Acknowledgments. Many thanks go to the anonymous reviewers for their detailed comments and suggestions. This work was supported by the National Key R&D Program of China with No. 2016YFB0800100, CAS Strategic Priority Research Program with No. XDA06010701, National Key Basic Research Project of China with No. 2011CB302400 and National Natural Science Foundation of China with No. 61671448, No. 61379139.

References

1. Ding, C., Xiao, G., Shan, W.: The Stability Theory of Stream Ciphers. LNCS, vol. 561. Springer, Heidelberg (1991)
2. Fu, F.-W., Niederreiter, H., Su, M.: The characterization of 2^n-periodic binary sequences with fixed 1-error linear complexity. In: Gong, G., Helleseth, T., Song, H.-Y., Yang, K. (eds.) SETA 2006. LNCS, vol. 4086, pp. 88–103. Springer, Heidelberg (2006). doi:10.1007/11863854_8

3. Games, R., Chan, A.: A fast algorithm for determining the complexity of a binary sequence with period 2^n (corresp.). IEEE Trans. Inf. Theory **29**(1), 144–146 (1983)
4. Kavuluru, R.: 2^n-periodic binary sequences with fixed k-error linear complexity for $k = 2$ or 3. In: Golomb, S.W., Parker, M.G., Pott, A., Winterhof, A. (eds.) SETA 2008. LNCS, vol. 5203, pp. 252–265. Springer, Heidelberg (2008). doi:10. 1007/978-3-540-85912-3_23
5. Kavuluru, R.: Characterization of 2^n-periodic binary sequences with fixed 2-error or 3-error linear complexity. Des. Codes Cryptogr. **53**(2), 75–97 (2009)
6. Kurosawa, K., Sato, F., Sakata, T., Kishimoto, W.: A relationship between linear complexity and k-error linear complexity. IEEE Trans. Inf. Theory **46**(2), 694–698 (2000)
7. Massey, J.L.: Shift-register synthesis and BCH decoding. IEEE Trans. Inf. Theory **15**(1), 122–127 (1969)
8. Meidl, W.: On the stability of 2^n-periodic binary sequences. IEEE Trans. Inf. Theory **51**(3), 1151–1155 (2005)
9. Ming, S.: Decomposing approach for error vectors of k-error linear complexity of certain periodic sequences. IEICE Trans. Fundam. Electr. Commun. Comput. Sci. **E97-A**(7), 1542–1555 (2014)
10. Rueppel, A.R.: Analysis and Design of Stream Ciphers. Communications and Control Engineering Series. Springer, Heidelberg (1986)
11. Stamp, M., Martin, C.F.: An algorithm for the k-error linear complexity of binary sequences with period 2^n. IEEE Trans. Inf. Theory **39**(4), 1398–1401 (1993)
12. Zhou, J.: A counterexample concerning the 3-error linear complexity of 2^n-periodic binary sequences. Des. Codes Cryptogr. **64**(3), 285–286 (2012)
13. Zhou, J., Liu, W.: The k-error linear complexity distribution for 2^n-periodic binary sequences. Des. Codes Cryptogr. **73**(1), 55–75 (2014)

The Variant of Remote Set Problem on Lattices

Wenwen Wang[1,2,3](✉), Kewei Lv[1,2](✉), and Jianing Liu[1,2,3]

[1] State Key Laboratory of Information Security,
Institute of Information Engineering, Chinese Academy of Sciences,
Beijing 100093, China
{wangwenwen,lvkewei,jianingliu}@iie.ac.cn
[2] Data Assurance Communication Security Research Center,
Chinese Academy of Sciences, Beijing 100093, China
[3] University of Chinese Academy Sciences, Beijing 100049, China

Abstract. In 2015, Haviv proposed the Remote Set Problem (RSP) on lattices and gave a deterministic algorithm to find a set containing a point which is $O(\sqrt{k/n})$ far from the lattice in ℓ_p norm for $2 \leq p \leq \infty$, where n is the lattice rank and k divides n. Inspired by it, we propose the variant of Remote Set Problem on Lattices (denoted by V-RSP) that only depends on parameter $\gamma \leq 1$. We obtain that the complexity classes that V-RSP belong to with the change of parameter γ. Using some elementary tools, we can solve V-RSP that can find a set containing a point which is $O(k/n)$ far from the lattice in any ℓ_p norm for $1 \leq p \leq \infty$. Furthermore, we also study relationships between ℓ_2 distance from a point to a lattice $\mathcal{L}$ and covering radius ($\rho^{(p)}(\mathcal{L})$), where $\rho^{(p)}(\mathcal{L})$ is defined with respect to the ℓ_p norm for $1 \leq p \leq \infty$, here, for $p = \infty$, our proof does not rely on Komlós Conjecture.

Keywords: Lattice · Equivalent norms · The variant of remote set problem · Hölder's inequality

1 Introduction

A lattice is a discrete additive subgroup of $\mathbb{R}^m$ and is the set of all integer linearly combinations of n linearly independent vectors $\boldsymbol{b}_1, \ldots, \boldsymbol{b}_n$ in $\mathbb{R}^m$, where n is the rank of the lattice, m is the dimension of the lattice and $\boldsymbol{b}_1, \ldots, \boldsymbol{b}_n$ is called a lattice basis. Gauss [7] gave an algorithm to find the shortest vector in any two dimension lattice that originated the study of lattices. Since then, many different lattice problems were proposed. In 1996, Ajtai [2] showed that finding relatively short nonzero vectors is as hard as approximating shortest vector problems in the worst case in a family of random lattice. These random lattices can be used for cryptography. Hence, the study of lattices gains a lot of attention from a computational point of view.

There are two classical problems in lattices. The first is the Shortest Vector Problem (SVP): given a lattice, find the shortest non-zero lattice vector. The second is the Closest Vector Problem (CVP): given a lattice and a target vector, find the closest lattice vector to the target vector.

© Springer International Publishing AG 2016
K.-Y. Lam et al. (Eds.): ICICS 2016, LNCS 9977, pp. 124–133, 2016.
DOI: 10.1007/978-3-319-50011-9_10

The covering radius $\rho^{(p)}(\mathcal{L})$ of lattice $\mathcal{L}$ is the maximum ℓ_p distance of a point in the linear span of $\mathcal{L}$ from the lattice, where $\rho^{(p)}(\mathcal{L})$ is measured with respect to the ℓ_p norm for $1 \leq p \leq \infty$. The covering radius problem is to find $\rho^{(p)}(\mathcal{L})$ for a given lattice $\mathcal{L}$. The Covering Radius Problem (CRP) is also an important lattice problem and the exact CRP is in Π_2 at the second level of the polynomial hierarchy. Computing the covering radius of a lattice is a classic problem in geometry of numbers, but it has received so far little attention from an algorithmic point of view. In 2004, Micciancio [16] showed that finding collision of some hash function can be reduced to approximate CRP of lattices, where CRP only is used to connect the average and worst case complexity of lattice problems. Motivated by [8], Guruswami et al. [10] initiated the study of computation complexity for CRP, and showed that CRP_2 lies in AM, $\text{CRP}_{\sqrt{n/\log n}}$ lies in coAM and $\text{CRP}_{\sqrt{n}}$ lies in $NP \cap coNP$ which implies that under Karp reductions $\text{CRP}_{\sqrt{n}}$ is not NP-hard unless $NP = coNP$. But they did not give some hardness results for CRP [10]. Peikert [18] showed that $\text{CRP}_{\sqrt{n}}$ lies in coNP in the ℓ_p norm for $2 \leq p \leq \infty$. The first hardness result for CRP was presented by Haviv and Regev, they proved that there exists some constant such that it is Π_2-hard in the ℓ_p norm for any sufficiently large value of p [12]. In 2015, Haviv [13] proposed the Remote Set Problem (RSP) on lattices which can be viewed as a generalized search variant of CRP. The goal of RSP is to find a set of points containing a point which is far from the lattice under a deterministic algorithm in ℓ_p norm for $2 \leq p \leq \infty$. By the deterministic polynomial time algorithm for RSP, Haviv showed that $\text{CRP}_{\sqrt{n/\log n}}$ lies in NP which improved the factor from [10], and proved that approximation GAPCRP can be reduced to approximation GAPCVP.

In the study of CRP, we usually find a point whose distance from the lattice approximates the covering radius. There is a deterministic construction of all the M^n linear combinations of the n basis vectors with all coefficients in $\{0, 1/M, \ldots, 1 - 1/M\}$ where M is an integer. Micciancio [10] showed that there exists at least one of them whose distance from the lattice approximates the covering radius to within a factor of $1 - 1/M$. In order to decrease the number of exponential points in the above construction [10], Haviv proposed RSP and gave a deterministic algorithm (see Sect. 3) that outputs $n/k \cdot 2^k$ linear combinations of vectors in basis with coefficient in $\{0, 1/2\}$ (i.e. $M = 2$) by partitioning the n basis vectors into n/k sets of size k [13]. The algorithm outputs a set of $n/k \cdot 2^k$ points containing a point whose ℓ_p distance from a lattice is at least $1/(2c_p) \cdot \sqrt{k/n} \cdot \rho^{(p)}(\mathcal{L})$ for $2 \leq p < \infty$, where c_p is a constant. For $p = \infty$, there is a similar result. Haviv analyzed RSP with respect to Banach spaces and obtained the results which hold for any ℓ_p norm for $2 \leq p \leq \infty$. Here, we will consider the variant of Remote Set Problem which is denoted by V-RSP with respect to any ℓ_p norm for $1 \leq p \leq \infty$.

Our Contributions. In this paper, we consider the variant of Remote Set Problem (V-RSP) on lattices. Using elementary method, we prove that V-RSP can be adapted to any ℓ_p norm for $1 \leq p \leq \infty$.

The Remote Set Problem [13] is defined and depends on two parameters d, γ to be minimized, where d is the size of the output set S by the algorithm for RSP and $\gamma \geq 1$ is the remoteness parameter for which S contains a point whose distance from $\mathcal{L}$ is at least $1/\gamma \cdot \rho^{(p)}(\mathcal{L})$. Here, we give the definition for V-RSP which only depends on remoteness parameter γ:

- $\gamma \leq 1$ is a parameter such that the algorithm finds a set containing a point whose distance from $\mathcal{L}$ is at least $\gamma \cdot \rho^{(p)}(\mathcal{L})$ for the input lattice $\mathcal{L}$ and γ.
- the size of the output set S by the algorithm can be represented by parameter γ: $|S| \leq O(n/(\alpha\gamma) \cdot M^{\alpha\gamma})$, where $\alpha = nM/(M-1)$ and $M \geq 2$ is an integer.

Our definition for V-RSP only depends on the parameter γ. The size of the output set by the algorithm for V-RSP is a function of γ. Therefore, we establish relationships between the size of the output set S and the remoteness parameter γ. The algorithm for RSP in [13] is also applied to solve V-RSP (see Algorithm 1). The algorithm for V-RSP outputs the set S of vectors as a linear combinations of the basis vectors with all coefficients in $\{0, 1/M, \ldots, 1 - 1/M\}$ where $M \geq 2$ by partitioning the n basis vectors into n/k sets of size $k = \lfloor (nM/c(M-1)) \cdot \gamma \rfloor \geq 1$. We show that the deterministic algorithm that on input rank n lattice $\mathcal{L}$ and $\gamma \leq 1$ outputs a set S of size $|S| \leq O(n/k \cdot M^k)$ containing at least one points which is $(1 - 1/M) \cdot k/n \cdot \rho^{(p)}(\mathcal{L})$ far from $\mathcal{L}$. Moreover, we show that the complexity classes that V-RSP belong to with the change of parameter γ. Using the triangle inequality of norm, the analysis for V-RSP can be adapted to any ℓ_p norm for $1 \leq p \leq \infty$. In the analysis of the algorithm for V-RSP, we use Hölder's Inequality to obtain that the output set containing a point has ℓ_2 distance from a lattice compared with the covering radius in any ℓ_p norm for $1 \leq p \leq \infty$. We also prove that the relationships between the output set containing a point has ℓ_2 distance from a lattice and $\rho^{(p)}(\mathcal{L})$ for $1 \leq p \leq \infty$. For $p = \infty$, we do not rely on Komlós Conjecture which is essential in [13]. We also obtain that the relationships between ℓ_p distance for $1 \leq p \leq \infty$ and $\rho^{(2)}(\mathcal{L})$.

Relation to Haviv's RSP. This paper is inspired by Haviv's, but differs from it in most of details. The definition for RSP in [13] depends on two parameters $d, \gamma \geq 1$ to be minimized, where d is the size of the set constructed and γ is the remoteness parameter. By the analysis the algorithm for RSP, Haviv showed that a deterministic time algorithm for RSP that on full-rank lattice $\mathcal{L}$ outputs a set S of points, at least one of which is $O(\sqrt{k/n}) \cdot \rho^{(p)}(\mathcal{L})$ in any ℓ_p norm for $2 \leq p \leq \infty$. Hence, the distance from the lattice of at least one of the points in S approximates the covering radius to within a factor of $O(\sqrt{k/n})$. Haviv also showed a polynomial time deterministic algorithm outputs a set of points, at least one of which is $\sqrt{\log n/n} \cdot \rho^{(p)}(\mathcal{L})$ far from $\mathcal{L}$ for $2 \leq p \leq \infty$. The proof techniques in [13] involved a theorem on balancing vectors [5] and six standard deviations theorem [19] of Spencer from Banach space theory, and specially depended on Komlós Conjecture for ℓ_∞ norm. All the analysis of Haviv's algorithm for RSP in [13] is hold in any ℓ_p norm for $2 \leq p \leq \infty$.

Our definition for V-RSP only depends on parameter $\gamma \leq 1$, the size of the set is bounded by γ and can not minimize arbitrarily. We prove that the output of the deterministic time algorithm for V-RSP contains a point in S whose distance from lattice $\mathcal{L}$ is at least $O(k/n) \cdot \rho^{(p)}(\mathcal{L})$ in any ℓ_p norm for $1 \leq p \leq \infty$. This implies that the distance of a point in S from the lattice approximates the covering radius to within a factor of $O(k/n)$. Moreover, when we choose $k = \lfloor M/(M-1) \cdot \sqrt{n \cdot \log_M n} \rfloor$, we also obtain that the set S containing a point which is $\sqrt{\log_M n/n} \cdot \rho^{(p)}(\mathcal{L})$ far from $\mathcal{L}$ for $1 \leq p \leq \infty$ in a deterministic time. The approximation factor is similar to Haviv's $\sqrt{\log n/n}$. We also analyze the complexity of V-RSP. The proof techniques for V-RSP only use some elementary inequalities involving triangle inequality of norm and Hölder's Inequality. And our results for V-RSP are adapted to any ℓ_p norm for $1 \leq p \leq \infty$.

Organization. The rest of the paper is organized as follows. In Sect. 2 we introduce basic notations about lattices and some important inequalities that we need in the paper. In Sect. 3 we propose the variant of Remote Set Problem (V-RSP) and analyze V-RSP.

2   Preliminaries

Let $\mathbb{R}^m$ be a m-dimensional Euclidean space. A norm $\| \cdot \|$ is a positive real-valued function on $\mathbb{R}^m$ that satisfies the triangle inequality, i.e., a function $\| \cdot \| : \mathbb{R}^m \longrightarrow \mathbb{R}$ such that

- $\|x\| \geq 0$ with equality only if $x = 0$.
- $\|kx\| = |k| \|x\|$.
- $\|x + y\| \leq \|x\| + \|y\|$.

for all $x, y \in \mathbb{R}^m$ and $k \in \mathbb{R}$. For $1 \leq p < \infty$, the ℓ_p norm of a vector $x = (x_1, x_2, \ldots, x_m) \in \mathbb{R}^m$ is defined as $\|x\|_p = (\sum_{i=1}^m |x_i|^p)^{1/p}$ and for $p = \infty$ the ℓ_∞ norm is defined as $\|x\|_\infty = \max_{1 \leq i \leq m} |x_i|$. The ℓ_p distance between two vector $x, y \in \mathbb{R}^m$ is defined as $dist_p(x, y) = \|x - y\|_p$. For any vector $x \in \mathbb{R}^m$ and any set $S \subseteq \mathbb{R}^m$, the ℓ_p distance from x to S is $dist_p(x, S) = \min_{y \in S} dist_p(x, y)$.

A lattice $\mathcal{L}$ is the set of all linear combinations that generated by n linearly independent vectors $b_1, \ldots, b_n$ in $\mathbb{R}^m (m \geq n)$, that is

$$\mathcal{L} = \{ \sum_{i=1}^n x_i b_i | x_i \in \mathbb{Z}, 1 \leq i \leq n \}.$$

The integer n is the rank of the lattice, m is the dimension of the lattice. The sequence of linear independent vectors $b_1, \ldots, b_n \in \mathbb{R}^m$ is called a basis of the lattice. We represent $b_1, \ldots, b_n$ by the matrix B of m rows and n columns, that is, $B = [b_1, \ldots, b_n] \in \mathbb{R}^{m \times n}$. The lattice $\mathcal{L}$ generated by a basis B is denoted by $\mathcal{L} = \mathcal{L}(B) = \{ Bx : x \in \mathbb{Z}^n \}$.

In the following, we consider the covering radius which is an important parameter associated with lattices.

Definition 1 (Covering Radius). *The covering radius of $\mathcal{L}$, denoted $\rho(\mathcal{L})$, is defined as the smallest radius ρ such that the (closed) spheres of radius ρ centered at all lattice points cover the entire space, i.e., any point in $span(\mathcal{L})$ is within distance ρ from the lattice.*

Formally, the covering radius $\rho^{(p)}(\mathcal{L})$ is defined as the maximum distance $dist_p(\boldsymbol{x}, \mathcal{L})$:

$$\rho^{(p)}(\mathcal{L}) = \max_{\boldsymbol{x} \in span(\mathcal{L})} dist_p(\boldsymbol{x}, \mathcal{L}),$$

where $\boldsymbol{x}$ ranges over the linear span of $\mathcal{L}$.

There exists a set of all the vector as a linear combinations of the basis vectors with all coefficients in $\{0, 1/M, \ldots, 1 - 1/M\}$. The following lemma shows that at least one of the points in the set is quite far from the lattice.

Lemma 1 [10]. *For every $1 \le p \le \infty$, any basis $\boldsymbol{B}$ and an integer $M > 0$, there exists a point*

$$\boldsymbol{v} = a_1 \boldsymbol{b}_1 + \cdots + a_n \boldsymbol{b}_n$$

such that $a_i \in \{0, 1/M, \ldots, 1 - 1/M\}$ for all i, and $dist_p(\boldsymbol{v}, \mathcal{L}) \ge (1 - 1/M) \cdot \rho^{(p)}(\mathcal{L})$.

The definition of the variant of Remote Set Problem (V-RSP) for any $1 \le p \le \infty$ and $\gamma \le 1$ is in the following.

Definition 2 (V-RSP$_\gamma^{(p)}$). *For an integer $M \ge 2$, given a lattice basis $\boldsymbol{B} \in \mathbb{Q}^{m \times n}$ and $\gamma \le 1$, the variant of Remote Set Problem is to find a set $S \subseteq span(\mathcal{L})$ of size $|S| \le O(n/(\alpha \gamma) \cdot M^{\alpha \gamma})$ such that S contains a point $\boldsymbol{v}$ satisfying*

$$dist_p(\boldsymbol{v}, \mathcal{L}) \ge \gamma \cdot \rho^{(p)}(\mathcal{L})$$

where $\alpha = nM/(M - 1)$.

The following inequalities are essential in this paper.

Lemma 2 (Equivalent Norms) [9]. *Let $\|\cdot\|_\alpha$ and $\|\cdot\|_\beta$ be two different norms on the same vector space V. There exists positive constants t, T such that*

$$t\|\boldsymbol{x}\|_\alpha \le \|\boldsymbol{x}\|_\beta \le T\|\boldsymbol{x}\|_\alpha$$

for any vector $\boldsymbol{x} \in V$.

Theorem 1 (Hölder's Inequality) [9]. *Fix an arbitrary norm $\|\cdot\|$ on $\mathbb{R}^m$, for any vector $\boldsymbol{x} \in \mathbb{R}^m$, we have the following inequalities:*

- *for any $1 \le p \le 2$, $\|\boldsymbol{x}\|_2 \le \|\boldsymbol{x}\|_p \le m^{1/p - 1/2}\|\boldsymbol{x}\|_2$,*
- *for any $2 < p < \infty$, $m^{1/p - 1/2}\|\boldsymbol{x}\|_2 \le \|\boldsymbol{x}\|_p \le \|\boldsymbol{x}\|_2$,*
- *for $p = \infty$, $\frac{1}{\sqrt{m}}\|\boldsymbol{x}\|_2 \le \|\boldsymbol{x}\|_\infty \le \|\boldsymbol{x}\|_2$.*

3   The Variant of Remote Set Problem

3.1   Algorithm for the Variant of Remote Set Problem

In this section, based on Definition 2, we use triangle inequality to analyze the algorithm for V-RSP which applies to any ℓ_p norm for $1 \le p \le \infty$.

Theorem 2. *For an integer $M \ge 2$, for every $1 \le p \le \infty$ and every $k = k(n,\gamma) = \lfloor \frac{nM}{c(M-1)}\gamma \rfloor \ge 1$, there exists a deterministic $M^k \cdot b^{O(1)}$ time algorithm for V-RSP$_\gamma^{(p)}$ that on input a lattice basis $\boldsymbol{B} \in \mathbb{Q}^{m \times n}$ and $\gamma \le 1$, outputs a set $\boldsymbol{S}$ of size $|\boldsymbol{S}| = O(n/k \cdot M^k) = O(n/(\alpha\gamma) \cdot M^{\alpha\gamma})$ containing a point which is quite far from a lattice, where $\alpha = nM/(M-1)$, n denotes lattice rank, m denotes lattice dimension, b is the input size, c is a constant.*

Proof. Our proof is similar to [13], but our technique is different since we only use the triangle inequality of norm. We will give full proof for completeness here.

Assume that $k = k(n,\gamma)$ divides n. First, we partition the lattice basis $\boldsymbol{B} = (\boldsymbol{b}_1, \boldsymbol{b}_2, \ldots, \boldsymbol{b}_n)$ into n/k sets of size k each, i.e., $\boldsymbol{B} = (\boldsymbol{B}_1, \boldsymbol{B}_2, \ldots, \boldsymbol{B}_{n/k})$. Then the algorithm outputs a set $\boldsymbol{S}$ containing $n/k \cdot M^k$ vectors in span$(\boldsymbol{B})$ that are linear combinations of vectors in $\boldsymbol{B}_i$ with coefficients in $\{0, 1/M, \ldots, 1 - 1/M\}$. These vectors must be in some $\boldsymbol{S}_i, i = 1, 2, \ldots, n/k$.

For every $1 \le i \le n/k$, $j = 1, 2, \ldots, k$,

$$\boldsymbol{S}_i = \{v | v = a_1 \boldsymbol{b}_{(i-1)k+1} + a_2 \boldsymbol{b}_{(i-1)k+2} + \cdots + a_k \boldsymbol{b}_{ik}\}$$

where $a_j \in \{0, 1/M, \ldots, 1 - 1/M\}$. The algorithm outputs $\boldsymbol{S} = \bigcup_{i=1}^{n/k} \boldsymbol{S}_i$. Hence, we have $|\boldsymbol{S}| \le n/k \cdot M^k$ and obtain $\boldsymbol{S}$ in time $M^k \cdot b^{O(1)}$, where b is the input size.

For $1 \le p \le \infty$, we claim that there exists a vector $\boldsymbol{w}$ in $\boldsymbol{S}$ such that ℓ_p distance from $\mathcal{L}(\boldsymbol{B})$ is at least $(1-1/M) \cdot k/n \cdot \rho^{(p)}(\mathcal{L}(\boldsymbol{B}))$, i.e., $dist_p(w, \mathcal{L}(\boldsymbol{B})) \ge (1 - 1/M) \cdot k/n \cdot \rho^{(p)}(\mathcal{L}(\boldsymbol{B}))$. Assume for contradiction that for every vector $\boldsymbol{v}$ in $\boldsymbol{S}$ there exists a lattice vector $\boldsymbol{y}$ such that

$$dist_p(\boldsymbol{v}, \boldsymbol{y}) < (1 - 1/M) \cdot k/n \cdot \rho^{(p)}(\mathcal{L}(\boldsymbol{B})).$$

By Lemma 1, there exists a point $\boldsymbol{v} = a_1 \boldsymbol{b}_1 + a_2 \boldsymbol{b}_2 + \cdots + a_n \boldsymbol{b}_n$ such that $a_i \in \{0, 1/M, \ldots, 1-1/M\}$ for all i and $dist_p(\boldsymbol{v}, \mathcal{L}(\boldsymbol{B})) \ge (1-1/M) \cdot \rho^{(p)}(\mathcal{L}(\boldsymbol{B}))$. Let

$$\boldsymbol{v} = \boldsymbol{v}_1 + \boldsymbol{v}_2 + \cdots + \boldsymbol{v}_{n/k}$$

where $\boldsymbol{v}_i = a_{(i-1)k+1} \boldsymbol{b}_{(i-1)k+1} + a_{(i-1)k+2} \boldsymbol{b}_{(i-1)k+2} + \cdots + a_{ik} \boldsymbol{b}_{ik}$, $a_j \in \{0, 1/M, \ldots, 1 - 1/M\}$ for $j = (i-1)k + 1, \ldots, ik, 1 \le i \le n/k$.

Clearly, $\boldsymbol{v}_i \in \boldsymbol{S}_i \subseteq \boldsymbol{S}$, by assumption that there exists a lattice vector $\boldsymbol{y}_i \in \mathcal{L}(\boldsymbol{B})$ such that

$$dist_p(\boldsymbol{v}_i, \boldsymbol{y}_i) = \|\boldsymbol{v}_i - \boldsymbol{y}_i\|_p < (1 - \frac{1}{M}) \cdot \frac{k}{n} \cdot \rho^{(p)}(\mathcal{L}(\boldsymbol{B})).$$

Algorithm 1. The Variant of Remote Set Problem ([13]).

Input:

A lattice basis $B = (B_1, B_2, \ldots, B_{n/k}) \in \mathbb{Q}^{m \times n}$, γ.

Output:

A set $S \subseteq span(B)$ of $n/k \cdot M^k$ vectors at least one of which is $(1 - 1/M) \cdot n/k \cdot \rho^{(p)}(\mathcal{L}(B))$ far from $\mathcal{L}(B)$.

For every $1 \leq i \leq n/k$

    1. Define $B_i = [b_{(i-1)k+1}, \ldots, b_{ik}]$.

    2. Construct the set

        $S_i = \{v | v = a_1 b_{(i-1)k+1} + a_2 b_{(i-1)k+2} + \cdots + a_k b_{ik}\}$,

    where $a_j \in \{0, 1/M, \ldots, 1 - 1/M\}$.

Return $S = \bigcup_{i=1}^{n/k} S_i$.

For every $1 \leq i \leq n/k$, let $\beta_i = v_i - y_i$. Using the triangle inequality, we have

$$\| \sum_{i=1}^{n/k} \beta_i \|_p \leq \|\beta_1\|_p + \|\beta_2\|_p + \cdots + \|\beta_{n/k}\|_p$$

$$< (1 - \frac{1}{M}) \cdot \frac{n}{k} \cdot \frac{k}{n} \cdot \rho^{(p)}(\mathcal{L}(B))$$

$$= (1 - \frac{1}{M}) \cdot \rho^{(p)}(\mathcal{L}(B)).$$

Since

$$v - \sum_{i=1}^{n/k} \beta_i = \sum_{i=1}^{n/k} v_i - \sum_{i=1}^{n/k} \beta_i = \sum_{i=1}^{n/k} y_i \in \mathcal{L}(B),$$

we have

$$dist_p(v, \mathcal{L}(B)) = dist_p(\sum_{i=1}^{n/k} \beta_i, \mathcal{L}(B))$$

$$\leq \| \sum_{i=1}^{n/k} \beta_i \|_p$$

$$< (1 - \frac{1}{M}) \cdot \rho^{(p)}(\mathcal{L}(B)).$$

This contradicts the choice of v. So, there exists a vector in S whose ℓ_p distance from $\mathcal{L}(B)$ is quite far.

Using the triangle inequality, the algorithm for V-RSP is also holding in any ℓ_p norm for $1 \leq p \leq \infty$ and solves the case of $1 \leq p < 2$. When $M = 2$, we can obtain a similar result to Haviv (see [13], Theorem 3.1), though our approximation factor is a little weaker. However, our techniques are simpler.

By choosing $k = \lfloor cM/(M - 1) \cdot \sqrt{n \log_M n} \rfloor$, where c is a constant and n is the lattice rank, we will derive that the output of our algorithm contains a point whose distance from lattice $\mathcal{L}$ is at least $\sqrt{\log_M n/n} \cdot \rho^{(p)}(\mathcal{L})$. This approximation factor is similar to Haviv's. We will describe in the following.

Corollary 1. *For an integer $M \geq 2$, for every $1 \leq p \leq \infty$ and $k = \lfloor cM/(M-1) \cdot \sqrt{n \log_M n} \rfloor$, there exists a deterministic time algorithm for V-RSP$_\gamma^{(p)}$ that on input a lattice $\boldsymbol{B} \in \mathbb{Q}^{m \times n}$ and $\gamma \leq 1$, outputs a set containing a point which is $\sqrt{\log_M n/n} \cdot \rho^{(p)}(\mathcal{L})$ far from lattice $\mathcal{L}$, where n denotes lattice rank and c is a constant.*

3.2   The Complexity Classes for V-RSP

We will analyze the complexity classes for V-RSP$_\gamma^{(p)}$ with the change of parameter γ, as stated in the following.

1.   For every $1 \leq p \leq \infty$ and $0 \leq \epsilon \leq 1$, for $\frac{1}{n}(1 - \frac{1}{M}) \leq \gamma \leq \frac{\log_M^\epsilon n}{n}(1 - \frac{1}{M})$, there exists a deterministic polynomial time algorithm for V-RSP$_\gamma^{(p)}$, and V-RSP$_\gamma^{(p)}$ lies in Class P.

2.   For every $1 \leq p \leq \infty$ and $\epsilon > 1$, for $\frac{\log_M n}{n}(1 - \frac{1}{M}) \leq \gamma \leq \frac{\log_M^\epsilon n}{n}(1 - \frac{1}{M})$, there exists a deterministic (single) exponential time algorithm for V-RSP$_\gamma^{(p)}$.

3.3   An Additional Property of V-RSP

By the Theorem 2, we show that the algorithm for V-RSP can find a set of points containing a point which is far from the lattice. We use the Hölder's Inequality in Theorem 1 to study the relationships between the ℓ_2 distance from a point of the output set to a lattice $\mathcal{L}$ and the covering radius ($\rho^{(p)}(\mathcal{L})$) of the lattice $\mathcal{L}$ for every $1 \leq p \leq \infty$. The case of $1 \leq p < 2$ is not mentioned in [13]. Specially, when $p = \infty$, we do not depend on Komlós Conjecture. Similar to [13], the following theorems are based on algorithm presented in the proof of Theorem 2.

Theorem 3. *For an integer $M \geq 2$, for every $1 \leq p \leq 2$ and every $k = k(n,\gamma) = \lfloor \frac{nM}{c(M-1)}\gamma \rfloor \geq 1$, there exists a deterministic $M^k \cdot b^{O(1)}$ time algorithm for V-RSP$_\gamma^{(p)}$ that on input a lattice basis $\boldsymbol{B} \in \mathbb{R}^m$ and $\gamma \leq 1$ outputs a set $\boldsymbol{S}$ of size $|\boldsymbol{S}| = O(n/k \cdot M^k) = O(n/(\alpha\gamma) \cdot M^{\alpha\gamma})$ containing a point whose ℓ_2 distance from $\mathcal{L}$ is at least $1/m^{1/p-1/2} \cdot (1 - 1/M) \cdot k/n \cdot \rho^{(p)}(\mathcal{L}(\boldsymbol{B}))$, where $\alpha = nM/(M-1)$, m denotes lattice dimension, b is the input size, c is a constant. For a special case of full-rank lattice $(m = n)$, one of the points whose ℓ_2 distance is at least $k/n^{1/p+1/2} \cdot (1 - 1/M) \cdot \rho^{(p)}(\mathcal{L}(\boldsymbol{B}))$.*

Theorem 4. *For an integer $M \geq 2$, for every $2 < p \leq \infty$ and every $k = k(n,\gamma) = \lfloor \frac{nM}{c(M-1)}\gamma \rfloor \geq 1$, there exists a deterministic $M^k \cdot b^{O(1)}$ time algorithm for V-RSP$_\gamma^{(p)}$ that on input a lattice $\boldsymbol{B} \in \mathbb{R}^m$ and $\gamma \leq 1$, outputs a set $\boldsymbol{S}$ of size $|\boldsymbol{S}| = O(n/k \cdot M^k) = O(n/(\alpha\gamma) \cdot M^{\alpha\gamma})$ containing a point whose ℓ_2 distance from $\mathcal{L}$ is at least $(1 - 1/M) \cdot k/n \cdot \rho^{(p)}(\mathcal{L}(\boldsymbol{B}))$, where $\alpha = nM/(M-1)$, m denotes lattice dimension, b is the input size, c is a constant.*

In the following, we study the relationships between the $\ell_p (1 \leq p \leq \infty)$ distance from a point of the output set to a lattice $\mathcal{L}$ and the covering radius $(\rho^{(2)}(\mathcal{L}))$ of the lattice $\mathcal{L}$.

Corollary 2. *For an integer $M \geq 2$, for every $1 \leq p \leq 2$ and every $k = k(n,\gamma) = \lfloor \frac{nM}{c(M-1)}\gamma \rfloor \geq 1$, there exists a deterministic $M^k \cdot b^{O(1)}$ time algorithm for V-RSP$_\gamma^{(p)}$ that on input a lattice $\mathbf{B} \in \mathbb{R}^m$ and $\gamma \leq 1$ outputs a set $\mathbf{S}$ of size $|\mathbf{S}| = O(n/k \cdot M^k)$ containing a point whose ℓ_p distance from $\mathcal{L}$ is at least $(1 - 1/M) \cdot k/n \cdot \rho^{(2)}(\mathcal{L}(\mathbf{B}))$. For every $2 < p < \infty$, one of points whose ℓ_p distance is at least $1/m^{1/p-1/2} \cdot (1 - 1/M) \cdot k/n \cdot \rho^{(2)}(\mathcal{L}(\mathbf{B}))$. For a the full-rank lattice $(m = n)$, one of the points whose ℓ_p distance is at least $k/n^{1/p+1/2} \cdot (1 - 1/M) \cdot \rho^{(2)}(\mathcal{L}(\mathbf{B}))$, where m denotes lattice dimension, b is the input size, c is a constant.*

Corollary 3. *For an integer $M \geq 2$, for every $p = \infty$ and every $k = k(n,\gamma) = \lfloor \frac{nM}{c(M-1)}\gamma \rfloor \geq 1$, there exists a deterministic $M^k \cdot b^{O(1)}$ time algorithm for V-RSP$_\gamma^{(p)}$ that on input a lattice $\mathbf{B} \in \mathbb{R}^m$ and $\gamma \leq 1$ outputs a set $\mathbf{S}$ of size $|\mathbf{S}| = O(n/k \cdot M^k)$ containing a point whose ℓ_p distance from $\mathcal{L}$ is at least $1/\sqrt{m} \cdot (1 - 1/M) \cdot k/n \cdot \rho^{(2)}(\mathcal{L}(\mathbf{B}))$, where m denotes lattice dimension, b is the input size, c is a constant.*

4   Conclusion

In our paper, we propose the variant of Remote Set Problem (V-RSP) which only relies on the parameter $\gamma \leq 1$. From the algorithm for RSP, we knew that the distance from the lattice of at least one of the point in the set $\mathbf{S}$ approximates the covering radius to within a factor of $O(\sqrt{k/n})$ in ℓ_p norm for $2 \leq p \leq \infty$. However, using some elementary tools, we obtain that the approximation is $O(k/n)$ in the algorithm for V-RSP in ℓ_p norm for $1 \leq p \leq \infty$. This introduces a $O(\sqrt{k/n})$ loss in the approximation factors. We also can get the same approximation factors at the cost of more time in the algorithm for V-RSP. Hence, there is an interesting problem to reduce the gap between RSP and V-RSP.

Acknowledgements. This work was supported by National Natural Science Foundation of China (Grant No. 61272039).

References

1. Aharonov, D., Regev, O.: Lattice problems in NP intersect coNP. J. ACM **52**(5), 749–765 (2005). Preliminary version in FOCS 2004
2. Ajtai, M.: Generating hard instances of lattice problems (extended abstract). In: 28th Annual ACM Symposium on the Theory of Computing (Philadelphia, PA, 1996), pp. 99–108. ACM, New York (1996)

3. Ajtai, M.: The shortest vector problem in ℓ_2 is NP-hard for randomized reductions (extended abstract). In: 30th ACM Symposium on the Theory of Computing, pp. 10-19 (1998)
4. Ajtai, M., Kumar, R., Sivakumar, D.: A Sieve algorithm for the shortest lattice vector problem. In: 33th ACM Symposium on Theory of Computing, pp. 601–610 (2001)
5. Banaszczyk, W.: Balancing vectors and Gaussian measures of n-dimensional convex bodies. Random Struct. Algorithm 12(4), 351–360 (1998)
6. Dinur, I., Kindler, G., Raz, R., Safra, S.: Approximating CVP to within almost-polynomial factors is NP-hard. Combinatorica 23(2), 205–243 (2003)
7. Gauss, C.F.: Disquisitiones Arithmeticae, Gerh. Fleischer Iun, Lipsia (1801)
8. Goldreich, O., Goldwasser, S.: On the limits of nonapproximability of lattice problems. J. Comput. Syst. Sci. 60(3), 540–563 (2000)
9. Griffel, D.H.: Applied Functional Analysis. Horwood Limited, Chichester (2002)
10. Guruswami, V., Micciancio, D., Regev, O.: The complexity of the covering radius problem on lattices and codes. Comput. Complex. 14(2), 90–121 (2005). Preliminary version in CCC 2004
11. Haviv, I., Regev, O.: Tensor-based hardness of the shortest vector problem to within almost polynomial factors. Theory Comput. 8, 513–531 (2012)
12. Haviv, I., Regev, O.: Hardness of the covering radius problem on lattices. Chicago J. Theoret. Comput. Sci. 04, 1–12 (2012)
13. Haviv, I.: The remote set problem on lattice. Comput. Complex. 24(1), 103–131 (2015)
14. Khot, S.: Hardness of approximating the shortest vector problem in lattices. J. ACM (JACM) 52(5), 789–808 (2005)
15. Lenstra, A., Lenstra, H., Lovász, L.: Factoring polynomials with rational coefficients. Math. Ann. 261, 515–534 (1982)
16. Micciancio, D.: Almost perfect lattices, the covering radius problem, and applications to Ajtai's connection factor. SIAM J. Comput 34, 118–169 (2004)
17. Micciancio, D., Voulgaris, P.: A deterministic single exponential time algorithm for most lattice problems based on Voronoi cell computation. Soc. Ind. Appl. Math., SIAM J. Comput. 42(3), 1364–1391 (2013)
18. Peikert, C.: Limits on the hardness of lattice problems in ℓ_p norms. Comput. Complex. 17(2), 300–335 (2008). Preliminary version in CCC 2007
19. Spencer, J.: Six standard deviations suffice. Trans. Am. Math. Soc. 289(2), 679–706 (1985)
20. Van Emde Boas, P.: Another NP-complete problem and the complexity of computing short vectors in a lattice. Technical report 8104, Department of Mathematics, University of Amsterdam, Netherlands (1981)

Compression-Based Integral Prior Classification for Improving Steganalysis

Viktor Monarev[1], Ilja Duplischev[2], and Andrey Pestunov[3(✉)]

[1] Institute of Computational Technologies SB RAS, Novosibirsk, Russia
viktor.monarev@gmail.com
[2] Novosibirsk State University, Novosibirsk, Russia
amfipter@gmail.com
[3] Novosibirsk State University of Economics and Management, Novosibirsk, Russia
pestunov@gmail.com

Abstract. We propose the integral prior classification approach for binary steganalysis which imply that several detectors are trained, and each detector is intended for processing only images with certain compression rate. In particular, the training set is splitted into several parts according to the images compression rate, then a corresponding number of detectors are trained, but each detector uses only an ascribed to it subset. The testing images are distributed between the detectors also according to their compression rate. We utilize BOSSbase 1.01 as benchmark data along with HUGO, WOW and S-UNIWARD as benchmark embedding algorithms. Comparison with state-of-the-art results demonstrated that, depending on the case, the integral prior classification allows to decrease the detection error by 0.05–0.16.

Keywords: Information hiding · Steganalysis · Support vector machine · Compression · HUGO · UNIWARD · WOW · Prior classification · SRM · PSRM

1 Introduction

The classic problem of steganalysis consists in distinguishing between empty and stego images via a bare detector; at that, all images are subject to processing. Recently, it was introduced an approach of how to exploit a prior classification in steganalysis [10], and, within it, there were proposed three possible methods of selecting a portion of the testing set such that a detection error, calculated over this subset, may be lower than that calculated over the whole set. In their paper, the authors also discussed an possibility of splitting the testing set into several subsets containing images with common (in some sense) properties and training an individual detector for each subset in order to decrease the detection error calculated over the whole testing set.

In this paper, we propose a compression-based method of how to turn this idea in practice. We suggest to split the training image set into several subsets according to their compression rate, then obtain a corresponding number of

© Springer International Publishing AG 2016
K.-Y. Lam et al. (Eds.): ICICS 2016, LNCS 9977, pp. 134–144, 2016.
DOI: 10.1007/978-3-319-50011-9_11

non-trained detectors, and train each of them utilizing a separate subset. During the testing phase, images with a certain compressing rate should be send to the detector, which has been trained on the images that have the close compression rate. The idea of using the compression rate as an indicator for the integral prior classification came from a well-known fact that noisy images are harder to steganalyze than plain ones, but noisiness is usually tightly correlated with entropy, and therefore with the compression rate. So, we guessed that the detectors for the noisy images should be better trained with noisy images, and the ones for the plain images should be trained with plain images.

The main hypothesis, which motivated our work, assumes that the detector preceded by the integral prior classification would be more accurate than the detector alone. It is worth mentioning, that compression is a very universal tool, which has been already used in steganalysis, see e.g. [2,8]; however, these papers are devoted to distinguishing either the basic LSB steganography or to creating quantitative steganalyzers, while the current paper focuses on binary detection of the content-adaptive embedding. Moreover, in the earlier papers, the data compression was exploited for developing the stego detectors themselves, while in the current paper we do not touch the detectors, and use the compression methods in order to perform the integral prior classification.

The principle difference between the single prior classification (introduced in [10]) and the integral prior classification (being introduced in this paper) consists in the fact that the single prior classification allows to select only *a part of the testing set* which would provide higher accuracy, while the integral prior classification enhances the accuracy estimated over *the whole testing set*. Thus, although the single prior classification may obtain a rather large subset, which would be sent into the steganalyzer, all the same, it discards other images. At the same time, the integral prior classification assumes that all the testing images are subject to processing by the detector, keeping us in the traditional scenario.

Using BOSSbase 1.01 [1] as benchmark data along with content-adaptive embedding methods HUGO [12], S-UNIWARD [5] and WOW [4] as benchmark embedding algorithms we compare our results against state-of-the-art due to Holub and Fridrich [6]. Our experiments have confirmed the above hypothesis and demonstrated that prepending the integral prior classification allows to decrease the detection error of the bare detector by 0.05–0.16. For the sake of clarity, we want to emphasize that the results of the current paper are compared against accuracy of the best bare detectors, and not with that of the detectors accompanied by the single prior classification, because the latter deals only with the part of the testing set, while the integral prior classification assumes that the detection error is calculated over the whole testing set.

2 Description of Integral Prior Classification

2.1 General Scheme

A general scheme of how to train the detectors using the integral prior classification is represented at the Fig. 1. At first, we need to split the training set

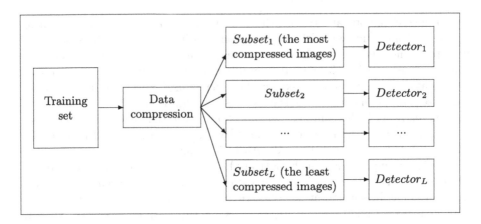

Fig. 1. The integral prior classification scheme

into subsets according to the compression rate in order to combine images with close compression rate in the same subsets. For instance, the first class contains the most compressed images, and the last class contains the least compressed images. The number of subsets would define the number of detectors for training. After the splitting, the detectors are trained: each detector is trained using the images from a certain subset. In particular, the first detector is trained using the first subset, the second detector is trained using the second subset etc.

During the testing phase, images are distributed between the detectors according to their compression rate, and each image is processed by the corresponding detector. Thus, unlike traditional bare detection scheme, which employs the detector alone, the integral prior classification assumes that the given image is sent to the detector which (we expect so), would provide the least detection error. Certainly, there may be some other ways of distributing the images (not only basing on the compression rate).

2.2   Detailed Description

In high-level steps, the detection with the integral prior classification is depicted at the Algorithm 1. The algorithm is injected with the training set $\mathcal{X}$ and the testing set $\mathcal{Y}$. Then a compression method $\texttt{Compress}(\,\cdot\,)$, a number of subsets L, along with their sizes, $size_1, \ldots, size_L$ ($size_1 + \ldots + size_L = |\mathcal{X}|$), and $size'_1, \ldots, size'_L$ ($size'_1 + \ldots + size'_L = |\mathcal{Y}|$), are chosen.

The SPLIT-SET function (see Algorithm 2) returns L non-intersected subsets which constitute a partition of the set Z. As you can see (Algorithm 1), this function is called twice: for splitting the training set $\mathcal{X}$ and for splitting the testing set $\mathcal{Y}$. The first step of this function is compressing every image $z \in \mathcal{Z}$ in order to obtain its size after compression $|\texttt{Compress}(z)|$. At the second step, the images are sorted according the this value (the sorted row we denote as follows: $z_{(1)}, z_{(2)}, \ldots, z_{(|\mathcal{Z}|)}$). And at last, the subsets are formed. The first $size_1$ images

---

DETECTION($\mathcal{X}$, $\mathcal{Y}$)

$\mathcal{X}$ — the training image set, $\mathcal{Y}$ — the testing image set.

1. Choose the compression function Compress($\cdot$);
2. Choose the number of detectors L;
3. Choose the sizes of the training subsets $size_l$, $l = \overline{1, L}$
   ($size_1 + \ldots + size_L = |\mathcal{X}|$);
4. Choose the sizes of the testing subsets $size'_l$, $l = \overline{1, L}$
   ($size'_1 + \ldots + size'_L = |\mathcal{Y}|$);
5. $(Subset_1, \ldots, Subset_L) :=$ SPLIT-SET($\mathcal{X}$, Compress($\cdot$), $size_1, \ldots, size_L$);
6. $(Detector_1, \ldots, Detector_L) :=$ TRAIN-DETECTORS($Subset_1, \ldots, Subset_L$);
7. $(Subset'_1, \ldots, Subset'_L) :=$ SPLIT-SET($\mathcal{Y}$, Compress($\cdot$), $size'_1, \ldots, size'_L$);
8. $\mathcal{Y}_{Empty} = \{\}$; $\mathcal{Y}_{Stego} = \{\}$;
9. ForEach $y \in \mathcal{Y}$
   (a) $detectorNumber :=$ DETECTOR-NUMBER(y, $Subset'_1, \ldots, Subset'_L$);
   (b) $detectionResult := Detector_{detectorNumber}(y)$;
   (c) If ($detectionResult = Empty$) $\mathcal{Y}_{Empty} := \mathcal{Y}_{Empty} \cup \{y\}$;
       Else $\mathcal{Y}_{Stego} := \mathcal{Y}_{Stego} \cup \{y\}$;

Result: $\mathcal{Y}_{Empty}$ — empty images (according to the detector);
$\mathcal{Y}_{Stego}$ — images with embedded information

Algorithm 1. High-level scheme of the detector with integral prior classification

are ascribed to the first subset, the next $size_2$ images are ascribed to the second subset, and so on; the last $size_L$ images are ascribed to the last subset.

Then the TRAIN-DETECTORS function (see Algorithm 3) receives L subsets and trains L detectors to distinguish between the empty and stego images. The detectors may be of different types, but, in steganography, usually the support vector machine or the ensemble classifier are employed. They utilize image features such as SRM [3], PSRM [6], SPAM [11] etc.

The testing phase is now divided into two stages: the prior classification stage and the detection stage. The prior classification stage consists in calling the DETECTOR-NUMBER function (see Algorithm 4), which returns the detector number for each image from the testing set $\mathcal{Y}$. This number is obtained according to the testing set splitting (see step 7 from the Algorithm 1) but there may be other ways of implementing it.

3   Experimental Results

We performed two types of experiments. Adjustment experiments aimed at searching for the better parameters, and benchmark experiment were performed with parameters, chosen during the adjustment experiments, and intended for comparing our results the state-of-the-art ones.

SPLIT-SET($\mathcal{Z}$, Compress($\cdot$), L, $size_1$, ..., $size_L$)
    $\mathcal{Z}$ — the image set to be splitted (the training or the testing set);
    Compress($\cdot$) — the compression function;
    L — the number of the subsets;
    $size_l$, $l = \overline{1, L}$ — sizes of the subsets ($size_1 + \ldots + size_L = |\mathcal{Z}|$).

1. Compress every image $z \in \mathcal{Z}$ and for each image obtain $|\text{Compress}(z)|$.
2. Sort the images according to the value $|\text{Compress}(z)|$ so, that $i < j$ means $|\text{Compres}(z_{(i)})| < |\text{Compress}(z_{(j)})|$.
3. Split the set $\mathcal{Z}$ into L subsets as follows:
    $Subset_1 = \{z_{(1)}, \ldots, z_{(size_1)}\}$;
    $Subset_2 = \{z_{(size_1+1)}, \ldots, z_{(size_1+size_2)}\}$;
    $Subset_3 = \{z_{(size_1+size_2+1)}, \ldots, z_{(size_1+size_2+size_3)}\}$;
    ...
    $Subset_L = \{z_{(size_1+\ldots+size_{L-1}+1)}, \ldots, z_{(|\mathcal{Z}|)}\}$.

Result: Subsets: $Subset_1$, $Subset_2$, ..., $Subset_L$.

Algorithm 2. Splitting the set into the several subsets according to their compression rate

---

TRAIN-DETECTORS(L, $Subset_1$, ..., $Subset_L$)
    L — the number of the detectors;
    $Subset_1$, ..., $Subset_L$ — the training subsets.

1. Obtain L non-trained detectors $Detector_1$, $Detector_2$, ..., $Detector_L$;
2. Train $Detector_l$ using the images from $Subset_l$, $l = \overline{1, L}$.

Result: The L trained detectors $Detector_1$, $Detector_2$, ..., $Detector_L$.

Algorithm 3. Detectors training scheme

DETECTOR-NUMBER(y, L, $Subset'_1$, $Subset'_2$, ..., $Subset'_L$)
    y — the image from the testing set;
    L — the number of the testing subsets;
    $Subset'_l$, $l = \overline{1, L}$ — the testing image set splitting. For $l = \overline{1, L}$

    If $y \in Subset'_l$
    $detectorNumber := l$;
Result: $detectorNumber$ — the detector which should process y.

Algorithm 4. Obtaining the number of a detector for the given image

---

3.1 Common Core of the Experiments

Images. During the adjustment experiments the image set from the Break Our Watermarking System 2 (BOWS2) contest [15] was utilized, and during the benchmark experiments—the BOSSbase 1.01 from the Break Our Steganographic System (BOSS) contest [1]. The BOWS2 image set consists of 10000 grayscale images in PGM format; the size of the images is 512 × 512. The well-known benchmark database BOSSbase 1.01 contains 10000 images captured by seven different cameras in RAW format. These images had been converted into 8-bit grayscale format, resized and cropped to the size 512 × 512 pixels.

Preparing the Training and the Testing Sets. The both bases, BOWS2 and BOSSbase, include 10000 images, therefore we prepared the corresponding training and testing sets in the same way. In order to prepare the training set $\mathcal{X}^p$ and the testing set $\mathcal{Y}^p$, where p identifies the embedding rate in bpp, the whole database was divided into two subsets $\mathcal{X}_0$ and $\mathcal{Y}_0$, where $|\mathcal{X}_0| = 7500$ and $|\mathcal{Y}_0| = 2500$. Then by random embedding p bpp into all the images from $\mathcal{X}_0$ and $\mathcal{Y}_0$ we obtained $\mathcal{X}_1^p$ and $\mathcal{Y}_1^p$ correspondingly. The training set was $\mathcal{X}^p = \mathcal{X}_0 \cup \mathcal{X}_1^p$ and the testing set $\mathcal{Y}^p = \mathcal{Y}_0 \cup \mathcal{Y}_1^p$. Thus, $|\mathcal{X}^p| = 15000$ and $|\mathcal{Y}^p| = 5000$. Both sets contain a half of empty images and a half of stego images. Further in the paper we omit the payload index p (it will not confuse the reader) and designate the training set as $\mathcal{X}$ and the testing set as $\mathcal{Y}$.

Compression Methods. We employed well-known lossless compression methods LZMA and PAQ. LZMA (Lempel-Ziv-Markov chain-Algorithm) is a method which uses a dictionary compression scheme [13]. We launched this archiver with the following script: "lzma -k -c -9". PAQ is based on the context mixing model and prediction by partial match [14]. The launching script in our experiments was "paq -11".

Detector. We employed a support vector machine as a detector of steganography. The Python implementation was taken from [16], where the default parameters were used except for the following: the linear kernel, shrinking—turned on, and the penalty parameter $C = 20000$.

Embedding Algorithms. In the benchmark experiments, we employed three embedding algorithms: HUGO, WOW and S-UNIWARD, because exactly these algorithms were used by Holub and Fridrich in their state-of-the-art paper [6]. HUGO (Highly Undetectable Steganography) is a content-adaptive algorithm based on so-called syndrome-trellis codes [12]. WOW (Wavelet Obtained Weights) uses wavelet-based distortion [4], and S-UNIWARD [5] is a simplified modification of WOW. In the adjusting experiments only HUGO was used.

Feature Set. We utilize Spatial Rich Model (SRM) features [3] as one of the most popular instruments for steganalysis. The newer Projection Spatial Rich Model features (PSRM) [6] only slightly decrease the detection error, but significantly increase complexity. SRM features have a total dimension of 34,671.

Detection Error. We measured detection accuracy in a standard manner via calculating the detection error $P_E = \frac{1}{2}(P_{FA} + P_{MD})$, where P_{FA} is the probability of false alarms, and P_{MD} is the probability of missed detections (see e.g. [3,7,9,11]).

3.2 Adjusting Experiments

The goal of this experimental phase is to choose parameters which will be used in the benchmark experiments in order to compare our results with the state-of-the-art. The task consists in choosing the following parameters: a compression method; a number of splitting classes (L); sizes of these subsets.

Due to a long training process of SVM it was infeasible to work over many possible values of the prior classification parameters in order to search for the very best of them. That is why we have chosen three reasonable numbers of the subsets, equal to 2, 3 and 5. The thresholds for the compression rate are determined by their sizes. Here 5 subsets are of the same size, and 2 or 3 subsets have been formed by aggregation of the least compressed subsets. Trying $L = 2$ and $L = 3$ we had hoped that training the detector on images which are harder to steganalyze would provide better accuracy. However, the Table 1 demonstrate that the best accuracy is provided by $L = 5$.

Table 1. The HUGO detection error (P_E) over the whole testing set and over the subsets separately. BOWS2 image set. Search for the best parameters

	Image set	LZMA compression			PAQ compression		
		0.1 bpp	0.2 bpp	0.4 bpp	0.1 bpp	0.2 bpp	0.4 bpp
$L = 2$, $size_1 = 3000$, $size_2 = 12000$, $size_1' = 1000$, $size_2' = 4000$							
Integral prior classification	$Subset_1'$	0.75	0.94	0.99	0.85	0.97	0.99
	$Subset_2'$	0.50	0.54	0.69	0.49	0.57	0.69
	Whole testing set	0.55	0.62	0.75	0.56	0.65	0.75
$L = 3$, $size_1 = size_2 = 3000$, $size_3 = 9000$, $size_1' = size_2' = 1000$, $size_3' = 3000$							
Integral prior classification	$Subset_1'$	0.75	0.94	0.99	0.85	0.97	0.99
	$Subset_2'$	0.67	0.85	0.95	0.65	0.89	0.97
	$Subset_3'$	0.50	0.55	0.67	0.51	0.54	0.64
	Whole testing set	0.58	0.69	0.79	0.60	0.69	0.77
$L = 5$, $size_1 = size_2 = size_3 = size_4 = size_5 = 3000$, $size_1' = size_2' = size_3' = size_4' = size_5' = 1000$							
Integral prior classification	$Subset_1'$	0.75	0.85	0.99	0.74	0.92	1.00
	$Subset_2'$	0.67	0.71	0.91	0.54	0.74	0.95
	$Subset_3'$	0.57	0.64	0.84	0.53	0.62	0.84
	$Subset_4'$	0.56	0.55	0.76	0.52	0.54	0.71
	$Subset_5'$	0.49	0.52	0.61	0.51	0.51	0.58
	Whole testing set	0.61	0.66	0.82	0.57	0.67	0.82
No prior classification		0.525	0.60	0.77	0.525	0.60	0.77

3.3   Benchmark Experiments

The goal of this section is to demonstrate that prepending the prior classification stage (aimed at choosing the appropriate detector for each image), enhances the stego detectors accuracy. We compare the detection error with the state-of-the-art data provided by Holub and Fridrich in [6]. Unlike us, they employed the ensemble classifier [7], which is known to be faster but slightly less accurate than support vector machine. In order to be more persuasive, we calculated the detection errors for our support vector machine implementation (without prior classification) and show that they are close to that for the ensemble classifier. Anyway, integral prior classification allows to exceed both results.

See Tables 2, 3 and 4, where this comparison is provided for HUGO, WOW and S-UNIWARD embedding algorithms correspondingly. Prior classification parameters are as follows (they were chosen during the adjusting experiments): PAQ compression method; $L = 5$; $size_1 = size_2 = size_3 = size_4 = size_5 = 3000$; $size'_1 = size'_2 = size'_3 = size'_4 = size'_5 = 1000$.

The results demonstrate that, depending on the case, the integral prior classification substantially increases the accuracy. The most impressing results (see HUGO 0.1 bpp, WOW 0.1 bpp, WOW 0.2 bpp, S-UNIWARD 0.1 bpp, S-UNIWARD 0.2 bpp, S-UNIWARD 0.4 bpp) provide the accuracy decrease for more than 0.1. In the Tables 2, 3 and 4, we mark out and type in bold those values which are compared against each other. In particular, we compare the detection errors obtained for the integral prior classification against the least errors among the errors of our support vector machine (SVM) implementation and two Fridrich and Holub results. For example, in the Table 2 for HUGO 0.1 bpp we compare 0.24 against 0.35, and in the Table 3 for WOW 0.4 bpp we compare 0.08 against 0.17. As you can see, if two implementations provide the same error they are both marked out.

Table 2. The HUGO detection error (P_E). BOSSbase 1.01

	Image set	0.1 bpp	0.2 bpp	0.4 bpp
Integral prior classification	$Subset'_1$	0.01	0.01	0.00
	$Subset'_2$	0.17	0.05	0.01
	$Subset'_3$	0.21	0.11	0.03
	$Subset'_4$	0.34	0.18	0.08
	$Subset'_5$	0.46	0.30	0.19
	Whole testing set	**0.24**	**0.13**	**0.06**
No prior classification (whole testing set)	Our implementation: SVM + SRM	**0.35**	0.27	0.15
	Holub and Fridrich [6]: Ensemble + SRM	0.36	0.25	0.12
	Holub and Fridrich [6]: Ensemble + PSRMQ1	**0.35**	**0.23**	**0.11**

Table 3. The WOW detection error (P_E). BOSSbase 1.01

	Image set	0.1 bpp	0.2 bpp	0.4 bpp
Integral prior classification	$Subset'_1$	0.02	0.01	0.00
	$Subset'_2$	0.20	0.08	0.01
	$Subset'_3$	0.25	0.13	0.06
	$Subset'_4$	0.30	0.18	0.11
	$Subset'_5$	0.44	0.29	0.20
	Whole testing set	**0.24**	**0.13**	**0.08**
No prior classification (whole testing set)	Our implementation: SVM + SRM	**0.38**	**0.29**	0.21
	Holub and Fridrich [6]: Ensemble + SRM	0.39	0.31	0.19
	Holub and Fridrich [6]: Ensemble + PSRMQ1	**0.38**	**0.29**	**0.17**

Table 4. The S-UNIWARD detection error (P_E). BOSSbase 1.01

	Image set	0.1 bpp	0.2 bpp	0.4 bpp
Integral prior classification	$Subset'_1$	0.01	0.00	0.00
	$Subset'_2$	0.21	0.04	0.00
	$Subset'_3$	0.29	0.14	0.02
	$Subset'_4$	0.33	0.20	0.11
	$Subset'_5$	0.41	0.37	0.16
	Whole testing set	**0.25**	**0.15**	**0.06**
No prior classification (whole testing set)	Our implementation: SVM + SRM	**0.37**	**0.30**	**0.17**
	Holub, Fridrich [6]: Ensemble + SRM	0.41	0.31	0.20
	Holub, Fridrich [6]: Ensemble + PSRMQ1	0.39	**0.30**	0.18

4   Conclusion

In this paper we have proposed the integral prior classification approach aimed at increasing the stego detectors accuracy. Although the basic idea of this approach is rather definite, it may have many possible implementations. For instance, it may be interesting (and, what is more important, it might lead to constructing even more accurate detectors) to classify images not according to their compression rates but some how else.

In the adjusting experiments we considered only three variants of the training image set splitting. Nevertheless, it was enough to reach the goal of our research and to demonstrate that prepending the integral prior classification before detection allows to exceed the accuracy of the state-of-the-art detectors. Thus, one of the possible future work directions may consist in conducting some theoretical research in order to elaborate recommendations of how to choose the number of subsets along with their size which would provide the better accuracy without necessity of heavy adjusting experiments.

It is worthwhile to notice, that in order to determine which detector would process which image, in the current implementation the testing set was splitted into several equal-size parts. However, it is not quite convenient if the testing images arrive one by one, unless we are able to wait until a sufficient quantity accumulates. That is why, in such a case the detector's number can be established according to the compression rates thresholds, instead of the testing set splitting.

The integral prior classification approach extends the single prior classification approach [10], which is intended for only selecting images which can be reliably detected and discards other images, though the selected images may constitute a rather large subset. The main idea of our extension is employing several detectors, each of which processes a certain testing subset or, in other words, images with special properties.

The efficiency of the integral prior classification has been demonstrated for HUGO, WOW and S-UNIWARD utilizing the BOSSbase 1.01 images. Depending on the payload and the embedding algorithm, the detection error decrease, comparing to the state-of-the-art, amounted to 0.05–0.16.

References

1. Bas, P., Filler, T., Pevný, T.: "Break our steganographic system": the ins and outs of organizing BOSS. In: Filler, T., Pevný, T., Craver, S., Ker, A. (eds.) IH 2011. LNCS, vol. 6958, pp. 59–70. Springer, Heidelberg (2011). doi:10.1007/978-3-642-24178-9_5
2. Boncelet, C., Marvel, L., Raqlin, A.: Compression-based steganalysis of LSB embedded images. In: Proceedings of SPIE, Security, Steganography, and Watermarking of Multimedia Contents VIII, vol. 6072, pp. 75-84 (2006)
3. Fridrich, J.: Rich models for steganalysis of digital images. IEEE Trans. Inf. Forensics Secur. **7**(3), 868–882 (2012)
4. Holub, V., Fridrich, J.: Designing steganographic distortion using directional filters. In: Proceedings of 4th IEEE International Workshop on Information Forensics and Security, pp. 234–239 (2012)
5. Holub, V., Fridrich, J.: Digital image steganography using universal distortion. In: Proceedings of 1st ACM Workshop, pp. 59–68 (2013)
6. Holub, V., Fridrich, J.: Random projections of residuals for digital image steganalysis. IEEE Trans. Inf. Forensics Secur. **8**(12), 1996–2006 (2013)
7. Kodovsky, J., Fridrich, J., Holub, V.: Ensemble classifiers for steganalysis of digital media. IEEE Trans. Inf. Forensics Secur. **7**(2), 434–444 (2011)
8. Monarev, V., Pestunov, A.: A new compression-based method for estimating LSB replacement rate in color and grayscale images. In: Proceedings of IEEE 7th International Conference on Intelligent Informationa Hiding and Multimedia Signal Processing, IIH-MSP, pp. 57–60 (2011)

9. Monarev, V., Pestunov, A.: A known-key scenario for steganalysis and a highly accurate detector within it. In: Proceedings of IEEE 10th International Conference on Intelligent Information Hiding and Multimedia Signal Processing, IIH-MSP, pp. 175–178 (2014)

10. Monarev, V., Pestunov, A.: Prior classification of stego containers as a new approach for enhancing steganalyzers accuracy. In: Qing, S., Okamoto, E., Kim, K., Liu, D. (eds.) ICICS 2015. LNCS, vol. 9543, pp. 445–457. Springer, Heidelberg (2016). doi:10.1007/978-3-319-29814-6_38

11. Pevny, T., Bas, P., Fridrich, J.: Steganalysis by subtractive pixel adjacency matrix. IEEE Trans. Inf. Forensics Secur. 5(2), 215–224 (2010)

12. Pevný, T., Filler, T., Bas, P.: Using high-dimensional image models to perform highly undetectable steganography. In: Böhme, R., Fong, P.W.L., Safavi-Naini, R. (eds.) IH 2010. LNCS, vol. 6387, pp. 161–177. Springer, Heidelberg (2010). doi:10.1007/978-3-642-16435-4_13

13. LZMA SDK (Software Development Kit). http://www.7-zip.org/sdk.html/

14. Large Text Compression Benchmark. http://mattmahoney.net/dc/text.html

15. Break Our Watermarking System, 2nd edn. http://bows2.ec-lille.fr/

16. scikit-learn: Machine Learning in Python. http://scikit-learn.org/

Group Verification Based Multiple-Differential Collision Attack

Changhai Ou[1,2], Zhu Wang[1(✉)], Degang Sun[1(✉)], Xinping Zhou[1,2], and Juan Ai[1,2]

[1] Institute of Information Engineering, Chinese Academy of Sciences, Beijing, China
{ouchanghai,wangzhu,sundegang,zhouxinping,aijuan}@iie.ac.cn
[2] University of Chinese Academy of Sciences, Beijing, China

Abstract. Bogdanov and Kizhvatov proposed the concept of test of chain, but they didn't give a practical scheme. Wang et al. proposed fault tolerant chain to enhance test of chain and gave a practical scheme. However, the attack efficiency of Correlation enhanced Collision Attack (CCA) is much lower than that of Correlation Power Analysis (CPA). A combination of CCA and CPA in fault tolerant chain proposed by Wang et al. may be unreasonable. Most importantly, when the threshold Thr_Δ introduced in Sect. 2.3 is large, the key recovery becomes very complex. Fault tolerant chain is unapplicable to this situation. In order to solve these problems, we propose a kind of new chain named group verification chain in this paper. We combine our group verification chain with MDCA and propose Group Verification based Multiple-Differential Collision Attack (GV-MDCA). Experiments on power trace set downloaded from the website DPA *contest v4* show that our group verification chain significantly improves the efficiency of fault tolerant chain.

Keywords: Group verification · Group verification chain · Collision attack · MDCA · GV-MDCA · DPA *contest v4* · Side channel attack

1 Introduction

There exist many kinds of leakages such as power consumption [7] and electromagnetic [2] when the cryptographic devices are on operation. Side channel attacks can be used to efficiently recover the key and pose serious threats to cryptographic implementation security. Side channel collision attack was firstly introduced in [13] against DES and extended in [12]. Nonlinear S-boxes are usually chosen as attack points. The linear parts such as MixColumns of AES, are also targeted in collision attack [12].

One advantage of collision attack is that it can help conquer the random masking of some AES implementations [3] and DES implementations [6]. Moradi et al. proposed MDCA based on binary voting and ternary voting [4]. Subsequently, he proposed CCA [9], which established the relationship among several key bytes using the collisions between different S-boxes. It is very efficient for

© Springer International Publishing AG 2016
K.-Y. Lam et al. (Eds.): ICICS 2016, LNCS 9977, pp. 145–156, 2016.
DOI: 10.1007/978-3-319-50011-9_12

CCA to attack the masking schemes such as Rotating S-boxes Masking (RSM) [10]. CCA directly uses the correlation coefficients between two columns of two different S-boxes, it doesn't relay on any hypothesis power leakage model. In 2012, Bogdanov and Kizhvatov combined CPA with collision attack, which was more efficient than both stand-alone CPA and collision attack [5]. Moreover, the concept of **test of chain** was given. However, there was no practical scheme given in their paper. Wang et al. proposed fault tolerant chain in [15]. As far as we know, fault tolerant chain is the only one practical scheme to enhance test of chain. So, in this paper, we just compare our scheme with fault tolerant chain.

Let k_a and k_b denote the ath and the bth key bytes respectively. Taking AES for example, CCA considers the relationship between two key bytes. However, any key byte falling outside the threshold Thr_k will result in very complex key recovery, since the attacker does not know which one is error. The scheme of Wang et al. can identify the specific error key byte. However, the scheme may be not a good one. Firstly, the efficiency of CCA is much lower than that of CPA, a combination of CCA and CPA is unreasonable. Secondly, the threshold Thr_Δ ($\Delta_{(k_a,k_b)} = k_a \oplus k_b$) of any two key bytes k_a and k_b is always set to 1, a lot of correct Δ values fall outside the threshold. This leads to failure of key recovery. Thirdly, the scheme uses only one $\Delta_{(k_a,k_b)}$ to identify the value of key byte k_b. If both $\Delta_{(k_a,k_b)}$ and k_b are wrong, but they still satisfy that $k_b = \Delta_{(k_a,k_b)} \oplus k_a$. Then, the scheme of Wang et al. will regard k_b as the correct key byte, which leads to the failure of key recovery. Actually, the probability of this situation is about 10% when $Thr_k = 2$ and reaches more than 70% when $Thr_k = 8$ (see Fig. 4).

In this paper, we propose group verification chain to enhance fault tolerant chain. We then combine MDCA with our group verification chain and propose Group Verification based MDCA (GV-MDCA). Two schemes named Frequency based GV-MDCA (FGV-MDCA) and Weight based GV-MDCA (WGV-MDCA) are given. Our scheme can successfully search the correct key in large thresholds and significantly improve the attack efficiency.

This paper is organized as follows. MDCA, CCA, Bogdanov and Kizhvatov's test of chain and fault tolerant chain proposed by Wang et al. are briefly introduced in Sect. 2. In Sect. 3, group verification chain is introduced. FGV-MDCA and WGV-MDCA are given in this section. Experiments are performed on power trace set *secmatv*1 downloaded from the website DPA *contest v*4 [1] in Sect. 4. Finally, we conclude this paper in Sect. 5.

2   Preliminaries

Bogdanov and Kizhvatov proposed linear collision attack in [5]. AES performs the 16 parallel SubBytes operations within the first round. A collision occurs if there are two S-boxes within the same AES encryption or with several AES encryptions accepting the same byte value as their input. $K = \{k_j\}_{j=1}^{16}$, $k_j \in F_{2^8}$ is the 16-byte subkey in the first round of AES. $P^i = \{p_j^i\}_{j=1}^{16}$, $p_j^i \in F_{2^8}$, are plaintexts, where i $=1,2,\ldots$ is the number of AES execution. If

$$S(p_{j_1}^{i_1} \oplus k_{j_1}) = S(p_{j_2}^{i_2} \oplus k_{j_2}), \tag{1}$$

a collision happens. The attacker obtains a linear equation

$$p_{j_1}^{i_1} \oplus p_{j_2}^{i_2} = k_{j_1} \oplus k_{j_2} = \Delta_{(k_{j_1}, k_{j_2})}. \tag{2}$$

Each equation is named a step of a chain [5].

2.1 Multiple Differential Collision Attack

The attacker will encounter a problem when the side channel collision theory is used in side channel attack. That is, how to detect collisions. Actually, the attacker can do this by comparing power traces of two S-boxes. For example, Bogdanov set a differential threshold in his MDCA. If the correlation coefficient of these two power traces was larger than the differential threshold, he deemed that a collision happened.

2.2 Correlation Enhanced Collision Attack

Moradi et al. divided power trace sections of each S-box into 256 classes according to their plaintext α from 0 to 255 [9]. Then, they averaged the power traces in each class and obtained 256 averaged power traces. Let M_j^α denote the averaged power trace of the jth Sbox where the jth plaintext byte are equal to α.

The value $\Delta_{(k_a, k_b)} = k_a \oplus k_b$ is a constant, since the key used in the cryptographic device is constant. Hence, a collision occurs whenever the ath and b^{th} plaintext bytes show the same difference. Moradi et al. guessed the difference $\Delta_{(k_a, k_b)}$ and verified their guess by detecting all collisions $p_a = \alpha$ and $p_b = \alpha \oplus \Delta_{(k_a, k_b)}$ for all $\alpha \in GF(2^8)$ [9]. To detect the correct $\Delta_{(k_a, k_b)}$, they calculated the correlation coefficient of M_a^α and $M_b^{\alpha \oplus \Delta_{(k_a, k_b)}}$ for all $\alpha \in GF(2^8)$. The correct difference $\Delta_{(k_a, k_b)}$ of two key bytes k_a and k_b is then given by:

$$\underset{\Delta_{(k_a, k_b)}}{\operatorname{argmax}} \rho(M_a^\alpha, M_b^{\alpha \oplus \Delta_{(k_a, k_b)}}). \tag{3}$$

The correlation coefficients are computed for each $\alpha \in GF(2^8)$. The correct $\Delta_{(k_a, k_b)}$ corresponds to the maximum correlation coefficient.

2.3 Test of Chain

Bogdanov and Kizhvatov defined test of chain in [5]. Suppose that the attacker uses CPA to obtain the 16 guessing key byte sequences $\{\xi_i | i = 1, 2, \cdots, 16\}$ of AES algorithm (as shown in Fig. 1). Specifically, he uses CCA to calculate $\Delta_{(k_a, k_b)}$ between any two key bytes k_a and k_b. He then sorts correlation coefficients for all possible guess key byte values in descending order.

Each vertical line denotes a sorted guessing key byte. Each black point in Fig. 1 denotes a possible guessing key byte value. Each line from ξ_a to ξ_b

$(1 \leq a < b \leq 16)$ denotes a step of a chain. For example, the red line from ξ_2 to ξ_3 denotes that the sixth guessing value of the second key byte and the first guessing value of the third key byte are in Thr_k, the corresponding $\Delta_{(k_2,k_3)}$ of these two guessing values is in Thr_Δ, too. Thr_k and Thr_Δ here are defined as the threshold of key byte values and the threshold of Δ. As shown in Fig. 1, there are 10 black points within Thr_k on each vertical line. So, Thr_k is set to 10 here. Thr_Δ is set in the same way. We only consider the guessing values in Thr_k on each list ξ_i. They are the most possible candidates of the key byte k_i.

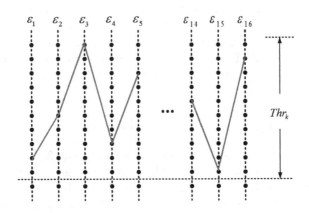

Fig. 1. Bogdanov and Kizhvatov's test of chain.

The chain is accepted if all key bytes of it are within the top m candidates. The chain is rejected if at least one key byte of it falls outside the m top candidates. m here is equal to Thr_k. In order to recover the full 16-byte key, the attacker usually hopes that a chain includes 15 steps as introduced in [5]. However, if a chain includes 15 steps, it is too long. The attacker has to calculate Δ between any two adjacent guessing key bytes. The complexity of computation is larger than exhausting all possible keys in Thr_k. For example, if Thr_k and Thr_Δ are set to 10 and 5 respectively, the attacker has to enumerate 10^{16} guessing keys in Thr_k by using brute-force attack. However, each step of a chain brings extra computation. The attacker has to enumerate all Δs in Thr_Δ. So, the computation complexity becomes $10^{16} * 5^{15}$.

2.4   Fault Tolerant Chain

Bogdanov and Kizhvatov did not give a practical scheme of their test of chain in [5]. The computation complexity of their test of chain is even greater than that of brute-force attack. For a chain, there may be several steps in the path from the free variable to the end. If an error happens in one of these steps, the key bytes computed in the following steps will be wrong, which will result in the failure of attack. Unfortunately, this kind of errors happen with non-negligible probability and lead to low efficiency of Bogdanov and Kizhvatov's attack.

Wang et al. constructed a new chain named fault-tolerant chain [15]. In their scheme, $k_i (i \geq 2)$ depends on only one key byte (i.e. k_1) instead of the other 14 key bytes. There are 15 chains from k_1 to k_i $(i = 2, \cdots, 16)$ (as shown in Fig. 2). Each chain only includes a step. This scheme greatly reduces the computation of test of chain proposed by Bogdanov and Kizhvatov [5]. Specifically, if the attacker enumerates all possible keys in the thresholds, the complexity is only $15 * (Thr_k)^2 * (Thr_\Delta)$ compared to $(Thr_k)^{16} * (Thr_\Delta)^{15}$ of test of chain.

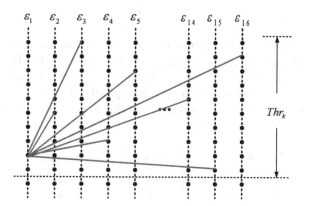

Fig. 2. Fault tolerant chain proposed by Wang et al.

Another advantage of fault tolerant chain is that, if k_i is wrong (under the threshold line), the attacker can still attempt to recover other ones. The error key bytes can still be exhausted. However, the threshold Thr_Δ of CCA is always set to 1 in their paper. Specifically, correlation coefficients of $\Delta_{(k_1,k_i)}$ of two key bytes k_1 and k_i are calculated using CCA. The 256 Δ values are sorted according to these correlation coefficients. Then the Δ corresponding to the maximum correlation coefficient is chosen as the candidate. Other Δ values in the $\Delta_{(k_1,k_i)}$ sequence are not taken into consideration. Actually, enlarging the threshold will lead to very complex key recovery. If $k_i = k_1 \oplus \Delta_{(k_1,k_i)}$ is under the threshold, they deduced that the chain is wrong. Subsequently, exhaustion is performed to find the correct key byte.

Moreover, if k_i and $\Delta_{(k_1,k_i)}$ are wrong and $k_i = k_1 \oplus \Delta_{(k_1,k_i)}$ is still satisfied, the attacker will regard the wrong guessing k_i as the correct key byte value. Actually, this kind of error happens with a high probability and increases with Thr_k. This is the main reason why the success rate declines in Fig. 4.

3   Group Verification Based MDCA

The Thr_Δ is always set to 1 in fault tolerant chain [15]. They did not discuss how to efficiently recover the key when $Thr_\Delta > 1$. In fact, enlarging Thr_Δ will result in very complex key recovery because of very huge key search space. In this case, the scheme of Wang et al. can't be applied any more.

3.1 Group Verification Chain

In this section, we introduce group verification chain, which can be used under the condition that both Thr_k and Thr_Δ are set largely. Group verification here is defined as the mutual verification among key bytes. Let ξ_i^k and $\xi_{\gamma+1}^t$ denote the kth and t^{th} guessing key values in ξ_i and $\xi_{\gamma+1}$. $\Delta_{(i,\gamma+1)}^m$ denotes the mth value in the $\Delta_{(i,\gamma+1)}$ sequence. If the equation

$$\xi_i^k \oplus \xi_{\gamma+1}^t = \Delta_{(i,\gamma+1)}^m \tag{4}$$

is satisfied, then we say that $\xi_{\gamma+1}^t$ can be verified by ξ_i^k. In our group verification chain, we do not care if ξ_i^k, $\xi_{\gamma+1}^t$ and $\Delta_{(i,\gamma+1)}^m$ are the correct key byte values and Δ value. Each candidate value can be verified by guessing values of other key bytes just like voting. When the support of a guessing key byte value is greater than the differential threshold, we deem that this is a good candidate.

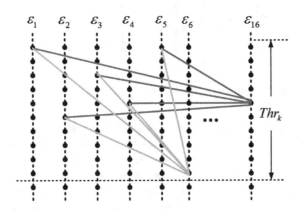

Fig. 3. Group verification chain.

Suppose that we use key byte values in $\xi_1, \cdots, \xi_5$ to verify guessing key byte values in $\xi_6, \cdots, \xi_{16}$ of AES algorithm (as shown in Fig. 3). 120 sequences of $\Delta_{(k_a,k_b)}$ between any two key bytes k_a and k_b are also calculated. The correct key byte values are effectively supported that the Eq. 4 is satisfied for most key values and Δs. Finally, the attacker gets the correct key.

3.2 Frequency Based GV-MDCA

Bogdanov proposed MDCA using binary voting and ternary voting [4], in which multiple difference is used for collision detection between any two S-boxes. Specifically, it is used to compare the power traces of two S-boxes to judge if collision has happened. In this paper, we deem that each S-box can be used as a key byte vote for other S-boxes.

There are 16 guessing key byte sequences $\{\xi_i | i = 1, 2, \cdots, 16\} \in GF(2^8)$ corresponding to S-boxes $1, \cdots, 16$ of AES algorithm. Let Y^{FGV} denote a decision threshold of possible key byte values. Suppose that we use the $1 \cdots \gamma$ key bytes to verify the $(\gamma + 1)^{th}$ key byte. Then, a Frequency based GV-MDCA (FGV-MDCA) can be defined as:

$$\Psi_{\xi_{\gamma+1}^t}^{FGV} = \begin{cases} 1 (\textbf{collision}), & \text{if } \Phi_{\xi_{\gamma+1}^t}^{FGV} > Y^{FGV} \\ 0 (\textbf{nocollision}), & \text{if } \Phi_{\xi_{\gamma+1}^t}^{FGV} < Y^{FGV} \end{cases} \tag{5}$$

where $\Psi_{\xi_{\gamma+1}^t}^{FGV}$ denotes that $\xi_{\gamma+1}^t$ is a candidate byte value in the sequence $\xi_{(\gamma+1)}$ and

$$\Phi_{\xi_{\gamma+1}^t}^{FGV} = \sum_{i=1}^{\gamma} \Theta(\xi_i^k, \xi_{\gamma+1}^t). \tag{6}$$

$\Theta(\xi_i^k, \xi_{\gamma+1}^t)$ here is defined as

$$\Theta(\xi_i^k, \xi_{\gamma+1}^t) = \begin{cases} 1, & \text{if } \xi_i^k \oplus \xi_{\gamma+1}^t = \Delta_{(i,\gamma+1)}^m \\ 0, & \text{else.} \end{cases} \tag{7}$$

The frequency of the correct byte values will be higher than these of wrong guessing key byte values in FGV-MDCA. This also shows that the correct key byte values obtain more support in the process of mutual verification, which makes them become obvious. The attacker can effectively restore the key by observing the frequencies of key byte values. He does not need to enumerate all possible key values within the threshold.

3.3   Weight Based GV-MDCA

Test of chain and fault tolerant chain introduced in Sect. 2, and our FGV-MDCA introduced in Sect. 3.2 use thresholds Thr_k and Thr_Δ. All possible keys within the thresholds are searched with the same probability. Obviously, this is unreasonable. The key values ranked in the front of $\{\xi_i | i = 1, 2, \cdots, 16\}$ should be enumerated with higher priority. A more accurate and higher efficient key search scheme named Weight Based GV-MDCA (WGV-MDCA) is proposed.

The attacker obtains key byte sequences and Δ sequences. The key byte values in the tops the sequences should be given higher weights. CPA is much more powerful than that of CCA in most cases. If we use moderate number of power traces, most of the correct byte values will be in the top of key byte sequences $\{\xi_i | i = 1, 2, \cdots, 16\}$. However, a number of correct Δ values are not in the top of their corresponding sequences when the same number of power traces are used. So, Δ values here become the most important factor of attack efficiency. So, we weigh key byte values referring to Δ sequences. Specifically, $\Theta(\xi_i^k, \xi_{\gamma+1}^t)$ here is defined as

$$\Theta(\xi_i^k, \xi_{\gamma+1}^t) = \begin{cases} Thr_\Delta - m, & \text{if } \xi_i^k \oplus \xi_{\gamma+1}^t = \Delta_{(i,\gamma+1)}^m \\ 0, & \text{else.} \end{cases} \tag{8}$$

For example, if Thr_Δ is set to 10 and m in Eq. 8 is 6 ($\Delta_{(i,\gamma+1)}^6$ is the sixth guessing value of the corresponding sequence of $\Delta_{(i,\gamma+1)}$). Then, $\Theta(\xi_i^k, \xi_{\gamma+1}^t)$ is 4. By using WGV-MDCA, the difference between the correct key and wrong keys becomes more obvious compared to FGV-MDCA.

3.4 The Differential Threshold

It is very hard to get a good value of Y^{FGV} in both FGV-MDCA and WGV-MDCA. This value is very different in these two schemes. We normalize each reordered sequence. If the attacker gives a large value to Y^{FGV}, the correct key byte value may be deleted. If he gives a small value to Y^{FGV}, there will be a lot of guessing keys be to enumerated. We set the differential threshold Y^{FGV} of our group verification chain to $\frac{1}{3}$. This value is achieved through experience.

4   Experimental Results

Our experiments are performed on an Rotating S-boxes Masking (RSM) [8] protected AES-256 implemented on the Side-channel Attack Standard Evaluation Board (SASEBO). 10000 power traces are downloaded from the webset of DPA contest v4 [1]. CCA is used to find the time samples of each S-box in the first round. To enhance the attack ability of CCA, Template Attack (TA) is combined with CCA. Then, we extract 4 interesting points from time interval of about a clock cycle suggested in [11].

We only compare our group verification chain with the fault tolerant chain proposed by Wang et al. [15]. Since fault tolerant chain is so far the only one practical scheme. $\xi_1, \cdots, \xi_7$ are used to verify guessing key byte values on $\xi_8, \cdots, \xi_{16}$. $\xi_{10}, \cdots, \xi_{16}$ are used to verify guessing key byte values on $\xi_1, \cdots, \xi_7$. Experimental results under different thresholds Thr_k, Thr_Δ and different numbers of power traces are given in Sects. 4.1, 4.2 and 4.3.

4.1   Experimental Results Under Different Thresholds Thr_k

Firstly, we compare our group verification chain (FGV-MDCA and WGV-MDCA) with fault tolerant chain under different thresholds Thr_k. Thr_Δ in fault tolerant chain is set to 1. This value is set to 5 in our FGV-MDCA and WGV-MDCA.

The success rate [14] of the 3 schemes are shown in Fig. 4. If $\Delta_{(k_1,k_b)}$ of two key bytes k_1 and k_b is wrong and there exist one or several wrong k_b that satisfy

$k_b = k_1 \oplus \Delta_{(k_1,k_b)}$. Then, the scheme of Wang et al. will considers k_b as the correct key byte value. This is the main reason of failure of key recovery.

The success rate of fault tolerant chain decreases with the increase of Thr_k, which is very high when $Thr_k \leq 2$ (as shown in Fig. 4). Since the probability of wrong key byte k_b satisfying $k_b = k_1 \oplus \Delta_{(k_1,k_b)}$ is small. With the increase of Thr_k, this probability increases. When $Thr_k = 2$, fault tolerant chain can get a success rate of about 0.90. However, this value is only about 0.44 when $Thr_k = 5$. When $Thr_k > 13$, the success rate is smaller than 0.10. That is to say, The larger the Thr_k, the harder for the attacker to get success.

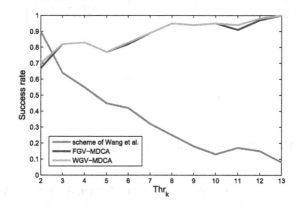

Fig. 4. Success rate under different Thr_k

The success rate of our FGV-MDCA and WGV-MDCA increases with Thr_k. When Thr_k is from 2 to 13, the success rate of FGV-MDCA and WGV-MDCA is from about 0.70 to about 1.00. When $Thr_k > 3$, the success rate of our FGV-MDCA and WGV-MDCA is greater than that of the scheme of Wang et al. This indicates that, the efficiency of group verification chain is slightly lower when Thr_k is small. With the increase of Thr_k, the correct key byte values fall within Thr_k and will be more effectively verified by group in our scheme.

Since Thr_Δ is set to 5, the success rate of FGV-MDCA and WGV-MDCA are very similar by only enlarging Thr_k.

4.2   Experimental Results Under Different Thresholds Thr_Δ

Secondly, we compare our FGV-MDCA and WGV-MDCA with the scheme of Wang et al. under different thresholds Thr_Δ. Thr_k here is set to 8. Thr_Δ of the scheme of Wang et al. is changed. Fault tolerant chain introduced in Sect. 2 can not be used in large Thr_Δ. We here enlarge this threshold. We then enumerate all possible chains that satisfy fault tolerant chain.

The success rate of the 3 schemes under different thresholds Thr_Δ are shown in Fig. 5. The success rate of fault tolerant chain is far lower than that of our

FGV-MDCA and WGV-MDCA. The success rate of fault tolerant chain does not significantly change with the increase of Thr_Δ. It ranges from 0.25 to 0.30 compared to from 0.8 to 1.00 of our FGV-MDCA and WGV-MDCA. The success rate of our FGV-MDCA and WGV-MDCA increase with Thr_Δ.

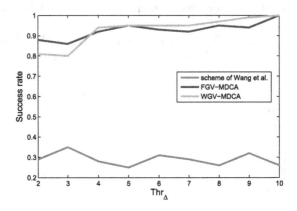

Fig. 5. Success rate under different thresholds Thr_Δ

When $Thr_\Delta = 2$, the success rate of FGV-MDCA and WGV-MDCA are about 0.87 and 0.82 respectively, both of which are significantly higher than that of the scheme of Wang et al. The success rate of FGV-MDCA is a little higher than that of WGV-MDCA when $Thr_\Delta < 4$. When $Thr_\Delta \geq 4$, the success rate of WGV-MDCA is higher than that of FGV-MDCA. The normalized weight of the correct key byte value in each reordered sequence $\{\xi_i | i = 1, 2, \cdots, 16\}$ in WGV-MDCA is more obvious than that in FGV-MDCA. This indicates that, the WGV-MDCA is more efficient than that of FGV-MDCA when Thr_Δ is large.

4.3   Experimental Results Under Different Numbers of Power Traces

Finally, we compare our FGV-MDCA and WGV-MDCA with the scheme of Wang et al. under the condition that different numbers of power traces are used. Thr_Δ is set to 5 and Thr_k is set to 8. Thr_Δ of the scheme of Wang et al. is still set to 1, since $Thr_\Delta > 1$ is very different from the fault tolerant chain.

When the number of power traces used in each repetition is from 60 to 170, the success rate of the 3 schemes are shown in Fig. 6. The success rate of the scheme of Wang et al. is far lower than that of our FGV-MDCA and WGV-MDCA. It ranges from 0 to 0.55 compared from 0.18 to 1.00 of our FGV-MDCA and from 0.37 to 1.00 of our WGV-MDCA. When the number of power traces used in each repetition is more than 150, the success rate of FGA-MDCA and WGA-MDCA is close to 1. However, the success rate of fault tolerant chain is only about 0.50 when about 170 power traces are used.

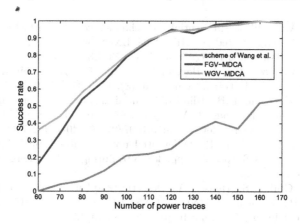

Fig. 6. Success rate under different numbers of power traces

The success rate of FGV-MDCA and WGV-MDCA is very close when more than 100 power traces are used in each repetition (as shown in Fig. 6). This is because, with the increase number of power traces, the locations of the correct key byte values and Δs fall in the top positions of $\{\xi_i | i = 1, 2, \cdots, 16\}$ and Δs sequences with higher probabilities.

5 Conclusions

In this paper, we propose group verification chain to enhance fault tolerant chain proposed by Wang et al. We combine MDCA and CCA to implement group verification chain and propose Group Verification based Multiple-Differential Collision Attack (GV-MDCA). Frequency based GV-MDCA (FGV-MDCA) and Weight based GV-MDCA (WGV-MDCA) are given. Experimental results performed on the power trace set of DPA *contest v*4 show that our group verification chain significantly improve the efficiency of fault tolerant chain.

Acknowledgment. This research is supported by the Nation Natural Science Foundation of China (No. 61372062).

References

1. Dpa contest. http://www.dpacontest.org/home/
2. Agrawal, D., Archambeault, B., Rao, J.R., Rohatgi, P.: The EM side—channel(s). In: Kaliski, B.S., Koç, K., Paar, C. (eds.) CHES 2002. LNCS, vol. 2523, pp. 29–45. Springer, Heidelberg (2003). doi:10.1007/3-540-36400-5_4
3. Biryukov, A., Khovratovich, D.: Two new techniques of side-channel cryptanalysis. In: Paillier, P., Verbauwhede, I. (eds.) CHES 2007. LNCS, vol. 4727, pp. 195–208. Springer, Heidelberg (2007). doi:10.1007/978-3-540-74735-2_14

4. Bogdanov, A.: Multiple-differential side-channel collision attacks on AES. In: Oswald, E., Rohatgi, P. (eds.) CHES 2008. LNCS, vol. 5154, pp. 30–44. Springer, Heidelberg (2008). doi:10.1007/978-3-540-85053-3_3

5. Bogdanov, A., Kizhvatov, I.: Beyond the limits of DPA: combined side-channel collision attacks. IEEE Trans. Comput. **61**(8), 1153–1164 (2012)

6. Handschuh, H., Preneel, B.: Blind differential cryptanalysis for enhanced power attacks. In: Biham, E., Youssef, A.M. (eds.) SAC 2006. LNCS, vol. 4356, pp. 163–173. Springer, Heidelberg (2007). doi:10.1007/978-3-540-74462-7_12

7. Kocher, P., Jaffe, J., Jun, B.: Differential power analysis. In: Wiener, M. (ed.) CRYPTO 1999. LNCS, vol. 1666, pp. 388–397. Springer, Heidelberg (1999). doi:10.1007/3-540-48405-1_25

8. Moradi, A., Guilley, S., Heuser, A.: Detecting hidden leakages. In: Boureanu, I., Owesarski, P., Vaudenay, S. (eds.) ACNS 2014. LNCS, vol. 8479, pp. 324–342. Springer, Heidelberg (2014). doi:10.1007/978-3-319-07536-5_20

9. Moradi, A., Mischke, O., Eisenbarth, T.: Correlation-enhanced power analysis collision attack. In: Mangard, S., Standaert, F.-X. (eds.) CHES 2010. LNCS, vol. 6225, pp. 125–139. Springer, Heidelberg (2010). doi:10.1007/978-3-642-15031-9_9

10. Nassar, M., Souissi, Y., Guilley, S., Danger, J.: RSM: A small and fast countermeasure for AES, secure against 1st and 2nd-order zero-offset SCAs. In: 2012 Design, Automation & Test in Europe Conference & Exhibition, DATE 2012, Dresden, Germany, 12–16 March 2012, pp. 1173–1178 (2012)

11. Rechberger, C., Oswald, E.: Practical template attacks. In: Lim, C.H., Yung, M. (eds.) WISA 2004. LNCS, vol. 3325, pp. 440–456. Springer, Heidelberg (2005). doi:10.1007/978-3-540-31815-6_35

12. Schramm, K., Leander, G., Felke, P., Paar, C.: A collision-attack on AES. In: Joye, M., Quisquater, J.-J. (eds.) CHES 2004. LNCS, vol. 3156, pp. 163–175. Springer, Heidelberg (2004). doi:10.1007/978-3-540-28632-5_12

13. Schramm, K., Wollinger, T., Paar, C.: A new class of collision attacks and its application to DES. In: Johansson, T. (ed.) FSE 2003. LNCS, vol. 2887, pp. 206–222. Springer, Heidelberg (2003). doi:10.1007/978-3-540-39887-5_16

14. Standaert, F.-X., Malkin, T.G., Yung, M.: A unified framework for the analysis of side-channel key recovery attacks. In: Joux, A. (ed.) EUROCRYPT 2009. LNCS, vol. 5479, pp. 443–461. Springer, Heidelberg (2009). doi:10.1007/978-3-642-01001-9_26

15. Wang, D., Wang, A., Zheng, X.: Fault-tolerant linear collision attack: a combination with correlation power analysis. In: Huang, X., Zhou, J. (eds.) ISPEC 2014. LNCS, vol. 8434, pp. 232–246. Springer, Heidelberg (2014). doi:10.1007/978-3-319-06320-1_18

Attack Behavior Analytics

A Transparent Learning Approach for Attack Prediction Based on User Behavior Analysis

Peizhi Shao[1], Jiuming Lu[1], Raymond K. Wong[1(✉)], and Wenzhuo Yang[2]

[1] School of Computer Science and Engineering, University of New South Wales,
Kensington, Australia
wong@cse.unsw.edu.au

[2] School of Computer Science and Engineering, Nanyang Technological University,
Singapore, Singapore

Abstract. User behavior can be used to determine vulnerable user actions and predict potential attacks. To our knowledge, much work has focused on finding vulnerable operations and disregarded reasoning/-explanations of its results. This paper proposes a transparent learning approach for user behavior analysis to address this issue. A user rating system is proposed to determine a security level of each user from several aspects, augmented with explanations of potential attacks based on his/her vulnerable user actions. This user rating model can be constructed by a semi-supervised learning classifier, and a rule mining algorithm can be applied to find hidden patterns and relations between user operations and potential attacks. With this approach, an organization can be aware of its weakness, and can better prepare for proactive attack defense or reactive responses.

Keywords: Transparent learning · Machine learning · User behavior analysis · Cybersecurity

1 Introduction

Cybersecurity (CS) is to study the processes and/or technologies that protect computers, programs, networks, and data from attacks, unauthorized access/change, or destruction. Cyber attacks are argued as the actions that attempt to bypass security mechanisms of computer systems [31]. A cyber attack detection is to identify individuals who try to use a computer system without authorization, or those who have access to the system but abuse their authorities [10]. Most attacks in general can be grouped into Denial of Service Attacks, Remote to Local Attacks, User to Root Attacks, and Probing [34].

Due to the increasing number of incidents of cyber attacks, CS has always been a critical issue concerned by every Internet user. Well-trained hackers make the traditional online security protection methods such as firewalls or virus detection software no longer effective. On the other hand, user behavior analysis (UBA) become a new area to detect online attacks and also perform real-time analysis based on user behavior and actions.

© Springer International Publishing AG 2016
K.-Y. Lam et al. (Eds.): ICICS 2016, LNCS 9977, pp. 159–172, 2016.
DOI: 10.1007/978-3-319-50011-9_13

For example, email is a main intermediary for spreading virus and Trojan horse. The attackers will widely spread emails containing worm programs to infect computers and networks. These emails usually have attractive subject, which draw user's attention and allure them to open them. For example the widely spread Verona virus, also known as Romeo & Juliet virus, contain the words like *I love you* or *sorry*. So if a user is easily attracted by these words and opens these emails from unknown senders, it is likely that they will be affected and cause security threat to their systems. For cautious users with good online behavior, they may check the sender email address and distinguish if an email is safe to open. In many cases these users may just delete these emails and blacklist he sender address.

Meanwhile, big data analysis has been widely used in commercial applications such like product recommendation, and UBA is used for identifying target customers for certain products. Recently, UBA has gained tractions in CS [26]. Compared with the traditional attack detection methods (which detect the actions of a certain attack or the existence of virus software or Trojan horse), UBA focuses on determining abnormal user actions based on their usual, normal activities. After that, warnings can then be generated and countermeasure can be implemented. In general, it is difficult for an attacker to imitate the original user's behavior. UBA can also be used to detect insider attacks, for example, an employee may illegally transfer the company data to other competitors for profit.

Since UBA allows users to implement preventive measures instead of detecting the attacks, CS companies have started adding UBA into their products/services. However, to the best of our knowledge, most UBA approaches focus on finding vulnerable user operations, and do not provide explanation or reasoning of their findings. In this paper, we propose a novel approach that is based on the concept of transparent learning, in which a prediction of attacks can be reasoned with explanations. As a result, an organization can be aware of its weakness, and can better prepare for proactive attack defense or reactive responses.

The rest of this paper is organized as follows. Section 2 summarizes related work and Sect. 3 presents our proposed approach. Section 4 describes an example to illustrate our approach and finally Sect. 5 concludes this paper.

2   Related Work

2.1   Machine Learning

There are plenty of works focusing on using different machine learning (ML) methods/models for detecting abnormal operations and predicting potential attacks in CS. For example, artificial neural networks were used in Cannady [11] to classify user operations into different categories of user misuses. Lippmann and Cunningham [21] proposed an Anomaly Detection System using keyword selection via articial neural networks. Bivens et al. [8] presented a complete Intrusion Detection System including the following stages: preprocessing, clustering the normal traffic, normalization, articial neural networks training and articial neural networks decision. Jemili et al. [15] suggested a framework using Bayesian network classifiers using nine features from the KDD 1999 data for anomaly detection and attack type recognition. Kruegel et al. [17] used a Bayesian network to classify events for OS calls. In Li et al. [20], an SVM classifier with an RBF kernel was used to classify the KDD 1999 dataset into predefined categories (Denial of service, Probe or Scan, User to root, Remote to local, and normal). Amiri et al. [2] used a least-square SVM to be faster son the same dataset. Some other ML models such as Hidden Markov Models [5] and Nave Bayes classifiers [35] have also been popular in CS, e.g., [3,16,25].

2.2   Rule Mining

Association rule Mining was introduced by Agrawal et al. [1] for discovering frequently appearing co-occurrences in supermarket data. Brahmi [9] applied the method to capture relationships between TCP/IP parameters and attack types. Zhengbing et al. [36] proposed a novel algorithm based on the signature apriori algorithm [14] to find new attack signatures from existing ones. Decision Trees such as ID3 [29] and C4.5 [30] are widely used for rule mining. Snort [24] is a well-known open-source tool using the signature-based approach. Kruegel and Toth [18] used DT to replace the misuse detection engine of Snort. Exposure [6,7] is a system using Weka J48 DT (an implementation of C4.5) as the classifier to detect domains that are involved in malicious activities. Inductive learning is a bottom-up approach that generates rules and theories from specific observations. Several ML algorithms such as DT are inductive, but when researchers refer to inductive learning, they usually mean Repeated Incremental Pruning to Produce Error Reduction [12] and the algorithm quasi-optimal [22]. Lee et al. [19] developed a framework using several ML techniques such as inductive learning, Association rule and Sequential pattern m ining to detect user misuses.

2.3   User Behavior Analysis

Researchers in [4] used UBA in CS. In [26], clustering algorithms such as Expectation Maximization, Density-Based Spatial Clustering of Applications with Noise, k-means have been used in UBA. A combination of these methods has also been discussed in [33]. Commercial products/services such as Lancope, Splunk, Solera have started including UBA in their offerings.

3   Our Approach

Unlike most existing UBA approaches, by following the concept of transparent learning, we use 2 independent modules working together. Firstly, a semi-supervised learning module is designed to rate a security risk of each user. The learning takes the rating that is a tuple of 3 scores that consider 3 different aspects, namely, constancy, accuracy and consistency, into account. Secondly, a rule mining module is used to identify hidden patterns between historic user operations and an attack, and is used to reason why the user is rated at a particular security level.

3.1 Transparent Learning

Transparent learning is a ML concept that aims at the transparency of ML models, algorithms and results. An ideal transparent learning technique is one that [32]:

– Produces models that a typical user can read, understand and modify.
– Uses algorithms that a typical user can understand and influence.
– Allows a user to incorporate domain knowledge when generating the models.

The main advantage of transparent learning is its interpretability. This is very important in CS, especially in understanding the reasons behind potential attack prediction. Most existing UBA systems can find potential vulnerabilities, but are unable to provide reasoning/explanations. This is because most of these systems are based on clustering or outlier detection, and many security experts may not understand why or how a prediction is made. To address this issue, we propose a transparent learning model containing 2 modules as shown in Fig. 1.

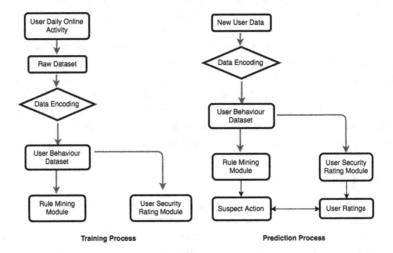

Fig. 1. The two main modules

3.2 User Security Rating Module

Based on user's daily online activities and the manner of using the computer, each user will be given a security rating. This rating indicates the probability that this user may lead to a threat to the system. This user behavior is a representation of one's personality and knowledge, and can be analysed from different aspects. Inspired by [13], we consider the following aspects when determining the rating:

Constancy – how long the user continuously maintains good online behavior. It indicates that the user has a good understanding of CS and/or the security policy of the company. It also illustrates the awareness of potential online attacks and will cautiously protect themselves from potential cyber attacks.

Accuracy – the frequency that a user makes security related mistake during online activities and the accuracy of the user to finish certain tasks. This shows the proficiency of the user. An experienced user is likely to have better security rating than a beginner.

Consistency – consistent usage patterns. If the user's online behavior is consistent. It is easy to be tracked and risk is also minimized.

3.3   Rule Mining Module

We base on an inductive learning algorithm called GOLEM [23] to develop a rule mining module. The algorithm works as follows. Firstly, it generates LGG [27,28] clauses from each pair of records. Then it picks the one that covering the maximum number of positive examples and considering reduction based on negative examples. Finally, it adds the reduced clause as a sub-rule into the final clause and mark the covered, positive examples. It repeats this process until all positive examples are covered.

GOLEM is a useful algorithm to find hidden rules between a set of facts and the results. However, in UBA, action frequency needs to be considered because frequent user actions should be more important than less frequent ones.

Algorithm 1. User Behavior Frequency GOLEM

Let ε^+ be a set of positive examples of user behavior records.
Let ε^- be a set of negative examples of user behavior records.
Let $M_h(\kappa)$ be an h-easy model of background knowledge κ.
Let s be a given sample limit.
Let $Pairs(s)$ be a random sample of pairs from ε^+.

Let $Lggs = \{C : \{\epsilon, \epsilon'\} \in Pairs(s) \text{ and } C = urlgg(\{\epsilon, \epsilon'\}) \text{ wrt } M_h(\kappa)$ and C consistent wrt $\varepsilon^-\}$
Let e be a specific operation in $lgg(\{\epsilon, \epsilon'\})$.
Let E be the operation type for operation e.
Let $f(E)$ be the frequency of the operation type E.
Let $ubfc$ of pair $\{\epsilon, \epsilon'\}$ be the product of $cover(lgg(\{\epsilon, \epsilon'\}))$ and the minimum $f(E)$ of $lgg(\{\epsilon, \epsilon'\})$.
Let S be the pair $\{\epsilon, \epsilon'\}$ whose $urlgg$ has the greatest $ubfc$ in $Lggs$.

DO
  $\varepsilon^+(S)$ be a random sample of size s from ε^+
  Let $Lggs = \{C : \epsilon' \in \varepsilon^+(S) \text{ and } C = urlgg(S \cup \{\epsilon'\}) \text{ consistent wrt } \varepsilon^-\}$
  Find ϵ' which produces the greatest $ubfc$ in $Lggs$.
  Let $S = S \cup \{\epsilon'\}$
  Let $\varepsilon^+ = \varepsilon^+ - cover(urlgg(S))$
WHILE covers more

Therefore, we extend the original GOLEM algorithm to User Behavior Frequency GOLEM (UBF-GOLEM). It is based on the notion of User Behavior Frequency Coverage (UBFC) - the product of the coverage of a specific operation and the frequency of this operation category. Then we change the LGG selection criteria from coverage based to UBFC based. The final algorithm is shown in Algorithm 1, and an example showing how GOLEM algorithm and UBF-GOLEM work is described in Sect. 4.

UBF-GOLEM is able to find hidden rules behind attack actions. For each attack action, we determine the most relevant operations that are related to an attack. After that, for attack prediction, vulnerable operations can be identified by comparing user operations with the generated rules.

4   An Illustrating Example

This section presents a simplified example to illustrate how the two modules work. Assume some worm virus spread from a domain called "virus.com". We first prepare the encoded raw data to generate the user security rating via a semi-supervised learning method.

4.1   Training the User Security Rating Module

Raw data from user online activities, such as log-on data, Device connection data, file transfer data, Http access data and Email data, are collected. Sample of these data is shown in Fig. 2.

Data Encoding. Each user will be given a rating that contains 3 scores by considering the 3 aspects (constancy, accuracy and consistency) mentioned in the previous subsection. Based on these scores, we can train a classifier to rate and rank (based on the likelihood and risk) of a particular user to be attacked.

Training. After the collected data are encoded into multi-dimensional numeric features, we then cluster the data using an unsupervised algorithm such as k-mean and Expectation Maximization. We then manually select and labeled some data for supervised learning the security risk of a user. Typical supervised ML algorithms, such as SVM, artificial neural networks or DT, can be used to train a classifier. We can then use the trained classifier to predict the remaining unlabeled data.

4.2   Using Inductive Learning

In the rule mining module, we classify the user operations into different types. The checkpoint for each action type is as shown in Table 1.

Log-on Data

Log-on id	date	user	pc	activity
X0W9-Q2DW16EI-1074QDVQ	01/02/2010 05:02:50	WCR0044	PC-9174	Logon
C2O4-Z2RH12FQ-9176MUEL	01/02/2010 05:19:09	WCR0044	PC-9174	Logoff

Device Data

Device id	date	user	pc	activity
W7U9-D6EJ66QR-5998NVVQ	01/02/2010 07:44:23	KBD0201	PC-5997	Connect
K3K6-K6PY61IC-7281YJRT	01/02/2010 07:45:55	BHV0556	PC-6254	Connect

File Data

File id	date	user	pc	filename	content
I7H0-J1BK99KL-0235UCYA	01/02/2010 05:16:32	WCR0044	PC-9174	N1Y38G35.doc	conqu...
V6C5-R5SW99WN-5752LTXJ	01/02/2010 05:16:39	WCR0044	PC-9174	L9RS8KW5.doc	Today...

Http Data

Http id	date	user	pc	url	content
G5W9-X4ZB41IJ-1699KNGR	01/02/2010 06:54:37	ACM0931	PC-5571	http://newegg.com	alone on they t1517 residual m7 73 sample subsequently c...
F2P0-H3GU35KC-5660VIYU	01/02/2010 06:55:09	ACM0931	PC-5571	http://megaclick.com .	parts dark would possibility 50 middle represent outer 3...

Email Data

Email id	date	user	pc	to	cc	bcc	from	size	attach	content
...	...	...	...	Ci..@dta...	Du...@dta...	El...@dta...	Re...@harr...	34113	3	...
...	...	...	...	Ca...@loc...			Ka...@dtaa..	46808	0	...

Fig. 2. Raw data sample

Example Data. For each user that has been attacked, we encode their data as discussed before. A snapshot of some positive examples is listed below:

```
[ Website_domain("virus.com"),
  Unusual_log_time(true),
  Website_domain("groupon.com"),
  Db_request_without_permission(false),
  Connect_too_long(false),
  Website_domain("google.com"),
  Get_file("1AFEEF45CB07F87C3D598ED8A5AA"),
  Website_domain("thepostgame.com"),
  Too_short_log(false) ]

[ Get_file("2351F8CD57177D4C1044D37460B"),
  Website_domain("imdb.com"),
  Receive_email_from("Glo34Hugh@hotmail.com"),
  Too_short_log(false),
  Db_request_without_permission(false),
  Connect_too_long(false),
  Connect_too_long(false),
  Send_email_to("ki77r089@gmail.com"),
  Send_email_to("mm63ld@gmail.com")]
```

```
[ Receive_email_from ("Kora_Guro@virus.com"),
  Receive_email_from ("Glo34Hugh@hotmail.com"),
  Too_short_log(false),
  Db_request_without_permission(false),
  Connect_too_long(false),
  Get_file("1AFEEF45CB07F87C3D598ED8A5AA"),
  Send_email_to("ki77r089@gmail.com"),
  Send_email_to("mm631d@gmail.com")]

[ Unusual_log_time(true),
  Website_domain("groupon.com"),
  Website_domain("imdb.com"),
  Connect_too_long(false),
  Connect_too_long(false),
  Get_file("1AFEEF45CB07F87C3D598ED8A5AA"),
  Too_short_log(false)]

[ Website_domain("virus.com"),
  Get_file("2351F8CD57177D4C1044D37460B"),
  Website_domain("groupon.com"),
  Too_short_log(false)]

[ Get_file("2351F8CD57177D4C1044D37460B"),
  Receive_email_from ("Kora_Guro@virus.com"),
  Unusual_log_time(true),
  Receive_email_from ("Glo34Hugh@hotmail.com"),
  Too_short_log(false),
  Db_request_without_permission(false),
  Connect_too_long(false),
  Website_domain("google.com"),
  Get_file("1AFEEF45CB07F87C3D598ED8A5AA"),
  Website_domain("thepostgame.com")]
```

Table 1. Data encoding

Online action	Checkpoint	Attribute data input
Log on PC	During work hours?	Unusual_log_time(true/false)
Log off PC	A short login session?	Too_short_log(true/false)
Web access	Website domain	Website_domain(''abc.com'')
Receive E-mail	Email sender	Receive_email_from(''xyz@abc.com'')
Send E-mail	Email receiver	Send_email_to(''xyz@abc.com'')
Login to database	Access permission?	Db_request_without_permission(true/false)
Log off database	Long login session?	Too_long_log(true/false)
Device connect	New device?	Device_first_connect(true/false)
Device disconnect	Long connection?	Connect_too_long(true/false)
File transfer from device	The file checksum	Get_file(''2351F8CD57177D4C1044D37460B'')
Download from website	The file checksum	Get_file(''1AFEEF45CB07F87C3D598ED8A5AA'')

Similarly, this is a snapshot of some negative examples from actions of users (that are not attacked):

```
[ Db_request_without_permission(false),
  Connect_too_long(false),
  Website_domain("google.com"),
  Get_file("1AFEEF45CB07F87C3D598ED8A5AA"),
  Website_domain("thepostgame.com"),
  Too_short_log(false)]

[ Website_domain("imdb.com"),
  Receive_email_from("Glo34Hugh@hotmail.com"),
  Too_short_log(false),
  Db_request_without_permission(false),
  Connect_too_long(false),
  Connect_too_long(false),
  Send_email_to("ki77r089@gmail.com"),
  Send_email_to("mm631d@gmail.com")]

[ Receive_email_from("Glo34Hugh@hotmail.com"),
  Too_short_log(false),
  Db_request_without_permission(false),
  Connect_too_long(false),
  Get_file("1AFEEF45CB07F87C3D598ED8A5AA"),
  Send_email_to("ki77r089@gmail.com"),
  Send_email_to("mm631d@gmail.com")]

[ Receive_email_from("Glo34Hugh@hotmail.com"),
  Too_short_log(false),
  Db_request_without_permission(false),
  Connect_too_long(false),
  Website_domain("google.com"),
  Get_file("1AFEEF45CB07F87C3D598ED8A5AA"),
  Send_email_to("ki77r089@gmail.com"),
  Send_email_to("mm163d@gmail.com"),
  Website_domain("thepostgame.com")]
```

And finally, this is a snapshot of some user actions that need to predict/determine if these are safe:

```
[ Get_file("2351F8CD57177D4C1044D37460B"),
  Website_domain("groupon.com"),
  Website_domain("imdb.com"),
  Receive_email_from("Glo34Hugh@hotmail.com")]

[ Receive_email_from("Kora_Guro@virus.com"),
  Unusual_log_time(true),
  Get_file("1AFEEF45CB07F87C3D598ED8A5AA"),
  Connect_too_long(false),
```

```
    Website_domain("google.com"),
    Send_email_to("mm63ld@gmail.com")]

[ Website_domain("virus.com"),
    Unusual_log_time(true),
    Receive_email_from("Glo34Hugh@hotmail.com"),
    Db_request_without_permission(false),
    Get_file("1AFEEF45CB07F87C3D598ED8A5AA"),
    Send_email_to("ki77r089@gmail.com")]
```

Rules Generated by GOLEM. Based on the example data listed before, the sub-rules generated from GOLEM are shown below. The coverage of each rule is also shown for each clause.

```
ROUND_1
Best_Rule:        [Get_file("2351F8CD57177D4C1044D37460B")]
Best_Cover:       3/6
2nd_Best_Rule:    [Website_domain("virus.com")]
2nd_Best_Cover:   2/6
ROUND_2
Best_Rule:        [Unusual_log_time(true),
                   Website_domain("groupon.com")]
Best_Cover:       2/3
2nd_Best_Rule:    [Website_domain("virus.com")]
2nd_Best_Cover:   1/3
ROUND_3
Best_Rule:        [Receive_email_from("Kora_Guro@virus.com")]
Best_Cover:       1/1
2nd_Best_Rule:    [Receive_email_from("Kora_Guro@virus.com")]
2nd_Best_Cover:   1/1
```

The rule generated for the attack is:

```
[Get_file("2351F8CD57177D4C1044D37460B")]
    OR
[Unusual_log_time(true) AND Website_domain("groupon.com")]
    OR
[Receive_email_from("Kora_Guro@virus.com")]
```

By applying the generated rule to the testing user actions, the result is shown in Table 2.

Table 2. GOLEM result

User	Potential attack	Vulnerable operations
User1	Virus	[Get_file("2351F8CD57177D4C1044D37460B")]
User2	Virus	[Receive_email_from("Kora_Guro@virus.com")]
User3	N/A	N/A

Rules Generated by UBF-GOLEM. Similarly to GOLEM, we apply UBF-GOLEM to the example data. There are 77 actions in all positive and negative examples. The top 3 frequent operations are: access website (16), send email (10) and get file (10). The rules are generated as follows:

```
ROUND_1
Best_Rule:      [website_domain("virus.com")]
Best_UBFC:      2/6 * 16/77
2nd_Best_Rule:  [Get_file("2351F8CD57177D4C1044D37460B")]
2nd_Best_UBFC:  3/6 * 10/77
ROUND_2
Best_Rule:      [Get_file("2351F8CD57177D4C1044D37460B")]
Best_UBFC:      2/4 * 10/77
2nd_Best_Rule:  [Receive_email_from("Kora_Guro@virus.com")]
2nd_Best_UBFC:  2/4 * 8/77
ROUND_3
Best_Rule:      [Receive_email_from("Kora_Guro@virus.com")]
Best_UBFC:      1/2 * 8/77
2nd_Best_Rule:  [Unusual_log_time(true),
                Website_domain("groupon.com")]
2nd_Best_UBFC:  1/2 * 7/77
ROUND_4
Best_Rule:      [Unusual_log_time(true),
                Website_domain("groupon.com")]
Best_UBFC:      1/1 * 7/77
2nd_Best_Rule:  [Unusual_log_time(true),
                Website_domain("groupon.com")]
2nd_Best_UBFC:  1/1 * 7/77
```

Furthermore, the rule generated for the attack is:

```
[website_domain("virus.com")]
    OR
[Get_file("2351F8CD57177D4C1044D37460B")]
    OR
[Receive_email_from("Kora_Guro@virus.com")]
    OR
[Unusual_log_time(true) AND Website_domain("groupon.com")]
```

Finally we can use the rules generated from UBF-GOLEM to determine the vulnerable actions from each user, as shown in Table 3.

UBF-GOLEM vs GOLEM. There are two advantages by using UBFC instead of a simple coverage for clause selection. Firstly, it considers the weights. The frequent operations should be more important as these operations have more chances to be attacked. Secondly, in GOLEM, if two clauses have the same coverage, the algorithm just chooses the first one. With UBFC, clauses with the same positive coverage can be ordered by UBF and this shall lead to more meaningful selection criteria.

Table 3. UBF-GOLEM result

User	Potential attack	Vulnerable operations
User1	Virus	[Get_file("2351F8CD57177D4C1044D37460B")]
User2	Virus	[Receive_email_from("Kora_Guro@virus.com")]
User3	Virus	[Website_domain("virus.com")]

In the example above, GOLEM generated rules ignore the potentially important sub-rule which is [website_domain("virus.com")]. This is because, for each sample incidence which is covered by more than one clause, only the best-covered one will be selected. For example, [website_domain("virus.com")] is the second best in the first two rounds, but it is ignored because all of its covered examples have been marked as covered by other sub-rules. However, [website_domain("virus.com")] is the most important sub-rule generated by UBF-GOLEM. This is because the website has the highest frequency of user operations, which makes its UBFC value larger than those from other sub-rules.

4.3 Discussions

Compared with other CS systems, our proposal focuses on supporting reasoning and determining relationships between an attack and user operations. Our approach determines the relationship between a threat and the user actions that may cause this threat. Based on the frequency and variety of these user operations, companies may consider adjusting their security policies accordingly. In our two module approach, the user security rating module provides each user a security rating, and the rule mining module is to determine potentially vulnerable operations performed by each user. This gives an idea on which individual or user group and also what operations need to be considered. When an attack happens, it will also be easier to locate and faster response to the attack.

5   Conclusions

User behavior is useful to predict potential attacks based on vulnerable user actions. Much work to date has focused on finding vulnerable operations instead of providing reasoning/explanations of its findings. In this paper, we have presented a transparent learning approach for UBA to address this issue. A user rating system is proposed to determine a security level of each user, with explanations of potential attacks based on his/her vulnerable user actions. A detailed example has been presented to illustrate how approach works. We believe that, with justifiable reasoning from our proposed approach, an organization can be aware of the weakness of its current system, and can better prepare for proactive attack defense or reactive responses.

References

1. Agrawal, R., Imieliński, T., Swami, A.: Mining association rules between sets of items in large databases. In: ACM Sigmod Record, vol. 22, pp. 207–216. ACM (1993)
2. Amiri, F., Yousefi, M.R., Lucas, C., Shakery, A., Yazdani, N.: Mutual information-based feature selection for intrusion detection systems. J. Netw. Comput. Appl. **34**(4), 1184–1199 (2011)
3. Ariu, D., Tronci, R., Giacinto, G.: HMMPayl: an intrusion detection system based on hidden Markov models. Comput. Secur. **30**(4), 221–241 (2011)
4. Asenjo, P.E.R.: Web user behavior analysis. Ph.D. thesis, Universidad De Chile (2011)
5. Baum, L.E., Eagon, J.A., et al.: An inequality with applications to statistical estimation for probabilistic functions of Markov processes and to a model for ecology. Bull. Amer. Math. Soc. **73**(3), 360–363 (1967)
6. Bilge, L., Kirda, E., Kruegel, C., Balduzzi, M.: EXPOSURE: finding malicious domains using passive DNS analysis. In: National Diabetes Services Scheme (NDSS) (2011)
7. Bilge, L., Sen, S., Balzarotti, D., Kirda, E., Kruegel, C.: EXPOSURE: a passive DNS analysis service to detect and report malicious domains. ACM Trans. Inf. Syst. Secur. (TISSEC) **16**(4), 14 (2014)
8. Bivens, A., Palagiri, C., Smith, R., Szymanski, B., Embrechts, M., et al.: Network-based intrusion detection using neural networks. Intell. Eng. Syst. Artif. Neural Netw. **12**(1), 579–584 (2002)
9. Brahmi, H., Brahmi, I., Ben Yahia, S.: OMC-IDS: at the cross-roads of OLAP mining and intrusion detection. In: Tan, P.-N., Chawla, S., Ho, C.K., Bailey, J. (eds.) PAKDD 2012. LNCS (LNAI), vol. 7302, pp. 13–24. Springer, Heidelberg (2012). doi:10.1007/978-3-642-30220-6_2
10. Buczak, A.L., Guven, E.: A survey of data mining and machine learning methods for cyber security intrusion detection. IEEE Commun. Surv. Tutor. **18**(2), 1153–1176 (2015)
11. Cannady, J.: Artificial neural networks for misuse detection. In: National Information Systems Security Conference, pp. 368–81 (1998)
12. Cohen, W.W.: Fast effective rule induction. In: Proceedings of the Twelfth International Conference on Machine Learning, pp. 115–123 (1995)
13. Digman, J.M.: Personality structure: emergence of the five-factor model. Annu. Rev. Psychol. **41**(1), 417–440 (1990)
14. Han, H., Lu, X.L., Ren, L.Y.: Using data mining to discover signatures in network-based intrusion detection. In: Proceedings of International Conference on Machine Learning and Cybernetics, vol. 1, pp. 13–17. IEEE (2002)
15. Jemili, F., Zaghdoud, M., Ahmed, M.B.: A framework for an adaptive intrusion detection system using Bayesian network. In: ISI, pp. 66–70 (2007)
16. Joshi, S.S., Phoha, V.V.: Investigating hidden Markov models capabilities in anomaly detection. In: Proceedings of the 43rd Annual Southeast Regional Conference, vol. 1, pp. 98–103. ACM (2005)
17. Kruegel, C., Mutz, D., Robertson, W., Valeur, F.: Bayesian event classification for intrusion detection. In: Proceedings 19th Annual Computer Security Applications Conference, pp. 14–23. IEEE (2003)
18. Kruegel, C., Toth, T.: Using decision trees to improve signature-based intrusion detection. In: Vigna, G., Kruegel, C., Jonsson, E. (eds.) RAID 2003. LNCS, vol. 2820, pp. 173–191. Springer, Heidelberg (2003). doi:10.1007/978-3-540-45248-5_10

19. Lee, W., Stolfo, S.J., Mok, K.W.: A data mining framework for building intrusion detection models. In: Proceedings of the 1999 IEEE Symposium on Security and Privacy, pp. 120–132. IEEE (1999)
20. Li, Y., Xia, J., Zhang, S., Yan, J., Ai, X., Dai, K.: An efficient intrusion detection system based on support vector machines and gradually feature removal method. Expert Syst. Appl. **39**(1), 424–430 (2012)
21. Lippmann, R.P., Cunningham, R.K.: Improving intrusion detection performance using keyword selection and neural networks. Comput. Netw. **34**(4), 597–603 (2000)
22. Michalski, R.S.: A theory and methodology of inductive learning. In: Michalski, R.S., Carbonell, J.G., Mitchell, T.M. (eds.) Machine Learning. Symbolic Computation, pp. 83–134. Springer, Heidelberg (1983)
23. Muggleton, S., Feng, C., et al.: Efficient Induction of Logic Programs. Turing Institute (1990)
24. Norton, M., Roelker, D.: SNORT 2.0: Hi-performance multi-rule inspection engine. Sourcefire Network Security Inc (2002)
25. Panda, M., Patra, M.R.: Network intrusion detection using naive bayes. Int. J. Comput. Sci. Netw. Secur. **7**(12), 258–263 (2007)
26. Pfleeger, S.L., Caputo, D.D.: Leveraging behavioral science to mitigate cyber security risk. Comput. Secur. **31**(4), 597–611 (2012)
27. Plotkin, G.: Automatic methods of inductive inference. Ph.D. thesis, The University of Edinburgh (1972)
28. Plotkin, G.D.: A further note on inductive generalization. In: Machine Intelligence, vol. 6, pp. 101–124. Edinburgh University Press (1971)
29. Quinlan, J.R.: Induction of decision trees. Mach. Learn. **1**(1), 81–106 (1986)
30. Quinlan, J.R.: C4. 5: Programs for Machine Learning. Elsevier, Amsterdam (2014)
31. Raiyn, J., et al.: A survey of cyber attack detection strategies. Int. J. Secur. Appl. **8**(1), 247–256 (2014)
32. Reiss, F.: Transparent Machine Learning for Information Extraction: State-of-the-Art and the Future (2015). http://www.emnlp.2015.org/tutorials/15/15_OptionalAttachment.pdf
33. Udantha, M., Ranathunga, S., Dias, G.: Modelling website user behaviors by combining the EM and DBSCAN algorithms. In: 2016 Moratuwa Engineering Research Conference (MERCon), pp. 168–173. IEEE (2016)
34. Uma, M., Padmavathi, G.: A survey on various cyber attacks and their classification. Int. J. Netw. Secur. **15**(5), 390–396 (2013)
35. Witten, I.H., Frank, E.: Data Mining: Practical Machine Learning Tools and Techniques. Morgan Kaufmann, Burlington (2005)
36. Zhengbing, H., Zhitang, L., Junqi, W.: A novel network intrusion detection system (NIDS) based on signatures search of data mining. In: First International Workshop on Knowledge Discovery and Data Mining (WKDD), pp. 10–16. IEEE (2008)

Application of Stylometry to DarkWeb Forum User Identification

Thanh Nghia Ho[(✉)] and Wee Keong Ng

Nanyang Technological University, Singapore, Singapore
hoth0002@e.ntu.edu.sg, wkn@pmail.ntu.edu.sg

Abstract. The fast growth of the cyberspace in recent years has served as a convenient channel for criminals to do their illegal businesses, especially in Dark Web - the hidden side of the Internet. The anonymous nature of Dark Web forums makes them ideal environments for criminal discussions. Ranging from government, security agencies to financial institutions, many parties are willing to trace the identities of the suspects through these online conversations. Dark Web participants usually have multiple accounts on various forums. On multiple occasions, being able to validate that multiple accounts on different Dark Web forums belong to the same person with high enough confidence allows us to combine various scattering pieces of information into a more concrete and advanced form of knowledge. Such knowledge will lead to actionable insights which are very useful for bringing the criminals to justice. In this paper, we examine the effectiveness of writing style analysis (stylometry) for linking multiple accounts in different Dark Web forums. Initial evaluations have shown that the proposed methodology is promisingly practicable, having a high potential to assist the investigators in exposing anonymous identities in cyber environments.

Keywords: Dark Web · Stylometry · Support vector machine

1 Introduction

Cybercrime is the act of exploiting Internet resources to commit illegal activities ranging from identity theft, drug sale, credit card stealth, and child pornography... It has been shown through past experiences that dealing with this crime wave is not a trivial task. The anonymous nature of the Internet and the ease to enter online criminal markets have greatly contributed to the dramatic increase in cybercrimes. According to Singapore Police Force (SPF) in its annual crime report in 2015, online commercial crimes are the main factor in the 4% rise of overall crime in Singapore. The existence of Dark Web further enhances the anonymity of online criminals. Unlike Surface Web, Dark Web can only be accessed using the TOR browser which provides a mechanism to hide surfing users' information from the Internet Service Providers (ISP). As a result, law enforcement agencies have difficulty in gathering as much information about the criminals on the Dark Web as in the Surface Web. However, there is no such

© Springer International Publishing AG 2016
K.-Y. Lam et al. (Eds.): ICICS 2016, LNCS 9977, pp. 173–183, 2016.
DOI: 10.1007/978-3-319-50011-9_14

thing as a perfect crime. The criminals may unconsciously leave some trails on the Internet in various forms of information, e.g. texts, images, and videos... These trails can provide valuable information which may help to reveal the criminal identities. In this research, we mainly focus on the analysis of criminal textual data in Dark Web forums. Specifically, we aim to profile Dark Web users by linking up their accounts on multiple Dark Web forums through writing style analysis. We consider, for example, a criminal selling drugs publicly in one Dark Web forum who also has another account with partial personal information on another Dark Web forum. The police can take advantage of that combined knowledge to carry out legal actions on the criminal.

In Sect. 2, we review the previous works that tackle the problem of authorship attribution. Section 3 provides an overview of the dataset that we use in this research. In Sect. 4, we formally introduce the aforementioned problem of authorship matching between users on multiple Dark Web forums. We present the main work, our novel authorship attribution algorithm, in Sect. 5. In Sect. 6, we evaluate our algorithm on a dataset collected from multiple Dark Web forums. Finally, in Sect. 7, we give a conclusion for this research and discuss a few potential future works.

2   Related Work

2.1   Dark Web Forums

Traditional Web search engines, including the powerful ones, such as Google and Bing, are unable to index everything on the Internet. In general, we can divide the Internet into two main parts: the visible layer (Surface Web) and the invisible layer (Deep Web). The Surface Web contains all searchable contents that are visible to the general public. In contrast to the Surface Web, the Deep Web is the section of the Internet whose contents have not been indexed by standard search engines. The Dark Web is classified as a small portion of the Deep Web that has been intentionally hidden and is inaccessible through standard web browsers such as Google Chrome, Mozilla Firefox, and Internet Explorer...

Dark Web forums are utilized by cybercriminals to set up secret trading networks and support the exchange of illegal goods and services. Criminals use Dark Web forums' screen names or aliases to communicate with others. In addition, the user's private identification information is usually not shown on those forums and there are no restrictions on the number of accounts a single user can create. In other words, a user can create several anonymous accounts on the same forum and this kind of feature creates multiple challenges to the security and intelligence organizations in tracing back the identity of the anonymous users. For example, on 3 November 2014, the then 18 years old Newcastle man Liam Lyburd was arrested because of his threat to carry out a mass-killing at Newcastle College on a Dark Web forum called "Evolution". The police discovered that he had used two different accounts with unique usernames ("The Joker" and "I Love My Anger") to express his admiration for Anders Breivik, who was sentenced 21 years in prison for killing 77 people in Norway, and Jaylen

Fryberg, who carried out a college attack in the US in which four students were killed [1].

The Dark Web and its danger to the society have extensively raised public awareness in recent years. A great number of parties, including the government and academic researchers, have paid serious attentions to this online threat. Although it is difficult to detect the activities of Dark Web participants, the hidden information in Dark Web forums represents a significant source of knowledge for law enforcement agencies. Accordingly, many researches have been carried out to study the Dark Web forum data. For example, Abbasi et al. [2] introduced a sentiment analysis framework to classify Dark Web forum opinions in both English and Arabic. Zhang et al. [3] created a Dark Web Forums Portal to collect and analyze data from multiple international Jihadist forums. However, few attempts have been made on Dark Web forum user's data integration and association between different forums.

2.2   Attribution Techniques

Amongst the authorship attribution techniques, statistical and machine learning methods are the two most frequently used ones. The former has gained a good reputation for its high level of accuracy [4]. However, there are some complications in these approaches, including the need for more stringent models and assumptions. The exponential growth in computer power over the past several years has promoted machine learning as a better candidate to solve the problem. Machine learning consists of a variety of different techniques such as Bayesian, decision tree, neural networks, k-nearest neighbors (k-NN), and support vector machines (SVMs)... Wang et al. [5] pointed out two huge advantages of machine learning compared to statistical methods. Firstly, machine learning techniques are more scalable as they can handle a larger number of features. Secondly, an acceptable tolerant degree to noise can be achieved with machine learning techniques. These advantages are crucial for working with online messages, which often involve classification of many authors and a large feature set.

SVM classification is the most popular machine learning approach in recent years due to its classification power and robustness. Diederich et al. first introduced SVM to the online text classification domain in 2000 [6] where experiments are based on newspaper articles. After that, in 2006, Zheng et. al. [7] has shown that SVM is far superior compared to other classification methods for authorship identification of online messages.

3   Corpora

There are many challenges associated with the data collection on Dark Web forums compared to Surface Web forums. Accessibility is a big issue as most Dark Web forums restrict their contents to the registered users. They are known as *password-protected* Web resources that require registration and login. In addition, some Dark Web forums provide the contents in the unlinked form.

"Unlinked content" referred to the online pages which are not linked to by other pages. This helps to limit the capabilities of web crawling programs. Hence, creating an effective crawling tool for Dark Web forums is a time-consuming and uneasy task. For the purpose of this research, we use an existing data source that is available online. The bulk of our data was obtained from a vast archive compiled by Gwern Branwen, who is an independent Dark Net Market (DNM) researcher. The archive contains data from more than 30 different Dark Web forums which are mostly in the HTML format.

4   Problem Specification

We define the authorship matching problem as the task to validate whether two accounts having the same username on multiple Dark Web forums belong to the same person or not through writing style analysis. Perito et al. [8] discovered an interesting fact that users have the tendency to use similar usernames for their accounts in different sites, e.g., "donald.trump" and "d.trump". Therefore, it seems that tracking different accounts of a user can be achieved by searching for similar usernames. However, this is not always the case. The chance that two different users coincidentally create accounts with the same username on two different forums is not rare. For example, two users who are the fans of Marvel comics/movies may create the accounts with the same username "spiderman".

In this paper, we propose a novel approach for performing authorship matching using stylometry and basic classification technique (SVM). The problem can become very complex if the users purposely alter their writing style in order to make sure that they are completely anonymous. Kacmarcik et al. [9] have explored different techniques of automatically obfuscating a document to preserve anonymity and found that the number of changes per 1000 words is too small to confound the standard approaches to authorship attribution. For this research, we assume that the authors do not attempt to hide their writing style when participating in online discussions on Dark Web forums.

5   Experiments

Most authorship experiments usually follow a similar machine learning pattern: the model is first trained on a set of texts (training set) and then tested on another set of texts (testing set). The evaluation is based on the accuracy of the testing phase. We apply the described train-and-test process to examine the effectiveness of our proposed authorship matching techniques by designing two different author-matching tasks.

In the first experiment, we collect all the posts of a user in the same Dark Web forum and split them into two parts with nearly equal size and evaluate the authorship matching between those two parts using the proposed framework. This experiment is used as the validation process for finding the best parameter values. We label this process as "Validation Phase".

After the "Validation Phase" is completed, we proceed to the "Testing Phase". In this experiment, we identify some users that have accounts on multiple Dark Web forums. For each user, we collect his/her posts in two arbitrary forums and evaluate the authorship matching between those two parts.

5.1 Message Collection

In the first step, we need to define the list of authors that we want to analyze and extract a set of forum messages posted by those authors from the Dark Web archived data. As the archived data is in HTML format, a data transformation step is required to convert the HTML documents into raw plain text documents. In each post block, there are many redundant components that we need to remove such as user's profile details, user's signature, and quoted post of another user... The preprocessor first parses an HTML document and returns the actual user's post contents. The parsing process is done with the help of "Beautiful Soup", a python library for HTML parsing.

5.2 Message Filtering

Real-world classification problems are influenced by several components. Among them, the presence of noises is a key factor. Noise is an unavoidable problem, which affects the quality of the data collection and data preparation processes. The performance of the authorship matching model built under such circumstances does not only depend on the quality of the training data, but also on its robustness against the noisy data. The noise in text data is defined as the undesired blocks of words which provide no or very little information and need to be removed in order to enhance the total quality of the classification process.

For Dark Web online messages between users, one of the most common "noise" which can be easily observed is known as users' PGP key. PGP stands for Pretty Good Privacy. PGP is most commonly used for data encryption and digital signatures. It adopts the public-key encryption mechanism in which a public key is used to encrypt the data and another separate private key is used to decrypt the encrypted data. Dark Web users usually make use of PGP to encrypt their sensitive information when doing illegal trading. Merchants on underground marketplaces usually provide own public key on their profile. Whenever other users want to trade goods or services from a merchant, they need to encrypt their shipping address using the public key provided by that merchant. In this way, only the merchant can decrypt and view the buyers' messages.

Another common "noise" that we need to consider comes from the hyperlinks (urls) that appear in the user's posts. Almost no user can memorize a long and difficult to remember url and retype it. In fact, users tend to copy/paste the url when they want to refer to an external source in their posts. Although each hyperlink is not directly typed by the authors, it still generates features for the stylometry process. For example, most of the feature set used in stylometry include bigrams and trigrams. The hyperlink usually begins with "http" or "https" and thus will create bigrams ("ht", "tt", "tp") and trigrams ("htt", "ttp"). These features contribute little to the stylometry process and may even affect the results badly if they dominate other features.

In addition, as our research mainly focuses on English text data, we need to remove the chunks of texts that are written in other languages. Language detection is performed using a Python module called "guess_language", which adopts a trigram-based algorithm. "guess_language" can detect over 60 languages, including non-alphabetical ones such as Japanese, Chinese, and Korean...

Last but not least, we need to remove duplicated paragraphs from the text documents. For example, some vendors tend to spam advertisements about their products or some admins may post the forum rules and guidelines multiple times to remind the users. Another common duplication problem comes from the user's forum signature. Most forums allow the users to add their unique signature in their user profile that is automatically appended to each of their posts. As a result, it reduces the exact length of the documents that are used in the classification. All the stylometry methods require some minimum number of words for both training and testing data. The more the duplications are present, the less effective the classification process become.

5.3   Feature Extraction

The purpose of the feature extraction process is to convert the raw text data into informative and non-redundant data representation to facilitate the subsequent learning step. The raw collected messages are in unstructured fragments, which are not ready to train with machine learning algorithms. Therefore, we first transform the original raw text data into structured representations of derived features. These features are referred hereafter as writing style features and include some special features which are not used in the authorship attribution of traditional writings. Because of the casual nature of the Web-based environment, authors are more likely to leave their own *writeprints* in their online conversations (email, chats, forum posts...). Many users try hard to differentiate themselves from others through unique and special online writing style. For example, some authors have the habit of ending the online posts with a smile emoticon ":)" because they think it's cool. In another case, some people, especially the non-native English speakers, tend to repeatedly use some misspelled words in their sentences, e.g. "absense", "noticable", "succesful"... For the Dark Web environment that we consider in this research, there are additional fingerprints that can be taken into accounts. For example, a drug-addicted person may mention a lot about a specific drug name or an active vendor will copy/paste an advertising of his product on multiple Dark Web forums. As a result, with a carefully selected set of features that can represent those fingerprints, the performance of the authorship matching can become reasonably good.

5.4   Validation Phase

We collected posts of 10 active users in different Dark Web forums from the Dark Web archive dataset. We defined the active users as the ones with at least 400 posts and around 6000 words (the contents must be written mostly in English). We denote this set as A. In this validation phase, we divide A into two parts, each of which contains half the posts of each user. We denote those two subsets of A as A_1 and A_2 respectively. We also collect posts of 99 other active users which are used as the fixed negative training dataset for both experiments and denote this set as C. The data in A_1 is used as the positive training data while the data in C provides the negative points which help to shape the classifiers. The desired result is 10 different classifiers for 10 testing users. Specifically, the classifier of each user U is constructed from the training dataset which contains posts of 100 authors (posts of 99 users in set C and posts of user U in A_1). The trained classifiers will be tested against the testing data in the set A_2 using different combinations of parameters. This experiment serves as the validation step which can help to determine the best parameter settings for our model.

5.5   Testing Phase

In the second experiment, for each user of the set A, we find another active account (having at least 400 posts with length around 6000 words) in a different Dark Web forum having the same username and collect all of his forum posts. We denote this set of data as B. The optimal model trained in the validation phase is applied to set B.

6   Discussions

Based on the fact that SVM only performs binary classification task, we apply the N two-way classification model, where N is equal to the number of testing authors. As a result, each SVM classification was applied N times on the testing set of documents. This is known as the one-against-all approach. To predict a new instance of the testing set, we choose the classifier with the largest decision function value. The generated results are in the form of confusion matrices, each matrix's size is $N \times N$. To evaluate the performance of this classification model, we compute the following metrics: recall (R), precision (P) and F_1 measure. F_1 is a popular measure that is frequently used in classification problems, where:

$$F_1 = \frac{2RP}{R + P}$$

For the first validation experiment, we apply the classification model using different SVM kernels. Basically, a kernel is a similarity function which we provide to a machine learning algorithm. It takes two inputs and estimates how similar they are. We carried out the experiment independently for each kernel type. The confusion matrices of all experiments are recorded. The row labels of each matrix are the names of the N classifiers used in the experiments (training authors) while the column labels are the N labeled testing documents. The number in each row (i, j) is the classifying decision value (distance to hyperplane) that the classifier in row i classifies the testing data of author in column j. The label (author) of each test document i is the highest value in column i which is highlighted in red color. After that, using the optimal kernel (which leads to the best accuracy), we apply the model to the testing dataset. The following tables (Tables 1, 2 and 3) show the results of the validation experiments using different kernels. The authors' usernames (labels) are abbreviated in order to protect their personal identity and privacy.

From the above results, we can observe that the linear and polynomial kernels can achieve 10/10 correct classifications. Table 4 shows the F_1 scores of the validation experiments.

In the next step, we carried out the test experiment using linear and polynomial kernels which achieved the perfect classification results for the first

Table 1. Validation experiment result (linear kernel)

	BM(t)	CW(t)	FT(t)	Ka(t)	Ta(t)	Zi(t)	cv(t)	ma(t)	mu(t)	ri(t)
BM(tr)	0.018	−1.154	−2.3	−1.91	−0.541	−0.776	0.777	−1.695	−1.467	−1.554
CW(tr)	−1.519	−0.321	−1.598	−2.091	−0.035	−1.079	−1.821	−2.18	−2.336	−1.858
FT(tr)	−1.507	−0.944	−0.407	−1.235	−1.634	−1.08	−1.272	−0.639	−1.005	−1.084
Ka(tr)	−1.943	−1.953	−1.226	0.144	−2.857	−1.888	−1.961	−0.611	−0.393	−0.91
Ta(tr)	−2.158	−2.541	−3.203	−3.628	1.582	−3.48	−2.795	−3.782	−3.865	−3.817
Zi(tr)	−1.813	−0.932	−1.387	−1.066	−4.126	0.816	−2.009	−1.02	−0.882	−0.722
cv(tr)	−0.927	−0.984	−1.413	−1.372	−0.959	−0.791	1.633	−1.329	−1.199	−1.132
ma(tr)	−1.64	−1.469	−1.082	−1.063	−2.783	−1.314	−1.633	0.531	−0.801	−1.382
mu(tr)	−2.443	−1.95	−1.232	−0.828	−5.082	−1.311	−2.812	−0.411	0.492	−1.1
ri(tr)	−1.624	−1.381	−1.485	−1.093	−1.734	−1.197	−0.709	−1.545	−1.289	0.544

Table 2. Validation experiment result (polynomial kernel)

	BM(t)	CW(t)	FT(t)	Ka(t)	Ta(t)	Zi(t)	cv(t)	ma(t)	mu(t)	ri(t)
BM(tr)	0.103	−1.16	−2.256	−1.85	−0.291	−0.79	0.924	−1.614	−1.423	−1.535
CW(tr)	−1.422	−0.446	−1.519	−1.986	−0.132	−1.134	−1.549	−2.043	−2.15	−1.742
FT(tr)	−1.589	−0.938	−0.377	−1.238	−2.058	−1.082	−1.309	−0.675	−1.007	−1.086
Ka(tr)	−2.083	−2.071	−1.229	0.127	−3.721	−1.918	−2.081	−0.704	−0.431	−0.927
Ta(tr)	−2.059	−2.365	−2.865	−3.157	1.696	−3.043	−2.559	−3.298	−3.318	−3.281
Zi(tr)	−1.912	−0.89	−1.418	−1.109	−5.624	0.868	−2.018	−1.091	−0.898	−0.749
cv(tr)	−0.914	−0.98	−1.374	−1.346	−0.954	−0.832	1.65	−1.296	−1.191	−1.141
ma(tr)	−1.757	−1.518	−1.067	−1.061	−3.709	−1.34	−1.752	0.588	−0.794	−1.424
mu(tr)	−2.703	−2.066	−1.198	−0.851	−7.206	−1.34	−3.192	−0.447	0.476	−1.093
ri(tr)	−1.732	−1.411	−1.478	−1.11	−2.259	−1.208	−0.678	−1.537	−1.285	0.539

Table 3. Validation experiment result (rbf kernel)

	BM(t)	CW(t)	FT(t)	Ka(t)	Ta(t)	Zi(t)	cv(t)	ma(t)	mu(t)	ri(t)
BM(tr)	−0.952	−0.995	−1.105	−1.061	−0.998	−0.986	−0.988	−1.003	−1.018	−1.031
CW(tr)	−1.02	−1.003	−1.001	−1.001	−0.989	−1	−0.989	−0.995	−0.999	−0.995
FT(tr)	−1	−1.019	−0.825	−0.976	−0.987	−1.015	−0.988	−0.971	−1.003	−0.954
Ka(tr)	−1.038	−1.056	−1.019	−0.71	−1.033	−1.062	−1.033	−0.986	−0.91	−0.981
Ta(tr)	−0.997	−1.008	−1.003	−1.003	−0.61	−0.999	−0.952	−0.977	−0.995	−0.979
Zi(tr)	−1.09	−1.091	−1.011	−0.956	−1.082	−0.79	−1.083	−1.068	−1.057	−1.012
cv(tr)	−0.936	−0.982	−1.015	−1	−0.963	−0.997	−0.423	−0.983	−0.995	−0.984
ma(tr)	−0.998	−1.006	−1.008	−1.006	−0.96	−1.008	−0.961	−0.374	−0.954	−0.991
mu(tr)	−1.021	−1.033	−1.069	−0.905	−1.019	−1.067	−1.02	−0.91	−0.66	−1.009
ri(tr)	−1.004	−1.041	−1.002	−0.947	−0.977	−1.036	−0.978	−1.007	−1.02	−0.393

Table 4. Validation experiments F_1 score

Kernel	F_1 **macro**	F_1 **micro**
Linear	1	1
Polynomial	1	1
Rbf	0.765	0.8

Table 5. Test experiment result (linear kernel)

	BM(t)	CW(t)	FT(t)	Ka(t)	Ta(t)	Zi(t)	cv(t)	ma(t)	mu(t)	ri(t)
BM(tr)	−0.073	−0.62	−2.023	−1.841	−1.204	−1.036	−0.328	−1.61	−1.177	−1.952
CW(tr)	−1.678	−0.686	−1.635	−2.254	−3.024	−1.48	−1.831	−2.608	−2.754	−2.58
FT(tr)	−1.39	−0.995	−0.662	−1.144	−1.468	−1.094	−1.14	−0.932	−1.169	−0.903
Ka(tr)	−2.119	−2.084	−1.632	0.164	−1.258	−1.793	−2.333	−0.519	−0.492	−0.649
Ta(tr)	−2.649	−3.012	−2.947	−3.417	−4.152	−3.083	−4.113	−4.027	−4.216	−4.571
Zi(tr)	−1.326	−0.36	−1.64	−1.532	−1.642	−0.063	−0.758	−0.967	−0.559	−0.551
cv(tr)	−1.004	−0.683	−1.585	−1.271	−1.306	−1.04	0.188	−1.273	−1.257	−1.371
ma(tr)	−1.588	−1.353	−1.324	−1.134	−1.411	−1.327	−1.342	−0.327	−0.946	−1.078
mu(tr)	−2.019	−2.043	−1.678	−0.899	−2.096	−1.681	−1.369	−0.616	0.831	−0.372
ri(tr)	−1.703	−1.419	−1.563	−1.011	−1.26	−1.27	−1.042	−1.415	−1.286	0.473

experiments. The results of this testing phase are recorded in Tables 5 and 6. Table 7 shows the F_1 scores of the test experiments.

The results show that there is not much difference between the performance of linear and polynomial kernels. Both can achieve 80% accuracy (8/10 correct classifications) which is a quite good result in authorship attribution domain.

Table 6. Test experiment result (polynomial kernel)

	BM(t)	CW(t)	FT(t)	Ka(t)	Ta(t)	Zi(t)	cv(t)	ma(t)	mu(t)	ri(t)
BM(tr)	−0.049	−0.623	−2.008	−1.801	−1.206	−1.042	−0.421	−1.55	−1.167	−1.824
CW(tr)	−1.546	−0.777	−1.518	−2.072	−2.583	−1.425	−1.778	−2.341	−2.451	−2.363
FT(tr)	−1.429	−0.994	−0.634	−1.151	−1.455	−1.099	−1.138	−0.944	−1.163	−0.925
Ka(tr)	−2.224	−2.162	−1.67	0.176	−1.238	−1.849	−2.28	−0.582	−0.551	−0.723
Ta(tr)	−2.455	−2.724	−2.679	−3.013	−3.532	−2.77	−3.486	−3.436	−3.538	−3.764
Zi(tr)	−1.334	−0.294	−1.701	−1.558	−1.625	0.002	−0.762	−1.013	−0.611	−0.656
cv(tr)	−1.005	−0.715	−1.535	−1.262	−1.315	−1.046	−0.075	−1.259	−1.249	−1.349
ma(tr)	−1.683	−1.382	−1.353	−1.138	−1.45	−1.357	−1.38	−0.303	−0.968	−1.103
mu(tr)	−2.15	−2.158	−1.707	−0.916	−2.139	−1.729	−1.44	−0.648	0.741	−0.447
ri(tr)	−1.779	−1.441	−1.574	−1.026	−1.314	−1.285	−1.077	−1.413	−1.287	0.255

Table 7. Test experiments F_1 score

Kernel	F_1 macro	F_1 micro
Linear	0.747	0.8
Polynomial	0.747	0.8

7 Conclusions and Future Work

In this research, we have built a framework for authorship matching based on features extracted from online messages in Dark Web forums. We have undertaken two separate experiments to evaluate the effectiveness of the proposed method. These experiments have shown that writing style can be used to attribute and correlate authorship between users on multiple Dark Web forums with high accuracy. The results of the experiments show that our method is comparable to all tested state-of-the-art methods. We believe that the proposed framework has the potential to aid the task of tracing secret cyber criminal identities that are hidden under the indexed surface webs.

However, there are some constraints associated with this research. Firstly, we only consider stylometric attributes that work at the character level, word level, sentence level, and document level. There are some other attributes that work at the phrase level, the clause level, and the paragraph level. These attributes, however, are not considered in this study. Given their properties, we can assume that these attributes should provide good results at least for the text summarization task. Secondly, as mentioned in previous chapters, we assume that no text obfuscation attempts are made by the users. The problem can be complicated if the users intentionally alter their writing style to avoid being undercovered by legal parties. Therefore, sophisticated techniques for detecting stylistic deception in written texts need to be integrated for handling such complex scenarios. Last but not least, the size of our test dataset (users who have at least two active accounts on different Dark Web forums) is small due to the limitations of the archived data that we use. We can overcome this problem by creating a data crawler to collect more data directly from Dark Web forums which can potentially help to increase the dimension of our test dataset.

In addition to the limitations of this research that we need to overcome, we have identified several promising research ideas based on the current study. There are two directions that can be considered as our potential future works.

(i) Firstly, as this study only focused on English messages, we plan to include more languages into our future researches.
(ii) Secondly, we will try to focus more on other features that are less related to writing style such as topic, posted date/location, user's forum signature, semantic features and apply this technique to find the correlations of users between dark webs and social networks.

References

1. DailyMail: Teen was hours away from columbine-style massacre at his old school: Ex-student, 19, 'stockpiled weapons and explosives including a 9mm pistol and five pipe bombs in a bid to carry out mass murder, July 2015
2. Abbasi, A., Chen, H.: Applying authorship analysis to arabic web content. In: Kantor, P., Muresan, G., Roberts, F., Zeng, D.D., Wang, F.-Y., Chen, H., Merkle, R.C. (eds.) ISI 2005. LNCS, vol. 3495, pp. 183–197. Springer, Heidelberg (2005). doi:10.1007/11427995_15
3. Zhang, Y., Zeng, S., Fan, L., Dang, Y., Larson, C.A., Chen, H.: Dark web forums portal: searching and analyzing jihadist forums. In: IEEE International Conference on Intelligence and Security Informatics ISI 2009, pp. 71–76. IEEE (2009)
4. Burrows, J.F.: Word-patterns and story-shapes: the statistical analysis of narrative style. Literary Linguist. Comput. 2(2), 61–70 (1987)
5. Wang, R.Y., Storey, V.C., Firth, C.P.: A framework for analysis of data quality research. IEEE Trans. Knowl. Data Eng. 7(4), 623–640 (1995)
6. Diederich, J., Kindermann, J., Leopold, E., Paass, G.: Authorship attribution with support vector machines. Appl. Intell. 19(1–2), 109–123 (2003)
7. Zheng, R., Li, J., Chen, H., Huang, Z.: A framework for authorship identification of online messages: writing-style features and classification techniques. J. Am. Soc. Inf. Sci. Technol. 57(3), 378–393 (2006)
8. Perito, D., Castelluccia, C., Kaafar, M.A., Manils, P.: How unique and traceable are usernames? In: Fischer-Hübner, S., Hopper, N. (eds.) PETS 2011. LNCS, vol. 6794, pp. 1–17. Springer, Heidelberg (2011). doi:10.1007/978-3-642-22263-4_1
9. Kacmarcik, G., Gamon, M.: Obfuscating document stylometry to preserve author anonymity. In: Proceedings of the COLING/ACL on Main Conference Poster Sessions, pp. 444–451. Association for Computational Linguistics (2006)

SECapacity: A Secure Capacity Scheduler in YARN

Chuntao Dong[1,2], Qingni Shen[1,2(✉)], Lijing Cheng[1,2], Yahui Yang[1,2], and Zhonghai Wu[1,2]

[1] School of Software and Microelectronics, Peking University, Beijing, China
{chuntaodong, morleycheng}@pku.edu.cn,
{qingnishen, yhyang, wuzh}@ss.pku.edu.cn
[2] MoE Key Lab of Network and Software Assurance,
Peking University, Beijing, China

Abstract. In this paper, aiming to the requirement that isolation of user's job and data security, we deeply analyze the mainstream computing framework Hadoop YARN, and start with the core module of YARN - resource scheduler. Using the existing label-based scheduling policy, we design and implement a SECapacity scheduler. Our main work including: First, according to the principle of least privilege, we propose a user-classification based scheduling policy, which divided users to several levels based on their attributes, then restrict which nodes could be used by this user according to the user level. Second, we design and implement a SECapacity scheduler to implement user-classification based scheduling. Third, we verify and analyze the effectiveness and efficiency of SECapacity scheduler, the results shows that SECapacity scheduler can ensure 100% isolation of users at different levels, and the performance overhead is about 6.95%.

Keywords: Big data platform · Hadoop · User-classification based scheduling · SECapacity scheduler

1 Introduction

Big data has rapidly developed into a hotspot, and big data analysis has been widely applied. In order to make good use of big data, academia and industry has proposed numerous techniques, such as Hadoop, Spark, Storm, and Graphlab etc., Hadoop has quickly become a major platform, which includes many technique as an ecosystem, such as MapReduce [2], YARN [8] and HDFS etc. With the development of big data applications, the security and privacy of big data have received sufficient attention. Due to the characteristics of big data and its complexity of processing, the security issues of big data are very complex and difficult to handle. The built-in security mechanism of Hadoop can only limit internal users to use resource legitimately. To ensure security and privacy of big data platform, academia and industry have proposed plenty of solutions. We will introduce these solutions in the related work of Sect. 2.

In this paper, first we analyze the security characteristics of big data platform and the related work. Then, we describe the threat scenario. Third, we refer to the principle

© Springer International Publishing AG 2016
K.-Y. Lam et al. (Eds.): ICICS 2016, LNCS 9977, pp. 184–194, 2016.
DOI: 10.1007/978-3-319-50011-9_15

of least privilege [3] and proposed SECapacity scheduler to enhance the isolation of tasks [1]. Fourth, we conduct a massive experiments to test performance and security of our SECapacity scheduler. Finally, we summarize our work and clarify the value of our work, illustrate the limitation of our work, and introduce our research in the future.

In this paper, **our main contributions** are summarized as following points:

(1) We proposed a user-classification based scheduling refer to the principle of least privilege, which can enhance isolation of user's job and protect data security.
(2) Based on user-classification based scheduling, we design and implement the SECapacity scheduler based on Capacity scheduler.
(3) We test the performance and analyze the security of SECapacity scheduler by conduct a series of experiments.

The rest of this paper is organized as follows. We introduce the background in Sect. 2, and describe the threat scenario in Sect. 3. In Sect. 4, we present the design details of SECapacity, and introduce the implementation details of SECapacity in Sect. 5. We then evaluate and analyze experimental results in Sect. 6. We conclude the paper in Sect. 7.

2 Background

This section provides the background information about security analysis of Hadoop, related work and the mechanism of Capacity scheduler.

2.1 Security Analysis

As a distributed computing platform, big data platform has its own advantages, as well as disadvantages in security. So we analyze it from the pros and cons.

Big data platform has native characteristic of security and robustness: (1) The distribution makes the platform more robustness. The entire system wouldn't be impact, when adversary attacks a single node or a small number of nodes; (2) In the big data environment, the value of a few number of data become less. It's not significant that malicious users just get the data on a single node; (3) Big data platform is constituted by thousands of storage and computing nodes, except for central node, the common nodes has no difference, it's not easy to find the valuable attack point among the nodes.

Big data platform also brings convenience to the attacker, so it's difficult to defend the threat: (1) The big data platform is consisted of thousands of storage and computing nodes, which makes it very difficult to detect and deal with intrusion timely. (2) The software on the big data platform uses the master - slave structure, it's hard to remove the feature of centralization. As long as there is such a pivot or management center node like ResourceManager or ApplicationMaster, it's easy to be attacked. (3) During data processing, because of the low value of single node, the attacker will target to steal data processing results to improve the attack efficiency.

2.2 Related Work

There are many security and privacy issues in the big data platform now. The academic have proposed many solutions to solve these issues. We will introduce several solutions in the part.

Indrajit Roy etc. present Airavat [7], a MapReduce-based system which provides strong security and privacy guarantees for distributed computations on sensitive data. Airavat is a novel integration of mandatory access control and differential privacy. Tien Tuan Anh Dinh etc. develop a solution which avoids using the expensive ORAM construction and ensure privacy preserving computation in MapReduce, and implement their solution in a system called M^2R [4]. Olga Ohrimenko etc. analyze the security of intermediate traffic between mappers and reducers, and they describe two provably-secure, practical solutions [6]. In the paper [9], the author present SecureMR, a practical service integrity assurance framework for MapReduce, which provide a set of practical security mechanisms that prevent replay and Denial of Service attacks, preserve the simplicity, applicability and scalability of MapReduce.

We summarize the current research work and find that there is few research focus on the security of data processing results. Therefore, we focus on the data leakage issue during the big data processing. The current solutions mainly focus on static data security and access security, but ignore the security and isolation of tasks. We detailedly describe the threat scenario and steal scheme in our previous work [5]. According to the security features of the big data platform, we select a systematic risk management strategy to enhance the security of the platform.

2.3 Capacity Scheduler

In this paper, we add the security scheduling strategy in Capacity scheduler of Hadoop to enhance the security. The Capacity scheduler is based on the ratio of memory using, but rarely consider of security issues. The main design and development of our work is using label-based-scheduling strategy [1].

Label-based Scheduling provides a method match the shared cluster resources on nodes to a queue. The node, which has the same label with the queue, can be used by this queue. Using label-based scheduling, an administrator can control exactly which nodes are chosen to run jobs submitted by different users and groups. It's useful for data locality and multi-tenancy use cases.

3 Threat Scenario

Because we have described the threat model that steal user's processing results and implement the solution in our previous work [5], we will only describe the threat scenario in this section.

Threat Model. We assume adversary is regarded as trusted but have malicious intentions. He tries to steal sensitive results from other user that he is not allowed to access. The threat model is depicted in Fig. 1. There are three types of entities:

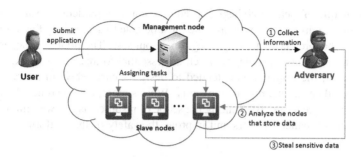

Fig. 1. The model of detecting the node storing the results

User: These entities have data to be stored in the cluster and interact with the Hadoop Cluster to manage their data and submit applications on the cluster.

Adversary: The adversary intends to steal the processed results of other users. He collects information and analyzes the nodes that store results.

Hadoop Cluster: The Hadoop cluster provides resources and services for users.

Based on the threat model, we proposed and implement the attack scheme [5]. The key of our scheme is confirm the node that storing the processed data. In general, the malicious want to running task on the node that the target user's job is running. In other words, lacking of job isolation mechanism lead to security problem in big data platform.

In this paper, we assume that the malicious user can control a few of nodes if they can deploy tasks on these nodes. Based on assume, the isolation mechanism of Hadoop is not enough to guarantee the security of the platform, we need to proposed a new solution at the platform level. So we design SECapacity Scheduler as a systematic risk management strategy to enhance the security of the platform.

4   SECapacity Scheduler

In this section, we introduce the details of the SECapacity Scheduler. First, we take an overview of the SECapacity. Then, we introduce the user-classification based scheduling strategy (UCBS). Third, we introduce the label based scheduling. At last, we proposed two scheme of UCBS.

4.1   Overview

According to the threat analysis, we knew that tasks of users and malicious users running on same node is not safe. We wish to separate the users from the malicious users, and isolate execution of their tasks. The scheduler limit the resource usage of each user, but don't limit the number of used nodes, user can apply for computing resources on any node. It is very easy to be utilized by malicious users. In the process of designing SECapacity scheduler, we take the least privilege as design principle.

The principle of Least Privilege [3] requires that in a particular abstraction layer of a computing environment, every module must be able to access only the information and resources that are necessary for its legitimate purpose. The principle means giving a user account only those privileges which are essential to that user's work.

In this paper, the principle is extended to design secure scheduling strategy. The scheduler should ensure the resource quantity. What's more, the scheduler should limit the scope of resource usage. By limiting the scope of resource usage, we limit influence scope of potential malicious users and improve the safety of the platform.

4.2   User-Classification Based Scheduling

According to the design principle, we face two problems: which user is a malicious user, and SECapacity scheduler take user as resource division unit will seriously affect the performance, so we proposed UCBS.

A. *User classification*

We need to identify potential malicious users among all the users. In order to describe our secure scheduling, we provide a reference user classification scheme. Our user classification scheme rating user according to attributes, and then divide all users into several levels on the basis of classification criteria. The classification criteria is determined by the administrator.

In our scheme, every user has four attributes, include user privilege, user resource quota, registration time and safety rating. The scores of these four attributes are represented by symbols U, R, T, and S, and rating criteria are shown in Table 1. According to rating criteria and the formula (1), we can give each user a score. Where a, b, c and d are parameters, we simplify all the parameters to 1.

$$G = a*U + b*R + c*T + d*S \tag{1}$$

If we take user as resource division unit will seriously affect the scheduling performance. So we propose a classification scheme to divide all users into several levels. The classification criteria is determined by the administrator. For example, assuming there are five users User1, User2, User3, User4 and User5 in the cluster, and the score

Table 1. User rating criteria

User property	User attribute classification and score evaluation criteria
User privilege	Super administrator = 50, Administrator = 10, Ordinary User = 1
User resource quota	User resource percentage of cluster resource
Registration time	Score of user registration time = $[Log_2T]$, T is the number of days
Safety rating based on behavior of users	Malicious behavior (such as tracking the other tasks) minus 10 score

of five users are: 21, 20, 31, 35 and 56. The classification criteria: 0–24 is level 1, 25–49 is level 2, and 50–75 is level 3.

B. *Resource classification*

According to the principle of least privilege, we limit the scope of nodes that user used. But we also need to ensure the "authority" of users, the "authority" is the resource quota of users. In the last part, we divide all users into several levels. We need to recalculate the total resource of users at the same level. Assuming that the number of nodes in the cluster is n, and the memory resource of each node is x, and there are m users U_1, $U_2...U_m$. The resource quota of m users is X_1, $X_2... X_m$. By user rating and user classification, m user are divided into K level L_1, $L_2... L_K$. The resource quota of all the users in level L_k ($0 \leq k \leq K$) is recorded as G_k, we use the formula (2) to calculate G_k.

$$Gk = \sum Xi, Ui \in Lk \tag{2}$$

Through the calculation, we can confirm the resource quota of K users are: G_1, $G_2... G_K$, then we use the formula (3) to calculate Nk, the number of nodes belong to level L_k ($0 \leq k \leq K$).

$$Nk = [Gi*n] \tag{3}$$

C. *Label based scheduling*

After divided all the users into several levels, we need to schedule the tasks to the corresponding nodes, we use label to achieve our scheduling goals. For convenience, we assume that every user monopolize a leaf queue. By configuring labels of queues and nodes, we schedule the tasks in the queue to the nodes that has the same labels with the queue. We proposed two isolation scheme as follows:

Node label setting policy: according to $N_k(0 \leq k \leq K)$, choose N_k nodes to set label k, and ensure the resource localization as much as possible.

4.3   The Scheme of Isolation Scheduling

According to the principle of least privilege, we proposed two schemes of isolation scheduling: complete isolation scheduling and range control scheduling.

Complete isolation scheduling: the jobs in the queue that has the label k can only use the nodes that has the same label with the queue.

Queue label setting policy: the queue that the user U_i belongs to should be set label k, $U_i \in L_k$, $0 \leq k \leq K$. We take the example that mentioned in the last part as example, its configuration scheme is as shown in the Fig. 2.

Range control scheduling: the jobs in the queue that has the label k can use the nodes that has the same label k and less than k.

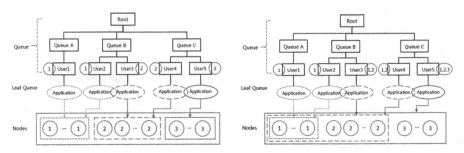

Fig. 2. Complete isolation scheduling scheme   **Fig. 3.** Range control scheduling scheme

Queue label setting policy: the queue that the user U_i belongs to should be set label 1, 2... k, $U_i \in L_k$, $0 \leq k \leq K$. We take the example that mentioned in the last part as ex-ample, its configuration scheme is as shown in the Fig. 3.

The detailed scheduling rules: users can use resources of lower levels users, but user can't use resource of higher level users. Users should firstly use resource that belong to their own level, we achieve this through starting resource preemption strategy.

5   Implementation

In this section we introduce the design and implementation of SECapacity scheduler. First we introduce the structure of SECapacity scheduler, then demonstrate the function and realization of each module in detail.

5.1   The Structure of SECapacity Scheduler

SECapacity scheduler is based on the Capacity scheduler of Hadoop 2.6.0, and using the label based scheduling. We implement the complete isolation scheduling in SECapacity scheduler. The structure of SECapacity scheduler is as shown in Fig. 4.

5.2   Function of Each Module

In this part, we will detailedly describe the function and implement of each module in the SECapacity Scheduler.

(1) **Queue and Node label management module:** rates and classify the user to generate the label configuration scheme. The module includes five components as follows:

User level management component rates all users and generates user classification scheme according to user's attributes. It has two function: initialization and updating.

Queue label management component is based on the user classification scheme to generate queue label configuration scheme.

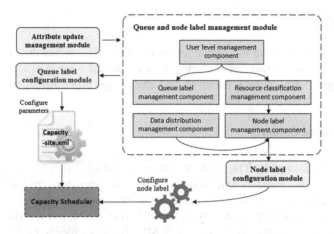

Fig. 4. The architecture of SECapacity scheduler

Resource classification management component calculates the total resource quota of each level's users according to the user classification scheme and the resource quota.

Data distribution management component uses the information of data blocks distribution to calculate the number of data blocks on each node.

Node label management component generates node label configuration scheme according to the nodes' number of each level and the distribution of all users' data block.

(2) **Attribute update management module** monitors user's attributes, and the changing of users and nodes in the cluster. According to these changes, it calls Queue & Node label management module to modify the classification of user, and generates a new queue and node label configuration scheme.

(3) **Queue label configuration module** uses the queue label configuration scheme to set the related configuration file. This module can automatically configure capacity-site.xml. This module mainly modifies the following parameters:

    (1) *yarn.scheduler.capacity.<queue-path>.accessible-node-labels*: decide which labels can be used by the *"queue-path"*.

    (2) *yarn.scheduler.capacity.<queue-path>.accessible-node-labels.<label>.capacity*: decide the available proportion of resources on the nodes labeled *"label"* which can be used by user in the queue named *"queue-path"*.

    (3) *yarn.scheduler.capacity.<queue-path>.accessible-node-labels.<label>.mamimum-capacity*: decide the upper bound of the resource labeled *"label"* which can be used by users in the queue named *"queue-path"*.

(4) **Node label configuration module** configures each node's label according to node label configuration scheme. This module uses node label configuration scheme to generate and run the configuration script.

6 Evaluation

In this section, we evaluate the performances of SECapacity Scheduler. We describe the experiment environment and scenarios, then conducted a series of experiments to test two schemes of isolation scheduling, and analyze the experimental results at last.

6.1 Experiment Scenario

Experiment Environment. The Hadoop cluster including 19 nodes, a master that deployment ResourceManager and NameNode, and 18 nodes that deployed DateNode and NodeManager. Every node using the local 64-bit Centos operation system with an Intel Core 7 processor running at 3.4 GHz, 4096 MB of RAM, and run Hadoop 2.6.0. We set up the size of every data block is 128 MB. The input files is 4.8 GB, and each block has 3 duplicates. To get the best performance in experiment, we assume there are three users and the quota of them is 33%, 33% and 34%. These three users are divided into three levels, and they execute the same job with the same size input files.

Setup. To test SECapacity scheduler, we need to configure the hadoop cluster. The configuration process includes the following four steps:

> *Step 1*: add system level label. According to the experimental scenario, we need to add three labels one, two and three. Execute command: *rmadmin -addToClusterNodeLabels one, two, three.*
>
> *Step 2:* label all nodes. The command is: *rmadmin -replaceLabelsOnNode yarn "nodeId = label".* In our experimental scenario, we configure six node with a same label.
>
> *Step 3:* configure the label recovery. The label information will be saved to the HDFS after the YARN restart.
>
> *Step 4:* according to the scheme of isolation scheduling, configure the capacity-scheduler.xml.

6.2 Performance Analysis

We mainly choose two **evaluation standard**: resource localization rate and runtime. The resource localization rate is the rate of map task running at the node that storing the input files. Dividing the cluster into several parts will reduce the resource localization rate and increase the runtime of job.

At first, we run 3 wordcount jobs that consists 39 map tasks and 1 reduce tasks to test the Capacity scheduler. In order to ensure the accuracy of experimental results, we run 20 experiments and calculate the average. A part of experiment results as shown in Table 2. Then, we also run 3 wordcount jobs that consists 39 map tasks and 1 reduce tasks in three levels to test the SECapacity scheduler. The nodes' number of each level is 6. A part of experiment results as shown in Table 3.

Table 2. The experiment results of capacity scheduler

Job	The first run		The second run		The third run	
	Runtime	Localization rate	Runtime	Localization rate	Runtime	Localization rate
Job 1	376	22/40	367	27/39	365	27/41
Job 4	384	23/41	336	30/41	359	31/41
Job 7	330	30/42	327	32/41	349	27/40

Table 3. The experiment results of SECapacity scheduler

Job	The first run		The second run		The third run	
	Runtime	Localization rate	Runtime	Localization rate	Runtime	Localization rate
Job 1	348	20/40	356	22/40	417	29/41
Job 4	361	22/40	374	18/40	430	27/42
Job 7	331	21/41	321	20/40	449	22/40

We summarize and analyze the results of Capacity scheduler and SECapacity scheduler in Table 4. By comparing the results, we find that the localization rate decline from 61.78%–71.65% to 49.32%–53.74%. The runtime rise from 336 s–367 s to 360 s–396 s, and rise 6.95% at average. According to the above results, we can get the conclusion that the runtime is associated with localization rate. We should improve the data distribution management component to increase the localization rate.

Table 4. Capacity scheduler vs. SECapacity scheduler

Job	Capacity scheduler		SECapacity scheduler		
	Runtime (s)	Localization rate (%)	The level of user that submit job	Runtime (s)	Localization rate (%)
Job 1	367	62.76	level 1	381	51.25
Job 2	372	61.78	level 1	369	53.74
Job 3	363	63.14	level 1	390	50.13
Job 4	358	70.12	level 2	394	52.50
Job 5	352	71.02	level 2	388	53.17
Job 6	364	69.35	level 2	396	50.37
Job 7	339	70.71	level 3	363	50.91
Job 8	344	70.13	level 3	376	49.32
Job 9	336	71.65	level 3	360	51.67

6.3 Security Analysis

If the level of a malicious user is higher than or equal to the level of users, users have the risk of information leakage, because a malicious user can apply for nodes that belongs to the other users. The SECapacity can only ensure safety and isolation of users at different levels, but can't protect users at the same level. So the SECapacity scheduler relay on the accuracy of user classification scheme. In the future work, we will ensure the safety and isolation of users at same levels.

7 Conclusion

In this paper, we propose a UCBS according to the principle of least privilege, and implement the scheduling strategy in SECapacity scheduler to enhance isolation of different level's jobs. Through the experiments, we verify the effectiveness and performance of SECapacity scheduler. The performance cost of our scheme is about 6.95%, and we don't need to modify Hadoop source directly. However, the effect of the SECapacity scheduler is highly dependent on the user classification scheme. We need to further improve our user classification scheme. Another problem is that SECapacity scheduler is poor at defend APT attacks, a malicious user can improve their permission through long-term hidden. We also need to solve the problem that how to defend against APT attack in the future work.

Acknowledgments. This work is supported by the National High Technology Research and Development Program ("863" Program) of China under Grant No. 2015AA016009, the National Natural Science Foundation of China under Grant No. 61232005, 61672062, and the Science and Technology Program of Shen Zhen, China under Grant No. JSGG20140516162852628.

References

1. Apache hadoop. http://hadoop.apache.org
2. Dean, J., Ghemawat, S.: MapReduce: simplified data processing on large clusters. In: Conference on Symposium on Operating Systems Design & Implementation, vol. 51, pp. 107–113. USENIX Association (2004)
3. Denning, P.J.: Fault tolerant operating systems. ACM Comput. Surv. 8(4), 359–389 (1976)
4. Dinh, T.T.A., Saxena, P., Chang, E.C., et al.: M^2R: enabling stronger privacy in mapreduce computation (2015)
5. Dong, C., Shen, Q., Li, W., Yang, Y., Wu, Z., Wan, X.: Eavesdropper: a framework for detecting the location of the processed result in hadoop. In: Qing, S., Okamoto, E., Kim, K., Liu, D. (eds.) ICICS 2015. LNCS, vol. 9543, pp. 458–466. Springer, Heidelberg (2016). doi:10.1007/978-3-319-29814-6_39
6. Ohrimenko, O., Costa, M., Fournet, C., et al.: Observing and preventing leakage in MapReduce. In: ACM SIGSAC Conference, pp. 1570–1581 (2015)
7. Roy, I., Setty, S.T.V., Kilzer, A., et al.: Airavat: security and privacy for MapReduce. In: Usenix Symposium on Networked Systems Design and Implementation, NSDI 2010, San Jose, pp. 297–312 (2010)
8. Vavilapalli, V.K., Murthy, A.C., Douglas, C., et al.: Apache hadoop YARN: yet another resource negotiator. In: Symposium on Cloud Computing, pp. 1–16 (2013)
9. Wei, W., Du, J., Yu, T., et al.: SecureMR: a service integrity assurance framework for MapReduce. In: Computer Security Applications Conference, pp. 73–82. IEEE (2009)

Authentication and Authorization

Integrity and Authenticity Protection with Selective Disclosure Control in the Cloud & IoT

Christoph Frädrich[2], Henrich C. Pöhls[1,2(✉)], Wolfgang Popp[2], Noëlle Rakotondravony[1,2], and Kai Samelin[3,4]

[1] Institute of IT-Security and Security Law, Passau, Germany
{hp,nr}@sec.uni-passau.de
[2] Chair of IT-Security, University of Passau, Passau, Germany
{fraedric,poppwolf}@fim.uni-passau.de
[3] IBM Research – Zurich, Rüschlikon, Switzerland
ksa@zurich.ibm.com
[4] TU Darmstadt, Darmstadt, Germany

Abstract. RSS allow the redaction of parts from signed data. Updatable RSS additionally enable the signatory to add new elements, while signatures can be merged by third parties under certain conditions.

We propose a framework for two new real-life application scenarios and implement it using an RSS with sufficient functionality on three different platforms, ranging from a potent cloud to a very resource-constrained Android device. Our evaluation shows impractical run time especially on the IoT device for the existing construction that was proven to be secure in the standard model. Thus, we provide an adjusted scheme with far better performance, which we prove to be secure in the random oracle model. Furthermore, we show how to increase performance using parallelization and several optimizations.

1 Introduction

Cryptographic protection of integrity using signatures gives us strong origin authentication for the data. To gain full end-to-end protection, and to verify the origin of the data, the signature has to be generated on the data gathering device. A drawback of standard digital signatures is that the signed data set cannot be split into parts to selectively disclose only required parts to protect the confidentiality of the unneeded data parts. Redactable signature schemes (RSS), a concept initially introduced by Steinfeld and Bull [24], and independently by

C. Frädrich, H.C. Pöhls, and W. Popp were supported by EU H2020 project PRISMACLOUD, grant agreement No. 644962. H.C. Pöhls was supported by EU FP7 project RERUM under grant agreement No. 609094. H.C. Pöhls, W. Popp, and N. Rakotondravony were supported by the Bavarian State Ministry of Education, Science and the Arts as part of the FORSEC research association. K. Samelin was supported by the EU ERC under grant PERCY No. 321310.

© Springer International Publishing AG 2016
K.-Y. Lam et al. (Eds.): ICICS 2016, LNCS 9977, pp. 197–213, 2016.
DOI: 10.1007/978-3-319-50011-9_16

Johnson et al. [12], offer a solution to the problem and "...model a situation where a censor can delete certain parts of a signed document without destroying the ability of the recipient to verify the integrity of the resulting (redacted) document." [12]. Clearly, this primitive has its merits whenever authentic data must be handled in a privacy friendly manner. However, despite their "obvious" usefulness, RSS did not gain the attention they deserve, most likely due to the lack of complete and convincing real-life application scenarios and a missing proof that they are truly practical.

Motivation. Our overall goal is to bring RSS to practice in a real-life application scenario. Namely, we applied RSS in two real-life use-cases and measured their performance. The two use cases that are described in more detail in Sect. 2 are: healthcare data and log entries. For medical data, or information that contains trade secrets, it is of paramount importance that the redacted parts do not leak from the redacted yet signed document. This property is called privacy, and means that a verifier must not be able to gain any knowledge about redacted elements without having access to them. In particular, we show how RSS can be used to ease managing data in a privacy friendly manner without any a-priori knowledge of the data's later usage or intended recipients. As RSS, in particular, keep the authenticity of the remaining data and are capable of identifying the signatory. This gives increased data quality assurance due to the possibility to verify the origin and the integrity of the data transmitted, and can even make the redacted data become acceptable as an evidence in court.

Contribution. We propose two privacy and authenticity preserving data workflows, sketched in Figs. 1 and 2. We found that the workflows can be instantiated with a suitable RSS, solving the problems related to data privacy and authenticity from the use cases. We back our finding by the evaluation of the actual performance in three very different environments: a constrained IoT device, a standard Android smart phone, and a powerful computing device as found in clouds. Interestingly, our evaluation shows that our approach is suitable for workflows involving cloud as well as the Android mobile phone under consideration, if implemented with care and certain optimizations, including some changes to the used RSS. Namely, the original RSS construction from [19] — cryptographically secure in the standard model — requires extensive primality tests. We reduce the cryptographic strength to the practically still useful random oracle model (ROM) to obtain usable and for many workflows satisfying performance. We provide a security proof of the altered construction.

State-of-the-Art. The concept of RSS has been introduced as "content extraction signatures" by Steinfeld et al. [24], and, in the same year, as "homomorphic signatures" [12] by Johnson et al. A security model for sets has been given by Miyazaki et al. [16]. Their ideas have been extended to work on trees [5,21], on lists [6,22], but also on arbitrary graphs [13]. A generalized security model was then derived by Derler et al. [9]. There are also schemes that offer *context-hiding*, a very strong privacy notion, and variations thereof [1,2]. Context-hiding

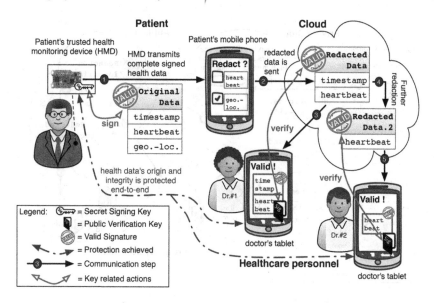

Fig. 1. Example workflow for e-health use-case: integrity and origin of remaining data remains verifiable and protected against active attacks; redaction needs no keys

schemes allow to generate signatures on derived sets with no possibility to detect whether these correspond to an already signed set in a statistical sense. However, all proposed schemes achieving this notion do not allow *updating* signatures, i.e., add new data, which is inherently required in our case. RSS have also been analyzed to allow this within the EU legal framework [18,25]. However, there is no work deploying more advanced RSS, which also allow *updating* signed data in a real-life context, even though there are some implementations, which evaluate less expressive constructions [20,23,27]. Of course, there is much additional related work which we cannot discuss due to space requirements. Ghosh et al. [11] provide a comprehensive overview.

2   Application Scenarios

In the first use-case (Fig. 1), healthcare data is gathered by a constrained, Internet-of-Things (IoT) like, yet certified and trusted, medical health monitoring device (HMD). The goal is to allow to share the resulting data with authenticity guarantees, e.g. that data was not maliciously modified and originated from a certain HMD. However, at the time of data generation and application of the integrity and authenticity protection, we do not know with whom we want to share which parts of the data being gathered. The workflow is as follows: The HMD senses the rate of the heartbeat and records it with a time stamp and a geo-location. When consulting the record, the medical personnel must be reassured that it was indeed taken by some HMD (e.g. certified medical equipment with a known good calibration) and not tampered (e.g. the patient faking to have

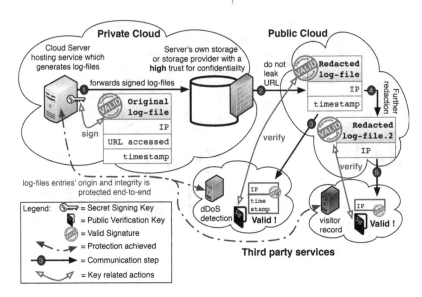

Fig. 2. Example workflow for the log-file use-case: origin and integrity of log-entries with limited information remains verifiable; redaction needs no keys

done exercises). For protection, each triplet (timestamp, heartbeat, geo.-loc.) is digitally signed on the HMD, using a secret signature generation key (sk) only known to that HMD. This is done for each new measurement; therefore the HMD not only signs but also *update* data. Communication step 1 shows that signed data is sent to the patient's mobile phone. The patient's personal Android smart phone then plays the role of the privacy-enhancing gateway and selects which data is forwarded to the healthcare provider. For example, the timestamps are made more coarse and the geo-location can be removed in certain user chosen areas. The patient entrusts his device and software to do these redactions. But the redaction itself requires no additional keys, the signature can be adjusted to fit the reduced data, e.g. geo.-location information is removed in the workflow depicted in Fig. 1. The redacted and still verifiably signed data is sent in step 2 to the healthcare provider. The provider can verify the received reduced data's adjusted signature on a cloud-based back-end. In step 3, it sends the data to a healthcare personnel's tablet computers. Additionally, the workflow allows to further reduce the data set. Thus, by redacting sensitive and unneeded information from the data first, any service in the cloud can further tailor the still authentic information into smaller packages. This is depicted by the communication steps 4 and 5 in Fig. 1. Overall, there are three important advantages from facilitating an RSS in this way:

– The workflow requires no interaction with the HMD to tailor the data after the production into different packages for different healthcare usages or different personal; still it allows any privacy-aware party to implement the need-to-know principle in an ad-hoc fashion.

- The workflow allows to verify that other than potential removal of more data, the data that is available has not been tampered with and originated from an identifiable HMD.
- The party or parties doing privacy preserving redactions are not required to be entrusted not to introduce other errors or even tamper the data.

Thus, the workflow achieves to keep a high data quality: The authenticity of the information shown to the healthcare personnel is protected even against a manipulation on the patient's smartphone, e.g., falsifying the heartbeat or geographic location to simulate jogging; and the origin is authenticated to be the certified HMD. This use-case has a small number of elements to be signed (<20) for each reading, but only *very* limited computing resources.

In the second use-case (Fig. 2), log-files of a service in the cloud are signed and thus are protected against unauthorized modifications when transferred to off-site storage services or other analyzing third party services. Here, our main requirement is again that certain unnecessary, or sensitive details from the log-file, e.g., an accessed URL[1], can be redacted. In a first step, the log-file's entry is generated by the service and the information of the IP, the accessed URL, and the time is added to a signed log file that is stored in the private cloud (communication step 1 in Fig. 2). Again, note that being able to directly handle adding new signed elements to an already signed set is very helpful in this scenario. In the example, the URL is treated as confidential and is removed in step 2 before the reduced information is then shared with several services that analyze log-files. In our example, a service for detection of distributed denial of service (dDoS) is provided with authentic tuples of IP and timestamp of the access to a certain service. By verifying the signature, the service provider that offers to detect distributed denial of services could know that it was not tampered and from which service it originated, i.e. mapping the pk to a known customer of the dDoS-detection service. An additional service could be to redact (step 4) and give the remaining information to other services. All the time, the authenticity of the remaining information can be retained in order to be still usable as forensic evidence or for data quality purposes. The second use-case is challenging due to a potentially large number of redactable elements in the log-files ($>1,000$), which we tackle by using cloud computing resources.

3   Cryptographic Preliminaries

For completeness of the paper, we re-state the cryptographic security properties needed for an RSS to be suitable in our scenario. We chose the construction by Pöhls and Samelin [19], as it is the only RSS achieving the required properties.

Notation. $\lambda \in \mathbb{N}$ denotes the security parameter. All algorithms take 1^λ as an (often implicit) additional input. We write $a \leftarrow A(x)$ if a is assigned the output

---

[1] By some data leakage prevention (DLP); depicted as 'firewall' in Fig. 2.

of algorithm A with input x. An algorithm is efficient if it runs in probabilistic polynomial time (ppt) in the length of its input. It may return a special error symbol $\bot \notin \{0,1\}^*$, denoting an exception. For the remainder of this paper, all algorithms are ppt if not explicitly mentioned otherwise. If we have a list, we require that we have an injective, and efficiently reversible, encoding which maps the list to $\{0,1\}^*$. For a set S, we assume, for notational reasons, a lexicographical ordering on the elements. A message space $\mathcal{M}$, and the randomness space $\mathcal{R}$, may implicitly depend on a corresponding public key. If not otherwise stated, we assume that $\mathcal{M} = \{0,1\}^*$ to reduce unhelpful boilerplate notation. A function $\nu : \mathbb{N} \to [0,1]$ is *negligible*, if it vanishes faster than every inverse polynomial, i.e., $\forall k \in \mathbb{N}, \exists n_0 \in \mathbb{N}$ such that $\nu(n) \leq n^{-k}, \forall n > n_0$. $||$ is a bit-concatenation.

The Strong-RSA Assumption. Let $(n, e', d, p, q) \leftarrow \mathsf{RSAKeyGen}(1^\lambda)$ be an RSA-key generator returning an RSA modulus $n = pq$, where p and q are random distinct (safe-) primes[2], $e' > 1$ an integer co-prime to $\varphi(n)$, and $d \equiv e'^{-1} \bmod \varphi(N)$. The flexible RSA problem associated to $\mathsf{RSAKeyGen}$ is, given n, and $y \leftarrow \mathbb{Z}_n^*$, to find x and e such that $x^e \equiv y \bmod N$, where e is also prime [3]. More formally, the Strong-RSA Assumption now states that for every PPT adversary $\mathcal{A}$, there exists a negligible function ϵ such that $\Pr[(n, e', d, p, q) \leftarrow \mathsf{RSAKeyGen}(1^\lambda), y \leftarrow \mathbb{Z}_n^*, (x, e) \leftarrow \mathcal{A}(n, y) : x^e \equiv y \bmod n] \leq \epsilon(\lambda)$ holds.

3.1   Cryptographic Accumulators ACC

A cryptographic accumulator ACC is a succinct, but not necessarily hiding [8,15], commitment to a potentially very large set S [3]. For each element $v \in S$ a witness (or proof) p_v can be generated which vouches v was really accumulated. A *trapdoor* accumulator allows to add new elements not priorly in the set S.

Definition 1 (Trapdoor Accumulators). *A cryptographic trapdoor accumulator ACC consists of four ppt algorithms:* $\mathsf{ACC} := (\mathsf{Gen}, \mathsf{Dig}, \mathsf{Proof}, \mathsf{Verf})$:

Gen. *This algorithm generates the key pair:* $(\mathsf{sk}_{\mathsf{ACC}}, \mathsf{pk}_{\mathsf{ACC}}) \leftarrow \mathsf{Gen}(1^\lambda)$
Dig. *On input of the set S to accumulate and the public parameters $\mathsf{pk}_{\mathsf{ACC}}$, it outputs an accumulator value* $a \leftarrow \mathsf{Dig}(\mathsf{pk}_{\mathsf{ACC}}, S)$
Proof. *This deterministic algorithm, on input of the secret key $\mathsf{sk}_{\mathsf{ACC}}$, the accumulator a, and a value v, outputs a witness p for v:* $p \leftarrow \mathsf{Proof}(\mathsf{sk}_{\mathsf{ACC}}, a, v)$
Verf. *On input of the public key $\mathsf{pk}_{\mathsf{ACC}}$, an accumulator a, a witness p, and a value v, it outputs a bit $d \in \{0,1\}$, indicating whether p is a valid witness for v w.r.t. a and $\mathsf{pk}_{\mathsf{ACC}}$:* $d \leftarrow \mathsf{Verf}(\mathsf{pk}_{\mathsf{ACC}}, a, v, p)$

Even though there is a proof algorithm, providing S at accumulator generation may speed up the algorithms for elements in S, if one knows $\mathsf{sk}_{\mathsf{ACC}}$.

---

[2] A prime p is safe, if $p = 2p' + 1$, where p' is also prime.

Security Model. Essentially, we require that an adversary cannot find a witness for an element for which it does not already know a proof. This has to hold even adaptively. For the formal definition of the required properties, such as correctness and collision-resistance, please see the full version or [19].

3.2 Mergeable and Updatable RSS (MRSS)

We now introduce mergeable and updatable MRSS, derived from Pöhls and Samelin [19].

Definition 2 (Mergeable and Updatable RSS (MRSS)). *A mergeable and updatable* MRSS *consists of six efficient algorithms. Let* MRSS := (*KeyGen, Sign, Verify, Redact, Update, Merge*), *such that:*

KeyGen. *The algorithm* KeyGen *outputs the public and private key of the signer, i.e.,* $(\mathsf{pk}, \mathsf{sk}) \leftarrow KeyGen(1^\lambda)$.

Sign. *The algorithm* Sign *gets as input the secret key* sk *and the set* $\mathcal{S}$. *It outputs* $(\sigma, \tau) \leftarrow Sign(\mathsf{sk}, \mathcal{S})$. *Here,* τ *is a tag.*

Verify. *The algorithm* Verify *outputs a bit* $d \in \{0, 1\}$ *indicating the correctness of the signature* σ, *w.r.t.* pk *and* τ, *protecting* $\mathcal{S}$. 1 *stands for a valid signature, while* 0 *indicates the opposite. In particular:* $d \leftarrow Verify(\mathsf{pk}, \mathcal{S}, \sigma, \tau)$.

Redact. *The algorithm* Redact *takes as input a set* $\mathcal{S}$, *the public key* pk *of the signer, a tag* τ, *and a valid signature* σ *and a set* $\mathcal{R} \subset \mathcal{S}$ *of elements to be redacted, outputting* $\sigma' \leftarrow Redact(\mathsf{pk}, \mathcal{S}, \sigma, \mathcal{R}, \tau)$. $\mathcal{R}$ *is allowed to be* $\emptyset$.

Update. *The algorithm* Update *takes as input a set/signature/tag tuple* $(\mathcal{S}, \sigma, \tau)$, sk *and a second set* $\mathcal{U}$. *It outputs* $\sigma' \leftarrow Update(\mathsf{sk}, \mathcal{S}, \sigma, \mathcal{U}, \tau)$.

Merge. *The algorithm* Merge *takes as input the public key* pk *of the signer, two sets* $\mathcal{S}$ *and* $\mathcal{V}$, *a tag* τ, *and the corresponding signatures* $\sigma_\mathcal{S}$ *and* $\sigma_\mathcal{V}$. *It outputs the merged signature* $\sigma_\mathcal{U} \leftarrow Merge(\mathsf{pk}, \mathcal{S}, \sigma_\mathcal{S}, \mathcal{V}, \sigma_\mathcal{V}, \tau)$.

Security Model. We now give a short overview of the security model. In a nutshell, an entity not having access to any secret keys must not be able to generate any signature which verifies for elements not endorsed by the signer, excluding merges under the same tag τ, and redactions (unforgeability). From the privacy perspective, which is arguably as important as the unforgeability requirement, we need some additional guarantees. In particular, we require that: (1) An outsider must neither be able to decide whether a given set was freshly signed or created by redacting or which elements have been added afterwards (update privacy/transparency). (2) An adversary must neither be able to decide whether a given signature was generated through a merge or freshly signed or which elements have been merged (merge privacy/transparency). (3) An adversary must neither be able to learn anything about redacted elements nor whether a signature is fresh or was created by a redaction (privacy/transparency).

Due to space requirements, the formal definitions of these security properties can be found in the full version of this paper or in [19].

Definition 3 (Secure MRSS). *We call an* MRSS *secure, if it is corect, unforge-able, transparent, private, merge transparent, merge private, update private, and update transparent* [19].

4   Constructions

The original paper's instantiation of ACC (as the major building block of the MRSS) was proven secure in the standard model [19]. We re-phrase the accumulator in the random-oracle model [4], as it offers better performance, after given the general instantiation of the MRSS.

The Construction by Pöhls and Samelin [19]. The basic ideas of the MRSS construction given in [19] is to start with an empty accumulator a generated for each key pair. For a signature, the public information of the accumulator $\mathsf{pk_{ACC}}$ is accompanied with the proofs for all the signed elements $v_i \in S$ and the updated accumulator value a. Apart from the elements, a tag τ is also accumulated making each signature linkable, and to allow updates and merging. For new signatures, a new tag is chosen.

Construction 1 (Updatable and Mergeable MRSS). *Let* MRSS := (*Key Gen, Sign, Verify, Redact, Update, Merge*) *such that:*

KeyGen. *The algorithm* KeyGen *generates the key pair in the following way:*
1. *Generate key pair required for* ACC, *i.e., run* $(\mathsf{sk_{ACC}}, \mathsf{pk_{ACC}}) \leftarrow Gen(1^\lambda)$
2. *Call* $a \leftarrow Dig(\mathsf{pk_{ACC}}, \emptyset)$
3. *Output* $(\mathsf{sk_{ACC}}, (\mathsf{pk_{ACC}}, a))$

Sign. *To sign a set S, perform the following steps:*
1. *Draw a tag* $\tau \in_R \{0,1\}^\lambda$
2. *Let* $p_\tau \leftarrow Proof(\mathsf{sk_{ACC}}, a, \tau)$
3. *Output* (σ, τ), *where* $\sigma = (p_\tau, \{(v_i, p_i) \mid v_i \in S \wedge p_i \leftarrow Proof(\mathsf{sk_{ACC}}, a, (v_i, \tau))\})$

Verify. *To verify signature* $\sigma = (p_\tau, \{(v_1, p_1), \ldots, (v_k, p_k)\})$ *with tag τ, perform:*
1. *For all $v_i \in S$ check that* $Verf(\mathsf{pk_{ACC}}, a, (v_i, \tau), p_i) = 1$
2. *Check that* $Verf(\mathsf{pk_{ACC}}, a, \tau, p_\tau) = 1$
3. *If* Verf *succeeded for all elements, output* 1, *otherwise* 0

Redact. *To redact a subset $\mathcal{R}$ from a valid signed set (S, σ) with tag τ, with $\mathcal{R} \subseteq S$, the algorithm performs the following steps:*
1. *Check the validity of σ using* Verify. *If σ is not valid, return* $\perp$
2. *Output σ', where* $\sigma' = (p_\tau, \{(v_i, p_i) \mid v_i \in S \setminus \mathcal{R}\})$

Update. *To update a valid signed set (S, σ) with tag τ by adding $\mathcal{U}$ and knowing* $\mathsf{sk_{ACC}}$, *the algorithm performs the following steps:*
1. *Verify σ w.r.t. τ using* Verify. *If σ is not valid, return* $\perp$
2. *Output σ', where* $\sigma' = (p_\tau, \{(v_i, p_i) \mid v_i \in S\} \cup \{(v_k, p_k) \mid v_k \in \mathcal{U}, p_k \leftarrow Proof(\mathsf{sk_{ACC}}, a, (v_k, \tau))\})$

Merge. *To merge two valid set/signature pairs $(\mathcal{S}, \sigma_\mathcal{S})$ and $(\mathcal{T}, \sigma_\mathcal{T})$ with an equal tag τ, the algorithm performs the following steps:*

1. *Verify $\sigma_\mathcal{S}$ and $\sigma_\mathcal{T}$ w.r.t. τ using* **Verify.** *If they do not verify, return $\bot$*
2. *Output $\sigma_\mathcal{U}$, where $\sigma_\mathcal{U} = (p_\tau, \{(v_i, p_i) \mid v_i \in \mathcal{S} \cup \mathcal{T}\})$, where p_i is taken from the corresponding signature*

Clearly, this construction is simple, yet fulfills all security requirements we need for our scenarios, if instantiated with a "good" accumulator. Moreover, Pöhls and Samelin have shown that the given construction is secure in the standard model if the strong RSA-Assumption holds [19], if used with their accumulator. However, the underlying hash-function needs to be division-intractable, whose only suitable instantiation seems to be mapping to primes in a collision-avoiding manner [7]. From an implementation perspective, this is too time-consuming, as we show in Sect. 5. We stress that Pöhls and Samelin already were aware of the fact that a signature-only based construction exists. However, as shown by Derler et al. [8], a lot of different accumulators exists, which may be used to achieve different or additional properties. We also leave this as open work, as for our applications scenarios trapdoor accumulators are enough.

4.1 Revisiting the Accumulator by Pöhls and Samelin

We now show that their construction is also secure in the random oracle model, as it offers far better efficiency, as we show in Sect. 5.

Trapdoor Accumulators ACC$'$. We now present the adjusted construction. Even though the changes are minimal (yet invasive), the resulting performance gain is significant. We therefore present the full scheme in detail next.

Construction 2 (Trapdoor-Accumulator ACC$'$). *Let $\mathcal{H} : \{0,1\}^* \to \{0,1\}^{\lambda-1}$ be a random oracle. Here, λ means the bit-length of the RSA modulus as proposed by Coron and Naccache [7]. Let* ACC$' := ($ Gen, Dig, Proof, Verf $)$ *such that:*

Gen. *Generate $n = pq$, where p and q are distinct safe primes using* RSAKeyGen. *Return $(\varphi(n), (n, \mathcal{H}))$, where $\varphi(pq) := (p-1) \cdot (q-1)$.*
Dig. *To improve efficiency, we use the build-in trapdoor. A new digest can therefore be drawn at random. Return $a \in_R \mathbb{Z}_n^\times$.*
Proof. *To generate a witness p_i for an element v_i, set $v_i' \leftarrow \mathcal{H}(v_i)\|1$. Output $p_i \leftarrow a^{v_i'^{-1} \pmod{\varphi(n)}} \bmod n$.*
Verf. *To check the correctness of a proof p w.r.t. an accumulator a, the public key* pk$_{\mathsf{ACC}}$, *and a value v, output 1, if $a \overset{?}{=} p^{\mathcal{H}(v)\|1} \pmod{n}$, and 0 otherwise.*

Theorem 1. *Construction 2 is secure in the random-oracle model, if the Strong-RSA Assumption holds.*

Proof. For construction 2, we only need to prove collision-resistance, while correctness is obvious. Essentially, the proof is the same as the one given by Gennaro et al. [10], but compressed. In a nutshell, we build an adversary $\mathcal{B}$ which uses $\mathcal{A}$ internally to break the Strong-RSA Assumption. Let q_h be an upper bound on the queries to the random oracle. Then, $\mathcal{B}$ draws a random index $i \in \{1, 2, \ldots, q_h\}$. It then draws q_h random bit-strings e_j of length $\lambda - 1$, and sets $e'_j \leftarrow e_j \| 1$. Then, it sets $p \leftarrow \prod_{j=1, i \neq j}^{q_h} e_j \bmod n$. If $\gcd(p, e_j) \neq 1$, abort. This abort only appears with negligible probability, as already shown by Gennaro et al. [7,10]. Then, $\mathcal{B}$ embeds the challenge (t, n) from the strong RSA-Experiment in the following way. It gives $(n, t^p \bmod n)$ to the adversary $\mathcal{A}$. For each query v_i, it sets the random oracle response to e'_i. If for v_i $(i \neq j)$ a witness is requested, it returns $t^{p/e'_i} \bmod n$. If, however, $i = j$, $\mathcal{B}$ has to abort. If $\mathcal{A}$ outputs (v^*, p^*) such that $t^p = p^{*v^*} \bmod n$, $\mathcal{B}$ calculates $ae'_j + bp = 1$ using EEA, and $r \leftarrow t^a p^{*b} \bmod n$. It outputs (e'_j, r) as its own solution. The probability of $\mathcal{B}$ winning is the same as $\mathcal{A}$ divided by q_h, ignoring negligible parts. $\square$

Theorem 2. *Construction 1 is secure if instantiated with the accumulator above (Construction 2).*

Proof. As the random oracle is still deterministic, the original proofs by Pöhls and Samelin [19] directly carry over without any modifications. $\square$

Clearly the full construction, inheriting from the given accumulator, is only secure in the random-oracle model. We stress that the same ideas hold for the signature-based construction given in the extended version of [19]. However, as already stated, an accumulator may offer better performance than the signature-based construction.

5   Implementation and Evaluation

We implemented both constructions of RSS described in Sect. 4 on three different platforms. The only known construction of a division-intractable hash-function includes expensive primality tests [7]. Henceforth, we refer to it as 'Prime'. Our new construction simply requires the hash's value to be odd and is henceforth denoted as 'Odd'. All hashes have been implemented as full-domain hashes using concatenation of shorter hash-outputs, as described by Bellare and Rogaway [4], paired with rejection sampling. Algorithm 1 shows the pseudo code for the implementation where FDH describes the full-domain hash and $\mathcal{H}$ a standard hash function such as SHA-512, but modeled as a random oracle. It is not hard to see that this implementation behaves like a random oracle, if $\mathcal{H}$ is a random oracle.

The crypto primitive was implemented in the C programming language for the constrained device RE-Mote and as a Java library for use in the cloud and on Android. Java was chosen because it is a widely used programming language and it provides many useful functionalities as well as existing cryptographic libraries. It also allowed us to re-use the same code base on both the Android and the cloud platform.

Data: Modulus n, a hash-function $\mathcal{H} : \{0,1\}^* \rightarrow \{0,1\}^\lambda$, a message $m \in \{0,1\}^*$
Result: An invertible hash h as defined
$c \leftarrow 0$;
$h \leftarrow \perp$;
$s \leftarrow \lfloor ((|n| - 1)/\lambda) \rfloor + 1$; $//|n|$ is the bit-length of n
while *true* **do**
    $h \leftarrow \mathcal{H}(m,c)||\mathcal{H}(m,c+1)||\ldots||\mathcal{H}(m,c+s-1)$;
    $h \leftarrow h \gg (s \cdot \lambda - |n| + 1)$; $//$shift out excessive bits
    if $\gcd(h||1, n) = 1$ $//h||1$ *is interpreted as a natural number* **then**
        | return $h||1$;
    end
    $c \leftarrow c + 1$;
end

Algorithm 1. Pseudocode of our FDH-Implementation

5.1 Our Platforms

The Android, Cloud and RE-Mote platforms are very different in terms of available computing power. On the one end, we have the very powerful cloud platform and on the other end, the resource constrained RE-Mote platform. The Android device's compute power is somewhere in between the two aforementioned ones.

A *cloud computer* uses multicore processors and has multiple gigabytes of RAM. In our implementation of the healthcare use-case, we used one Intel Core i7-4790 quad-core processor clocked at 3.60 GHz to 4.00 GHz with 16 GB of RAM and Oracle's JVM in version 1.8.0.92.

We used a Motorola Moto G (3rd Gen.) smart phone as the *Android device* for our implementation. It has a Qualcomm Snapdragon 410 quad-core processor clocked at 1.4 GHz with 1 GB RAM and was running Android Version 6.0.

The RE-Mote is a *resource-constrained IoT platform* that has been designed for applications with additional cryptographic support for increased security and privacy [17, 26] and still offers a low power consumption. It is based on a CC2538 ARM Cortex-M3, with up to 512 KB of programmable flash and 32 KB of RAM.

5.2 MRSS Key Generation is Done in the Cloud

The generation of keys in both of our use-cases solely happens in the cloud (see Table 1 for performance). Still, providing a complete PKI was out of scope of our implementation. Nevertheless, our Java library needs access to the keys. We tackled this problem by loading the keys from a Java keystore, which is based on the keystore provided by the Bouncy Castle [14] crypto library. In the healthcare scenario this is due to the high need for computation power: the search for large safe-primes on the constrained device could easily take a couple of days and we foresee these keys to be provided or indeed generated during a burn-in phase of the certified HMD. In the cloud scenario the cloud service signs.

5.3 MRSS in the Cloud

To use the computing power of the cloud environment to full advantage, we implemented parallelized versions of the sign, update and verify algorithms. Namely, these three algorithms perform modular arithmetics and compute cryptographic hashes. This is more computationally intensive than removing elements from a given set, which is what the merge and redact algorithms do. To no surprise the merge and redact operations are very fast compared to the sign, update and verify operations. Thus, we did not put effort into parallelizing merge and redact. Sign, update and verify perform computations on every element of a given set or message. This calculation is on one element only and it is independent[3] from the calculations on all other elements of the message. Using this knowledge allowed us to parallelize sign, update and verify; using Java we carried out the computation on each element of the set in parallel.

5.4 MRSS on a Mobile Phone

As we were only interested in performance measurements and not in user interaction with the RSS, we implemented a bare-bone Android application without a graphical user interface. This application reused the Java RSS library that we already developed and implemented for the cloud. All cryptographic algorithms and the testing benchmarks used for the cloud platform were implemented also on Android, except those concerning key generation. Key generation tests were excluded since in our framework only the public keys are needed for verification. The quad core CPU of the Motorola Moto G allowed us to use the parallelization features provided by our Java RSS library, which sped up the tests significantly but diminished the usability of the mobile phone because no optimizations in that regard were made, as this was not important for the test application.

5.5 MRSS on a Constrained Device

The sign and verify algorithms are implemented in the C programming language, compatible with the Contiki operating system ran by the RE-Mote device. We used the different functions provided by an existing Elliptic Curve Cryptography library[4] for the manipulation of numbers of large size. These functions implement arithmetical operations on big integers.

To tackle the considerable amount of time required by the safe prime generation algorithm, we generated the keys externally and hard coded the values on the RE-Mote device. The implementation on the RE-Mote is not as fast as we hoped, but there is still room for improvement. In particular, we could use a better optimized function for modular exponentiation, since this is the most expensive calculation in RSS and also called very often. Another limitation of the RE-Mote is its small RAM size, which made it impossible to sign or verify large messages.

---

[3] Does not need a result of a previous calculation.
[4] https://github.com/oriolpinol/contiki.

Table 1. Runtime in seconds of the KeyGen, Redact, Merge operations

	Cloud		Mobile		RE-Mote	
	2,048	4,096	2,048	4,096	2,048	4,096
KeyGen	122.4	4,336.0	–	–	–	–
Redact[a]	0.27×10^{-3}	0.19×10^{-3}	5.87×10^{-3}	4.17×10^{-3}	insuff. RAM	insuff. RAM
Merge[b]	0.08×10^{-3}	0.06×10^{-3}	1.32×10^{-3}	2.813×10^{-3}	insuff. RAM	insuff. RAM

[a] Redact 500 elements of 1,000-element message
[b] Merge two 500-element messages

5.6 Evaluation

For every test, we varied different parameters like the security parameter λ and different levels of parallelization as well as using the 'Prime' and 'Odd' hash function implementations. On the constrained device we used a message with 4 redactable elements. For the mobile phone and the cloud we used for the 'Prime' version a message with 100 elements and for those using the 'Odd' version of the hash function, we used 100 and 1,000 elements. We decided not to run tests with 1,000 elements when using the original —'Prime'— version of the hash function, because these tests were painfully slow. Tests which took longer than 12 h ($>0.5d$) were stopped as such a runtime makes the scheme impractical to use.

The Construction 2 checks if the given message and signature verifies before calling the actual merge, update and redact routines. However, we disabled signature verification in these algorithms to gain a better impression of how fast or slow these operations are, because otherwise it would have also included the verification runtime. For a full runtime of update, merge and redact one must add the runtime of the verification algorithm on top.

Tables 1, 2, 3 and 4 show the detailed results of our performance measurements. These tables show an average runtime of four repetitions of every test.

Observations. Most important of all, we found that using the revised hash function, that does not require primality tests, denoted as 'Odd', allowed to achieve an average speedup of 1,100 times compared to the originally proposed one, denoted 'Prime'. Figure 3 shows this very impressive speedup as well as how the construction of MRSS scales excellently on multi-core CPUs.

Further, the test results show that—as expected—the runtime of operations increases linearly with the number of elements in a message. Additionally, it can be noted that the redact and merge operations are extremely fast independent of the used security parameter. Regarding the update and sign operation, we expected update to be slightly faster, since sign needs to additionally process the tag. However, this did not show in the results. Also the linearity of the selected RSS shows its practicality regarding update: updating n elements to a small message is equally fast as updating the same amount to a large message.

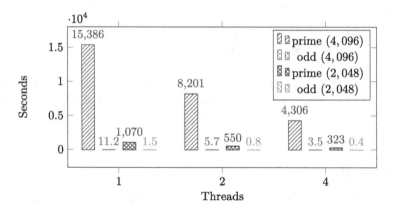

Fig. 3. Runtime in seconds of signing a 100-element message with 4,096 and 2,048 bit keys on an Intel Core i7-4790 CPU

Table 2. Average runtime in seconds of signing 100- and 1,000-element messages

Sign		Threads/λ							
		1		2		4		8	
		2,048	4,096	2,048	4,096	2,048	4,096	2,048	4,096
Cloud	Prime (100)	1,070.0	15,386.0	550.0	8,201.0	323.0	4,306.0	294.0	4,161.0
	Odd (100)	1.5	11.2	0.8	5.7	0.4	3.5	0.4	3.0
	Odd (1,000)	15.0	111.0	8.1	56.3	4.5	31.3	3.9	28.8
Mobile	Prime (100)	>0.5d	>0.5d	>0.5d	>0.5d	>0.5d	>0.5d	–	–
	Odd (100)	13.4	93.5	6.7	47.6	3.7	25.1	–	–
	Odd (1,000)	132.0	925.0	65.9	465.0	34.3	254.0	–	–
RE-Mote	Prime (4)	>0.5d	>0.5d	–	–	–	–	–	–
	Odd (4)	962.0	>0.5d	–	–	–	–	–	–

Table 3. Average runtime in seconds of updating 100 and 1,000 elements to a message

Update		Threads/λ							
		1		2		4		8	
		2,048	4,096	2,048	4,096	2,048	4,096	2,048	4,096
Cloud	Prime (100)	1,022.0	15,996.0	526.0	8,157.0	310.0	4,548.0	270.0	4,327.0
	Odd (100)	1.5	11.1	0.8	5.6	0.5	3.0	0.4	2.9
	Odd (1,000)	15.0	111.0	8.1	56.1	4.5	31.5	3.9	28.7
Mobile	Prime (100)	>0.5d	>0.5d	>0.5d	>0.5d	>0.5d	>0.5d	–	–
	Odd (100)	13.2	92.6	6.6	46.5	4.0	24.7	–	–
	Odd (1,000)	132.0	925.0	65.7	462.0	38.3	279.0	–	–

Table 4. Average runtime in seconds of verifying 100- and 1,000-element messages

Verify		Threads/λ							
		1		2		4		8	
		2,048	4,096	2,048	4,096	2,048	4,096	2,048	4,096
Cloud	Prime (100)	1,047.0	18,911.0	553.0	9,724.0	334.0	5,416.0	300.0	5,080.0
	Odd (100)	1.5	11.1	0.9	5.6	0.5	3.2	0.4	3.0
	Odd (1,000)	14.7	110.0	7.4	55.3	4.8	30.4	3.8	28.6
Mobile	Prime (100)	$>0.5d$	$>0.5d$	$>0.5d$	$>0.5d$	$>0.5d$	$>0.5d$	–	–
	Odd (100)	13.0	92.9	6.6	47.2	3.7	24.8	–	–
	Odd (1,000)	130.0	919.0	64.8	461.0	35.7	269.0	–	–
RE-Mote	Prime (4)	$>0.5d$	$>0.5d$	–	–	–	–	–	–
	Odd (4)	951.0	$>0.5d$	–	–	–	–	–	–

6 Conclusion

We presented two use cases where Redactable Signature Schemes (RSS) can be used to a great advantage of all involved parties. With the given building blocks and our adjusted accumulator, we proved that the existing construction—which is taken from the standard model to the random oracle model—becomes practical. We gave exact runtimes for the old and adjusted construction in two real world applications on three very diverse hardware platforms. Our proof of concept implementation on the three platforms showed the infeasibility of the construction in the standard model due to excessive runtime for all operations, whereas the construction in the random oracle model offers practical runtimes on cloud and mobile devices. On the constrained device even the adjusted algorithm already runs for several minutes for only a small number of elements. However no factorisation co-processor was used for any speed-up and the used type of arithmetics are known to be slow on constrained devices. For IoT, future work is to look for usable elliptic curve based redactable signature constructions.

References

1. Ahn, J.H., Boneh, D., Camenisch, J., Hohenberger, S., Shelat, A., Waters, B.: Computing on authenticated data. Cryptology ePrint Archive, Report 2011/096 (2011). http://eprint.iacr.org/
2. Attrapadung, N., Libert, B., Peters, T.: Computing on authenticated data: new privacy definitions and constructions. In: Wang, X., Sako, K. (eds.) ASIACRYPT 2012. LNCS, vol. 7658, pp. 367–385. Springer, Heidelberg (2012). doi:10.1007/978-3-642-34961-4_23
3. Barić, N., Pfitzmann, B.: Collision-free accumulators and fail-stop signature schemes without trees. In: Fumy, W. (ed.) EUROCRYPT 1997. LNCS, vol. 1233, pp. 480–494. Springer, Heidelberg (1997). doi:10.1007/3-540-69053-0_33
4. Bellare, M., Rogaway, P.: Random oracles are practical: a paradigm for designing efficient protocols. In: CCS, pp. 62–73 (1993)

5. Brzuska, C., et al.: Redactable signatures for tree-structured data: definitions and constructions. In: Zhou, J., Yung, M. (eds.) ACNS 2010. LNCS, vol. 6123, pp. 87–104. Springer, Heidelberg (2010). doi:10.1007/978-3-642-13708-2_6

6. Chang, E.-C., Lim, C.L., Xu, J.: Short redactable signatures using random trees. In: Fischlin, M. (ed.) CT-RSA 2009. LNCS, vol. 5473, pp. 133–147. Springer, Heidelberg (2009). doi:10.1007/978-3-642-00862-7_9

7. Coron, J.-S., Naccache, D.: Security analysis of the Gennaro-Halevi-Rabin signature scheme. In: Preneel, B. (ed.) EUROCRYPT 2000. LNCS, vol. 1807, pp. 91–101. Springer, Heidelberg (2000). doi:10.1007/3-540-45539-6_7

8. Derler, D., Hanser, C., Slamanig, D.: Revisiting cryptographic accumulators, additional properties and relations to other primitives. In: Nyberg, K. (ed.) CT-RSA 2015. LNCS, vol. 9048, pp. 127–144. Springer, Heidelberg (2015). doi:10.1007/978-3-319-16715-2_7

9. Derler, D., Pöhls, H.C., Samelin, K., Slamanig, D.: A general framework for redactable signatures and new constructions. In: Kwon, S., Yun, A. (eds.) ICISC 2015. LNCS, vol. 9558, pp. 3–19. Springer, Heidelberg (2016). doi:10.1007/978-3-319-30840-1_1

10. Gennaro, R., Halevi, S., Rabin, T.: Secure hash-and-sign signatures without the random oracle. In: Stern, J. (ed.) EUROCRYPT 1999. LNCS, vol. 1592, pp. 123–139. Springer, Heidelberg (1999). doi:10.1007/3-540-48910-X_9

11. Ghosh, E., Ohrimenko, O., Tamassia, R.: Verifiable member and order queries on a list in zero-knowledge. IACR Cryptology ePrint Archive, p. 632 (2014)

12. Johnson, R., Molnar, D., Song, D., Wagner, D.: Homomorphic signature schemes. In: Preneel, B. (ed.) CT-RSA 2002. LNCS, vol. 2271, pp. 244–262. Springer, Heidelberg (2002). doi:10.1007/3-540-45760-7_17

13. Kundu, A., Bertino, E.: Privacy-preserving authentication of trees and graphs. Int. J. Inf. Secur. 12(6), 467–494 (2013). doi:10.1007/s10207-013-0198-5

14. Legion of the Bouncy Castle Inc: The legion of the bouncy castle. https://bouncycastle.org/specifications.html, October 2016

15. de Meer, H., Liedel, M., Pöhls, H.C., Posegga, J., Samelin, K.: Indistinguishability of one-way accumulators. Technical report MIP-1210, University of Passau (2012)

16. Miyazaki, K., Hanaoka, G., Imai, H.: Digitally signed document sanitizing scheme based on bilinear maps. In: AsiaCCS, pp. 343–354 (2006)

17. Pöhls, H.C., Angelakis, V., Suppan, S., Fischer, K., Oikonomou, G., Tragos, E.Z., Rodriguez, R.D., Mouroutis, T.: Rerum: building a reliable IoT upon privacy- and security- enabled smart objects. In: IEEE WCNC (2014)

18. Pöhls, H.C., Höhne, F.: The role of data integrity in EU digital signature legislation — achieving statutory trust for sanitizable signature schemes. In: Meadows, C., Fernandez-Gago, C. (eds.) STM 2011. LNCS, vol. 7170, pp. 175–192. Springer, Heidelberg (2012). doi:10.1007/978-3-642-29963-6_13

19. Pöhls, H.C., Samelin, K.: On updatable redactable signatures. In: Boureanu, I., Owesarski, P., Vaudenay, S. (eds.) ACNS 2014. LNCS, vol. 8479, pp. 457–475. Springer, Heidelberg (2014). doi:10.1007/978-3-319-07536-5_27

20. Pöhls, H.C., Samelin, K., Posegga, J.: Sanitizable signatures in XML signature — performance, mixing properties, and revisiting the property of transparency. In: Lopez, J., Tsudik, G. (eds.) ACNS 2011. LNCS, vol. 6715, pp. 166–182. Springer, Heidelberg (2011). doi:10.1007/978-3-642-21554-4_10

21. Samelin, K., Pöhls, H.C., Bilzhause, A., Posegga, J., de Meer, H.: On structural signatures for tree data structures. In: Bao, F., Samarati, P., Zhou, J. (eds.) ACNS 2012. LNCS, vol. 7341, pp. 171–187. Springer, Heidelberg (2012). doi:10.1007/978-3-642-31284-7_11

22. Samelin, K., Pöhls, H.C., Bilzhause, A., Posegga, J., de Meer, H.: Redactable signatures for independent removal of structure and content. In: Ryan, M.D., Smyth, B., Wang, G. (eds.) ISPEC 2012. LNCS, vol. 7232, pp. 17–33. Springer, Heidelberg (2012). doi:10.1007/978-3-642-29101-2_2

23. Slamanig, D., Stingl, C.: Disclosing verifiable partial information of signed CDA documents using generalized redactable signatures. In: Healthcom, pp. 146–152 (2009)

24. Steinfeld, R., Bull, L., Zheng, Y.: Content extraction signatures. In: Kim, K. (ed.) ICISC 2002. LNCS, vol. 2288, pp. 163–205. Springer, Heidelberg (2002). doi:10.1007/3-540-45861-1_22

25. Stranacher, K., Krnjic, V., Zefferer, T.: Trust and reliability for public sector data. In: Proceedings of International Conference on e-Business and e-Government, vol. 73, pp. 124–132 (2013)

26. Tragos, E.Z., Angelakis, V., Fragkiadakis, A., Gundlegard, D., Nechifor, S., Oikonomou, G., Pöhls, H.C., Gavras, A.: Enabling reliable and secure IOT-based smart city applications. In: IEEE PERCOM, pp. 111–116 (2014)

27. Wu, Z.-Y., Hsueh, C.-W., Tsai, C.-Y., Lai, F., Lee, H.-C., Chung, Y.: Redactable signatures for signed CDA documents. J. Med. Syst. **36**(3), 1795–1808 (2012). doi:10.1007/s10916-010-9639-0

MultiPol: Towards a Multi-policy Authorization Framework for RESTful Interfaces in the Cloud

Yang Luo[1], Tian Puyang[1], Wu Luo[1], Qingni Shen[1],
Anbang Ruan[2], and Zhonghai Wu[1(✉)]

[1] Peking University, Beijing, China
{luoyang,puyangsky,lwyeluo,qingnishen,wuzh}@pku.edu.cn
[2] University of Oxford, Oxford, UK
anbang.ruan@cs.ox.ac.uk

Abstract. Recently a large number of existing cloud systems adopt representational state transfer (REST) as the interface of their services. The end users or even components inside the cloud invoke RESTful calls to perform various actions. The authorization mechanisms of the existing clouds fail to supply two key elements: unified access control and flexible support for different policies. Moreover, different clouds usually provide distinct access control concepts and policy languages. This might cause confusion for customers whose business is distributed in multiple clouds. In this paper, we propose a multi-policy authorization framework called MultiPol to support various access control policies for OpenStack. The end users can customize or even integrate different policies together to form a single decision via logical connectors. This paper presents the design and implementation of MultiPol, including a new service called Policy Service and an attachment module called Request Filter. Experiments on OpenStack show that MultiPol has improved the flexibility and security of policy management without affecting other services. Meantime, the average performance overhead is as low as 7.8%, which is acceptable for practical use. Since MultiPol is built on REST, it is also adaptive to other clouds which also provide RESTful interfaces.

Keywords: Representational state transfer · Access control · OpenStack · Multi-policy

1 Introduction

Cloud computing has become a revolutionary force for enterprises to reduce their costs by using on-demand computational infrastructures [1–3]. Although being the most widely-adopted open sourced cloud, OpenStack failed to provide adequate consideration on security, especially the access control area. Presently, the critical role of single sign-on in providing cloud security has been well demonstrated by keystone, a standalone authentication service, yet the access control mechanism of OpenStack is still unable to provide strong security. Locally stored policy is used to enforce access control for almost all OpenStack services, and

© Springer International Publishing AG 2016
K.-Y. Lam et al. (Eds.): ICICS 2016, LNCS 9977, pp. 214–226, 2016.
DOI: 10.1007/978-3-319-50011-9_17

the policy is built in, which disallows anyone to modify it except cloud service provider itself. From the perspective of access control, attribute-based access control (ABAC) [4,5] is readily adopted by OpenStack and role-based access control (RBAC) [6] is partially supported as well. However, these models are hard-coded into the cloud and lack adequate flexibility to be customized. The above implementation has several limitations as an approach for providing cloud access control. First, the policy is currently decentralized. All access controls are restricted within the scope of a physical host. A policy supervisor has to suffer preparing a policy for each service and manually deploying them to all cloud nodes, the process of which can be quite unfriendly and error-prone. Second, the security hook code is a headache for developers. A part of the permission checks are even hard-coded into the platform. If a cloud customer is unwilling to use the built-in security policy and desires to customize his own, there will be no way for him to achieve this.

To solve the above-mentioned issues, in this paper, we propose an authorization framework called multiple-policy framework (MultiPol). It includes a stand-alone service called `Policy Service`, and an attachment module called `Request Filter` which is required to be attached to other OpenStack services to filter the requests sent to them (we state it as "attached" not "patched" because it is highly loose-coupled with other services). With the MultiPol framework, each representational state transfer (REST) [7] request towards the cloud (including requests sent by not only outside consumers but also the cloud infrastructure itself) is filtered by `Request Filter` first. `Request Filter` then validates it by sending its security contexts to `Policy Service`, which will make a proper decision based on policy enforcement. If `Policy Service` says yes to this access, the request will be permitted by `Request Filter` to reach the demanded service. Otherwise `Request Filter` will reject it by returning an error. The MultiPol framework highlights the achievement of decoupling access controls from functionalities of cloud in code level, which facilitates both cloud service providers and tenant administrators to have a global view on their security perimeters: the entire cloud or an individual tenant. And the security settings, especially policy configurations can be modified through the unified `Policy Service` interface. Policy Service manages multiple policies provided by both cloud providers and consumers. Several calls are provided by `Policy Service` and `Request Filter` as a part of the framework. We have implemented the security framework based on the latest OpenStack Mitaka [8]. Despite the fact that OpenStack employs REST as its primary interface, the MultiPol framework is general enough to be applied to other kind of interfaces, like simple object access protocol (SOAP), etc.

The remainder of this paper is organized as follows. Section 2 elaborates on the background. Section 3 presents the design of MultiPol framework. Section 4 brings the implementation. Section 5 describes experimental results. Section 6 concludes this paper.

2   Background

For the past few years, there has been a considerable interest in environments that support multiple and complex access control policies [9–13]. Access control as a service (ACaaS), proposed in [14] by Wu et al., provided a new cloud service to enforce a comprehensive and fine-grained access control. It is claimed to support multiple access control models, whereas there is no evidence that this approach applies to the models except RBAC. And this work is highly based on IAM provided by AWS, which makes it difficult to apply for other clouds. OpenStack access control (OSAC), proposed in [15] by Tang et al., has presented a formalized description for conceptions in keystone, such as domains and projects in addition to roles. It further proposed a domain trust extension for OSAC to facilitate secure cross-domain authorization. This work is orthogonal to ours, since it mainly focuses on the enhancement of keystone. The domain trust decision made by OSAC can be used as a policy condition in MultiPol, which increases the granularity of access controls. So our work can be well integrated together. The work proposed in [16] by Jin et al., has defined a formal ABAC specification suitable for infrastructure as a service (IaaS) and implemented it in OpenStack. It includes two models: the operational model $IaaS_{op}$ and the administrative model $IaaS_{ad}$, which provide fine-grained access control for tenants. However, this work only focuses on isolated tenants, cross-tenant access control is not supported. Moreover, their model is bundled with ABAC, which lacks the flexibility for cloud users to design a policy which is based on a customized model. The existing solutions usually follow a path by trying to progress in terms of expressiveness and functionality. However, a vast majority of them remain merely academic and lack practical acceptance owing to their complexity in usage or computation. So instead of making a universal policy model applicable for all scenarios, we try to narrow down the scope to the most popular cloud systems. And we found that recently, REST [7] has become the most widely-accepted interface standard for the clouds.

Systems that conform to the constraints of REST can be called RESTful. RESTful systems typically, but not always, communicate over hypertext transfer protocol (HTTP) with methods like `GET`, `POST`, `PUT` and `DELETE` that web browsers use to retrieve web pages and send data to remote servers.

As being an abstract architectural style instead of a strictly defined protocol, REST does not seek to specify the accurate syntax on the request form. This fairly results in the current numerous implementations respectively from different service providers. However, based on the analysis upon the interface design from mainstream web services in the marketplace, we can extract the representative elements for a typical RESTful request. A standard request form (SRF) is defined from those elements to ensure that the vast majority of the RESTful requests would fit in it. The MultiPol framework accepts the input of SRF requests to ensure it can be seamlessly applied to a control system using the SRF. Now we present the definition of SRF as below:

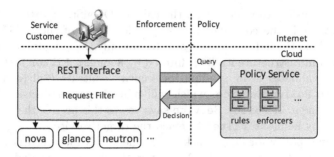

Fig. 1. Architecture of multiPol authorization framework

```
Verb
{http|https}://DomainName[/Version]/Object/
```

Verb: the HTTP method, possible values are GET, POST, PUT and DELETE.
DomainName: the domain name of the cloud service provider.
Version: the version of the REST interface this request is asking for. Offering version numbers in REST calls is usually a good design for maintaining multiple API versions simultaneously.
Object: the part of the path in the URI, which identifies the resource. It is generally an ordered list of strings separated by /.

It is notable that as an essential part for an access behavior, the **subject** does not show up in the SRF. This is due to the fact that the **subject** is usually implicitly embedded in the HTTP header, or represented by an access token retrieved in the previous authentication step. Therefore, this entity needs to be obtained according to the specific implementation. An example of a policy rule for RESTful interfaces is shown below.

```
Subject, Object, Verb -> Effect
```

In the above expression, **Effect** is the authorization decision that the policy declares to enforce. To support both positive and negative authorizations, **Effect** can be assigned to either **Allow** or **Deny**. Finally, the entire hierarchy of the RESTful policy syntax can be described in backus-naur form like below:

```
Policy ::= [Version,] Rules
Rules ::= {Rule}
Rule ::= Subject, Object, Verb -> Effect
Verb ::= GET | POST | PUT | DELETE
Effect ::= Allow | Deny
```

3   MultiPol Design

The architecture of the MultiPol authorization framework is shown in Fig. 1. We divide it into two parts: **Request Filter** and **Policy Service**. **Request**

`Filter` is responsible to intercept all the calls to OpenStack's REST interface. `Policy Service` is the container of policy rules. Each of the REST requests towards the cloud (including requests sent by not only the outside consumers but also the cloud infrastructure itself) is filtered by `Request Filter` first. `Request Filter` then validates it by sending its security contexts (`Subject`, `Object`, `Verb`, etc.) to `Policy Service`, which will make a proper decision based on policy enforcement. If `Policy Service` says yes to this access, the request will be permitted by `Request Filter` to reach the target service.

The original policy for OpenStack is a single JSON file called `policy.json` locally stored on the service node. A number of rules are provided in that file and are supposed to be globally enforced for every cloud user, including cloud administrators. A user cannot specify his own policy rules or make changes to the original policy enforcement mechanism. This structure was poorly designed and failed to meet policy customization demands from both consumer and cloud provider's perspectives. Therefore, the MultiPol framework intends to solve this issue. In the MultiPol framework, two types of policy are designed as below:

Global Policy. This type of policy is provided by the cloud provider. It can be enforced on all tenants across the whole cloud, and only cloud administrator can modify it. A global policy is public to be viewed and used by all cloud users, just like the built-in types for a VM instance.

Customer Policy. This type of policy is configurable on the consumer side. It only applies within a tenant-wide scope, and a tenant's administrator can modify it, while other tenants can neither view nor change it.

The MultiPol framework is based on metadata, which is a file that describes the multiple policies and organizes them into a tree structure. Policies can be nested, the inner policy is called a "sub policy" of the outer one, the outmost policy is the root of the policy tree and will be enforced by MultiPol in a depth-first manner. Policy is composed of a number of fields including name, type, enforcer, version and rules, which are described in the Table 1.

When we talk about a security policy, we do not quite distinguish between practical policy rules or just the enforcing logic for this sort of policy. MultiPol has clarified these conceptions by defining them as rules and enforcer. A security system that supports multiple policies typically allows its users to design their policy rules. However, the underlying enforcement logic of them is usually unchangeable. MultiPol makes it customizable even for cloud users to offer maximum flexibility. In OpenStack, policy enforcement was originally implemented as a module called `policy.py`, which can be viewed as an enforcer for different policy languages including the original ABAC policy. We refactor it by extracting out the shared logic of a general enforcer into an inheritable base class, so MultiPol can support multiple policies. A policy language author for the MultiPol should write his own enforcer in accordance with the base class declarations. These declarations can be simplified as below:

- **Input**: request vector (subject, object, verb), policy rules
- **Output**: decision (`permit|deny`)

Table 1. The fields of a multiPol policy

Fild	Meaning	
Name	The identifier for the policy, must be unique within the metadata	
Type	A flag tells whether the policy is provided by cloud provider itself, possible values are:	
	Global	This policy is provided by the cloud provider itself, customer can just refer to it by name
	Customer	This is a user-customized policy, and the customer has to specify its content. This value is by default
Enforcer	The processing logic for this policy, output ips decision, possible values are:	
	Default	The original ABAC policy enforcer adopted by policy.json
	op-and	The intersection enforcer, meaning all sub policies will be composed in a deny-override manner
	op-or	The union enforcer, meaning all sub policy decisions will be composed in an allow-override manner
	all-pass	A special enforcer that permits all accesses
	all-forbid	A special enforcer that denies all accesses
	custom	A cloud user can customize a policy enforcer on his own
Version	A descriptive string that indicates the current version of the policy	
Rules	This field's meaning varies based on different situations:	
	When *enforcer* = all-pass or all-forbid	This field will be omitted
	When *enforcer* = op-and or op-or	This field will be a name list of its sub policies
	other conditions	The field will be the rules of the policy

Through this mechanism, a cloud user can customize their own security module by submitting his policy to the cloud. Since enforcer is essentially Python code, the cloud provider is required to provide some sorts of code examine measures for uploaded enforcer files to ensure there are no malicious code included.

4   Implementation

4.1   Request Filter

As a part of the MultiPol framework, `Request Filter` serves as an extension to target services to provide access controls for them. OpenStack typically provides its services based on web server gateway interface specification (WSGI). This standard specifies a structure called filter chain, which is an extension mechanism that supports the preprocessing and filtering of incoming requests before they arrive to the application side. Keystone has utilized these filters to offer authentication for the cloud. Thus a natural way to think about it would be implementing `Request Filter` as a WSGI filter as well. It is called `multipol_enforce` and exactly located after `keystonecontext` (keystone's middleware). We believe this is an optimal place as access control always comes after authentication.

Request Filter attempts to reduce invasiveness to other services by limiting modification of Request Filter to a couple of lines of configuration, so no existing code change is involved. The following code fragment shows Request Filter's modification in nova's configuration: */etc/nova/api-paste.ini.*

```
[composite:openstack_compute_api_v2]
keystone = compute_req_id faultwrap sizelimit authtoken keystonecontext
multipol_enforce ratelimit osapi_compute_app_v2
keystone_nolimit = compute_req_id faultwrap sizelimit authtoken
keystonecontext multipol_enforce osapi_compute_app_v2
[filter:multipol_enforce]
paste.filter_factory = multipol.rf.enforce:Multipol Enforce.factory
```

Request Filter normally queries for a security decision each time when needed. This manner will bring additional time overhead, mainly the network latency. To alleviate this situation, a cache module is provided in Request Filter for each decision from Policy Service. So that a new request can just use the cached result, instead of accessing Policy Service again. If cache misses, Request Filter then queries Policy Service for decision making, and newly obtained ruling result will be buffered in the cache.

4.2   Policy Service

Policy Service is the newly proposed service which plays a crucial part in the MultiPol enforcement framework. It provides access controls for all functions calls to the REST interfaces of the cloud. The structure of Policy Service is shown in Fig. 2. It primarily composes of three parts:

- API Module: serves as a REST interface of the Policy Service.
- Verify Module: consults access rules in the policy and determines an access ruling result in response to the verify query from Request Filter.
- Update Module: manages the storage of all policies in the Policy Service, controls the policy updates and also provides a functionality to send notifications to Request Filter for events like cache wiping.

Additionally, a database and a message queue are also required by Policy Service just like other services. The database is currently only used for storing metadata about the policy. The practical policy rules are stored on disk. The message queue is used to provide communications among API Module, Verify Module and Update Module.

It is worth noting that the Policy Service can be deployed on multiple nodes just as other services do, so requests to Policy Service API will be load-balanced to gain performance and avoid single point failures.

Since Policy Service is also provided as a service, its interfaces also require to be access controlled by Request Filter. This means that all requests to functions provided by Policy Service will be mediated by Policy Service itself. This kind of manner might cause deadlock if not handled correctly:

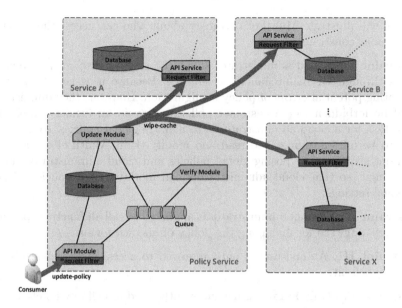

Fig. 2. The components of `Policy Service`

a function call to `Policy Service` asks for a permission from `Policy Service`. It is easy to see that the `verify` operation will cause an endless loop of calling and it requires to be specially handled to interrupt the loop. A rational solution is letting `Request Filter` act differently for this function: instead of querying `Policy Service` for decision, `Request Filter` only performs a local check to ensure the caller is checking his own access rights. Since the caller context of a `verify` call just comes from the request context which has been authenticated by keystone, this prevents a malicious user to fake another user's identity and peep at other's access rights by testing against the `verify` function.

`Update Module` is the handler for policy update matters, including managing policy storage, enforcing policy constraints and calling `Request Filter` for purpose like cache wiping.

Since multiple policies are supported in `Policy Service`, first we need to design the storage arrangement to hold these policies. A good implementation is storing the policies based on their types. Global policies are cloud-wide functioned and should be stored in a top-level path like `/etc/multipol/`. While customer policies are only restricted to tenants and should be stored in a tenant-specific path like `/etc/multipol/customer_policy/%TENANT_ID%/` (where `%TENANT_ID%` represents the tenant identifier). The filename of a policy is identical with its occurrence in the metadata, so the enforcer can easily find the related policy files by parsing the metadata. Since a policy name in a metadata is unique, there will not be a filename conflict in the storage stage. For convenience, we refer to policy, enforcer, metadata together as policy in this paper.

Next we will illustrate MultiPol's strategy about who can access the policy. It includes four constraints:

Constraint I. A cloud administrator should be privileged to read all tenants' policies through for maintenance convenience. Because it is helpful for troubleshooting potential errors of policy configuration. However, the administrator should be forbidden to set customer policies to avoid an insider attack. The second task for a cloud administrator is to manage global policies, so he is supposed to be fully authorized to read and modify them. MultiPol enforces this constraint straightly by posing global policies and cloud administrators in the same tenant, so that cloud administrators can modify global policies without additional settings.

Constraint II. A tenant administrator is approved to call all functions provided by `Policy Service` for managing the policy of his own tenant.

Constraint III. An end-user is only approved to access resources in his own tenant by default.

Constraint IV. Only `Policy Service` is authorized to call any functions provided by `Request Filter`.

Based on the above constraints, we can deduce several global policies, which can be enforced by the MultiPol framework for all the cloud users:

- `enable`: the policy enabling the rights for the administrators to configure their policies. This policy is based on `Constraint I` and `Constraint II` and enforced by `Policy Service`.
- `restrict`: the policy to ensure users can only have rights to access resources belonging to their own tenants, so unauthorized access is restricted. This policy is based on `Constraint III` and enforced by `Policy Service`.
- `self-protect`: the policy to ensure functions provided by `Request Filter` cannot be invoked by any other code except `Policy Service`. This policy is based on `Constraint IV`. It is notable that this policy is directly enforced by `Request Filter` to avoid the above mentioned deadlock.

5   Experiments

This section shows how we implement MultiPol enforcement framework in the OpenStack cloud and evaluate its performance and usability.

5.1   Performance

We used tempest [17] for benchmarking. We compared the standard OpenStack Mitaka cloud against an alternative with the MultiPol framework applied (for both `Request Filter`'s cache off and on). The results are shown in Table 2. The additional time introduced by the security framework is acceptable, as the average cost was 14.2% for cache disabled, and 7.8% for cache enabled.

Table 2. Tempest benchmarks, time in seconds

Service	Mitaka	MultiPol	%Overhead	MultiPol+Cache	%Overhead
Nova	643.85	709.31	10.2%	697.27	8.3%
Glance	246.34	288.71	17.2%	275.13	11.7%
Neutron	238.16	268.95	12.9%	253.34	6.4%
Cinder	157.22	199.33	26.8%	175.71	11.8%
Heat	324.35	371.28	14.5%	349.68	7.8%
Ceilometer	698.63	723.32	3.5%	706.14	1.1%

This overhead is primarily due to the communication delays between `Policy Service` and `Request Filter`. The worst case was 26.8% for cache disabled and 11.8% for cache enabled in cinder. This result is expected because of the relatively small amount of time consumed in each glance call compared to the execution of permission checking. The effect of MultiPol to ceilometer is not obvious due to fewer operations needed to be access controlled. The average additional cost per function call is close to 121 ms, which is a fairly small figure compared with the delay across a large-scale public network like Internet.

Since the cache mechanism in `Request Filter` is a critical component, it is important to evaluate its memory usage. A record in the cache is stored in a format like a vector, which contains information of `Subject`, `Object` and `Verb`. The calculation shows that one record requires 150 Bytes on average. To be more intuitive, we use Tempest to test all commands of OpenStack nova. The size of used cache turns out to be 68.5 KBytes after running 403 tests. Let us assume that the usage of an individual user roughly equals to a Tempest test. If the size of cache is 1 GBytes, a cloud based on Openstack with one nova API service can support nearly 15000 users (1G/68.5K). This capacity is adequate for practical use. Moreover, we can utilize a caching algorithm like least recently used (LRU) to delete a couple of records when the cache size exceeds a preset threshold,

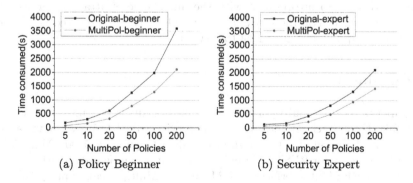

(a) Policy Beginner (b) Security Expert

Fig. 3. Comparison of time consumed on designing of two different policies

such as 85 %. Therefore, the size of cache required by `Request Filter` is affordable, which cannot affect the usage of the MultiPol enforcement framework.

5.2 Usability

We analyzed the total time consumed in the policy designing process conducted by end-users at different degrees (e.g., policy beginners and security experts). The results are shown in Fig. 3. MultiPol has mitigated almost 41.3% efforts for a beginner and 32.1% for security expert on the average. This is because MultiPol allows to use different policies, and we have provided some built-in policy enforcers like ABAC, RBAC, etc. So the users can just choose to write the policy they are familiar with. Moreover, MultiPol has provided a standard request form shared by all kinds of REST interfaces. No matter how many REST systems a customer needs to manage, he only needs to learn the basic elements of access control once, like subject, object, verb, etc. It saves a large number of efforts by reducing the learning time for different policies.

From the developers' perspective, We also give a rough estimate of the scale and complexity of adding centralized security enforcement to OpenStack. In summary, `Request Filter`'s code modification to a service was only limited to several Python code files, summing up to hundreds of LOC. And those components increased in size less than 1.5% (except `Policy Service`). Besides these code modifications, we also examined other types of changes involved, like configuration changes, data changes, etc. Since `Request Filter` is designed to be a WSGI attachment, this needs a couple of lines of modifications in the configuration of that service.

The changes required to implement the MultiPol framework did not involve any modifications to the existing Python code or RESTful calls. A couple of calls are provided by `Policy Service` to support policy management for both cloud consumers and service providers. Furthermore, an internal call is extended on `Request Filter` for cache wiping. Despite the fact that `Request Filter`'s call is sharing the same RESTful interface with the attached service, it does not actually increase invasiveness since they are straightly handled by `Request Filter` and have no involvement with the inner logic of attached service. All applications that run on the stock OpenStack cloud can be executed unchanged on a cloud equipped with MultiPol framework.

6 Conclusion

This paper proposes a multi-policy access control framework called MultiPol for clouds like OpenStack. It includes a new service called `Policy Service` and an attachment module for target services called `Request Filter`. MultiPol is especially designed for RESTful interfaces, so that it can be used in other clouds that support RESTful interfaces too. Meantime, Multipol can express different policies by providing the enforcer mechanism. It utilizes cache to minimize the performance overhead of remote permission checking. The experimental results on OpenStack Mitaka indicate the average enforcement overhead is 7.8%, which is an acceptable result.

Acknowledgment. We thank the reviewers for their help improving this paper. This work was supported by the National High Technology Research and Development Program ("863" Program) of China under Grant No. 2015AA016009, the National Natural Science Foundation of China under Grant No. 61232005, 61672062, and the Science and Technology Program of ShenZhen, China under Grant No. JSGG20140516162852628.

References

1. Crago, S., Dunn, K., Eads, P., Hochstein, L., Kang, D.-I., Kang, M., Modium, D., Singh, K., Suh, J., Walters, J.P.: Heterogeneous cloud computing. In: 2011 IEEE International Conference on Cluster Computing (CLUSTER), pp. 378–385. IEEE (2011)
2. Subashini, S., Kavitha, V.: A survey on security issues in service delivery models of cloud computing. J. Netw. Comput. Appl. **34**(1), 1–11 (2011)
3. Takabi, H., Joshi, J.B., Ahn, G.-J.: Security and privacy challenges in cloud computing environments. IEEE Secur. Privacy **6**, 24–31 (2010)
4. Yuan, E., Tong, J.: Attributed based access control (ABAC) for web services. In: Proceedings of 2005 IEEE International Conference on Web Services, ICWS 2005. IEEE (2005)
5. Hu, V.C., Kuhn, D.R., Ferraiolo, D.F.: Attribute-based access control. Computer **2**, 85–88 (2015)
6. Sandhu, R.S., Coyne, E.J., Feinstein, H.L., Youman, C.E.: Role-based access control models. Computer **2**, 38–47 (1996)
7. Fielding, R.T.: Architectural styles and the design of network-based software architectures. Ph.D. dissertation, University of California, Irvine (2000)
8. OpenStack: Openstack mitaka (2016). https://www.openstack.org/software/mitaka
9. Ribeiro, C., Zúquete, A., Ferreira, P., Guedes, P.: SPL: an access control language for security policies with complex constraints. In: Network and Distributed System Security Symposium (NDSS01), pp. 89–107 (2001)
10. Bertino, E., Jajodia, S., Samarati, P.: Supporting multiple access control policies in database systems. In: Proceedings of 1996 IEEE Symposium on Security and Privacy, vol. 1996, pp. 94–107. IEEE (1996)
11. Carney, M., Loe, B.: A comparison of methods for implementing adaptive security policies. In: Proceedings of the Seventh USENIX Security Symposium, pp. 1–14 (1998)
12. Jajodia, S., Samarati, P., Subrahmanian, V., Bertino, E.: A unified framework for enforcing multiple access control policies. ACM Sigmod Record **26**(2), 474–485 (1997)
13. Minsky, N.H., Ungureanu, V.: Unified support for heterogeneous security policies in distributed systems. In: 7th USENIX Security Symposium, pp. 131–142 (1998)
14. Wu, R., Zhang, X., Ahn, G.-J., Sharifi, H., Xie, H.: Acaas: access control as a service for iaas cloud. In: 2013 International Conference on Social Computing (SocialCom), pp. 423–428. IEEE (2013)
15. Tang, B., Sandhu, R.: Extending openstack access control with domain trust. In: Au, M.H., Carminati, B., Kuo, C.-C.J. (eds.) NSS 2014. LNCS, vol. 8792, pp. 54–69. Springer, Heidelberg (2014). doi:10.1007/978-3-319-11698-3_5

16. Jin, X., Krishnan, R., Sandhu, R.: Role and attribute based collaborative admin-istration of intra-tenant cloud iaaS. In: 2014 International Conference on Collabo-rative Computing: Networking, Applications and Worksharing (CollaborateCom), pp. 261–274. IEEE (2014)
17. OpenStack, Openstack tempest (2016). https://github.com/openstack/tempest

Provably Secure Identity-Based Identification and Signature Schemes with Parallel-PVR

Bo Song and Yiming Zhao[✉]

Laboratory of Cryptography and Information Security,
Fudan University, Shanghai, China
{songb15,zhym}@fudan.edu.cn

Abstract. Identity-based identification and signature (IBI/IBS) schemes are two of the most fundamental cryptographic primitives with greatly simplified public key management. Meanwhile, code-based cryptography is one of few alternatives supposed to be secure in a post-quantum world, so several code-based IBI/IBS schemes have been proposed. However, with increasingly profound researches on coding theory, the security reduction and efficiency of such schemes have been invalidated and challenged. In this paper, we construct provably secure IBI/IBS schemes from code assumptions against impersonation under active and concurrent attacks through PVR signature and Or-proof technique. We also present the parallel-PVR technique to decrease parameter values while maintaining the standard security level. Compared to other code-based IBI/IBS schemes, our schemes achieve not only preferable public parameter size, private key size, communication cost and signature length due to better parameter choices, but also provably secure.

Keywords: Identity-based cryptography · Code-based cryptography · Syndrome decoding · Parallel-CFS · PVR signature · Or-proof

1 Introduction

Public key management is one of the most critical issues on multi-party communications and public key cryptography. In 1984, Shamir [24] introduced identity-based public key cryptography, which largely simplifies the management of public keys for the authentication of users. The key point is that the public key of a user can be his identity *id*, i.e., public information about that user, such as a name, a phone number, or an e-mail address. Therefore, it is very appealing to make fundamental cryptographic primitives, i.e., identification protocol and digital signature, gain such advantages [4,15,18].

With identity-based identification and signature (IBI/IBS) schemes, people could prove their identities and the authenticity of their messages to others without specific public keys [15]. After identity initialization, no further interaction with the authority is required during the identity verification. A list of valid identities is not necessary. Literally unlimited number of identities can

© Springer International Publishing AG 2016
K.-Y. Lam et al. (Eds.): ICICS 2016, LNCS 9977, pp. 227–238, 2016.
DOI: 10.1007/978-3-319-50011-9_18

join the system. Meanwhile the confidentiality and integrity of the identity are kept regardless of the number of verification. It make possible to digitize identity cards, passports, credit cards and other indispensable identity tools in the modern society with availability and provable security.

At the same time, with the development of quantum computers and other attacks on number factoring or discrete logarithm problems [3,27], *code-based cryptography* represents one of few alternatives supposed to be secure under such circumstance. McEliece [20] proposed the first code-based public cryptosystem in 1978. Since then, as we never put all eggs in one basket, a wide range of code-based cryptographic primitives has been proposed, such as digital signatures, identification protocols and hash functions [21]. Moreover, compared to traditional cryptosystems, many of them also show the advantage on fast computation [11,21]. In 2009, Cayrel et al. [7] proposed first code-based IBI/IBS schemes, or the mCFS-Stern scheme. It can be regarded as a combination of the CFS signature scheme [9] and the Stern identification protocol [25,26]. There are several improved mCFS-Stern schemes are proposed since then [2,28].

However, with the development of code-based cryptography, security and efficiency issues on the mCFS-Stern scheme have arisen. Firstly, Faugère et al. [12] developed a high rate distinguisher for Goppa codes so that the security proof of mCFS-Stern scheme is invalidated. Secondly, Bleichenbacher [17] showed an attack based on the Generalized Birthday Algorithm [19]. It decreases the security level from $2^{\frac{mt}{2}}$ to $2^{\frac{mt}{3}}$ so that increased parameters are required to maintain a required security level, i.e., 2^{80}. Thirdly, other improved mCFS-Stern schemes, either using quasi-dyadic Goppa codes in the user key extraction algorithm [2] or modifying the Stern protocol so that the cheating probability of each round reduced from $\frac{2}{3}$ to $\frac{1}{2}$ [1,8], are vulnerable to the very recent structural attack on quasi-cyclic (QC) or quasi-dyadic (QD) alternant/Goppa codes [13].

Our Contribution. In this paper, we first propose provably secure identity-based identification and signature schemes with the PVR signature [23] technique applied in the user key extraction algorithm. It does not rely on the indistinguishability between a binary Goppa code and a random code, whereas it is required in the CFS signature scheme and has been invalidated by the distinguisher. Moreover, we present the parallel-PVR technique, inspired by the parallel-CFS technique [16]. It decreases the value of parameters while maintaining the standard security level, which used to be highly influenced by the Bleichenbacher attack. It also might be of an independent interest in the code-based digital signature. Finally, we adapt the Or-proof technique [18,28] to our schemes so that they are secure against impersonation under active and concurrent attacks (id-imp-ca) instead of passive attacks (id-imp-pa). Currently, our schemes are the only code-based IBI/IBS schemes which are provably secure and they also achieve better efficiency compared to the mCFS-Stern scheme.

The paper is organized as follows: In Sect. 2, we provide some preliminaries. We propose basic provably secure IBI/IBS schemes from code assumptions in Sect. 3. In Sect. 4, we further optimize our schemes with parallel-PVR and improve their security level. We discuss the parameters in Sect. 5 and conclude in Sect. 6.

2   Preliminaries

We first provide some backgrounds and notions for code-based cryptography and then review the definition of identity-based identification and signature schemes in this section.

2.1   Code-Based Cryptography

Let C denotes a binary linear-error correcting code of length $n = 2^m$ and dimension k, or a $[n, k]$ code is a subspace of dimension k of $\mathbb{F}_2^n$. The elements of the set C are called *codewords*. A generator matrix G of a $[n, k]$ code C is a matrix whose rows form a basis of C. A *parity check matrix* H of C is an $(n - k) \times n$ matrix whose rows form a basis of the orthogonal complement of C. The *syndrome* of a vector $x \in \mathbb{F}_2^n$ with respect to H is the vector $Hx^T \in \mathbb{F}_2^{n-k}$. The error correcting capability of the code is $t \leqslant \lceil \frac{d-1}{2} \rceil$, where d is the minimum Hamming distance of C. The Hamming distance between two words refers to the number of coordinates where they differ. The Hamming weight of a vector x, or wt(x), is the number of non-zero entries. We use the symbol $\overset{\$}{\leftarrow}$ to denote the uniformly random selection, and use the symbol $\|$ to denote the concatenation.

The Bounded Decoding Problem (BD). Let n and k be two positive integers and $n \geqslant k$.

Input. $s \overset{\$}{\leftarrow} \mathbb{F}_2^{n-k}$, $\omega = \frac{n-k}{\log_2 n}$, and $H \overset{\$}{\leftarrow} \mathbb{F}_2^{(n-k) \times n}$.
Find. a word $x \in \mathbb{F}_2^n$ such that wt$(x) \leqslant \omega$ and $Hx^T = s$.

The BD problem is showed to be NP-complete in [5]. The advantage of a probabilistic polynomial-time (PPT) algorithm solving the BD problem for $[n, k]$ code should be negligible.

Randomized Courtois-Finiasz-Sendrier Signature Scheme. Courtois et al. [9] first proposed a practical code-based signature scheme, or the *CFS* scheme. Dallot [10] proposed a randomized variant *mCFS* and proved mCFS is strongly unforgeable under chosen message attack at that time. The scheme works as follows:

Key Generation. Set $t = \frac{n-k}{\log_2 n}$. The private key is a $(n - k) \times n$ parity check matrix H of a t-error correcting Goppa code, a non-singular matrix Q and a permutation matrix P. The public key is the $(n - k) \times n$ matrix $\tilde{H} = QHP$.
Sign.
1. $i \overset{\$}{\leftarrow} \mathbb{F}_2^{n-k}$
2. Use the decoding algorithm to decode $Q^{-1}h(m\|i)$. h is a cryptographic hash function and m is the signing message.
3. If the decoding result $x' = \perp$, go back to step 1. It needs $t!$ decodings on average.

   4. Output $(i, x = x'P)$.
Verify.
   1. Compute $s' = \tilde{H}x^T$ and $s = h(m\|i)$.
   2. If $s' = s$ and $\mathrm{wt}(x) \leqslant t$, then the signature is valid; otherwise return false.

The security reduction of the scheme relies on the indistinguishability between a binary Goppa code and a random code. However, it is invalidated by a high rate distinguisher for Goppa codes [12]. Recently, Mathew et al. [23] proposed the PVR signature scheme. Which altered the key-construct of the CFS signature and presented a formal proof of PVR without such assumption. Meanwhile, Bleichenbacher [17] showed an attack so that it has to increase the parameters of CFS such as m and t to achieve the same security level. Finiasz proposed the Parallel-CFS [16], which resisted such attack through performing multiple complete-decoding-based signing processes.

The Stern Identification Scheme. Stern [25, 26] proposed a standard identification scheme based on error-correcting codes. Given a random public $(n-k) \times n$ matrix H over $\mathbb{F}_2$. Each user P receives a secret key x of n bits and $\mathrm{wt}(x) = t$. The public key of P is $s = Hx^T$. To prove to a verifier V that the prover P is the user corresponding to the public key s, P runs the following identification protocol with his secret key x:

Commitment. P randomly chooses $y \in \mathbb{F}_2^n$ and a permutation σ of $\{1, 2, \cdots, n\}$. P sends to V the commitments c_1, c_2, and c_3 such that: $c_1 = h(\sigma\|Hy^T); c_2 = h(\sigma(y)); c_3 = h(\sigma(y \oplus x))$, where h denotes a cryptographic hash function.
Challenge. V randomly sends $b \in \{0, 1, 2\}$ to P.
Answer.
   If $b = 0$: P reveals y and σ.
   If $b = 1$: P reveals $(y \oplus x)$ and σ.
   If $b = 2$: P reveals $\sigma(y)$ and $\sigma(x)$.
Verification.
   If $b = 0$: V verifies that c_1, c_2 have been honestly calculated.
   If $b = 1$: V verifies that c_1, c_3 have been honestly calculated.
   If $b = 2$: V verifies that c_2, c_3 have been honestly calculated, and $\mathrm{wt}(\sigma(x))$ is t.
Repeat. Repeat the above four steps for γ times so that the expected security level is reached.

Remark 1. During the verification step, if b equals 1, Hy^T can be directly derived from $H(y \oplus x)^T$ through: $Hy^T = H(y \oplus x)^T \oplus Hx^T = H(y \oplus x)^T \oplus s$.

Theorem 1. *The Stern identification protocol (P, V) is a proof of knowledge system with knowledge error $(\frac{2}{3})^\gamma$[26].*

2.2 Identity-Based Identification and Signature

In this section, we review the definition and security model for an identity-based identification scheme (IBI) following [4,28]. An identity-based signature scheme (IBS) can be derived from IBI through Fiat-Shamir heuristic [15].

IBI Definition. An identity-based identification scheme $\mathcal{IBI}$ = (MKGen, UKGen, $\overline{P}$, $\overline{V}$) consists of four PPT algorithms as follows:

Master key generation algorithm (MKGen). It takes 1^κ as input, where κ is the security parameter. It returns a pair of the system public parameters mpk, and the master secret key msk, which is known only to a master entity.
User key extraction algorithm (UKGen). It takes msk and an identity $id \in \{0,1\}^*$ as inputs. It returns a user secret key $usk[id]$.
Interactive identification protocol ($\overline{P}$, $\overline{V}$). The prover P with identity id runs algorithm $\overline{P}$ with initial state $usk[id]$, and the verifier V runs $\overline{V}$ with (mpk, id). When $\overline{V}$ returns 'accept' or 'reject', the protocol ends.

Completeness: For all $\kappa \in \mathbb{N}$, $id \in \{0,1\}^*$, $(mpk, msk) \leftarrow$ MKGen(1^κ), and $usk[id] \leftarrow$ UKGen(msk, i), the protocol between $\overline{P}$ with initial state $usk[id]$ and $\overline{V}$ with (mpk, id) always ends with $\overline{V}$ outputing 'accept'.

Security Models. There are three security models, i.e., impersonation under passive (id-imp-pa) attacks, active (id-imp-aa), and concurrent (id-imp-ca) attacks. The id-imp-pa secure implies the adversary can query the conversation between P and V while the id-imp-aa/ca secure implies the adversary acts a malicious V to communicate with P. The id-imp-ca security implies the adversary can concurrently issue proving queries instead of only one interactive query at a time for the id-imp-aa secure. The formal definitions will be shown in the full paper due to page limitation.

Code-Based IBI Schemes. Cayrel et al. [7] proposed the first IBI scheme from code assumption with security proof. It combines the mCFS signature scheme and the Stern identification protocol (mCFS-Stern) as follows:

MKGen. Set mpk and msk as the public parameters and the private key of mCFS scheme respectively.
UKGen. Generate a mCFS signature (i, x) of the identity id. Set $usk[id] = (i, x)$.
Interactive identification protocol. P first sends i to V. Then P is initialized with x and V is initialized with $h(id\|i)$. P communicates with V through the Stern identification protocol.

Cayrel et al. [7] show the mCFS-Stern scheme is id-imp-pa secure. Moreover, Yang et al. [28] proved the scheme also implies id-imp-aa secure. To achieve id-imp-ca secure, Yang et al. also proposed a new variant of the mCFS-Stern scheme, which introduced the OR-proof technique [18].

Theorem 2. *Yang's identification protocol (P, V) is a proof of knowledge system with knowledge error $(\frac{2}{3})^\gamma$* [28].

Remark 2. It should be noticed that the user key extraction of the mCFS-Stern scheme cannot resist the Bleichenbacher attack and the security proof relies on the indistinguishability between a binary Goppa code and a random code, which has been already invalidated.

Fiat-Shamir Heuristic and IBS Schemes. According to Bellare et al. [4], identity-based signature (IBS) schemes could be constructed from convertible standard signatures or IBI schemes through Fiat and Shamir Heuristic. Unfortunately, code-based signature schemes, e.g., mCFS signature, are not convertible since no trapdoor samplable relation has been found to fit the key generation of existing signature schemes. Therefore, we adopt the latter method to construct IBS schemes.

Fiat and Shamir [15] proposed a general paradigm to drive a secure signature scheme from an identification scheme. Specifically, given a identification scheme with the commitment α, the challenge bit β, and the response γ, the signature for the message m is the transcript (α, β, γ), where $\beta = h(\alpha, n)$ and h is a cryptographic hash function. The verifier verifies the signature as V in the identification scheme. The paradigm will be used to derive the IBS schemes from our IBI schemes in the paper without security loss [22].

3   Provably Secure IBI/IBS Schemes

In this section, we propose a provably secure identity-based identification scheme, the PVR-Stern scheme. It is id-imp-pa secure and the security reduction is no longer depending on the indistinguishability between Goppa codes and random codes through the PVR signature technique. We describe the scheme as follows:

Master key generation. Based on the input parameter 1^κ, choose parameters n, k, $t = \frac{n-k}{\log 2n}$, $n' = n - k + 1$, and a cryptographic hash functions $\mathcal{G}$: $\mathbb{F}_2^{n-k} \times \{0,1\}^n \to \mathbb{F}_2^{n'}$. Select a $(n-k) \times n$ parity check matrix H of a t-error correcting binary Goppa code. Select a $n \times n$ permutation matrix P. Select a vector $a \xleftarrow{\$} \mathbb{F}_2^{n'}$. Select a vector $b \xleftarrow{\$} \mathbb{F}_2^n$. Compute a $(n-k) \times n'$ matrix H' such that $H'a^T = 0$. Select a full-rank matrix $Q' \xleftarrow{\$} \mathbb{F}_2^{n' \times (n-k)}$, such that it makes a $(n-k) \times (n-k)$ matrix $Q = H'Q'$ invertible. Generate a $n' \times n$ parity check matrix $\tilde{H} = Q'HP \oplus a^T b$. If $\tilde{H}$ is not full-rank, choose another b to re-generate $\tilde{H}$ until it is full-rank. The master secret key $msk = (H, P, Q, H')$ and the master public parameters $mpk = (\tilde{H}, n, k, t, n', \mathcal{G})$.

User key extraction. Select $i \xleftarrow{\$} \mathbb{F}_2^{n-k}$. Using the decoding algorithm to decode $Q^{-1}H'\mathcal{G}(i, id)^T$. If the decoding result x' is not found, then go back to select i again. When x' is found, $x = P^T x'$, where $\mathrm{wt}(x)$ is t or less. The user public key is $\mathcal{G}(i, id)$, and the corresponding user secret key, $usk[id]$ is x.

Interactive identification protocol. P first sends i to V. Then P is initialized with x and V is initialized with $\mathcal{G}(id\|i)$. P communicates with V through the Stern identification protocol.

3.1   Security

Theorem 3. *The PVR-Stern scheme is secure under passive attacks in the random oracle model.*

Proof. The proof adapts the reduction of the mCFS-Stern scheme [7] and the PVR signature scheme [23]. We show a skeleton of the proof due to the page limitation, and a detail proof will be given in the full paper.

The proof follows through a series of games. Game 0 is the standard id-imp-pa game, and $\Pr[X_0] = \mathrm{Adv}_{\mathcal{A}}^{\mathrm{id-imp-pa}}(\kappa)$. Game 1 simulates the hash oracle for $\mathcal{G}$ and the user key extraction oracle. The incoherence between the simulation of two oracles causes failure with a negligible probability ϵ. Therefore, $|\Pr[X_0] - \Pr[X_1]| \leqslant \epsilon$. Game 2 changes the user key extraction algorithm, it replaces H with R and $\tilde{H}$ with R', where $R'^T = [R^T|z^T]$, $R \xleftarrow{\$} \mathbb{F}_2^{(n-k)\times n}$, and $z \xleftarrow{\$} \mathbb{F}_2^n$. The adversary $\mathcal{A}$ can differentiate between Game 3 and Game 2 only if he can distinguish the random matrix R' from $\tilde{H}$. Since a, b, H' are secret and b cannot be identified from $\tilde{H}$ [23], such differentiation happens with negligible probability. *Instead of depending on the probability to distinguish the Goppa code and the random code,* $\Pr[X_2] = \Pr[X_1]$. Game 3 selects a random index as the target identity index, and $\Pr[X_3] = \Pr[X_2]$. Game 4 modifies the winning condition so that if the impersonating identity is not equal to the target identity, then the game is aborted. $\Pr[X_4] = \frac{\Pr[X_3]}{c}$, where c is a constant related to the number of queries. Game 5 answers conversation queries on the target identity, and $\Pr[X_5] = \Pr[X_4]$. Based on Theorem 1, it can be calculated that $\mathrm{Adv}_{\mathcal{A}}^{\mathrm{id-imp-pa}}(\kappa) = \Pr[X_0]$ is equivalent to the advantage of breaking the BD problem. Therefore, the PVR-Stern scheme is id-imp-pa secure. Actually, it also implies id-imp-aa secure with the proof of [28].

4   IBI/IBS Schemes with Parallel-PVR

The PVR-Stern scheme is id-imp-pa/aa secure and the parameter choice depends on the Bleichenbacher attack, which decreases the security level from $2^{\frac{mt}{2}}$ to $2^{\frac{mt}{3}}$. In this section, we propose the Parallel-PVR-caStern scheme. We first convert from the original counter-based PVR for the user key generation to complete decoding based PVR, so that we can construct parallel-PVR for better efficiency. Then we improve the security from id-imp-pa/aa secure to id-imp-ca secure through the OR-proof technique. We describe the scheme as follows:

Master key generation. The master key generation algorithm of Parallel-PVR-caStern is identical to that of PVR-Stern except for some additional public parameters: cryptographic hash functions $\mathcal{G}_1, \cdots, \mathcal{G}_\lambda : \{0,1\}^n \to \mathbb{F}_2^{n'}$, injective mapping ϕ, parallel degree λ and additional weight δ for complete decoding such that $\binom{n}{t+\delta} > n^t$. The master secret key $msk = (H, P, Q, H')$ and the master public parameters $mpk = (\tilde{H}, n, k, t, n', \lambda, \mathcal{G}_1, \cdots, \mathcal{G}_\lambda, \phi, \delta)$.

User key extraction. For λ signatures for the user identity id in parallel, compute $s'_i = \mathcal{G}_i(id)$, where $i \in \{1, 2, \cdots, \lambda\}$, and compute $s_i = H' s'^T_i$. Search all error patterns of $\phi_\delta(j)$ weight δ, compute $s_{j,i} = s_i + \tilde{H}\phi_\delta(j)^T$, and then apply the decoding algorithm to the $s_{j,i}$ where the result is $P^T Decode_H(Q^{-1}s_{j,i})$. Once the decodable syndrome $s_{j_0,i}$ is found, then we have found a $p'_{j_0,i}$ such that $\tilde{H}\phi_t(p'_{j_0,i})^T = s_{j_0,i}$. The ith signature for the user identity id is $p_{j_0,i} = \phi^{-1}_{t+\delta}(\phi_t(p'_{j_0,i}) + \phi_\delta(j))$ such that $\tilde{H}\phi_{t+\delta}(p_{j_0,i})^T = \mathcal{G}_i(id)$. Then the parallel signature for the user identity id is $x = (p_{j_0,1}\|\cdots\|p_{j_0,\lambda})$.

Run the above process twice to generate two different parallel signatures x_0 and x_1 for the user identity id, and toss a coin ϖ. The user public key is $(\mathcal{G}_1(id)\|\cdots\|\mathcal{G}_\lambda(id))$ and the corresponding user secret key $usk[id]$ is (ϖ, x_ϖ).

Interactive identification protocol. For each $i \in \{1, 2, \cdots, \lambda\}$, the prover P is initialized with $\varpi, p_{j_0,i} \in x_\varpi$ to verify $\tilde{H}\phi_{t+\delta}(p_{j_0,i})^T = \mathcal{G}_i(id)$, and the verifier V is initialized with the $\mathcal{G}_i(id)$. The detail is as follows:

Commitment. Based on $\mathcal{G}_i(id)$ and $p_{j_0,i}$, calculate c^ϖ_1, c^ϖ_2, and c^ϖ_3 according to the original Stern identification protocol. P randomly choose $b_{1-\varpi}, b'_{1-\varpi} \in \{0, 1, 2\}$. Based on the values of $b_{1-\varpi}$ and $b'_{1-\varpi}$, select one of three impersonation strategies for Stern protocol listed follow and calculate corresponding $c^{1-\varpi}_1, c^{1-\varpi}_2$, and $c^{1-\varpi}_3$:

1. If $b_{1-\varpi}$ and $b'_{1-\varpi}$ are not 0, change y in the original commitment to $y \oplus \phi_{t+\delta}(p_{j_0,i})$.
2. If $b_{1-\varpi}$ and $b'_{1-\varpi}$ are not 1, change $\phi_{t+\delta}(p_{j_0,i})$ in the original commitment to a random vector v where $wt(v) = t$.
3. If $b_{1-\varpi}$ and $b'_{1-\varpi}$ are not 2, change $y \oplus \phi_{t+\delta}(p_{j_0,i})$ in the original commitment to $v \oplus y$ where $\tilde{H}v^T = \mathcal{G}_i(id)$ and $wt(v)$ is arbitrary.

P sends $(c^0_1, c^0_2, c^0_3, c^1_1, c^1_2, c^1_3)$ to V.

Challenge. V randomly sends $b \in \{0, 1, 2\}$ to P.

Answer. P calculates $b_\varpi = b - b_{1-\varpi} \mod 3$ and $b'_\varpi = b - b'_{1-\varpi} \mod 3$. Based on b_ϖ and b'_ϖ, P calculates two responses r_ϖ and r'_ϖ respectively according to the original Stern protocol. Based on $b_{1-\varpi}$ and $b'_{1-\varpi}$, P calculates two responses $r_{1-\varpi}$ and $r'_{1-\varpi}$ respectively according to the chosen impersonation strategy. P then sends (b_0, b_1, b'_0, b'_1) to V.

Check. V checks whether $b_0 \neq b'_0$, $b_1 \neq b'_1$, $b_0 + b_1 = b \mod 3$, and $b'_0 + b'_1 = b \mod 3$. V then randomly sends $\rho \in \{0, 1\}$ to P.

Response. If ρ is 0, P sends r_0 and r_1. If ρ is 1, P sends r'_0 and r'_1.

Verification. If ρ is 0, V checks r_0 and r_1. If ρ is 1, P checks r'_0 and r'_1.

Repeat. Repeat the above four steps for γ times so that the expected security level is reached.

Remark 3. In the practical implementation, the parity matrix $\tilde{H}$ may be hidden with the support and the generator polynomial of the Goppa code in the master key generation algorithm according to [6,16]. Since the calculation of $\tilde{H}$ is a key point to avoid the assumption on the indistinguishability between Goppa codes and random codes, we still use original notions here for clarity.

4.1 Security

We first consider the security of the PVR-caStern scheme, which could be regarded as a special case of the Parallel-PVR-caStern scheme whose λ is always equal to one. Then we show the security of the Parallel-PVR-caStern scheme.

Theorem 4. *The PVR-caStern scheme is secure against impersonation under active and concurrent attacks in the random oracle model.*

The proof is obtained by contradiction and adapting the proofs by [14,18]. If there is an adversary $\mathcal{A}$ who can win the id-imp-ca game with non-negligible probability, then we can construct an adversary $\mathcal{F}$ who can win the id-imp-pa game with non-negligible probability. We will show the proof in the full paper due to the page limitation.

Theorem 5. *The Parallel-PVR-caStern scheme is secure against impersonation under active and concurrent attacks in the random oracle model.*

Proof. Based on Theorem 4, for each $i \in \{1, 2, \cdots, \lambda\}$, the i-th identification is secure under concurrent attacks in the random oracle model. Finiasz [16] has proposed that the parallel signatures keep a practical selection of parameters without the loss of security when the signing message (user identity here) is consistency, i.e., λ different cryptographic hashes for a user identity id constitute the user public key. Hence, since the PVR-caStern scheme is id-imp-ca secure, the Parallel-PVR-caStern scheme is id-imp-ca secure.

5   Parameters and Security

We compare the costs and sizes of the mCFS-Stern scheme and our four schemes the as shown in Table 1. Our schemes differ in the ability to resist the Bleichenbacher attack (with/without parallel-PVR) and the security level (id-imp-pa/id-imp-ca). The mCFS-Stern scheme is not provably secure while our schemes are all provably secure. For each scheme in the table, the upper row shows the asymptotic sizes and costs, and the lower row presents the estimated costs and sizes with the parameters suggested by [7,16,17,23] to achieve a security level of about 2^{80}. Specifically, for the schemes without parallel-PVR, $m = \log_2 n = 20$ and $t = 12$, otherwise, $m = 18$, $t = 9$, $\lambda = 2$, and $\delta = 2$. For IBI schemes, the γ for communication cost is 58, and for converted IBS schemes through Fiat-Shamir paradigm, the γ for signature length is 280.

Parallel-PVR based schemes seem to cost more for their multiple signature and communication procedure, but they actually decrease the parameters values, especially for m and t. It shows that, with parallel-PVR, it improves a lot on mpk size, msk size, usk size, communication cost and signature length with few costs

Table 1. The asymptotic and estimated costs and sizes of our IBI/IBS schemes and the mCFS-Stern scheme.

Scheme	mpk Size	msk Size	usk Size	usk Cost	Communi- cation Cost	Signature Length	Security
mCFS-Stern	$tm2^m$	tm	tm	$t!t^2m^2$	$2^m\gamma$	$2^m\gamma$	Not provably secure
	30MB	240	240	2^{45}	2^{26}	35MB	
PVR-Stern	$tm2^m$	tm	tm	$t!t^2m^3$	$2^m\gamma$	$2^m\gamma$	$2^{\frac{tm}{3}}$
	30MB	240	240	2^{49}	2^{26}	35MB	2^{80}
PVR-caStern	$tm2^m$	tm	tm	$t!t^2m^3$	$2^{m+1}\gamma$	$2^{m+1}\gamma$	$2^{\frac{tm}{3}}$
	30MB	240	240	2^{49}	2^{27}	70MB	2^{80}
Parallel-PVR-Stern	$tm2^m$	tm	λtm	$\lambda t!t^2m^3$	$\lambda 2^m\gamma$	$\lambda 2^m\gamma$	$2^{tm\frac{2^\lambda-1}{2^{\lambda+1}-1}}$
	5MB	162	324	2^{38}	2^{25}	18MB	2^{77}
Parallel-PVR-caStern	$tm2^m$	tm	λtm	$\lambda t!t^2m^3$	$\lambda 2^{m+1}\gamma$	$\lambda 2^{m+1}\gamma$	$2^{tm\frac{2^\lambda-1}{2^{\lambda+1}-1}}$
	5MB	162	324	2^{38}	2^{26}	35MB	2^{77}

The mCFS-Stern scheme is the base scheme and our four schemes differ in the ability to resist the Bleichenbacher attack (with/without parallel-PVR) and the security level (id-imp-pa/id-imp-ca). For each scheme in the table, the upper row shows the asymptotic sizes and costs with the code length m, the error correcting capability t, the number of repetition γ, and the degree of parallelism λ. The lower row presents the estimated sizes (in bits) and costs (in the number of computations) with the parameters suggested by [7,16,17,23].

of usk size since the security level is optimized to $2^{tm\frac{2^\lambda-1}{2^{\lambda+1}-1}}$. If id-imp-ca secure is required, the communication cost and signature length will be double compared to the lower security level. It can be concluded that our schemes improve the efficiency of the mCFS-Stern scheme while maintaining the provable security.

6   Conclusion

In this paper, we propose identity-based identification and signature schemes from code assumptions with parallel-PVR. They are not only provably secure against impersonation under active and concurrent attacks but also have better efficiency.

It is worth noting that it still need lots of works to study more robust assumptions on coding theory and construct broader identity-based cryptosystems from code assumptions. Also, we will make more efforts to achieve better system parameters so that code-based schemes will be more practical.

Acknowledgments. Many thanks go to the anonymous reviewers. This paper is supported by the National Natural Science Foundation of China (Grant No.61572136).

References

1. Aguilar, C., Gaborit, P., Schrek, J.: A new zero-knowledge code based identification scheme with reduced communication. In: Proceedings of IEEE Information Theory Workshop, pp. 648–652. IEEE (2011)

2. Yousfi Alaoui, S.M., Cayrel, P.-L., Mohammed, M.: Improved identity-based identification and signature schemes using Quasi-Dyadic Goppa codes. In: Kim, T., Adeli, H., Robles, R.J., Balitanas, M. (eds.) ISA 2011. CCIS, vol. 200, pp. 146–155. Springer, Heidelberg (2011). doi:10.1007/978-3-642-23141-4_14

3. Barbulescu, R., Gaudry, P., Joux, A., Thomé, E.: A heuristic Quasi-polynomial algorithm for discrete logarithm in finite fields of small characteristic. In: Nguyen, P.Q., Oswald, E. (eds.) EUROCRYPT 2014. LNCS, vol. 8441, pp. 1–16. Springer, Heidelberg (2014). doi:10.1007/978-3-642-55220-5_1

4. Bellare, M., Namprempre, C., Neven, G.: Security proofs for identity-based identification and signature schemes. J. Cryptol. 22(1), 1–61 (2009)

5. Berlekamp, E.R., McEliece, R.J., Van Tilborg, H.C.: On the inherent intractability of certain coding problems. IEEE Trans. Inf. Theor. 24(3), 384–386 (1978)

6. Biswas, B., Sendrier, N.: McEliece cryptosystem implementation: theory and practice. In: Buchmann, J., Ding, J. (eds.) PQCrypto 2008. LNCS, vol. 5299, pp. 47–62. Springer, Heidelberg (2008). doi:10.1007/978-3-540-88403-3_4

7. Cayrel, P.L., Gaborit, P., Galindo, D., Girault, M.: Improved identity-based identification using correcting codes. CoRR, abs/0903.0069 (2009)

8. Cayrel, P.-L., Véron, P., Yousfi Alaoui, S.M.: A zero-knowledge identification scheme based on the q-ary syndrome decoding problem. In: Biryukov, A., Gong, G., Stinson, D.R. (eds.) SAC 2010. LNCS, vol. 6544, pp. 171–186. Springer, Heidelberg (2011). doi:10.1007/978-3-642-19574-7_12

9. Courtois, N.T., Finiasz, M., Sendrier, N.: How to achieve a McEliece-based digital signature scheme. In: Boyd, C. (ed.) ASIACRYPT 2001. LNCS, vol. 2248, pp. 157–174. Springer, Heidelberg (2001). doi:10.1007/3-540-45682-1_10

10. Dallot, L.: Towards a concrete security proof of courtois, finiasz and sendrier signature scheme. In: Lucks, S., Sadeghi, A.-R., Wolf, C. (eds.) WEWoRC 2007. LNCS, vol. 4945, pp. 65–77. Springer, Heidelberg (2008). doi:10.1007/978-3-540-88353-1_6

11. Ezerman, M.F., Lee, H.T., Ling, S., Nguyen, K., Wang, H.: A provably secure group signature scheme from code-based assumptions. In: Iwata, T., Cheon, J.H. (eds.) ASIACRYPT 2015. LNCS, vol. 9452, pp. 260–285. Springer, Heidelberg (2015). doi:10.1007/978-3-662-48797-6_12

12. Faugere, J.C., Gauthier-Umana, V., Otmani, A., Perret, L., Tillich, J.P.: A distinguisher for high-rate McEliece cryptosystems. IEEE Trans. Inf. Theor. 59(10), 6830–6844 (2013)

13. Faugere, J.C., Otmani, A., Perret, L., De Portzamparc, F., Tillich, J.P.: Folding alternant and Goppa codes with non-trivial automorphism groups. IEEE Trans. Inf. Theor. 62(1), 184–198 (2016)

14. Feige, U., Shamir, A.: Witness indistinguishable and witness hiding protocols. In: Proceedings of ACM Symposium on Theory of Computing, pp. 416–426. ACM (1990)

15. Fiat, A., Shamir, A.: How to prove yourself: practical solutions to identification and signature problems. In: Odlyzko, A.M. (ed.) CRYPTO 1986. LNCS, vol. 263, pp. 186–194. Springer, Heidelberg (1987). doi:10.1007/3-540-47721-7_12

16. Finiasz, M.: Parallel-CFS. In: Biryukov, A., Gong, G., Stinson, D.R. (eds.) SAC 2010. LNCS, vol. 6544, pp. 159–170. Springer, Heidelberg (2011). doi:10.1007/978-3-642-19574-7_11

17. Finiasz, M., Sendrier, N.: Security bounds for the design of code-based cryptosystems. In: Matsui, M. (ed.) ASIACRYPT 2009. LNCS, vol. 5912, pp. 88–105. Springer, Heidelberg (2009). doi:10.1007/978-3-642-10366-7_6

18. Fujioka, A., Saito, T., Xagawa, K.: Security enhancements by OR-proof in identity-based identification. In: Bao, F., Samarati, P., Zhou, J. (eds.) ACNS 2012. LNCS, vol. 7341, pp. 135–152. Springer, Heidelberg (2012). doi:10.1007/978-3-642-31284-7_9

19. Girault, M., Cohen, R., Campana, M.: A generalized birthday attack. In: Barstow, D., Brauer, W., Brinch Hansen, P., Gries, D., Luckham, D., Moler, C., Pnueli, A., Seegmüller, G., Stoer, J., Wirth, N., Günther, C.G. (eds.) EUROCRYPT 1988. LNCS, vol. 330, pp. 129–156. Springer, Heidelberg (1988). doi:10.1007/3-540-45961-8_12

20. McEliece, R.: A public-key cryptosystem based on algebraic. JPL DSN Prog. Rep. **4244**, 114–116 (1978)

21. Overbeck, R., Sendrier, N.: Code-based cryptography. In: Bernstein, D.J., Buchmann, J., Dahmen, E. (eds.) Post-Quantum Cryptography, pp. 95–145. Springer, Heidelberg (2009)

22. Pointcheval, D., Stern, J.: Security proofs for signature schemes. In: Maurer, U. (ed.) EUROCRYPT 1996. LNCS, vol. 1070, pp. 387–398. Springer, Heidelberg (1996). doi:10.1007/3-540-68339-9_33

23. Preetha Mathew, K., Vasant, S., Rangan, C.P.: On provably secure code-based signature and signcryption scheme. IACR Cryptology ePrint Archive 2012, vol. 585 (2012)

24. Shamir, A.: Identity-based cryptosystems and signature schemes. In: Blakley, G.R., Chaum, D. (eds.) CRYPTO 1984. LNCS, vol. 196, pp. 47–53. Springer, Heidelberg (1985). doi:10.1007/3-540-39568-7_5

25. Stern, J.: A new identification scheme based on syndrome decoding. In: Stinson, D.R. (ed.) CRYPTO 1993. LNCS, vol. 773, pp. 13–21. Springer, Heidelberg (1994). doi:10.1007/3-540-48329-2_2

26. Stern, J.: A new paradigm for public key identification. IEEE Trans. Inf. Theor. **42**(6), 1757–1768 (1996)

27. Vandersypen, L.M., Steffen, M., Breyta, G., Yannoni, C.S., Sherwood, M.H., Chuang, I.L.: Experimental realization of Shor's quantum factoring algorithm using nuclear magnetic resonance. Nature **414**(6866), 883–887 (2001)

28. Yang, G., Tan, C.H., Mu, Y., Susilo, W., Wong, D.S.: Identity based identification from algebraic coding theory. Theor. Comput. Sci. **520**, 51–61 (2014)

Engineering Issues of Cryptographic and Security Systems

Assessment of Efficient Fingerprint Image Protection Principles Using Different Types of AFIS

Martin Draschl, Jutta Hämmerle-Uhl, and Andreas Uhl$^{(\boxtimes)}$

Visual Computing and Security Lab (VISEL), Department of Computer Sciences,
University of Salzburg, Salzburg, Austria
uhl@cosy.sbg.ac.at

Abstract. Biometric system security requires cryptographic protection of sample data under certain circumstances. We assess the impact of low complexity selective encryption schemes applied to JPEG2000 compressed fingerprint data when protected data is subjected to different types of automated fingerprint recognition schemes (AFIS). Results indicate that the obtained security is highly dependent on the type of AFIS applied, but also on the progression order of the underlying JPEG2000 codestream. Still we are able to identify general trends independent of the applied AFIS and determined by the chosen progression order, thus enabling the design of generic protection principles.

1 Introduction

The International Organisation for Standardisation (ISO) specifies biometric data to be recorded and stored in (raw) image form (ISO/IEC 19794 specifies JPEG2000 [1] for lossy fingerprint image compression), not only in extracted templates (e.g. minutiae-lists or iris-codes). On the one hand, such deployments benefit from future improvements (e.g. in feature extraction stage) which can be easily incorporated without re-enrollment of registered users. On the other hand, since biometric templates may depend on patent-registered algorithms, databases of raw images enable more interoperability and vendor neutrality. These facts motivate detailed investigations and optimisations of image compression in biometrics (see e.g. for face detection and iris recognition [2,3]) in order to provide an efficient storage and rapid transmission of biometric records.

In (distributed) biometric recognition, biometric sample data is sent from the acquisition device to the authentication component and can eventually be read by an eavesdropper on the channel. Also, biometric enrollment sample databases as mentioned before can be compromised and the data misused in fraudulent manner. Therefore, these data, often stored as JPEG2000 data as described before, require cryptographic protection for storage and transmission.

In this paper, taking into account the restrictions of biometric cryptosystems, cancelable biometrics, and homomorphic encryption techniques (these are

© Springer International Publishing AG 2016
K.-Y. Lam et al. (Eds.): ICICS 2016, LNCS 9977, pp. 241–253, 2016.
DOI: 10.1007/978-3-319-50011-9_19

designed to support template security as well as matching and partially suffer from questionable security and high computational demand), we investigate options for a lightweight encryption scheme for JPEG2000 compressed fingerprint data. In particular we consider the interplay between applying different types of automated fingerprint identification systems (AFIS) to the protected data and the achieved level of security/data protection when the JPEG2000 data is given in different progression orders. It is important to notice that, being based on classical AES encryption, matching in the encrypted domain is not supported. However, our proposed technique offers extremely low computational effort and there is absolutely no impact on recognition accuracy once the data are decrypted. Still, in case a full AES encryption of the data is feasible in terms of computational resources, this option is always preferable due to unquestioned security. Thus the investigated approach is especially useful for protection of transmission between sensor and feature extraction/matching modules when involving low-powered devices and for the encryption of vast user sample datasets (like present in the Unique Identification Authority of India's (UID) Aadhaar project) where matching in the encrypted domain is not an absolute prerequisite for sensible deployment.

Section 2 introduces principles of encrypting JPEG2000 data and specifically describes the approach as applied in this paper. Fingerprint recognition schemes as used in the paper are sketched in Sect. 3. Section 4 describes experiments, where we systematically assess the security of the proposed encryption scheme by applying different types of fingerprint recognition schemes to the (attacked) encrypted data. Section 5 presents the conclusions of this paper.

2   Efficient Encryption of Fingerprint Data

2.1   JPEG2000 Encryption in the Biometric Context

A large variety of custom image and video encryption schemes have been developed over the last years [4,5], many of them being motivated by the potential reduction of computational effort as compared to full encryption (see e.g. a depreciated scheme for fingerprint image encryption [6]). Reducing computational encryption effort is of interest in the context of biometric systems in case either weak hardware (e.g. mobile sensing devices) or large quantities of data (e.g. nation-wide sample databases) are involved.

However, when encrypting a JPEG2000 file (or any other media file) in a non format-compliant manner it is not possible to assess the security of the chosen encryption strategy since the encrypted file can not be interpreted by decoding soft- or hardware (this specifically applies to selective or partial encryption schemes which protect a specific part of a codestream only). But for assessing security (e.g. applying corresponding image quality metrics, or, as done in the present paper, attempting to use the protected data in the target application context), encrypted visual data usually need to be decoded and converted back into pictorial information.

Thus, an actual biometric system will opt to employ a non format-compliant encryption variant in its deployment installation (e.g. to decrease computational cost or to disable common decoders to interpret the data). However, we will consider the corresponding format-compliant counterpart to facilitate security assessment of the chosen scheme (while the results are equally valid for the corresponding non-compliant variants).

For JPEG2000, [7] provides a comprehensive survey of encryption schemes. In our target application context, only bitstream oriented techniques are appropriate, i.e. encryption is applied to the JPEG2000 compressed data, as fingerprint data might be compressed right after acquisition but encrypted much later. We consider encryption of packet body data in this work, while additional packet header encryption may be used to further strengthen the schemes discussed [8].

2.2 Selective JPEG2000 Encryption Approaches

In the following, we introduce a systematic approach to assess selective encryption techniques wrt. the question how to apply encryption to different parts of the JPEG2000 codestream.

We aim to achieve format compliance to enable security assessment as discussed above, while actual encryption schemes deployed in practice would not care about format compliance (while still following the same approaches where and to which extent encryption should be applied). Each packet within the JPEG2000 code stream eventually contains start of packet header (SOP) and end of packet header (EOP) markers. For this purpose, the used encoding software, i.e. JJ2000, is executed with the $-Psop$ and $-Peph$ options which enable these optional markers. These markers are used for orientation within the file and for excluding all header information from the encryption process. Additional care must be taken when replacing the packet data with the generated encrypted bytes. If the result of the encryption operation results in a value of a SOP or EOP header marker (or any other non-admissible packet value), a second encryption iteration is conducted to maintain format-compliance [9].

In the following, we introduce a specific type of selective encryption methodology, i.e. "Windowed Encryption", which is used to accurately spot the encryption location in the JPEG2000 bitstream with the biggest impact (in our context on matching rates when AFIS-based recognition is applied to encrypted data). In recent work [10] we have compared different ways how to apply encryption to different parts of a fingerprint-image JPEG2000 codestream, specifically focusing on the question if encryption should preferably be applied to one single chunk of data right at the start of the codestream ("Absolute Encryption") or if it is better to encrypt smaller contiguous chunks distributed over the packets of the codestream ("Sequential Encryption" and "Distributed Encryption"). While the corresponding results indicate highest security for the approach distributing the encryption as uniformly as possible across the codestream (thus favoring "Distributed Encryption"), experiments have been limited to the minutiae-based NIST NBIS AFIS system and have ignored the question which are the most sensitive, i.e. confidentiality-relevant, parts of the codestream. In applying

"Windowed Encryption" we will look into the question if the location of the most sensitive parts of the JPEG2000 codestream depends on (i) the AFIS employed to attempt recognition on the protected data and (ii) the progression order of the JPEG2000 codestream. The latter question has been discussed in general JPEG2000 selective encryption schemes and it has been found that the choice of either protecting layer progressive or resolution progressive JPEG2000 codestreams indeed has a significant impact wrt. the confidentiality achieved [11].

"Windowed Encryption" as shown in Fig. 1 is operated by moving a fixed window (of the size of one percent of the filesize in our experiments) across the packet data, the percentage of encrypted data does not change during the experiments. Instead, only the position of the one percent window is changed in one percent steps within packet data.

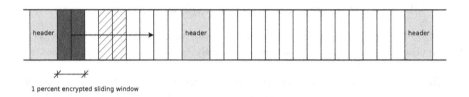

1 percent encrypted sliding window

Fig. 1. Windowed Encryption mode

In this manner, recognition experiments on the protected data reveal the parts of the JPEG2000 codestream that contains the most "valuable" fingerprint information exploited by the different AFIS for matching purposes, i.e. that is most sensitive if protected by encryption.

Security Assessment. When assessing the security of format compliantly encrypted visual data, the data can simply be decoded with the encrypted parts (called "direct decoding"). Due to format compliance, this is possible with any given decoding scheme, however, the encrypted parts introduce noise-type distortion into the data which kind of overlay the visual information still present in the data (see Fig. 3). An informed attacker can certainly do better than this naive approach. Therefore, a highly efficient attack is obtained when removing the encrypted parts before decoding and replacing them by suited data minimising error metrics (termed "replacement attack [12]") which has been successfully conducted in the JPEG2000 context [11]. This can be done most efficiently using codec specific error concealment tools, which treat encrypted data like any type of bitstream error ("error concealment attack"). The JJ2000 version used in the experiments includes the patches and enhancements to JPEG2000 error concealment provided by [13]. It fixes issues within the error concealment code found in the original code and improves results noticeably. The basic version of JJ2000 uses a simple resetting strategy as error concealment method while the version used enables JJ2000 to reset the coefficients on bitplane basis.

As visible in Fig. 3 even after error concealment attacks ridge and valley information can still be present, which could be improved further with fingerprint specific quality enhancement techniques (images like those displayed cannot be assumed to be sufficiently secured). Thus, the final design goal for a secure fingerprint encryption scheme is to get rid of this residual ridge information.

The general assessment of the security of low quality encrypted visual data is difficult. Although classical image and video quality metrics (IVQM) like SSIM or even PSNR have been repeatedly applied to such data, it has been shown recently that this does not correlate well to human perception [14]. Also, IVQM specifically developed to assess the security (i.e. confidentiality/protection level) of encrypted visual data have been recently shown not to meet the design expectations [15]. Moreover, the general quality appearance to human observers is not at all relevant in our setting. Only the assessment of forensic fingerprint experts would make sense in terms of human judgement.

However, in our case, security assessment does not need to rely on human specialists – since our application context is highly specific and well defined, we apply fingerprint recognition algorithms (AFIS) to the protected data to verify if the protection is sufficiently strong to prevent the use of the encrypted fingerprint data in an automated recognition context.

3   Fingerprint Recognition

Different types of fingerprint recognition schemes react differently to image degradations. Therefore, we will consider fundamentally different types of fingerprint feature extraction and matching schemes, based on the discriminative characteristics fingerprints do contain [16]:

Correlation-Based Matcher: These approaches use the fingerprint images in their entirety, the global ridge and valley structure of a fingerprint is decisive. Images are correlated at different rotational and translational alignments, image transform techniques may be utilised for that purpose. As a representative of this class, we use a custom implementation of the phase only correlation (POC) matcher [17] the details of which are described in recent work [18].

Ridge Feature-Based Matcher: Matching algorithms in this category deal with the overall ridge and valley structure in the fingerprint, yet in a localised manner. Characteristics like local ridge orientation or local ridge frequency are used to generate a set of appropriate features representing the individual fingerprint. As a representative of the ridge feature-based matcher type we use a custom implementation of the fingercode approach (FC) [19] the details of which are described in recent work [18].

Minutiae-Based Matcher: The set of minutiae within each fingerprint is determined and stored as list, each minutia being represented (at least) by its location and direction. The matching process then basically tries to establish an optimal alignment between the minutiae sets of two fingerprints to be matched, resulting in a maximum number of pairings between minutiae from one set with compatible ones from the other set. As the representative of the minutiae-based matcher type we use *mindtct* and *bozorth3* from the "NIST Biometric Image Software" (NBIS) package (available at http://fingerprint.nist.gov/NBIS/) for minutiae detection and matching, respectively.

4 Experiments

4.1 Experimental Settings

All experiments are based on images taken from databases of the Fingerprint Verification Competition (FVC). In particular, our results are based on set B of all 4 datasets of the years 2000, 2002 and 2004. Set B contains a subset of 10 fingers (8 imprints each) of each of the four datasets in each year, thus leading to 120 fingers overall. This strategy is chosen to have a high diversity of fingerprint sensors represented in the data.

Images are compressed into lossless JPEG2000 format using JJ2000 in layer progressive and resolution progressive ordering. Subsequently they are encrypted using the different positions in "Windowed Encryption" by shifting the encryption window across the data as described and subsequently either directly decoded or decoded with enabled error concealment with the JJ2000 variant mentioned [13].

The procedure used for matching the decoded/encrypted fingerprint images is chosen to be the same as FVC demands for performance evaluation. In a first run, every sample of a finger is matched against all other samples of the same finger from that dataset. Symmetric matches are not taken into account. Based on this run the False Non Match Rate (FNMR) is calculated. A second run is performed matching the first impression of each finger against all other first images of all fingers from that dataset. Again symmetric matches are not evaluated. The results of these matches are used for the calculation of the False Matching Rate (FMR). Overall, we will consider equal error rate (EER) and receiver operating curves (ROC) to compare the protection capabilities of the different encryption schemes. Obviously, higher EER correspond to better data protection as well as worse ROC behaviour is preferred for better data protection. Windowed Encryption experiments involve all three AFIS types described.

4.2 Experimental Results

In the following, we will apply Windowed Encryption and will assess the sensitivity towards location of the protected data when using different types of AFIS. Figure 2 shows the ROC behaviour of the three recognition schemes when applied to plain (unprotected, i.e. unencrypted) data. NBIS exhibits the best behaviour except for very low FNMR where FC is better, POC exhibits the worst behaviour, except for high FNMR, where it is superior to FC.

In Fig. 3 image examples for Windowed Encryption are given where encryption starts right at the first packet data and only 0.5% of the bitstream are

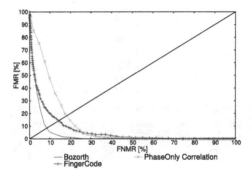

Fig. 2. ROC - Reference matches set B

encrypted. The visual impression confirms that error concealment indeed is able to reveal data which seems to be protected under direct decoding. This fact has been already observed [10] and its implication for fingerprint image security under partial encryption has been extensively discussed.

Fig. 3. Encryption Examples - original, 0.5% encrypted with direct reconstruction and error concealment, respectively.

The first results are obtained when encrypting layer progressive JPEG2000 codestreams. Figure 4 shows the effects of Windowed Encryption using NBIS for recognition. Results are very clear in that the further the encryption window is moved away from the bitstream start, the less secure the scheme gets. This is true for direct decoding as well as for error concealment. When encrypting data at positions starting at 10% of the data or later, recognition "degrades" to the unprotected case (see Fig. 2) for direct decoding, the same is true at 8% or later for error concealment. It is obvious that in general, conducting an error concealment attack only slightly reduces security.

Figure 5 exhibits a fairly different behaviour for FC. For direct encoding, recognition is "down" to the unprotected behaviour already when starting encryption at 6% or later. Additionally, is turns out to be more secure to encrypt starting at 2% data as compared to starting at 1%. Apart from that, the "natural order" (i.e. less secure when encrypting parts farther away from the codestream start) is preserved. The more significant differences however are seen

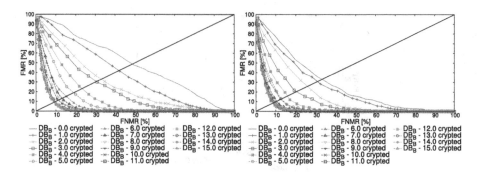

Fig. 4. ROC - Windowed Encryption (NBIS) - direct reconstruction vs. error concealment attack.

when error concealment is used. FC is obviously very well capable to handle encrypted data and apart from encrypting right from the bitstrems start, almost no protection at all can be achieved. This result indicates that different types of recognition schemes are able to handle encrypted data to a very different extent (here, robustness of FC is clearly superior to NBIS for the encryption effects introduced).

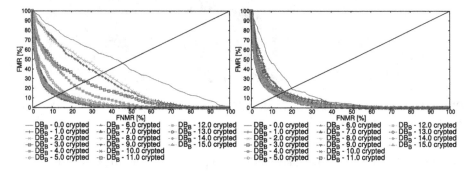

Fig. 5. ROC - Windowed Encryption (FC) - direct reconstruction vs. error concealment attack.

Figure 6 visualises the POC results. For direct decoding, degradation to unprotected behaviour is also seen for encryption starts at 6% of the data or later. Apart from a slight mingling of 1% and 2% start position, applying encryption closer to the start of the data leads to more secure results. For error concealment, degradation to unprotected behaviour is found at the same position and the relative ordering is entirely following the bitstream ordering, however, all variants are significantly less secure as compared to direct decoding.

Table 1 only looks at the EERs (i.e. a single point at the ROC curve), but already comparing layer progressive and resolution progressive ordering in two subsequent lines. The numerical values for layer progressive codestream ordering

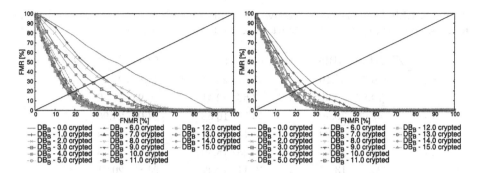

Fig. 6. ROC - Windowed Encryption (POC) - direct reconstruction vs. error concealment attack.

of course confirm the graphical results as displayed in Figs. 4, 5 and 6. However,
for the resolution progressive ordering, we notice significant differences as follows.
Obviously, contrasting to the layer progression mode, the data most important
for AFIS is not located at the start of the codestream, but, depending on the
actual AFIS and decoding variant (direct vs. error concealment) considered,
either at 3% or 4% of the data. It is also interesting to note that there is not
a single peak in the EER values but there is a second local maximum in the
area of 11%–13% of the data, less distinct for the error concealment decoding
case. The locations of these peaks point to the position of the first data packets
in layer progression ordering. Despite all the differences spotted, it gets obvious
that the positions of the most sensitive areas in the JPEG2000 codestream are
not depending on the actual AFIS employed.

Another clear difference is the best protection (i.e. highest EER) achieved by
the different AFIS: For error concealment decoding, layer progressive ordering
achieves EERs of 33% (NBIS), 20% (FC), and 28% (POC), while resolution progressive decoding results in maxima at 24% (NBIS), 18% (FC), and 24% (POC),
respectively. Thus, it gets clear that for an equal extent of protection, more data
needs to be encrypted in resolution progressive ordering. The same tendency
is observed for direct decoding, where layer progressive ordering achieves 49%
(NBIS), 46% (FC), and 45% (POC), while resolution progressive decoding results
in maxima at 39% (NBIS), 32% (FC), and 35% (POC), respectively.

Figure 7 shows the effects of Windowed Encryption applied to resolution progressive codestream ordering using NBIS for recognition. The overall impression
is similar compared to the layer progressive mode (Fig. 4) with two significant
differences: First, results do degrade quicker to the unprotected case when moving away from the best settings, and second, the best results are achieved when
starting to encrypt at 3% or 4% of the data (both for direct as well as error
concealment decoding). The next best settings are positioning the encryption
window at 2%, 5%, and 12% of the data.

The high robustness of FC wrt. partial codestream encryption is confirmed
also for resolution progressive ordering as shown in Fig. 8. Compared to the layer

Table 1. EER [%] - Layer progressive (first line for each start value) vs. resolution progressive (second line for each start value) codestream ordering.

start [%]	NBIS	NBIS err.conc	FC	FC err.conc	POC	POC err.conc
0.0	48.70	33.10	45.97	20.11	44.88	28.37
	19.87	9.52	13.66	12.41	26.93	21.39
1.0	42.00	30.80	33.77	16.58	34.08	24.96
	16.70	9.29	13.15	13.04	21.81	18.76
2.0	32.97	25.83	36.28	15.40	33.06	22.53
	25.34	13.83	19.11	12.42	24.83	20.81
3.0	30.46	20.33	26.64	15.16	28.95	22.32
	39.31	21.86	32.10	15.32	32.89	21.54
4.0	23.17	15.79	21.82	13.57	25.27	22.03
	37.51	23.94	32.47	17.76	35.48	23.87
5.0	18.94	12.76	15.89	13.72	21.19	20.04
	24.57	16.29	17.87	13.67	23.23	19.99
6.0	15.24	12.37	14.20	13.25	19.92	19.01
	12.23	11.39	14.35	13.25	17.97	19.21
7.0	13.08	10.41	13.81	13.68	18.63	18.99
	10.40	9.74	13.33	13.30	17.57	17.79
8.0	12.13	9.93	12.38	13.14	16.91	17.94
	15.06	11.68	17.84	14.78	22.29	18.40
9.0	11.26	9.49	12.64	13.28	17.26	18.28
	19.08	12.23	18.58	12.69	21.29	18.09
10.0	9.60	8.93	12.64	14.93	17.26	18.89
	15.63	11.43	16.91	14.56	21.41	18.52
11.0	9.59	9.26	12.65	12.89	19.25	17.59
	21.52	14.08	23.30	15.34	27.98	19.92
12.0	9.40	9.02	12.83	13.63	17.69	17.80
	24.56	14.21	22.50	13.85	26.23	20.26
13.0	9.21	8.68	14.08	13.45	17.50	17.49
	20.65	14.22	19.47	14.74	24.37	19.50
14.0	9.37	9.02	13.24	13.62	18.51	18.29
	15.41	12.33	14.83	13.24	20.15	18.89
15.0	9.22	8.40	13.76	14.86	18.41	18.63
	12.48	10.09	13.41	15.24	18.97	17.98

progressive case (as shown in Fig. 5), even higher robustness is exhibited and for error concealment decoding, not even a single setting provides a sensible level of

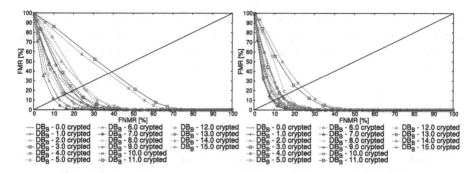

Fig. 7. ROC - Windowed Encryption (NBIS) - direct reconstruction vs. error concealment attack for resolution progressive mode.

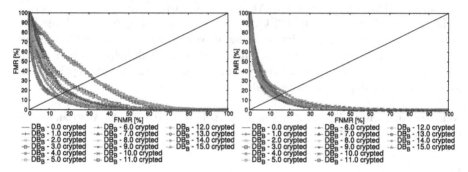

Fig. 8. ROC - Windowed Encryption (FC) - direct reconstruction vs. error concealment attack for resolution progressive mode.

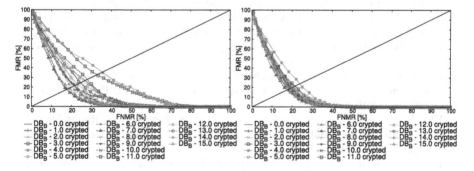

Fig. 9. ROC - Windowed Encryption (POC) - direct reconstruction vs. error concealment attack for resolution progressive mode.

protection. Again, when starting to encrypt at 3% or 4% of the data the best results are achieved.

Finally, Fig. 9 shows the results of POC when applied to protected codestream data in resolution progressive ordering. The same trends may be observed:

Best protection is achieved for starting to encrypt at 3% or 4% of the data, protection level is worse compared to layer progressive codestream ordering (compare Fig. 6), and under error concealment decoding, the protection level is negligible.

5 Conclusion

We have compared various approaches to apply selective/partial encryption to fingerprint data compressed into JPEG2000 format. Evaluations are done by comparing recognition performance on encrypted data. We have found that sensitivity/robustness against partially encrypted data is highly dependent on the actual recognition scheme used and does not correspond to the recognition performance ranking of the different AFIS seen on clear data. Moreover, there is a significant difference if the JPEG2000 codestream is organised in layer progressive or resolution progressive ordering, however, the observed differences are identical for all three types of AFIS. These first results will help to finally design AFIS recognition system aware encryption schemes with low encryption complexity and decent protection capability.

Acknowledgments. This work has been partially supported by the Austrian Science Fund, project No. 27776.

References

1. Taubman, D., Marcellin, M.: JPEG2000 – Image Compression Fundamentals Standards and Practice. Kluwer Academic Publishers, New York (2002)
2. Elmer, P., Lupp, A., Sprenger, S., Thaler, R., Uhl, A.: Exploring compression impact on face detection using haar-like features. In: Paulsen, R.R., Pedersen, K.S. (eds.) SCIA 2015. LNCS, vol. 9127, pp. 53–64. Springer, Heidelberg (2015). doi:10.1007/978-3-319-19665-7_5
3. Ives, R.W., Bishop, D., Du, Y., Belcher, C.: Iris recognition: the consequences of image compression. EURASIP J. Adv. Sig. Process. 2010 Article ID 680845 (2010). doi:10.1155/2010/680845
4. Uhl, A., Pommer, A.: Image and Video Encryption. From Digital Rights Management to Secured Personal Communication. Advances in Information Security, vol. 15. Springer, Heidelberg (2005)
5. Lian, S.: Multimedia Content Encryption: Techniques and Applications. CRC Press, Boca Raton (2008)
6. Engel, D., Pschernig, E., Uhl, A.: An analysis of lightweight encryption schemes for fingerprint images. IEEE Trans. Inf. Forensics Secur. **3**(2), 173–182 (2008)
7. Engel, D., Stütz, T., Uhl, A.: A survey on JPEG2000 encryption. Multimedia Syst. **15**(4), 243–270 (2009)
8. Engel, D., Stütz, T., Uhl, A.: Format-compliant JPEG2000 encryption with combined packet header and packet body protection. In: Proceedings of ACM Multimedia and Security Workshop, MM-SEC 2007, pp. 87–95. ACM, New York, September 2007

9. Stütz, T., Uhl, A.: On format-compliant iterative encryption of JPEG2000. In: Proceedings of the Eighth IEEE International Symposium on Multimedia (ISM 2006), pp. 985–990. IEEE Computer Society, San Diego, December 2006

10. Draschl, M., Hämmerle-Uhl, J., Uhl, A.: Efficient fingerprint image protection principles using selective JPEG2000 encryption. In: Proceedings of the 1st Workshop on Sensing, Processing and Learning for Intelligent Machines (SPLINE 2016), Aalborg, Denmark, pp. 1–6 (2016)

11. Norcen, R., Uhl, A.: Selective encryption of the JPEG2000 bitstream. In: Lioy, A., Mazzocchi, D. (eds.) CMS 2003. LNCS, vol. 2828, pp. 194–204. Springer, Heidelberg (2003). doi:10.1007/978-3-540-45184-6_16

12. Podesser, M., Schmidt, H.P., Uhl, A.: Selective bitplane encryption for secure transmission of image data in mobile environments. In: CD-ROM Proceedings of the 5th IEEE Nordic Signal Processing Symposium (NORSIG 2002), Tromso-Trondheim, Norway, IEEE Norway Section file cr1037.pdf, October 2002

13. Stütz, T., Uhl, A.: On JPEG2000 error concealment attacks. In: Wada, T., Huang, F., Lin, S. (eds.) PSIVT 2009. LNCS, vol. 5414, pp. 851–861. Springer, Heidelberg (2009). doi:10.1007/978-3-540-92957-4_74

14. Hofbauer, H., Uhl, A.: Visual quality indices and low quality images. In: IEEE 2nd European Workshop on Visual Information Processing, Paris, France, pp. 171–176, July 2010

15. Hofbauer, H., Uhl, A.: Identifying deficits of visual security metrics for images. Sig. Process.: Image Commun. **46**, 60–75 (2016)

16. Maltoni, D., Maio, D., Jain, A., Prabhakar, S.: Handbook of Fingerprint Recognition, 2nd edn. Springer, Heidelberg (2009)

17. Koichi, I., Hiroshi, N., Koji, K., Takafumi, A., Tatsuo, H.: A fingerprint matching algorithm using phase-only correlation. IEICE Trans. Fundam. **E87-A**(3), 682–691 (2004)

18. Hämmerle-Uhl, J., Pober, M., Uhl, A.: Towards a standardised testsuite to assess fingerprint matching robustness: the StirMark toolkit – cross-feature type comparisons. In: Decker, B., Dittmann, J., Kraetzer, C., Vielhauer, C. (eds.) CMS 2013. LNCS, vol. 8099, pp. 3–17. Springer, Heidelberg (2013). doi:10.1007/978-3-642-40779-6_1

19. Jain, A.K., Prabhakar, S., Hong, L., Pankanti, S.: Filterbank-based fingerprint matching. IEEE Trans. Image Process. **9**(5), 846–859 (2000)

Medical Record System Using Blockchain, Big Data and Tokenization

Paul Tak Shing Liu[1,2(✉)]

[1] Social Mind Analytics (Research and Technology) Limited,
Hong Kong, China
ogmaster2011@gmail.com
[2] Maximus Consulting (Hong Kong) Limited, Hong Kong, China

Abstract. This paper will discuss the major aspects of medical records, blockchain and big data. In turn, it will discuss the advantage and disadvantage of using blockchain on medical records storage and retrieval. It will also discuss the alternatives of using blockchain and big data techniques. Different aspects of medical records will be investigated briefly: (1) integrity, (2) viewing control, (3) viewing approval, (4) western medicine and chinese medicine practice, (5) storage size and duration, (6) deletion and purge, (7) file format conversion, (8) data migration, (9) report interpretation, etc. Characteristics of blockchain and big data analytics will be explored briefly with description. A conclusion will summarize the approaches. References will be provided for further research and investigation.

Keywords: Medical record · Blockchain · Big data analytic · Tokenization

1 Introduction

Medical Record. To improve our medical service for our patients around the world we must have a readily available standardized medical record history any time anywhere. We must also overcome the following challenges: (1) record type, (2) storage, (3) medical records and reports, (4) ownership and reading right, (5) data security, (6) western medical practice and Chinese medical practice, (7) patient's right of knowledge.

Medical record types include text reports, word documents, images, videos and data. They are all important in our medical history. They are all in different formats with possible free style.

Central storage is important too. It is because many doctors may not have their own or may have different medical record systems. Record formats may pose a challenge sometimes. Nevertheless, many formats can now be converted from one to another or vice versa. Yet another problem, forever increasing storage due to forever increasing number of reports/files is caused by the continuous contribution of reports or records from medical doctors or patients. All old reports or records must be archived regularly and must be transferred to new storage media from time to time.

© Springer International Publishing AG 2016
K.-Y. Lam et al. (Eds.): ICICS 2016, LNCS 9977, pp. 254–261, 2016.
DOI: 10.1007/978-3-319-50011-9_20

Medical test result interpretation, diagnosis, treatments and recovering progress are medical reports prepared by medical professionals or medical doctors. Test result interpretation will be given by professional medical personnel in free style writing. However, those interpretations may be in different presentation styles and in free style writing. Similarly, diagnostics will be given in writing by medical doctor. They involve free style writing and can be difficult to be interpreted by both machine and patient. Medical treatments will be given in writing by medical doctor. They involve free style writing too and can be very different from doctor to doctor. Different doctor may also use different dosages for similar treatment. Recovering progress of patient will be observed and recorded in writing by medical doctor. Those progress reports too involve free style writing and are difficult to be interpreted by machine and patient. Also, extra patient data and recovering progress can be contributed and inputted by patient through web interface from time to time into medical record system. These extra data and reports are vital to every patient's recovering process and are important to medical doctor's diagnosis. Nonetheless, patients may use very different wordings and very free style writing too.

Medical record ownership and record sharing among doctors is extremely controversy within medical community. Many doctors worry about possible lawsuit initiation by others or even by patient if things go wrong. Medical related legal matter or lawsuit may incur from time to time. Therefore, all documents generated must be properly stored and must be produced to court in whole if requested. All records must not be tampered. All records must not be deleted for whatever reason.

Data security is important. It is necessary to protect the privacy of both patient and medical doctor. All kinds of IT security measures must be implemented for data protection. Many doctor's medical reports actually need some kind of data security. For example, IT security, backup, data recovery, etc. All these could jack up their clinic operation cost.

Patient's right of reading reports can be very tricky. Since all medical reports are owned by medical doctors, medical doctor has the right not to share the medical reports to anyone, including patients. All accesses must require the consent from the report owner which is the doctor. Report reading right may also induce lawsuit which is most worried by medical doctor. Report reading right for other medical personnel can be conditionally limited by report owner. It all depends on who will read the medical report. That medical personnel must require pre-arranged consent from the report owner. Can patient and/or other medical personnel view the patient's medical history without directly accessing the medical reports owned by other doctors? This is very important in a way that patient's conditions can be properly accessed without the jeopardy of delay due to the tedious requesting process of consent from other doctors.

Western medical doctor and Chinese medical doctor are very much different in terms of practice and report writing. Their reports must require proper translation back and forth. Simply translating Chinese into English is definitely not enough. It also need certain qualitative translation on medical terms.

If a medical doctor retires, what can we do with all the medical reports owned by that specific doctor? It is a tricky question. Besides, that specific medical doctor may want to release all medical reports with conditions. However, that doctor may want to retain the secrecy of those reports. On the other hand, other doctors may not want to take up the responsibility of all those medical reports in case of possible lawsuits.

Finally, patients should have right to know who has viewed the related reports about specific patient. This is to avoid unauthorized access to patient's privacy. At the same time, patient should be able to report unauthorized access to his/her own medical history.

HK eHealth. There are few other criteria imposed by ehealth system (eHR) by Hong Kong government [1]. Those include (1) government-led, (2) data privacy and security, (3) not compulsory, (4) open and pre-defined common standards, (5) building block approach. Every record access of patient's record will be recorded and notification will be sent to corresponding patient. The record data are very restricted, including lab tests, x-ray, etc. Medical doctor's reports may not be there. All authorized medical personnel may read patient's records if corresponding patient agrees.

Blockchain. In electronic currency world, blockchain has been very popular for bit-coin transaction settlement as a public ledger [2]. However, blockchain itself has its own limitation and criteria. They are summarized as followed.

Blockchain can prevent duplicated transactions by accepting the very first arrived transaction for specific unspent electronic currency and rejecting other transactions for that unspent currency immediately thereafter. The inverse hash calculation used by the proof of work will reinforce such status for the long run. This is the heart of blockchain. It can then be extended to prevent duplication of work. Duplication of work can be avoided and can be detected immediately through the digital signature of the duplicated records. However, it is not possible, through digital signature, to detect similar, but different, records or files.

The proof of work uses the inverse calculation of hash value [3, 4]. The inverse hash calculation is difficult and the direct hash calculation is simple. Blockchain then forces transaction settlement or any electronic work to include the inverse hash calculation. Then direct hash calculation will be used to verify that the transaction settlement work has been completed.

Blockchain can prevent the deletion of work. Deletion or tampering of work will be notified in the chain if the direct calculation of the hash value of specific block is inconsistent.

Blockchain cannot reverse the work or transaction settlement. The reverse of work is not possible because it is not possible to recalculate the hash value of specific individual block without the recalculation of all hash values of all other blocks thereafter. However, unfortunately, this part of the whole protocol is mostly hacked since bitcoin's birth.

The guarantee of the existence of data records or files is not easy. If only digital signature is used, it cannot guarantee the existence of records or files. If the original piece of document is not within a specific block, there is no way to guarantee the existence of such document within specific system or internet or world wide web.

Big Data Analytics. Big data, nowadays, can achieve many things using artificial intelligence techniques. Popularity analytic tells which item or group of items is most popular from the data sources. With popularity analytic, we can detect similarity or closeness among topics within large volume of data. Groups of items (or topics) can be system generated using closeness relationship formulation. Or they can be assigned by user. Sentiment analytic tells the positive or negative feeling towards specific item or topic. It can also tell the percentage towards positive feeling and the percentage towards negative feeling. Aspect mining tells the characteristics of specific item. Both popularity and sentiment analytics can be performed on specific aspect. Prediction of future public behavior towards specific item, or person can be performed in the near future. Strategy and action suggestions for specific item or person can be formulated thereafter.

Tokenization. Tokenization is very important in this respect of medical reports sharing. Token will not depend on operating systems and does not include content within. The storage server can examine the validity of the token before sending out the required report(s). The report owner can sign the request token sent by specific viewer with confidence.

2 Development Approaches

The following proposed features summarize what can be implemented to overcome the challenges described in introduction section for the development of a reasonably sound and safe medical record system that will benefit most patients.

Medical record types, formats and storage are the first few challenges in the whole development cycle. They can be resolved by today's technology without much challenge. Whether we use off the shelf ready-made software or customer-designed system, it is never a challenge right now. It is always good to have a centralized system with backup in different locations for data storage, new data insertion or instant data record reading. Different channels can be established for accepting documents or multi-media files. Standardization can be achieved by converting all files into a couple reading formats.

All medical tests, test interpretation, diagnosis, treatment and recovering progress reports are important data records or files. A general medical report system can utilize different channels for accepting the data or files. A web based good looking user interface can be developed for such purpose. It can upload individual files or a batch of files. As for the data or progress reports contributed by patients can be inputed through web based interfacing portal.

All uploaded data files and records can now be saved to a centralized storage area or database for future retrieval. All records or files must be digitally signed by owners/contributors and must designate the possible viewing counterparties. Each record will be used later for either patient's view, or original medical doctor's review, or be reviewed by other medical doctors for further diagnosis and treatment, or be retrieved by court for judicial process.

Next, we should consider measure to reduce the risk of purge and modification unintentionally or intentionally. We can implement blockchain mechanism directly on the medical reports.

Database, backup and duplicated hardware have been used historically to protect data from the risk of tampering. Hash value and digital signature or blind signature of each record can further reinforce protection tampering [5].

Blockchain mechanism can be implemented for all the encrypted medical data records and files [6–8]. Encryption of medical record or file is needed for further protection from unauthorized access. In turn, blind signature can be used for integrity check of the original medical record or file. In order that each record or file is not being deleted or tampered, each encrypted record or file should be included serially inside the blockchain implemented. At the same time, the blind signatures should also be included for the proof of genuine of each record. Many proposed medical record blockchain implementations only include the digital signature of each record or file. The use of digital signature can avoid the record or file being tampered. However, it cannot avoid the deletion of specific file or record without any notice from system. A modified blockchain can be implemented to further enhance the integrity of all the records/files encapsulated inside the chain. A modified blockchain can include randomly selected hash values of blocks from the chain. This can constantly check the integrity of each record/file from the chain. In turn, it ensures the existence of each record/file in the long run [9].

Data security can be implemented with ease using state of art IT security and control technology. Tokenization can be utilized to send reading authorization to whoever medical personnel who needs reading specific report. Token can contain specific authorization command without directly containing specific record/file.

Forever increasing number of records or files can be a headache in the long run to storage, operation and archiving. To copy the whole blockchain from old storage device to new storage device is not difficult but tedious. However, if any of the file format is going to be outdated and needs conversion, it is going to be chaos. Not only the file needs conversion, but also the digital signatures and hash values need recalculation too. To change or delete record/file, one can neither delete nor purge specific record/file in blockchain. This is one of the underlying criteria of blockchain technology. The owner can only invalidate the old record/file and add a new one to overlay on top of the old record/file which cannot be deleted or purged. However, the old record/file will be there forever. Similar to bitcoin transaction settlement, old transaction will be there forever and new transaction will replace the old one. To update the old record is similar to spending specific electronic currency note. Instead, owner must spend the old record and create a new record with different format. From storage point of view, records/files must be transferred to new storage from time to time. Old records/files must be converted to new reading formats regularly. In turn, both hash values and digital signatures must be regenerated and the old records/files must be invalidated at some point of time regularly. This could further increase the overall size of the blockchain exponentially. Therefore, we must decide at the very beginning that we have to use certain reading formats forever. Besides, we may also need to create a separate blockchain to facilitate migration purpose.

Although forever increasing number of records poses a big challenge, there may be an alternative design [10]. Blockchain itself cannot be deleted partly. The whole thing is built forever. We can only delete or purge the whole chain at the same time. If we want to delete or purge some records or files or reports in the near future, we must design it at the very beginning. Since patients will die one day, after certain period of time, the passed away patients' records should be cleared forever or archived in another storage for later retrieval for research. One possibility is to build many blockchains for different groups of patients. The grouping can base on age, or geographic location, or hospitals/clinics, etc. Then, at certain point of time, when all patients within one blockchain are deceased, we can remove or archive the whole blockchain directly without hesitation. Otherwise, we must be prepared for forever increasing storage in the long run.

Reading right for patient requires either a pre-written report for patient only or a universal standard interpretation of all reports written by medical doctors. Since all reports are written by human medical doctors, all the wordings can be very much different for the same thing. Therefore, one possibility is to use big data technique to re-interpret all reports for patients. The actual original reports must have original medical doctor's signed consent before being released to patients due to lawsuit concern from medical doctors. However, big data analytic can give a very brief statistical summary of each report of specific patient. Big data technique can also display the patients' medical conditions over a time line in a graphical view. This is essentially important for patients and other medical doctors in the long run. Other medical doctors may need such systematic time line for diagnosis and treatment.

For big data analytic to work properly, all records must not be encrypted. Therefore, it is important to strip off the identity of patient from medical record or file before use. A separate database for big data analytic is needed for further isolation. However, we can still use certain serial number for backward association with specific patient if needed.

For retiring medical doctors, medical report ownership can be assigned to another professional or to the system for further reading right management. Although it may be not preferable from patients' point of view, it is a second best option. Many other arrangements can be developed thereafter.

Translation from Chinese medical doctor's report into western medical doctor's reading style, or vice versa, is a very difficult challenge to be solved. It is that the underlying philosophy of both western medical doctor and Chinese doctor are very much different. It is necessary to do a thorough research on terms interpretation to have an accurate translation back and forth. However, if there are reports for similar diagnosis and treatment coming from both western medical doctors and Chinese medical doctors, big data can still make an approximate association of terms coming from both sides. Then it may be possible to make translation using big data analytics. The more reports the system has, the more accurate association it can make. It will be ongoing research and tedious work. However, big data will provide an immediate viable approach to such difficulty.

Although it is possible to detect duplicated pieces of work, it is not so easy to prevent similar, but different, pieces of work. With digital signature of every piece of document, we can easily detect duplication. However, even a slight change in specific document, a different digital signature will be generated and cannot be associated with the original document. Fortunately, we can use big data analytic to detect similarity between two documents in a large volume of works. Although big data analytic is not fool proof technique, its approximation is more than enough.

Blockchain is a very good choice for present and previous works by others which concentrate on the integrity of medical reports without worrying about many other factors. However, in the long run, blockchain related application development will hit a solid wall very soon when number of medical data records or files hits a larger volume. They will need to fix a lot of challenges mentioned in previous section. It is a lot better to prepare for the worst cases to come. Blockchain can protect the integrity. However, it cannot guarantee the existence or the interpretation of the reports. It cannot control the viewing right. It cannot solve the challenges of outdating formats. It cannot handle forever increasing storage size. It cannot handle deletion or purge. Blockchain is not everything. We need other technologies to supplement any design.

Hong Kong government has its own electronic health system (eHR). The system philosophically is similar. However, the data types are not comprehensive enough. It does not consider other important factors. It may not be very useful for most patients and medical doctors. Technologically, eHR does not use blockchain technology and is a centralized system. Patients cannot contribute their data to the system either. The system eHR is still a very primitive design. It needs much further improvement.

Finally, the system should implement a reading log on all patient's medical records. This log can be a database table or can also be a blockchain which will avoid log record tampering or deletion.

3   Conclusion

In this paper, the actual design of sharing medical records system is explored. Every aspect of medical records is studied briefly. The characteristics of blockchain are explained on its pros and cons. Big data analytic has its own capabilities and is explained briefly in introduction. Medical records sharing system's integrity, deletion and purge, record sharing, storage, format conversion, data migration, interpretation and standardization are examined. Different approaches to overcome all human related challenges are suggested in this paper with confidence. The use of blockchain is very important. However, other technologies, big data analytics and tokenization, are very much needed to supplement the original design. Although actual implementation is not put into production, the approaches should be practical enough. Each suggestion gives some details and reasons behind the technical direction. Hope that this will stimulate further research and development for the benefit of patients as well as general medical community.

References

1. Hong Kong Government. Electronic Health Record Sharing System (2016). http://www. ehealth.gov.hk/en/home/index.html
2. Franco, P.: Understanding Bitcoin – Cryptography Engineering and Economics. Wiley, Hoboken (2015)

3. Stallings, W.: Cryptography and Network Security – Principles and Practice, 6th edn. Pearson, London (2014)
4. Milne, J.S.: Elliptic Curves, Kea Books (2006)
5. Chaum, D.: Blind signatures for untraceable payments. In: Advances in Cryptology: Proceedings of CRYPTO 1982 (1982)
6. Forde, B.: MedRec: Electronic Medical Records on the Blockchain, 2 July 2016. https://www.pubpub.org/pub/medrec
7. Everington, J.: Du to use blockchain for health records, 30 May 2016. http://www.thenational.ae/business/technology/du-to-use-blockchain-for-health-records
8. Scott, M.: The Future of Medical Records: Two Blockchain Experts Weigh In, 1 May 2016. https://btcmanager.com/news/the-future-of-medical-records-two-blockchain-experts-weigh-in/
9. Ekblaw, A., Azaria, A., Vieira, T., Lippman, A.: MedRec: Medical Data Management on the Blockchain, 11 August 2016. https://medium.com/mit-media-lab-digital-currency-initiative/medrec-electronic-medical-records-on-the-blockchain-c2d7e1bc7d09#.wj7tr2fvq
10. Yessi Bello Perez (@yessi_kbello). Medical Records Project Wins Top Prize at Blockchain Hackathon, 10 November 2015. http://www.coindesk.com/medvault-wins-e5000-at-deloitte-sponsored-blockchain-hackathon/

Is it Good or Bad? Disclosure of Medical Ailments on Twitter

B.S. Vidyalakshmi and Raymond Wong(✉)

School of Computer Science and Engineering,
University of New South Wales, Sydney, Australia
wong@cse.unsw.edu.au

Abstract. Health discussions is among the top topic of discussion on social network. Numerous studies have turned to Twitter to collect their own dataset of tweets containing health mentions, for analysis. In this work we analyze Twitter dataset containing health mentions and find if it is good or bad to discuss health conditions on Twitter. Tweets with health mention could disclose health condition of the twitterer or of an associate. Health mention can be used as a joke or may be a news article raising awareness. Before mining Twitter for health mentions, it is important to understand the context or theme of the tweet. We propose to categorize the tweets into categories, with each category representing a different theme. We analyze the Twitter dataset with health mentions as a whole and analyze the twitter dataset categorized to find the advantages and disadvantages of the health mentions on Twitter.

1 Background

According to the Pew internet project, eight in ten internet users look online for health information, making it the third most popular online pursuit[1]. With the pervasive use of internet and social networks in particular, opinions and discussions is not restricted to people whom we know offline but includes online friends too [17]. According to a survey[2], among the top 10 topics people discuss on the web, health discussions was the top topic. Given these understanding, health information also forms a strong case for study using tweets.

With 6000 tweets generated on an average per second[3], it is next to impossible to gain any knowledge out of this huge data store without first bifurcating the health related tweets from non-health related ones. While most works using health mentions on Twitter use keywords to collect their dataset, some additionally filter the collected dataset to clean it before further analysis.

Works on health mentions in Twitter (health mention is health condition or disease mentioned as part of the tweet) have concentrated on finding Personal health mentions [34], Secondary health mentions [2], being able to predict Flu

---

[1] http://www.pewinternet.org/2011/02/01/health-topics-2/.
[2] http://www.synthesio.com/blog/the-10-most-popular-topics-on-the-web/.
[3] http://www.internetlivestats.com/twitter-statistics/.

© Springer International Publishing AG 2016
K.-Y. Lam et al. (Eds.): ICICS 2016, LNCS 9977, pp. 262–277, 2016.
DOI: 10.1007/978-3-319-50011-9_21

and other disease trends in the general population from a given location [1, 3, 19, 28], creating awareness and removing misconceptions about a disease [26, 32]. The first step in gaining such knowledge from Twitter health mentions is to appropriately collect the tweets by finding the tweets that should and should not be part of the dataset with one way being through classifying them appropriately. Many works classify tweets into positive/negative tweets, utilizing the positive ones for further analysis while other works classify them into multiple categories before further analysis.

In this paper, we focus on health mentions on Twitter in general and decompose it into several categories of health mentions including Personal and Secondary health mentions, View and Awareness, Spam, LOL, News, Information seeking and Conversations. To categorize the data we use Q methodology. We go further and investigate the knowledge that can be gained by classifying the health mention tweets into each category. We analyze each category to envisage its usefulness and contend that categories theme can be further tuned based on the nature of knowledge that is expected to be gained and depending on the end user domain - be it medical, political, governance, and such.

Numerous works have utilized health mentions on Twitter with some works mapping to advantages of health mentions such as awareness campaigns and virtual support groups, with other works mapping to disadvantages of health mentions such as Personal and Secondary health mentions leading to privacy leaks. In this work, we ask the question *Are health mentions on Twitter Good or Bad?* Hence, we analyze both the advantages and disadvantages of health mentions on Twitter. Health mentions on Twitter may belong to multiple contexts and hence the categorization. In this work, in order to categorize the tweets, we have highlighted the importance of understanding the pitfalls in identifying the contexts of health mentions to classify them accordingly.

This work utilizes a Twitter dataset collected over a period of 10 months, containing 79 million tweets for analysis. Initially, health mentions are analyzed using training dataset (Labelled_500 dataset) to come up with themes for categories. By using a compound classifier consisting of Naive Bayes, Support Vector Machines (SVM) and Random Forrest classifiers, tweets from Test dataset are classified into the categories. Further analysis is carried out on each category to find the pitfalls, advantages and disadvantages.

The contributions of this work are:

- Propose a method to classify tweets using a small training set using a compound classifier there by achieving improved accuracy as compared to individual classifiers
- Investigate the advantages and disadvantages of health mentions in Twitter
- Analyze the pitfalls in identifying and segregating misleading health mentions in tweets from Twitter

The rest of the paper is organized as follows. In Sect. 2, data collection and tweet filtering are explained. Categorization is discussed in Sect. 3. Sections 4, 5 and 6 respectively highlight the pitfalls, advantages and disadvantages of health mentions in Twitter. Section 7 concludes and point out some of the directions for future work.

2   Data Filtering for Health Mention Tweets

We considered Twitter social network for the health mentions study due to its easy accessibility and relatively low number of private accounts[4], restricting tweet gathering from them. The collected Twitter corpus consists of 79 million tweets with 709 tweets on average per user. The tweets contains 9 million hashtags in total. The data was collected between 1 January 2010 to 20 October 2010. 79 million tweets were filtered to obtain tweets that contain a mention of disease or health condition in its message or hashtag yielding the health mention corpus.

We collected tweets that contained health mentions either in hashtags or in message content. To ensure that we filtered all tweets related to health mentions, hashtags of tweets containing health mentions were filtered first. Works on hashtags show that they carry a lot of value in their one word [9,29]. In this work, hashtags describing each health related mention was guided by the hashtags from Symplur project, specifically the Symplur healthcare hashtags project[5]. The project presents an exhaustive source of the Twitter hashtags related to diseases, health conditions, and other personal health related topics. The Symplur hashtag project contained 495 hashtags for diseases and health conditions as at May 2016[6].

Majority of tweets do not contain any hashtags associated with them [29]. Hence, the message content of the tweets were filtered with Symplur hashtags providing the source of words. The hashtags were split into meaningful chunks where ever they made sense e.g., #Heartattack would be split as Heart attack, #HighBloodPressure as High Blood Pressure. By restricting searching for tweets containing all the split words (or unsplit word as a single word), we ensured that as much spam was blocked as possible.

Filtering for health mentions yields 146265 distinct tweets out of 79 million tweets, which forms the Test dataset. The number of distinct users are 32031 with an average of 4.5 tweets per user. Tweets were filtered for English only tweets.

The filtered health mention corpus contains 264 diseases and health conditions mentioned as part of tweets out of a possible 495 in 146265 tweets. Table 1 lists the top 30 diseases and health conditions. It can be noted that 14 out of the top 30 of diseases and health conditions are part of the medical expenditure panel survey that lists the common health issues[7].

---

[4] http://temp.beevolve.com/twitter-statistics/.

[5] http://www.symplur.com/healthcare-hashtags/.

[6] http://www.symplur.com/healthcare-hashtags/diseases/.

[7] http://meps.ahrq.gov/mepsweb/.

Table 1. Top 30 health mentions with percentage in test dataset

Health condition	%	Health condition	%
AIDS	3.76	Allergies	<1
HIV	3.43	Stroke	<1
Flu	2.70	Obesity	<1
Diabetes	2.56	UTI	<1
Alzheimer	2.02	Anxiety	<1
Suicide	1.80	Lupus	<1
STD	1.63	Malaria	<1
Breast cancer	1.49	Dementia	<1
OCD	1.08	Herpes	<1
Depression	0.96	Migraine	<1
Bald	0.64	Dengue	<1
Prostate cancer	0.53	Fracture	<1
Autism	0.51	Asthma	<1
ADHD	0.51	Heartattack	<1
Bipolar	<1	Lymphoma	<1

3   Health Mentions Categorized

Need for Categorization. According to a survey[8], among the top 10 topics people discuss on the web, health discussions was the top topic. These health mentions on a large scale corpus, such as twitter messages from millions of people, provide a source that can be analyzed further to gain knowledge. Twitterers tweeting health mentions may be engaging in personal health discussion or that of a close friend or relative. They may also be discussing the general health concerns of a particular season from their geolocation or the discussion could be media events broadcast on news outlets. Using health mentions as a way of joke is not uncommon (e.g., *I might as well smoke get lung cancer and die. Lol. Martn is funny*). Health advocates and advocates spreading awareness about diseases use social networks, such as Twitter, for furthering their agenda of raising awareness. Making use of URL embedding feature of tweets, scamsters use Twitter to lead their followers to fraudulent or advertisement website. As such, health mentions in tweets can be used for any one or all of these purposes. Understanding the context in which the health mention has been used is important before further analysis can be carried out on health mention corpus.

Health mentions have been a source to gain knowledge about the general population e.g., Flu trends [1,3,19,28]. Multiple studies into health mentions concentrate on a specific category of health mentions. Detecting Personal health mentions on twitter [34], health mentions of a third person [2], raising awareness

---

[8] http://www.synthesio.com/blog/the-10-most-popular-topics-on-the-web/.

about a particular disease [32] or finding the user understanding about the medical treatments [26]. Each of these studies construct their datasets from twitter based on the problem being studied, there by categorizing the twitter dataset. These studies endorse that health mentions on twitter belong to multiple contexts/categories.

Another advantage of categorization, is learning to avoid categories that should be filtered out and not be part of health corpus. Keyword based data extraction from Twitter [1–3, 7, 12, 19, 26, 28, 34], for the purpose of further analysis comes with the risk of containing all the tweets containing the keywords. Some of these tweets are essentially Spam or LOL tweets which contain a health condition or disease as part of the message but not in health context. Hence, after the data extraction from twitter, most of the works employ one of the two strategies to further filter out such tweets from health corpus - (i) Classify the tweets into related (or Positive tweets) and unrelated (or Negative) tweets [3, 12, 34] or (ii) Ad-hoc filtering using keywords [2, 26] based on the purpose for which health mention corpus is collected (e.g., word Cancer appears in tweets about astrology for the cancer sign while the same word also denotes a disease, hence astrology tweets are filtered out in [2]). We contend that Spam and LOL tweets can be further analyzed to find the features and keywords necessary to filter out such tweets from health mention corpus. We can also gain knowledge on health conditions or diseases that are more prone to Spam and LOL's than others.

Given these understanding about the need for categorization, we first categorize and then further analyze the health corpus, to gain knowledge in terms of advantages and disadvantages of using health mentions in Twitter. We analyze the pitfalls that provide a source of knowledge to filter out unrelated tweets containing health mentions from the health mention corpus.

Categorization. To categorize the health mention tweets, Q methodology was applied. Q methodology provides a way to improve the understanding of human perspectives [23] and has also been used to explore people's health seeking behavior [27]. Q methodology has also been applied to health mention corpus of Twitter [26].

We randomly chose 500 tweets that had a disease or health condition mentioned in the tweet to construct Labelled_500 dataset. Two researchers classified the tweets into major categories using the Q methodology. Researchers then discussed to identify the final set of categories with each category having a theme at its centre. Each tweet aligns to one category.

Recent work by [34] have shown that a classifier trained for health mentions of some diseases or conditions can effectively classify tweets containing health mentions of different diseases and conditions. Given this understanding, we randomly chose 500 tweets belonging to multiple health mentions for manual labelling. The distribution of tweets into different categories are as given in Fig. 1 on the Labelled_500 dataset.

We use three well known text classifiers to train the tweets using Labelled_500 dataset. Multinomial Naive Bayes [21], Support Vector Machine with stochastic

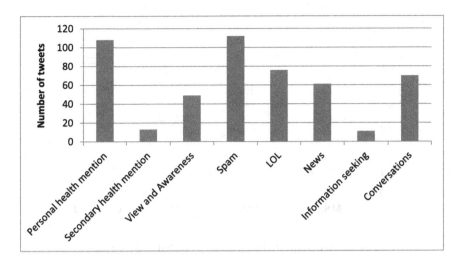

Fig. 1. Tweet distribution among categories of Labelled_500 dataset

gradient descent (SGD) learning [35] and Random Forrest [6] classifiers from the scikit-learn python module are the three classifiers used. These classifiers have been shown to be effective on short texts like tweets [24,25]. Naive Bayes, Support Vector Machine and Random Forrest gave the highest F-measure on tweets for detecting influenza reports in experiments carried out by Aramaki *et al.* [3], substantiating the effectiveness of the three classifiers on short texts.

To enhance the feature set of the classifier algorithms, we used the below features along with a matrix of TF-IDF features of tweets. Effectiveness of these features for short-text have been verified by earlier works [5,11,18].

- Punctuation and emoticons - These can convey the emotions of the twitterer which can be used for classification e.g., *oh no! first lamarcus gets hurt a couple days ago, now steve blake is in hospital for pneumonia!* :(
- @usernames, http links - Known http links can be used for filtering out the tweets belonging to non-health related contexts. e.g., http://twittascope. com/twittascope/?sign=4. Tweet containing Cancer keyword, but Cancer here refers to sun sign. @ and http links also act as features more relevant to Spam, Conversations categorization.

This work does not propose a new automatic classifier of tweets into categories. But, to ensure all the tweets belong to the categories that they have been classified into, we built a compound classifier consisting of all the three classifiers. Only those tweets were chosen as belonging to a category when all three classifiers predicted the same category label to a tweet. All other tweets were discarded. This was to ensure that further analysis of tweets of each category was as accurate as possible. It is important to note that, since each classifier uses the same features from the trained Labelled_500 dataset, there is a possibility of all three classifiers getting a tweet category label wrong.

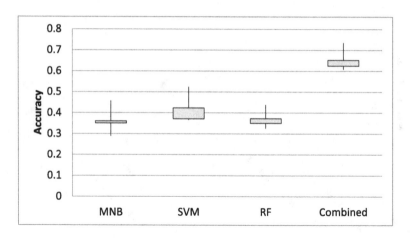

Fig. 2. Accuracy of classifiers on Labelled_500 dataset

We perform 10 runs on the Labelled_500 dataset and report the accuracy in Fig. 2. Though combined classifier discards tweets which do not find consensus among the three classifiers leading to a smaller dataset, the accuracy gain against individual classifiers, warrant the use of combined classifier.

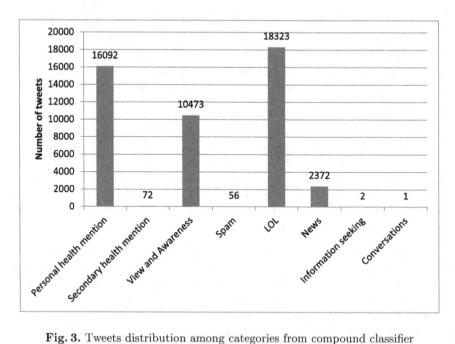

Fig. 3. Tweets distribution among categories from compound classifier

After training on the Labelled_500 dataset, applying combined classifier on the Test dataset of 146265 tweets resulted in a dataset consisting of 47391 tweets where all the three classifiers predicted the same label. The number of tweets' distribution among different categories are as seen in Fig. 3.

While Personal, Awareness and LOL have the highest distribution with News having a notable number among the categories, the proposed method of using the classifiers with TF-IDF, punctuation, emoji's and http links does not yield identification of tweets from Conversations, Information seeking, Spam and Secondary health mention categories.

We discuss the pitfalls faced in identifying each category and in particular the Spams, Conversations, Information seeking categories in the following Sections.

4   Pitfalls in Collecting Health Mention Corpus

Health mentions on Twitter can provide a dataset that can be mined in real-time if required, through API's. Before collecting health mention dataset for specific analysis purposes, it is important to understand the tweets that are not related to health but still find their way into the dataset by the mere mention of health conditions in the tweet text or in the hashtags of tweets.

Many feature selection methods and NLP techniques have been utilized for short text classification on Twitter containing health mentions. Some have used only those health conditions that are less prone to wrong mentions under LOL's or Spam for data collection like Cancer tweets [2] or H1N1 or Swine Flu tweets [7]. Others have used NLP techniques such as stemming, Lemma forms, Punctuation and Emoji's [10,12,34] to filter out such tweets.

Aramaki *et al.* [3] in their work, note that a tweet containing words *influenza* or *flu*, may not mean the twitterer has got the flu, instead it might just contain the health mention e.g., *Influenza is now raging throughout Japan*. Such works corroborate our contention of the requirement to understand the context of tweet use and understand the pitfalls in health data collection, before further analysis is carried on them.

As seen from Fig. 1, the manually labelled dataset of Labelled_500, contains a fair share of Spam, News, Secondary health mentions and Conversations while the combined classifier cannot automatically identify them as seen in Fig. 3. We analyze the health mentions belonging to these categories in particular to find the reasons for difficulty in identifying them. We also analyze LOL category as it has the highest distribution of tweets through combined categories.

Spamming is often targeted [13], where a health condition revealed by the twitterer could be used as a front to misleading the twitterer to spam sites promoting alternative medicines and therapies e.g., *Fight everyday stress & anxiety with a new nutritional supplement. Try Zanexis* -http://tr.im/gAGx. Spam category also contains those tweets that have been wrongly classified as health related tweets e.g., 1. *Im gonna miss 2009 its lik this year flu by :'(* or e.g., 2. *Looks like I'm done in the suicide pool (Denver). Woulda lost with my other choice this week, too..* Using keywords of diseases to capture diseases and health condition tweets would need to find ways to block such tweets from creeping into health mention corpus. While, Spam category accounts for 11% in Labelled_500 dataset Fig. 1, the distribution in the test dataset is less than 1%.

Health mentions can also be used as metaphors, sarcasm or as a joke/LOL about a situation. These tweets, with disease and health condition keyword, do not form part of the health mentions corpus. While some health conditions are hardly used as adjectives, some are prone to be used as a joke e.g., Baldness finds 12 genuine mentions versus 16 mentions used as joke/adjective in the Labelled_500 health corpus. Fever is another such condition which is often used as adjective e.g., *It's 2010, swine flu is over! It's all about BIEBER FEVER!!!!! ! LOL...RT NOW!!!.* Though, this tweet contains two health mentions it should not be part of the health corpus. While Baldness and Fever are used as adjectives, UTI and Fracture find their use to be less than 0.5% in LOL category in Test dataset.

We analyzed the tweets classified through the three classifiers belonging to Spam and LOL categories. Top 5 health mentions in Spamming category are shown in Table 2. Cancer also finds a mention in Top 5, but, we removed those messages talking about horoscope cancer, due to the excessive number leading to a skewed dataset similar to earlier work on Cancer [2]. All the Spam tweets detected contained a http link. It should be noted that messages that are wrongly classified as Spam but without a http link, have not been categorized into this category. Table 3 gives the top 10 health mentions of the LOL category. The list contains well known diseases being used as a joke in tweets. Though, these does not give an exhaustive list of health mentions used under the two categories, they nevertheless provide an indication of the problem faced in health mention corpus collection.

Table 2. Top 5 health mentions in Spam category

Health mention	Percentage
Dialysis	87.72
Acne	3.51
Alzheimer	3.51
Allergy	3.51
STD	1.75

News also finds a part in the health mention tweets (5% in the Test dataset, refer Fig. 3). News from news sites about major health breakthroughs, current health crisis,from a particular geographical location or general news consisting of health keywords are all part of this category tweets. News stories from a particular location posted by a twitterer could reveal some association of the twitterer with that location, leading to privacy breaches.

Table 3. Top 10 health mentions in LOL category

Health mention	Percentage
Breast cancer	9.37
AIDS	9.12
Flu	8.99
Diabetes	7.68
HIV	5.22
Suicide	3.90
STD	3.89
Bald	3.03
Depression	2.96
OCD	2.63

Though tweets from Conversations category are part of the health mentions corpus used for further analysis, it finds a mention in Pitfalls due to the ambiguity in the subject (person implicated) of health mention in conversations. A tweet such as *@ddxxxxo Im sick with the flu too! And Im watching Princess Protection Program on the couch! Haha! Well I hope you feel better! Byee! <3* would implicate both the twitterers in conversation to be sick with flu while *@faxxxxx don't u hate tht depression..ugh it always sucks* is a conversation about a health condition which does not attribute the condition to any of the twitterers in conversation, and hence is a general conversation.

Table 4. Conversations

Conversations	Percentage
General conversations	32.43
Personal health mention conversations	28.38
Secondary health mention conversations	39.19

We analyzed the Labelled_500 dataset used for training to find all conversations. It is as seen in Table 4. As can be seen nearly 28% of conversations, though conversations, are essentially Personal health mention and 39% are Secondary health mentions with only 32% belonging to the Conversations category of Labelled_500 dataset. Conversations have to be carefully classified into either Personal or Secondary health mentions due to the ambiguity involved in attributing the health mention to a twitterer or classifying it as a health mention in a conversation without implicating anyone.

5   Advantages of Health Mentions in Twitter

Using health mentions in tweets, multiple research works have aimed at finding the spread of a disease [1,3,19] along with user concern about a disease [28,30]. These works collect data mainly using keywords to identify the health mention tweets. Since most of these works rely on self-reported and secondary reported tweets, a majority of the tweets belong to Personal or Secondary category [3] with tweets from News category also contributing [30] to it.

Health mention tweets also draws health advocates and every day twitterers to support the health campaigns promoted by local government (e.g., effects of drugs[9]), [16,36] or individual person or group of people e.g., Movember campaigns. There have been many studies about using social media as a venue for raising awareness about health issues among general public [20,32]. Twitterers could also opine their views about health conditions which affect them, their immediate circle of family or friends. Awareness and Views category along with Information seeking category would form a part of health mention corpus that can be analyzed for the success/failure of an awareness campaign or to design an awareness campaign.

Tweets from Awareness category provide a way of measuring the amount of success a campaign has had by measuring the frequency and geographical spread of a campaign and support for it, by twitterers. Since Twitter users do not necessarily represent the general public, success or improvement strategies of campaigns designed specifically for social media could be analyzed through tweets belonging to this category.

Top 10 health mentions from the View and Awareness category is given in Table 5. Of the Top 3 health mentions, Breast Cancer has a month dedicated to create awareness, Diabetes and AIDS have days for creating awareness with the best known awareness event being the *BCAM campaign* for breast cancer [31].

Since people express their views about a particular disease or condition through health mention tweets, analyzing these tweets can provide a crowd based source on which the need for a campaign aimed at removing the misunderstanding could be designed e.g., study by Scanfeld *et al.* [26] highlight the use of Twitter to find the misuse or misunderstanding surrounding the use of antibiotics.

Information seeking tweets are those that raise health related questions seeking answers. This category contained least number of tweets overall (6.6% of Labelled_500 and <1% from Test dataset). Though information seeking does not endorse the seeker to be suffering from the health condition about which the question speaks, an analysis of tweets may point to Personal health condition or that of someone associated with the information seeker, along with understanding or misunderstanding regarding a health condition.

Health mentions on twitter have also been used as virtual support groups as well as for knowledge sharing [4]. Twitter based community of practice has been

---

[9] http://www.drugs.health.gov.au/.

Table 5. Top 10 health mentions in view and awareness category

Health mention	Percentage
Breast cancer	16.07
Diabetes	13.01
AIDS	10.65
HIV	5.24
Prostate cancer	4.41
Alzheimer	3.29
Obesity	1.57
Cancer survivors	1.13
Epilepsy	0.86
Lupus	0.74

analyzed [33] which shows the interactions to be within general consumers and within providers of health information.

Thus health mention on Twitter could be used for designing awareness campaigns along with measuring its success or failure. It could also be used for providing virtual support communities.

6 Disadvantages of Health Mentions in Twitter

Personally Identifiable Information (PII) and sensitive information leak through short texts of social networks, such as Twitter has been well documented [8,22]. Health condition is a sensitive topic. The health mentions of Personal, Secondary, News and Conversations categories are more privacy sensitive than the rest of the categories due to the possibility of identifying the subject (person) of health mention in the tweet.

Personal health status mentions on social network, such as Twitter, when corroborated with other publicly available information about the twitterer, from public forums or other social networks can lead to PII leak as shown by multiple works [8,14,15]. Personal health mention on Twitter has been studied by Yin et al. [34], who observe that as much as 44% of tweets containing health mention keywords disclose Personal health status. The dataset used in this work, had as much as 34% of the users disclose Personal health status.

Secondary health mentions and Conversations, which divulge health information about a third person also leads to infringement of individual's privacy. Anderson et al. [2] in their study on Secondary sharing of sensitive health issue (cancer in their study) highlight retweeting of primary twitterer's health mention, without their explicit consent. In our dataset we found less than 1% percent of tweets were Secondary health mentions as identified by the compound classifier. As discussed earlier in Sect. 4, conversations contribute to Secondary health mentions with as much as 39% of conversations being Secondary health mentions. As part of our future work, we would like to find a way to classify the conversations alone, with Secondary mentions in conversations classified as Secondary health mentions.

With less than 10% of users having protected accounts on Twitter[10], followers and followings of twitterer are publicly available. The subject (third person) of health mention in Secondary and Conversation tweets can thus be identified using followers or followings. Hence, a health mention about another twitterer could lead to sensitive information being leaked.

In Test dataset, top 10 health mentions of Personal health status category finds some overlap with the top 10 health mentions of the Secondary health mentions category as shown in Table 6. We found that both the categories contain disclosures of serious health conditions, unlike [34], which found Secondary health mentions to be disclosing more serious health conditions.

Table 6. Top 10 health mentions in personal and secondary categories, with overlap between the categories *italicized*

Personal category	Secondary category
Depression	Stroke
Allergies	Cancer
OCD	Herpes
Bipolar	Malaria
STD	*AIDS*
AIDS	*Flu*
Migraine	*Allergies*
HIV	*HIV*
Flu	*Anxiety*
Anxiety	Eating disorder

With geotagging feature enabling addition of explicit geographical coordinates to the tweets, there is a steady increase in users providing location information (Locations can be exact or relative, such as cities). As per a survey, the geolocation tagged tweets rose from less than 1%[11] in 2010 to around 6%[12] in 2013 who voluntarily opted in for location information broadcast. Our dataset, collected back in 2010, contains location information for 2 percent of the 79 million tweets. In addition to voluntary disclosure, using user's hometown, time zone and language among others, an application *Twitter2GIS* showed that

---

[10] http://techcrunch.com/2009/10/05/twitter-data-analysis-an-investors-perspective-2/.

[11] http://thenextweb.com/2010/01/15/twitter-geofail-023-tweets-geotagged/.

[12] http://www.esecurityplanet.com/network-security/study-finds-one-in-five-tweets-discloses-the-users-location.html.

through Twitter API and Google's Geocoding API, 20 percent twitterer's location could be discovered to an accuracy of street level or better. In this context, health mentions, along with location information pose additional threat to individual's privacy through sensitive information and PII leak.

7 Conclusion and Future Work

This work analyzes the health mentions in messages and hashtags of Twitter. Health mention tweets are classified into different categories based on the contexts of their use. In this work health mention tweets were collected by utilizing health mentions as keywords. The Pitfalls involved in using keyword based filtering without understanding the context of theme of the tweet has been discussed which highlights the need to categorize the tweets. These pitfalls, in turn provide an invaluable knowledge from which health mention tweets can be further filtered for spurious tweets containing health mentions. We discuss the advantages and disadvantages of health mentions on Twitter, there by trying to answer the question - is it good or bad to have health mentions in tweets?

We would like to incorporate the knowledge gained from this work to improve the existing automatic classifiers of health mention tweets. It is also important to note that slang has not been considered as part of the literature to filter health mention tweets. User generated content is often prone to misspellings and slangs. We would like to consider this in health mentions filtering as part of our future work.

References

1. Achrekar, H., Gandhe, A., Lazarus, R., Yu, S.-H., Liu, B.: Predicting flu trends using Twitter data. In IEEE Conference on Computer Communications Workshops (INFOCOM WKSHPS), pp. 702–707 (2011)
2. Anderson, M.D., Adams, J.A., Hooten, E.R., Cancerous tweets,: socially sharing sensitive health information. In IEEE International Conference on Systems, Man and Cybernetics (SMC), pp. 648–653 (2014)
3. Aramaki, E., Maskawa, S., Morita, M., Twitter catches the flu: detecting influenza epidemics using Twitter. In Proceedings of the ACL Conference on Empirical Methods in Natural Language Processing, pp. 1568–1576 (2011)
4. Attai, D.J., Cowher, M.S., Al-Hamadani, M., Schoger, J.M., Staley, A.C., Landercasper, J.: Twitter social media is an effective tool for breast cancer patient education, support,: patient-reported outcomes by survey. J. Med. Internet Res. 17(7) (2015)
5. Banerjee, N., Chakraborty, D., Joshi, A., Mittal, S., Rai, A., Ravindran, B.: Towards analyzing micro-blogs for detection and classification of real-time intentions. In: International AAAI Conference on Web and Social Media (ICWSM) (2012)
6. Breiman, L.: Random forests. Mach. Learn. 45(1), 5–32 (2001)
7. Chew, C., Eysenbach, G.: Pandemics in the age of Twitter: content analysis of tweets during the 2009 H1N1 outbreak. PloS One 5(11), e14118 (2010)

8. Correa, D., Sureka, A., Sethi, R.: Whacky!-what anyone could know about you from Twitter. In: IEEE Tenth Annual International Conference on Privacy, Security and Trust (PST), pp. 43–50 (2012)
9. Cunha, E., Magno, G., Comarela, G., Almeida, V., Gonçalves, M.A., Benevenuto, F.: Analyzing the dynamic evolution of hashtags on Twitter: a language-based approach. In: Proceedings of the ACL Workshop on Languages in Social Media, pp. 58–65 (2011)
10. Davidov, D., Tsur, O., Rappoport, A.: Enhanced sentiment learning using Twitter hashtags, smileys. In: Proceedings of the Twenty third International ACL Conference on Computational Linguistics: Observation of Strains, pp. 241–249 (2010)
11. Davidov, D., Tsur, O., Rappoport, A.: Semi-supervised recognition of sarcastic sentences in Twitter and Amazon. In: Proceedings of the Fourteenth ACL Conference on Computational Natural Language Learning, pp. 107–116 (2010)
12. Doan, S., Ohno-Machado, L., Collier, N.: Enhancing Twitter data analysis with simple semantic filtering,: example in tracking influenza-like illnesses. In: IEEE Second International Conference on Healthcare Informatics, Imaging and Systems Biology (HISB), pp. 62–71 (2012)
13. Ghosh, S., Viswanath, B., Kooti, F., Sharma, N.K., Korlam, G., Benevenuto, F., Ganguly, N., Gummadi, K.P.: Understanding and combating link farming in the Twitter social network. In: Proceedings of the Twenty first International ACM Conference on World Wide Web, pp. 61–70 (2012)
14. Goga, O.: Matching user accounts across online social networks: methods and applications. Ph.D. thesis, LIP6-Laboratoire d'Informatique de Paris 6 (2014)
15. Jamuna, G.: I know your family: a hybrid information retrieval approach to extract family information from microblogs. Ph.D. thesis, University of Kansas (2014)
16. Jenine, K.H.: Local health department use of Twitter to disseminate diabetes information, united states. Preventing Chronic Dis. **10** (2013)
17. Kumar, R., Novak, J., Tomkins, A.: Structure, evolution of online social networks. In: Link Mining: Models, Algorithms, and Applications, pp. 337–357. Springer, Heidelberg (2010)
18. Lamb, A., Paul, M.J., Dredze, M.: Separating fact from fear: tracking flu infections on Twitter. In: Proceedings of HLT-NAACL, pp. 789–795 (2013)
19. Lampos, V., Cristianini, N.: Tracking the flu pandemic by monitoring the social web. In: IEEE Second International Workshop on Cognitive Information Processing (CIP), pp. 411–416 (2010)
20. Lorie Donelle, R.N.: Health tweets,: an exploration of health promotion on Twitter. Online J. Issues Nurs. **17**(3), 1–16A (2012)
21. Manning, C.D., Raghavan, P., Schütze, H., et al.: Introduction to Information Retrieval. Cambridge University Press, Cambridge (2008)
22. Mao, H., Shuai, X., Kapadia, A.: Loose tweets,: an analysis of privacy leaks on Twitter. In: Proceedings of the Tenth Annual ACM Workshop on Privacy in the Electronic Society, pp. 1–12 (2011)
23. McKeown, B., Dan Thomas, B.: Q Methodology, vol. 66. Sage Publications, Thousand Oaks (2013)
24. Meij, E., Weerkamp, W., de Rijke, M.: Adding semantics to microblog posts. In: Proceedings of the Fifth ACM International Conference on Web Search and Data Mining, pp. 563–572 (2012)
25. Nishida, K., Hoshide, T., Fujimura, K.: Improving tweet stream classification by detecting changes in word probability. In: Proceedings of the Thirty Fiftth International ACM SIGIR Conference on Research and Development in Information Retrieval, pp. 971–980 (2012)

26. Scanfeld, D., Scanfeld, V., Larson, E.L.: Dissemination of health information through social networks: Twitter and antibiotics. Am. J. Infect. Control **38**(3), 182–188 (2010)
27. Shabila, N.P., Al-Tawil, N.G., Al-Hadithi, T.S., Sondorp, E.: Using q-methodology to explore peoples health seeking behavior and perception of the quality of primary care services. BMC Public Health **14**(1), 1 (2014)
28. Signorini, A., Segre, A.M., Polgreen, P.M.: The use of Twitter to track levels of disease activity and public concern in the us during the influenza A H1N1 pandemic. PloS One **6**(5), e19467 (2011)
29. Suh, B., Hong, L., Pirolli, P., Chi, E.H.: Want to be retweeted? large scale analytics on factors impacting retweet in Twitter network. In IEEE Second International Conference on Social Computing (socialcom), pp. 177–184 (2010)
30. Szomszor, M., Kostkova, P., Louis, C.S.: Twitter informatics,: tracking and understanding public reaction during the 2009 swine flu pandemic. In: IEEE/WIC/ACM International Conference on Web Intelligence and Intelligent Agent Technology (WI-IAT), vol. 1, pp. 320–323 (2011)
31. Thackeray, R., Burton, S.H., Giraud-Carrier, C., Rollins, S.R., Draper, C.R.: Using Twitter for breast cancer prevention: an analysis of breast cancer awareness month. BMC Cancer **13**(1), 1 (2013)
32. Songhua, X., Markson, C., Costello, K.L., Xing, C.Y., Demissie, K., Llanos, A.A.: Leveraging social media to promote public health knowledge: example of cancer awareness via Twitter. JMIR Public Health Surveill. **2**(1), e17 (2016)
33. Xu, W.W., Chiu, I.-H., Chen, Y., Mukherjee, T.: Twitter hashtags for health: applying network and content analyses to understand the health knowledge sharing in a Twitter-based community of practice. Qual. Quant. **49**(4), 1361–1380 (2015)
34. Yin, Z., Fabbri, D., Trent Rosenbloom, S., Malin, B.: A scalable framework to detect personal health mentions on Twitter. J. Med. Internet Res. **17**(6), e138 (2015)
35. Zhang, T.: Solving large scale linear prediction problems using stochastic gradient descent algorithms. In: Proceedings of the Twenty First International ACM Conference on Machine Learning, p. 116 (2004)
36. Abedalthagafi, M., Mar, F.A., Almalki, T., Kutbi, A.H., Harris-Brown, T., Harbarth, S., Balkhy, H.H., Paterson, D.L., Hasanain, R.A.: The potential role of social media platforms in community awareness of antibiotic use in the gulf cooperation council states: luxury or necessity? J. Med. Internet Res. **17**(10), e233 (2015)

Weaknesses in Security Considerations Related to Chaos-Based Image Encryption

Thomas Hütter, Mario Preishuber, Jutta Hämmerle-Uhl, and Andreas Uhl$^{(\boxtimes)}$

Visual Computing and Security Lab (VISEL), Department of Computer Sciences,
University of Salzburg, Salzburg, Austria
andreas.uhl@sbg.ac.at

Abstract. Over the past years an enormous variety of different chaos-based image and video encryption algorithms have been proposed and published. While any algorithm published undergoes some more or less strict experimental security analysis, many of those schemes are being broken in subsequent publications. In this work it is shown that three issues wrt. chaos-based encryption security considerations severely question the soundness of these techniques. It is experimentally demonstrated that obviously weak (i.e. insecure) encryption schemes do not consistently fail commonly used tests to assess chaos-based encryption security and thus, passing these test is only a necessary condition for a secure scheme, but by no means a sufficient one. Security analysis of chaos-based encryption schemes needs to be entirely reconsidered.

1 Introduction

In the mid 1990's scientists around the world started research in the field of chaos-based image encryption, inspired by the work of Scharinger and Pichler [20] who applied the Baker map [6] to the discrete case of 2D image encryption and by the work of Fridrich [9] who extended the discretised map to 3D and composed it with a diffusion mechanism. Since then, new chaos-based image and video encryption schemes have been proposed at an almost weekly basis and a large number of corresponding publications is observed in many conferences and journals (see Table 1 for example), and the flood does not seem to be about to stop.

We concentrate on chaos-based encryption techniques applying discretised 2D chaotic maps iteratively to image matrices directly (which are also considered experimentally, i.e. [9,20]) and do not cover techniques which XOR the visual data with pseudo-random sequences generated by chaos-based random number generators (e.g. [32]).

In this work, we will look into three security-related weaknesses of chaos-based image and video encryption schemes as follows.

1st Weakness: Security-related Motivation – a major motivation often stated for chaos-based image and video encryption is a security concern when applying cryptographically secure ciphers to images with their intrinsic features

© Springer International Publishing AG 2016
K.-Y. Lam et al. (Eds.): ICICS 2016, LNCS 9977, pp. 278–291, 2016.
DOI: 10.1007/978-3-319-50011-9_22

in particular "high redundancy and strong correlations among adjacent pixels" [26]. In order to justify this concern, it is common in chaos-based image and video encryption literature to refer to the Handbook of Applied Cryptography [17]. Indeed, this resource contains several analyses which apply to encrypting redundant data. First, with respect to practical security concerns, it is stated that redundant plaintext data causes problems for synchronous stream ciphers and block ciphers with small block size, which are prone to dictionary attacks in case of using non-chaining modes like ECB. Obviously, this does not pose a security problem when applying AES in CFB mode to visual data for example. Second, with respect to a more theoretical security concern, there is a close interconnection between the redundancy of plaintext data and the unicity distance, a fact which suggests plaintext data to be as random as possible (which is not the case for classical visual data like image and video data of course). However, todays state-of-the-art encryption schemes are expected to be secure regardless of the data being encrypted. Indeed, the minimum level of security typically expected is ciphertext indistinguishability under a chosen-plaintext attack (IND-CPA). This requires that, even if an adversary may choose the messages being encrypted, (s)he still cannot distinguish the encrypted output from a random bitstring (of equal length). Currently, no attacks have been published that would violate the IND-CPA assumption wrt. AES for example. If an encryption system is severely broken, eventually the nature of the data being encrypted might affect the ability of an attacker to exploit the system's weakness. In that case, any system for which that is the case would be regarded as hopelessly insecure and unsuitable for use today. Therefore, the motivation to use chaos-based encryption for visual data instead of encryption with a cryptographically strong cipher for security reasons cannot be justified.

2nd Weakness: Many broken Algorithms – an extensive analysis of security problems in chaos-based encryption schemes in general, including an analysis of problems with selecting specific chaotic maps is given in [5] and [24] lists several principles of cryptoanalysing chaos-based encryption. A recent review on chaos-based image encryption [18] contains a good selection of papers demonstrating successful cryptanalysis of published chaos-based image encryption schemes and also [33] provides a corresponding survey-like section on successful cryptanalyses. Some examples for the classical "crypto game" in chaos-based image and video encryption, i.e. proposing techniques, which are subsequently broken and enhanced in further work (among them proposals in top quality journals, e.g. [19,31]) are given in Table 1.

Regarding the two chaos-based schemes considered experimentally also the highly referenced paper by Fridrich [9] was subject to cryptanalysis. The paper

Table 1. Examples for the crypto game in chaos-based image encryption.

Proposed technique ...	[3]	[3]	[7]	[12]	[31]	[25]	[29]	[10]	[19]	[11]	[27]	[9]	[9]
Broken/improved by ...	[4]	[15]	[14]	[22]	[33]	[2]	[1]	[13]	[13]	[8]	[30]	[16]	[23]

proposes an encryption scheme which is based on chaotic confusion and pixel diffusion in several iterations. Analysis of this algorithm has been done by [16] and [23]. They conduct a brute force attack, known- and selected plaintext attacks, as well as chosen-ciphertext attacks showing security problems in the algorithm.

Of course, the large amount of broken chaos-based encryption schemes gives rise to the question if current security assessment as done by the proposing authors is indeed sound (and of course, it is not in most cases as we will demonstrate).

3rd Weakness: Insufficient Security Analysis Methodology – the third security-related weakness, intrinsically linked with the second one, is a lack of systematic and sound methodology for security analysis. Of course, a weak security analysis will automatically lead to many algorithms being broken (see second weakness). While any chaos-based encryption algorithm published undergoes some more or less strict experimental security analysis, suggesting its high security standard, many of those schemes are being broken in subsequent publications (see previous subsection). The security analysis conducted in most corresponding publications usually consists of a set of (statistical) measurements applied to encrypted visual data, e.g. computing characteristics like correlation property, sequence tests, entropy or color value distribution. Other methods like NPCR and UACI [28] are used to show the resistance against differential or linear attacks like chosen-plaintext or known-plaintext attacks. Furthermore, NPCR is also used to show key sensitivity of an encryption algorithm. The first problem with this approach is that in many papers, only a limited set of images is used to derive the results and often, only some graphics are shown to qualitatively "prove" a specific property based on an example (e.g. histograms or correlation plots). The second problem, even more severe, is that even if properly conducted on sufficient data and underpinned with quantitative results, passing these tests is only a necessary condition for a secure scheme, but by no means a sufficient one. This will be shown in the remaining part of this work.

Section 2 describes the set of (insecure) image encryption algorithms and security "metrics" used in our experimental analysis. In Sect. 3 results wrt. to security analysis are presented and discussed, while Sect. 4 presents the conclusions which fundamentally question motivations and security analyses of many chaos-based algorithms for visual data encryption.

2   Encryption Algorithms and Security Assessment Metrics

To foster reproducible research, all software written for this paper, including image encryption techniques, security assessment metrics and the experimental framework, are open source and freely available at GitHub: https://github.com/mpreis/seth. Software is implemented in C++. We used the CImg library (http://cimg.sourceforge.net) to handle images.

2.1   Encryption Techniques

Baker's Map. The Baker's map [6] is the probably best known chaotic map. An image is split vertically, stretched horizontally and the resulting pieces are stapled on top of each other. The number of times and the position where the image is split can be chosen arbitrarily and is used as key. This map can be applied to an image as follows [9]:

Define a sequence $n_1, n_2, \ldots, n_k$ where k is the number of rectangles the image is split into. Each n_i must divide the image width N without remainder and $n_1 + \cdots + n_k = N$. Furthermore, $N_i = n_1 + \cdots + n_i$ and $N_0 = 0$.

Let r with $N_{i-1} \leq r < N_i$ and s with $0 \leq s < N$ a pixel in an $N \times N$ image. Then this pixel $(r, \ s)$ is mapped to: (with $q_i = \frac{N}{n_i}$)

$$B(r, s) = \left(\left(q_i * (r - N_i) + (s \mod q_i) \right), \left(\frac{s - (s \mod q_i)}{q_i + N_i} \right) \right) \qquad (1)$$

So far, the algorithm is just a permutation of pixels. To distribute the gray values a substitution is added in the following manner.

Let $(r, \ s)$ be a pixel with gray value g_{rs} which is mapped to $B(r, \ s)$ with gray value $h(r, \ s, g_{rs})$. So, the new gray value depends on the pixel position and the former gray value. A possible way to calculate the new value is the following, where L is the number of gray values:

$$h(r, \ s, g_{rs}) = (g_{rs} + r * s) \mod L \qquad (2)$$

Baker's map may be applied several times. The number of iterations used in our experiments is a random number between 10 and 45. To determine the number of slices we generate a set of n random numbers until the sum of these numbers is equal or greater than the width of the image. If the sum is greater than the image width, the last value is replaced by the image width minus the sum of the $n - 1$ previous values. Each number indicates the width of a single slice.

XOR-Followers. In this approach, deliberately designed to be insecure, a bit is transformed dependent on its following bits. Let k be the length of an arbitrary bitstream key. XOR the next k bits of the current bit with the key and store the resulting bitstream. Then, XOR all bits of this bitstream to get a new bit which is XORed with the current bit. The key space of this algorithm is the worst one considered and the encryption process can also be interpreted as follows. XOR-followers uses the next k bits of an image to calculate the new value of the actual bit. This scheme corresponds to applying a "one-time pad" (OPT) encryption, where the OTP is constructed from the local image content and a fixed key. Obviously, this encryption scheme can not be considered as secure.

We generate a random number which determines the length of the key used for the XOR-followers encryption. There is a minimum length of 8 and a maximum of 256 in our experiments. The next step is to generate a key of length k which is done by taking k random numbers modulo 2.

(a) Original   (b)   XOR-followers (c) XOR short key (d) XOR short key
                (256 bit key)   pixel (256 bit key)   MSB (256 bit key)

Fig. 1. Lena image encrypted.

XOR Short Key is implemented in pixel-mode (encrypts an image pixel by pixel starting at the most significant bit and ends up at the least significant bit) and MSB-mode (encrypts for every pixel of an image at first the most significant bit (MSB), then for every pixel position MSB-1 and so on).

Instead of creating a one time pad to be used as keystream, this approach simply uses a short key which is XORed repetitively with the image content by shifting the key across the image. In our implementation a short key corresponds to an integer number in its binary representation. An integer number leads to a key space of 2^{32} which is way to small to resist brute-force attacks.

The key is a randomly chosen integer number without any bounds. This scheme is known to be severely insecure, especially on highly redundant data (the most well known attack is termed "counting coincidences" [21]).

Figure 1 illustrates the encryption of the Lena image with some example configurations. The visual impression of the ciphertexts shown already strongly indicates the almost negligible level of security achieved.

2.2   Security Assessment Metrics

In this section we describe well known security assessment metrics that are used in the majority of papers on chaos-based image and video encryption to experimentally proof the security of their encryption schemes. We have chosen the tests by analysing the experimental section of several papers that propose a chaos-based encryption scheme, see also Table 1.

Correlation Property. Start with selecting N randomly chosen couples of adjacent pixels from the cipher image. This has to be done three times, for the horizontal, vertical and diagonal correlation property. Then, the correlation coefficient r_{xy} of two adjacent pixels is calculated as follows:

$$E(x) = \frac{1}{N} \sum_i^N x_i, \ D(x) = \frac{1}{N} \sum_i^N (x_i - E(x))^2$$

$$cov(x,y) = \frac{1}{N} \sum_i^N (x_i - E(x)) * (y_i - E(y)), \ r_{xy} = \frac{cov(x,y)}{\sqrt{D(x)} * \sqrt{D(y)}} \tag{3}$$

x, y are gray values of two adjacent pixels. The correlation coefficient r_{xy} is a value between -1 and 1, where 1 and -1 means highly correlated and 0 uncorrelated. Because neighboring pixels in images are highly correlated, this coefficient should approximate 0 for encrypted images to avoid statistical attacks.

Gray Scale Histogram Uniformity. Considering a gray scale histogram of an image one can see a pattern corresponding to the distribution of the relative frequency of the occurring grey values. It is important for an encrypted image to have a different histogram than the original image in particular a uniformly distributed one. We use the variance of the entries of the grey value histogram bins to measure the extent of uniform distribution of an image's histogram. 0 would be a totally uniformly distributed histogram, which would be the optimum for an encrypted image.

NPCR. The number of pixel change rate (NPCR) measures the relative number of different pixels in two images I_1 (original) and I_2 (encrypted) and is calculated by the following equation:

$$NPCR = \frac{\sum_{i,j} D(i,j)}{\text{number of pixels}} * 100\% \tag{4}$$

where

$$D(i,j) = \begin{cases} 0, & I_1(i,j) = I_2(i,j) \\ 1, & \text{otherwise} \end{cases} \tag{5}$$

The higher the better for security, with a maximum of 100%.

UACI. Like NPCR, the unified average changing intensity (UACI) is also used to show the difference of two images I_1 (original) and I_2 (encrypted) and is calculated as follows:

$$UACI = \frac{\sum_{i,j} \frac{I_1(i,j) - I_2(i,j)}{\text{tonal range}}}{\text{number of pixels}} * 100\% \tag{6}$$

The result is also in percent, this means the higher the better, with a maximum of 100% but usually values are much lower and highly depend on image content.

3   Experimental Evaluation

3.1   Experimental Setup

Images and Naming. For all our experiments we used the images of the USC-SIPI image database maintained by the University of Southern California and a dataset of standard test images maintained by the University of Granada, overall 128 images. These databases are freely available at http://sipi.usc.edu/database/ and http://decsai.ugr.es/cvg/CG/base.htm. The used images are of size 512×512 and 8bpp grey scale. We applied each encryption technique to each image and executed each test as described in Sect. 2.2. For each test on every encryption scheme we computed the mean and standard deviation over all images applying 100 randomly selected keys per image. For our visual illustrations we use the famous Lena image which is part of our image pool. In the following section we use shortcuts for the encryption algorithms. Baker's map is denoted *baker*. The substitution-mode of the Baker's map is called *baker-sub*. Further, *xor-key-pix* is used if XOR short key is in pixel-mode and *xor-key-msb* if it is used in MSB-mode. The numbers (*8, 32* or *256*) at the end of a term indicate the key-length in bit. The XOR followers algorithm is denoted *xor-followers* and again we append the key-length.

3.2   Evaluation Results

To provide qualitative results, we use exemplary illustrations of computed values based on the Lena image. Note that this is only meant to visualise basic properties but does not provide any conclusive information, since these visualisations are based on a single image and key only. Quantitative results computed over all images using 100 random keys for each image are provided in tabular form, listing mean values and standard deviation.

Correlation Property Test. In the illustrations, we just focus on the correlation of vertically adjacent pixel pairs. Figure 2a shows the correlation of the original Lena image. As expected, there is a strong dependency, which is indicated by the clustering of the plotted pixel pairs along a diagonal.

Figure 2b illustrates the correlation of Lena encrypted with the XOR short key algorithm in pixel-mode. As we see there are several areas with a higher concentration of pixel pairs. The most significant concentration is along the diagonal, like in the original Lena image. The pixel pairs are not uniformly distributed. This means there are still dependencies among the pixels. The result for the XOR short key algorithm in MSB-mode is not better.

Figure 2c shows the correlation of vertical pixel pairs using the XOR-followers algorithm to encrypt the Lena image. The result is slightly better than the result of XOR short key. Nevertheless, most of the pixel pairs can be found along the diagonals. This shows that there are dependencies between pixel pairs, and this leads to a higher correlation property as also shown by Table 2.

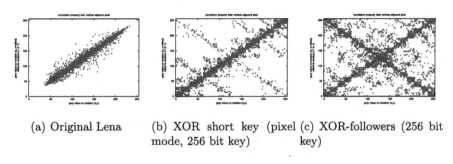

(a) Original Lena   (b) XOR short key (pixel (c) XOR-followers (256 bit
                        mode, 256 bit key)   key)

Fig. 2. Correlation property (vertical).

Table 2 shows the quantitative results of the correlation property computed over all images using the considered encryption schemes. Results basically confirm all visual observation made above. Simplistic algorithms like XOR short key or XOR-followers with short key length lead to poor numerical results also supporting the illustrations. The correlation property of XOR-followers with 256 bit key is ≈ 0.04. If we compare this with the result of the Baker's map, which is 0.002984, we see a large difference. In terms of correlation, chaos-based schemes lead to superior results compared to the deliberately insecure schemes.

Table 2. Average correlation properties over all tested images.

Encryption	Vertical horizontal diagonal			Vertical horizontal diagonal		
	Mean			(Standard deviation)		
xor-key-pix-8	0.710550	0.387219	0.347165	(0.021387)	(0.060259)	(0.054845)
xor-key-pix-32	0.715003	0.397949	0.356478	(0.018945)	(0.039519)	(0.037896)
xor-key-pix-256	0.714619	0.399354	0.357709	(0.018529)	(0.034743)	(0.03362)
xor-key-msb-8	0.886602	0.874574	0.809875	(0.008905)	(0.011872)	(0.023852)
xor-key-msb-32	0.886792	0.874621	0.810086	(0.008856)	(0.011891)	(0.02381)
xor-key-msb-256	0.886764	0.874547	0.810003	(0.008872)	(0.011905)	(0.023846)
xor-followers-8	0.146756	0.146240	0.124010	(0.0374)	(0.038542)	(0.031647)
xor-followers-32	0.073218	0.088525	0.055907	(0.032644)	(0.026302)	(0.023301)
xor-followers-256	0.049615	0.060557	0.033824	(0.025877)	(0.01439)	(0.012841)
baker-sub	0.003207	0.000050	0.000018	(0.001295)	(0.000208)	(0.000202)
baker	0.002984	0.000100	0.000072	(0.00132)	(0.000276)	(0.000262)

Contrasting to other metrics, standard deviation is not larger for worse encryption schemes (see e.g. rather low standard deviation for XOR short key algorithms even for short key length).

Grey Scale Histogram. Figure 3 shows the grey scale histogram of the original Lena image. As expected the grey scale values are not uniformly distributed in

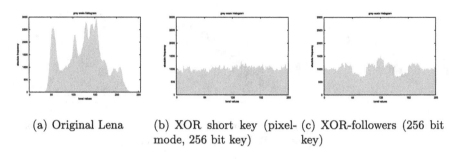

   (a) Original Lena   (b) XOR short key (pixel- (c) XOR-followers (256 bit
                           mode, 256 bit key)   key)

Fig. 3. Grey scale histograms.

the original. As shown in the figure there are several spikes and there are values which are not attained in the original image.

The XOR short key algorithm influences the grey scale values and changes their distribution in the histogram. Therefore, the values are much better distributed than in the original image, which is shown in Fig. 3b. However, we are far from achieving a perfectly flat histogram.

The grey scale histogram of the XOR-followers algorithm shows uniform distribution of the grey scale values only to a medium extent. If we take a closer look we see that there are several spikes which seam to occur periodically, see Fig. 3c. Again, the distribution is not as smooth as would be expected from a perfect algorithm.

Table 3 shows the corresponding quantitative results, i.e. average variance of the grey scale histogram bins over all images. A small value indicates that the gray scale values of an image are uniformly distributed. This test confirms the qualitative results of the displayed grey scale histograms and reports excellent values for Baker's map in substitution mode only. However, the deliberately insecure schemes are still clearly superior to the "pure" chaotic scheme without substitution (both in terms of mean and standard deviation). There is a mix of XOR-followers and XOR short key in pixel mode found as group of second best techniques, where longer keys do not necessarily provide better results.

So far, we have observed inconsistencies wrt. algorithm ranking concerning different metrics: While for the correlation values, both chaos-based encryption schemes deliver better values compared to the deliberately insecure variants, for the histogram-bin variance only Baker's map in substitution mode is better than those algorithms. The permutation-only chaotic scheme is the worst one. Also, the ranking among XOR-followers and the variants of XOR short key is not consistent among the two metrics discussed so far.

NPCR and UACI. NPCR values have their theoretical maximum at 100% while for UACI there is no theoretical maximum, however it is evident that higher values are better. Taking a look at Table 4 we see that the NPCR values of XOR short key in MSB-mode are the worst ones. All other values are above 99%, except for the permutation only chaos-based scheme, the best mean value

Table 3. Grey-scale histogram bin variance.

Encryption	Mean variance	Standard deviation
xor-key-pix-8	5745.642493	6787449468.58157
xor-key-pix-32	5393.119154	15956913550.987
xor-key-pix-256	2075.310975	19580730.204758
xor-key-msb-8	1029635.438768	173086477183998
xor-key-msb-32	1159182.716775	203421440346693
xor-key-msb-256	1100090.429456	189863134653252
xor-followers-8	2924.137718	212041579.480851
xor-followers-32	23195.459391	2735952915334.39
xor-followers-256	21408.063662	3244132007115.65
baker-sub	6.330361	238.709062
baker	2086390.600900	351119352268353

is attained by the XOR-followers with 32 bit key (only the standard deviation is larger compared to Baker's map with substitution). When comparing the computed values with our illustrative encrypted image examples, we note that in the example of the XOR-followers image there are some parts which likely correspond to contours – even though, this approach leads to a very good NPCR value. If we compare the visual encryption result and the NPCR value of the XOR short key algorithm we notice that Lena is still recognisable in both variants. In MSB-mode, as expected, we get a bad NPCR result, but the pixel-mode reaches a value over 99 percent. The NPCR value of XOR short key and XOR-followers algorithms turns out to be independent of the key length.

Table 4 presents the results the UACI test as well. Algorithms with good results in the NPCR test, also exhibit good results result in the UACI test, however, UACI seems to be more discriminative. Baker's map stays under 20 percent, which is one of the worst results. Interestingly, XOR followers with a 32 bit key again performs best with an UACI of 32.9. The XOR short key algorithm in pixel mode gives very poor values. That is remarkable, because this XOR short key variant has an NPCR value over 99 percent. The results show, that the key-length does not lead to better result for XOR short key and XOR followers. We conclude that most of the NPCR test results are confirmed by the UACI test. Encryption schemes with a solid NPCR result also pass at the UACI test, except for XOR short key.

Summarising, NPCR and UACI exhibit further weaknesses: XOR-followers with 32 bit key, an obviously weak encryption scheme, results in the best values. Second, the chaos-based scheme with permutation-only is only better as XOR short key schemes in pixel mode (UACI) or MSB mode (NPCR). UACI is the only metric which does not rate XOR short key in MSB mode as the worst algorithm group. And third, maybe worst, NPCR does not clearly detect (values still beyond 99%) encryption schemes clearly exhibiting visual defects. An

Table 4. Average UACI and NPCR test results.

Encryption	UACI	NPCR	UACI	NPCR
	Mean		(Standard deviation)	
xor-key-pix-8	16.521567	99.241211	(18.667307)	(43.775804)
xor-key-pix-32	16.102003	99.089111	(6.047226)	(7.907319)
xor-key-pix-256	16.122123	99.036255	(2.554497)	(1.115388)
xor-key-msb-8	22.266539	49.492188	(620.447027)	(2499.937434)
xor-key-msb-32	22.337422	49.960938	(613.269976)	(2500.193802)
xosr-key-msb-256	22.544910	50.289062	(617.188992)	(2500.111764)
xor-followers-8	27.916054	99.519661	(65.655065)	(0.062579)
xor-followers-32	32.908797	99.652940	(32.978066)	(2.081644)
xor-followers-256	30.150691	99.455602	(59.791081)	(0.861717)
baker-sub	31.948774	99.608591	(14.196343)	(0.000165)
baker	19.527519	97.055924	(70.996208)	(53.389462)

additional issue with UACI is that even well performing technique exhibit very large standard deviation, indicating a significant dependence on image nature and structure.

4   Conclusion

We have identified and discussed three weaknesses in security-related issues wrt. chaos-based image and video encryption. First, we demonstrate that a commonly used motivation to employ these encryption primitives instead of classical, cryptographically strong ciphers is not valid as modern encryption primitives – for which the IND-CPA assumption is supposed to be valid – do not exhibit the claimed weaknesses when it comes to encrypting highly redundant and correlated data (like image data). Second, an obvious weakness is the high number of broken chaos-based image and video encryption schemes. More severe, typically this fact is ignored in manuscripts proposing new schemes in which of course it should be made clear in how far a new cipher is able to withstand all the demonstrated attacks against related schemes. Third, we were able to experimentally demonstrate that deliberately chosen low-security encryption schemes do not clearly fail a battery of tests for experimental security evaluation, which are commonly used to assess chaos-based encryption schemes for visual data. In particular, we have noticed that

– for NPCR and UACI, XOR-followers with 32 bit key (almost ridiculously low security) is ranked superior to all chaos-based encryption variants;
– for most security "metrics" deliberately weak schemes are rated superior to the permutation-only chaos-based cipher;

- the ranking among the considered encryption algorithms and their variants based on the metrics' values is not at all consistent and thus does not seem to allow any implication about the level of security achieved;
- even visually obvious security deficits are not detected by all metrics considered;
- a very high standard deviation can be observed for many metrics (in many cases associated with low quality mean) emphasising the importance of using large scale image sets and key spaces in experimentation.

Therefore, the commonly used way to experimentally assess security of these schemes is severely questioned since it has to be clear that even passing these tests is necessary for security, but is by no means a sufficient criterion (as spectacularly demonstrated by the multitude of broken algorithms passing these tests).

Acknowledgement. This work has been partially supported by the Austrian Science Fund, project no. 27776.

References

1. Ahmad, M., Imran, R., Shazhad, A.: Cryptanalysis of image encryption algorithm based on fractional-order lorenz-like chaotic system. In: Satapathy, S.C., Govardhan, A., Raju, K.S., Mandal, J.K. (eds.) Emerging ICT for Bridging the Future - Proceedings of the 49th Annual Convention of the Computer Society of India CSI Volume 2. AISC, vol. 338, pp. 381–388. Springer, Heidelberg (2015). doi:10.1007/978-3-319-13731-5_41
2. Ahmad, M.: Cryptanalysis of chaos based secure satellite imagery cryptosystem. In: Aluru, S., Bandyopadhyay, S., Catalyurek, U.V., Dubhashi, D.P., Jones, P.H., Parashar, M., Schmidt, B. (eds.) IC3 2011. CCIS, vol. 168, pp. 81–91. Springer, Heidelberg (2011). doi:10.1007/978-3-642-22606-9_12
3. Alvarez, E., Fernandez, A., García, P., Jiménez, J., Marcano, A.: New approach to chaotic encryption. Phys. Lett. A **263**(4), 373–375 (1999)
4. Alvarez, E., Montoya, F., Romera, M., Pastor, G.: Cryptanalysis of a chaotic encryption system. Phys. Lett. A **276**(4), 191–196 (2000)
5. Alvarez, G., Amigó, J.M., Arroyo, D., Li, S.: Lessons learnt from the cryptanalysis of chaos-based ciphers. In: Kocarev, L., Lian, S. (eds.) Chaos-Based Cryptography: Theory, Algorithms and Applications. Studies in Computational Intelligence, vol. 354, pp. 257–295. Springer, Heidelberg (2011). doi:10.1007/978-3-642-20542-2_8
6. Balatoni, J., Renji, A.: On the notion of entropy (Hungarian). Publ. Math. Inst. Hung. Acad. Sci. **1**(9), 9–40 (1956)
7. Chen, R., Lu, W., Lai, J.: Image encryption using progressive cellular automata substitution and SCAN. In: Proceeding of IEEE International Symposium on Circuits and Systems, vol. 2, pp. 1690–1693 (2005)
8. Cokal, C., Solak, E.: Cryptanalysis of a chaos-based image encryption algorithm. Phys. Lett. A **373**, 1357–1360 (2009)
9. Fridrich, J.: Image encryption based on chaotic maps. In: 1997 IEEE International Conference on Systems, Man, and Cybernetics, 1997. Computational Cybernetics and Simulation, vol. 2, pp. 1105–1110. IEEE (1997)

10. Gao, T., Chen, Z.: A new image encryption algorithm based on hyper-chaos. Phys. Lett. A **372**(4), 394–400 (2008)
11. Guan, Z.H., Huang, F., Guan, W.: Chaos-based image encryption algorithm. Phys. Lett. A **346**(1), 153–157 (2005)
12. Hussain, I., Shah, T., Gondal, M.A.: Image encryption algorithm based on total shuffling scheme and chaotic s-box transformation. J. Vibr. Control **20**(14), 2133–2136 (2014)
13. Jeng, F.G., Huang, W.L., Chen, T.H.: Cryptanalysis and improvement of two hyper-chaos-based image encryption schemes. Sig. Process.: Image Commun. **34**, 45–51 (2015)
14. Li, C., Lo, K.-T.: Cryptanalysis of an image encryption scheme using cellular automata substitution and SCAN. In: Qiu, G., Lam, K.M., Kiya, H., Xue, X.-Y., Kuo, C.-C.J., Lew, M.S. (eds.) PCM 2010. LNCS, vol. 6297, pp. 601–610. Springer, Heidelberg (2010). doi:10.1007/978-3-642-15702-8_55
15. Li, S., Mou, X., Cai, Y.: Improving security of a chaotic encryption approach. Phys. Lett. A **290**(3–4), 127–133 (2001)
16. Lian, S., Sun, J., Wang, Z.: Security analysis of a chaos-based image encryption algorithm. Phys. A: Stat. Mech. Appl. **351**(2), 645–661 (2005)
17. Menezes, A.J., Vanstone, S.A., van Oorschot, P.C.: Handbook of Applied Cryptography (5th printing). CRC Press, Boca Raton (2001)
18. Mishra, M., Mankar, V.: Review on chaotic sequences based cryptography and cryptanalysis. Int. J. Electron. Eng. **3**(2), 189–194 (2011)
19. Rhouma, R., Belghith, S.: Cryptanalysis of a new image encryption algorithm based on hyper-chaos. Phys. Lett. A **372**(38), 5973–5978 (2008)
20. Scharinger, J., Pichler, F.: Efficient image encryption based on chaotic maps. In: Proceedings of the 20th Workshop of the Austrian Association for Pattern Recognition (OAGM/AAPR 1996) on Pattern Recognition. pp. 159–170. Oldenbourg Verlag, Munich (1996)
21. Schneier, B.: Applied Cryptography: Protocols, Algorithms and Source Code in C, 2nd edn. Wiley, Hoboken (1996)
22. Sharma, P.K., Ahmad, M., Khan, P.M.: Cryptanalysis of image encryption algorithm based on pixel shuffling and chaotic S-box transformation. In: Mauri, J.L., Thampi, S.M., Rawat, D.B., Jin, D. (eds.) SSCC 2014. CCIS, vol. 467, pp. 173–181. Springer, Heidelberg (2014). doi:10.1007/978-3-662-44966-0_16
23. Solak, E., Cokal, C., Yildiz, O., Biyikoglu, T.: Cryptanalysis of Fridrich's chaotic image encryption. Int. J. Bifurc. Chaos **20**(5), 1405–1413 (2010)
24. Solak, E.: Cryptanalysis of chaotic ciphers. In: Kocarev, L., Lian, S. (eds.) Chaos-Based Cryptography: Theory, Algorithms and Applications. Studies in Computational Intelligence, vol. 354, pp. 227–256. Springer, Heidelberg (2011). doi:10.1007/978-3-642-20542-2_7
25. Usama, M., Khan, M., Alghathbar, K., Lee, C.: Chaos-based secure satellite imagery cryptosystem. Comput. Math. Appl. **60**(2), 326–337 (2010)
26. Wang, X., Teng, L., Qi, X.: A novel colour image encryption algorithm based on chaos. Sig. Process. **92**(4), 1101–1108 (2012)
27. Wang, X., Guo, K.: A new image alternate encryption algorithm based on chaotic map. Nonlinear Dyn. **76**(4), 1943–1950 (2014)
28. Wu, Y., Noonan, J., Again, S.: NPCR and UACI randomness tests for image encryption. Cyber J.: J. Sel. Areas Telecommun. (JSAT) **4**, 31–38 (2011)
29. Xu, Y., Wang, H., Li, Y., Pei, B.: Image encryption based on synchronization of fractional chaotic systems. Commun. Nonlinear Sci. Numer. Simul. **19**(10), 3735–3744 (2014)

30. Yap, W.S., Phan, R.C.W., Yau, W.C., Heng, S.H.: Cryptanalysis of a new image alternate encryption algorithm based on chaotic map. Nonlinear Dyn. **80**(3), 1483–1491 (2015)
31. Ye, G.D.: Image scrambling encryption algorithm of pixel bit based on chaos map. Pattern Recogn. Lett. **31**, 347–354 (2010)
32. Yen, J.C., Chen, H.C., Wu, S.M.: Design and implementation of a new cryptographic system for multimedia transmission. In: IEEE International Symposium on Circuits and Systems, ISCAS 2005, pp. 6126–6129. IEEE (2005)
33. Zhao, L., Adhikari, A., Xiao, D., Sakurai, K.: Cryptanalysis on an image scrambling encryption scheme based on pixel bit. In: Kim, H.-J., Shi, Y.Q., Barni, M. (eds.) IWDW 2010. LNCS, vol. 6526, pp. 45–59. Springer, Heidelberg (2011). doi:10.1007/978-3-642-18405-5_5

Low-Cost Hardware Implementation of Elliptic Curve Cryptography for General Prime Fields

Yuan Ma[1,2]([✉]), Qinglong Zhang[3], Zongbin Liu[1,2],
Chenyang Tu[1,2], and Jingqiang Lin[1,2]

[1] Data Assurance and Communication Security Research Center,
Chinese Academy of Sciences, Beijing, China
{yma,zbliu,chytu,linjq}@is.ac.cn
[2] State Key Laboratory of Information Security,
Institute of Information Engineering,
Chinese Academy of Sciences, Beijing, China
[3] Huawei Technologies, Zhejiang, China
ql.zhang@huawei.com

Abstract. In resource-constrained applications, elliptic curve cryptography (ECC) is preferable for the property of shorter key size with comparable security. Binary extension fields are usually used for area-optimized implementations, since the complex carry-propagation logics are avoided over these fields. However, efficient ECC implementations over (general) prime fields are still challenging for low-area constraint. As a popular implementation platform for cryptographic algorithms, Field Programmable Gate Array (FPGA) attracts more and more attentions for these applications due to its nice properties of flexibility and short development cycle. In this paper, we propose a compact and efficient arithmetic logical unit (ALU) by highly integrating the functions of Montgomery modular multiplications, additions and subtractions over general prime fields. Then we design a low-cost hardware architecture for generic elliptic curve point multiplications for FPGA platforms. Experimental results indicate that the implementation only occupies 105 Slices, 2 DSP blocks and 2 BRAMs in Spartan-6 FPGA. To the best of our knowledge, our implementation is the smallest for general prime fields in FPGAs.

Keywords: Elliptic curve cryptography · Low-cost · FPGA · Implementation

1 Introduction

Low-cost cryptographic implementations have been more and more attractive for modern applications. A low-cost implementation also means the reduction of

Q. Zhang—This work was performed while the second author was in Chinese Academy of Sciences.

© Springer International Publishing AG 2016
K.-Y. Lam et al. (Eds.): ICICS 2016, LNCS 9977, pp. 292–306, 2016.
DOI: 10.1007/978-3-319-50011-9_23

consumed resources and power, which is necessary for these constrained scenarios. Although the available resources are strictly constrained, public-key cryptography (PKC) involving burdensome arithmetic is usually required due to its advantages over symmetric cryptography. Compared with RSA or other PKC algorithms over finite fields, elliptic curve cryptography (ECC) uses a much shorter key to achieve an equivalent level of security. Therefore, ECC implementations are preferred for resource-constrained applications owing to the lower computational complexity and other nice properties such as reduced storage and power consumption. Compared with software and ASIC (Application Specific Integrated Circuit) implementations of ECC, FPGA implementation is a better choice in the trade-off between execution speed and development period. In addition, FPGAs are often used as the early-validation platforms for the ASICs, thus have important research values.

ECC designs can be roughly split into two categories: over (extended) binary fields $\mathbb{F}_{2^n}$ and over prime fields $\mathbb{F}_p$, and also some designs support both the two. The first category offers better performance and lower resource consumption, mostly because no carry is propagated in the field structure. That is why most area-optimized designs focus on binary field implementations. Nevertheless, prime fields also have significant value either in the applications, such as digital signature generation, or in the standards of elliptic curves [4,5,16]. The NIST curves over binary or prime fields have significant advantages in area and speed for hardware implementations, as fast reduction methods can be adopted and the parameters are fixed. Therefore, most of the low-area targeted designs [1,6,8,11,18,19,21,23] (especially in ASICs) are focusing on these standardized curves. These implementations are efficient for elliptic curve point multiplications (ECPMs), but for further applications (such as digital signature generation), they are hard to be complete these functions alone. For example, the Elliptic Curve Digital Signature Algorithm (ECDSA) needs another prime (the order of the base point) field operations for the final operation, but fast reduction methods cannot be applicable for that prime which is not special. Existing implementations based on the fast reduction have to specifically add the scheduling instructions and improve the hardware arithmetic unit for supporting the signature generation, such as [18].

In this paper, in order to better support the applications based on ECC (such as curve transition, or signature generation and key agreement which require the operations over another prime field) for area-constrained scenarios, we propose a low-cost hardware ECC implementation for general prime fields based on Montgomery modular multiplications. Besides supporting the operation over another prime field under the same curve, the implementation also supports the transition of different curves (of the same length) without reconfiguration. For example, if needed, the user can switch the underlying curve from the NIST curve P-256 to the SM2 elliptic curve (Chinese ECC standard [16]) through writing new parameters for meeting certain demands.

The implementation is constructed based on our proposed prime-field arithmetic logical unit (ALU) for modular arithmetic, which is able to perform the operations of Montgomery modular multiplications, additions and subtractions with high compatibility. For the sake of efficiency, the ALU is designed to be a high-radix architecture. Particularly, we employ Shift Register Look-up Table (SRLs) in FPGAs to implement long registers to minimize the occupied area, and eliminate the operations between additions/subtractions and Montgomery multiplications to decrease the control circuits. Furthermore, we maximize the frequency of the ALU with the help of the dedicated DSP (Digital Signal Processing) blocks in modern FPGAs, and the execution efficiency of the ECC implementation is significantly improved. In the higher level, we optimize the scheduling process in the point addition to improve the use efficiency of the ALU. Finally, we implement the design in Spartan-6 FPGA platform. The design only occupies 105 Slices, 2 DSP blocks and 2 BRAMs in Spartan-6 FPGA with a low computation latency. Comparison results indicate that our implementation outperforms the existing works in FPGAs over prime fields in the aspect of area, and a lot of logic Slices or dedicated cores are saved.

The rest of this paper is organized as follows. Section 2 presents the preliminaries for elliptic curve cryptography. Section 3 describes the hardware architectures of the ALU and the ECC processor. Section 4 gives implementation results in FPGAs. Section 5 presents the comparison results with related work. Section 6 concludes the paper.

2   Elliptic Curve Cryptography

The elliptic curve is defined over a field $\mathbb{K}$ given by the Weierstrass equation:

$$E : y^2 + a_1 xy + a_3 y = x^3 + a_2 x^2 + a_4 x + a_6. \tag{1}$$

In the case of the characteristic $Char(\mathbb{K}) \neq 2, 3$, the general Weierstrass equation is simplified to

$$E : y^2 = x^3 + ax + b. \tag{2}$$

In [14], Montgomery developed an original technique to compute multiples of points on an elliptic curve, as shown in Algorithm 1. His technique is based on the fact that the sum of two points whose difference is a known point can be computed without the y-coordinates of the two points. For each iteration in the Montgomery ladder algorithm, $Q_1 - Q_0$ always equals to the base point P, thus can be preset as a constant in advance. As the speed is not the primary optimization goal, we do not adopt more efficient algorithms such as NAF (Nonadjacent Form) or window-based algorithms, but employ the Montgomery ladder algorithm whose control is simpler. In addition, the method is resistant against Simple Power Analysis (SPA).

Let $P = (x_1, y_1)$ and $Q = (x_2, y_2) \in E(\mathbb{F}_q)$ with $P \neq \pm Q$, and $P + Q = (x_3, y_3)$, $2P = (x_4, y_4)$. Given the point $P - Q = (x', y')$, the x-coordinates of $P + Q$ and $2P$ satisfy [2]:

$$x_3 = \frac{2(x_1 + x_2)(x_1 x_2 + a) + 4b}{(x_1 - x_2)^2} - x', \tag{3}$$

Algorithm 1. Montgomery ladder algorithm for point multiplication

---

Input: $P \in E(\mathbb{F}_q)$, $k = (k_{l-1}, ..., k_1, k_0)$ with $k_{l-1} = 1$
Output: kP
1: $Q_0 = P$; $Q_1 = 2P$
2: **for** $i = l - 2$ down **to** 0 **do**
3:     **if** $k_i = 0$ **then**
4:         $Q_1 = Q_0 + Q_1$; $Q_0 = 2Q_0$
5:     **else**
6:         $Q_0 = Q_0 + Q_1$; $Q_1 = 2Q_1$
7:     **end if**
8: **end for**
9: return (Q_0)

---

and

$$x_4 = \frac{(x_1^2 - a)^2 - 8bx_1}{4(x_1^3 + ax_1 + b)}. \tag{4}$$

The formulas for point addition and point doubling require a field inversion and several field multiplications. If inversion in $\mathbb{K}$ is significantly more expensive than multiplication, then it may be advantageous to represent points using projective coordinates.

The projective point $(X : Y : Z)$, $Z \neq 0$, corresponds to the affine point $(X/Z, Y/Z)$. The projective equation of the elliptic curve is

$$Y^2 Z = X^3 + aXZ^2 + bZ^3.$$

The point at infinity ∞ corresponds to $(0 : 1 : 0)$, while the negative of $(X : Y : Z)$ is $(X : -Y : Z)$. Under the standard projective coordinate, these equations becomes [10]:

$$Z_3 = (X_1 Z_2 + X_2 Z_1)^2, \tag{5}$$
$$X_3 = 2(X_1 Z_2 + X_2 Z_1)(X_1 X_2 + aZ_1 Z_2) + 4bZ_1^2 Z_2^2 - x' Z_3, \tag{6}$$
$$Z_4 = 4Z_1(X_1^3 + aX_1 Z_1^2 + bZ_1^3), \tag{7}$$
$$X_4 = (X_1^2 + aZ_1^2)^2 - 8bX_1 Z_1^3. \tag{8}$$

In some cases (such as public key generation), the y-coordinate is required. The y-coordinate of P can be deduced by:

$$y_1 = \frac{2b + (a + x' x_1)(x' + x_1) - x_2(x' - x_1)^2}{2y'}.$$

Note that y' is the y-coordinate of the base point that is known in advance in Algorithm 1, so $(2y')^{-1}$ can be pre-computed and the inversion is replaced by a multiplication in the equation.

In the original ladder, the addition and doubling are computed separately. For sake of efficiency, Izu et al. [9] encapsulated these formulae into one formula, which outputs x-coordinate values of $P + Q$ and $2P$ on inputs P and Q. With a projective version of the x-coordinate-only formulae, X_3, Z_3, X_4, Z_4 can be computed with 17 multiplications and 18 additions. The number of auxiliary variables for the formulae is 7. The y-coordinate recovery algorithm requires 13 multiplications and 7 additions and 7 auxiliary variables [9]. For one ECPM, the y-coordinate recovery is only performed once, thus has negligible impact on the execution efficiency.

3   Hardware Architecture

In general, the compact ECC architecture is usually composed of four parts: the ALU for finite-field arithmetic, data memory, program memory and other control circuits. The core of the design is to simplify the ALU operations and further utilize the ALU efficiently for elliptic curves arithmetic. In this section, we first propose a compact and efficient ALU architecture based on a series of design policies, and then design a low-cost ECC architecture.

3.1   ALU Design

Design Policy. The design of an ALU is crucial for ECC implementations. The purpose of our design is to construct a compact and area-saving architecture. To achieve this goal, we establish the following design policy for the circuit architecture.

1. To support the operations of general prime fields or generic curves rather than specific curves (such as NIST curves) in order to guarantee the flexibility.
2. To set the bus width of the input/output signals to no more than 16 bits in order to simplify the control, and to use single-port RAM rather than dual-port RAM.
3. To integrate all the prime-field operations to use the same computing circuit in order to save consumed resources.
4. To specifically enrich the ALU functions to optimize the scheduling process inside the elliptic curve arithmetic.

Item (1) ensures the flexibility of the ECC implementation, so that it is not only suitable for the NIST primes (such as P-192, P-256) but also for the operations over general prime fields. Item (2) guarantees lower-resource consumption when using RAMs. With narrower width and single port RAM, smaller area of control circuits are consumed. The use of single-port RAM is to improve the transportability of the architecture. Item (3) makes the same circuit perform modular multiplication, addition and subtraction by configuration, which improves the utilization. Item (4) enhances the efficiency for calculating point addition and doubling, as some involved specific operations can be optimally executed by the ALU.

Modular Arithmetic. According to the design policy (1), we choose Montgomery multiplication as the underlying modular multiplication algorithm, rather than the fast reduction method which is only available for pseudo Mersenne primes such as NIST standardized primes [5]. Montgomery multiplication is a method to perform modular multiplication without the need to perform division by the modulus [13]. A version of Montgomery's algorithm [17] is given as Algorithm 2. This algorithm avoids multiplication and addition in quotient determination to simplify the computation.

Algorithm 2. Montgomery multiplication algorithm with simplified quotient determination [17]

Input:

A modulus $M > 2$ with $\gcd(M,2) = 1$ and positive integers w, n such that $4\widetilde{M} < 2^{wn}$, where $\widetilde{M}$ is given by $\widetilde{M} = (\bar{M} \bmod 2^w)M$.

Integer R^{-1}, where $(2^{wn}R^{-1})\bmod M = 1$

Integer $\bar{M}$, where $(-M\bar{M})\bmod 2^w = 1$

Integer multiplicand A, where $0 \leq A \leq 2\widetilde{M}$

Integer multiplier $B = \sum_{i=0}^{n}(2^w)^i b_i$, where digit $b_n = 0, b_i \in \{0,1,\ldots,2^w - 1\}$ for $0 \leq i < n$ and $0 \leq B \leq 2\widetilde{M}$

Output:

An integer S_{n+1} where $S_{n+1} \equiv ABR^{-1}(\bmod M)$ and $0 \leq S_{n+1} \leq 2\widetilde{M}$

1: $S_0 = 0$;
2: **for** $i = 0$ **to** n **do**
3:     $q_i = S_i \bmod 2^w$;
4:     $S_{i+1} = S_i \text{ div } 2^w + q_i M' + b_i A$, where $M' = (\widetilde{M} + 1) \text{ div } 2^w$;
5: **end for**
6: **return** S_{n+1}

On the observation from Algorithm 2, the step to calculate S_{i+1} is crucial for this modular multiplication. In order to make this algorithm suitable for hardware implementation, we propose a processing method which uses two w-bit multipliers and a few adders, as shown in Algorithm 3. The long integer S_i and M' are split into w-bit blocks. The remaining inputs appearing in Algorithm 2 are omitted.

In Algorithm 3, S_i and M' are divided into n w-bit blocks. S_i is represented as: $S_i = \{S_i^{(n-1)}, S_i^{(n-2)}, \ldots, S_i^{(0)}\}$. During the initialization procedure, S_0 and $(w+1)$-bit $Carry$ are set to be zero. After the initialization, there are two loops to complete the Montgomery multiplication. For the operands A and B, the outer loop is responsible for the split of B and the inner loop controls the use of w-bit a_j. The most resource consuming calculation is in the inner loop, and this calculation is involved with two w-bit multipliers and an addition with four addends. Since the inner loop consumes n clocks and the outer loop has $(n+1)$ times, it takes $n(n+1)$ clocks to finish one Montgomery multiplication.

Algorithm 3. Processing method for the compact design of Montgomery multiplication

---

Input:
   $A, B, M' = \{m'_{n-1}, \ldots, m'_0\}$
Output:
   $S_{n+1} \equiv ABR^{-1}(\mod M)$ and $0 \leq S_{n+1} \leq 2\widetilde{M}$.
1: $S_0 = 0, Carry = \{w+1\}'b0;$
2: **for** $i = 0$ **to** n **do**
3:      $q_i = S_i^{(0)};$
4:    **for** $j = 0$ **to** $n-1$ **do**
5:      $\{Carry, S_{i+1}^{(j)}\} = S_i^{(j+1)} + Carry + q_i m'_j + b_i a_j;$
6:    **end for**
7: **end for**
8: **return** S_{n+1}

Based on the processing method, we add the modular addition and subtraction function by using the existing accumulator in the multiplier. In fact, the Montgomery multiplication has the function of reduction by expanding R. For example, for any input $A, B < 4\widetilde{M}$, when $R = 2^{wn} > 4 \times 4\widetilde{M} = 16\widetilde{M}$, the final result still satisfies $0 < S_{n+1} < 2\widetilde{M}$. Therefore, we do not perform the reduction of the addition results, but only to guarantee the multiplier input in the range of $(0, 4\widetilde{M})$. For modular subtraction, we need to add integer multiples of M to the subtraction result when it is negative. The algorithm for modular addition and subtraction is shown in Algorithm 4.

Algorithm 4. Modular addition and subtraction sharing the circuit of Montgomery multiplication

---

Input: $A, B, \widetilde{M},$
        operation flag $sub \in \{0, 1\}$ denotes a subtraction when $sub = 1$ and addition otherwise;
Output: S
1: $S = 0, Carry = (w+1)'b0;$
2: **for** $j = 0$ **to** $n-1$ **do**
3:    $\{Carry, S^{(j)}\} = Carry + b_j \oplus \{sub\} + a_j + (j == 0?1 : 0);$
4: **end for**
5: **while** $Carry \neq 0$ **do**
6:    $\{Carry, S\} = \{Carry, S\} + \widetilde{M};$
7: **end while**
8: **return** S

In the initialization of Algorithm 4, S_0 and $(w+1)$-bit $Carry$ are set to zero. According to the operation flag sub, the accumulator can complete both addition and subtraction. When the operation is modular addition, after the n-time loop, the operation is completed. When the operation is modular subtraction, the XOR operation is activated and '1' is added in the first round. Furthermore, if $Carry$ is not zero after the iteration, which means the final result of S is negative, it requires extra additions with $\widetilde{M}$ until S is positive.

Design Architecture. The ALU architecture integrating Montgomery multiplication, addition and subtraction operations is depicted as Fig. 1. According the design policy (2), only one data input port is allowed for the ALU. There are three logic calculation units: two w-bit multipliers and one adder with four inputs. Also, there are two long shift registers which are used for storing M' and the computed result S, and these two registers are shifted w-bit every clock. Here, we carefully minimize the number of states of the shift registers to reduce the control circuits for these massive registers.

The data flow of the multiplication in the ALU is explained as follows. Before the first modular multiplication, we should load the modulus into the shift register M' and the bus width of this data input port is w, so it takes nearly $(n-1)$-time shifts to finish the loading. Note that the loading operation is only executed once at the beginning of the prime field computation. Algorithm 3 is performed after rightmost w-bit b_0 into the ALU register. Then $a_0, a_1, \cdots, a_{n-1}$ successively enter the left multiplier unit of the ALU figure. The width of the addition result is $2w+1$ bit, where the higher $w+1$ bits are fed back to the adder in the next cycle and the rest are put into the S shift registers. Due to the one extra cycle for loading b_i, the total clock cycles for one multiplication increases to $(n+1)^2$.

The addition and subtraction shares the same accumulator of the ALU. The configuration is easily completed by using the multiplexers which are responsible for switching the values of sub and zero. Another advantage of the ALU structure is that it can perform the operation $\alpha A \pm \beta B$, where $\alpha, \beta \in [0, 2^w - 1]$ and $\beta \equiv 1$ for subtraction. The function is more powerful by combining Algorithm 4, as the result can be immediately input to the ALU for Montgomery multiplication without modular reduction gradually. This is useful to merge the adjacent additions and subtractions in point addition and doubling algorithms, thus saves program commands and consumed time. The required clock cycles for one-time addition/subtraction is $2(n+1)$.

3.2   FPGA Optimization

In modern FPGAs, the dedicated resources and multifunctional logics allows us to further improve the efficiency of the ALU.

Maximizing Frequency. The maximum frequency of the ALU is limited due to the long critical path, which consists of one multiplier, one adder of four numbers and some multiplexers, as shown in Fig. 1. This could reduce the compatibility of the ALU (or the ECC implementation) with high-speed modules that run at a high frequency in the same FPGA. Therefore, we maximize the frequency of

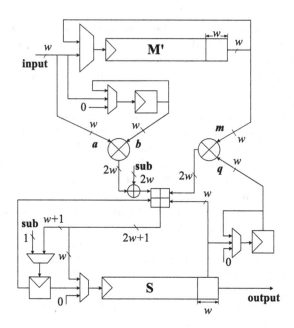

Fig. 1. The ALU architecture

the ALU with the help of the dedicated DSP (Digital Signal Processing) blocks in modern FPGAs, which also significantly improves the execution efficiency of the ECC implementation. In our targeted FPGA platform Xilinx Spartan-6, the DPS block named DSP48A1 is able to perform (mixed) multiplications and subtractions/additions efficiently, and the frequency can achieve very high by inserting the registers (i.e., pipeline) inside DSP blocks.

In the pipeline setting up, to guarantee that the result is computed in each loop after the pipeline is filled, we shall recognize that which variables can be known in advance and which ones cannot be. The critical data path of the ALU in the i-round j-loop is represented as:

$$\{Carry, S_{i+1}^{(j)}\} = Carry + S_i^{(j+1)} + q_i * m_j' + a_i * b_j,$$

where the variables except for $Carry$ for the next loop are known before the end of the current loop, thus can be pre-computed. In addition, the result of $a_i * b_j$ should be negated for the subtraction operation (b_j always equals 1 for the subtraction), and we also put the negation operation into the DSP blocks by being subtracted with w-bit 1's.

The data path with pipelines inside DSP blocks is depicted as Fig. 2, which contains two DSP blocks with a three-stage pipeline. The stage latencies are balanced to maximize the frequency. In the 1st stage, the two multiplications are performed. The negation and the addition operations are processed in the 2nd stage, and the two DSP blocks are connected using the cascade connection ports PCOUT and PCIN to decrease the wire delay. The remain three-number addition is performed in the 3rd stage. After the frequency optimization, the maximum frequency of ALU is improved to 200 MHz in our experiment, which is nearly three times than the original. The execution time of the multiplication or addition/subtraction sightly increases by two clock cycles that is caused by filling up the pipeline.

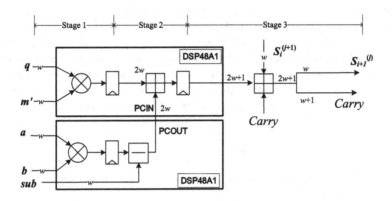

Fig. 2. The optimized data path with pipelines

Minimizing Area. In the ALU, the main consumed resources are divides into three parts: multiplier and adder units, the long shift registers, and the control circuit, and we have put some addition operations in the DSP blocks to improve the resource utilization. Here we further employ the SRLs in FPGAs to implement the long shift registers. SRLs are one type of LUTs that can efficiently implement shift registers. One 6-input SRL can compose 1-bit-width and 64-bit-depth shift registers, while it requires 64 registers in the non-optimizing manner. In addition, as we mentioned, the two groups of shift registers (S and M in Fig. 1) have only two states: suspending and shifting, except for the heading registers that have different inputs. For SRL implementations, each SRL has an input to control the inside registers shifting or not. Therefore, these registers can be efficiently implemented in FPGAs with a ultra-low cost.

3.3 ECC Architecture

Based on the ALU design and the Montgomery ladder algorithm for point multiplication, we design our ECC architecture by utilizing decoders and program commands to control all the required operations over prime fields. The ECC architecture is designed as shown in Fig. 3. Except for the ALU module, two memories are deployed in the architecture. One is the PROGRAM ROM and the other is a DATA RAM which is used for storing intermediate values, the constants, and the final results.

Point multiplication is composed of a series of point addition and point doubling. After the mix of modular multiplications and additions by utilizing the multiple-and-addition function of the ALU, one point addition and doubling needs 17 modular multiplications and 12 modular addition/subtraction. For each modular multiplication or modular addition/subtraction, there is a command to indicate the type of this operator, the addresses for the operands of this operator. Therefore, for one point addition and point doubling there are 29 commands in total and there is a decoder to determine which command is used for next calculation according to k. In order to simplify the decoder, we have two sets of commands in the PROGRAM ROM, one set of 29 commands is for the case in which k_i is 0, and the other set of 29 commands is for the case in which k_i is 1.

Modular inversion is required for transferring the projective coordinates to affine ones or generating the signature. In our implementation, the operation is carried out by utilizing the ALU, and the commands are also stored in the ROM of Fig. 3. We take advantage of Fermat's little theorem to calculate the inversion, which is

$$a^{p-2} \equiv a^{-1} \bmod p. \tag{9}$$

Hence, the operation of modular inversion just consumes a few extra memory and control circuits.

4   Hardware Implementation

In this section, we implement the 256-bit ECC architecture in Xilinx FPGAs, and evaluate its area and efficiency.

4.1   Efficiency

For demonstration purposes, we implement 256-bit ECPM of generic curves over prime fields in FPGAs. The parameters of the ALU and ECC processor are set as follows. The modulus M has 256-bit length, the width $w = 16$, $n = 18$, and $R = 2^{wn} = 2^{288}$. Hence, the total number of processing cycles for a modular multiplication and addition/subtraction is $(n+1)^2+2 = 363$ and $2(n+1)+2 = 40$,

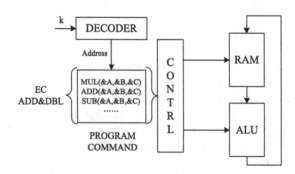

Fig. 3. The ECC architecture

respectively. The RAM size is set to 256-bit depth and 16-bit width (256×16), and the program ROM size is 128×16.

For 256-bit ECPM, the required clock cycles of $w = 16$ for different operations are listed in Table 1. One 256-bit ECPM has at most 256 point addition & doubling operations for Montgomery ladder algorithm. The inversion in the ECPM is only considered once. The y-coordinate is also calculated at the end of ECPM. As a result, the 256-bit ECPM for generic curves can be completed in about 1847 K clock cycles for $w = 16$.

Table 1. Required clock cycles for the operations ($w = 16$)

Operation	MUL	ADD/SUB	Point ADD & DBL	INV	Other	ECPM
Clock cycles	363	40	6651	139392	5362	1847410

4.2 FPGA Implementation

We implement the ECC processor on Xilinx Spartan-6 (XC6SLX45T-4) and Spartan-3E (XC3S100E-5) FPGAs. The two FPGAs are both low-cost-application oriented, while the latter is an old device which is useful for the fair comparison with previous work. The post place and route (PAR) implementation results by ISE 14.6 are shown in Table 2. Note that the differences between internal structure of the two FPGAs make the consumed logics seemingly significantly different. One Slice in Spartan-3E contains two 4-input LUTs and two flip-flops, while the Slice in Spartan-6 contains four 6-input LUTs and four flip-flops. The multiplier resources are multi-functional DSP units in Spartan-6, while they are multiplier hardcores (MULT) in Spartan-3E. It is noted that the functions that were completed in DSP blocks are implemented using LUT logics in Spartan-3E.

Table 2. PAR results of the ECC processor in FPGAs

Device	Resource					Speed	
	LUT	Flip-flop	Slice	DSP/MULT	BRAM	Frequency	ECPM latency
Spartan-6	332	372	105	2	2	200.4 MHz	9.2 ms
Spartan-3E	520	392	350	2	2	145.6 MHz	12.7 ms

On Spartan-3E FPGA, 350 Slices, 2 MULTs, and 2 BRAMs are occupied to implement our ECC architecture with $w = 16$, including 520 LUTs and 392 Flip-flops. The maximum frequency on Spartan-3E is 145.6 MHz, and it needs 12.7 ms to finish one ECPM. In Spartan-6 FPGA, it costs only 105 Slices (including 332 6-input LUTs and 382 flip-flops), 2 DSP blocks and 2 BRAMs. One ECPM consumes only 9.2 ms with $w = 16$ in Spartan-6. From these results, it is observed that our low-cost ECC architecture has an excellent performance in FPGAs: very small area with a low computation latency.

5   Related Work and Comparison

Many low-cost ECC implementations are targeted to ASICs. Because the area is extremely constrained and the application is specific, the ASIC implementations use standardized curves that support the fast reduction, such as [1,6,8,11,18,23]. Different with their underlying methods, we choose the Montgomery multiplication as the modular method, which is more complex than the fast reduction, but is more flexible. This allows us to support generic curves or different prime fields under the same curve without reconfiguration. Hence, we do not perform the comparison with ASIC implementations due to the differences in the underlying platform and the design goal.

Table 3. Comparison of ECC implementations in FPGAs (256-bit prime field)

Work	FPGA	Curve	Slice	MULT/DSP	BRAM	Freq. (MHz)	Latency (ms)
This work (16 bit)	Spartan-6	any	105	2	2	200.4	9.2
	Spartan-3E	any	350	2	2	145.6	12.7
Vliegen [22] (16 bit)	Virtex-2 Pro	any	1832	2	9	108.2	29.83
Varchola [21] (16 bit)	Virtex-2 Pro	P-256	773	1	3	210.0	10.02
Roy [19]	Spartan-6	P-256	72	8	24	156.25	12.2
McIvor [3]	Virtex-2 Pro	any	15755	256	0	39.5	3.84
Tawalbeh [12]	Virtex-5	any	20000	0	0	200	1.66
Ghosh [20]	Virtex-4	any	13661	0	0	43	9.2
Guillermin [15]	Stratix II	any	9177ALM	96	0	157.2	0.68
Ma [24]	Virtex-5	any	1725	37	10	291	0.38
Güneysu [7]	Virtex-4	P-256	1715	32	11	490	0.45

Table 3 lists related works for ECC implementations in FPGAs, where the former three [19,21,22] focused on compact implementations and others [3,7,12,15,20,24] on high-speed implementations. Especially, [7,19,21] optimized the implementation efficiency for NIST prime P-256. Vliegen *et al.* [22] presented a compact FPGA-based architecture for ECC over prime fields by using the coarsely integrated operand scanning (CIOS) method of Montgomery multiplication. The architecture is available for any prime-field curve, but the occupied area is large. Varchola *et al.* [21] optimized the computational unit using fast reduction for the NIST primes, and obtained a very high frequency and relative small area (773 Slices in Virtex-2 Pro). Targeting generic curves, our optimized ECC architecture has a significant lower area than these two works. As Virtex-2 family FPGAs are not recommended by Xilinx, we choose Spartan-3E FPGA, which has a similar structure of Virtex-2 Pro, to perform the comparison. In our implementation, only 350 Slices with 2 MULTs and 2 BRAMs are consumed, thus more than half of the resources are saved in the comparison with [22] and [21]. Roy et al. [19] recently present a single instruction based light ECC processor coupled with dedicated hardcores of the FPGAs for NIST P-256. The implementation only occupies 72 Slices, but the consumed DSP blocks and BRAMs are relatively more (8 DSP blocks and 24 BRAMs). Therefore, our implementation achieves a good balance in the consumed logics and hardcores. Furthermore, thanks to the optimization inside DSP blocks, our ECC implementation is able to run at a high frequency and compute the ECPM for general prime fields with a low latency.

6 Conclusion

In this paper, we propose a very low-cost ECC implementation for general prime fields. In the architecture design, we efficiently integrate all the prime operations into the compact ALU, and specifically optimize its functions for elliptic curve arithmetic. In the architecture implementation, we further adopt platform-targeted optimization techniques, such as pipeline inside DSP blocks and SRL implementation in FPGAs, and this allows us to further reduce the area of the implementation and improve the efficiency. Experimental results indicate that the implementation only occupies 105 Slices, 2 DSP blocks and 2 BRAMs in Spartan-6 FPGA. In future work, we will add the countermeasures into the implementation to resist side channel attacks.

Acknowledgments. We thank the anonymous reviewers of SAC 2016 and ICICS 2016 for their invaluable suggestions and comments. This work was partially supported by National Basic Research Program of China (973 Program No. 2013CB338001), National Natural Science Foundation of China (No. 61602476, No. 61402470) and Strategy Pilot Project of Chinese Academy of Sciences (No. XDA06010702).

References

1. Bosmans, J., Roy, S.S., Järvinen, K., Verbauwhede, I.: A tiny coprocessor for elliptic curve cryptography over the 256-bit NIST prime field. In: 29th International Conference on VLSI Design and 15th International Conference on Embedded Systems, VLSID 2016, Kolkata, India, 4–8 January 2016, pp. 523–528 (2016)
2. Brier, É., Joye, M.: Weierstraß elliptic curves and side-channel attacks. In: Naccache, D., Paillier, P. (eds.) PKC 2002. LNCS, vol. 2274, pp. 335–345. Springer, Heidelberg (2002). doi:10.1007/3-540-45664-3_24
3. McIvor, C., McLoone, M., McCanny, J.: An FPGA elliptic curve cryptographic accelerator over GF(p). In: Irish Signals and Systems Conference (ISSC), pp. 589–594 (2004)
4. Cericom Research: Standards for Efficient Cryptography - SEC-1: Elliptic curve cryptography (2000). www.secg.org/sec1-v2.pdf
5. Cericom Research: Standards for Efficient Cryptography - SEC-2: Recommended Elliptic Curve Domain Parameters (2000). www.secg.org/SEC2-Ver-1.0.pdf
6. Furbass, F., Wolkerstorfer, J.: ECC processor with low die size for rfid applications. In: International Symposium on Circuits and Systems (ISCAS) 2007, pp. 1835–1838. IEEE (2007)
7. Güneysu, T., Paar, C.: Ultra high performance ECC over NIST primes on commercial FPGAs. In: Oswald, E., Rohatgi, P. (eds.) CHES 2008. LNCS, vol. 5154, pp. 62–78. Springer, Heidelberg (2008). doi:10.1007/978-3-540-85053-3_5

8. Hutter, M., Feldhofer, M., Plos, T.: An ECDSA processor for RFID authentication. In: Ors Yalcin, S.B. (ed.) RFIDSec 2010. LNCS, vol. 6370, pp. 189–202. Springer, Heidelberg (2010). doi:10.1007/978-3-642-16822-2_16

9. Izu, T., Möller, B., Takagi, T.: Improved elliptic curve multiplication methods resistant against side channel attacks. In: Menezes, A., Sarkar, P. (eds.) INDOCRYPT 2002. LNCS, vol. 2551, pp. 296–313. Springer, Heidelberg (2002). doi:10.1007/3-540-36231-2_24

10. Izu, T., Takagi, T.: A fast parallel elliptic curve multiplication resistant against side channel attacks. In: Naccache, D., Paillier, P. (eds.) PKC 2002. LNCS, vol. 2274, pp. 280–296. Springer, Heidelberg (2002). doi:10.1007/3-540-45664-3_20

11. Kern, T., Feldhofer, M.: Low-resource ECDSA implementation for passive RFID tags. In: 17th IEEE International Conference on Electronics, Circuits, and Systems, ICECS 2010, Athens, Greece, 12–15. pp. 1236–1239, December 2010

12. Tawalbeh, L., Mohammad, A., Gutub, A.: Efficient FPGA implementation of a programmable architecture for GF(p) elliptic curve crypto computations. J. Sig. Process. Syst. **59**(3), 233–244 (2010)

13. Montgomery, P.L.: Modular multiplication without trial division. Math. Comput. **44**(170), 519–521 (1985)

14. Montgomery, P.L.: Speeding the pollard and elliptic curve methods of factorization. Math. Comput. **48**(177), 243–264 (1987)

15. Guillermin, N.: A high speed coprocessor for elliptic curvescalar multiplications over Fp. Cryptographic Hardw. Embed. Syst. (CHES) **2010**, 48–64 (2010)

16. Office of State Commercial Cryptography Administration: Public Key Cryptographic Algorithm SM2 Based on Elliptic Curves (2012, in Chinese). http://www.oscca.gov.cn/UpFile/2010122214822692.pdf

17. Orup, H.: Simplifying quotient determination in high-radix modular multiplication. In: IEEE Symposium on Computer Arithmetic, pp. 193–199 (1995)

18. Pessl, P., Hutter, M.: Curved tags - a low-resource ECDSA implementation tailored for RFID. Radio Freq. Ident.: Secur. Priv. Issues (RFIDSec) **2014**, 156–172 (2014)

19. Roy, D.B., Das, P., Mukhopadhyay, D.: ECC on Your fingertips: a single instruction approach for lightweight ECC design in $GF(p)$. In: Dunkelman, O., Keliher, L. (eds.) SAC 2015. LNCS, vol. 9566, pp. 161–177. Springer, Heidelberg (2016). doi:10.1007/978-3-319-31301-6_9

20. Ghosh, S., Alam, M., Chowdhury, D.R., Gupta, I.S.: Parallel crypto-devices for GF(p) elliptic curve multiplication resistant against side channel attacks. In: Comput. Electr. Eng. pp. 329–338 (2009)

21. Varchola, M., Guneysu, T., Mischke, O.: Microecc: a lightweight reconfigurable elliptic curve crypto-processor. In: International Conference on Reconfigurable Computing and FPGAs (ReConFig) 2011, pp. 204–210. IEEE (2011)

22. Vliegen, J., Mentens, N., Genoe, J., Braeken, A., Kubera, S., Touhafi, A., Verbauwhede, I.: A compact fpga-based architecture for elliptic curve cryptography over prime fields. In: International Conference on Application-Specific Systems Architectures and Processors (ASAP) 2010, pp. 313–316. IEEE (2010)

23. Wenger, E., Feldhofer, M., Felber, N.: Low-resource hardware design of an elliptic curve processor for contactless devices. In: Chung, Y., Yung, M. (eds.) WISA 2010. LNCS, vol. 6513, pp. 92–106. Springer, Heidelberg (2011). doi:10.1007/978-3-642-17955-6_7

24. Ma, Y., Liu, Z., Pan, W., Jing, J.: A high-speed elliptic curve cryptographic processor for generic curves over Fp. Sel. Areas Crypt. (SAC) **2013**, 421–437 (2014)

Differential Fault Analysis on Midori

Wei Cheng[1,2], Yongbin Zhou[1,2(✉)], and Laurent Sauvage[3]

[1] State Key Laboratory of Information Security, Institute of Information Engineering,
Chinese Academy of Sciences, No. 89A Minzhuang Road, Beijing 100093, China
{chengwei,zhouyongbin}@iie.ac.cn
[2] University of Chinese Academy of Sciences,
No. 19A Yuquan Road, Beijing 100049, China
[3] Institute Mines-Tlcom, Telecom ParisTech, CNRS LTCI, Paris, France
laurent.sauvage@telecom-paristech.fr

Abstract. Midori is an energy-efficient lightweight block cipher published by Banik et al. in ASIACRYPT 2015, which consists of two variants with block sizes of 64-bit and 128-bit, respectively. In this paper, a new method is proposed to exploit cell-oriented fault propagation patterns in recognizing appropriate faulty ciphertexts and fault positions, which poses a serious threat to practical security of Midori. In light of this, we present a Differential Fault Attack against the Midori using cell-oriented fault model. Specifically, by inducing two random cell faults into the input of the antepenultimate round, our attack reduces the secret key search space from 2^{128} to 2^{32} for Midori-128 and from 2^{128} to 2^{80} for Midori-64, respectively. Our experiments confirmed that two faulty ciphertexts induced into the input of antepenultimate round could recover twelve in sixteen cells of subkey with over 80% probability.

Keywords: Lightweight cipher · Differential fault analysis · Cell-oriented fault propagation · Midori

1 Introduction

In recent years, Internet of Things (IoT) as a new information network technology is booming, accompanied by an endless stream of new devices including Smart-Home devices, wearable devices, medical implants and other battery operated portable equipments. These devices always produce, process, transfer and store private information such as wearable equipments, or even security-critically control over people's lives like heart pacemakers. Inevitably, there is growing concern about their actual security. Fortunately, the cryptographic technique is a reliable way to meet these security requirements. As a result, the resource-constrained devices like RFID tags and sensing nodes used in the IoT have drawn a great attention on the lightweight cipher, which is featured with low latency, small areas, low energy consumption and hardware-friendly design. In this flourishing field, several lightweight block ciphers have been proposed in the last few years, including HIGHT [1], CLEFIA [2], PRESENT [3], KATAN [4], PRINCE [5], LED [6], Piccolo [7], SIMON/SPECK [8], Midori [9] and so on.

© Springer International Publishing AG 2016
K.-Y. Lam et al. (Eds.): ICICS 2016, LNCS 9977, pp. 307–317, 2016.
DOI: 10.1007/978-3-319-50011-9_24

Midori is published in the ASIACRYPT 2015 by Banik [9] et al. with two variants Midori-64 and Midori-128, both of them optimized with the energy consumption criterion. The optimizing work mainly consist of replacing the 8-bit Sboxes with 4-bit Sboxes and using almost MDS (Maximum Distance Separable) binary matrices instead of MDS matrices. By adopting this energy-efficient architecture, Midori seems to be a promising cipher with low latency and small areas at the same time. However, the security (mathematical security and practical security) of lightweight cipher is vital as it is the key to protect our security-sensitive information inside the IoT devices from attackers. On one hand, several literatures have studied the mathematical security of Midori by means of classical cryptanalysis, including differential/linear cryptanalysis [9], impossible differential cryptanalysis [10], meet-in-middle attack [11], truncated differential and related-key differential attacks [12]. Nonetheless, these cryptanalysis haven't identified any serious weakness with respect to mathematical properties. On the other hand, the practical security also plays a key role for security, but for Midori, there is no public literature studied its practical security so far.

Other than classical cryptanalysis, differential fault attack (DFA) is a typical cryptanalysis on cryptographic devices (implementations). It was first proposed by Biham and Shamir [13] against DES-like cryptosystem. After that, several similar attacks have been proposed to analyze the AES [14–16], Triple-DES [17], SMS4 [18,19], LED [20] et al. In essence, the DFA exploits the subtle relationships between the secret key and the behavior information under malfunctions to launch a key recovery attack. Typically, it derives information about the secret key by the differential between correct and faulty ciphertext (with the same plaintext). Thus, besides selecting a suitable fault model, the key to a DFA in practical is to determine whether the success of fault injection. All these aforementioned DFA methods haven't pointed out how to filter the proper faulty ciphertexts. As the DFA method described in [16], although it only need one faulty ciphertext to recover the 128-bit secret key, there is a huge difficulty to discriminate and sort out the applicable faulty ciphertext. On the other hand, the determination of the fault location also influences the analysis complexity. If it is unknown, the exhaustive method is needed to cover all possibilities, thus the computational complexity will be multiplied. Therefore, if the precise positions could be deduced straightly by the faulty and correct ciphertexts, the attacking complexity would be decreased dramatically. For Midori, the almost MDS matrix used in its permutation-layer gives us an unexpected convenience to solve both filtering and positioning problems, thus from a security point of view, this feature poses the great threat to its practical security against attacks like DFAs.

In this paper, we firstly illustrate an crucial vulnerability in Midori caused by the almost MDS binary matrix. We begin with investigating the fault propagation property of single fault induced in the antepenultimate round of encryption, then examine the differential of correct and faulty ciphertext, and analyze the positions of nonzero differentials. Some distinct patterns emerge, which connects the faulty position and the nonzero-differential positions, and these patterns could be exploited to deduce the corrupted positions. This fact also suggests that the tradeoffs must be taken between security and the performance metrics like latency, energy consumption by (lightweight) cipher designers. Based on this observation, we propose a new cell-oriented differential fault analysis method against both Midori-64 and Midori-128, as they adopt the same overall structure. Our attack adopts cell-oriented fault model, and the fault injection position could be inferred only using correct and faulty ciphertext. By retrieving the related subkeys, our method reduces the secret key search space by 2^{48} and 2^{96} only using two faulty ciphertexts for Midori-64 and Midori-128, respectively.

The rest of this paper is organized as follows. Section 2 briefly introduces the block cipher Midori. Section 3 investigates the cell-oriented fault propagation of Midori. Then Sect. 4 proposes our DFA method, and Sect. 5 summarizes the attacking complexity and experiments. Finally Sect. 6 concludes the paper.

2 Description of Block Cipher Midori

Midori consists of two variants, Midori-64 and Midori-128. Their block sizes n are 64-bit and 128-bit respectively, and the key sizes are 128-bit for both. Midori adopts a typical Substitution-Permutation Network structure, its state matrix is a 4×4 cell-matrix, where the cell sizes m are 4-bit and 8-bit for Midori-64 and Midori-128, respectively. The state matrix S is defined as follows:

$$S = \begin{pmatrix} s_0 & s_4 & s_8 & s_{12} \\ s_1 & s_5 & s_9 & s_{13} \\ s_2 & s_6 & s_{10} & s_{14} \\ s_3 & s_7 & s_{11} & s_{15} \end{pmatrix},$$

where $s_0, s_1, \ldots, s_{15}$ are sixteen cells. Midori is composed of encryption, decryption and key schedule, its overall structure of encryption is depicted as Fig. 1. And the comparison of two variants of Midori is tabulated as Table 1.

Table 1. The comparison of two Midori variants

	Block size(n)	Cell size(m)	Key size	Number of rounds(R)
Midori-64	64	4	128	16
Midori-128	128	8	128	20

2.1 Encryption and Decryption

For Midori, its encryption and decryption consist of R rounds of round function. Each of it consists of four transformations including *SubCell*, *ShuffleCell*, *MixColumn* and *KeyAdd*. The plaintext is divided into 16 cells and rearranged into the state matrix S. The overall structure of encryption is pictured as Fig. 1 and these four transformations are described in the following.

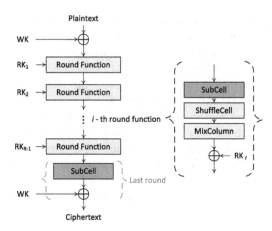

Fig. 1. Overall structure of Midori (Encryption), $R = 16$ for Midori-64 and $R = 20$ for Midori-128. WK is the whitening key and RK_i is the round key.

- $SubCell(SuC)$: For Midori-64, apply the 4-bit Sb_0 to the state matrix S for each cell: $s_i \leftarrow Sb_0(s_i)$. Similarly, for Midori-128, the 4-bit Sb_0 is replaced by 8-bit Sboxes (composed by two 4-bit Sb_1 and two bit-permutations [9]): SSb_0, SSb_1, SSb_2, SSb_3, namely, $s_i \leftarrow SSb_{i \bmod 4}(s_i)$, where $0 \le i \le 15$.
- $ShuffleCell(ShC)$: Each cell of the state S is permuted as follows:
  $(s_0, s_1, \ldots, s_{15}) \leftarrow (s_0, s_{10}, s_5, s_{15}, s_{14}, s_4, s_{11}, s_1, s_9, s_3, s_{12}, s_6, s_7, s_{13}, s_2, s_8)$
- $MixColumn(MC)$: M is applied to every $4m$-bit column of the state matrix S, i.e., ${}^t(s_i, s_{i+1}, s_{i+2}, s_{i+3}) \leftarrow M \cdot {}^t(s_i, s_{i+1}, s_{i+2}, s_{i+3})$ and $i = 0, 4, 8, 12$. Here M and its inverse matrix M' are defined as:

$$M = M' = \begin{pmatrix} 0 & 1 & 1 & 1 \\ 1 & 0 & 1 & 1 \\ 1 & 1 & 0 & 1 \\ 1 & 1 & 1 & 0 \end{pmatrix}$$

- $KeyAdd(AK)$: The i-th n-bit round key RK_i is XORed to a state matrix S.

Table 2. 4-bit bijective Sbox Sb_0 and Sb_1 in hexadecimal form [9]

	0	1	2	3	4	5	6	7	8	9	A	B	C	D	E	F
Sb_0	C	A	D	3	E	B	F	7	8	9	1	5	0	2	4	6
Sb_1	1	0	5	3	E	2	F	7	D	A	9	B	C	8	4	6

The decryption procedure shares the whole structure with encryption except that the $ShuffleCell$ is replaced by its inverse and the order of the round keys RK_i is from R to 0 (Fig. 1).

2.2   Key Schedule

For Midori-64, the 128-bit secret key K is the concatenation of two 64-bit keys K_0 and K_1, thus the $WK = K_0 \oplus K_1$ and the round key $RK_i = K_{(i-1) \mod 2} \oplus \alpha_{i-1}$, where $1 \leq i \leq 15$. For Midori-128, $WK = K$ and $RK_i = K \oplus \beta_{i-1}$, where $1 \leq i \leq 19$. Note that α_i, β_i are both constants, and $\alpha_i = \beta_i$ for $0 \leq i \leq 14$.

2.3   Notations

The following notations were used throughout the rest of the paper.

- X^i, X^i_j: X^i is the output of the (i)-th round, $i = 1, 2, \ldots, R$, thus X^0 is defined as the plaintext and $X^R = C$ is the ciphertext. X^i_j is the j-th cell of X^i, $j = 0, 1, \ldots, 15$.
- SuC^i, ShC^i, MC^i, AK^i: these are the state matrix after $SubCell$, $ShuffleCell$, $MixColumn$ and $KeyAdd$ of the i-th round, respectively. Namely, $AK^R = X^R$ is the ciphertext.
- RK^i: the round key used in the i-th round function, $i = 1, 2, \ldots, R - 1$, and $RK^0 = WK$, $RK^R = WK$.
- ΔX: the difference of two state matrixes X and X'.

3   Cell-Oriented Fault Propagation Analysis

In this section, we investigate the propagation of one cell-oriented fault induced into the input of $(R\text{-}2)$-th round function.

3.1   Fault Propagation in Last Three Rounds

Due to the simple diffusion pattern of inducing fault into the input of last round and penultimate round, we focus on the single cell-oriented random fault injected into the input of antepenultimate round. As depicted in Fig. 2, the single cell fault f induced before the antepenultimate round is changed into f' after $SubCell$, and remains unchanged after $ShuffleCell$, then the other three cells in the same column are infected with identical differential f', which stay the same after $KeyAdd$ transformation. The refreshing of differential values in the $(R\text{-}1)$-th round is similar to $(R\text{-}2)$-th round, and then trivial in R-th round because of omitted permutation-layer in the last round. Thus the output differentials equal to the XOR of correct ciphertext and faulty ciphertext or two faulty ciphertexts.

3.2   Cell-Oriented Fault Propagation Patterns

Distinct association patterns could be observed between the positions of nonzero-differentials and the position of single cell-oriented fault. Specifically, as pictured in Fig. 3, each cell of faults induced in the input of antepenultimate round results in nine faulty cells with unique patterns. Apparently, these patterns could be

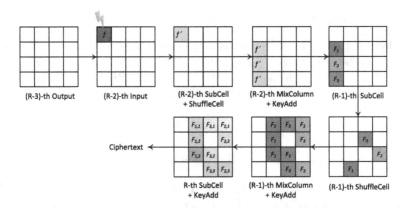

Fig. 2. The fault propagation of last three rounds, fault is induced into the first cell of state matrix. f, f', F_i, and $F_{i,j}$ are the differentials of two corresponding intermediates, where $i, j = 1, 2, 3$.

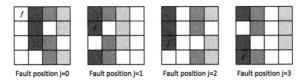

Fault position j=0   Fault position j=1   Fault position j=2   Fault position j=3

Fig. 3. The fault propagation patterns of four cells in the first column, f is the faulty differential and its position is corresponding to the fault injection position.

straightforwardly inferred only requiring the correct ciphertext and faulty ciphertext. That is, the position of corrupted cell in state matrix S could be uniquely determined. The essential reason of this pattern is caused by the almost MDS matrix applied in the permutation layer of Midori. The fault propagation patterns of four cells in the first state matrix column are depicted as Fig. 3 (fault position j = 0 is detailed in Fig. 2).

In Midori, all design choices are made to save energy consumption, including using 4×4 almost MDS binary matrices instead of 4×4 MDS matrices. However, because the branch number of almost MDS matrices [9] is 4, one nonzero active input leads to three nonzero active outputs in the same column, and nine nonzero active outputs after two rounds transformations. As a result, the diffusing effect is weak enough to find distinct patterns of faulty positions. Compared to MDS matrix applied in the AES (Advanced Encryption Standard), after two rounds of round function, one nonzero active input leads to sixteen nonzero active outputs, therefore, no obvious association patterns between the fault injection position and nonzero differential positions in output.

In the view of practical security, this energy-efficient almost MDS matrix gives rise to a vulnerability, especially faced with differential fault attacks. This fact demonstrates that the tradeoffs must be taken between security and the performance metrics like latency, energy consumption by (lightweight) cipher designers. For practical security, the full diffusion MDS matrix is evidently more preferable than almost MDS matrix for SPN-structure ciphers.

4   Cell-Oriented Differential Fault Analysis on Midori

As pictured in Fig. 2, the fault propagation patterns are clear. Let us denote the correct ciphertext $C = X^R = AK^R$ and faulty ciphertext $C' = X'^R = AK'^R$, then we have the differential $\triangle C$ that

$$\triangle C = C \oplus C' = X^R \oplus X'^R \tag{1}$$

For the $(R\text{-}1)$-th round, the output differential has three nonzero values which equal to F_1, F_2, F_3, respectively. Thus, due to the involution property of Sboxes applied in the Midori, for F_1, we have following four equations:

$$\begin{aligned}
F_1 &= SuC(C_4 \oplus RK_4^R) \oplus SuC(C_4' \oplus RK_4^R) \\
F_1 &= SuC(C_5 \oplus RK_5^R) \oplus SuC(C_5' \oplus RK_5^R) \\
F_1 &= SuC(C_6 \oplus RK_6^R) \oplus SuC(C_6' \oplus RK_6^R) \\
0 &= SuC(C_7 \oplus RK_7^R) \oplus SuC(C_7' \oplus RK_7^R)
\end{aligned} \tag{2}$$

where $F_1 \in \mathbb{F}_{2^m}$, $m = 4$ for Midori-64 and $m = 8$ for Midori-128. These four equations can be solved for three subkey cells RK_4^R, RK_5^R, RK_6^R. The key search space of this triple of key cells is reduced to an expected value of 2^m from $(2^m)^3 = 2^{3m}$. Similar equations could be deduced for F_2 and F_3, thus after combination of these three classes of equations, the whole key search space related to F_1, F_2 and F_3 is reduced to 2^{3m} from 2^{9m}.

By continuing this method, and X^{R-2} is the output of $(R\text{-}2)$-th round, then its first column is:

$$\begin{aligned}
X_0^{R-2} &= SuC(SuC(C_1 \oplus RK_1^R) \oplus RK_1^{R-1} \oplus SuC(C_2 \oplus RK_2^R) \\
&\quad \oplus RK_2^{R-1} \oplus SuC(C_3 \oplus RK_3^R) \oplus RK_3^{R-1}) \\
X_1^{R-2} &= SuC(SuC(C_4 \oplus RK_4^R) \oplus RK_4^{R-1} \oplus SuC(C_5 \oplus RK_5^R) \\
&\quad \oplus RK_5^{R-1} \oplus SuC(C_6 \oplus RK_6^R) \oplus RK_6^{R-1}) \\
X_2^{R-2} &= SuC(SuC(C_{12} \oplus RK_{12}^R) \oplus RK_{12}^{R-1} \oplus SuC(C_{13} \oplus RK_{13}^R) \\
&\quad \oplus RK_{13}^{R-1} \oplus SuC(C_{15} \oplus RK_{15}^R) \oplus RK_{15}^{R-1}) \\
X_3^{R-2} &= SuC(SuC(C_8 \oplus RK_8^R) \oplus RK_8^{R-1} \oplus SuC(C_{10} \oplus RK_{10}^R) \\
&\quad \oplus RK_{10}^{R-1} \oplus SuC(C_{11} \oplus RK_{11}^R) \oplus RK_{11}^{R-1})
\end{aligned} \tag{3}$$

Thus considering its cell-oriented differentials in the output of $(R\text{-}2)$-th round:

$$\begin{aligned}
0 &= \triangle X_0^{R-2} = X_0^{R-2} \oplus X_0'^{R-2} \\
f' &= \triangle X_1^{R-2} = X_1^{R-2} \oplus X_1'^{R-2} \\
f' &= \triangle X_2^{R-2} = X_2^{R-2} \oplus X_2'^{R-2} \\
f' &= \triangle X_3^{R-2} = X_3^{R-2} \oplus X_3'^{R-2}
\end{aligned} \tag{4}$$

Consequently, the interrelation between subkey cells in the equations further reduce the subkey search space. Apparently, for the first cell output of $(R-3)$-th round and its nonzero differential are:

$$X_0^{R-3} = SuC(X_1^{R-2} \oplus RK_1^{R-2} \oplus X_2^{R-2} \oplus RK_2^{R-2} \oplus X_3^{R-2} \oplus RK_3^{R-2})$$
$$f = X_0^{R-3} \oplus X_0'^{R-3} \tag{5}$$

With combination of equations Eqs. 2, 4 and 5, only twelve cells of subkey essentially involve nonzero differential operations, resulting that the key search space is reduced to an expected decrease value of 2^{12m}.

5   Attacking Complexity and Experimental Results

5.1   Attacking Complexity

In essence, differential fault analysis utilizes the interrelationship of input differential and output differential in the $SubCell$. For Midori, its relationship is defined as follows [18]:

$$INs(\triangle x, \triangle y) = \{zi | zi \in \mathbb{F}_{2^m}, SuC(zi) \oplus SuC(zi \oplus \triangle x) = \triangle y\}$$
$$Ns(\triangle x, \triangle y) = \#\{zi | zi \in \mathbb{F}_{2^m}, SuC(zi) \oplus SuC(zi \oplus \triangle x) = \triangle y\} \tag{6}$$

then for Midori's last round $SubCell$, using the first equation of Eq. 2, $\triangle x = C_4 \oplus C_4'$, $\triangle y = F_1$, then the candidates of subkey cell could be recovered using $RK_4^R = C_4 \oplus INs$. Candidates of other subkey cells could be derived similarly.

Note that the maximum differential probability [9] of $SubCell$ are 2^{-2}, namely, maximum of Ns equals to $16 \times 2^{-2} = 4$ for Midori-64 and $256 \times 2^{-2} = 64$ for Midori-128. That is, for fixed $\triangle x, \triangle y$, the maximum number of subkey cell candidates should be 4 and 64 for Midori-64 and Midori-128, respectively. Specifically, for Sb_0, Sb_1 separately used in Midori-64 and Midori-128, if $Ns(\triangle x, \triangle y)$ is not null, then it equals 2 with probability of 75.0% (72/96) and 85.71% (90/105) for Sb_1. Due to the $SubCell$ of Midori-128 is constructed by Sb_1, if it is divided into two of Sb_1, the attacking complexity could be reduced dramatically.

Since at least two faults are required to uniquely determine the subkey cell candidates in equations Eq. 2, we derive intersection of subkey cell candidates using multiple faults induced in the same rounds (optional). Given that two faults are induced in the same cell position of $(R-2)$-th input, three nonzero differentials are obtained by pairing combination. Therefore, for Midori-128, at least two faulty ciphertexts are required to recover nine cells of RK^R and three cells of RK^{R-1}. Considering that $RK^{R-1} = RK^{R-1} \oplus \beta_{R-2}$ and $K = WK = RK^R$, hence twelve cells of secret key K could be deduced, its secret key search space is reduced to 2^{32} from 2^{128} at best. For Midori-64, two faulty ciphertexts could only recover nine cells of RK^R and three cells of RK^{R-1}, thus secret key search space decreases by an expected value of 2^{48} ($= 2^{12m}$).

5.2   Experimental Results

We implemented our attack on a PC using Matlab R2014b (64-bit) with 2.60 GHz CPU and 4 GB memory. The fault injection was simulated by software commands. We use the equations similar to Eq. 2 to illustrate our attack which is applied to Midori-64. Two simulated faults were induced into the first cell of $(R\text{-}1)$-th input, namely X_0^{R-2} and the corrupted value is kept unknown.

Table 3. Subkey cell recovery for RK_1^R, RK_2^R and RK_3^R using two faulty ciphertexts

	cNum = 1	cNum = 2	cNum = 4	Proportion of cNum = 1	Time latency(s)
RK_1^R	92	4	9	87.62%	0.2381
RK_2^R	86	10	9	81.90%	0.2389
RK_3^R	86	10	9	81.90%	0.2629

*cNum = #{Candidates} denotes the number of subkey cell candidates. The first three columns denote the number of possible combinations of two distinct differentials satisfying cNum = 1, cNum = 2 and cNum = 3, respectively.

Considering that $Ns(\triangle x, \triangle y)$ of Sb_0, the number of nonzero input $\triangle x$ equals 15, thus all combinations of two distinct differentials only have $105 \ (= 15 \times 14/2)$ elements. In consequence, as tabulated in Table 3, three subkey cells of RK^R could be recovered with over 80% probability only using two faulty ciphertexts.

On the basis of above experiments, for Midori-128, the attacking complexity in practice is estimated to $2^9 \cdot (3e^2 + 3e) \ (= 12 \cdot C_{(e+1)}^2 \cdot 2^8)$, where e denotes the number of faults induced in the same cell position. For Midori-64, with the same setting, the attacking is estimated to $2^5 \cdot (3e^2 + 3e)$.

6   Conclusions

In this paper, based on the cell-oriented fault propagation patterns existing in Midori, we presented a differential fault analysis method against its two variants Midori-64 and Midori-128. Our method straightly exploits these patterns to uniquely determine the corrupted positions, resulting in its low attacking complexity. Especially, secret key search space is reduced from 2^{128} to 2^{32} for Midori-128 and from 2^{128} to 2^{80} for Midori-64, respectively. In addition, our experimental results confirms that the almost MDS matrix used in its permutation layer resulting in a vulnerability, which could be utilized by practical attacks like DFAs. This result evidently provides a new design advice to cipher designers.

Acknowledgments. This work was supported in part by National Natural Science Foundation of China (Grant No. 61272478, No. 61472416 and No. 61632020) and Strategic Priority Research Program of the Chinese Academy of Sciences (Grant No. XDA06010701 and XDA06010703).

References

1. Hong, D., Sung, J., Hong, S., Lim, J., Lee, S., Koo, B.-S., Lee, C., Chang, D., Lee, J., Jeong, K., Kim, H., Kim, J., Chee, S.: HIGHT: a new block cipher suitable for low-resource device. In: Goubin, L., Matsui, M. (eds.) CHES 2006. LNCS, vol. 4249, pp. 46–59. Springer, Heidelberg (2006). doi:10.1007/11894063_4

2. Shirai, T., Shibutani, K., Akishita, T., Moriai, S., Iwata, T.: The 128-bit blockcipher CLEFIA (extended abstract). In: Biryukov, A. (ed.) FSE 2007. LNCS, vol. 4593, pp. 181–195. Springer, Heidelberg (2007). doi:10.1007/978-3-540-74619-5_12

3. Bogdanov, A., Knudsen, L.R., Leander, G., Paar, C., Poschmann, A., Robshaw, M.J.B., Seurin, Y., Vikkelsoe, C.: PRESENT: An ultra-lightweight block cipher. In: Paillier, P., Verbauwhede, I. (eds.) CHES 2007. LNCS, vol. 4727, pp. 450–466. Springer, Heidelberg (2007). doi:10.1007/978-3-540-74735-2_31

4. Cannière, C., Dunkelman, O., Knežević, M.: KATAN and KTANTAN — a family of small and efficient hardware-oriented block ciphers. In: Clavier, C., Gaj, K. (eds.) CHES 2009. LNCS, vol. 5747, pp. 272–288. Springer, Heidelberg (2009). doi:10.1007/978-3-642-04138-9_20

5. Borghoff, J., Canteaut, A., Güneysu, T., Kavun, E.B., Knezevic, M., Knudsen, L.R., Leander, G., Nikov, V., Paar, C., Rechberger, C., Rombouts, P., Thomsen, S.S., Yalçın, T.: PRINCE – a low-latency block cipher for pervasive computing applications. In: Wang, X., Sako, K. (eds.) ASIACRYPT 2012. LNCS, vol. 7658, pp. 208–225. Springer, Heidelberg (2012). doi:10.1007/978-3-642-34961-4_14

6. Guo, J., Peyrin, T., Poschmann, A., Robshaw, M.: The LED block cipher. In: Preneel, B., Takagi, T. (eds.) CHES 2011. LNCS, vol. 6917, pp. 326–341. Springer, Heidelberg (2011). doi:10.1007/978-3-642-23951-9_22

7. Shibutani, K., Isobe, T., Hiwatari, H., Mitsuda, A., Akishita, T., Shirai, T.: Piccolo: an ultra-lightweight blockcipher. In: Preneel, B., Takagi, T. (eds.) CHES 2011. LNCS, vol. 6917, pp. 342–357. Springer, Heidelberg (2011). doi:10.1007/978-3-642-23951-9_23

8. Ray, B., Douglas, S., Jason, S., Stefan, T.-C., Bryan, W., Louis, W.: The SIMON and SPECK Families of Lightweight Block Ciphers. Cryptology ePrint Archive, Report 2013/404 (2013). http://eprint.iacr.org/

9. Banik, S., Bogdanov, A., Isobe, T., Shibutani, K., Hiwatari, H., Akishita, T., Regazzoni, F.: Midori: a block cipher for low energy. In: Iwata, T., Cheon, J.H. (eds.) ASIACRYPT 2015. LNCS, vol. 9453, pp. 411–436. Springer, Heidelberg (2015). doi:10.1007/978-3-662-48800-3_17

10. Cheng, Z., Wang, X.: Impossible Differential Cryptanalysis of Midori. Cryptology ePrint Archive, Report 2016/535 (2016). http://eprint.iacr.org/

11. Lin, L., Wu, W.: Meet-in-the-Middle Attacks on Reduced-Round Midori-64. Cryptology ePrint Archive, Report 2015/1165 (2015). http://eprint.iacr.org/

12. Dong, X., Shen, Y.: Cryptanalysis of Reduced-Round Midori64 Block Cipher. Cryptology ePrint Archive, Report 2016/676 (2016). http://eprint.iacr.org/

13. Biham, E., Shamir, A.: Differential cryptanalysis of DES-like cryptosystems. In: Menezes, A.J., Vanstone, S.A. (eds.) CRYPTO 1990. LNCS, vol. 537, pp. 2–21. Springer, Heidelberg (1991). doi:10.1007/3-540-38424-3_1

14. Giraud, C.: DFA on AES. In: Dobbertin, H., Rijmen, V., Sowa, A. (eds.) AES 2004. LNCS, vol. 3373, pp. 27–41. Springer, Heidelberg (2005). doi:10.1007/11506447_4

15. Mukhopadhyay, D.: An improved fault based attack of the advanced encryption standard. In: Preneel, B. (ed.) AFRICACRYPT 2009. LNCS, vol. 5580, pp. 421–434. Springer, Heidelberg (2009). doi:10.1007/978-3-642-02384-2_26

16. Tunstall, M., Mukhopadhyay, D., Ali, S.: Differential fault analysis of the advanced encryption standard using a single fault. In: Ardagna, C.A., Zhou, J. (eds.) WISTP 2011. LNCS, vol. 6633, pp. 224–233. Springer, Heidelberg (2011). doi:10.1007/978-3-642-21040-2_15

17. Hemme, L.: A differential fault attack against early rounds of (triple-)DES. In: Joye, M., Quisquater, J.-J. (eds.) CHES 2004. LNCS, vol. 3156, pp. 254–267. Springer, Heidelberg (2004). doi:10.1007/978-3-540-28632-5_19

18. Li, R., Sun, B., Li, C., You, J.: Differential fault analysis on SMS4 using a single fault. J. Inf. Process. Lett. **111**(4), 156–163 (2011)

19. Wu, W., Zhang, L.: Differential fault analysis on SMS4. J. Int. J. Comput. Intell. Syst. **9**, 011 (2006)

20. Li, W., Gu, D., Xia, X., Zhao, C., Liu, Z., Liu, Y., Wang, Q.: Single byte differential fault analysis on the LED lightweight cipher in the wireless sensor network. J. Int. J. Comput. Intell. Syst. **5**(5), 896–904 (2012)

Privacy Protection

Private Boolean Query Processing on Encrypted Data

Hoang Giang Do$^{(\boxtimes)}$ and Wee Keong Ng

School of Computer Science and Engineering, Nanyang Technological University,
Singapore, Singapore
do0004ng@e.ntu.edu.sg, wkn@pmail.ntu.edu.sg

Abstract. Outsourcing the data to the clouds offers an opportunity to drastically reduce costs of storing and processing data. On the other hand, it deprives the data owners of direct control over their data and that introduces new privacy risks. Data encryption has been introduced to tackle the data confidentiality issue. However, data encryption also brings a new challenge of query processing over encrypted data. Recently, solutions for supporting query over encrypted data have been developed. However, they are either failing to support complex queries or insecure regarding certain security requirements (i.e. access patterns, query privacy). In this paper, we propose a novel privacy-preserving query processing framework to support boolean queries over encrypted data. Our framework utilizes Bloom filter and additive homomorphic encryption to systematically derive the query evaluation results in a privacy-preserving manner. We theoretically and empirically analyze the performance of the proposed protocols and demonstrate their practical values.

1 Introduction

The cloud computing paradigm has offered the user an opportunity to drastically reduce costs of storing and processing data. Outsourcing data storage as well as data management to the clouds is useful in many services including law enforcement, finance, healthcare, etc. However, data outsourcing deprives the data owners of direct control over their data, and it brings new crucial security risks.

Since there are many possibilities for data leakage to occur at the server side, the user should not fully trust the clouds for data privacy. One possibility comes from corrupted employees who do not follow privacy policies. They may intentionally or unintentionally reveal sensitive information such as personal health records, financial transaction, or personal voice, etc. Even when the cloud service provider claims to enforce sufficient policies on such privacy violence, there are still chances that cloud computing systems may be vulnerable to external malicious attacks. Once intrusions take place, any single detail of these sensitive data will be publicly exposed. Finally, due to privacy regulations of different countries, the cloud data may be required to be shared with a certain third party. Therefore, storing plaintext data in the cloud might lead to full exposure of your data.

© Springer International Publishing AG 2016
K.-Y. Lam et al. (Eds.): ICICS 2016, LNCS 9977, pp. 321–332, 2016.
DOI: 10.1007/978-3-319-50011-9_25

Data encryption has been introduced to tackle the problem of data confidentiality on the clouds. However, at the same time, it also creates a new challenge of data usability over remotely encrypted data. While the data owner should have the ability to query and obtain useful data when needed, the simple encryption method is insufficient for the basic requirement. There are different approaches to address this problem of privacy preserving encrypted data retrieval in the clouds. They include (i) downloading the entire dataset and doing a local search on the decrypted data or (ii) encrypting the data by a searchable encryption method and performing searching over the encrypted data with the aid of the cloud server. Since the first approach is not feasible as it incurs heavy communicational and computational cost on the end-user, the latter has gained significant attention in recent years. Following this direction, various methods have been proposed for evaluating search queries over encrypted data. However, most of the existing works focus on the problem of single keyword matching and inherently, are not suitable to execute complex queries.

In this paper, we study the problem of supporting an important class of complex search operations: boolean keyword retrieval. We consider a scenario where an encrypted dataset contains a number of encrypted documents. Each document is associated with a certain set of keywords. An authorized user is able to perform search queries which are the combination of logic predicates on the keyword set. The output of the query processing is the index set of satisfied documents and nothing else to the data consumer. During the query processing, not only the outsourced data are kept private from the clouds, but also the user's input query remains in confidentiality.

We organize the paper as follows: In the next section, we review the existing works on secure query processing over encrypted data. Section 3 describes our problem statement, data model, and query model as well as the requirements for the designed framework. Section 4 reviews the necessary building blocks which are Bloom Filters and additively homomorphic public-key encryption scheme (i.e. the Pailliers encryption scheme). The proposed solution for complex boolean query processing on encrypted data is presented in Sect. 5. The section systematically discusses four stages of the solution. Section 6 presents our experimental evaluations of the proposed sub-protocols. The final section discusses future works and concludes the paper.

2   Related Work

There are two general approaches that tackle the problem of secure query processing over encrypted data without downloading the entire dataset. The first approach deploys tamper-proof trusted hardware (which is either trusted or certified by the clients) on the cloud-side. The hardware provides a secure environment that allows the cloud to perform secure operations over the data in critical query processing stages. Along this direction, Bajaj and Sion [1] leveraged the existence of trusted hardware to design TrustedDB, an outsourced database prototype that allows a client to execute SQL queries with privacy and under regulatory compliance constraints. However, the secure hardware is very expensive and may not be suitable for general cloud computing paradigm which typically makes use of cheap commodity machines.

The second approach makes use of cryptographic protocols to perform operations over the encrypted data. Song et al. [14] proposed the first searchable symmetric-key encryption. Goh [9] provided the first security definition for searchable symmetric encryption and presented a Bloom-filter based solution with linear complexity. Curtmola et al. [5] introduced the notion of adaptive semantic security for symmetric searchable encryption together with a sub-linear time and sub-linear space constructions. These techniques only support single keyword search, and not suitable for complex queries.

Boneh and Waters [3] presented a new cryptographic primitive called hidden vector encryption that allows evaluating conjunctive queries over encrypted data. The method also supports general subset and range queries. However, it is worth to note that their technique is very expensive when data domain is large and complex to implement. Do and Ng [7] proposed another scheme that can handle conjunctive keywords search and multidimensional range queries by performing prefix encoding before encryption. We note that the methods are only suitable for conjunctive queries, but not directly applicable to disjunctive queries. Moreover, almost all existing techniques fail to provide rigorous privacy protection due to access pattern leakage. Islam et al. [11] showed that data access pattern leakage could lead to the disclosure of a significant amount of sensitive information. In our proposed protocol, we design a secure protocol that not only preserves query privacy but also keep the access patterns in confidentiality.

3   Definitions and Assumptions

3.1   Problem Statement

In our problem settings, we consider three different parties: the data owner, the cloud and the data consumer. Let D denote Alice's data with n documents. Each document is associated with a certain set of keywords that enable to search or retrieve it efficiently. We assume that the data owner wishes to encrypt D using his/her own key and outsources the encrypted data to a cloud so that latter an authorized data consumer is able to search on the encrypted data. The input query is represented by a logical combination (i.e. negation, conjunction, and disjunction) of the keyword predicates. At the same time, several security issues should be addressed such as data confidentiality, the privacy of query content, etc.

Formally, let $W = \{0,1\}^*$ be a universe of words and $D \subseteq W$ be corpus. Let $Kw = \{w_1, \cdots, w_n\}$ denote a set of searchable keywords. The keyword set Kw is publicly known (hence it is called a common reference keyword set). While Kw can be any the searchable property set of the corpus D, for simplicity, we assume the problem as a general boolean keyword search. That means $Kw \subseteq D$ and the predicate $d(w_i) = 1$ if and only if the document d contains the keyword w_i. Otherwise, $d(w_i) = 0$.

A boolean query q_K contains keyword predicate and a set of logical expressions $\wedge, \vee, \neg$. Let $d_C = \{d^{(1)}, \ldots, d^{(n)}\}$ be n documents stored in a server C. With a set of keywords $K \subseteq Kw$, we define a query $q_K : d \rightarrow \{0, 1\}$ that takes a document d as input and outputs 1, if and only if d matches the criteria.

3.2 Security Assumptions

In this paper, we assume that the data owner, the cloud and the data consumer are semi-honest. The cloud server will correctly follow the protocol specification, however, at the same time, it is also curious about stored data as well as the query content. In general, a secure complex boolean query should meet the following privacy requirements:

- Data Confidentiality. The data are encrypted by a provably secure cryptosystem. Besides, during the query processing, the cloud should not gain any new knowledge on the stored data.
- Query Privacy. At any point of time, the data consumer's query should never be revealed to the cloud and the data owner.
- Access Pattern Privacy. Data access patterns of the data consumer should not be disclosed to the cloud and the data owner. Data access patterns are the information of the documents satisfy the query (even the attackers do not know the query content).
- End-user's Privacy. At the end of the query processing protocol, only the satisfied results should be revealed to the data consumer and nothing else.

4   Building Blocks

4.1   Bloom Filter

Bloom filter [2] provides a way to probabilistically represent set membership of elements using a small amount of space, even when the universe set is large. It represents a set $S = \{s_1, \ldots, s_n\}$ of n element by a space-efficient m-element array $B = \{B[1], B[2], \ldots, B[m]\}$. A random set of hash functions $h_1, \ldots, h_t$, where each function $h_i : \{0, 1\}^* \rightarrow [0, \ldots, m]$ are chosen to associate with the Bloom filter B.

The filter algorithm is constructed as follows. The bit array B is initially set to 0. For each element $s_i \in S$, the bits corresponding to the positions $h_1(s_i), h_2(s_i), \ldots, h_t(s_i)$ are set. The same bit in the array may be set several times without any restriction. Figure 1 depicts how an element is inserted into a Bloom filter.

After the Bloom filter is constructed, membership queries can be easily answered. To determine whether an element x belongs to the set S, we check all the bits corresponding to the positions $h_1(s), h_2(s), \ldots, h_t(s)$. If at least one bit is 0, then $x \notin S$ for sure. Otherwise, we conclude that $x \in S$. Actually, a false positive may occur when an element $x \notin S$ is recognized as an element of the set. However, mathematical analysis shows that the probability when the algorithm returning 1 for $x \notin S$ is approximately $(1 - e^{\frac{-tn}{m}})^t$, which is small enough for the practical use.

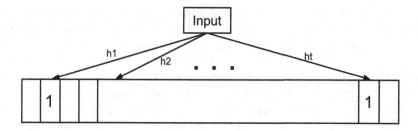

Fig. 1. Bloom filter insertion

4.2   Additive Homomorphic Encryption

A homomorphic encryption scheme is a cryptosystem that allows arithmetic operations to be performed on the cirphertext without decryption or knowing the actual values. Consider two operators $\times$ and $+$ on the ciphertext and plaintext domain, respectively, if m_1 and m_2 are two plaintext elements, an additive homomorphic scheme Enc satisfies

$$Enc(m_1) \times Enc(m_2) = Enc(m_1 + m_2).$$

Efficient additive homomorphic cryptosystems have been proposed such as the Pallier cryptosystem [12], or the Damgard and Jurik cryptosystem [6] which is length-flexible Paillier's encryption scheme. We emphasize that any additive homomorphic encryption scheme that satisfies the above properties can be utilized to implement our proposed framework. However, for simplicity, we assume that the additive homomorphic encryption we are using in this paper is the Paillier cryptosystem. The security of the Paillier encryption scheme relies on the computational hardness assumption of a novel mathematical problem called the composite residuosity. The decision version of this problem class assumes that no polynomial time algorithms can distinguish N-th residues modulo N^2 with non-negligible probability. We refer to the reader [12] for more details.

4.3   Oblivious Transfer and OT Extension

Oblivious transfer (OT) is a major building block for designing a number of secure computation protocols. The protocol consists of two parties: the receiver and the sender. The basic 1-out-of 2 OT_1^2 allows the receiver choose either one from two input of the senders without learning anything regarding the other. OT_1^2 was introduced by Even *et al.* [8] as a generalization of Rabin "oblivious transfer" [13]. Brassard *et al.* [4] further extended OT_1^2 to 1-out-of n OT_1^n where the receiver is able to obtain one from n messages possessed by the sender. Since then, many efficient protocols for OT with different security assumptions have been proposed over the years. k-out of n OT_n^k scheme is the final form of OT schemes and the one we make use in our solution. In it, from n encrypted messages sent by the sender, the chooser can obtain k of them which he had chosen without the senders knowledge about which part of the messages can be obtained by him. While it is clear that OT_n^k can be constructed by applying k repetitions of OT_1^n, there have been more efficient protocols. Wu *et al.* [15] introduced two-lock cryptosystems to improve the efficiency of OT_n^k protocol from $O(kn)$ to $O(k + n)$. Recently, Guo *et al.* [10] proposed a cryptographic concept called subset membership encryption and applied it to construct two round OT_n^k protocol against semi-honest adversaries. The algorithm only requires the communication cost of $O(n)$ for the sender and $O(k)$ for the receiver.

5   Proposed Framework

5.1   System Overview

As mentioned in Sect. 3, the data owner outsources a corpus D of encrypted documents so that later the data consumer is able to perform complex boolean keyword queries. A query is represented by logical expressions $\wedge, \vee, \neg$ of boolean keyword predicates q_k. The results of the query are the indices of satisfied documents.

This paper explicitly assumes that each document d_i is associated with a subset $S^{(i)} \subseteq K$ of keywords. For simplicity, we assume that each document has the same number of associated keywords. For each document, we represent these associated keywords by a Bloom-filter of size m. Let $\{h_1, h_2, \ldots, h_t\}$ be independently keyed hash functions. A keyed hash function h_i inputs a secret key from key space K and a keyword k and outputs an integer in the range of $[1, \ldots, m]$. The preprocessing stage when the data owner prepares the data and uploads them to the cloud is described as follows:

1. The data owner generates a secret pseudorandom function F mapping an integer to a random key in the key space K.
2. For each document $d^{(i)}$, the data owner does the following:
   - Generating a key for hash functions: $k^{(i)} \leftarrow F(i)$.
   - Creating a Bloom-filter $B^{(i)}$ associated the documents.
   - Inserting the document keyword set $S^{(i)}$ into Bloom-filter $B^{(i)}$ with the hash functions: $h_1, h_2, ..., h_t$ using the key $k^{(i)}$. Concretely, for each keyword $w_j^{(i)}$ of the document $d^{(i)}$, we set the bit $h_1(k^{(i)}, w_j^{(i)}), \ldots,$ $h_t(k^{(i)}, w_j^{(i)})$ in Bloom-filter $B^{(i)}$.
   - Encrypting the content of the document by a standard cryptosystem (i.e. AES).
3. The data owner sends the encrypted dataset as well as the Bloom-fiters for all encrypted documents to the cloud server.
4. The data owner shares the secret function F with the authorized data consumer.

Let D' denote the outsourced data of the data owner. D' consists of multiple records and each of them has the following form:

$$\Big\langle \text{Document index, Encrypted content, Bloom Filter data} \Big\rangle$$

Two arbitrary documents have two different Bloom filters which are generated by two different sets of hash functions (i.e. different keys for keyed hash functions). Moreover, the keys are generated by a pseudorandom function F. The input of F is the index of the document. Hence, with the view of Bloom filters data, the cloud cannot make any conclusion about the associated keyword sets.

Now consider an authorized data consumer (which would typically be authorized by the data owner) who wants to securely retrieve data from D' in the cloud. The satisfied documents are defined by his/her private boolean query. The query phase consists of three stages as the following:

- Secure Single Keyword Evaluation - In this stage, the data consumer evaluates a single keyword query for each encrypted document. The output of this stage is the encryption of either 1 or 0, depending on whether the document contains the keyword.
- Secure Complex Boolean Query Evaluation - Based on the results of the previous stage, the data consumer collaborates with the cloud to compute the result of the complex logical combination of boolean predicates. Again, the output of this stage is the encryption of either 1 or 0 depending on whether the document satisfies the input query.
- Retrieval of Output Data - At this stage, the data consumer collaborates with the cloud to securely retrieve the indices of satisfied documents, and obtains the final documents by private information retrieval or oblivious RAM with known indices.

5.2   Secure Single Keyword Evaluation

We consider the scenario of evaluating a single boolean predicate $q_k(d)$ for each document d in the encrypted data corpus D'. More concretely, we propose an algorithm to answer the query whether a particular encrypted document d contains a given keyword k.

We denote Alice, S, Bob be the data owner, the cloud, and the data consumer respectively. Let (pk, sk) be the Paillier key pair of S, and $Enc(\cdot)$ be the encryption under public key pk. Protocol 1 describes the algorithm that inputs an index i, and a keyword w and outputs an encrypted bit b. $b = 1$ if the document contains the keyword and 0 otherwise. The result is held by Bob but remains encrypted under S's public key pk.

In line 5 of Protocol 1, Bob and S collaboratively compute the mulitplication operation on the encrypted data. In this protocol (i.e. SecMul), Bob holds two private encrypted inputs $(Enc(x), Enc(y))$ and S keeps the Paillier secret key sk, where x and y are unknown to both two parties. The output of $SecMul(Enc(x), Enc(y))$ is $Enc(x \times y)$ and revealed only to Bob. The protocol $SecMul$ is presented in Protocol 2. Regarding the definition of $SecMul$ (i.e. Protocol 2), Bob iteratively computes the product of $\prod Enc(B^{(i)}[h_j(k, w)])$ in the encrypted form for $j = 1, \ldots, t$. The product equals to 1 if any only if all the bits of $\{Enc(B^{(i)}[h_j(k, w)])\}$ are set and 0 otherwise. Hence, the correctness of the protocol follows that observation.

Protocol 1. Secure Single Keyword Evaluation

Input: Integer i denotes the index of document $d^{(i)}$, keyword w, pk is Pailier public key of S

Output: Encrypted bit $Enc(b)$, where $b = q(w, d^{(i)})$ - whether $d^{(i)}$ contain w

1 S encrypts each bit in the Bloom filter $B^{(i)}$ by its Pailier public key;
2 Bob generates key $k = F(i)$;
3 S and Bob perform (t, m) oblivious transfer to send encrypted
   $\{Enc(B^{(i)}[h_j(k, w)])\}$ to Bob, $j = \overline{1, t}$;
4 Bob computes $r = Enc(1)$;
5 For each correspoding bit $h_j(k, w)$, Bob computes
   $r = SecMul(r, Enc(B^{(i)}[h_j(k, w)]))$;
6 Bob outputs r.

Regarding in line 1, 2 of Protocol 1, S is required to encrypt the Bloom filter sets each time for a single keyword evaluation. However, since a complex boolean query normally contains multiple of keyword evaluations, one time Bloom filters encryption and communication for a query are sufficient. The protocol requires n encrypted bit transfers for the Bloom filter and $2 \times t$ encrypted integer communication for t *Secure Multiplication* rounds.

Protocol 2. Secure Multiplication

Input: Bob holds $(Enc(x), Enc(y))$, and S holds the private key sk

Output: Bob holds $Enc(x \times y)$

1 Bob generates two random number r, s;
2 Bob computes $Enc(x + r), Enc(y + s)$ sends them to S;
3 S decrypts and obtains $x + r$, $y + s$;
4 S computes $(x + r)(y + s)$ and send $Enc((x + r)(y + s))$ to Bob;
5 Bob computes
   $Enc(x \times y) = Enc((x + r)(y + s)) - Enc(x \times s) - Enc(y \times r) - Enc(r \times s)$.

The computations at line 2, 5 of Protocol 2 are simply performed by the homomorphic property of Paillier encryption. During the protocol, Bob only works on encrypted data, while the server receives two random numbers. Hence, no information regarding x and y is gained by *Bob* and S. The correctness of the protocol is trivial as $(x + r)(y + s) = x \times y + x \times s + y \times r + r \times s$. The protocol requires 2 encrypted integer transfer for communication cost. Bob has to perform 5 multiplicative operations and 5 exponential operations in the ciphertext space.

5.3   Secure Complex Boolean Query Evaluation

At this stage, Bob holds the encrypted result of the evaluation for each document with each keyword appearing in the private query. This sub-section discusses three basic primitives that operate on the encrypted inputs of the stage. With these primitives, Bob has the capability to compute the encryption of the desired bit result for each document's query evaluation. The output of this stage is a single encrypted bit for each document. That single bit indicates whether the document satisfied the query.

Inputs of the three primitives are either one single encrypted bit (NOT operation) or two encrypted bits (AND and OR operations). The descriptions of them are presented as follows:

1. $\neg$ (NOT) - It is straightforward to derive the formula for bit negation operation: $Enc(\neg x) = Enc(1) - Enc(x)$. Clearly, the operation leaks no information regarding the encrypted bit x to both the cloud S and Bob. It requires 1 exponential operation and 1 multiplicative operation. Clearly, the protocol leaks no information to Bob and S, since S receives no more data while Bob only works on his inputs which are encrypted data.
2. $\wedge$ (AND) - Because $x \wedge y = x \times y$ for any two bits x, y. The primitive is exactly the same with the description of SecMul (Protocol 2). The protocol requires 5 multiplicative operations and 5 exponential operations in the ciphertext space. The security of the protocol follows the analysis of Secure Multiplication (i.e. Protocol 2).
3. $\vee$ (OR) - Since $x \vee y = x + y - x \times y$, we can derive the definition of the OR primitive as in the Protocol 3. The protocol requires 7 multiplicative operations and 6 exponential operations in the ciphertext space. During the protocol, the data that Bob and S receive are exactly the same with those received during Protocol 2, hence, Bob and S gain nothing after the protocol execution.

Protocol 3. Secure OR Operation

Input: Bob holds $(Enc(x), Enc(y))$, and S holds the private key sk
Output: Bob holds $Enc(x \vee y)$
1 Bob and S collaboratively compute $Enc(x \times y)$ using protocol 2 ;
2 Bob computes $r = Enc(x) + Enc(y) - Enc(x \times y)$;
3 Bob outputs r;

5.4 Secure Retrieval of Output Data

Following the output of the Secure complex boolean query evaluation stage, Bob has the evaluation result (in encrypted form) for the combination of all predicates in the input on each data records. The goal of this stage is to utilize these results to reveal the raw evaluation result to Bob. The results are the indices of satisfied records. It is still worthy to point out that after this final stage, Bob can obtain only the result and nothing else, at the same time S gain nothing regarding Bob's query.

Let denote (pkB, skB) as Bob's Paillier key pair, and $Enc(pkB, \cdot)$ as the encryption using Bob's public key. The process of Secure retrieval of output data is presented in Protocol 4.

Protocol 4. Secure Retrieval of Output Data

Input: Bob holds $Enc(b_i)$- the encrypted evaluation result of each document,
Output: Bob holds S_r the set of statisfied indices

1 For each index id_i
    (1.1) S sends $Enc(id_i)$ to Bob.
    (1.2) Bob and S compute $Enc(b_i \times id_i) = SecMul(Enc(b_i), Enc(id_i))$
    (1.3) Bob generates a random integer r_i, and computes $Enc(b_i \times id_i + r_i)$
    (1.4) Bob sends $Enc(b_i \times id_i + r_i)$ and $Enc(pkB, r_i)$ to S.
    (1.5) S decrypts to get $b_i \times id_i + r_i$
    (1.6) S generates a random integer s_i and encrypts $Enc(pkB, b_i \times id_i + r_i + s_i)$
    (1.7) S computes $Enc(pkB, s_i + r_i)$;
2 S sends pairs of $\{Enc(pkB, b_i \times id_i + r_i + s_i), Enc(pkB, s_i + r_i)\}$ to Bob in a random order;
3 Bob decrypts and computes $p_i = b_i \times id_i$;
4 If $p_i \neq 0$, Bob adds p_i to S_r;
5 Bob outputs S_r;

At line 1.4, the cloud S receives $Enc(pkB, r_i)$ (encrypted by Bob's public key) and a random number $b_i \times id_i + r_i$ for each document. Clearly, it learns nothing regarding the evaluation results of Bob's input query. On the other hand, Bob recieves two random number $b_i \times id_i + r_i + s_i$ and $s_i + r_i$ for document id_i, the only information he obtains is $b_i \times id_i$ and nothing else.

6   Implemetation

We implemented and calculated the CPU time required to run the sub-protocols that we propose in Sect. 5. Our experiments were conducted on a Windows 10.0 machines with a processor 3.0 GHz and 16 GB RAM. We used Paillier cryptosystem as the underlying additive homomorphic encryption scheme and implemented the proposed sub-protocols in Java. In order to make all the same subprotocol to play the similar role, we implemented a simplified version of Secure Retrieval of Output Data (i.e. Protocol 4) protocol. In this simplified version, we consider there is only one document. As the result of the assumption, the output of the sub-protocol is either 0 or the index of the single document. Table 1 shows the processing time of four sub-protocols with different Paillier encryption key sizes.

While the specification of secure OR protocol requires 4 more multiplicative operations compared to secure AND protocol in the ciphertext space, the result shows that there is not much difference between the running times of secure AND and secure OR. On the other hands, we note that the running time of

Table 1. Running times of different sub-protocols in our implementation

Key size	Secure negation	Secure AND	Secure OR	Secure retrieval
512	4 ms	20 ms	22 ms	38 ms
1024	17 ms	73 ms	86 ms	150 ms
2048	81 ms	517 ms	558 ms	1090 ms

secure Negation is significantly larger than the difference between the previous two protocol. That means the encryption/decryption operations are more computationally expensive than performing arithmetic calculations on the ciphertext space. If we fix the Paillier encryption key size to 1024 bits, we note that the running times of secure retrieval of output data is 150 milliseconds, hence, we can easily handle thousands of data records in a reasonable time (i.e. 30 min). However, we observed that the computation cost of the sub-protocols increases by almost a factor of 7 when the Paillier key size is doubled.

7 Conclusion and Future Work

Thanks to various benefits (i.e. such as cost-efficiency and flexibility), outsourcing data storage and operational services to clouds has gained significant attention from both industry and academia. However, due to privacy concerns, data are typically encrypted before being outsourced. On the other hand, data encryption brings new challenges to both academia and industry which is query processing over encrypted data. Various techniques have been proposed to securely perform data retrieval over encrypted data. However, these techniques are either not directly applicable for evaluating complex queries over encrypted data or insecure regarding certain security requirements.

This paper presents a framework to securely evaluate boolean queries over encrypted data in the cloud. We applied Bloom filter and additive homomorphic encryption to construct a secure single keyword evaluation. We also presented an efficient mechanism to systematically combine the evaluation results of individual predicates to compute the corresponding query evaluation result. Our protocol not only protects data confidentiality and privacy of users input query but also hides the access patterns of the queries. The experimental results show that our protocol is practical for a small and medium size of data. As future work, we will design, implement and evaluate our protocols in parallel paradigms such as Map-Reduce or GPU. We also plan to extend our solutions to address other adversary models, such as fully malicious adversaries.

References

1. Bajaj, S., Sion, R.: TrustedDB: a trusted hardware based database with privacy and data confidentiality. In: Proceedings of the ACM SIGMOD International Conference on Management of Data, SIGMOD 2011, Athens, Greece (2011)

2. Bloom, B.H.: Space/time trade-offs in hash coding with allowable errors. Commun. ACM **13**(7), 422–426 (1970)

3. Boneh, D., Waters, B.: Conjunctive, subset, and range queries on encrypted data. IACR Cryptology ePrint Archive 2006 (2006)

4. Brassard, G., Crépeau, C., Robert, J.-M.: All-or-nothing disclosure of secrets. In: Odlyzko, A.M. (ed.) CRYPTO 1986. LNCS, vol. 263, pp. 234–238. Springer, Heidelberg (1987). doi:10.1007/3-540-47721-7_17

5. Curtmola, R., Garay, J.A., Kamara, S., Ostrovsky, R.: Searchable symmetric encryption: improved definitions and efficient constructions. In: Proceedings of the 13th ACM Conference on Computer and Communications Security, CCS 2006, Alexandria, VA, USA (2006)

6. Damgård, I., Jurik, M.: A generalisation, a simplification and some applications of paillier's probabilistic public-key system. In: Kim, K. (ed.) PKC 2001. LNCS, vol. 1992, pp. 119–136. Springer, Heidelberg (2001). doi:10.1007/3-540-44586-2_9

7. Do, H.G., Ng, W.K.: Privacy-preserving approach for sharing and processing intrusion alert data. In: Tenth IEEE International Conference on Intelligent Sensors, Sensor Networks and Information Processing, ISSNIP 2015, Singapore (2015)

8. Even, S., Goldreich, O., Lempel, A.: A randomized protocol for signing contracts. Commun. ACM **28**(6), 637–647 (1985)

9. Goh, E.: Secure indexes. IACR Cryptology ePrint Archive (2003)

10. Guo, F., Mu, Y., Susilo, W.: Subset membership encryption and its applications to oblivious transfer. IEEE Trans. Inf. Forensics Secur. **9**(7), 1098–1107 (2014)

11. Islam, M.S., Kuzu, M., Kantarcioglu, M.: Access pattern disclosure on searchable encryption: ramification, attack and mitigation. In: 19th Annual Network and Distributed System Security Symposium, NDSS 2012, San Diego, California, USA (2012)

12. Paillier, P.: Public-key cryptosystems based on composite degree residuosity classes. In: Stern, J. (ed.) EUROCRYPT 1999. LNCS, vol. 1592, pp. 223–238. Springer, Heidelberg (1999). doi:10.1007/3-540-48910-X_16

13. Rabin, M.O.: How to exchange secrets with oblivious transfer. IACR Cryptology ePrint Archive 2005 (2005)

14. Song, D.X., Wagner, D., Perrig, A.: Practical techniques for searches on encrypted data. In: 2000 IEEE Symposium on Security and Privacy, Berkeley, California, USA (2000)

15. Wu, Q.-H., Zhang, J.-H., Wang, Y.-M.: Practical t-out-n oblivious transfer and its applications. In: Qing, S., Gollmann, D., Zhou, J. (eds.) ICICS 2003. LNCS, vol. 2836, pp. 226–237. Springer, Heidelberg (2003). doi:10.1007/978-3-540-39927-8_21

Privacy Leakage via Attribute Inference in Directed Social Networks

Raymond K. Wong[✉] and B.S. Vidyalakshmi

School of Computer Science and Engineering, University of New South Wales,
Sydney, Australia
wong@cse.unsw.edu.au

Abstract. Social networking has become a frequent activity for most
internet users. Profile attribute inference research has gained popularity due to its importance in social network privacy. While many social
networks are in the form of directed networks, most attribute inference approaches are based on undirected networks. Aimed at a directed
social network, we propose an algorithm utilising the concepts of tie-
strength and co-profiling attribute with circles. We propose to infer both
attributes and circles iteratively, by propagating the known attribute values of followers and followings within certain circles. With the ability to
follow or be followed by any user, the possibility of many weak links being
formed is high. We utilize tie-strength to address this and differentiate
each user's influence in the ego user attribute inference. Experiments
show the superior performance of our proposed approach over the state
of the art method.

1   Introduction

Social networking has become one of the most popular internet activities online
with nearly 74% of online adults using social networking sites, as per a recent
study[1]. Profile creation in the popular social networks (Facebook, Twitter,
Google+, LinkedIn) requires users to give out their personal information, with
only a few fields (e.g., name) being mandatory and the rest being optional (e.g.,
college, age, relationship status). Many studies [5,17] have highlighted the privacy aspect of giving out these personal information and how users navigate
around these through proxies, not filling in the attributes or hiding important
profile information from being publicly visible. Study on Google+ [8], reported
that as much as 70% of the users do not provide any attributes while another
Google+ study [14] reported only about 10% of the users provide more than
six attributes. A study on Twitter [12] reported only about 20% of users having
provided their home cities. These studies confirm the norm of leaving attributes
unfilled or making the attributes publicly invisible.

This paper focuses on privacy leakage of personal information even user's
and/or friends' attributes are not completely filled or publicly visible. Furthermore, research into attribute inference of a user have concentrated on utilising

---

[1] http://www.pewinternet.org/fact-sheets/social-networking-fact-sheet/.

© Springer International Publishing AG 2016
K.-Y. Lam et al. (Eds.): ICICS 2016, LNCS 9977, pp. 333–346, 2016.
DOI: 10.1007/978-3-319-50011-9_26

available information that the user himself has publicly disclosed, albeit partially, along with information from the linked users (followers/followings) who may have made their information publicly available. We concentrate on an ego network which is a subnetwork inside a social network, consisting of the ego user (whose attributes are to be inferred), his linked users and the links between them.

Model: Multiple research works have utilised the disclosed attributes by the ego and by the users linked to the ego in inferring ego user attributes and identifying the circles to which users belong. Attribute inference work [16], using Facebook, proposed that friends share all attributes with the ego if they belong to a community (or circle). Circle detection works [10, 21] substantiate this understanding to be flawed by empirically confirming that friends belonging to a circle share only one or a few attributes with the ego. Attribute-Circle Dependency [11], captures this concept of a circle created with friends sharing the same college (i.e., classmates) and another circle created with friends sharing the same employer (i.e., colleagues). Hence, the knowledge of circle can help in attribute inference. Since circle information is publicly unavailable, [11] proposed to co-profile the circle members and then the ego attributes. However, they neglected the aspect of ego user being strongly connected to some while weakly connected to the others. In fact, [3] pointed at users tending to preferentially attach and spend time on creating and maintaining those relationships in which they are interested in. Research into tie-strength measurement point at the often neglected aspect of low cost of link formation that can lead to networks with heterogeneous relationship strengths (e.g., acquaintances and best friends mixed together) [20]. Works [15, 19] also point at another dimension to link creation, that of users feeling obliged to link with users. Hence, to address this, in our current work, we utilize tie-strength as a proxy to measure the influence of each linked user in ego user attribute inference. In our approach for addressing the attribute inference from social neighbours, we utilise the concepts of Influence (I) of linked users, Attribute-Circle dependency and model it into a cost function which is iteratively updated until the cost cannot be further minimised, to arrive at the ego user attribute values. With studies reporting that a majority of users leave their attributes unfilled or publicly invisible [8, 12], we assume all attributes of the ego user have to be inferred.

Attribute Inference in Directed vs Undirected Networks: An ego network in directed social networks consists of linked users who are directly connected to the ego user through a follower or following link. Directed social networks provide the ability to follow any user without the need for the followed user to either provide explicit consent to be followed or reciprocate the friendship. This ability, though beneficial, has a risk attached to it due to attribute inference capabilities from attributes of the followers and/or followings.

Attribute inference works so far have not differentiated attribute inference in directed and undirected networks [11, 16]. Though [8] use Google+, a directed social network, they convert the directed network into undirected network by keeping only bi-directional links (friends subnetwork). (In this paper, we use the standard terminology used in research into social network graph, *friend node* - to mean a node who follows the ego user and the ego user follows the node back). This is the general norm due to the inherent belief that only mutual friendships give out the true reason for connecting over a social network [8]. We show, further, through experiments that this belief is not beneficial in the case of attribute inference. In a social network where the reciprocity of linking is not essential (directed social network), if the attribute inference is still feasible and is better than the converted undirected social network, the magnitude of risk to privacy is amplified. Hence, in this work, we would like to concentrate on attribute inference in directed network and compare results obtained between directed social network and undirected social network obtained by converting directed network. As far as our knowledge goes, this is the first work to give a detailed account of using followers subnetwork (followers and links only), following subnetwork (following users and links only), or all links subnetwork (followers and following links) along with friends subnetwork for attribute inference in a directed social network.

Experiments and Results: Similar to work that utilise partial social graph for attribute inference [4], partial ego network (a partial social graph) in the form of follower subnetwork or following subnetwork is shown to be capable of attribute inference in directed social network. Experimental results show the proposed method to be better than the Co-profiling approach [11] which is the previous best method of attribute inference bettering works [13,16,22,23].

We present results for attribute inference when attributes are inferred together and when attributes are inferred separately. It is important to note that the works so far [11,13,16,22,23] have concentrated on inferring each attribute separately. Though, inference accuracy of attributes inferred separately is greater than the inference accuracy of attributes inferred together, the later approach can provide gains in terms of run-time as all attributes are inferred together.

The rest of the paper is organised as follows. We define the problem in Sect. 2 and present the proposed method in Sect. 3. We then show the experimental results in Sect. 4 and conclude the paper in Sect. 5.

2   Problem Abstraction

In our work to infer attributes of a user in a directed social network, we propose to concentrate on a user's *ego network*. We study the problem of inferring attributes of the ego user v_0 in a subnetwork of followers, following, friends and all_links each of which have been constructed considering followers, followings, friends and all linked_user's for each ego user. These can be considered as four datasets which are constructed for every ego network.

Figure 1 shows a sample *ego network* which is a subnetwork inside a social network consisting of the *ego* node v_0, nodes connected to the ego node

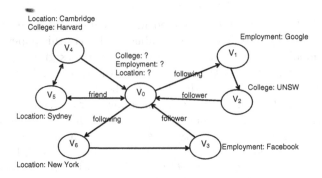

Fig. 1. A sample ego network

(e.g., v_1, v_2, v_3), directed links between ego and the nodes (e.g., (v_0, v_1), (v_2, v_0)) as also the links between the nodes (e.g., (v_1, v_2), (v_6, v_3)). The vertices (or nodes) V and edges E (or links) forming the social network, can be represented as a directed graph $G = (V, E)$ where edge E is formed by a directed link starting from vertex v_i and ending at vertex v_j represented as the pair (v_i, v_j). The nodes except the ego user are denoted by V' and the links between the nodes belonging to V' are represented by E' with $E' \subset E$ and $V' \cup v^0 = V$. We call users belonging to V' as *linked_users* who are linked to the ego user v_0 through a follower or following link. Since the problem setting addresses attribute inference in directed social networks, the directionality of the link is of importance. Therefore, Link $(v_i, v_j) \neq (v_j, v_i)$.

Each node represents a social network user, who creates a profile with various attributes describing the user. In this work we infer categorical attributes college, employment and location. Proposed method can be extended to include non-categorical attributes (skills, bio), by clustering them into categorical attributes before applying attribute inference. A_p denotes attribute p to be inferred and $a_{i,p}$ denotes its value for user v_i. We assume that each user has a single value for the attribute in question (e.g., user has worked only at Google). This can be extended to include multivalued attributes by considering the top-n results of attribute inference for the user instead of the top value alone.

In the ego user v_0's ego network, some of the users have all the attributes filled in while some have filled only a few of their attributes with the majority rest leaving all attributes unfilled or publicly invisible. Users who have filled in only a few attributes are called *Partially Labelled users* (denoted as P), while users who have filled all the attributes are called *Labelled users* (denoted as L), with the users who have no attributes filled in, called the *Unlabelled users*, (denoted as U). As described in Sect. 1, we assume $v_0 \in U$.

3   Proposed Solution for Attribute Inference

3.1   Concepts

Given an ego user and the network structure formed by ego's links with the nodes in his ego network, the aim is to infer ego users' attributes from the known attributes of the linked_users. In an ego network, the circles to which linked_users belong is unknown and so are some or all of their attributes. A circle can be considered as user grouping suggested by the Social network provider or explicitly grouped by the ego user. It is called as *Circles* in Google+ while it is called *Lists* in Facebook and Twitter. Works on circle detection [10,21] empirically confirm users belonging to a circle share one or a few attributes. With the understanding that both circle and attributes can be co-profiled as both are dependent on each other, the co-profiling approach was proposed by Li et al. [11] which bettered all the existing methods for attribute inference [13,16,22]. Hence, our starting point was their work. Two concepts that formed the basis of their work, which we continue to use, are Attribute-Circle dependency (Concept 1) and Circle-Connection dependency (Concept 2).

In social networks, some users may be strongly connected (through preferentially attaching) to the ego user while some form casual links (obligatory links). This forms the basis of research into finding differing tie-strengths between users [7,20]. We use the concept of tie-strength to find the Influence (I) of each linked_user in attribute inference unlike [11] which gives each linked_user and his attributes equal importance.

Thus, the concepts that form the basis of our model are Attribute-Circle dependency (Concept 1) and Influence (Concept 3) of linked_user. Even though Circle-Connection dependency (Concept 2) is part of the model, Concept 2's inclusion into the cost function of attribute inference is shown to have no effect on attribute inference. Concept 3 (Influence I) of each linked_user is measured through tie-strength between the ego and the linked_user. Tie-strength offers the concept of users being strongly connected to some users while weakly connected to others. Research into tie-strength measurement point at the often neglected aspect of low cost of link formation that can lead to networks with heterogeneous relationship strengths (e.g., acquaintances and best friends mixed together) [20]. We propose to use tie-strength normalized as Influence (I) by including it in cost function used for ego user attribute inference.

3.2   Notation

f_i represents the *attribute vector* of a given user v_i with each dimension of the attribute vector representing a candidate value of an attribute. An attribute vector $< 0, 1, 0, 1, 1, 1 >$ represents a candidate vector set <Harvard, UNSW, Facebook, Google, Sydney, New York>, with 1 representing the presence of the attribute and 0 the absence. The candidate attribute values used in inferring ego user's attribute are obtained by the known attribute values of the L and P users. The value of the yth dimension of f_i, denoted as $f_{i,y}$ is a real number greater than 0, indicating the likelihood of this attribute value being the attribute value of v_i. The L and P users $\{v_i \in L, P\}$ have $f_{i,y} = 1$ for an observed attribute value. The f_i is an unknown vector for unlabelled user $\{v_i \in U\}$ initially and is determined through the proposed algorithm.

The circle to which a user v_i belongs to called *circle assignment*, denoted by x_i, can be a value between 1 to K with K denoting the number of circles. A circle

C_t is given as $\left\{ v_i \in V' | x_i = t \right\}$. We model each linked_user as belonging to one circle in a given ego network in this work and do not consider circle overlapping as part of this work.

The attribute value that is associated with a circle (the common attribute value) is denoted by an *association vector* w_t for each circle C_t. w_t is a binary vector with $\{w_{t,y} \in 0/1\}$ for a given dimension y indicating its association with the circle C_t. Using the example mentioned above, $< 1, 0, 0, 0, 0, 0 >$ indicates the users in C_t share one attribute value with the ego, indicating, they all study at Harvard and have other attributes different from ego.

The Influence (I) of a linked_user provides the information about which linked_user should influence more than the other in inferring ego user attributes. Within the circle to which a linked_user belongs, Circle level Influence ($I_{i \equiv C_t}$) provides the influence of the linked_user f_i and Global level Influence ($I_{i \equiv L_i}$) provides the overall influence of the linked_user irrespective of the circle to which he belongs.

3.3   Model

As suggested by Attribute-Circle dependency and Circle Influence, if two users v_i and v_j belong to the same circle C_t, their attribute vectors should be close on the dimension of associate attribute value w_t of the circle. If v_i and v_j share same relationship with the ego user v_0 and have the same relationship t, then their influence within the circle C_t, should also be close. Thus, minimizing the squared distance measure we arrive at $\sum\limits_{e_{ij} \in E', v_i, v_j \in C_t} (w_t \cdot (f_i \cdot I_{i \equiv C_t} - f_j \cdot I_{j \equiv C_t}))^2 + \sum\limits_{v_i \in C_t} (w_t \cdot$ $(f_0 \cdot 1 - f_i \cdot I_{i \equiv C_t}))^2$ where f_i and f_j denote the attribute vectors and $I_{i \equiv C_t}, I_{j \equiv C_t}$ denote tie-strength normalized into Influence (I) of v_i, v_j respectively, with w_t representing the associate attribute vector of circle C_t.

The L and P users provide the explicit knowledge in establishing the associate attribute value of a circle. As such, the associate attribute value w_t, of a circle C_t, should be the value shared by many L and P users and Global Influence ($I_{i \equiv L_i}$) should be similar which is to minimize $\sum\limits_{v_i \in L, P \cap C_t} I_{i \equiv L_i} \cdot (w_t \cdot f_i - 1)^2$. Circle-Connection dependency, is given by $\sum\limits_{e_{ij} \in E', x_i != x_j} 1$, which is to minimize the inter circle connections between linked_users. This is also included into the cost function. Thus, we arrive at the cost function as in Eq. 1.

$$\sum_{t=1}^{K} \{ \sum_{e_{ij} \in E', v_i, v_j \in C_t} (w_t \cdot (f_i \cdot I_{i \equiv C_t} - f_j \cdot I_{j \equiv C_t}))^2$$

$$+ \sum_{v_i \in C_t} (w_t \cdot (f_0 \cdot 1 - f_i \cdot I_{i \equiv C_t}))^2 \}$$

$$+ \sum_{t=1}^{K} \sum_{v_i \in L, P \cap C_t} I_{i \equiv L_i} \cdot (w_t \cdot f_i - 1)^2 + \sum_{e_{ij} \in E', x_i != x_j} 1 \tag{1}$$

3.4   Algorithm

In order to infer the attribute values using the known (ego network structure, tie-strength), partially known (attribute values of some nodes of the ego network) and unknown (circles) information, the unknown values have to be initialized in the first step after which the algorithm can be applied. By initializing the unknown variables and with the knowledge of known variables, we intend to minimize the cost function given by Eq. 1 and iteratively update the unknown variables till convergence, similar to co-ordinate descent method. We update the unknown variables, i.e., circles C_t, the associated circle value w_t, the attribute vectors of the ego user f_0 and Unlabelled users $f_i \in U$. One variable is iteratively updated while keeping others constant as part of the algorithm.

Initialization: The L and P users attribute vector f_i is known and the Unlabelled users' attribute vector and the ego user v_0's attribute vector is unknown. We initialise the Unlabelled users attribute vectors to 0.5 on all dimensions ($f_i = 0.5, \forall f_i \in U$). Since, the number of circles and the circle membership is unknown in our dataset, we initialised the number of circles and the circle membership through the community detection algorithm [1], known as Louvain method. We chose [1] as it works on both directed (all_links, follower, following subnetworks) and undirected networks (friends subnetwork) as is the case in our setting, unlike the algorithm [2] used for community detection in [11], that works only on undirected networks.

Step 1 - Attribute Vector: To update the attribute vectors f_i of Unlabelled users ($f_i \in U$), and f_0 of the ego user, we keep the association vector w_t and the circle assignment x_i constant. This reduces the Eq. 1 to a quadratic function as given by Eq. 2. We obtain the first order partial derivate for f_i and f_0 from the quadratic equation, keeping all the other variables constant to arrive at Eqs. 3 and 4. f_0 and f_i are iteratively updated until convergence using co-ordinate descent method, similar to the attribute inference work by [11].

   Only $f_{i,y}$ of f_i and $f_{0,y}$ of f_0 are updated considering w_t, the association vector of Circle C_t, has only one non-zero dimension $w_{t,y}$. It is important to note that attributes are propagated only within the circle based on their attribute vector f_i and Influence (I).

$$
\sum_{t=1}^{K} \Big\{ \sum_{e_{ij} \in E', v_i, v_j \in C_t} (w_t \cdot (f_i \cdot I_{i \equiv C_t} - f_j \cdot I_{j \equiv C_t}))^2
$$
$$
+ \sum_{v_i \in C_t} (w_t \cdot (f_0 \cdot 1 - f_i \cdot I_{i \equiv C_t}))^2 \Big\} \tag{2}
$$

$$
f_{i,y} = \frac{f_{0,y} + \sum_{e_{ij} \in E', v_j \in C_t} f_{j,y} \cdot I_{j \equiv C_t}}{1 + \sum_{e_{ij} \in E', v_j \in C_t} 1}, v_i \in U \cap C_t, w_{t,y} = 1 \tag{3}
$$

$$f_{0,y} = \frac{\sum_{t=1,w_t,y=1}^{K} \sum_{v_j \in C_t} f_{j,y} \cdot I_{j \equiv C_t}}{\sum_{t=1,w_t,y=1}^{K} \sum_{v_j \in C_t} 1}, w_{t,y} = 1, \forall t = 1,...K \qquad (4)$$

Step 2 - Circle Assignment: Circle assignment x_i, of each linked_user is updated iteratively keeping the other two variables, the attribute vector f_i and the associate attribute w_t of each circle C_t constant. Intuitively, in every iteration, a given linked_user v_i belongs to that circle x_i, which minimizes the objective function given by Eq. 1 the most else remain in the current circle if no other assignment can reduce it. Equation 5 tries to find the circle C_t, for an Unlabelled user $v_i \in U$, such that there are many connections within C_t, with similar Influence $I_{i \equiv C_t}$ as the current circle with which user is associated. Equation 6 finds the circle for a Labelled or Partially Labelled user $v_i \in \{L, P\}$, accounting the prior knowledge of f_i and Influence $I_{i \equiv L_i}$. Intuitively, if v_i's, attribute vector f_i, has the associate attribute value w_t of a circle, then the user should belong to that circle. Influence $I_{i \equiv L_i}$ in Eq. 5, sees to it that, a user does not belong to that circle whose associate attribute value w_t, is not held by f_i of $v_i \in \{L, P\}$. Hence, the value of the Influence $I_{i \equiv L_i}$, should be large.

$$x_i = \arg \max_{t=1,...,K} [\sum_{e_{ij} \in E', v_j \in C_t} (1 - (w_t \cdot (f_i \cdot I_{i \equiv C_t} - f_j \cdot I_{j \equiv C_t}))^2)$$
$$- (w_t \cdot (f_0 \cdot 1 - f_i \cdot I_{i \equiv C_t}))^2], v_i \in U \qquad (5)$$

$$x_i = \arg \max_{t=1,...,K} [\sum_{e_{ij} \in E', v_j \in C_t} (1 - (w_t \cdot (f_i \cdot I_{i \equiv C_t} - f_j \cdot I_{j \equiv C_t}))^2)$$
$$- (w_t \cdot (f_0 \cdot 1 - f_i \cdot I_{i \equiv C_t}))^2 - (I_{i \equiv L_i} \cdot (w_t \cdot f_i - 1)^2)], v_i \in L, P \qquad (6)$$

Step 3 - Associate Attribute Value of a Circle: Keeping the circle assignment C_t and the attribute vector f_i of each user v_i fixed, we find the associate attribute value w_t of each circle, with the assumption that each circle has only one attribute value or dimension as 1. With a finite number of dimensions for the attribute values, we select the attribute value that best minimizes the objective function given by Eq. 1.

4   Experiments

4.1   Dataset

We used Google+ social network to evaluate the attribute inference performance of the proposed method. We chose Google+ as it is mid-way between the more popular counterparts, Facebook and Twitter, inheriting the best of both the worlds in it [14]. A total of 154 ego users and their direct followers and following links were crawled using Google+ API resulting in a total of 39860 Google+ users who had made their profiles public between April 2015 to July 2015 and

Oct 2015 to Nov 2015. Since, we infer ego user's attributes college, employment and current location, we crawled these attributes of all the users, if they were publicly available. The dataset consists of 18815 colleges, 37009 employers and 9426 current locations for attributes and a total of 539777 links from 39860 Google+ users.

In a real world setting, the number of linked_users who provide their attributes varies. Hence, as part of the experiments we inferred ego user attributes with different percentages (10%, 20%, 30% and 100%) of Labelled and Partially Labelled users. It has been shown from previous works on attribute inference [11, 16] that attributes of as little as 20% of linked_users is sufficient to infer ego user attributes with significant accuracy. Hence, we continue to hold 20% as the standard percentage of known linked_users against which attribute inference is tested.

Directed vs Undirected Social Networks – Works into attribute inference so far have concentrated on either using undirected networks [4, 11, 16] and generalizing it to both directed and undirected networks. Though few of the works use directed networks, they convert the directed networks into undirected networks by retaining only two-way links and two-way linked nodes as part of the dataset [8]. We do not resort to convert the directed Google+ data into undirected dataset by retaining links (v_i, v_j) if and only if both edges (v_i, v_j) and (v_j, v_i) exist in the ego network. This was done in order to find the attribute inference ability with an ego follower subnetwork or an ego following subnetwork. But, by keeping all the links, there is a possibility of having many spurious links or spammers in the ego network. We are aware that there is a wealth of research in identifying and removing spammers from social networks [6, 9, 18]. The spamming activity is targeted and hence this targeted spamming will place the ego user at a risk of his attributes being exposed easily. It has also been noted in these studies that bringing down these spammer accounts will only be temporary and a complete spam block is not a realistic expectation for any social network. Hence, we chose to retain all the links for attribute inference.

It is important to note that we could not find any previous works using follower, following, or all_links subnetworks for attribute inference. Hence, to facilitate comparing our proposed method with previous works, we convert the Google+ dataset into an undirected network by retaining two-way links and two-way linked nodes to obtain the *friend subnetwork*. First, we present the results on converted undirected network or friend subnetwork. We then present the results of attribute inference on follower, following and all_links subnetworks by keeping the directedness of the links intact i.e., on directed network.

Baseline – We compare our proposed method with co-profiling approach for attribute inference by Li et al. [11] which has been shown to be better than the previous methods of attribute inference [13, 16, 22, 23]. As such, we compare our work with co-profiling approach for attribute inference [11]. Co-profiling approach (here after referred to as CP), infers both circle and attributes together as (i) both are dependant on each other and (ii) both necessitate inferring due to being missing or absent publicly in a social network. CP proposes that users within a circle share one or a few attributes. Some users known attributes are propogated within circles to determine the attributes of unlabelled friends and the ego user. We implemented the algorithm of CP and as part of the experiments, we tested it with the optimal parameter values as described in the paper.

Attribute Inference Strategy – Works so far have resorted to inferring ego user attributes independently, i.e., inferring one attribute for each run of the experiments. Except for CP which can take multiple attributes as input for inference, works by [13,16,22,23] infer attributes independently. Since the proposed method can infer attributes independently and together, as part of the experiments we infer attributes using both approaches. We report the results for the proposed method as well as the baseline method of CP for both attribute inference approaches.

4.2   Experiment Results

We compare the proposed method with CP on friend subnetwork dataset and present the results in this section.

Table 1. Attribute inference accuracy with 20% Labelled and Partially Labelled users

Proposed method	College	Employment	Location
Mean	0.288	0.152	0.240
Variance	4E-04	3E-05	0E+00
Co-profiling method	College	Employment	Location
Mean	0.195	0.121	0.195
Variance	6E-04	9E-04	2E-03

Table 1 provides the results of attribute inference with 20% of Labelled and Partially Labelled linked_users. We ran the attribute inference multiple times to avail mean and variances of the inference accuracy. Figures 2 and 3 provide the attribute inference results of the proposed method and CP. While Fig. 2 gives the inference accuracy of attributes inferred together, inference accuracy of attributes inferred independently is given in Fig. 3. We have the following observations.

Observation 1: Attribute inference accuracy of the proposed method is better across 10%, 20%, 30% and 100% of Labelled and Partially Labelled linked_users, when compared to CP as seen in Figs. 2 and 3. Proposed method utilizes influence of users in place of static parameters used in CP. Result shows the ability

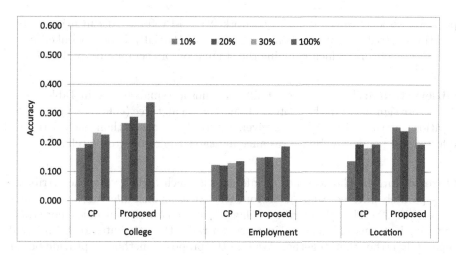

Fig. 2. Attribute inference accuracy of Co-Profiling (CP) and the proposed method with attributes inferred together

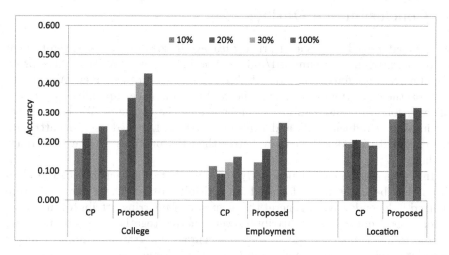

Fig. 3. Attribute inference accuracy of Co-Profiling (CP) and the proposed method with attributes inferred independently

of the proposed method which takes advantage of the available mutual friend information to infer the Influence (I) and utilize it in attribute propagation and circle's associate attribute determination, thus yielding better accuracy.

Observation 2: Accuracy of CP increases with the increase in Labelled users from 10% to 20% and then stagnates with no considerable increase in accuracy for 30% and 100%. Labelled users, who have filled in all three attributes is around 25% in our dataset while Labelled users is shown to be much lesser than 20% from previous work on directed social network [8]. Co-Profiling fails in utilizing the additional attribute information in the form of Partially Labelled linked_users in the ego network, which explains the stagnation of accuracy beyond 20%.

Observation 3: The variances of different runs are small as seen in Table 1. It is even more significant in the context of inference of all three (college, employment, location) attributes together as given by Table 1, rather than each attribute inferred independently. Small variance indicates the results to be reliable.

Observation 4: The accuracy of inference is much higher when the attributes are separately inferred (Fig. 3), one for each run, as against inferring all attributes at once (Fig. 2). Though inferring each attribute separately consumes more time, the gain in terms of accuracy increase warrants the attributes to be inferred separately rather than together. We find the proposed method to provide better accuracy than CP in both the cases.

5 Conclusion and Outlook

We have addressed the issue of privacy leakage in social networks, even though many user attributes are unfilled/hidden. Specifically, we have studied the problem of attribute inference in a directed social network in this paper. We concentrate on the ego network of a user and find the inference capabilities of friend, follower, following and all_links subnetworks of the ego user. We have shown the impact of influence (I) and utilising Partially Labelled users in attribute inference, with inference accuracy better than the previous attribute inference method.

Inferring attributes independently (one attribute for each run of the algorithm) has been the norm followed by multiple works. When attributes were inferred independently, in general the accuracy of inferring attributes increased or remained similar to when attributes were inferred together. Though, inferring attributes independently provides better accuracy, inferring attributes together provides an alternative with gains in terms of run-time.

As our future work, we would like to test the inference capabilities on other social networks and on the impact of inherent make-up of nodes. We would like to incorporate overlapping and hierarchical circles where a user may belong to multiple circles. Finally we would also like to test the proposed method on ego networks of larger sizes.

References

1. Blondel, V.D., Guillaume, J.-L., Lambiotte, R., Lefebvre, E.: Fast unfolding of communities in large networks. J. Stat. Mech. Theory Exp. **10**(10), 008 (2008)
2. Clauset, A., Newman, M.E., Moore, C.: Finding community structure in very large networks. Phys. Rev. E **70**(6), 066111 (2004)

3. Dindia, K., Canary, D.J.: Definitions and theoretical perspectives on maintaining relationships. J. Soc. Pers. Relatsh. **10**(2), 163–173 (1993)
4. Dougnon, R.Y., Fournier-Viger, P., Nkambou, R.: Inferring user profiles in online social networks using a partial social graph. In: Barbosa, D., Milios, E. (eds.) CANADIAN AI 2015. LNCS (LNAI), vol. 9091, pp. 84–99. Springer, Heidelberg (2015). doi:10.1007/978-3-319-18356-5_8
5. Ellison, N.B., Vitak, J., Steinfield, C., Gray, R., Lampe, C.: Negotiating privacy concerns and social capital needs in a social media environment. In: Trepte, S., Reinecke, L. (eds.) Privacy Online, pp. 19–32. Springer, Heidelberg (2011)
6. Ghosh, S., Viswanath, B., Kooti, F., Sharma, N.K., Korlam, G., Benevenuto, F., Ganguly, N., Gummadi, K.P.: Understanding and combating link farming in the twitter social network. In: Proceedings of the 21st International Conference on World Wide Web, pp. 61–70. ACM (2012)
7. Gilbert, E., Karahalios, K.: Predicting tie strength with social media. In: Proceedings of the SIGCHI Conference on Human Factors in Computing Systems, pp. 211–220. ACM (2009)
8. Gong, N.Z., Talwalkar, A., Mackey, L., Huang, L., Shin, E.C.R., Stefanov, E., Shi, E.R., Song, D.: Joint link prediction and attribute inference using a social-attribute network. ACM Trans. Intell. Syst. Technol. (TIST) **5**(2), 27 (2014)
9. Lee, K., Caverlee, J., Webb, S.: Uncovering social spammers: social honeypots+ machine learning. In: Proceedings of the 33rd International ACM SIGIR Conference on Research and Development in Information Retrieval, pp. 435–442. ACM (2010)
10. Leskovec, J., Mcauley, J.J.: Learning to discover social circles in ego networks. In: Advances in Neural Information Processing Systems, pp. 539–547 (2012)
11. Li, R., Wang, C., Chang, K.C.-C.: User profiling in an ego network: co-profiling attributes and relationships. In: Proceedings of the 23rd International Conference on World Wide Web, pp. 819–830 (2014)
12. Li, R., Wang, S., Deng, H., Wang, R., Chang, K.C.-C.: Towards social user profiling: unified and discriminative influence model for inferring home locations. In: Proceedings of the 18th ACM SIGKDD International Conference on Knowledge Discovery and Data Mining, pp. 1023–1031. ACM (2012)
13. Macskassy, S.A., Provost, F.: A simple relational classifier. In: Workshop on Multi-Relational Data Mining (MRDM-2003), p. 64. Citeseer
14. Magno, G., Comarela, G., Saez-Trumper, D., Cha, M., Almeida, V.: New kid on the block: exploring the Google+ social graph. In: Proceedings of the 2012 ACM Conference on Internet Measurement Conference, pp. 159–170. ACM (2012)
15. Mislove, A., Koppula, H.S., Gummadi, K.P., Druschel, P., Bhattacharjee, B.: Growth of the flickr social network. In: Proceedings of the First Workshop on Online Social Networks, pp. 25–30. ACM (2008)
16. Mislove, A., Viswanath, B., Gummadi, K.P., Druschel, P.: You are who you know: inferring user profiles in online social networks. In: Proceedings of the Third ACM International Conference on Web Search and Data Mining, pp. 251–260. ACM (2010)
17. Raynes-Goldie, K.: Aliases, creeping, wall cleaning: understanding privacy in the age of Facebook. First Monday **15**(1) (2010)
18. Stringhini, G., Kruegel, C., Vigna, G.: Detecting spammers on social networks. In: Proceedings of the 26th Annual Computer Security Applications Conference, pp. 1–9. ACM (2010)

19. Viswanath, B., Mislove, A., Cha, M., Gummadi, K.P.: On the evolution of user interaction in Facebook. In: Proceedings of the 2nd ACM Workshop on Online Social Networks, pp. 37–42. ACM (2009)
20. Xiang, R., Neville, J., Rogati, M.: Modeling relationship strength in online social networks. In: Proceedings of the 19th International Conference on World Wide Web, pp. 981–990. ACM (2010)
21. Yang, J., McAuley, J., Leskovec, J.: Community detection in networks with node attributes. In: Proceedings of the 2013 IEEE 13th International Conference on Data Mining (ICDM), pp. 1151–1156. IEEE (2013)
22. Zhou, D., Bousquet, O., Lal, T.N., Weston, J., Schölkopf, B.: Learning with local and global consistency. Adv. Neural Inf. Process. Syst. **16**(16), 321–328 (2004)
23. Zhu, X., Ghahramani, Z., Lafferty, J., et al.: Semi-supervised learning using Gaussian fields and harmonic functions. In: ICML, vol. 3, pp. 912–919 (2003)

DynaEgo: Privacy-Preserving Collaborative Filtering Recommender System Based on Social-Aware Differential Privacy

Shen Yan[1,2,3], Shiran Pan[1,2,3], Wen-Tao Zhu[1,2(✉)], and Keke Chen[4]

[1] State Key Laboratory of Information Security,
Institute of Information Engineering, Chinese Academy of Sciences, Beijing, China
{yanshen,panshiran}@iie.ac.cn, wtzhu@ieee.org
[2] Data Assurance and Communication Security Research Center,
Chinese Academy of Sciences, Beijing, China
[3] University of Chinese Academy of Sciences, Beijing, China
[4] Data Intensive Analysis and Computing (DIAC) Lab, Kno.e.sis Center,
Wright State University, Dayton, OH, USA
keke.chen@wright.edu

Abstract. Collaborative filtering plays an important role in online recommender systems, which provide personalized services to consumers by collecting and analyzing their rating histories. At the same time, such personalization may unfavorably incur privacy leakage, which has motivated the development of privacy-preserving collaborative filtering (PPCF) mechanisms. Most previous research efforts more or less impair the quality of recommendation. In this paper, we propose a social-aware algorithm called DynaEgo to improve the performance of PPCF. DynaEgo utilizes the principle of differential privacy as well as the social relationships to adaptively modify users' rating histories to prevent exact user information from being leaked. Theoretical analysis is provided to validate our scheme. Experiments on a real data set also show that DynaEgo outperforms existent solutions in terms of both privacy protection and recommendation quality.

Keywords: Social networks · Privacy preserving · Recommender system · Collaborative filtering · Differential privacy

1 Introduction

Recommender systems [1] are widely used in e-commerce and online social networks, suggesting products, movies, music, etc. to consumers. Recommender systems are designed to provide personalized suggestions on items to consumers. Collaborative filtering (CF) plays an important role in recommender systems, which makes recommendations by collecting suggestions from similar users (user-based) or similar items (item-based).

However, the tendency towards personalization has raised privacy concerns [2]. To address this problem, privacy-preserving collaborative filtering (PPCF)

© Springer International Publishing AG 2016
K.-Y. Lam et al. (Eds.): ICICS 2016, LNCS 9977, pp. 347–357, 2016.
DOI: 10.1007/978-3-319-50011-9_27

methods have been proposed, most of which employ traditional approaches such as cryptography, obfuscation, and perturbation. These approaches either induce great computation cost or provide insufficient privacy protection, thus impairing the performance in practical applications. In 2006, Dwork [3] proposed the notion of differential privacy (DP), which provides a quantifiable measurement of privacy. McSherry and Mironov [4] first introduced DP into CF. They constructed a private covariance matrix to randomize each user's ratings. In the context of the recommender systems, DP ensures that no user would be able to guess whether certain items appear in other users' rating histories.

Unfortunately, former methods fail to resist the k nearest neighbors (kNN) attack, which was first proposed by Calandrino et al. [5]. In the kNN attack, the adversary can infer the rating history of the target user by creating fake users. The success of the attack is due to that CF reveals users' preferences explicitly or implicitly, so the attacker can take advantage of the preferences to infer more information. Existent PPCF schemes only obscure the values of ratings, but not protect users' preferences. To address the problem, Guerraoui et al. [6] proposed D2P, which strengthens the notion of DP in recommender systems by creating a perturbed rating history named *AlterEgo* for each user. The perturbation process of D2P is highly dependent on subjectively selected parameters, which makes the privacy level non-intuitive and hard to control.

To improve both the privacy protection and the recommendation quality of former solutions, we introduce social relationships to PPCF schemes. Although social relationships have been widely used in recommender systems to boost the accuracy of recommendation, little work adopts it to provide effective privacy protection. In practice, users tend to share similar tastes with their close friends. So, substituting users's ratings with their friends' rating histories will obscure the exact ratings while keeping high utility. The import of social relationship information calls for us to customize the perturbed rating histories for different users. Therefore, the modified rating histories in our scheme are generated dynamically, which vary with the user who is receiving recommendations. We call our dynamically modified rating history *DyEgo*, and correspondingly name our scheme DynaEgo.

The rest of the paper is organized as follows. Section 2 introduces the preliminaries. In Sect. 3, we present our construction along with the theoretical analysis on privacy preserving. Section 4 reports the experimental results on a real data set called Epinions. Section 5 concludes this paper.

2   Preliminaries

2.1   Notation

Let $U = \{u_1, u_2, ..., u_n\}$ be a set of users and $I = \{t_1, t_2, ..., t_m\}$ be a set of items. The rating histories data set D can be represented as an $n \times m$ matrix, which can be decomposed into row vectors P_i and column vectors R_i. Specifically, the row vector $P_i = [r_{i1}, r_{i2}, ..., r_{im}]$ corresponds to the user u_i's rating history, and r_{ij} denotes the rating that user u_i gave to item t_j. The column vector

$R_i = [r_{1i}, r_{2i}, ..., r_{ni}]$ is composed of the ratings that t_i has received. For an item t_j that has not been rated by u_i, $r_{ij} = 0$. $sim(u_i, u_j)$ represents the similarity between users, and $itemsim(t_i, t_j)$ is the similarity between items. Empirical analysis indicates that Pearson correlation coefficient (Eq. 1) and Cosine similarity (Eq. 2) outperform other measurements, respectively:

$$sim(u_i, u_j) = \frac{\sum_{k=1}^{m}(P_i^{(k)} - \bar{P}_i)(P_j^{(k)} - \bar{P}_j)}{\sqrt{\sum_{k=1}^{m}(P_i^{(k)} - \bar{P}_i)^2 \sum_{k=1}^{m}(P_j^{(k)} - \bar{P}_j)^2}}, \tag{1}$$

$$itemsim(t_i, t_j) = \frac{\sum_{k=1}^{n} R_i^{(k)} \cdot R_j^{(k)}}{\sqrt{\sum_{k=1}^{n} R_i^{(k)} \sum_{k=1}^{n} R_j^{(k)}}}. \tag{2}$$

2.2 Differential Privacy

Definition 1 (ϵ-Differential Privacy). *A random function M satisfies ϵ- differential privacy if for all neighboring data sets D and D', and for all outputs t of this randomized function, the following statement holds:*

$$\frac{\Pr(M(D) = t)}{\Pr(M(D') = t)} \leq \exp(\epsilon), \ where \ \exp(\epsilon) \triangleq e^{\epsilon},$$

Two data sets D and D' are said to be neighbors if they are different in at most one item. ϵ is the privacy protection parameter which controls the amount of distinction induced by two neighboring data sets. A smaller value of ϵ ensures a stronger privacy guarantee.

Two main mechanisms are usually used to achieve DP: the *Laplace* mechanism [7] and the *Exponential* mechanism [8]. The *Laplace* mechanism is only suitable for numeric outputs, while the *Exponential* mechanism is designed to address the privacy issues in scenarios of entity outputs.

Definition 2 (Exponential Mechanism). *Let $q(r)$ be a score function of data set D that measures the score of output $r \in D$. The mechanism M satisfies ϵ-differential privacy if $M(D)$ outputs r with the probability:*

$$\Pr(M(D) = r) = \frac{\exp(\epsilon q(r)/(2\Delta q))}{\sum_{r \in D} \exp(\epsilon q(r)/(2\Delta q))},$$

where Δq is the global sensitivity of q.

Definition 3 (Global Sensitivity). *The global sensitivity Δq of a function q is the maximum absolute difference obtained on the output over all neighboring data sets:*

$$\Delta q = \max_{D \sim D'} |q(D) - q(D')|.$$

Definition 4 (Composition Property [8]). *The sequential application of mechanisms M_i, each giving ϵ_i-differential privacy, gives $\sum \epsilon_i$-differential privacy.*

2.3 *k*NN Attack

The *k*NN attack assumes that the attacker knows m elements in P_t (i.e., partial rating history of u_t), which may be obtained by methods like social engineering. Then the attacker wants to infer the remaining items that u_t has rated.

The process of the *k*NN attack can be summarized as follows. The attacker creates k fake users (i.e., sybils), and assigns the partial rating history of u_t to each sybil's rating history. Then, with high probability, the k most similar users of each sybil will consist of u_t and the other $k - 1$ sybils. The attacker inspects the list of items recommended to any of the sybils. Any item which appears in the list must have been rated by u_t.

2.4 Related Work

Former DP based PPCF solutions utilized DP mechanisms in various ways. McSherry and Mironov [4] proposed the first DP-based PPCF mechanism, which adds *Laplace* noise to the covariance matrix. PNCF [9] adopted the *Exponential* mechanism to select the neighbors, and add *Laplace* noise to the computation results. Zhu and Sun [10] proposed a mechanism based on the *Exponential* mechanism and designed a low sensitivity metric to measure the similarity.

Another method to adopt DP into PPCF is creating perturbed rating histories, e.g., *AlterEgo* in D2P [6]. In D2P scheme, the *AlterEgo* remains unchanged once created. In addition, the perturbation mechanism of D2P greatly depends on subjectively chosen parameters. Different from D2P, our proposal DynaEgo depends on the *Exponential* mechanism of DP, and employs social relationships to dynamically modify the rating histories.

3 DynaEgo Recommender

3.1 System Model

In this paper, we consider a general user-based CF recommender system, consisting of two parties: the service provider and the users. The service provider is trusted, storing users' rating histories and the social relationships data. There may be some malicious users in the system, who aim to infer other users' rating histories. The malicious users conduct the *k*NN attack. u_a is the active user, who is receiving recommendations. The service provider leverages k most similar users' rating histories to suggest items to u_a.

As Fig. 1 shows, DynaEgo relies on the *DyEgos* to make recommendations. The *DyEgos* are adaptively imitational rating histories. DynaEgo operates in three phases: Grouping phase, Modification phase, and Recommendation phase. The Recommendation phase is the same as the traditional CF algorithm, except using the *DyEgos* rather than the exact rating histories. Thus we only introduce the first two phases in detail below.

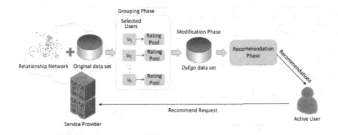

Fig. 1. The DynaEgo recommender scheme.

3.2   Grouping Phase

The Grouping phase consists of two steps. We select s users as the $SelectedUsers$ at first, then create a $RatingPool$ for each user in $SelectedUsers$.

$SelectedUsers$ are s users who have the most similar rating histories to u_a, where $s > k$ (k is the size of neighbors). To reduce the computation cost, only the rating histories of the $SelectedUsers$ will be substituted. Then, we create a $RatingPool$ for each u_i in $SelectedUsers$. We use the $Exponential$ mechanism of DP to randomly select h users for u_i, and add their ratings into the $RatingPool$ of u_i. More specifically, $sim(\cdot)$ acts as the score function, and $\Delta sim = 1$.

Algorithm 1 illustrates the process of creating the $RatingPool$ for a user u_t in $SelectedUsers$.

Algorithm 1. Grouping Function

Input: u_t, U, h, I
Output: $RatingPool_t$
  $UserPool = \{\}$
  for $i = 1 : h$ **do**
    Sample a user $u \in U$ with probability: $\dfrac{\exp(\epsilon_1 \cdot sim(u,u_t)/2)}{\sum_{u \in U} \exp(\epsilon_1 \cdot sim(u,u_t)/2)}$
    $UserPool.add(u)$, $U = U \backslash u$
  end for
  for u_i in $UserPool$ **do**
    for t_j in I **do**
      if $r_{ij} \neq 0$ **then**
        $RatingPool_t.add(r_{ij})$
      end if
    end for
  end for

3.3   Modification Phase

Our scheme relies on the $RatingPools$ obtained from the Grouping phase to create $DyEgos$ by the $Exponential$ mechanism. For users not in $SelectedUsers$, their $DyEgos$ are their real rating histories. Algorithm 2 shows the process of

---

Algorithm 2. Modification Function

Input: P_t, α, $RatingPool_t$
Output: $DyEgo_t$

$q(r_{ij}, r_{xy}) = \alpha \cdot trust(u_i, u_x) + (1 - \alpha) \cdot itemsim(t_j, t_y)$
  for r_{ij} in P_t **do**
    Sample a rating $r_{xy} \in RatingPool_t$ with probability:

$$\frac{\exp(\epsilon_2 \cdot q(r_{ij}, r_{xy})/2)}{\sum_{r_{xy} \in RatingPool_t} \exp(\epsilon_2 \cdot q(r_{ij}, r_{xy})/2)}$$

  $DyEgo_t.add(r_{xy})$
  end for

---

creating $DyEgo$ for u_t. The social information is used to design the score function. It is believed that users with more common friends are more likely to have similar tastes. So we use the percentage of common friends (Eq. 3) to measure the trust relationship.

$$trust(u_i, u_j) = \frac{|F(u_i) \cap F(u_j)|}{|F(u_i) \cup F(u_j)|}. \tag{3}$$

Here, function $F(\cdot)$ returns the friend list of the user. $|F(u_i) \cap F(u_j)|$ is the number of common friends of u_i and u_j, and $|F(u_i) \cup F(u_j)|$ is the number of total friends of u_i and u_j.

According to Algorithm 2, we set the score function as $\alpha \cdot trust(u_i, u_y) + (1 - \alpha) \cdot itemsim(t_j, t_x)$, where $\alpha \in (0, 1)$ is the parameter indicating the weight of social information in perturbations.

3.4 Theoretical Analysis

Theorem 1. *The recommendation mechanism M based on **DynaEgo** satisfies $(\epsilon_1 + \epsilon_2)$-differential privacy, where ϵ_1 and ϵ_2 are privacy parameters in Grouping phase and Modification phase, respectively.*

First, we present lemmas and corollaries needed to prove Theorem 1.

Lemma 1. *We denote $SUB(i, j)$ the event of substituting element i with j in a user's rating history. For three arbitrary elements i, j, and k, where $i \neq j$, the following inequality holds:*

$$\frac{\Pr(SUB(i, k))}{\Pr(SUB(j, k))} \leq \exp(\epsilon_2),$$

where ϵ_2 is the privacy parameter in Modification phase.

The correctness of Lemma 1 can be easily derived from Definition 2 and Algorithm 2.

Lemma 2. *Let P_i denote the original rating history of user u_i, whereas P_i' and P_i are neighbors. PS is a privacy preserving mechanism which creates the DyEgo P_{iE} of u_i. Then, we have:*

$$\frac{\Pr(PS(P_i, P_{iE}))}{\Pr(PS(P_i', P_{iE}))} \leq \exp(\epsilon_2).$$

Proof. Let $P_i = [r_{i1}, r_{i2}, ..., r_{ik}, ..., r_{im}]$. Without loss of generality, we assume that P_i and P_i' only differ in the first element, i.e., $P_i' = [r_{i1}', r_{i2}, ..., r_{ik}, ..., r_{im}]$. r_{ik}^{π} denotes the permutation of the rating r_{ik}.

Based on the fact that every element is replaced independently, we get:

$$\Pr(PS(P_i, P_{iE})) = \prod_{k=1}^{m} \Pr(SUB(r_{ik}, r_{ik}^{\pi})), \tag{4}$$

$$\Pr(PS(P_i', P_{iE})) = \Pr(SUB(r_{i1}', r_{i1}^{\pi})) \cdot \prod_{k=2}^{m} \Pr(SUB(r_{ik}, r_{ik}^{\pi})). \tag{5}$$

Now, from Eqs. 4 and 5, we have:

$$\frac{\Pr(PS(P_i, P_{iE}))}{\Pr(PS(P_i', P_{iE}))} = \frac{\Pr(SUB(r_{i1}, r_{i1}^{\pi})) \cdot \prod_{k=2}^{m} \Pr(SUB(r_{ik}, r_{ik}^{\pi}))}{\Pr(SUB(r_{i1}', r_{i1}^{\pi})) \cdot \prod_{k=2}^{m} \Pr(SUB(r_{ik}, r_{ik}^{\pi}))}.$$

So, according to Lemma 1, we can get:

$$\frac{\Pr(PS(P_i, P_{iE}))}{\Pr(PS(P_i', P_{iE}))} = \frac{\Pr(SUB(r_{i1}, r_{i1}^{\pi})) \cdot \prod_{k=2}^{m} \Pr(SUB(r_{ik}, r_{ik}^{\pi}))}{\Pr(SUB(r_{i1}', r_{i1}^{\pi})) \cdot \prod_{k=2}^{m} \Pr(SUB(r_{ik}, r_{ik}^{\pi}))}$$
$$\leq \frac{\exp(\epsilon_2 \Pr(SUB(r_{i1}', r_{i1}^{\pi})) \cdot \prod_{k=2}^{m} \Pr(SUB(r_{ik}, r_{ik}^{\pi}))}{\Pr(SUB(r_{i1}', r_{i1}^{\pi})) \cdot \prod_{k=2}^{m} \Pr(SUB(r_{ik}, r_{ik}^{\pi}))} = \exp(\epsilon_2).$$

$\square$

Corollary 1. *For any two neighboring original rating histories data sets D, D', and an arbitrary DyEgo data set D^r, we denote $DS(D, D^r)$ as the function of substituting D^r for D. Then, we have:*

$$\frac{\Pr(DS(D, D^r))}{\Pr(DS(D', D^r))} \leq \exp(\epsilon_1 + \epsilon_2).$$

Proof. The process of building *DyEgo* set is composed of two phases: Creating the *RatingPool* and Modification phase. According to Lemma 2, the Modification phase satisfies ϵ_2-differential privacy. If the process of creating the *RatingPool* satisfies ϵ_1-differential privacy, the construction of *DyEgo* data set satisfies $(\epsilon_1 + \epsilon_2)$-differential privacy due to the composition property of DP. $\square$

Proof of Theorem 1. Let M the mechanism based on DynaEgo, and M' is an arbitrary recommendation algorithm. We denote Rec as the recommendations given to u_a. So, Theorem 1 can be rewritten as:

$$\frac{\Pr(M(D, u_a) = Rec)}{\Pr(M(D', u_a) = Rec)} \leq \exp(\epsilon_1 + \epsilon_2).$$

In addition, we have:

$$\Pr(M(D, u_a) = Rec) = \sum_{D^r} \Pr(DS(D, D^r)) \Pr(M'(D^r, u_a) = Rec), \quad (6)$$

$$\Pr(M(D', u_a) = Rec) = \sum_{D^r} \Pr(DS(D', D^r)) \Pr(M'(D^r, u_a) = Rec). \quad (7)$$

From Eqs. 6, 7, and Corollary 1, we can get:

$$\frac{\Pr(M(D, u_a) = Rec)}{\Pr(M(D', u_a) = Rec)} = \frac{\sum_{D^r} \Pr(DS(D, D^r)) \Pr(M'(D^r, u_a) = Rec)}{\sum_{D^r} \Pr(DS(D', D^r)) \Pr(M'(D^r, u_a) = Rec)}$$

$$\leq \frac{\sum_{D^r} \exp(\epsilon_1 + \epsilon_2) \Pr(DS(D', D^r)) \Pr(M'(D^r, u_a) = Rec)}{\sum_{D^r} \Pr(DS(D', D^r)) \Pr(M'(D^r, u_a) = Rec)} = \exp(\epsilon_1 + \epsilon_2).$$

Therefore, we can conclude that M satisfies $(\epsilon_1 + \epsilon_2)$-differential privacy. □

4   Experimental Evaluation

4.1   Setup

Data Set. We evaluate DynaEgo with the Epinions[1] data set. The Epinions data set consists of ratings given by 49,290 users over 139,738 items, and each rating ranges from 1 to 5. In addition, Epinions provides the social relationship data. In this paper, we use a subset of the Epinions data set with ratings given by 100 users over 500 items and the corresponding social relationship data, which shares the same size with the data set in [6].

Parameter Selection. The performance of PPCF varies with the privacy parameter ϵ. In our experiments, we set $\epsilon = 2$. According to [6], in D2P, ϵ is decided by three parameters: λ, p, and p^*. We set $\lambda = 0.5$, $p = 0.8$, and $p^* = 0.01$, which ensure that $\epsilon = 2$. Whereas in PNCF, the parameter ϵ can be selected directly. In our scheme, the privacy parameters ϵ_1 and ϵ_2 in Grouping phase and Modification phase are 1, ensuring the overall mechanism satisfies 2-differential privacy. In addition, without loss of generality, we set the size of $SelectedUsers$ twice as large as the neighbors' size, i.e., $s = 2k$. $h = 10$, and $\alpha = 0.2$.

4.2   Utility Evaluation

This section examines the utility performance of DynaEgo. We conduct experiments by defining different size of neighbors. We apply the traditional user-based CF as the baseline, and then compare DynaEgo with D2P and PNCF.

We measure the recommendation quality in terms of classification accuracy metrics (CAM) [11]. CAM measures the frequency with which a recommender makes correct or incorrect decisions about whether an item should be recommended. In CAM evaluation, parts of u_a's ratings are deleted, and we observe

---

[1] http://www.trustlet.org/epinions.html.

how well the recommendations match the real rating record. The recommender system selects the top-5 items as the recommendations. We compare the F_1-Score of the PPCF schemes and the non-private CF. The experiment for each mechanism is repeated for 50 times to eliminate the impact of randomization.

According to Fig. 2, DynaEgo maintains the F_1-Score larger than 0.6, which indicates that DynaEgo maintain a high recommendation quality. Specifically, when #$neighbor = 15$, DynaEgo achieves an F_1-Score of 0.628, which outperforms the results of D2P (0.462) and PNCF (0.508) by 36% and 24%, respectively.

4.3   Privacy Evaluation

We use the *SuccessRate* of the kNN attack as the metric, which indicates the percentage of inferences that are correct (i.e., the items that u_t has rated).

We consider a recommender system with the configuration of 10 neighbors. An attacker creates 10 sybils, each of whom owns a rating history with parts of u_t's rating history (i.e., the auxiliary knowledge). Ideally, each sybil has a neighborhood consisting of u_t plus 9 other sybils. However, in PPCF schemes, the sybil cannot obtain neighbors as expected, due to the introduced perturbation.

In Fig. 3, each point represents the average value of *SuccessRate* from 50 repeated experiments. It may seem strange at the first sight that the *SuccessRate* decreases with the increase of auxiliary information. In fact, in PPCF schemes, more auxiliary knowledge increases the probability of other sybils rather than the target user appearing in the neighbors. Since sybil user's rating history does not have any information about u_t's remaining rating history, the increase of sybil users in neighbors has a negative effect on the inferences.

For the non-private scheme, the *SuccessRate* of kNN attack is 1.0, which indicates that the kNN attack always succeed. In PPCF schemes, the *SuccessRate* falls significantly. Compared with other PPCF schemes, DynaEgo has lower *SuccessRate* regardless the percentage of auxiliary knowledge of the attacker.

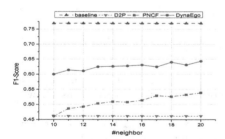

Fig. 2. Utility comparison between D2P, PNCF, and DynaEgo

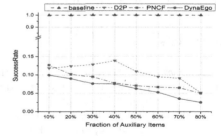

Fig. 3. Resistance of D2P, PNCF, and DynaEgo to the kNN attack.

4.4   Effect of Social Relationship Weight (α)

We vary the value of parameter α from 0.1 to 0.9 to observe the change of F_1-Score and SuccessRate, with the configuration of 80% auxiliary items and 15 neighbors. The larger α is, the bigger impact the social relationship will have.

Table 1. Effect of α on privacy and utility

α	0.1	0.2	0.3	0.4	0.5	0.6	0.7	0.8	0.9
F_1-Score	0.625385	0.622308	0.613846	0.612308	**0.607692**	0.618461	0.621026	0.625385	0.627692
SuccessRate	0.024365	0.021989	0.022166	0.019447	**0.017265**	0.021544	0.022121	0.021825	0.024005

Table 1 indicates that when $\alpha = 0.5$, our scheme will have the best resistance to the kNN attack and a correspondingly lower F_1-Score value. The privacy protection degrades when α approaches 0.1 or 0.9.

5   Conclusions

In this paper, we have proposed a social-aware PPCF scheme called DynaEgo. The main idea of DynaEgo is substituting users' rating histories adaptively, which adopts the *Exponential* mechanism of DP. Additionally, social relationships are used to design the score function. To evaluate the performance of our scheme, we have conducted experiments on the Epinions data set. The results show that DynaEgo outperforms existent solutions in both utility and privacy protection. Since DynaEgo is independent of any specific recommendation algorithm, it can be applied to all recommender systems that are based on users' rating histories.

Acknowledgment. This work was supported by the National Natural Science Foundation of China under Grant 61272479, the National 973 Program of China under Grant 2013CB338001, and the Strategic Priority Research Program of Chinese Academy of Sciences under Grant XDA06010702.

References

1. Adomavicius, G., Tuzhilin, A.: Toward the next generation of recommender systems: a survey of the state-of-the-art and possible extensions. IEEE Trans. Knowl. Data Eng. **17**(6), 734–749 (2005)
2. Ramakrishnan, N., Keller, B.J., Mirza, B.J., Grama, A.Y., Karypis, G.: Privacy risks in recommender systems. IEEE Internet Comput. **5**(6), 54 (2001)
3. Dwork, C.: Differential privacy. In: Bugliesi, M., Preneel, B., Sassone, V., Wegener, I. (eds.) ICALP 2006. LNCS, vol. 4052, pp. 1–12. Springer, Heidelberg (2006). doi:10.1007/11787006_1
4. McSherry, F., Mironov, I.: Differentially private recommender systems: building privacy into the net. In: 15th ACM SIGKDD International Conference on Knowledge Discovery and Data Mining (KDD 2009), pp. 627–636. ACM (2009)

5. Calandrino, J.A., Kilzer, A., Narayanan, A., Felten, E.W., Shmatikov, V.: You might also like: privacy risks of collaborative filtering. In: 32nd IEEE Symposium on Security and Privacy (S&P 2011), pp. 231–246. IEEE (2011)

6. Guerraoui, R., Kermarrec, A.M., Patra, R., Taziki, M.: D2P: distance-based differential privacy in recommenders. Proc. VLDB Endow. **8**(8), 862–873 (2015)

7. Dwork, C., McSherry, F., Nissim, K., Smith, A.: Calibrating noise to sensitivity in private data analysis. In: Halevi, S., Rabin, T. (eds.) TCC 2006. LNCS, vol. 3876, pp. 265–284. Springer, Heidelberg (2006). doi:10.1007/11681878_14

8. McSherry, F., Talwar, K.: Mechanism design via differential privacy. In: 48th Annual IEEE Symposium on Foundations of Computer Science (FOCS 2007), pp. 94–103. IEEE (2007)

9. Zhu, T., Li, G., Ren, Y., Zhou, W., Xiong, P.: Differential privacy for neighborhood-based collaborative filtering. In: 2013 IEEE/ACM International Conference on Advances in Social Networks Analysis and Mining (ASONAM 2013), pp. 752–759. ACM (2013)

10. Zhu, X., Sun, Y.: Differential privacy for collaborative filtering recommender algorithm. In: 2nd ACM International Workshop on Security and Privacy Analytics, pp. 9–16. ACM (2016)

11. Herlocker, J.L., Konstan, J.A., Terveen, L.G., Riedl, J.T.: Evaluating collaborative filtering recommender systems. ACM Trans. Inf. Syst. (TOIS) **22**(1), 5–53 (2004)

Risk Evaluation and Security

A Comprehensive Study of Co-residence Threat in Multi-tenant Public PaaS Clouds

Weijuan Zhang[1,2,3,4], Xiaoqi Jia[1,2,3,4], Chang Wang[2,3,4], Shengzhi Zhang[5],
Qingjia Huang[2,3,4(✉)], Mingsheng Wang[1,2], and Peng Liu[6]

[1] State Key Laboratory of Information Security,
Institute of Information Engineering, CAS, Beijing, China
{zhangweijuan,jiaxiaoqi,wangmingsheng}@iie.ac.cn
[2] University of Chinese Academy of Sciences, Beijing, China
[3] Key Laboratory of Network Assessment Technology, IIE, CAS, Beijing, China
{wangchang,huangqingjia}@iie.ac.cn
[4] Beijing Key Laboratory of Network Security and Protection Technology,
Beijing, China
[5] School of Computing, Florida Institute of Technology, Melbourne, USA
zhangs@fit.edu
[6] College of Information Sciences and Technology,
The Pennsylvania State University, State College, USA
pliu@ist.psu.edu

Abstract. Public Platform-as-a-Service (PaaS) clouds are always multi-tenant. Applications from different tenants may reside on the same physical machine, which introduces the risk of sharing physical resources with a potentially malicious application. This gives the malicious application the chance to extract secret information of other tenants via side-channels. Though large numbers of researchers focus on the information extraction, there are few studies on the co-residence threat in public clouds, especially PaaS clouds. In this paper, we in detail studied the co-residence threat of public PaaS clouds. Firstly, we investigate the characteristics of different PaaS clouds and implement a memory bus based covert-channel detection method that works for various PaaS cloud platforms. Secondly, we study three popular PaaS clouds Amazon Elastic Beanstalk, IBM Bluemix and OpenShift, to identify the co-residence threat in their placement policies. We evaluate several placement variables (e.g., application type, number of the instances, time launched, data center region, etc.) to study their influence on achieving co-residence. The results show that all the three PaaS clouds are vulnerable to the co-residence threat and the application type plays an important role in achieving co-residence on container-based PaaS clouds. At last, we present an efficient launch strategy to achieve co-residence with the victim on public PaaS clouds.

Keywords: PaaS cloud · Co-resident · Memory bus · Co-residence threat · Multi-tenant

© Springer International Publishing AG 2016
K.-Y. Lam et al. (Eds.): ICICS 2016, LNCS 9977, pp. 361–375, 2016.
DOI: 10.1007/978-3-319-50011-9_28

1   Introduction

Cloud computing develops rapidly in recent years and public PaaS cloud plays an important role in the cloud service market. Report from Synergy Research Group [1] shows that across six key cloud services and infrastructure market segments, operator and vendor revenues of 2015 had grown by 28% on an annualized basis. The report also says public IaaS (Infrastructure-as-a-Service)/PaaS services had the highest growth rate of 51%, nearly twice the average level. The global market for PaaS is projected to reach US $7.5 billion by 2020 [2]. PaaS cloud provides the environment to rapidly develop and deploy applications for the developers. It saves the developers' effort to build up the complicated environment each time and bypasses the maintenance of the underlying infrastructure and services. The public PaaS clouds are usually multi-tenant due to the resource consolidation needs of cloud service providers. PaaS cloud often leverages OS-based techniques such as process protect mechanisms or Linux containers (LXC) to isolate tenants, which is a light-weighted virtualization and takes less resources compared to hypervisor-based techniques common in IaaS clouds.

However, multi-tenancy in public clouds enables co-resident attacks [3]. If an attacker has successfully launched an instance[1] co-resident with the victim, i.e., on the same physical machine, the attacker can then implement attacks to break the logical isolation between tenants and extract secret information from the victim. One of the most notable attacks is the side-channel attack that breaks the virtualization isolation boundary by actively monitoring shared resource usage, e.g., utilizing performance degradation [4,5] to influence the victims, or using Last-Level-Caches (LLCs), local storage disks or memory bus [3,6–10] to obtain useful information.

To successfully implement co-resident attack, there are two main steps: the first step is to achieve co-residence with the victim, which includes a launch strategy (to follow some policies when the attacker creates instances) together with co-residence detection (to detect whether the launched instances have achieved co-residence with the victim); the second step is the information extraction. Existing researches focus on the second step of the attack, that is how to exploit the shared resources to steal other tenants' secret information, such as private key [11,12] or password reset link [10]. Recently, researchers have begun to study the effort made by the adversary to attain co-residence with victim instances. Varadarajan et al. [8] investigated the placement vulnerabilities of three IaaS clouds (Amazon EC2, GCE and Microsoft Azure) and quantitatively evaluated their susceptibility to co-location attacks. Zhang et al. [9] gave a measurement study on the co-residence threat inside Amazon EC2.

For the multi-tenant public PaaS clouds however, little has been done to investigate the potential co-residence issue. Although Varadarajan et al. [8] briefly discussed the co-residence problem of the PaaS cloud Heroku in their

---

[1] In IaaS cloud, "instance" typically refers to an instantiated VM. While in this paper, it refers to a service unit provided to the tenants by the PaaS cloud providers, which is usually an application development/runtime environment.

work, no proof-of-concept prototype has been proposed. Zhang et al. [10] simply tested the PaaS cloud DotCloud and OpenShift to show it is possible to accomplish co-residence but did not give further analysis on co-residence threat, since the paper mainly focused on the information extraction step of the co-resident attack. To the best of our knowledge, this is the first study to systematically assess the co-residence threat of multi-tenant public PaaS clouds.

Since the instance isolation mechanisms (e.g., container-based or application-based) in PaaS clouds can be different from the ones (VM-based) in IaaS clouds, we believe that the findings about the co-residence threat of IaaS clouds cannot be simply "borrowed" to summarize the characteristics of PaaS specific co-residence problem. Also, the placement variables that may influence co-residence in PaaS clouds are not completely the same with IaaS clouds. For example, the application type, which is a new feature and may play a key role in co-residence analysis does not exist in VM-based IaaS clouds. What's more, due to the relative small size of the service unit, the co-residence threats in PaaS clouds cannot be the same with the ones in IaaS clouds. All in all, we believe the PaaS specific co-residence threats have unique characteristics yet to be uncovered. This work seeks to provide new understanding about these unique characteristics.

In this paper, we study the co-residence threat of three popular public PaaS clouds Amazon Elastic Beanstalk [13], IBM Bluemix [14] and OpenShift [15]. A memory bus contention based covert channel is implemented to detect co-residence. The main contributions of our paper are: (1) We investigate the isolation mechanism of three popular PaaS clouds and identify the co-residence threat in their placement policies. We find that, for the container-based PaaS clouds, the application type (e.g., Python or Node.js) plays an important role in achieving co-residence. (2) We test several other placement variables, such as the number of the instances, time launched and data center region, to study their influence on achieving co-residence in PaaS clouds. (3) According to the experimental results, we propose a launch strategy to achieve co-residence with the victim using least effort.

The remaining of the paper is organized as follows. Section 2 presents the background and the problem statement. Section 3 proposes the co-residence detection technique used in our tests as well as the experimental methodology. In Sect. 4 we discuss the experimental results. Section 5 describes the related work and Sect. 6 concludes the paper.

2   Problem Statement

2.1   Public PaaS Clouds

PaaS is a virtualization based cloud that hosts numerous customer programs in the same machine simultaneously to reduce the overall costs. Since public PaaS clouds are usually multi-tenant, isolation between tenants is essential for the security. Two of the common isolation mechanisms are VM-based isolation and container-based isolation used in a variety of PaaS systems. Some PaaS clouds give each customer a separate IaaS VM instance, e.g., the Amazon Elastic

Beanstalk, thereby leveraging the isolation offered by modern virtualization. However, some PaaS clouds utilize the container to isolate different instances. A container is always a group of processes that are isolated from other groups via distinct kernel namespaces and resource allocation quotas (so-called control groups or cgroups). A popular open-source project, Docker [16], which has been adopted by several PaaS offerings (e.g., OpenShift, IBM Bluemix, etc.), is built on top of facilities provided by the Linux kernel and does not require a complete operating system (OS).

In the PaaS service model, cloud provider offers the customers various execution environments (e.g., PHP, Ruby, Node.js, Java, etc.). The customers can upload the applications' executables or source code to the environment, which is deployed in a provider-managed OS. This OS may run on a physical machine or within a guest VM on a public IaaS platform such as Amazon EC2. Before uploading an application, the customer should first apply for a corresponding execution environment. For example, if the customer wants to deploy a Python application to the PaaS clouds, she should first apply for a Python instance on the cloud and then push her source code into the instance. The host OS manages the source usage of all the instances deployed on it.

2.2   Motivation

There are mainly three reasons motivating us to study the co-residence threat of PaaS clouds: (1) Due to the different cloud architectures, the placement policies of the container-based PaaS cloud may be different from the IaaS clouds. We have a key observation that containers of the same type usually boot from the same image while for VMs, each VM must have a separate image. This means that application types could play a critical role in achieving co-residence. (2) The co-residency security problems of the PaaS cloud are more serious than the IaaS cloud. The service unit (e.g., a container or simply an application) of the PaaS cloud is much smaller than that of the IaaS cloud in most cases, so there are more chances for instances in the PaaS cloud to achieve co-residence. (3) The weak isolation mechanisms between PaaS cloud instances introduce more security problems. For example, in a docker container, the attacker is able to gain information of the entire system, such as modules, interrupts, memory usage and etc. These information can be used as logical side-channels for co-residency detection. Even worse, two containers of the same application type may boot from the same image, which gives the attacker the chance to launch the flush-reload attacks [10,11]. In summary, it is necessary to study the co-residence threat of the PaaS clouds independently rather than simply follow the previous research results of the IaaS clouds.

The placement policies of the cloud determine how hard it is to achieve co-residence. In this paper, we plan to study the co-residence threats residing in the placement policies of PaaS clouds from the following aspects: (1) How much effort is needed to achieve co-residence with a single target or a set of targets in both container-based and VM-based PaaS clouds? Is it cheap or expensive? (2) Does application type really play a critical role in container-based PaaS clouds' co-residence threat analysis? (3) How do the control knobs (number of the instances, launch time, etc.) identified by IaaS co-residence threat analysis influence the PaaS cloud? (4) Is there any chance for the attacker to achieve co-residence with the victim using less effort?

2.3   Threat Model

To achieve co-residence with the victim there are two steps: a launch strategy to create attacker's instances and a co-residence detection. We do not consider the following information extraction attack after attaining co-residence. The focus of our work is to search for the launch strategies that an adversary can follow to increase the chance of co-residency with the victim instances. We assume the victim instances provide external service interfaces to the customers and the attacker has normal right to use the public PaaS clouds just like any other regular customers. Also, we assume the cloud providers and the cloud platforms are trusted.

3   Experimental Methodology

3.1   Co-residence Detection

Memory Bus Contention Based Co-residence Detection. We adopt the memory bus contention technique [7] to detect co-residence in this paper. The contention of the memory bus is used as a covert channel. If one of the instance locks the memory bus regularly, it slows down other instances of using the bus, such as fetching data from the DRAM. Processors always lock the memory bus through atomic memory operations. However, modern x86 processors support atomic memory operations and maintain their atomicity using cache coherence protocols, which may not need to lock the memory bus. But when an atomic memory operation extends across two cache-lines, the x86 processor will lock the memory bus [17]. We utilize this feature to implement the detection to ensure the detection works on different CPU architectures.

In our implementation, the memory bus covert channel is between a *lock process* and a *probe process*. The two processes run in separate instances. The *lock process* creates a memory buffer and uses pointer arithmetic to force atomic operations on unaligned memory addresses, which will cause atomic operations across two cache-lines regularly. This indirectly locks the memory bus even on all modern processor architectures [7]. The *probe process* creates a memory buffer, accesses it frequently, and measures the time taken to access the memory. Before accessing the buffer, it first flushes the memory using the *clflush*[2] instruction. The *clflush* instruction evicts the specific memory line from all the cache hierarchy, including the L1, L2 and the shared LLC. This ensures the following probe operation will hit the memory and use the memory bus. Thus, if the memory

---

[2] The clflush instruction takes a virtual address as the operand and will flush all cachelines with the corresponding physical address out of the entire cache hierarchy.

bus is locked, the *probe process* will take longer time to finish probing the buffer memory. Otherwise, the time is shorter. We combine the memory bus contention and the *clflush* instruction to make the detection more accurate. It works even when the cache size of the machine is unknown.

Threshold. We use a *threshold* to determine when the change in the *probe process* performance indicates co-residency. In each test, we run the *probe process* in one instance and keep the *lock process* idle at first. The performance measured by this run is the *baseline* performance without contention. Then the *probe process* and the *lock process* are run together. We test the public PaaS cloud Amazon Elastic Beanstalk, IBM Bluemix, OpenShift as well as a local machine. The configurations of the physical machines are shown in Table 1 and the test results are shown in Table 2.

In order to measure the effectiveness of the memory bus covert channel we run tests in our local machine. The result shows that the blocking of the memory bus can significantly slowdown the *probe process* of accessing the memory. The performance degradation is as high as 5.4x (Table 2). The local hardware architecture has multi sockets (Table 1). We didn't pin the process to a particular CPU or core. We run as many as 100 samples in the test to let the processes have the chance to run on the same socket or on different sockets. The results do not demonstrate obvious difference. That means the detection method works even when the co-resident instances are running on cores on different sockets, which is also concluded by Varadarajan et al. [8].

Also, across these hardware configurations (Table 1) on the public clouds, we repeat the test for 100 times and find no obvious difference either. We observed a performance degradation of at least 3.2x (Table 2) compared to not running memory locking process (i.e., a baseline). The following tests in this paper are started with a conservative threshold of 4x for Amazon Elastic Beanstalk, 3.5x for Bluemix and 2.5x for OpenShift to minimize false positives.

Table 1. Machine configurations.

Cloud provider	Machine architecture	Clock (GHz)	LLC (MB)	Cores/CPU	Socket
Local machine	Intel xeon E5-4610	2.40	15	6	2
Elastic beanstalk	Intel xeon E5-2670 v2	2.50	25	10	2
Bluemix	Intel xeon E5-2690 v3	2.60	30	12	2
OpenShift	Intel xeon E5-2670 v2	2.50	25	10	2

Reducing Noise. The sources of noise come from the neighboring instances of the attacker or victim. Any noise could affect the performance of the *probe process* with and without the block signal and result in misdetection. To reduce the noise, we switch between with and without the block signal in each test and compare the difference to determine co-residency. Also, we take 20 samples of each measurement and only when the time difference is stable all the time, the instances can be detected as co-resident.

Table 2. Memory probing tests with/without the block process. *Times* represent the ratio of co-residency time to the baseline. The time unit is 10^7 CPU cycles.

Cloud provider	Isolation	Baseline	Co-resident	Times
Local machine	Process	112	610	5.45
Elastic beanstalk	Xen VM	109	556	5.46
Bluemix	Docker container	121	516	4.26
OpenShift	Docker container	115	372	3.23

3.2 Experimental Design

The success of the co-residence attack refers to the fact that there is at least one attack instance achieves co-residence with the victim instances. There are several placement variables such as cloud provider, application type, number of the instances, time launched and data center region that may influence the success of the attack. We study the effect of each placement variable on the premise of the other variables.

When studying the effect of application types, we choose Python and Node.js applications for OpenShift and Amazon Elastic Beanstalk, while for the Bluemix, we use two different docker images to launch containers. When studying the effect of number of instances, we varies the number of victim instances as well as the number of attack instances. Since many clouds support auto scaling to ensure load balance when running an application, e.g., a web server, the attacker has the chance to enforce the victim to launch more instances through increasing the workload of the application.

The delay from the time when the victim has finished launching its instances to the time when the attacker begins to launch instances is used to define the *time interval* between attacker and victim. For example, if the attack instances are created exactly at the time when the victim has finished his instances' creation, the time interval is 0; if the attack instances are created 1 h later after the victim instances are created, the time interval is 1 h. We use the default instance sizes in our tests, that is t2.small on Amazon Elastic Beanstalk, small gear on OpenShift and docker container on Bluemix, because co-residence detection doesn't need too much resource. The default data center regions are: us-east-1 for OpenShift, us-west-1a for Amazon Elastic Beanstalk, US South for Bluemix, unless otherwise noted.

We use the APIs of the PaaS clouds to implement auto test. Each cloud has the CLI tools running in Linux, e.g., *eb* for Amazon Elastic Beanstalk, *rhc* for OpenShift, *cf* for Bluemix. We used a single, local Intel Core i5-3470 machine to launch instances, log instance information and run the co-residency detection test suite. We crafted several scripts to implement auto creation, deletion and test of the instances. All these experiments were conducted over 2 months between April 2016 to June 2016.

4   Co-residence Threat Study

In this section, we present our measurement on placement and quantification of achieving co-residence in PaaS cloud Amazon Elastic Beanstalk, IBM Bluemix and OpenShift. At first, we test the three clouds for the threat of co-residence (Sect. 4.1). Then we investigate whether the application type plays an important role in achieving co-residence in container-based PaaS clouds (Sect. 4.2). Next up, we study how the other placement variables influence co-residence attacks (Sects. 4.3, 4.4 and 4.5) and finally summarise our findings (Sect. 4.6).

4.1   The Effort Taken to Achieve Co-residence with a Particular Target

In this section, we test the effort needed by an adversary to obtain co-residence with a single victim instance. After a target victim instance was launched, the adversary launched attack instances one-at-a-time sequentially until one obtained co-residence with the victim as indicated by the detection method. The attack instances and the victim instance have the same application type. In this test, there is a chance that the attack will never succeed if the machine where the victim instance runs has reached its upper limit. We treat the result as *valid* only if the co-residence is achieved within 200 attack instances (the valid rate with varying thresholds will be studied in the future). We repeat the trials until ten valid results are obtained. Table 3 shows the number of attack instances needed to obtain co-residence with a single victim. From the experiment results we can see that, co-residence phenomenon with one single victim commonly happens on all the three popular PaaS clouds. In Bluemix, only a few attack instances are needed to obtain co-residence. The results also show that Bluemix has the smallest variance of the results, while Amazon Elastic Beanstalk and OpenShift's variance is relatively higher, which means higher randomness in the number of attack instances.

Table 3. Distribution of the number of attack instances that are needed to obtain co-residence with a single victim. Results are ten times of test on each cloud. The time interval is 0.

Cloud provider	Value of ten tests	Mean	S.D	Min	Median	Max
Bluemix	1 5 2 2 4 2 2 4 1 2	2.5	1.35	1	2	5
OpenShift	37 37 15 11 36 18 17 32 27 31	26.1	9.97	11	29	37
Amazon	56 37 13 53 23 44 4 8 15 21	27.4	18.82	4	22	56

4.2   Effect of the Type of Instances

The victim instance could have the same application type with the attacker (all Python) or different (e.g., victim instance is Node.js and attack instances are Python). We study how the application types influence co-residence in this part.

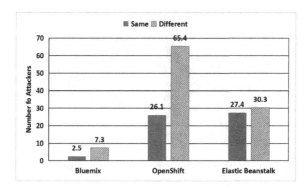

Fig. 1. The average number of attack instances needed to obtain co-residence with a single victim. *Same* means the victim and the attackers are the same application type. *Different* means the victim and the attackers are different application types. Results are the average of ten tests on each cloud. The time interval is 0.

Bluemix and OpenShift are container-based PaaS clouds while Amazon Elastic Beanstalk is a VM based PaaS cloud. Figure 1 shows the average number of attack instances needed to obtain co-residence with a single victim. From the experiment results we can see that, for Bluemix and OpenShift, it is obviously easier to achieve co-residence with the victim using the same application type than different application types. While for the Amazon Elastic Beanstalk, there is no obvious difference. The reason should be the different isolation mechanisms between instances. This indicates that using the instances of the same application type as the victim to attack will increase the chance of co-residence in container-based PaaS clouds.

Bluemix has the weakest resistance to co-resident attack of the three clouds. Sometimes only one attack instance is enough. Since it is too easy for Bluemix to achieve co-residence, it can be predicted that in the following experiments (ten victim instances or more), the co-residency achievement will be much easier. So we will not talk about the Bluemix in the following experiments any more.

4.3 Effect of the Number of Instances

We observe the placement behavior varying the number of victim and attacker instances in this part. Intuitively, we expect the chances of co-residence to increase with the increasing number of attack or victim instances. All the tests use the same application type (Python) and the time interval is 0. The experiment results are the average of ten times tests.

At first, we keep all the placement variables constant including the number of attack instances (fixed to 30) and then vary the number of victim instances (10, 20, 30) to observe how the number of victim instances influences the results of co-residency. As is shown in Fig. 2-(a), for both OpenShift and Amazon Elastic Beanstalk we observe that, the more victim instances, the higher co-residency chance. Similarly, we also see an increase in the chances of co-residency with

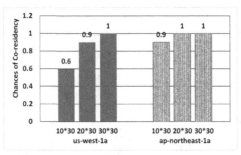

(a) Vary the number of victim instances

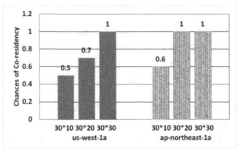

(b) Vary the number of attack instances

Fig. 2. Chances of co-residency with varying number of instances. (a) Fixing the number of attack instances to 30 and varying the number of victim instances; (b) Fixing the number of victim instances to 30 and varying the number of attack instances. All these results are from one data center region (OpenShift: us-east-1, Amazon Elastic Beanstalk: us-west-1a).

increasing number of attack instances (10, 20, 30) across both of the cloud providers (as shown in Fig. 2-(b)). So we can conclude that, the chance of co-residency increases as the increase of the number of attacker or victim instances.

4.4 Effect of the Time Interval

In this section, we want to find the answer to the questions that how quickly an attacker should launch her instances after the victim instances are launched, and whether there is any increase in chance associated with the time interval or whether the result can help an adversary to design better launch strategies? We launch 20 victim instances at the beginning and after every certain time delay (e.g., 0 h, 1 h, 2 h, etc.), we launch 20 attack instances and do the co-residency detection and then remove them. We keep the other placement variables constant and repeat the test for ten times.

Figure 3 shows the chances of co-residency with varying delays between victim and attack instance launches. The experimental results have no obvious regularity. For OpenShift, the success rate reaches maximum at time interval 0 h, 1 h and 8 h while minimum at time interval 32 h. For Amazon Elastic Beanstalk,

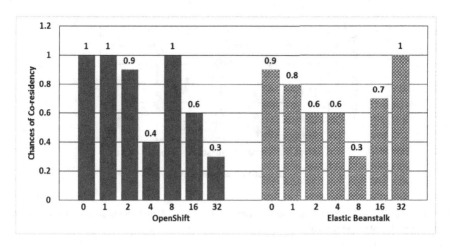

Fig. 3. Chances of co-residency with varying delays between victim and attacker instances launches. All these results are from one data center region (OpenShift: us-east-1, Amazon Elastic Beanstalk: us-west-1a).

the success rate reaches maximum at time interval 32 h, while minimum at time interval 8 h. With smaller interval (within 1 h), the adversary has relatively high chance to attack successfully. We did not find the chance of co-residency drops to zero during the detection. We speculate that the reason could be that some neighboring instances on the victim's machine were terminated though some may be created.

4.5 Effect of the Data Center Region

We only compared the different regions of Amazon Elastic Beanstalk (the us-west-1a and ap-northeast-1a) in this section since OpenShift is built on Amazon EC2 and we believe they have the same regularity. All the tests use the same application type (Python) and the delay is 0. The experiment results are the average of ten times tests. Ap-northeast-1a is less popular than us-west-1a and has relatively fewer machines, so we expect higher success rate. Figure 4 shows that, no matter at any circumstances, attack instances in ap-northeast-1a have the same or more chance of achieving co-residence with the victim instances than the ones in us-west-1a, as we expected.

4.6 Summary of the Co-residence Threat

Through the experiment results we can find that: (1) All three clouds examined by us show weak resistance against co-resident attacks. In the Bluemix PaaS cloud, only a few attack instances are needed to obtain co-residence with a particular target. Even in the worse observed cases, one hundred attack instances are always sufficient in Amazon and OpenShift. This indicates the cost of such co-resident attack can be really low. In fact, we spend only a little money for

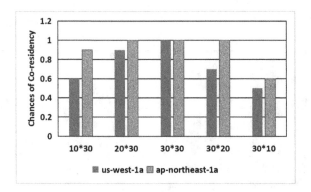

Fig. 4. Chances of co-residency with varying number of instances in different regions of Amazon Elastic Beanstalk.

Amazon Elastic Beanstalk during the tests. For the other two PaaS clouds, we can finish all the tests for free by applying a number of accounts. (2) Application types really play a critical role in achieving co-residence in container based PaaS clouds. When an adversary uses the instances of the same application type as the victim to attack in container-based PaaS clouds Bluemix and OpenShift, the success rate is higher. (3) In the study of the other placement variables that may influence co-residence possibility we find that, increasing the number of victim instances or attack instances will help increase the chance of co-residency in clouds OpenShift and Amazon. Besides, though in the long term of time delay we did not find any regularity in the chance of achieving co-residence, we find that in the delay within 1 h the adversary has relatively higher chance to attack successfully. Also in the less popular region of Amazon with less physical servers, the attacker has more chance achieving co-residence with the victim.

Therefore, to improve the success rate in co-resident attacks, the adversary should launch instances of the same type as the victim and try to increase the number of victim or attack instances. Also a smaller region and shorter time interval will help the attack. The adversary can first trigger a scale-up event on target victim by increasing its workload, which will cause more victim instances to launch. Afterwards, the adversary can launch multiple instances and may observe some of them achieve co-residence with the newly launched victim instances.

4.7 Discussion

Although the test is done in a way that we control both the attack instances and the target instances, we believe the results can reflect the real placement policy of the PaaS clouds. Also, the co-residence detection can be implemented without controlling the victim instances. For example, the attacker can run *lock process* in the attack instance and then trigger the victim to access the memory by requesting large size web pages from the target web application as described in [8]. Through analyzing the response time of the web requests the attacker can infer whether he has achieved co-residence with the victim instance or not.

What's more, there are other placement variables that we haven't test in this paper, such as the time of the day, the size of the instances, the threshold of valid results (mentioned in Sect. 4.1) and other PaaS cloud platforms. We plan to investigate their effects on co-resident attack in our future work.

5   Related Work

Co-residence Detection. Techniques for co-residency detection have been studied by many pioneers. They categorize these techniques into two classes: the *side-channel* detection and *covert-channel* detection [8].

The side-channel detection is done by the attacker without the help of the victim. There are network based side-channel detection method, for example, network round-trip timing side-channel was used by Ristenpart et al. [3] to detect co-residency, Bates et al. [18] proposed a side-channel for co-residency detection by causing network traffic congestion in the host NICs from attacker-controlled VMs. There are also time based side-channel detection, e.g., Zhang et al. [19] developed a system called HomeAlone to enable VMs to detect third-party VMs using timing side-channels in the last level caches, Varadarajan et al. [8] used a timing side-channel based on memory bus blocking to detect co-residency when study placement vulnerability in different clouds.

Unlike the side-channel detection, the covert-channel detection needs the victim's cooperation. Ristenpart et al. [3] use coarse-grained covert-channels in CPU caches and hard disk drives for co-residency confirmation. Xu et al. [6] established covert-channels in shared LLC between two colluding VMs in the public clouds. Zhang et al. [10] also use the LLC as the covert-channel to detect co-residency on PaaS clouds. There are also researches [7–9] exploited memory bus as a covert-channel on modern x86 processors, in which the sender issues atomic operations on memory blocks spanning multiple cache lines to cause memory bus locking or similar effects on recent processors. Inci et al. [20] compared three co-residence detection methods LLC software profiling, LLC covert channel and memory bus locking for their efficiency on detecting co-location and showed that the LLC software profiling technique worked no matter with or without the cooperation from the victim. We use the memory bus as the covert-channel in our paper, by adding a *clflush* instruction to the receiver to ensure the always hitting of the memory without thinking about the cache size.

Co-residence Threat Studies. The co-residence problem was first proposed by Ristenpart et al. [3], which showed that a malicious cloud tenant may place one of his VMs on the same machine as a target VM. Their study was followed by Xu et al. [6] and further extended by Herzberg et al. [21]. Xu et al. [9] investigated how Amazon EC2 evolved in VM placement, network management, and Virtual Private Cloud (VPC), conducted a systematic measurement study of co-residence threats in Amazon EC2. Varadarajan et al. [8] studied placement vulnerabilities in the context of VPC on EC2, as well as on Azure and GCE. There are also studies about new VM placement policies, Han et al. [22,23] and

Azar et al. [24], which are used to defend against placement attacks. However, all of these researches focus on IaaS clouds placement problems.

Varadarajan et al. [8] have briefly mentioned the placement problem of the PaaS clouds. They take Heroku as an example in their work and use logical side-channel to determine co-residency. Zhang et al. [10] also simply tested the PaaS cloud DotCloud and OpenShift to show it is not too difficult to accomplish co-residency. However, none of them gave further analyse of the co-residence threat in public PaaS clouds, which is just our purpose of this paper.

6   Conclusion

In this paper we studied the co-residence threat of the multi-tenant public PaaS clouds. We analyzed the characteristics of different public PaaS clouds and implemented a memory bus based covert-channel co-residency detection method. Using the detection method we investigated three popular public PaaS clouds Bluemix, OpenShift and Amazon Elastic Beanstalk to identify the potential co-residence threat. We find that it is straightforward and cost-efficient to achieve co-residence on the three public PaaS clouds. It even costs no money to achieve co-residence in Bluemix and OpenShift. Also application type plays a critical role in container-based PaaS clouds' co-residence threat analysis. Finally, based on our finding, we presented the strategy to achieve co-residence with least effort.

Acknowledgement. We would like to thank Zeyi Liu and the anonymous reviewers for their insightful and detailed comments. This paper was supported by National Natural Science Foundation of China (NSFC) under Grant No. 61100228 and the project Core Electronic Devices, High-end Generic Chips and Basic Software (No. 2015ZX01029101-001). Peng Liu was supported by NSF CNS-1422594 and NSF SBE-1422215.

References

1. 2015 Review Shows $110 billion Cloud Market Growing at 28% Annually (2016). https://www.srgresearch.com/articles/2015-review-shows-110-billion-cloud-market-growing-28-annually. Accessed 3 Mar 2016
2. Platform as a service - a global strategic business report (2015). http://www.strategyr.com/MCP-7070.asp. Accessed 3 Mar 2016
3. Ristenpart, T., Tromer, E., Shacham, H., Savage, S.: Hey, you, get off of my cloud,: exploring information leakage in third-party compute clouds. In: Proceedings of the 16th ACM Conference on Computer and Communications Security, pp. 199–212. ACM (2009)
4. Varadarajan, V., Kooburat, T., Farley, B., Ristenpart, T., Swift, M.M.: Resource-freeing attacks: improve your cloud performance (at your neighbor's expense). In: Proceedings of the 2012 ACM Conference on Computer and Communications Security, pp. 281–292. ACM (2012)
5. Zhou, F., Goel, M., Desnoyers, P., Sundaram, R.: Scheduler vulnerabilities and attacks in cloud computing. arXiv preprint arXiv:1103.0759 (2011)

6. Xu, Y., Bailey, M., Jahanian, F., Joshi, K., Hiltunen, M., Schlichting, R.: An exploration of L2 cache covert channels in virtualized environments. In: Proceedings of the 3rd ACM Workshop on Cloud Computing Security Workshop, pp. 29–40. ACM (2011)

7. Wu, Z., Xu, Z., Wang, H.: Whispers in the hyper-space: high-speed covert channel attacks in the cloud. In: Presented as Part of the 21st USENIX Security Symposium (USENIX Security 12), pp. 159–173 (2012)

8. Varadarajan, V., Zhang, Y., Ristenpart, T., Swift, M.: A placement vulnerability study in multi-tenant public clouds. In: 24th USENIX Security Symposium (USENIX Security 2015), pp. 913–928 (2015)

9. Xu, Z., Wang, H., Wu, Z.: A measurement study on co-residence threat inside the cloud. In: 24th USENIX Security Symposium (USENIX Security 2015), pp. 929–944 (2015)

10. Zhang, Y., Juels, A., Reiter, M.K., Ristenpart, T.: Cross-tenant side-channel attacks in paas clouds. In: Proceedings of the 2014 ACM SIGSAC Conference on Computer and Communications Security, pp. 990–1003. ACM (2014)

11. Yarom, Y., Falkner, K.: Flush+reload: a high resolution, low noise, L3 cacheside-channel attack. In: 23rd USENIX Security Symposium (USENIX Security 2014), pp. 719–732 (2014)

12. Zhang, Y., Juels, A., Reiter, M.K., Ristenpart, T.: Cross-vm side channels and their use to extract private keys. In: Proceedings of the 2012 ACM Conference on Computer and Communications Security, pp. 305–316. ACM (2012)

13. Amazon. https://aws.amazon.com/cn/. Accessed 23 Apr 2016

14. Bluemix. https://new-console.ng.bluemix.net/. Accessed 23 Apr 2016

15. Openshift. https://developers.openshift.com/. Accessed 23 Apr 2016

16. Docker. https://www.docker.io/. Accessed 23 Apr 2016

17. Guide, P.: Intel® 64 and IA-32 architectures software developers manual (2011)

18. Bates, A., Mood, B., Pletcher, J., Pruse, H., Valafar, M., Butler, K.: Detecting co-residency with active traffic analysis techniques. In: Proceedings of the 2012 ACM Workshop on Cloud Computing Security Workshop, pp. 1–12. ACM (2012)

19. Zhang, Y., Juels, A., Oprea, A., Reiter, M.K.: Homealone: co-residency detection in the cloud via side-channel analysis. In: 2011 IEEE Symposium on Security and Privacy (SP), pp. 313–328. IEEE (2011)

20. Inci, M.S., Gulmezoglu, B., Eisenbarth, T., Sunar, B.: Co-location detection on the cloud (2016)

21. Herzberg, A., Shulman, H., Ullrich, J., Weippl, E.: Cloudoscopy: services discovery and topology mapping. In: Proceedings of the 2013 ACM Workshop on Cloud Computing Security Workshop, pp. 113–122. ACM (2013)

22. Han, Y., Alpcan, T., Chan, J., Leckie, C.: Security games for virtual machine allocation in cloud computing. In: Das, S.K., Nita-Rotaru, C., Kantarcioglu, M. (eds.) GameSec 2013. LNCS, vol. 8252, pp. 99–118. Springer, Heidelberg (2013). doi:10.1007/978-3-319-02786-9_7

23. Han, Y., Chan, J., Alpcan, T., Leckie, C.: Virtual machine allocation policies against co-resident attacks in cloud computing. In: 2014 IEEE International Conference on Communications (ICC), pp. 786–792. IEEE (2014)

24. Azar, Y., Kamara, S., Menache, I., Raykova, M., Shepard, B.: Co-location-resistant clouds. In: Proceedings of the 6th Edition of the ACM Workshop on Cloud Computing Security, pp. 9–20. ACM (2014)

The Threat of Virtualization: Hypervisor-Based Rootkits on the ARM Architecture

Robert Buhren$^{(\boxtimes)}$, Julian Vetter, and Jan Nordholz

Technical University Berlin, Berlin, Germany
{robert,julian,jnordholz}@sec.t-labs.tu-berlin.de

Abstract. The virtualization capabilities of today's systems offer rootkits excellent hideouts, where they are fairly immune to countermeasures. In this paper, we evaluate the vulnerability to hypervisor-based rootkits of ARM-based platforms, considering both ARMv7 and ARMv8. We implement a proof-of-concept rootkit to prove the validity of our findings. We then detail the anatomy of an attack wherein a hypervisor rootkit and a userspace process collaborate to undermine the isolation properties enforced by the Linux kernel. Based on our discoveries, we explore the possibilities of mitigating each attack vector. Finally, we discuss methods to detect such highly privileged rootkits so as to conceive more effective countermeasures.

Keywords: Rootkit · Hypervisor · ARM · Virtualization

1 Introduction

In the ongoing malware arms race, adversaries try not only to take over systems but retain control over the system for as long as possible. As higher privileged levels implement the abstractions and define the boundaries that all lower privileged layers have to adhere to, sophisticated attacks always try to infect the highest privileged layer of a system, ideally a higher privileged layer than the one used by the defender's detection mechanism.

Soon after virtualization extensions by Intel and AMD publicly appeared in 2005 King et al. [16] proposed the first VM-based rootkit in 2006. The technique then became famous under the name *Bluepill* [19,20], whereby an adversary installs a malicious hypervisor during normal execution of the OS to take control over all system resources. On the ARM architecture, just like on the x86 architecture before, the arms race is well underway. A considerable number of rootkits exist (e.g. [8,22,23]) that infiltrate the OS kernel and maintain control over the system. However, the question whether the technique of VM-based rootkits is applicable on the ARM architecture remains open.

In this paper, we want to address the open research question as to whether the construction of a hypervisor rootkit is feasible on the ARM architecture. First we are going to answer whether it is possible to install a rootkit into the

© Springer International Publishing AG 2016
K.-Y. Lam et al. (Eds.): ICICS 2016, LNCS 9977, pp. 376–391, 2016.
DOI: 10.1007/978-3-319-50011-9_29

hypervisor mode to subvert a running OS kernel. Moreover, we answer the question concerning the detectability of the rootkit. Previous work has thoroughly discussed the detectability of hypervisors on the x86 architecture [13,15,21,26]. However, because of the fundamental differences in the design of the virtualization extensions between ARM and x86, the earlier findings cannot be simply extrapolated.

Contribution. We make the following contributions: (1) We determined three attack vectors on currently deployed Linux systems that allow us to install a rootkit into the hypervisor mode and subvert the running OS. Each vector is applicable in a different scenario, which proves the versatility of the attack, and allows us to attack a broad range of devices. (2) We built a very small rootkit that is installed into hypervisor mode to gain full system control and optionally provide malicious services. The rootkit image is a mere 16 kB in size, with 95 % attributed to page table data and alignment. (3) We evaluated our rootkit and discuss potential detection mechanisms. We identify a new and reliable way to detect it by exploiting characteristics of the ARM TLB. (4) We present a number of mitigation techniques to seal the hypervisor mode and prevent our attack.

2   ARM Virtualization

This section introduces the ARM virtualization extensions as far as needed to understand the remainder of the paper. Well-experienced readers may skip ahead but should note our preference for ARMv8 terminology (see below).

Version 7 and earlier versions of the ARM architecture define seven execution modes. One of these is unprivileged and operates at *privilege level 0* (PL0), whereas the other six are privileged and collectively referred to as *privilege level 1* (PL1). ARMv8 combines the privileged execution modes into a single one, thus allowing for simpler exception and interrupt handler code. It also slightly changes nomenclature and coins the new term *exception level*, but leaves the numbering and their meaning basically unmodified, thus renaming PL0 to EL0 and PL1 to EL1. In addition systems with virtualization extensions have an additional execution mode. This mode is located in the new privilege level EL2 (PL2 for ARMv7), placed above EL0 and EL1.

The ARM architecture provides an additional separation concept that is orthogonal to privilege levels. TrustZone [3,6] introduces the notion of a "secure world", which mirrors the privilege levels of the classical "non-secure world". In addition, a new execution mode, monitor mode (*mon*), facilitates the switch between the two worlds. There is one notable difference though between ARMv7 and ARMv8 with respect to TrustZone. As the world switch component was classically provided by the Secure OS as well, *mon* mode was added to the ARMv7 PL1 modes, and switching between secure *svc* and *mon* was seamlessly possible. ARMv8 moved the monitor mode into a level of its own at the top of the hierarchy, EL3, so that it can no longer be entered freely from the secure world. This has implications for one of our attack vectors.

As both terms PL and EL mean virtually the same, we have chosen to stick with "EL" for the remainder of this paper, i.e. we prefer ARMv8 terminology. Unless stated otherwise, all statements apply to both ARMv7 (with PL substituted in place of EL) and ARMv8.

3 Attack Model

In the following section, we discuss the assumptions and requirements for our attack as well as the scope and focus of the attacks.

In the considered attack scenario, depicted in Fig. 1, an adversary first gains control of a user-level process (Fig. 1 ①) and then manages to exploit a kernel vulnerability (Fig. 1 ②). Vulnerabilities in the Linux kernel appear frequently enough [9] to make our assumptions sound. Once having kernel access, the adversary is able to manipulate the OS at will, but he is still visible to the OS and exposed to scanners executing directly in kernel mode or as a highly privileged process. Therefore, the adversary hides by moving to the more privileged hypervisor mode ③. From there, he can put away the OS into a virtual machine, eliminating the risks of being detected from an EL1 scanner (Fig. 1 ④). During the infection phase, the rootkit is briefly exposed to a scanner running in EL1; however, as we show later in the paper (Sect. 8), the time frame is small.

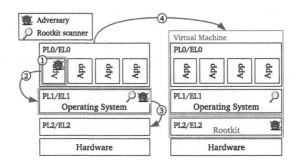

Fig. 1. From a compromised application (①), an adversary compromises the OS kernel (②). Then he gains hypervisor privileges (③) before the victim OS is put away into a VM (④).

4 Entering EL2

In the following, we describe several ways to plant code into EL2. The key observation is that being able to overwrite the exception vector table address for EL2 is sufficient for that end. After the adversary has placed his own base address, he can easily trigger an exception from EL1 that traps into EL2, executing one of his planted handler vectors. So each of the following attack vectors manages to overwrite the value contained in **VBAR_EL2**, thus enabling the adversary to gain control on the next EL2 intercept.

We want to note that except for attack vector 3, all described attack vectors were tested on both an ARMv7 and ARMv8 processor[1].

Attack Vector 1 - Linux Hypervisor Stub. Current versions of the Linux kernel check the EL they are booted into. If they find themselves in EL2, they install a stub vector table address before dropping down to EL1. The purpose of this stub is to allow a type-II hypervisor implementation (e.g. KVM) to install its own vector table, thus gaining the world switch capabilities required for its hypervisor duties. This stub only consists of four lines of assembly, which provide support for querying and writing the vector table base address. KVM uses this facility in the following way. It stores its EL2 vector table at some memory location and loads the base address into register r0. Then it executes the hvc instruction. The stub simply copies r0 to VBAR_EL2 and returns. All subsequent calls after this installation procedure are then handled by KVM's vector table. Thus KVM has acquired EL2 privileges and can use these to control and switch between virtual machines.

The installation of the stub vector table depends only on the bootup EL, Linux provides no way to turn it off. If no KVM module is available or the adversary can mount his attack before KVM is loaded, this provides easy control over EL2.

Attack Vector 2 - KVM Hyp Call Function. The KVM hypervisor on ARM uses "split-mode" virtualization [10,11], i.e., parts of the hypervisor code run in EL1. Only code that explicitly needs access to functionality that is only present in the hypervisor mode runs in EL2. The EL1 part is called "high-visor" and the EL2 part is called "low-visor". The "host" Linux is still running in EL1. When KVM is loaded, it installs its own VBAR_EL2, using the previously mentioned hypervisor stub. This prevents an adversary from planting his own code. However, KVM also offers the possibility for the Linux kernel to provide a function pointer to the "low-visor" running in EL2[2], i.e. there is no well defined API between low- and high-visor, but arbitrary code execution in EL2 is always possible. This mechanism can be used to trivially replace the exception vector table for EL2.

Attack Vector 3 - Migrate Linux to Non-secure (ARMv7 only). Some systems run their normal world OS completely in the secure world. This simplifies the system deployment because the bootloader does not have to configure the secure world and then switch to the normal (non-secure) world. When the system does not need the secure world, this seems like a valid scenario. In the secure world all, registers are named exactly the same as their non-secure counterparts. Therefore, an OS can either run in secure or non-secure EL1 without any changes.

However, as the secure EL1 has control over the non-secure EL2, an adversary running in secure EL1 can manipulate registers belonging to the non-secure EL2.

---

[1] Attack vector 3 only works on the ARMv7 architecture due to changes in the design of the processor modes (for details refer to Sect. 2).

[2] This function is defined as kvm_call_hyp on both ARMv7 and ARMv8.

But after installing itself into non-secure EL2, the adversary does not have any control over the OS yet, because it is still running in secure EL1. So first the OS has to be migrated from secure EL1 to non-secure EL1. Apart from copying register values from their secure counterpart, the adversary has to configure the interrupt controller so that all interrupts arrive in the normal world instead of in the secure world. After duplicating the processor state and installing his malicious code, the adversary can resume the execution in the non-secure EL1. The state duplication is the critical step for this attack vector. Installing code into EL2 afterwards is trivial because all EL2 registers are writable from secure EL1.

5   EL2 Rootkit Requirements

In order to design a hypervisor-based rootkit (a rootkit that runs in EL2), we identified three crucial aspects. These are: *Resilience*, *Evading detection* and *Availability*. Each point is addressed in the following section.

5.1   Resilience

Even though the rootkit executes in EL2, the code pages of the rootkit are memory pages managed by the *victim OS*. To prevent the *victim OS* from modifying or removing these pages, the rootkit must use a stage 2 page table. This stage 2 page table then contains the entire physical address space, except for the pages occupied by the rootkit. However, as the *victim OS* is unaware that these pages have been repurposed, it might still try to use them. The rootkit must therefore handle these accesses appropriately. The rootkit can back virtual pages with identical contents with only one physical page, freeing the duplicates for the rootkit. This is similar to the well-established *Kernel Samepage Merging* [7]. Accesses to these pages do not trap and thus perform at native speed; however, the unexpected side-effects of the duplicity of the page may lead to confusion or a crash of the *victim OS*.

Another alternative is to leave its own pages unmapped in the stage 2 page table. This would lead to a stage 2 data abort, which transfers control to the rootkit. The rootkit could now return fake data to the *victim OS* on a read operation and ignore write operations to these pages. Accesses to these pages are vastly reduced in performance, and a write test would reveal the fake. However, timing effects can be hidden and this method could be implemented with minimum complexity.

5.2   Evading Detection

A sufficiently sophisticated rootkit scanner running in EL1 could detect a rootkit in EL2 in a number of ways. In this section, we discuss the approaches we could employ to obfuscate the rootkit and hide it from a scanner.

Performance Counters. The ARM performance counters [4,5] can be programmed to specifically count instructions executed in EL2 which would reveal the presence of a rootkit. However, the ARM architecture allows EL2 to trap all coprocessor instructions, among them the performance counters. To hide its presence, the rootkit simply has to trap and emulate the sensitive performance monitor registers and provide unsuspicious response values. Thus the *victim OS* would still be able to use the performance monitor infrastructure, but the presence of the rootkit would not be revealed.

DMA. Some peripherals have the ability to access memory directly (DMA). A suspecting *victim OS* could reprogram hardware peripherals to directly write to any physical address, effectively bypassing the stage 2 translation. Such a mechanism threatens the rootkit. On hardware platforms that contain an ARM System Memory Management Unit (SMMU [18]), the rootkit could easily prevent DMA access to its own pages. It would do so by preventing the *victim OS* to manage the SMMU, emulating SMMU accesses by producing fake responses, and then programming the SMMU to restrict DMA access to those pages still available to the *victim OS*. On hardware platforms without an SMMU, the rootkit would have to emulate every DMA-capable device – third-party DMA controllers as well as first-party DMA devices, e.g. SD/MMC controllers – to prevent its memory from being disclosed or overwritten.

System Emulation. Many system control interfaces on ARM platforms are memory mapped. For example, the interrupt controller interface exposes the current interrupt configuration state. The *victim OS* could use this to look for discrepancies to its own expected interrupt state. It could thus discover the EL2 timer, which the rootkit might employ for its periodic execution. In order to hide these activities, accesses to the interrupt controller have to be emulated.

Time. As described before, some system control interfaces and peripherals have to be emulated by the rootkit. However, the increased access latencies due to emulation can be measured by a scanner in EL1. To prevent this, the rootkit has to present a virtualized timer to the *victim OS*. Newer versions of the Linux kernel already use the ARM EL1 virtual timer interface. This allows the rootkit to transparently warp the time for the *victim OS*.

In case the *victim OS* uses the EL1 physical timer, the rootkit can trap all accesses to these timer registers and emulate the "time warp" by reporting lower values. If auxiliary timers (like additional ARM SP804 [2] peripherals) exist on the system, the rootkit has to emulate accesses to those as well. Since the *victim OS* has no access to an independent clock source on the system, it cannot reliably determine how much wall time has passed since its last measurement. The only chance for a scanner to detect the rootkit is with the reference of an external time source. To reveal the presence of a rootkit in EL2 using an external time source, a sophisticated scanner could induce a large amount of traps into EL2. This could be done by accessing coprocessor registers which are emulated by the rootkit. Also, the *victim OS* could trigger large amounts of interrupts that have to be handled by the rootkit. Due to the time warping the discrepancy between the local time and the external time grows with each entry in EL2. Section 8 discusses the effectiveness of such a scanner in more detail.

Cache and TLB. ARM allows SoC designers to use several levels of caches, but most common are just two levels, a dedicated L1 cache for each core and a L2 cache shared among all cores. Since the cache is shared between all privilege levels, a scanner could notice a performance slow down because not all cache lines are available to the *victim OS*.

As described in Sect. 5.1, the rootkit would want to use a stage 2 page table to prevent the *victim OS* from accessing the memory pages of the rootkit. The stage 2 page table translations are cached in a dedicated part of the TLB (Translation Lookaside Buffer), the IPA (Intermediate Physical Address) cache. The IPA cache is transparent and fetches translation just like the normal TLB (for stage 1 translations), but only for stage 2 page table translations. Thus, a scanner could exploit this fact and try to measure artifacts originating from IPA cache hits or misses.

5.3   Availability

To perform its malicious tasks, a rootkit must gain control. A rootkit can run in two different modes of operation, which we have termed *proactive* and *reactive*. Whether a rootkit operates in *reactive* or *proactive* mode has implications on detectability, runtime and implementation complexity.

Proactive execution requires a time source to periodically gain control. A periodic timer interrupt that is routed to EL2 can be configured in such a way that the rootkit can perform its malicious operation. ARM's interrupt controller, however, does not provide a mechanism to selectively route interrupts to EL1 or EL2. Therefore, in the *proactive* model, all interrupts have to be intercepted by the rootkit. The rootkit then has to filter out its EL2 timer events and deliver all other interrupts to the *victim OS*. This approach is more complex to implement and increases interrupt latency. However, it is perfectly suited for data exfiltration attacks where keystrokes or other user actions are monitored during phases of platform activity and later transmitted to an external command-and-control entity when the platform would otherwise be idle.

Reactive execution is a less invasive approach because the rootkit would only react to certain stimuli from within the *victim OS*. Inside the *victim OS*, the adversary would want to run an unsuspiciously looking program in EL0 (without any specific user permissions) that communicates directly with the rootkit in EL2. However, most traps that can be configured to target EL2 can only originate in EL1 (and not EL0), e.g. the hvc instruction. Execution of such an instruction in EL0 is considered undefined and would simply be reported to EL1. This makes it difficult for a program running in EL0 to communicate directly with the rootkit in EL2, without notifying the *victim OS* in EL1.

One of the few exceptions are the deprecated Jazelle[3] instructions. These instructions can be executed in EL0 and directly trap into EL2. ARMv7 mandates that any system implementing the ARM virtualization extensions must provide an empty Jazelle implementation. This implementation only includes a few Jazelle control registers and the bxj instruction. The specification also mandates that this bxj instruction must behave exactly like a bx instruction. Even though the Jazelle implementation is not fully implemented anymore, the *HSTR* register still provides the option to trap accesses to Jazelle functionality to EL2. Thus, in the *reactive* execution mode, the rootkit would enable trapping of the Jazelle instructions into EL2. Now an EL0 application is able to trigger EL2 traps by executing a bxj instruction without notifying the *victim OS* in EL1.

The *reactive* approach is much easier to implement than the *proactive* model, and it has almost zero overhead during regular system activity. However, it is more suited for externally triggered attacks. For example, an unsuspicious application with network connectivity could allow an adversary to invade the platform, quickly elevate his privileges by activating the rookit, steal sensitive pieces of information, and deprivilege itself again all by signalling the rootkit with the previously described Jazelle functionality.

6   EL2 Rootkit Implementation

Based on the previously defined requirements on *resilience, detectability* and *availability*, we implemented a rootkit, which we called *rHV*. Of course, a real attack would comprise the transition from EL0 to EL1 first, which would rely on a real vulnerability in the Linux kernel. For simplicity, we implemented a kernel module to load our *rHV* code directly into EL1. The kernel module provides a device node where we supply our *rHV* binary, along with a number to signal the kernel module which attack vector to use. The kernel module then exploits the specified attack vector to deploy *rHV*.

Once *rHV* is deployed, its execution is split into two parts. The *initialization phase* starts immediately when *rHV* is loaded. Depending on the attack vector, the *initialization phase* starts in secure EL1 (Attack vector 3) or directly in EL2 (Attack vectors 1 and 2). After the initialization phase, *rHV* enters *runtime phase*, where *rHV* provides its malicious service.

Initialization Phase. In the initialization phase, *rHV* checks whether the processor's current security state is secure. If this is the case, *Attack vector 3 - Migrate Linux to non-secure* (see Sect. 4) is used. To do this, *rHV* copies a number of registers from the secure to their non-secure counterpart. Additionally, the interrupt controller is configured in such a way that all interrupts are routed to the non-secure world.

---

[3] Jazelle is a special processor instruction set for native execution of Java bytecode found in earlier ARM cores.

As discussed in Sect. 5.1, for a rootkit to be *resilient*, it has to control accesses to main memory. For *rHV*, we decided to stick with the solution to trap accesses to pages which are occupied by *rHV* itself and emulate read/write accesses to these pages. So the second step of the initialization code, after the migration is finished, is to setup a stage 2 page table. In our experiments, we tested different stage 2 page table layouts (from a single 1 GByte mapping entry for the entire address space up to 4 KBytes entries) to verify the impact through the stage 2 page table and the IPA cache on the overall system performance. Results with the different stage 2 page table layouts are provided in Sect. 8. Once the stage 2 page table is constructed and activated, *rHV* jumps to the third step of the initialization phase.

As already described in Sect. 5.2, certain performance monitoring registers can be configured to reveal the presence of *rHV*. Therefore, we configured the hardware so that all accesses to these registers trap into EL2. We implemented emulation code to reflect the real values of the registers but ignored write accesses to them.

We implemented two versions of *rHV*, one for the *reactive* mode and one for the *proactive* mode, because the mode has influence on the layout of the stage 2 page table. In *reactive* mode, *rHV* does not need access to the interrupt controller, so it can just forward the interfaces to the *victim OS*. No additional entries in the stage 2 page table are necessary. In *proactive* mode, however, *rHV* has to handle timer interrupts. Thus, accesses from the *victim OS* to the interrupt controller must be prevented. Instead, the stage 2 page table gets an entry for a virtual interrupt controller interface, which is presented to the *victim OS*. Finally, *rHV* also enables the EL2 timer to gain periodic control.

Runtime Phase. As discussed in Sect. 5.3, we implemented both modes of operation *reactive* and *proactive*. The implications on the overall system performance based on the execution mode are provided in Sect. 8.

Independent from the fact whether *rHV* runs in *proactive* or *reactive* mode, a number of operations need to be done. First, the cycles the CPU spends in EL2 mode must not be visible to the *victim OS*. Recent versions of the Linux kernel already use the virtual timer infrastructure, which makes it easy to warp the time for the *victim OS*. *rHV* warps the guest timer in the following manner: upon each entry into EL2, the current time value is saved. Upon exiting EL2, the *rHV* again reads the current time value. The difference of these values is then stored in the appropriate offset register (CNTVOFF). The ARM virtualized timer infrastructure automatically subtracts the value of this offset register whenever the *victim OS* reads its ("virtual") time. Thus, the time spent in EL2 mode is no longer detectable from EL1.

In addition to the time warping, which is necessary in both modes of operation, in *proactive* mode, *rHV* also has to handle interrupts. In order to use a dedicated timer for EL2, all interrupts must be trapped into EL2. Upon each interrupt, *rHV* checks whether the interrupt originated from the EL2 timer or not. In the latter case, the interrupt is simply forwarded to the *victim OS*; otherwise *rHV* handles the interrupt itself and performs its malicious operation. Afterwards, execution is resumed in the *victim OS*.

7   Malicious Service

Once rHV has taken control of EL2, it can provide services to adversary-controllable EL0 services. We implemented a simple privilege escalation service as a proof-of-concept to show the feasibility of the approach. However, more sophisticated services are conceivable as rHV's power over the system is unconfined.

Our malicious service consists of a combination of code that executes in EL2 (residing in rHV) and a malicious app running in EL0. The idea is that the malicious app, which executes with normal user privileges, requests elevation to root, performs modifications to the installed OS or extracts sensitive information, and is deprivileged again. In the *proactive* case, rHV uses the dedicated EL2 timer to gain control and uses this timeslot to check whether the malicious EL0 process is currently running. We use the kernel structure reconstruction method to search for the `task_struct` of our malicious app. When its presence is detected by comparing certain identifiers, e.g., the process name, the rHV replaces the UID of the task with zero, thus granting root privileges.

A process that suddenly executes with root privileges might raise suspicion. A component in EL1 might recognize this change; therefore, the rHV resets the UID to its original value when the next interrupt occurs. With this mechanism, we make sure that no reschedule happens while the malicious process is executing.

In the *reactive model*, rHV is invoked with the `bxj` instruction. If the general purpose registers contain the correct magic values, rHV uses the same method as mentioned before to find the `task_struct` and then sets the UID to zero. Otherwise, the instruction is simply emulated as `bx`.

8   Evaluation and Countermeasures

The effectiveness of any rootkit heavily depends on the stealthiness. As described in Sect. 5, some transitions from EL1 into EL2 are inevitable. Thus, in this section, we evaluate how long certain operations take and discuss the effectiveness of scanners trying to detect the presence of rHV. We also analyze the overhead of the two-stage MMU translation process. All tests were conducted on a Cubieboard 2 [1].

A rootkit scanner could try to uncover rHV through the induced performance overhead (e.g., when rHV runs *proactive* all interrupts cause the CPU to trap into EL2). Also the 2 stage page table translations introduce overhead that a scanner could try to measure. To estimate the effectiveness of such a scanner, we performed a number of standard system benchmarks. With the lmbench [17] benchmarking suite, we measured rHV's impact on these low level operations. Table 1 shows the results. Column 1 describes the performed benchmark, the other columns show the results in the respective setups. We performed each benchmark 50 times and calculated the mean values and their respective standard deviation. The mean values show a slight, but noticeable performance overhead in the rHV setups. However, the high standard deviation values render the mean value difference almost undetectable. In order to further analyze the

Table 1. lmbench benchmarks (results are in microseconds).

Benchmark	Linux		rHV (proactive)		rHV (reactive)	
	mean	std. dev	mean	std. dev	mean	std. dev
lat_ctx 2	58.1050	4.8200	59.2100	5.6957	58.8400	4.6556
lat_ctx 4	64.3100	4.3080	65.8950	5.3935	65.8300	4.3352
lat_ctx 8	66.0458	4.4091	68.2240	5.1715	67.6644	4.3407
lat syscall	0.2785	0.0018	0.2787	0.0007	0.2785	0.0014
lat read	0.6623	0.0015	0.6628	0.0015	0.6625	0.0015
lat write	0.4779	0.0009	0.4788	0.0010	0.4781	0.0009
lat_pipe	12.5509	0.6583	12.6093	0.7291	12.8524	0.8827
lat_select	15.7479	0.0061	15.7526	0.0074	15.7502	0.0076

detectability, we verified that the measurement results indeed follow a Gaussian distribution by running 500 iterations of the lmbench context switch benchmark. We then extrapolated Gaussian curves from the mean values and standard deviations from Table 1 and compared native against *rHV*-controlled execution (see Fig. 2).

From these graphs, it is evident that a scanner would require a vast number of measurements and exact knowledge of the distribution parameters of both clean and infected systems to reliably discern whether *rHV* is indeed running on a platform.

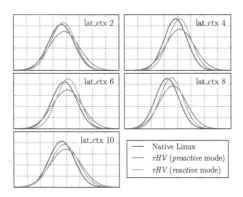

Fig. 2. Comparison of the distributions of context switch benchmarks.

Clock Drift. Another approach is to measure the clock drift that is induced by *rHV*. As described in Sect. 5.2, *rHV* hides the clock cycles that the CPU spends in EL2. In combination with an external time source, a scanner could exploit this effect to reveal the discrepancy between the local clock and the external clock source. Since the scanner can not know when *rHV* actually executes, it would enforce traps into EL2 to reveal the clock drift. This could be done by e.g. multiple executions of a `bxj` instruction in the *reactive* setup or by utilizing a peripheral to trigger a large number of interrupts in the *proactive* setup. Figure 3 depicts the drift of the local clock compared to an external clock, e.g. NTP. Assuming an NTP accuracy of ~5 ms over an internet connection the clock drift introduced by *rHV* becomes visible after 60.000 traps into EL2, which could be either an execution of `bxj` or an interrupt handled by *rHV*.

In both cases, a huge number of events is necessary in order to build a scanner that could reliably discern between a native and an *rHV*-infected system. Although not implemented by us, we argue that *rHV* could be retrofitted with an "alarm mechanism" that detects unusually large numbers of EL2 traps and activates appropriate countermeasures to evade detection (e.g. switching from *proactive* to *reactive* execution).

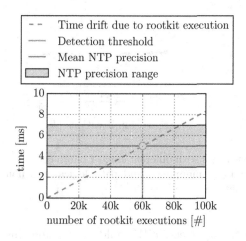

Fig. 3. Detectability of *rHV* in *reactive* execution based on time drift.

Stage 2 MMU. As mentioned in Sect. 5.2, *rHV* might employ a stage 2 page table to hide itself. This two-step translation process costs additional time, which *rHV* cannot hide, as there is (quite intentionally) no trap. In order to illustrate and quantify this effect, we built a separate bare-metal setup. We chose two sets of sixteen memory locations each, one of them pathological to the TLB due to its limited associativity on the Cortex-A7. These sixteen locations are then accessed in a tight loop and the total time is measured, flushing the TLB before the first iteration. The resulting graph is shown in Fig. 4.

We can observe that for low loop iteration counts, the major contributing factor is the stage 2 page table walk caused by the initial TLB flush. However we will have to assume that the IPA cache is warm when the scanner operates, so we cannot assume that this effect will be directly visible. The figure shows that for higher loop iteration counts, the access times average out, even for a stage 2 pagetable consisting of 2 MBytes entries. If, on the other hand, the scanner knows and exerts an access pattern that requires continuous walks, the effect is indeed detectable, regardless of the current TLB state, as the "s2_2m_pat" curve shows. This pattern is however highly dependent on the stage 2 entries and requires e.g. for 2 MBytes mappings access to locations that are at least 512 MBytes apart.

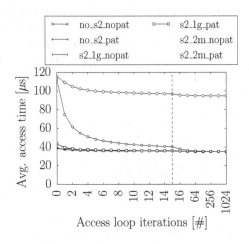

Fig. 4. Memory access times with different stage 2 parameters (s2 and no_s2), different mapping sizes (1g and 2 m mappings) and pathological and non-pathological access patterns (pat and nopat).

As this is an intrinsic effect, *rHV* could only evade this by resorting to a different hiding strategy or by employing more complex paging schemes, e.g. adaptive mechanisms as discussed by Wang et al. in [24].

9 Attack Vector Prevention

In this section, we describe several ways to prevent *rHV* or any other malware from occupying EL2. In general, the countermeasures are different depending on whether our attack should be prevented in an already deployed system or if it is possible to replace components with recompiled versions.

If the user has full control over the platform, and the system firmware boots into secure EL1, the SCR.HCE could be set to zero, disabling the hvc instruction. The bootloader could also directly switch to EL1 mode in the non-secure world, giving Linux no chance to install its hyp stub vectors into EL2. This way, EL2 is sealed and cannot be entered directly anymore. However, these fixes require changes to the boot chain, which is usually under vendor control. Additionally, boot software would have to know whether virtualization extension lockdown is desired, which requires development of an appropriate mechanism, e.g., a flag in the EL1 OS image, or a runtime EL3 service which irrevocably disables EL2 until reset.

If EL2 is still unsealed when EL3 (or secure EL1 on ARMv7) has been left and the general purpose OS starts up, it is complicated to get EL2 sealed. It is remarkable that EL2 itself offers no way to disable hvc functionality. In these cases where disabling EL2 is impossible, the best bet is to make it unusable.

One approach might be to set VBAR_EL2 to an invalid location. As hvc itself cannot be enabled, this still leaves an opportunity for a denial of service attack, as execution of that instruction would then lead to an endless exception loop. An improved attempt might thus install a "nop" vector table, which just executes eret (exception return) for every EL2 trap it receives. This strategy suffers from the problem that the vector table has to be located in physical memory, and all of physical memory is accessible to EL1. Thus an adversary could again find the location of this vector table, overwrite its entries, and gain EL2 control again.

Finally, the defender could create a stage 2 page table of his own to protect his lockdown EL2 vector table from being manipulated from EL1. Accesses to this range would then either result in stage 2 page faults, which the lockdown hypervisor could reflect to EL1, or could be backed by invalid physical addresses or emulated so that EL1 just sees garbage data.

The Linux hyp stub was added to the kernel soon after Linux kernel release v3.6. Many Android devices still run kernel versions lower then v3.6 (e.g. v3.0 or v3.4). These devices then have a completely uninitialized EL2 mode. To prevent an adversary from exploiting this entry (Sect. 4), an administrator or a user can seal EL2 as described for attack vector 1.

10 Related Work

Soon after Intel and AMD released their respective virtualization extensions King et al. [16] proposed a new form of malware that resides in a virtual machine. The suggested malware, dubbed VMBR (Virtual Machine Based Rootkit), runs in a VM on top of an existing hypervisor, such as Virtual PC or VMWare Workstation. With the help of the underlying hypervisor, they implemented a number of malicious services to spy on a victim OS. In the same year, Rutkowska [19] set out the *Bluepill* concept. Her attack leverages AMD's virtualization extension to move the operating system into a virtual machine *on-the-fly*. In 2008, Wojtczuk and Rutkowska [20, 25] also showed how to attack Xen using different DMA capable devices (e.g. network card), which are controlled by the privileged domain Dom0. They use these devices from Dom0 to overwrite parts of the Xen hypervisor, installing a backdoor.

A number of mitigation techniques have been proposed to detect and prevent the subversion of system software (OS or hypervisor) on x86 based processors. Garfinkel et al. [15] discuss the detectability of hypervisors from within a guest. Based on a number of discrepancies (CPU interface, timing, resources, etc.), they argue that the prevention of detecting a hypervisor from within a guest

OS is infeasible and fundamentally in conflict with the technical limitations of virtualized platforms. In the same year, Franklin et al. [14] proposed a technique to detect the presence of a hypervisor on a target system. Their approach exploits hypervisor timing dependencies to elicit measurable hypervisor overhead.

On the ARM architecture, David et al. [12] and Zhang et al. [27] proposed hardware-assisted rootkits. Both leverage architectural features to hide their rootkits. The Cloaker rootkit [12] uses an alternative VBAR address to regularly gain control. On every exception that traps into a privileged mode, the rootkit gains control. As soon as the rootkit has performed its malicious task, it jumps to the original exception vector to stay stealthy. The CacheKit rootkit, as described in [27], uses the ARM cache lockdown feature to solely stay in the L2 cache. The authors claim that rootkit scanners that only scan the main memory are unable to detect the rootkit.

11   Conclusion

In this paper, we showed that an adversary can gain control over the EL2 processor mode on ARM to install a highly privileged rootkit. This EL2 rootkit is very hard to detect and to remove because it has full control over all system resources and can easily spy on the OS kernel as well as user applications. In a proof-of-concept implementation, we showed what a malicious service utilizing the capabilities of rHV could look like. We evaluated our rootkit and showed that most of the obvious detection mechanisms (e.g. time drift, memory access times, etc.) would not work on such a EL2 rootkit. However, with the IPA cache we identified a unique and reliable a way to detect it nevertheless. We also discussed a number of mechanisms to seal the EL2 mode and to prevent malicious software from installing itself into EL2 entirely.

We believe that EL2 should be sealed if an operating system does not intend to make use of the virtualization capabilities of the device. This ensures that no malware can gain higher privileges than the OS kernel itself and thus escape detection.

References

1. Cubieboard 2. http://cubieboard.org/model/cb2/. Accessed 06 May 2015
2. ARM Dual-Timer Module (SP804). Technical Reference Manual, January 2004
3. ARM Security Technology - Building a Secure System using TrustZone Technology. Whitepaper, April 2009
4. ARM Architecture Reference Manual. ARMv7-A and ARMv7-R edition. Whitepaper, July 2012
5. ARM Architecture Reference Manual ARMv8, for ARMv8-A architecture profile. Whitepaper, July 2014
6. Alves, T., Felton, D.: Trustzone: integrated hardware and software security-enabling trusted computing in embedded systems. White paper, arm, July 2004
7. Arcangeli, A., Eidus, I., Wright, C.: Increasing memory density by using KSM. In: Proceedings of the Linux Symposium, pp. 19–28. Citeseer (2009)

8. Coppola, M.: Suterusu rootkit: inline kernel function hooking on x86 and arm, January 2013. http://poppopret.org/2013/01/07/suterusu-rootkit-inline-kernel-function-hooking-on-x86-and-arm/. Accessed 08 Mar 2016
9. CVE, Details: The ultimate security vulnerabilty datasource: Linux Kernel: Vulnerability Statistics, March 2016. https://www.cvedetails.com/product/47/Linux-Linux-Kernel.html?vendor_id=33. Accessed 29 Mar 2016
10. Dall, C., Nieh, J.: KVM/ARM: Experiences Building the Linux ARM Hypervisor (2013)
11. Dall, C., Nieh, J.: KVM/ARM: The Design and Implementation of the Linux ARM Hypervisor, pp. 333–347 (2014)
12. David, F.M., Chan, E.M., Carlyle, J.C., Campbell, R.H.: Cloaker: hardware supported rootkit concealment. In: IEEE Symposium on Security and Privacy, SP 2008, pp. 296–310. IEEE (2008)
13. Franklin, J., Luk, M., McCune, J.M.: Detecting the presence of a vmm through side-effect analysis 15–712 project final report. Selected Project Reports, Fall 2005 Advanced OS & Distributed Systems (15–712), p. 7 (2005)
14. Franklin, J., Luk, M., McCune, J.M., Seshadri, A., Perrig, A., van Doorn, L.: Towards sound detection of virtual machines. In: Botnet Detection, pp. 89–116. Springer, Heidelberg (2008)
15. Garfinkel, T., Adams, K., Warfield, A., Franklin, J.: Compatibility is not transparency: Vmm detection myths and realities. In: HotOS (2007)
16. King, S.T., Chen, P.M.: SubVirt: implementing malware with virtual machines. In: 2006 IEEE Symposium on Security and Privacy, p. 14. IEEE (2006)
17. McVoy, L.W., Staelin, C., et al.: lmbench: portable tools for performance analysis. In: USENIX Annual Technical Conference, San Diego, CA, USA, pp. 279–294 (1996)
18. Mijat, R., Nightingale, A.: Virtualization is coming to a platform near you. ARM White Paper (2011)
19. Rutkowska, J.: Introducing blue pill. The official blog of the invisiblethings. org 22 (2006)
20. Rutkowska, J., Tereshkin, A.: Bluepilling the xen hypervisor. Black Hat USA (2008)
21. Sharifi, M., Salimi, H., Saberi, A., Gharibshah, J.: VMM detection using privilege rings and benchmark execution times. Int. J. Commun. Netw. Distrib. Syst. **11**(3), 310–326 (2013)
22. trimpsyw,: adore-ng - linux rootkit adapted for 2.6 and 3.x, October 2014. https://github.com/trimpsyw/adore-ng. Accessed 08 Mar 2016
23. unixfreaxjp,: MMD-0028-2014 - Fuzzy reversing a new China ELF Linux/XOR. DDoS, September 2014. http://blog.malwaremustdie.org/2014/09/mmd-0028-2014-fuzzy-reversing-new-china.html. Accessed 08 Mar 2016
24. Wang, X., Zang, J., Wang, Z., Luo, Y., Li, X.: Selective hardware/software memory virtualization. ACM SIGPLAN Not. **46**(7), 217–226 (2011)
25. Wojtczuk, R.: Subverting the xen hypervisor. Citeseer (2008)
26. Xiao, J., Lu, L., Huang, H., Wang, H.: Hyperprobe: towards virtual machine extrospection. In: 29th LISA, pp. 1–12. USENIX Association (2015)
27. Zhang, N., Sun, H., Sun, K., Lou, W., Hou, Y.T.: Cachekit: evading memory introspection using cache incoherence. In: 2016 IEEE European Symposium on Security and Privacy. IEEE (2016)

Towards Trustworthy Smart Cyber-Physical Systems

M.W. David[1]([⊠]), C.R. Yerkes[1], M.E. Simmons[1],
and W. Franceschini[2]

[1] National Intelligence University, Washington D.C., USA
{michael.david_cntr,christopher.yerkes,
mitchell.simmons2}@dodiis.mil
[2] U.S. Army General Staff, Washington, D.C., USA
wilfredo.franceschini.mil@mail.mil

Abstract. This paper looks at issues facing the design and operation of trusted, smart cyber-physical systems (CPS). It does this within the context of current efforts related to developing trusted hardware and software, and identifies issues related to those efforts. The paper also looks at several emerging technologies related to wireless systems, artificial intelligence and security analytics; and assesses how they may be leveraged to advance the goals of current and future efforts to create, operate and maintain trusted smart CPS. The views expressed do not reflect the official policy or position of the National Intelligence University, the Department of Defense, the U.S. Intelligence Community, or the U.S. Government.

Keywords: Cyber-physical systems · Internet of Things · Trustworthiness · Wireless · Artificial intelligence · Security analytics

1 Introduction

"We can establish trust among a small group of people known to us, but it's harder to achieve trusting relationships on a larger scale" [1]. Vinton Cerf made this comment in a brief commentary back in 2010 when addressing the topic of trust and the Internet. It was true then, and even more relevant now due to continued rapid development and expansion of global supply chains, wireless networks, smart phones and devices, Big Data and data science. A system of trust is imperative to the exchange of all data and communications [2]. As noted by Huang et. al., it is challenging for computer scientists to build metrics-based trust models applicable in large scale; for instance, attempting to codify social sciences' thrust concepts into Pretty Good Privacy (PGP) signature chains [3]. A more recent publication by Huang describes how the Internet of Things (IoT), together with cloud computing, mobile computing, and social computing, will lead to novel Cyber Physical Social Smart Systems (CPS3), such as smart supply chains, smart manufacturing, smart cities, smart product life cycle management.., and so on [4]. However, without strong security foundations, moving beyond traditional protection mechanism—lightweight cryptography, secure protocols, and privacy assurance—, malicious hacks and or glitches in the IoT will outweigh any of its benefits [5].

© Springer International Publishing AG 2016
K.-Y. Lam et al. (Eds.): ICICS 2016, LNCS 9977, pp. 392–399, 2016.
DOI: 10.1007/978-3-319-50011-9_30

Developers must evaluate current technologies and security protocols and decide if adaptations or entirely new designs will better accomplish the desired security goals. We need to consider IoT cybersecurity problems from a perspective of IoT. In general, although security may not turn out to be a real obstacle in the implementation of IoT, the adoption will have wider and deeper impacts on the general population because it will be immersed into our daily lives. The United States government has undertaken a number of measures and programs in order to deal with its needs for trusted systems. This paper describes some of these activities in order to provide awareness, as well as stimulate dialog and research that will support the goals and objectives of these activities.

2 Trusted Software and Hardware Activities

2.1 The Software and Supply Chain Assurance Forum

Due to repeated cyber based intrusions into critical infrastructure, U.S. Presidential Executive Order (EO) 13636 was issued in 2013, and Section 8(e) required the Department of Defense (DoD) and General Services Administration (GSA) to submit recommendations to the President on improving the cybersecurity and resilience of the nation through the Federal Acquisition System [6]. The EO 13636 vision was to improve cyber security of critical infrastructure through greater government and private sector partnerships. It resulted in a DoD-GSA Report, entitled "*Improving Cyberse-curity and Resilience Through Acquisition*", which makes six acquisition reform recommendations and identifies issues relevant to implementation [7]. With EO 13636 and the Report as its backdrop, the Software and Supply Chain Assurance (SSCA) Forum has explored how public and private sector organizations through greater partnering arrangements are addressing various aspects of supply chain risk through their procurement activities and what further improvements might be made in the future.

2.2 Trusted Access Programs

The National Security Agency created its Trusted Access Program Office (TAPO) for the DoD and the U.S. Intelligence Community (IC) to provide guaranteed access to trusted microelectronics technologies for their critical national security based system needs. TAPO's objectives are to provide the DoD and the IC a trusted supplier path for [8]:

- Guaranteed access to trusted foundry suppliers for mission applications.
- Ability to fabricate classified designs up to the secret level.
- Access for low volume customers to leading edge technology.
- Quick turnaround times for prototyping and production.
- Technology support through industry partnership.

The DoD created its own Trusted Defense Systems Strategy based on DoD Instruction 5200.44 in November 2012, which was updated in August 2016, to provide additional focus on cybersecurity. DoDI 5200.44 establishes policy and assigns responsibilities to minimize the risk that DoD's warfighting mission capability will be impaired due to vulnerabilities in system design or sabotage, or subversion of a system's mission critical functions or critical components, as defined in this Instruction, by foreign intelligence, terrorists, or other hostile elements. This is also extended to include all spare or replacement parts and software upgrades to those mission critical functions or critical components over their full life cycles. Basically, the intent is to achieve Trusted Systems and Networks (TSN) [9].

In a related activity, the goal of Defense Advanced Research Project Agency's (DARPA) Supply Chain Hardware Integrity for Electronics Defense (SHIELD) program is to eliminate counterfeit integrated circuits from the electronics supply chain by making counterfeiting unprofitable from a complexity and time perspective. SHIELD seeks to combine NSA-level encryption, sensors, near-field power and communications into a microscopic-scale chip capable of being inserted into the packaging of an integrated circuit. This 100×100 μm "dielet" will act as a hardware root of trust, detecting any attempt to access or reverse engineer the dielet. Authentication of the integrated circuit will be achieved by an external probe that provides power to the dielet to establish a secure link between the dielet and a server, and the designed fragility of the dielet also makes it inherently more tamper resistant from physical removal or alternation [10].

3 Artificial Intelligence and Security Analytics

Security and trust have been a unique challenge in the design and adoption of information systems since the early days of their development. Unintentional and intentional vulnerabilities can be imbedded deep within the design of our hardware and software. This design challenge has been exacerbated and become increasingly more complex as our technology has moved from standalone hardware into the age of distributed and tightly networked information systems. With advances in and infusion of artificial intelligence (AI) technology as it applies to autonomous vehicles, weapon systems, and intelligent personal assistants, as well as a host of other systems, the issue of trust will undoubtedly persist [11, 12].

Trust in AI systems can be sectioned into three broad categories: (1) Integrity of Data, (2) Integrity of AI Algorithms and Hardware at an operational level, and (3) Integrity of Hardware and Software Design. Both Data Integrity and Integrity of Design are broadly covered under the Trusted Software and Hardware Activities section of this paper. Much of the trust work in this area depends on development of trusted hardware manufacturing, software development and supply chains.

The unique aspects of trust in AI systems, for instance, the integrity of algorithms and hardware, has garnered much recent attention. Several prominent technology developers and scientists, including Elon Musk, Bill Gates and Stephen Hawking, have expressed concern that AI could pose an existential threat to mankind, in an open letter on *Research Priorities for Robust and Beneficial Artificial Intelligence* [13]. One hundred and fifty AI scientists and technologists call for research on the societal impacts of advanced AI. This concern has also reached the highest levels of government with the White House Office of Science and Technology Policy releasing a June 2016 *Request for Information on Preparing for the Future of Artificial Intelligence*

[14]. One of the primary concerns is that AI systems of the future are expected to learn and develop with little or no human intervention in an autonomous fashion mimicking the behavior of living organisms. Automated machine decision processes could potentially be developed that lack the ethical conceptual frameworks of human decision processes.

Entirely new models of trust and security will be required to address this concern as technology develops. Frameworks of machine-to-machine trust will need to be conceptualized, designed and implemented. Situations never before encountered, the bane of the designer, will inevitably be part of the process. As AI algorithms play an ever increasing role in our lives we will need to understand how trust, security and advanced automation interplay.

As noted in the introduction, we also need to consider the IoT, and the enormous amounts of data and security problems it creates, from an IoT perspective. That being said, it may be somewhat difficult to describe the perspective of IoT. One view suggested by the Potomac Institute for Policy Studies (PIPS) is a redefined "data, information, knowledge, and wisdom" (or DIKW) framework. PIPS has proposed a framework or thought process to apply to IoT issues. The construct is intended to assist analysts in understanding intelligence, regardless of source, in terms of distinct levels of complex thinking to measures individuals' unique physical or behavioral characteristics in order to recognize or authenticate their identity [15].

As already mentioned, the wide adoption of the IoT and other cyber-physical systems will have significant impacts, and inevitably, unexpected consequences. With respect to Big Data, CPS devices are expected to generate an unprecedented flood of "real world information," possibly pushing current Big Data architectures to new limits [16]. Advances in machine learning and AI will likely alleviate scalability challenges, but the aggregation and correlation of CPS Big Data involving real-world entities and people will raise privacy and security concerns.

4 Emerging Technologies

Since the scope of this paper is limited, the intention is to only touch on two items in this section, and both are related to wireless systems.

The first is related to research on wireless product design and fabrications at Finland's Aalto University's Radio Science and Engineering. They have reportedly developed a method that allows 50 year old analog technology antennas to shift into the digital world. Antennas are typically tuned only to a few frequencies but using multiple smaller antennas can, with the help of advanced digital electronics, operate digitally with any frequency thus making them reconfigurable to changing environments such as intentional jamming or background interference. The removal of a larger antenna in exchange for smaller ones makes phone design much less complex. This could possibly allow for larger phone screens, lengthen battery life, and facilitate increased data transfer speeds from 100 to 1,000 times faster. Furthermore, this new antenna concept permits the creation of more compact antennas with better radiation efficiency and thus greater range of use from the base systems. Due to the correlation of greater radiation efficiency to greater distances, this means a lower cost physical network to operate and maintain [17]. A paper entitled "Concept for Frequency Reconfigurable Antenna Based on Distributed Transceivers" describing the principles of the method has been published in IEEE's *Antennas and Wireless Propagation Letters* [18].

The Defense Advanced Research Projects Agency (DARPA), which serves as a key research arm of the Department of Defense, is focused on wireless systems to exploit the power of the IoT to help the U.S. dominate battlefields. DARPA is funding the development of sensors and artificial intelligence systems that could help break into, extract and analyze information from, enemy devices and communication systems. The components and systems will arm the U.S. with more data to analyze enemy moves and strategy.

DARPA has some interesting projects, as stated by a collaborating company representative supporting a DARPA program. "They are talking about going into any situation and extracting information at any time, [with] artificial intelligence systems that can attack and hack any network," said Jim McGregor, principal analyst at Tirias Research [19]. The DARPA program mentioned plans to fund the development of sensors and electromagnetic systems that could access point-to-point wired and wireless communications, even ones that are not linked to the internet.

In another initiative, DARPA announced the intent to develop components that can operate in a dynamic and contested electromagnetic spectrum by leveraging machine learning for spectral reasoning. The same announcement acknowledges that "extensive heterogeneous sensor arrays" will be part of future conflicts, therefore, DoD needs tactical sensors with "novel sensing modalities", higher performance, and lower costs."

It should be noted that not all DARPA research comes to fruition or reaches operational capability. However, the goal of being able to identify and select relevant data at the front end of the collection cycle, would certainly contribute to being able to predict or respond to an emerging situation.

In addition to leveraging technology to enhance warfare, DARPA is interested in developing the knowhow for detecting and recovering from cyber-attacks on US critical infrastructure. The Rapid Attack Detection, Isolation and Characterization System (RADICS) program will research early detection of cyber threats against the power grid and how to reduce the time required to restore service [20]. Understandably, technological breakthroughs in industrial control systems (ICS) cybersecurity—e.g. threat detection and/or machine-to-machine data analytics—are expected to propagate to CPS and the IoT.

5 Dealing with the Issues and Recommendations for Future Research

Academia and industry are working hard to develop tools and technologies to deal with some of the issues raised above.

For example, in the area of Artificial Intelligence and security analytics, IBM Research and the University of Maryland Baltimore County (UMBC) have launched a project to collaborate on the advancement of cognitive cybersecurity. Traditional security systems can ingest the massive amount of security data but the ability to process it for exploitation is lacking. By exploring the intersection of cybersecurity and cognitive technology, the IBM-UMBC team hopes to better exploit this large amount of security data and evolve how security professionals and technologies collaborate to help overcome cyber threats. The project involves the creation of the Accelerated Cognitive Cybersecurity Laboratory (ACCL) which is opening in the Fall of 2016. The lab will work to advance the application of cognitive computing to cybersecurity through data analytics and machine learning. It will also explore the optimization of computer power for very large data throughput [21].

In relation to the trusted hardware and software issue, several interesting proposals have been made by academic and industrial researchers. For example, Columbia University has proposed a new Trojan detection tool called FANCI (Functional Analysis for Nearly-unused Circuit Identification). It is part of a proposal designed to discover backdoors in hardware designs prior to the fabrication using functional analysis. If backdoors can be detected statically, then the design can be fixed or rejected before it is sent to the market [22].

Interestingly, researchers in China are also looking into the area of trust verification and the hardware Trojan issue. They have proposed a tool called FASTrust (Feature Analysis for Third-Party IP Trust Verification). It is designed to address shortcomings in existing hardware trust verification techniques, which suffer from high computational complexity, low extensibility and inability to detect implicitly-triggered hardware Trojans (HT). Reportedly, it is different from existing HT detection methods, and lab results show that FASTrust is able to detect all HTs from TrustHub benchmarks and DeTrust benchmarks [23].

Researchers in India are also working on trusted systems and Trojan detection schemes. In one case, the focus is on Advanced Encryption Standard (AES) related hardware. They note that an adversary may insert hardware Trojans to destroy a system at some future time or leak the confidential information or secret keys it is supposed to protect [24].

The above items offer some solutions for specific issues, but in the IoT we are dealing not only with systems-of-systems, but multiple smart cyber-physical systems. All the way from DARPA's "dielet" to Smart Cities, all of these devices produce huge volumes of data, and we must leverage artificial intelligence and machine learning to take advantage of it. As noted by Dr. J.A. Stankovic, new research problems arise due to the large scale of interconnectedness between devices, and the increased volume of connections to the physical world. To deal with this, more cooperation is needed between the research communities in order to advance the underlying technologies in the right direction, and create, operate and maintain trusted smart CPS [25].

References

1. Cerf, V.G.: Trust and the internet. IEEE Internet Comput. **14**(5), 95–96 (2010)
2. Abelson, H., Anderson, R., Bellovin, S.M., Benaloh, J., Blaze, M., Diffie, W., Gilmore, J., et al.: Keys under doormats: mandating insecurity by requiring government access to all data and communications. J. Cybersecurity **1**(1), 69–79 (2015)

3. Huang, J., Nicol, D.: A formal-semantics-based calculus of trust. IEEE Internet Comput. **14** (5), 38–46 (2010)

4. Huang, J., Seck, M.D., Gheorghe, A.: Towards trustworthy smart cyber-physical-social systems in the era of internet of things. In: 2016 11th System of Systems Engineering Conference (SoSE), pp. 1–6. IEEE (2016). https://fs.wp.odu.edu/j2huang/wp-content/uploads/sites/.../SoSE2016-CPS3Trust.pdf. (Accessed 5 Sep 2016)

5. Roman, R., Najera, P., Lopez, J.: Securing the internet of things. Comput. **44**(9), 51–58 (2011). http://ieeexplore.ieee.org/stamp/stamp.jsp?arnumber=6017172. (Accessed 18 Sep 2016)

6. Exec. Order No. 13636, 3 C.F.R (February 2013). https://www.gpo.gov/fdsys/pkg/FR-2013-02-19/pdf/2013-03915.pdf (Accessed 5 Sep 2016)

7. Department of Defense and General Services Administration (GSA). Improving Cybersecurity and Resilience Through Acquisition. Report, pp. 1–23 (2013). http://www.gsa.gov/portal/mediald/185367/fileName/IMPROVING_CYBERSECURITY_AND_RESILIENCE_THROUGH_ACQUISITION.action. (Accessed 5 Sep 2016)

8. National Security Agency (NSA). https://www.nsa.gov/business/programs/tapo.shtml

9. Department of Defense Instruction 5200.44. www.dtic.mil/whs/directives/corres/pdf/520044p.pdf. (Accessed 17 Sep 2016)

10. Defense Advanced Research Projects Agency (DARPA) SHILED Program. http://www.darpa.mil/program/supply-chain-hardware-integrity-for-electronics-defense

11. Karger, P.A., Schell, R.R.: Multics security evaluation: vulnerability analysis. In: Proceedings of the 18th Annual Computer Security Applications Conference, pp. 127–146. IEEE (2002)

12. Thompson, K.: Reflections on trusting trust. Commun. ACM **27**(8), 761–763 (1984). http://dl.acm.org/citation.cfm?id=358210

13. Russell, S., Dewey, D., Tegmark, M.: Research priorities for robust and beneficial artificial intelligence. AI Mag. 105–114 (2015)

14. Office of Science and Technology, The White House. https://www.whitehouse.gov/webform/rfi-preparing-future-artificial-intelligence

15. Potomac Institute for Policy Studies. http://www.potomacinstitute.org/images/studies/DIKWIntelligence2AugFINAL.pdf. (Accessed 5 Sep 2016)

16. Jara, A.J., Genoud, D., Bocchi, Y.: Big data for cyber physical systems: an analysis of challenges, solutions and opportunities. In: 2014 Eighth International Conference on Innovative Mobile and Internet Service in Ubiquitous Computing Innovative Mobile and Internet Services in Ubiquitous Computing (IMIS), pp. 376–380. IEEE (2014)

17. Aalto University Press Release: new digital antenna could revolutionize the future of mobile phones. http://www.aalto.fi/en/current/news/2016-08-31-002/

18. Hannula, J.-M., Holopainen, J., Viikari, V.: Concept for frequency reconfigurable antenna based on distributed transceivers. IEEE Antennas Wirel. Propag. Lett., 24 August 2016 (2016). http://dx.doi.org/10.1109/LAWP.2016.2602006. (Accessed 18 Sep 2016)

19. Narayan, S.: DARPA See IoT and AI as ways to dominate new wars. http://www.techgig.com/tech-news/editors-pick/DARPA-sees-IoT-and-AI-as-weapons-to-dominate-wars-63910

20. Defense Advanced Research Projects Agency (DARPA): Rapid Attack Detection, Isolation and Characterization Systems (RADICS). Advertisement. FedBizOpps.gov., 11 December 2015. https://www.fbo.gov/index?s=opportunity&mode=form&id=cecbcd2b6ae554c874b4b3a326887949&tab=core&_cview=1

21. Rao, J.R.: IBM and UMBC Collaborate to Advance Cognitive Cybersecurity. In: News Release, May 10, 2016. IBM News Room (2016). http://www-03.ibm.com/press/us/en/pressrelease/49684.wss. (Accessed 17 Sep 2016)

22. Waksman, A., Suozzo, M., Sethumadhavan, S.: FANCI: identification of stealthy malicious logic using boolean functional analysis. In: Proceedings of the 2013 ACM SIGSAC Conference on Computer and Communications Security, pp. 697–708. ACM (2013). http://www.cs.columbia.edu/~simha/preprint_ccs13.pdf
23. Yao, S., Chen, X., Zhang, J., Liu, Q., Wang, J., Xu, Q., Wang, Y., Yang, H.: FASTrust: feature analysis for third-party IP trust verification. In: 2015 IEEE International Test Conference (ITC), pp. 1–10. IEEE (2015)
24. Kumar, K.S., Chanamala, R., Sahoo, S.R., Mahapatra, K.K.: An improved AES hardware Trojan benchmark to validate Trojan detection schemes in an ASIC design flow. In: 2015 19th International Symposium on VLSI Design and Test (VDAT), pp. 1–6. IEEE (2015)
25. Stankovic, J.A.: Research directions for the internet of things. IEEE Internet of Things J. **1** (1), 3–9 (2014)

Key Management and Language-Based Security

Vulnerability and Enhancement on Bluetooth Pairing and Link Key Generation Scheme for Security Modes 2 and 3

Da-Zhi Sun[1,2(⊠)] and Xiao-Hong Li[1]

[1] School of Computer Science and Technology,
Tianjin University, No. 135, Yaguan Road, Tianjin Haihe Education Park,
Tianjin 300350, People's Republic of China
{sundazhi,xiaohongli}@tju.edu.cn
[2] State Key Laboratory of Information Security,
Institute of Information Engineering, Chinese Academy of Sciences,
Beijing 100093, People's Republic of China

Abstract. According to adopted Bluetooth standard specifications, we examine the security of the pairing and link key generation scheme for Security Modes 2 and 3. The contribution is threefold. (1) It is demonstrated that the pairing and link key generation scheme for Security Modes 2 and 3 suffers the known-key attack. That is, the attacker without any long-term secret key is able to impersonate the targeted Bluetooth device at any time, once he obtains a short-term secret key, i.e., the initialization key, in its previous successful run. (2) An improved scheme is therefore proposed to overcome the known-key attack. (3) A security model is also presented to check the improved scheme. The improved scheme provably prevents the known-key attack on the original pairing and link key generation scheme for Security Modes 2 and 3. In addition, the improved scheme is more efficient than the original pairing and link key generation scheme.

Keywords: Bluetooth standard · Pairing · Link key generation · Known-key attack · Security model · Bluetooth device

1 Introduction

The Bluetooth technology [1] aims to universal short-range and low-power wireless connectivity between common devices installed with Bluetooth hardware and software modules. Nowadays, Bluetooth modules are integrated in most smartphones, wireless headsets, and many notebook computers and vehicles.

Owing to the ubiquitousness of Bluetooth devices and their network, the security solutions are necessary to safeguard the Bluetooth applications under the hostile environments [2–8]. Since the Bluetooth network is not an IP-based network, the Bluetooth network can not directly apply IP-based standard security solutions, such as IPSec or Secure Socket Layer/Transport Layer Security (SSL/TLS). Additionally, because of the low cost and small-sized design, Bluetooth devices always cannot provide enough computation, memory, and electric power resources to implement the

© Springer International Publishing AG 2016
K.-Y. Lam et al. (Eds.): ICICS 2016, LNCS 9977, pp. 403–417, 2016.
DOI: 10.1007/978-3-319-50011-9_31

resource intensive security mechanisms. In this situation, the Bluetooth standard [9] brings forward the exchanging key, authentication, and confidentiality mechanisms to protect Bluetooth devices and their network in a secure manner.

1.1   Security Architecture of Bluetooth Network

According to the Bluetooth standard [9–11], four security modes are designed to achieve different security requirements of the Bluetooth device. Each Bluetooth device must operate in one of these modes, called Security Modes 1 through 4. Each Bluetooth specification version can support one or multiple (not all) security modes. Security Mode 1 does not provide any sort of security. Except for Security Mode 1, Security Modes 2, 3, and 4 are all mainly composed of three crucial security functions, i.e., the pairing and link key generation procedure, the authentication procedure, and the confidentiality procedure. The pairing and link key generation procedure aims to form a pair of trusted Bluetooth devices. The authentication procedure is to validate the legitimate identity claimed by the Bluetooth device itself. The confidentiality procedure offers a separate confidential service to the data transmitted between the Bluetooth devices. Security Modes 2 and 4 belong to the service-level-enforced security mode, where security procedures are initiated after physical and logical link setup. In contrast, Security Mode 3 is the link level-enforced security mode. It means that a Bluetooth device initiates security procedures before the physical link is fully established.

The crucial task in Security Modes 2, 3, and 4 is to generate and distribute the link keys among the Bluetooth devices, because the subsequent security procedures require depending on them to achieve the security goals. In fact, the link key dominates the security of the Bluetooth network system. The exchange of the link keys need employ the pairing and link key generation procedure and takes place during the initialization phase.

1.2   Related Work and Our Contribution

In order to establish the link key, Security Modes 2 and 3 [9–11] make use of the same pairing and link key generation scheme called the Personal Identification Number (PIN) pairing. To our best knowledge, no security analysis and enhanced method are dedicated to the pairing and link key generation scheme for Security Modes 2 and 3.

In this paper, we investigate the security of the pairing and link key generation scheme for Security Modes 2 and 3 in adopted Bluetooth standard specifications [10, 11]. Our contribution is threefold. (1) It is demonstrated that the pairing and link key generation scheme for Security Modes 2 and 3 suffers the known-key attack. That is, the attacker without any long-term secret key is able to impersonate the targeted Bluetooth device at any time, once he obtains a short-term secret key, i.e., the initialization key, in its previous successful run. (2) An improved scheme is therefore proposed to overcome the known-key attack. (3) A security model is also presented to check the improved scheme. The improved scheme provably prevents the known-key attack on the original pairing and link key generation scheme for Security Modes 2 and 3. In addition, the improved scheme is more efficient than the original pairing and link key generation scheme.

2   Review of Standard Scheme

In the PIN pairing for Security Modes 2 and 3 [10, 11], the PIN code used in Bluetooth pairing can vary between 1 and 16 bytes of binary or, more commonly, alphanumeric characters. For the PIN pairing, two Bluetooth devices simultaneously derive link keys, when the user(s) enter an identical secret PIN into one or both devices, depending on the configuration and device type. The PIN entry and key derivation can be illustrated as Fig. 1 and depicted as follows.

Step 1. A Bluetooth device, denoted as device 1, senses other Bluetooth devices in its communication range, and then detects a Bluetooth device, denoted as device 2.

Step 2. Device 1 generates a 128-bit random number IN_RAND and acquires the PIN number from the user or the application, and then sends the IN_RAND to device 2.

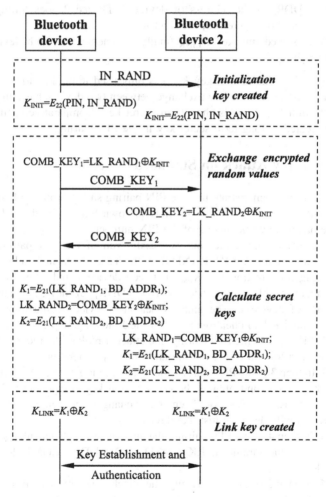

Fig. 1. Link key generation and authentication from PIN.

Device 2 gets the same PIN number from the user or the application. Both device 1 and device 2 compute the 128-bit initialization key $K_{INIT} = E_{22}(PIN, IN\_RAND)$, where E_{22} based on the encryption function SAFER+ is the key generation function.

Step 3. Device 1 computes the combination key component $COMB\_KEY_1 = LK\_RAND_1 \oplus K_{INIT}$, where LK_RAND_1 is its local random number and $\oplus$ denotes the bit-wise exclusive-OR operator. Similarly, device 2 computes the combination key component $COMB\_KEY_2 = LK\_RAND_2 \oplus K_{INIT}$, where LK_RAND_2 also is its local random number. Then, these two devices exchange the values $COMB\_KEY_1$ and $COMB\_KEY_2$ each other.

Step 4. Device 1 can calculate the 128-bit secret key $K_1 = E_{21}(LK\_RAND_1, BD\_ADDR_1)$, where BD_ADDR_1 is its address and E_{21} based on the encryption function SAFER+ is another key generation function. In order to obtain the secret key K_2, device 1 first acquires the value LK_RAND_2 by computing $COMB\_KEY_2 \oplus K_{INIT}$, and then also computes the 128-bit secret key $K_2 = E_{21}(LK\_RAND_2, BD\_ADDR_2)$, where BD_ADDR_2 is the address of device 2. Device 2 goes through the similar process to obtain both secret keys K_1 and K_2.

Step 5. A shared link key K_{LINK} finally is generated on both devices by simply computing $K_1 \oplus K_2$.

Note that the initialization key K_{INIT} is only used in the initialization process and need be discarded when the key exchange between two devices has completed. Hence, the initialization key K_{INIT} is short-term secret key. Comparatively, the number PIN should be treated as long-term secret key in the PIN pairing.

3   Known-Key Attack on Standard Scheme

In this section, we demonstrate that the PIN pairing suffers from the known-key attack [12–15]. That is, the attacker can generate his own link key with a Bluetooth device though he has no any knowledge of the PIN number.

Assume that during a previous successful run of the PIN pairing, the attacker records the random number IN_RAND from the insecure channel and further learns the corresponding initialization key K_{INIT} between device 1 and device 2. Also, assume that the attacker obtains the address BD_ADDR_1 of device 1 and the address BD_ADDR_2 of device 2. The attacker searches device 2, and then can arbitrarily impersonate device 1 to cheat device 2 by the following steps.

Step 1. In Step 2 of the PIN pairing, the attacker replays the recorded IN_RAND to device 2 to start his run of the pairing and link key generation.

Step 2. In Step 3 of the PIN pairing, the attacker randomly generates his own random number LK_RAND_1 and obtains the combination key component $COMB\_KEY_1$ by computing $LK\_RAND_1 \oplus K_{INIT}$. Then, he exchanges the values $COMB\_KEY_1$ and $COMB\_KEY_2$ with device 2 just like device 1.

Step 3. In Step 4 of the PIN pairing, the attacker similarly calculates the secret keys K_1 and K_2 using the parameters LK_RAND_1, BD_ADDR_1, $COMB\_KEY_2$, K_{INIT}, and BD_ADDR_2.

Step 4. In Step 5 of the PIN pairing, the attacker gets his shared link key K_{LINK} by computing $K_1 \oplus K_2$.

To impersonate device 1, the attacker reuses the previous initialization key K_{INIT} in his own run. Note that device 2 should share the initialization key with the attacker after Step 2 of the PIN pairing. The reason is that device 2 computes the initialization key K_{INIT} by $E_{22}(PIN, IN\_RAND)$, and inputs PIN and IN_RAND are all same as those of the previous run. Since both the attacker and device 2 use the same K_{INIT}, they should subsequently compute the same LK_RAND_1, LK_RAND_2, K_1, and K_2. In the end, the attacker and device 2 share the link key K_{LINK}. Figure 2 depicts the proposed attack using the previous IN_RAND and the corresponding K_{INIT}.

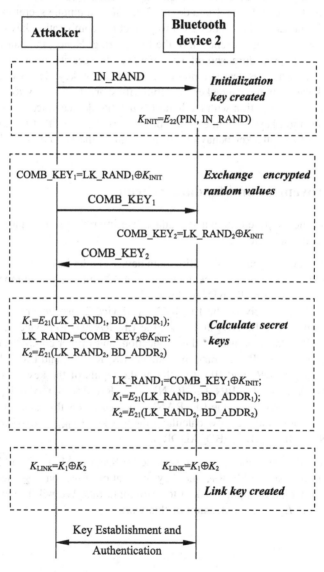

Fig. 2. Known-key attack on link key generation and authentication from PIN.

Comment.

(1) In analyzing the pairing and link key generation scheme, the potential impact of compromise of various types of keying material should be considered, even if such compromise is not normally expected (see [16]). In particular, the effect of the compromise of past secret key should be considered. Therefore, it is reasonable to assume that the ephemeral initialization key K_{INIT} in past run can be compromised. In fact, the known-key security is a desirable security attribute for the pairing and link key generation scheme.

(2) According to the Bluetooth standard specifications [10, 11], each run of the PIN pairing between device 1 and device 2 produces a unique secret initialization key. The initialization key is designed to protect the combination key components and the link key in the current run of the PIN pairing. Hence, the pairing and link key generation procedure should still achieve its security goal in the face of an attacker, who has learned previous initialization key. However, the proposed attack shows that the attacker can arbitrarily share the link key K_{LINK} and establish the secure connection with the honest Bluetooth device, once he knows a previous initialization key and some public parameters. It means that the initialization key fails to limit attacker behaviors in the event of the key compromise.

4   Improvement on Standard Scheme

To prevent the proposed known-key attack, we improve the PIN pairing for Security Modes 2 and 3 as follows.

Step 1. Device 1 senses other Bluetooth devices under its communication range and detects device 2. Further, device 1 generates a 128-bit random number LK_RAND_1, and then sends the LK_RAND_1 to device 2.

Step 2. Upon receiving the LK_RAND_1, device 2 also generates another 128-bit random number LK_RAND_2 and sends the LK_RAND_2 to device 1. Then, device 2 obtains the PIN from the user or the application, and further computes the 128-bit link key K_{LINK} using the PIN, the random numbers LK_RAND_1 and LK_RAND_2, and their addresses BD_ADDR_1 and BD_ADDR_2 as the inputs of the key generation function E_{22}. That is, $K_{LINK} = E_{22}(PIN, LK\_RAND_1, LK\_RAND_2, BD\_ADDR_1, BD\_ADDR_2)$.

Step 3. Upon receiving the LK_RAND_2, device 1 gets the same PIN from the user or the application, and then also calculates the link key $K_{LINK} = E_{22}(PIN, LK\_RAND_1, LK\_RAND_2, BD\_ADDR_1, BD\_ADDR_2)$.

Figure 3 describes the improved scheme for Security Modes 2 and 3. Based on the encryption function SAFER+, the key generation function E_{22} needs slightly to increase the length of input to adapt to extra input bits. We will propose the modified version of the E_{22} in the extension of this work.

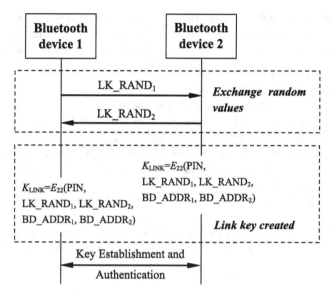

Fig. 3. Improvement on link key generation and authentication from PIN.

5   Security Evaluation of Our Improvement

In this section, we present the security model and the corresponding analysis result. We say that a real-valued function ε: N $\rightarrow$ R is negligible if for every constant $c > 0$ there exists an integer $k_c > 0$ such that $\varepsilon(k) < k^{-c}$ for all $k > k_c$. A function n is non-negligible if it is not a negligible function.

5.1   Pairing and Link Key Generation Scheme

Let $U = \{1, 2, \ldots, n\}$ be the set of Bluetooth devices (probabilistic polynomial-time machines) in the Bluetooth network system. Here, the attacker is not included as those devices. We consider that the pairing and link key generation schemes are collections of interactive procedures, run concurrently by these Bluetooth devices. Schemes specify a particular processing of incoming messages and the generation of outgoing messages. Schemes are initially triggered at a device by an external "call" and later by the arrival of messages. Upon each of these events, and according to the scheme specification, the scheme processes information and may generate and transmit a message and/or wait for the next message to arrive. We call each copy of a scheme run at a device as a session. Practically, a session is an interactive subroutine executed inside a device. Each session at a given device creates a local state for that session during execution, and produces local outputs by that device. This output can be a quantity, e.g., a link key, returned to the calling program, or the recording of a scheme event, such as a successful or failed termination. When a session ends its run, we call it complete and assume that its local state is erased. More specifically, we formally describe the pairing and link key generation scheme as follows.

Definition 1. A pairing and link key generation scheme is a probabilistic polynomial-time computable function Π, which specifies how honest Bluetooth devices behave. The domain and range of the function Π is as follows. Π takes as input:

1^k: the security parameter $k \in N$ expressed in the unary notation.

$i \in U$: the device identity of sender.

$j \in U$: the device identity of intended recipient.

K_{ij}: the key material, which includes the shared secret keys between i and j and the corresponding public parameters of both i and j.

tran: a transcript is the message received by i in the current run of the scheme.

Let $\{0, 1\}^*$ denote the set of finite binary strings. $\Pi(1^k, i, j, K_{ij}, tran)$ outputs a triple (x, δ, K_{LINK}), where

$x \in \{0, 1\}^* \cup \{*\}$ is the next message to be sent from i to j, and $\{*\}$ means no message is sent;

$\delta \in \{\text{Accept, Reject}, *\}$ is i's current decision, and $*$ says no decision yet reached;

K_{LINK} is the link key and may be a null to indicate no link key yet generated.

5.2   Attacker Ability

The attacker is able to observe all communication between any two devices. Also, he may initiate sessions with any devices at the same time, engage in multiple sessions with the same device, and ask a device to enter a session with itself. Furthermore, he can possibly ask a device to reveal its shared secret keys. Informally, a pairing and link key generation scheme under such a powerful model ensures the secret key secure if no attacker can learn anything about the shared link key computed by two uncorrupted devices i and j after their corresponding session. Here, the uncorrupted device means that its long-term secret key PIN has not been revealed.

We assume that an attacker E is a probabilistic polynomial-time Turing Machine taking as the input of the security parameter 1^k and the directory of all device public information. Let T be some polynomial function and $n_s = T(k)$. E has access to a collection of oracles:

$$\{\Pi_{i,j}^s : i \in U, j \in U, s \in \{1, 2, \ldots, n_s\}\}.$$

Oracle $\Pi_{i,j}^s$ behaves as the device i carrying out a scheme session in the belief that it is communicating with j for the sth time. Each oracle $\Pi_{i,j}^s$ maintains its own variable *tran* to store its view of the run so far. Each oracle $\Pi_{i,j}^s$ takes as initial inputs the security parameter 1^k, the PIN assigned to both device i and device j, a *tran* value of a empty string λ, and the directory of all available device public information. E is allowed to make two types of queries of its oracles as follows.

Send$(\Pi_{i,j}^s, x) \rightarrow x'$: the Send query represents that E gives a particular oracle $\Pi_{i,j}^s$ the message x as input, and then receives the oracle answer x' as output. Clearly, the output is meant to be sent to the counterpart. E starts a session with the query Send$(\Pi_{i,j}^s, \lambda)$, i.e., E wishes to initiate the session by sending the empty string λ to the oracle. If E uses the Send query to transmit the last message x in the session, he will receive a null as output, i.e., Send$(\prod_{i,j}^{s}, x) \rightarrow$ null.

Reveal$(\prod_{i,j}^{s}) \rightarrow K$: the Reveal query tells a particular oracle $\prod_{i,j}^{s}$ to reveal whatever all short-term secret keys it currently holds, such as the initialization key and the link key.

To maintain the scheme experiment defined above, the Bluetooth network system is responsible for running a scheme Π in the presence of an attacker E. It needs to point out that all oracles' copies of i's public address value BD_ADDR$_i$ in their public directories are updated according to the current state of the Bluetooth network system. In addition, the system need be initialized by an instantiation function. We define it as follows.

Setup(1^k): (1) Run a secure algorithm Gen(1^k) to generate the long-term secret keys PIN and the corresponding addresses BD_ADDR for all devices; (2) Initialize all oracles $\prod_{i,j}^{s}$, secretly distribute the long-term secret keys PIN to all $\prod_{i,j}^{s}$, and publicly send the corresponding addresses BD_ADDR to all $\prod_{i,j}^{s}$; (3) Start E on the input of the security parameter 1^k and the list of all device addresses.

5.3   Matching Conversations

To characterize secure mutual authentication between two Bluetooth devices, we employ the notion of matching conversations [17–19].

According to the pairing and link key generation scheme, a conversation of oracle $\prod_{i,j}^{s}$ is a sequence of timely ordered messages. Let $\tau_1 < \tau_2 < \ldots < \tau_R$ (for some positive integer R) be a time sequence recorded by $\prod_{i,j}^{s}$, when it converses. The conversation can be written by the following sequence:

$$(\tau_1, x_1, x_1'),\ (\tau_2, x_2, x_2'),\ \ldots,\ (\tau_R, x_R, x_R').$$

This sequence encodes that at time τ_1, oracle $\prod_{i,j}^{s}$ was asked x_1 and responded with x'_1, and then, at some later time $\tau_2 > \tau_1$, the oracle $\prod_{i,j}^{s}$ was asked x_2 and responded with x'_2, and so on, until, finally, at time τ_R, it was asked x_R and responded with x'_R. Moreover, if $x_1 = \lambda$, we call an initiator oracle; else if x_1 is any other string, we call a responder oracle. For simplicity, we focus on the case, where R is even. Now, the matching conversations can be defined as follows.

Definition 2. Fix a number of moves R $= 2\rho$. Run Π in the presence of attacker and consider two oracles $\prod_{i,j}^{s}$ and $\prod_{j,i}^{t}$ that engage in conversations *conv* and *conv'*, respectively.

(1) We say that *conv'* is a matching conversation to *conv* if there exist $\tau_0 < \tau_1 < \tau_2 < \ldots < \tau_R$ and $x_1, x'_1, x_2, x'_2, \ldots, x_\rho, x'_\rho$, such that *conv* is prefixed by

$$(\tau_0, \lambda, x_1),\ (\tau_2, x'_1, x_2),\ (\tau_4, x'_2, x_3), \ldots, (\tau_{2\rho}, x'_\rho, null)$$

and *conv'* is prefixed by

$$\left(\tau_1, x_1, x_1'\right), \left(\tau_3, x_2, x_2'\right), \left(\tau_5, x_3, x_3'\right), \ldots, \left(\tau_{2\rho-1}, x_\rho, x_\rho'\right).$$

(2) We say that *conv* is a matching conversation to *conv'* if there exist $\tau_0 < \tau_1 < \tau_2 < \ldots < \tau_{R-1}$ and $x_1, x'_1, x_2, x'_2, \ldots, x_\rho, x'_\rho$, such that *conv'* is prefixed by

$$\left(\tau_1, x_1, x_1'\right), \left(\tau_3, x_2, x_2'\right), \left(\tau_5, x_3, x_3'\right), \ldots, \left(\tau_{2\rho-1}, x_\rho, x_\rho'\right)$$

and *conv* is prefixed by

$$\left(\tau_0, \lambda, x_1\right), \left(\tau_2, x_1', x_2\right), \left(\tau_4, x_2', x_3\right), \ldots, \left(\tau_{2\rho-2}, x_{\rho-1}', x_\rho\right).$$

Let *No-Matching^E(k)* be the event that there exist i, j, and s such that oracle $\prod_{i,j}^s$ accepted and there is no oracle $\prod_{j,i}^t$, which engaged in a matching conversation. When the probability of the *No-Matching^E(k)* is negligible, the attacker cannot mount any attack more harmful than acting honestly just like a wire.

5.4 Attack Game

To examine the security of the secret keys, we present an attack game for the pairing and link key generation scheme inspired by the classic secure key distribution game [17, 18]. We describe the attack game in Fig. 4. The goal of the attacker E in this game is to distinguish the link key K_{LINK} generated by a fresh oracle $\prod_{i,j}^s$ from a random secret number with the same bit length. In other word, the attacker E's job is to guess the random bit b based on the output of Test($\prod_{i,j}^s$). Here, the fresh oracle $\prod_{i,j}^s$ means that the attacker E is allowed to call the Send queries to $\prod_{i,j}^s$, but never uses the Reveal query to disclose the short-term secret keys in $\prod_{i,j}^s$. An attacker E with the parameters k, r, and f is denoted by $E[k, r, f]$, where k is the security parameter, and r and f respectively are the numbers of Send and Reveal queries in the learning phase. The variables r and f can be bounded by polynomials in the security parameter k.

5.5 Definition of Security

Let $E[k, r, f]$ play the attack game $G_A^{Indis\_K_{LINK}}[k, r, f]$. We can define

$$advantage^E(k) = \left| \Pr\left[E \text{ wins } G_A^{Indis\_K_{LINK}}[k, r, f]\right] - \frac{1}{2} \right|. \tag{1}$$

Attack Game $G_A^{Indis - K_{LINK}}[k, r, f]$

Phase1 : Initialization

Call the instantiation function Setup(1^k) to setup a Bluetooth network system.

Phase 2:Learning

The attacker E may do the following in any interleaved order :

(1) Make Send queries for any scheme oracles, without exceeding r overall queries.

(2) Make Reveal queries for any scheme oracles, without exceeding f overall queries.

Phase 3 : Challenge

(1) E selects a fresh oracle $\prod_{i,j}^{s}$ and still is allowed to make Send queries for the $\prod_{i,j}^{s}$.

(2) E asks the $\prod_{i,j}^{s}$ a single new query Test ($\prod_{i,j}^{s}$).

(3) To answer the Test query, the oracle does as follows.

(3.1) Flip a fair coin $b \leftarrow \{0,1\}$.

(3.2) Return the link key K_{LINK} if $b = 0$, or else return a random key sample K_{Sam} from the key space if $b = 1$.

(4) E outputs his guess bit b' based on the output of the Test ($\prod_{i,j}^{s}$).

Game result : E wins $G_A^{Indis - K_{LINK}}$ if $b' = b$.

Fig. 4. The parameterized attack game for pairing and link key generation.

With forenamed definitions and notions, we can now formally define the scheme security as follows.

Definition 3. A pairing and link key generation scheme is secure if:

(1) The scheme successfully distributes the link key in the absence of an attacker.
(2) (Optional) The probability of No-Matching^E(k) is negligible (This is the mandatory rule, when the scheme provides the key confirmation).
(3) Let $E[k, r, f]$ be any polynomial-time attacker. Then, advantage^E(k) is negligible.

According to Definition 3, the original pairing and link key generation scheme in Security Modes 2 and 3 is insecure. In the attack game $G_A^{Indis - K_{LINK}}[k, r, f]$, E can call a query Send($\prod_{1,2}^{s-1}, \lambda$) to start the session and then obtain the IN_RAND from device 1 in Phase 2 of the attack game. E further calls a Send($\prod_{2,1}^{s-1}$, IN_RAND) query to transmit the IN_RAND to device 2. Similarly, E can respectively get and transmit the COMB_KEY$_1$ and COMB_KEY$_2$ to finish the session. Next, E calls the query Reveal($\prod_{1,2}^{s-1}$) to disclose the K_{INIT}. At this time, E finishes Phase 2 of the attack game. To start Phase 3 of the attack game, E can call a query Send($\prod_{2,1}^s$, IN_RAND) to transmit the previous IN_RAND to device 2. Then, E generates his random number LK_RAND$_1$ and computes the combination key component COMB_KEY$_1$ = LK_RAND$_1 \oplus K_{INIT}$. To finish the session, E sends the COMB_KEY$_1$ to device 2 by using a query Send($\prod_{2,1}^s$, COMB_KEY$_1$) and gets the COMB_KEY$_2$ from device 2. Now, E computes LK_RAND$_2$ = COMB_KEY$_2 \oplus K_{INIT}$ and derives the link key K_{LINK} by E_{21}(LK_RAND$_1$, BD_ADDR$_1$)$\oplus E_{21}$(LK_RAND$_2$, BD_ADDR$_2$). E can call the query Test($\prod_{2,1}^s$). If the output of the query Test($\prod_{2,1}^s$) is equal to the K_{LINK}, then E guesses $b' = 0$; else he guesses $b' = 1$. Obviously, we know that $\Pr\left[E \text{ wins } G_A^{Indis\_K_{LINK}}[k, r, f]\right] = 1$ and $advantage^E(k) = 1/2$. It concludes that $advantage^E(k)$ is non-negligible.

5.6   Security Result of Our Improvement

Theorem 1. Let k be the security parameter. Assume that the key generation function E_{22} is a pseudorandom function family with the security parameter specified above. That is, the domain of the E_{22} is $\{1, 0\}^{L(k)}$ and its range is $\{1, 0\}^k$, where $L(k)$ is polynomially bounded function of the security parameter k. Also, assume that the LK_RAND$_1$ and LK_RAND$_2$ are all random numbers with k-bit length. Then, our improvement described in Fig. 3 is a secure pairing and link key generation scheme.

The proof of Theorem 1 needs to use the standard security assumption of pseudorandom function. We do not provide the proof details here and remain for the extension of this work.

6   Performance Evaluation of Our Improvement

To verify the improved scheme, we use MATLAB Simulink to build the test bed and find that the improved scheme is practical for the Bluetooth network system using its Bluetooth communication of the Instrument Control Toolbox. The improved scheme for Security Modes 2 and 3 can be employed in different Bluetooth-enabled devices and potentially implemented in the service level or the link level of the Bluetooth network systems. Therefore, for the common measure of the scheme performance, we further compare the improved scheme with the original pairing and link key generation scheme. Here, both schemes are designed for the same security goal of the Bluetooth device.

In the implementation complexity concern, the improved scheme requires the random number generator to generate LK_RAND$_1$ and LK_RAND$_2$ and the key generation function E_{22} to derive the link key. Comparatively, the original scheme also needs the random number generator to generate IN_RAND, LK_RAND$_1$, and LK_RAND$_2$, but two key generation functions E_{21} and E_{22} to derive the initialization key and the link key.

As for the communication cost, the improved scheme requires two message inter-actions to finish a session, compared with three message interactions in the original scheme. Moreover, the improved scheme need exchange data LK_RAND_1, LK_RAND_2, while the original scheme need exchange data IN_RAND, $COMB\_KEY_1$, and $COMB\_KEY_2$. Therefore, communication cost of a session is $128 + 128 = 256$ bits in the improved scheme and $128 + 128 + 128 = 384$ bits in the original scheme.

As far as the computation cost is concerned, the improved scheme needs one computation of the key generation function to get the link key in each Bluetooth device side. But, the original scheme employs three computations to achieve the same task. Furthermore, the original scheme requires three extra exclusive-OR operations.

For the storage cost, we only consider the long-standing values. Clearly, both schemes require storing their addresses BD_ADDR_1 and BD_ADDR_2. According to the Bluetooth standard, the address for the device is the 48-bit address.

We summarize the performance results of the improved scheme and the original scheme in Table 1. It shows that the improved scheme is more efficient than the original scheme. This is a desirable feature due to the limited hardware resources of Bluetooth devices.

Table 1. Performance comparison: our improved scheme vs original scheme.

Cost	Our improved scheme	Original scheme
Implementation complexity	Medium –	Medium
Communication	256 bits	384 bits
Computation	1 H[a]	3H + 3XOR[b]
Storage	96 bits	96 bits

[a]H denotes the key generation function computation
[b]XOR denotes the exclusive-OR operation

7 Conclusions

The pairing and link key generation scheme for Security Modes 2 and 3 is widely applied in the Bluetooth devices, because the scheme stands in the core specification of the Bluetooth standard. The scheme should provide strong secure assurance, i.e., the known-key security, in fear of vulnerabilities and abuse mounting. Such security requirement for the scheme is reinforced by the possibility of more and more Bluetooth device abuses in the real world applications [20–22]. We therefore believe that our results are a steady step to enhancing Bluetooth security solutions.

We do not consider the security of the pairing and link key generation scheme for Security Mode 4. It might be interesting to investigate this problem in the future. Moreover, our future work will examine and repair the security flaws in the authentication procedure and the confidentiality procedure of the Bluetooth standard.

Acknowledgments. We thank the anonymous reviewers for their useful comments. The work of Dr. Da-Zhi Sun was supported in part by the State Scholarship Fund of the China Scholarship Council, in part by the Open Project of Shanghai Key Laboratory of Trustworthy Computing under Grant No. 07dz22304201402, and in part by National Natural Science Foundation of China under Grant Nos. 61003306 and 61272106.

References

1. Bluetooth Special Interest Group (SIG) (2016). https://www.bluetooth.org/en-us
2. Hager, C.T., Midkiff, S.F.: An analysis of Bluetooth security vulnerabilities. In: Proceedings of IEEE Wireless Communications and Networking Conference-WCNC 2003, New Orleans, LA, USA, vol. 3, pp. 1825–1831. IEEE Communications Society (2003)
3. Wong, F.-L., Stajano, F., Clulow, J.: Repairing the Bluetooth pairing protocol. In: Christianson, B., Crispo, B., Malcolm, James, A., Roe, M. (eds.) Security Protocols 2005. LNCS, vol. 4631, pp. 31–45. Springer, Heidelberg (2007). doi:10.1007/978-3-540-77156-2_4
4. Lindell, A.Y.: Comparison-based key exchange and the security of the numeric comparison mode in Bluetooth v2.1. In: Fischlin, M. (ed.) CT-RSA 2009. LNCS, vol. 5473, pp. 66–83. Springer, Heidelberg (2009). doi:10.1007/978-3-642-00862-7_5
5. Haataja, K., Toivanen, P.: Two practical man-in-the-middle attacks on Bluetooth secure simple pairing and countermeasures. IEEE Trans. Wireless Commun. 9(1), 384–392 (2010)
6. Phan, R.C.-W., Mingard, P.: Analyzing the secure simple pairing in Bluetooth v4.0. Wireless Pers. Commun. **64**(4), 719–737 (2012)
7. Xu, J.F., Zhang, T., Lin, D., Mao, Y., Liu, X.N., Chen, S.W., Shao, S., Tian, B., Yi, S.W.: Pairing and authentication security technologies in low-power Bluetooth. In: Proceedings of the 2013 IEEE International Conference on Green Computing and Communications-GreenCom, the 2013 IEEE International Conference on Internet of Things-iThings, the 2013 IEEE International Conference on and IEEE Cyber, Physical and Social Computing-CPSCom, Beijing, China, pp. 1081–1085. IEEE Computer Society (2013)
8. Mandal, B.K., Bhattacharyya, D., Kim, T.H.: An architecture design for wireless authentication security in Bluetooth network. Int. J. Secur. Appl. **8**(3), 1–8 (2014)
9. Padgette, J., Scarfone, K., Chen, L.: Guide to Bluetooth security: recommendations of the National Institute of Standards and Technology. National Institute of Standards and Technology (NIST), U.S. Department of Commerce, Special Publication 800-121 Revision 1 June 2012. http://csrc.nist.gov/publications/nistpubs/800-121-rev1/sp800-121_rev1.pdf
10. Specification of the Bluetooth System, Covered Core Package Version: 4.2, Master Table of Contents & Compliance Requirements, Bluetooth SIG Proprietary, December 2014. https://www.bluetooth.com/specifications/adopted-specifications
11. Specification of the Bluetooth System, Supplement to the Bluetooth Core Specification, CSSv6, Bluetooth SIG Proprietary, July 2015. https://www.bluetooth.com/specifications/adopted-specifications
12. Diffie, W., van Oorschot, P., Wiener, M.: Authentication and authenticated key exchanges. Des. Codes Crypt. **2**(2), 107–125 (1992)
13. Canetti, R., Krawczyk, H.: Analysis of key-exchange protocols and their use for building secure channels. In: Pfitzmann, B. (ed.) EUROCRYPT 2001. LNCS, vol. 2045, pp. 453–474. Springer, Heidelberg (2001). doi:10.1007/3-540-44987-6_28
14. Fujioka, A., Suzuki, K., Xagawa, K., Yoneyama, K.: Strongly secure authenticated key exchange from factoring, codes, and lattices. Des. Codes Crypt. **76**(3), 469–504 (2015)

15. Wang, D., Wang, N., Wang, P., Qing, S.H.: Preserving privacy for free: efficient and provably secure two-factor authentication scheme with user anonymity. Inf. Sci. **321**, 162–178 (2015)

16. Menezes, A., van Oorschot, P., Vanstone, S.: Handbook of Applied Cryptography, pp. 489–534. CRC Press, Boca Raton (1997)

17. Bellare, M., Rogaway, P.: Entity authentication and key distribution. In: Stinson, D.R. (ed.) CRYPTO 1993. LNCS, vol. 773, pp. 232–249. Springer, Heidelberg (1994). doi:10.1007/3-540-48329-2_21

18. Blake-Wilson, S., Johnson, D., Menezes, A.: Key agreement protocols and their security analysis. In: Darnell, M. (ed.) Cryptography and Coding 1997. LNCS, vol. 1355, pp. 30–45. Springer, Heidelberg (1997). doi:10.1007/BFb0024447

19. Sun, D.-Z., Li, J.-X., Feng, Z.-Y., Cao, Z.-F., Xu, G.-Q.: On the security and improvement of a two-factor user authentication scheme in wireless sensor networks. Pers. Ubiquit. Comput. **17**(5), 895–905 (2013)

20. Talasila, M., Curtmola, R., Borcea, C.: Collaborative Bluetooth-based location authentication on smart phones. Pervasive Mob. Comput. **17**(Part A), 43–62 (2015)

21. Sun, J.C., Zhang, R., Jin, X.C., Zhang, Y.C.: SecureFind: secure and privacy-preserving object finding via mobile crowdsourcing. IEEE Trans. Wireless Commun. **15**(3), 1716–1728 (2016)

22. Farina, P., Cambiaso, E., Papaleo, G., Aiello, M.: Are mobile botnets a possible threat? The case of SlowBot Net. Comput. Secur. **58**, 268–283 (2016)

Optimizing Secure Computation Programs with Private Conditionals

Peeter Laud[1]([⊠]) and Alisa Pankova[1,2,3]

[1] Cybernetica AS, Tartu, Estonia
{peeter.laud,alisa.pankova}@cyber.ee
[2] Software Technologies and Applications Competence Centre (STACC),
Tartu, Estonia
[3] University of Tartu, Tartu, Estonia

Abstract. Secure computation platforms are often provided with a programming language that allows a developer to write privacy-preserving applications and hides away the underlying cryptographic details. The control flow of these programs is expensive to hide, hence branching on private values is often disallowed. The application programmers have to specify their programs in terms of allowed constructions, either using *ad-hoc* methods to avoid such branchings, or the general methodology of executing all branches and obliviously selecting the effects of one at the end. There may be compiler support for the latter.

The execution of all branches introduces significant computational overhead. If the branches perform similar private operations, then it may make sense to compute repeating patterns only once, even though the necessary bookkeeping also has overheads. In this paper, we propose a program optimization doing exactly that, allowing the overhead of private conditionals to be reduced. The optimization is quite general, and can be applied to various privacy-preserving platforms.

1 Introduction

There exist a number of sufficiently practical methods for privacy-preserving computations [1–3], as well as secure computation platforms implementing these methods [4–7]. To facilitate the use of such platforms, and to hide the cryptographic details from the application programmer, the platforms allow the compilation of protocols from higher-level descriptions, where the latter are specified in some domain-specific language [4,8–11] or in a subset of some general language, e.g. C, possibly with extra privacy annotations [12,13]. Operations with private values are compiled to protocols transforming the representations of inputs of these operations to the representation of the output.

In secure multiparty computation (SMC) protocol sets based on secret sharing [2,3,14,15], the involved parties are usually partitioned into input, computation, and output parties [16]. The computation parties are holding the private values in secret-shared form between them, and are performing the bulk of computation and communication. In this setting, if- and switch-statements with

© Springer International Publishing AG 2016
K.-Y. Lam et al. (Eds.): ICICS 2016, LNCS 9977, pp. 418–430, 2016.
DOI: 10.1007/978-3-319-50011-9_32

private conditions are among unsupported operations. Namely, the taken branch should not be revealed to anyone, but it is difficult to hide the control flow of the program. Instead of choosing the right branch, all the branches are executed, and the final values of all program variables are chosen obliviously from the outcomes of all branches [13,17]. This introduces a significant overhead. An obvious optimization idea, which has not received much attention so far except for [18] in a different setting, is to locate similar operations in different branches and try to fuse them into one. The operation is not trivial, because the gathering of inputs to fused operations introduces additional oblivious choices.

In this work, we consider a simple imperative language with variables typed "public" and "private", invoking secure protocols to process private data. The use of expressions typed "private" is allowed in the conditions of if and switch statements. We translate a program written in this language into a computational circuit and optimize it, trying to fuse together the sets of operations, where the outcome of at most one of them is used in any concrete execution. Our optimization is based on *mixed integer linear programming*, but some greedy heuristics are proposed as well for better performance. Our optimization is very generic and can be applied on the program level, without decomposing high-level operations to arithmetic or boolean circuits. We do the optimization for some simple programs with private conditionals, and evaluate them top of the Sharemind SMC platform [14], showing that the optimization is indeed useful in practice.

2   Preliminaries

Secure Computation. There is a computing party (or several parties) whose task is to compute some function on secret inputs, without being allowed to infer any information about the inputs and/or the outputs. The inputs for such a function may be either encrypted on secret shared among several computing parties.

Languages for Secure Computation. A privacy-preserving application is often described as a higher level functionality, without taking into account the underlying cryptographic protocols. Existing platforms usually come with a language [4,13,14,19] to program such applications. A program looks very similar to an ordinary imperative language (such as Java, Python, or C), but it does much more, as it is being compiled to a sequence of cryptographic protocols.

Mixed Integer Linear Programming [20]. A *mixed integer linear programming* is an optimization task stated as

$$\text{minimize } \mathbf{c}^{\mathrm{T}} \cdot \mathbf{x}, \text{ s.t } A\mathbf{x} \leq \mathbf{b}, \mathbf{x} \geq \mathbf{0}, x_i \in \{0,1\} \text{ for } i \in \mathcal{I}, \tag{1}$$

where $\mathbf{x} \in \mathbb{R}^n$ is a vector of variables that are optimized, and the quantities $A \in \mathbb{R}^{m \times n}, \mathbf{b} \in \mathbb{R}^n, \mathbf{c} \in \mathbb{R}^n, \mathcal{I} \subseteq \{1, \ldots, n\}$ are the parameters defining the task.

3 Related Work

There are a number of languages for specifying privacy-preserving applications to be run on top of secure computation platforms. These may be either domain-specific languages [4,8,10] or variants of general-purpose languages [12]. Often these languages do not offer support for private conditionals.

The support of private conditionals is present in SMCL [9], as well as in newer languages and frameworks, such as PICCO [13], Obliv-C [21], Wysteria [22], SCVM [23], or the DSL embedded in Haskell by Mitchell et al. [11]. A necessary precondition of making private conditions possible is forbidding any public side effects inside the private branches (such as assignments to public variables or termination), since that may leak information about which branch has been executed. All the branches are executed simultaneously, and the value of each variable that could have been modified in at least one branch is updated by selecting its value obliviously. Planul and Mitchell [17] have more thoroughly investigated the leakage through conditionals. They have formally defined the transformation for executing all branches and investigated the limits of its applicability to programs that have potentially non-terminating sub-programs.

The existing compilers that support private conditionals by executing both branches do not attempt to reduce the computational overhead of such execution. We are aware of only a single optimization attempt targeted towards this sort of inefficiencies [18], but the details of their setting are quite different from ours. They are targeting privacy-preserving applications running on top of garbled circuits (GC), building a circuit into which all circuits representing the branches can be embedded. Their technique significantly depends on what can be hidden by the GC protocols about the details of the circuits. Our approach is more generic and applies at the language level.

4 Programs and Circuits

The Imperative Language with Private Conditionals. We start from a simple imperative language, which is just a list of assignments and conditional statements. The variables x in the language are typed either as public or private, these types also flow to expressions. Namely, the expression $f(e_1, \ldots, e_n)$ is private iff at least one of e_i is private. The special operation declassify turns a private expression to a public one. An assignment of a private expression to a public variable is not allowed. Only private variables may be assigned inside the branches of private conditions [13,17]. The syntax c denotes compile-time constants.

$$prog ::= stmt$$
$$f ::= arithmetic\ blackbox\ function$$
$$exp ::= x^{\text{pub}} \mid x^{\text{priv}} \mid c \mid f(\ exp^* \ ) \mid \texttt{declassify}(\ exp\ )$$
$$stmt ::= x := exp \mid \texttt{skip} \mid stmt\ ;\ stmt \mid \texttt{if}\ exp\ \texttt{then}\ stmt\ \texttt{else}\ stmt$$

During the execution of a program on top of a secure computation platform, public values are known by all computation parties, while private values are either encrypted or secret-shared among them [8]. An *arithmetic blackbox function* is an arithmetic, or relational, or boolean, etc. operation, for which we have implementations for all partitionings of its arguments into public and private values. E.g. for integer multiplication, we have the multiplication of public values, as well as protocols to multiply two private values, as well as a public and a private value [14].

Computational Circuits. Due to the existence of private conditionals, the programs written in this language need to be translated into computational circuits before execution. These circuits are not convenient for expressing looping constructs. Also, our optimizations so far do not handle loops. For this reason, we have left them out of the language. We note that loops with public conditions could in principle be handled inside private conditionals [13].

A computation circuit is a directed acyclic graph where each node is assigned a value that can be computed from its immediate predecessors, except the input nodes which obtain their values externally.

Definition 1. *Let Var be the set of program variables. A computational circuit is defined as a set of gates $G = \{g_1, \ldots, g_m\}$ for some $m \in \mathbb{N}$, where each gate $g \in G$ is defined as $g = (op, [v_1, \ldots, v_n])$:*

- *op is the operation that the gate computes (an arithmetic blackbox function of the secure computation platform);*
- *$[v_1, \ldots, v_n]$ for $v_i \in G \cup Var$ is the list of the arguments to which the operation op is applied when the gate is evaluated.*

For $g = (op, args) \in G$, we write $\mathsf{op}^G(g) = op$, and $\mathsf{args}^G(g) = args$.

The circuits that we work on are going to contain gates whose operation is the *oblivious choice*; such gates are introduced while transforming out private conditionals. Such a gate g has $\mathsf{op}^G(g) = oc$, $\mathsf{args}^G(g) = [b_1, v_1, \ldots, b_n, v_n])$, and it returns the output of v_i iff the output of b_i is 1. If there is no such b_i, then it outputs 0. It works on the assumption that at most one gate b_i outputs 1.

Transforming Programs to Circuits. Each assignment $y := f(x_1, \ldots, x_n)$ of the initial program can be viewed as single circuit computing a set of gates G defined by the description of f on inputs $x_1, \ldots, x_n$. A sequence of assignments is put together into a single circuit using circuit composition.

```
if b:
    x := 2;
else:
    x := x + y;
    y := 5*y;
```

$\Rightarrow$

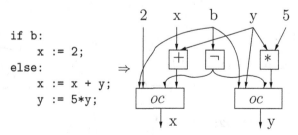

Fig. 1. Example of program transformation

If the program statement is not an assignment, but a private conditional statement, all its branches are first transformed to independent circuits G_i. Let g_i^y be the gate of G_i that outputs the value of y. The value of each variable y is then selected obliviously amongst the output vertices $g_i^y \in G_i$, where the choice bit b_i of g_i^y is the condition of executing the i-th branch. So far, the transformation is similar to the related work [13,17]. An example of transforming a conditional statement to a circuit is given in Fig. 1.

5   Optimizing the Circuit

Let G be a computational circuit. Without loss of generality, let $G = \{1, \ldots, n\}$. The *weakest precondition* ϕ_g^G of evaluating a gate $g \in G$ is a boolean expression over the conditional variables, such that $\phi_g^G = 1$ iff the gate g is evaluated for the given valuation of conditional variables.

The main idea of our optimization is the following. Let $g_1, \ldots, g_k \in G$ be the gates such that $\mathsf{args}^G(g_i) = [x_1^i, \ldots, x_n^i]$, and $\mathsf{op}^G(g_i) = op$ for all i. Let $\phi_{g_1}^G, \ldots, \phi_{g_k}^G$ be mutually exclusive. This happens for example if each g_i belongs to a distinct branch of a set of nested conditional statements. In this case, we can *fuse* the gates $g_1, \ldots, g_k$ into a single gate g that computes the same operation op, choosing each of its inputs x_j obliviously amongst $x_j^1, \ldots, x_j^k$. This introduces n new oblivious choice gates, but leaves just one gate g computing op. An example of optimizing a circuit of two branches is given in Fig. 2.

As discussed in Sect. 4, private branches are not allowed to assign to public variables, so we are fusing only private gates. Hence such a transformation does not affect any public variables through which some additional data might have leaked, and it does not modify the privacy of the initial program.

5.1   High-Level Overview

Preprocessing. First, we look for the pairs of mutually exclusive gates. Find the weakest precondition ϕ_i^G of each gate i. For $i, j \in G$, define $\mathsf{mex}^G(i,j) = 1$ iff $(i = j) \vee (\phi_i^G \wedge \phi_j^G$ is unsatisfiable). For a correct (but not necessarily optimal) solution, it suffices to find only a subset of mutually excluding pairs.

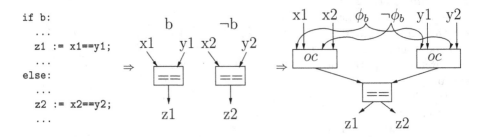

Fig. 2. An example of gate fusing

Since fusing forces all the gate arguments to become chosen obliviously, all the inputs of a fused gate in general are treated as private. Depending on the secure computation platform and the particular operation, this may formally change the gate operation, possibly becoming more expensive, or even unsupported. We define $\mathsf{mex}^G(i, j) = 0$ for the gates i or j that have any public inputs, and whose cost may change if these inputs become private.

Plan. We partition the gates into disjoint sets C_k, planning to leave only one gate in each C_k after the optimization. The following conditions should hold:

- $\forall i, j \in C_k : i \neq j \implies \mathsf{mex}^G(i, j) = 1$: we fuse only mutually exclusive gates, so that indeed at most one gate of C_k will actually be evaluated.
- $\forall i, j \in C_k : \mathsf{op}^G(i) = \mathsf{op}^G(j)$: only the same operation gates are fused.
- Let $E := \{(C_i, C_j) \mid \exists k, \ell : k \in C_i, \ell \in C_j, \ell \in \mathsf{args}^G(k)\}$. The relation $(C_i, C_j) \in E$ denotes that C_j should be evaluated strictly before C_i. We require that the graph $(\{C_k\}_k, E)$ should be acyclic.

If we treat the gates G as vertices, and the relation $\mathsf{mex}^G(i, j)$ as edges, we get that C_k are disjoint cliques on this graph. A possible fusing of gates into a clique is shown in Fig. 3, where the gray lines connect the gates for which $\mathsf{mex}^G(i, j)$ holds, and the shaded gates are treated as a single clique.

To ensure that the optimized circuit is acyclic, define the following predicates, that can be easily derived from the initial circuit:

- $\mathsf{pred}^G(i, k) = 1$ iff $k \in \mathsf{args}^G(i)$;
- $\mathsf{cpred}^G(i, k) = 1$ iff $k \in \phi_i^G$.

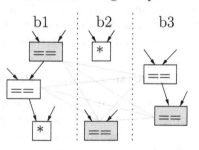

Fig. 3. Fusing gates into cliques

The predicate $\mathsf{pred}^G(i, k)$ is true just if k is an immediate predecessor of i in G. The predicate $\mathsf{cpred}^G(i, k)$ is true if k is used to compute the weakest precondition of i. This means that k does not have to be computed strictly before i in general. However, if i is fused with some other gate, we will need the value of k for computing the choice of the arguments of i, and in this case k has to be computed strictly before i. We call k a *conditional* predecessor of i.

The number of cliques may vary between 1 and $|G|$. For simplicity, we assume that we always have exactly $|G|$ cliques, and some of them may just be left empty. We denote the clique $\{i_1, \ldots, i_k\}$ by C_j, where $j = \min(i_1, \ldots, i_k)$ is the *representative* of the clique C_j, which is the only gate of C_j left after the fusing.

Transformation. The plan gives us a collection of sets of gates C_j, each having gates of certain operation op_j. Consider any $C_j = \{g_1, \ldots, g_{m_j}\}$. Let the inputs of the gate g_i be $x_1^i, \ldots, x_n^i$. Let b_i be the wire that outputs the value of ϕ_i^G.

Introduce n new oblivious choice gates $v_\ell = (oc, [b_1, x_\ell^1, \ldots, b_{m_j}, x_\ell^{m_j}])$ for $\ell \in [n]$. Add a new gate $g = (op_j, [v_1, \ldots, v_n])$. Discard all the gates g_i. Any gate in the rest of the circuit that has used some g_i as an input should now use g instead.

The Cost. In a privacy-preserving application, each gate operation corresponds to some cryptographic protocol. In SMC platforms, such protocols require communication between the parties. We choose the total number of communicated bits as the cost. This metric is additive w.r.t the cost of individual gates. We note that introducing new oblivious choices may increase the number of rounds.

Greedy Construction of Cliques. First, we propose some simple heuristic optimizations of the cost. The gates G are partitioned into subsets, grouped by their operation. These subsets are sorted according to the cost of their operation, so that more expensive gates come first. The subsets are turned into cliques one by one, starting from the most expensive operation. A clique C_k is formed only if it is valid and is not in contradiction with already formed cliques, i.e.:

- any two gates $i, j \in C_k$ satisfy $\mathsf{mex}^G(i, j) = 1$;
- no $i \in C_k$ has already been included into some other clique;
- C_k does not introduce cycles.

We use two main greedy strategies for forming a set of cliques for a particular subset of gates. The first one merges the largest possible clique first. The second one merges the cliques pairwise, trying to form as many cliques as possible.

5.2   Reduction to an Integer Programming Task

As an alternative to greedy algorithms, we reduce the gate fusing task to an integer program and solve it using an external solver (such as [24]).

We consider mixed integer programs of the form (1), defined as a tuple $(A, \mathbf{b}, \mathbf{c}, \mathcal{I})$. We describe how these quantities are constructed from G.

Variables. The core of our optimization are the variables that affect the cost of the transformed circuit. We also need some variables that help to avoid cycles. For all $i, j \in G$, we define the following variables:

- $g_i^j \in \{0, 1\}$, $g_i^j = 1$ iff g_i belongs to the clique C_j.
  The gate j will be the representative of C_j. Namely, $g_j^j = 1$ iff C_j is non-empty. Fixing the representative reduces the number of symmetric solutions significantly. This also allows us to compute the cost of all the cliques.
- $\ell_j \in \mathbb{R}$ is the circuit topological level on which the gate j is evaluated. All the gates with the same level are evaluated simultaneously. Each gate must have a strictly larger level than all its predecessors.
- $c_j \in \{0, 1\}$, $c_j = 1$ iff the gate g_j is fused with some other gate.
  Each gate should have a strictly larger level than all its *conditional* predecessors iff it is merged with some other gate.

Cost Function. We minimize the value $\sum_{j=1}^{|G|} cost(\mathsf{op}^G(j)) \cdot g_j^j$, which is the total cost of the gates left after fusing, except the new oblivious choice gates, and the new boolean operations possibly introduced for the weakest preconditions. This is sufficient as far as the cost of the oblivious choice and the bit operations is smaller than the cost of the gate operation being merged.

Inequality Constraints. The constraints $A\mathbf{x} \leq \mathbf{b}$ state the relations between the variables. Since $A\mathbf{x} \geq \mathbf{b}$ can be expressed as $-A\mathbf{x} \leq -\mathbf{b}$, we may as well use $\leq, \geq,$ and $=$ relations in the constraints.

Building Blocks. We describe how some logical statements are encoded as sets of constraints. Their correctness can be easily verified by case distinction.

Multiplication by a bit. $z = x \cdot y$ for $x \in \{0, 1\}$, $y, z \in \mathbb{R}$, where C is a known
   upper bound on y. We denote this set of constraints $\mathcal{P}(C, x, y, z)$.
- $C \cdot x + y - z \leq C$;
- $C \cdot x - y + z \leq C$;
- $C \cdot x - z \geq 0$.

Threshold. $y = 1$ if $\sum_{x \in \mathcal{X}} x \geq A$, and $y = 0$ otherwise, for $\forall x \in \mathcal{X} : x \in \{0, 1\}$,
   $y \in \mathbb{R}$, some constant A. We denote this set of constraints $\mathcal{F}(A, \mathcal{X}, y)$.
- $\mathcal{P}(1, y, x, z_x)$ for all $x \in \mathcal{X}$, where z_x are fresh variable names;
- $A \cdot y - \sum_{x \in \mathcal{X}} z_x \leq 0$;
- $\sum_{x \in \mathcal{X}} x - \sum_{x \in \mathcal{X}} z_x + (A - 1)y \geq (A - 1)$.

Implication of inequality. $(z = 1) \implies (x - y \geq A)$ for $z \in \{0, 1\}$, $x, y \in \mathbb{R}$,
   some constant A, where C is a known upper bound on x, y. We denote this
   constraint by $\mathcal{G}(C, A, x, y, z)$.
- $(C + A) \cdot z + y - x \geq C$.

Structural Constraints. These ensure that the fusing forms a correct graph.

1. Only mutually exclusive gates may belong to the same clique.
   $g_i^j + g_k^j \leq 1$ for $i, k \in G$, $\neg\mathsf{mex}^G(i, k)$.
2. Each gate belongs to exactly one clique.
   $\sum_{j=1}^{|G|} g_i^j = 1$ for all $i \in G$.
3. If the clique C_j is non-empty, then it contains the gate j. This makes gate j
   the representative of C_j.
   $g_j^j - g_i^j \geq 0$ for all $i, j \in G$.
4. We assign an operation to each clique, based on its representative: $\mathsf{op}^G(C_j) = \mathsf{op}^G(j)$. The gate i may to belong to C_j only if $\mathsf{op}^G(C_j) = \mathsf{op}^G(i)$.
   $g_i^j = 0$ if $\mathsf{op}^G(i) \neq \mathsf{op}^G(j)$.
5. Prevent from fusing gates with cost 0, reducing the search space.
   $g_j^j = 1$ for all j such that $cost(\mathsf{op}^G(j)) = 0$.

6. The cliques are not allowed to form cycles. We assign a level ℓ_i to each gate i. If k is a predecessor of i, then $\ell_k < \ell_i$. To avoid degenerate solutions to the ILP, we introduce some difference between the levels: $\ell_i - \ell_k \geq 1$. If a gate i belongs to the clique C_j, then $\ell_i = \ell_j$. We take $|G|$ as the maximal value for ℓ_i, since we need at most $|G|$ distinct levels.

(a) $\ell_i - \ell_k \geq 1$ for all $i, k \in G$, $\mathsf{pred}^G(i, k)$;

(b) $\mathcal{G}(|G|, 0, \ell_i, \ell_j, g_i^j)$, $\mathcal{G}(|G|, 0, \ell_j, \ell_i, g_i^j)$ for all $i, j \in G$;

(c) $\ell_i \geq 0, \ell_i \leq |G|$.

We need to take into account the conditional predecessors. Let $c_j = 1$ iff the gate j is fused with some other gate. That is, either $g_j^j = 0$ (j belongs to some other clique), or $\sum_{i \in G, i \neq j} g_i^j \geq 1$ (there is some other gate in C_j).

(d) $d_j = (1 - g_j^j)$ for all $j \in G$;

(e) $\mathcal{F}(1, \{d_j\} \cup \{g_i^j \mid i \in G, i \neq j\}, c_j)$ for all $j \in G$;

Finally, if $c_i = 1$ (i is fused with some other gate), then $l_k - l_i \geq 1$ (i is computed strictly before its conditional predecessor k).

(f) $\mathcal{G}(|G|, 1, \ell_i, \ell_k, c_i)$ for all $i, k \in G$, $\mathsf{cpred}^G(i, k)$;

Binary Constraints. Dealing with a mixed integer program, we need to state explicitly that $g_i^j \in \{0, 1\}$ for all $i, j \in G$. The condition $c_j \in \{0, 1\}$ may remain implicit, as it follows from $g_i^j \in \{0, 1\}$ and the inequality constraints for c_j.

6   Implementation and Evaluation

We have implemented the transformation of the program to a circuit, the optimizations, and the transformation of the circuit according to the obtained set of cliques in SWI-Prolog [25]. The ILP is solved externally by the GLPK solver [24].

The optimizations have been tested on small programs. Since we are dealing with a relatively new problem, there are no good test sets, and we had to invent some sample programs ourselves. In general, the programs with private conditionals are related to evaluation of decision diagrams with private decisions. We provide five different programs, each with its own specificity.

- loan (31 gates, integer): A simple binary decision tree, which decides whether a person should be given a loan, based on its background. Only the comparisons that are needed for making decisions are fused.
- sqrt (123 gates, integer): Uses binary search to compute the square root of an integer. Since the input is private, it makes a fixed number of iterations. The division by 2 is on purpose inserted into both branches, modified in such a way that it cannot be trivially outlined without arithmetic theory.
- driver (53 gates, floating point [26]): We took the decision tree that is applied to certain parameters of a piece of music in order to check how well it wakes up a sleepy car driver [27], assuming a privacy-preserving setting of this task. Some decisions require more complex operations, such as logarithms and inverses.

- stats (68 gates, floating point): choosing a particular statistical test may depend on the type of data (ordinal, binary). Here we assume that the decision bits (which analysis to choose) are already given, but are private. The program chooses amongst the Student t-test, the Wilcoxon test, the Welch test, and the χ^2 test, whose privacy-preserving implementations are taken from [28].
- erf (335 gates, integer): The program evaluates the error function of a floating point number, which is represented as a triple (sign, significand, exponent) of integers [26]. The implementation is taken from [29]. The method chosen to compute the answer depends on the range in which the initial input is located.

All our programs are vectorized. During optimization, we treated vector operations as single gates. We ran the optimizer on a Lenovo X201i laptop with a 4-core Intel Core i3 2.4 GHz processor and 4 GB of RAM running Ubuntu 12.04. The optimization times are given in the Table 1. The rows correspond to different strategies, where lp_1 is the ILP approach described in Sect. 5.2, and lp_2 is an extended ILP that takes into account the new oblivious choice gates, and the gates computing weakest preconditions. The columns are the programs, where the numbers after the program name (for stats and erf) specify the depths of the subcircuits into which the gates were merged before optimization, being treated as single gates. In general, there was little variation in optimization times for depths of 2 or more. The greatest difference was noted for stats and erf, where the optimization time was significantly larger without constructing the subcircuits first. The overhead comes mainly from looking at all possible pairs of mutually exclusive gates. The details of lp_2, as well as the construction of subcircuits from gates, are given in the full version of this paper [30].

Table 1. Optimization times

	Times (ms)					Times (s)	
	driver	sqrt	loan	stats, 0	stats, 1–5	erf, 0	erf, 1–7
greed	75–125	495–571	41–53	103–123	181–185	43.5	2.5–8.5
lp_1	118–181	584–780	83–97	142–170	292	47	2.9–8.2
lp_2	171–381	593–1300	115–121	214–262	16291	47.6	15.3–52.5

We compiled the optimized graphs into programs, executed them on Sharemind (three servers on a local 1 Gbps network; the speed of the network is the bottleneck in these tests) and measured their running time. Each test was run 100 times on $n = 10$, $n = 10^3$ inputs, and 10 times on $n = 10^6$ inputs. The summary of the results is given in Table 2. For each program, we give the runtime range of its optimized versions, the runtime of the non-optimized version, and which strategies have been the best and the worst. Here greed$_1$ is the strategy that chooses the largest clique first, and greed$_2$ fuses the gates pairwise.

Since the runtime depends also on the number of rounds that we did not optimize, our results are not good for small inputs. However, as the total

Table 2. Execution times

$n = 10$	driver	sqrt	loan	erf	stats
Time (ms)	156–193	71–77	12–15	85–121	1700–1750
w/o opt.	156	73	16	91	1760
Best strat.	$greed_1$	depth 0	depth 0	depth 1,5+	lp_1, lp_2
Worst strat.	$greed_1$ depth 0	depth 1	$greed_2$ depth 0	depth 2–4	$greed_1$, $greed_2$

$n = 10^3$	driver	sqrt	loan	erf
Time (ms)	588–809	249–291	32–41	275–334
w/o opt.	705	283	51	316
Best strat.	lp_1, lp_2, $greed_1$	depth 0	depth 0	depth 1,4+
Worst strat.	$greed_1$ depth 0	$greed_1$ depth 3	$greed_2$ depth 0	depth 2,3

$n = 10^6$	driver	sqrt	loan	erf	stats, $n = 100$
Time (s)	200–336	97–120	10–14	95–111	136–146
w/o opt.	256	121	19.5	108	148
Best strat.	lp_1, lp_2, $greed_1$	depth 0	depth 0	depth 1,4+	No preference
Worst strat.	$greed_1$ depth 0	depth 2+	$greed_2$ depth 0	depth 2,3	No preference

amount of communication and computation increases, our optimized programs are becoming more advantageous. While greedy approaches may outperform ILP approaches for smaller inputs, ILP is more stable for large inputs.

In general, it is preferable not to merge the initial gates into subcircuits (take depth 0). The greedy strategies work quite well for the given programs, but their results are too unpredictable and can be very good as well as very bad. The results of ILP are in general better. In practice, it would be good to estimate the approximate runtime of the program before it is actually executed, so that we could take the best variant. Our optimizations seem to be most useful for library functions, where several different optimized versions can be compiled and benchmarked before choosing the final one.

7   Conclusion

We have presented a generic optimization for programs written in imperative languages for privacy-preserving computation platforms. We have benchmarked some programs on Sharemind, and see that we indeed can obtain better runtimes. As future work, we might consider decomposing blackbox operations deeper into subprotocols, allowing to partially fuse different blackbox operations.

Acknowledgements. Supported by Estonian Research Council, grant IUT27-1.

References

1. Yao, A.C.: Protocols for secure computations (extended abstract). In: CSF 1982, pp. 160–164. IEEE Computer Society (1982)

2. Goldreich, O., Micali, S., Wigderson, A.: How to play any mental game or a completeness theorem for protocols with honest majority. In: Aho, A.V. (ed.) STOC 1987, pp. 218–229. ACM (1987)

3. Cramer, R., Damgård, I., Maurer, U.: General secure multi-party computation from any linear secret-sharing scheme. In: Preneel, B. (ed.) EUROCRYPT 2000. LNCS, vol. 1807, pp. 316–334. Springer, Heidelberg (2000). doi:10.1007/3-540-45539-6_22

4. Malkhi, D., Nisan, N., Pinkas, B., Sella, Y.: Fairplay - a secure two-party computation system. In: SSYM 2004, USENIX Security Symposium, Berkeley, CA, USA, pp. 287–302. USENIX Association (2004)

5. Bogdanov, D., Laur, S., Willemson, J.: Sharemind: a framework for fast privacy-preserving computations. In: Jajodia, S., Lopez, J. (eds.) ESORICS 2008. LNCS, vol. 5283, pp. 192–206. Springer, Heidelberg (2008). doi:10.1007/978-3-540-88313-5_13

6. Burkhart, M., Strasser, M., Many, D., Dimitropoulos, X.: SEPIA: privacy-preserving aggregation of multi-domain network events and statistics. In: SSYM 2010, USENIX Security Symposium, Washington, DC, USA, pp. 223–239. USENIX Association (2010)

7. Demmler, D., Schneider, T., Zohner, M.: ABY - a framework for efficient mixed-protocol secure two-party computation. In: NDSS 2015. The Internet Society (2015)

8. Bogdanov, D., Laud, P., Randmets, J.: Domain-polymorphic programming of privacy-preserving applications. In: Russo, A., Tripp, O. (eds.) PLAS@ECOOP 2014, p. 53. ACM (2014)

9. Nielsen, J.D., Schwartzbach, M.I.: A domain-specific programming language for secure multiparty computation. In: Hicks, M.W. (ed.) PLAS 2007, pp. 21–30. ACM (2007)

10. Schröpfer, A., Kerschbaum, F., Müller, G.: L1 - an intermediate language for mixed-protocol secure computation. In: COMPSAC 2011, pp. 298–307. IEEE Computer Society (2011)

11. Mitchell, J.C., Sharma, R., Stefan, D., Zimmerman, J.: Information-flow control for programming on encrypted data. In: Chong, S. (ed.) CSF 2012, pp. 45–60. IEEE Computer Society (2012)

12. Franz, M., Holzer, A., Katzenbeisser, S., Schallhart, C., Veith, H.: CBMC-GC: an ANSI C compiler for secure two-party computations. In: Cohen, A. (ed.) CC 2014. LNCS, vol. 8409, pp. 244–249. Springer, Heidelberg (2014). doi:10.1007/978-3-642-54807-9_15

13. Zhang, Y., Steele, A., Blanton, M.: PICCO: a general-purpose compiler for private distributed computation. In: Sadeghi, A.-R., Gligor, V.D., Yung, M. (eds.) CCS 2013, pp. 813–826. ACM (2013)

14. Bogdanov, D., Niitsoo, M., Toft, T., Willemson, J.: High-performance secure multi-party computation for data mining applications. Int. J. Inf. Secur. 11, 403–418 (2012). doi:10.1007/s10207-012-0177-2

15. Damgård, I., Pastro, V., Smart, N., Zakarias, S.: Multiparty computation from somewhat homomorphic encryption. In: Safavi-Naini, R., Canetti, R. (eds.) CRYPTO 2012. LNCS, vol. 7417, pp. 643–662. Springer, Heidelberg (2012). doi:10.1007/978-3-642-32009-5_38

16. Pruulmann-Vengerfeldt, P., Kamm, L., Talviste, R., Laud, P., Bogdanov, D.: Capability Model, UaESMC Deliverable 1.1, March 2012

17. Planul, J., Mitchell, J.C.: Oblivious program execution and path-sensitive non-interference. In: CSF 2013, pp. 66–80. IEEE (2013)

18. Kennedy, W.S., Kolesnikov, V., Wilfong, G.: Overlaying circuit clauses for secure computation. Cryptology ePrint Archive, Report 2016/685 (2016). http://eprint. iacr.org/2016/685

19. Damgård, I., Geisler, M., Krøigaard, M., Nielsen, J.B.: Asynchronous multiparty computation: theory and implementation. In: Jarecki, S., Tsudik, G. (eds.) PKC 2009. LNCS, vol. 5443, pp. 160–179. Springer, Heidelberg (2009). doi:10.1007/ 978-3-642-00468-1_10

20. Schrijver, A.: Theory of Linear and Integer Programming. Wiley Series in Discrete Mathematics & Optimization. Wiley, Chichester (1998)

21. Zahur, S., Evans, D.: Obliv-C: a language for extensible data-oblivious computation. Cryptology ePrint Archive, Report 2015/1153 (2015). http://eprint.iacr.org/ 2015/1153

22. Rastogi, A., Hammer, M.A., Hicks, M.W.: Wysteria: a programming language for generic, mixed-mode multiparty computations. In: SP 2014, pp. 655–670, IEEE Computer Society (2014)

23. Liu, C., Huang, Y., Shi, E., Katz, J., Hicks, M.W.: Automating efficient RAM-model secure computation. In: SP 2014, pp. 623–638, IEEE Computer Society (2014)

24. GLPK: GNU Linear Programming Kit. http://www.gnu.org/software/glpk

25. Wielemaker, J., Schrijvers, T., Triska, M., Lager, T.: SWI-Prolog. Theory Pract. Log. Program. 12, 67–96 (2012)

26. Kamm, L., Willemson, J.: Secure floating point arithmetic and private satellite collision analysis. Int. J. Inf. Secur. 14, 531–548 (2015). doi:10.1007/ s10207-014-0271-8

27. Liu, N.-H., Chiang, C.-Y., Hsu, H.-M.: Improving driver alertness through music selection using a mobile EEG to detect brainwaves. Sensors 13, 8199–8221 (2013)

28. Bogdanov, D., Kamm, L., Laur, S., Sokk, V.: Rmind: a tool for cryptographically secure statistical analysis. Cryptology ePrint Archive, Report 2014/512 (2014). http://eprint.iacr.org/2014/512

29. Krips, T., Willemson, J.: Hybrid model of fixed and floating point numbers in secure multiparty computations. In: Chow, S.S.M., Camenisch, J., Hui, L.C.K., Yiu, S.M. (eds.) ISC 2014. LNCS, vol. 8783, pp. 179–197. Springer, Heidelberg (2014). doi:10.1007/978-3-319-13257-0_11

30. Laud, P., Pankova, A.: Optimizing secure computation programs with private conditionals (full version). Cryptology ePrint Archive, Report 2016/942 (2016). http://eprint.iacr.org/2016/942

Automated Security Proof of Cryptographic Support Commands in TPM 2.0

Weijin Wang[1,2]([✉]), Yu Qin[1], Bo Yang[1,2], Yingjun Zhang[1,2], and Dengguo Feng[1,3]

[1] TCA, Institute of Software, Chinese Academy of Sciences, Beijing, China
{wangweijin,qin_yu,yangbo,zhangyingjun,feng}@tca.iscas.ac.cn
[2] University of Chinese Academy of Sciences, Beijing, China
[3] SKLCS, Institute of Software, Chinese Academy of Sciences, Beijing, China

Abstract. Trusted Platform Module (TPM) is a physical chip that enables trust in a computing platform and makes the platform achieve more security than software alone. In TPM 2.0, the cryptographic primitives are exposed for general purpose use. Since several logical attacks on the TPM commands have been reported by formal methods, we want to formally analyze the newly-added commands in TPM 2.0. However, we adopt a peculiar but interesting formal approach that can get a provable-security result for the cryptographic support commands.

In this paper, we propose a security model for the cryptographic support commands in TPM 2.0. This model utilizes the notion of modern cryptography and is expressed in a formal approach using a probabilistic polynomial-time process calculus. The security policy can be automatically proved by a formal analysis tool CryptoVerif.

Keywords: Formal method · Trusted computing · TPM 2.0 · Cryptographic support commands · CryptoVerif

1 Introduction

In order to obtain security assurance, many computing platforms or embedded devices make use of cryptographic devices, such as Trusted Platform Modules (TPM), Hardware Security Modules (HSM), to provide essential cryptographic operations. These cryptographic devices protect cryptographic keys in the untrusted environment from physical tampering attacks. Applications running on this environment can communicate with the cryptographic devices via various programming interfaces that are called cryptographic APIs.

Starting 2006, many new PCs/laptops have been sold with a TPM chip built in. TPM technology also has been developed by industry to protect computing infrastructure and billions of end points. For instance, Microsoft has its Windows 10 equipped with TPM technology. Moreover, TPM 2.0 Library Specification was approved as a formal international standard under ISO/IEC [10].

We refer to the cryptographic APIs in TPM 2.0 specifications [15] as cryptographic support commands, including symmetric/asymmetric encryption,

© Springer International Publishing AG 2016
K.-Y. Lam et al. (Eds.): ICICS 2016, LNCS 9977, pp. 431–441, 2016.
DOI: 10.1007/978-3-319-50011-9_33

HMAC and signature, etc. To our knowledge, there are no previous formal-analysis works that focus on these new-added commands. But plenty of works have been done in related fields (i.e., formal analysis of APIs), such as TPM 2.0 key management commands [13,18], TPM 2.0 authentication commands [14,16] or PKCS #11 cryptographic APIs [9,11].

Most of the early works of API analysis aim to find flaws or attacks. Some vulnerabilities have been found, such as the attack on the key duplication mechanism of TPM 2.0 [18]. However, some other research works aim to provide the provable security guarantee for API framework. Cortier and Steel [7] presented a new symmetric key management API framework which has a formal security policy and manual proofs of security in the symbolic model. Daubignard et al. [8] extended their work with asymmetric cryptography. Cachin and Chandran [5] presented a novel, provably secure, cryptographic API interface. They used the notion of modern cryptography to manually prove the security policy of the API interface and then provided an emulation of the security policy in the PKCS #11 interface. Then Chu and Feng [6] used their method to prove the security of TPM 2.0 cryptography APIs (but not a formally-analyzed way). Recently, Scerri and Stanley-Oakes [12] presented an analysis of key wrapping APIs with generic policies and used their result to propose a secure refinement of PKCS #11. Their work obtains computational guarantees by a indirect way that uses symbolic formalism to prove computational security statements.

Following up this research line, we want to provide provable security guarantee for the newly-added cryptographic support commands in TPM 2.0, and the most interesting aspect is that we attempt to gain an automated result. Specifically, we model the relevant cryptographic support commands in TPM 2.0 specification. Then similar to the work of Cachin and Chandran, we define the security of commands in the notion of modern cryptography via a game running between a challenger and an adversary. The adversary may try to break the security of the commands by distinguishing left-world encryption from right-world encryption or by contradicting the integrity of the authentication operations. Finally we express the model in a probabilistic polynomial-time process calculus and automatically prove it by a formal analysis tool – CryptoVerif.

Note that our model cannot be treated as a complete solution although we show how to prove the commands in TPM 2.0 with suitable abstractions. For example, we omit abstracting the attribute *duplication* used for duplication commands in the key structure. As the paper of Cachin and Chandran said, the higher level goal of this line of research is "To lay a foundation for the design of future token interfaces with provable security guarantees".

2   Cryptographic Support Commands in TPM 2.0

In TPM 2.0, the cryptographic primitives are exposed for general purpose use, hence the cryptographic support commands appear. To use the commands, keys are critical. A key has a public area and a sensitive area, and both areas consist of some elements. In this section, we will describe the key structure firstly, and then introduce the commands w.r.t our work.

2.1 Key Structure Elements

Each key has two components. The first is a public area that contains the attributes of the key and a public identity. The second is the sensitive area that contains the elements that require TPM protections. The elements of a key structure related to our work are described in Table 1.

Table 1. Key structure elements

Area	Field	Description
Public	*type*	TPM_ALG_SYMCIPHER, TPM_ALG_RSA, TPM_ALG_ECC
	Attribute	usage: *sign, decrypt, restricted*
	unique	For an asymmetric key, this will be the public key. For a symmetric key, this will be the hash value of the sensitive area.
Sensitive	*sensitive*	For an asymmetric key, this is the private key. For a symmetric key, this is the key
	seedValue	For an storage key, this is the seed to generate the protection values for the child keys. For a symmetric key, this is an obfuscation value

2.2 Cryptographic Support Commands

The TPM 2.0 exposes the cryptographic primitives for general purpose use. Here we explain these commands, together with key creation commands.

TPM2_CreatePrimary. This command is used to create a SRK (Storage Root Key). But it will not return the sensitive area, which never leaves the TPM.

TPM2_Create. This command is used to create a key that is generated with values from the TPM RNG.

TPM2_Load. This command is used to load a created key into TPM.

TPM2_EncryptDecrypt. This command performs symmetric encryption or decryption.

TPM2_RSA_Encrypt. This command performs RSA encryption.

TPM2_RSA_Decrypt. This command performs RSA decryption.

TPM2_HMAC. This command performs an HMAC on the supplied data, which can be seen as symmetric signature.

TPM2_Sign. This command causes the TPM to sign a externally provided hash with a asymmetric signing key.

TPM2_VerifySignature. This command uses loaded keys to validate a symmetric or asymmetric signature on a message.

Note that in the TPM specification, ECC is not used directly for encryption. Therefore, there are not explicit commands for ECC encryption here.

3 Security Definition

We define the security of cryptographic support commands in the way that is similar in spirit to Cachin and Chandran [5], who adopt the notion of modern cryptography via a game played between a challenger $\mathcal{C}$ and an adversary $\mathcal{A}$.

Specifically, We assume a challenger $\mathcal{C}$ owns a TPM implementing all commands described in Session 2. The challenger initializes this TPM and chooses the challenge key set $\mathcal{CK} \subseteq \mathbb{K}$ from the initialized TPM. The adversary can make any queries to the challenger. The set $\mathcal{AK} \subseteq \mathbb{K}$ denotes the key generated or derived by the adversary.

Initial. The challenger $\mathcal{C}$ initializes a TPM, chooses the challenge key set $\mathcal{CK}$ (consists of a storage root key SRK a symmetric key SK, an asymmetric key pair PK, a parent key WK, a MAC key MK, a signing key pair SSK). It sends the handles of these keys to adversary $\mathcal{A}$, together with public keys if they exist. In the end, $\mathcal{C}$ picks a bit b at random.

Phase 1. The adversary $\mathcal{A}$ makes queries on cryptographic support commands defined in Sect. 2 for any $K, L \in \mathbb{K}$, and the created keys must be added to the set $\mathcal{AK}$ indicating that they belong to the adversary.

Challenge. The adversary $\mathcal{A}$ submits two messages m_0 and m_1 to challenger $\mathcal{C}$ and obtains a ciphertext under the key in $\mathcal{CK}$.

1. Test symmetric encryption (**testSENC**,m_0,m_1): $\mathcal{C}$ verifies that the input messages have not been queried in Phase 1 first and then executes operation $c^* \leftarrow$ **TPM2_EncryptDecrypt**$(SK, encrypt, m_b)$ and returns c^*.
2. Test asymmetric encryption (**testPENC**,m_0,m_1): $\mathcal{C}$ also verifies that the input messages have not been queried in Phase 1 first. Then he executes operation $\bar{c}^* \leftarrow$ **TPM2_RSA_Encrypt**(PK, m_b) and responds with $\bar{c}^*$.

For other challenges from the adversary $\mathcal{A}$, The challenger $\mathcal{C}$ calls the corresponding commands and responds with what the commands output.

Phase 2. The adversary $\mathcal{A}$ continues to make queries on the commands as done in Phase 1, but is explicitly forbidden to query the return values c^* and $\bar{c}^*$.

Final Phase. In the end, $\mathcal{A}$ proceeds as follows:

1. $\mathcal{A}$ outputs a bit b', its guess as to the value of b. The advantage of $\mathcal{A}$ can be defined as $\alpha_1 = |\Pr[b' = b] - \frac{1}{2}|$.
2. $\mathcal{A}$ outputs (m', t') for $MK \in \mathcal{CK}$ such that t' was never returned by $\mathcal{C}$ in a query **TPM2_HMAC**(MK, m'). The advantage of $\mathcal{A}$ can be defined as $\alpha_2 = |\Pr[\textbf{TPM2\_VerifySignature}(MK, m', t') = true]|$.
3. $\mathcal{A}$ outputs (m'', s'') for $SSK \in \mathcal{CK}$ such that s'' was never returned by $\mathcal{C}$ in a query **TPM2_Sign**(SSK, m''). The advantage of $\mathcal{A}$ can be defined as $\alpha_3 = |\Pr[\textbf{TPM2\_VerifySignature}(SSK, m'', s'') = true]|$.
4. $\mathcal{A}$ outputs a key blob $(K', (w', l'))$ such that (w', l') can be successfully loaded as K' by the TPM while K' was never created by the creation command **TPM2_Create**. The advantage of $\mathcal{A}$ can be defined as $\alpha_4 = |\Pr[\textbf{TPM2\_Load}(SSK, (w', l')) = K']|$.

Definition 1. *The Cryptographic Support Commands in TPM 2.0 are secure if the advantages $\alpha_1, \alpha_2, \alpha_3, \alpha_4$ are negligible for all efficient adversaries $\mathcal{A}$.*

4 Proving the Security in CryptoVerif

In this section, we want to prove that the cryptographic support commands satisfy **Definition** 1 by CryptoVerif. Before that, we give a brief overview of CryptoVerif and then model the commands and security definition in CryptoVerif's calculus. The results will be presented in the end. Note that the complete input of CryptoVerif will appear in [17].

4.1 CryptoVerif Basics

There are two main approaches to the verification of cryptographic protocols. One approach is known as the computational model and another approach is known as the symbolic or Dalev-Yao model. The CryptoVerif, proposed by Blanchet [2–4], can directly prove security properties of cryptographic protocols in the computational model.

CryptoVerif builts proofs by sequences of games. It starts from the initial game given as input, which represents the protocol to prove in interaction with an adversary (real mode). Then, it transforms this game step by step using a set of predefined game transformations, such that each game is indistinguishable from the previous one. CryptoVerif transforms one game into another by applying the security definition of a cryptographic primitive or by applying syntactic transformations. In the last game of a proof sequence the desired security properties should be obvious (ideal mode).

CryptoVerif is sound: whatever indications the user gives, when the prover shows a security property of the protocol, the property indeed holds assuming the given hypotheses on the cryptographic primitives.

4.2 Modelling the Game in CryptoVerif

We adopt a probabilistic polynomial-time process calculus (CryptoVerif's calculus) to model the game defined in Session 3. Before this, we will identify the key structure and some tricks in expressing the commands.

CryptoVerif provides tables for persistent storage. Processes may populate and access tables, but deletion is forbidden. Therefore, to express key structure, we declare a table *keystruct*:

   table *keystruct*(handle, keytype, bool, keyseed1, keyseed2)

The handle,keytype represents the key handle and key type according to the literal meaning. The keytype $\in$ {srkey,symmetric,asymmetric,wrap,mac,signature} captures two fields *type* and *usage* in the TPM key structure elements. For example, if the keytype is an asymmetric encryption key (i.e., =asymmetric), then correspondingly $type = TPM\_ALG\_RSA$ and $descrypt = SET$ in the TPM key structure. The Boolean flag `bool` is an assistant flag to help our process identify whether the corresponding key can be stored outside. It is not a real field in the structure. We add this flag for convenience in the decision condition of the process. We use key seed instead of key value. This is equivalent to what we describe in Sect. 2, since either symmetric key or asymmetric key pair can be generated by a key seed (using a key generation algorithm). Hence `keyseed1` corresponds to field $unique$ and $sensitive$. The second key seed `keyseed2` corresponds to the field $seedValue$.

The command **TPM2_Create** requires that the new key must be under protection of its father key via a wrapping operation. However, the father key may also be created by this command. CryptoVerif's calculus cannot handle the complex state transition and control flow. Therefore, we model this command into two separate process: $TPM2\_CreateK$ and $TPM2\_CreateWrap$. The former is used to model the process of generating a new key. The later is used to model the wrapping process of the new key by its father key. More details is below.

Modelling the Initial Phase. The oracle $Ogen$ described in Table 2 generates the challenge key set $C\mathbb{K}$ and chooses a random bit b. It returns the key handles and public keys, therefore, immediately corresponding to the initial phase of our description.

Table 2. Initial phase

$Ogen():=iv1 \xleftarrow{R} keyseed; iv2 \xleftarrow{R} keyseed; srkhd \xleftarrow{R} handle;$
insert $keystruct(SRK, srkey, false, RNG(SPS, iv1), RNG(SPS, iv2));$
$ks \xleftarrow{R} keyseed; k \leftarrow kgen(ks); SK \xleftarrow{R} handle;$
......
$b \xleftarrow{R} bool;$
return $(SRK, SK, PK, pk, WK, MK, SSK, spk);$

The SPS is a seed persistently stored in a TPM. We use a function RNG to model different key generated from the same seed SPS. Since the SRK is never stored off the TPM in any form, we set the boolean flag `bool` $= false$.

Modelling Phase 1 & 2. The processes named after the cryptographic support commands allow the adversary $\mathcal{C}$ to perform requests, capturing Phase 1 & 2 of our description. Note that we do not distinguish between Phase 1 & 2. This is acceptable since both Phase 1 and Phase 2 are in parallel with the challenge phase in our formalization. These processes provide some oracles for modelling the capacity of adversary to invoke the commands. For limited space, we present some of them, which are described in Table 3.

The processes $TPM2\_CreateK$ and $TPM2\_CreateWrap$ model the create operation. The former presents in the table. It provides an oracle OCK waiting

Table 3. Phase 1 & 2

Let TPM2_CreateK =
  foreach $i_C K \leq q_C K$ **do** OCK($ktype$: $keytype$):=
  if $ktype = asymmetric$ **then** (
      $pks' \xleftarrow{R} keyseed$; $pk' \leftarrow pkgen(pks')$; $sk' \leftarrow skgen(pks')$; $PK' \xleftarrow{R} handle$;
      insert keystruct(PK', $asymmetric$, $true$, pks', $obfuscation$);
      return (PK', pk'))
  else if $ktype = ...$

Let TPM2_RSA_Encrypt =
  foreach $i_{PE} \leq q_{PE}$ **do** OSE(PK_3 : $handle$, pm_3 : $pcleartext$):=
  get keystruct($= PK_3$, $= asymmetric$, $= true$, pks_3, $= obfuscation$) **in**
  $pk_3 \leftarrow pkgen(ks_3)$; $pr_3 \xleftarrow{R} pseed$;
  return($\mathcal{PE}(pm_3, pk_3, pr_3)$).

Let TPM2_RSA_Decrypt =
  foreach $i_{PD} \leq q_{PD}$ **do** OSD(PK_4 : $handle$, pc_4 : $pciphertext$):=
  find $u \leq N$ **suchthat defined**($pc_1[u]$) && ($pc_4 = pc_1[u]$) **then end else**
  get keystruct($= PK_4$, $= asymmetric$, $= true$, pks_4, $= obfuscation$) **in**
  $sk_4 \leftarrow skgen(pks_4)$;
  return($\mathcal{PD}(pc_4, sk_4)$).

---

for a message $ktype$ from $\mathcal{C}$ and then generates a corresponding key according to $ktype$ and returns the key handle and public portion. The attribute **type** of the new key is set to be $ktype$ and **bool** is set to be $true$.

The process *TPM2_RSA_Encrypt* provides an asymmetric encryption oracle OPE waiting for a query on a plaintext pm to be encrypted by PK_3. It looks up the encryption key (i.e., a key seed that can generates public key) with handle PK_3 in $keystruct$. Then it encrypts the plaintext using the public key and returns the ciphertext. The process *TPM2_RSA_Decrypt* provides a decryption oracle OPD waiting for a query on a ciphertext pc_4 to be decrypted by the private key of PK_4 and returns the corresponding plaintext. The *find* clause guarantees the challenge ciphertext would not be queried to the decryption oracle.

Modelling the Challenge Phase. The Challenge phase models the test oracles for challenger $\mathcal{C}$. The adversary $\mathcal{A}$ tries to break the security of the cryptographic support commands by confirming which world he was talking to (the world of $b = 0$ and the world of $b = 1$), or creating a forged tag or signature to against the integrity of the authentication operations. Therefore, the adversary would make a query (m_0, m_1) to its oracles, and whenever he does, the oracle computes the return value depending on the pre-selected random boolean value b. The adversary would make a query to its authentication oracles as well and get the return value in favor of a forgery. We also present part of the Challenge phase, as described in Table 4.

The process *testPENC* models a test oracle taking a tuple (pm_0, pm_1) as input from $\mathcal{A}$ and returning the asymmetric encrypted value of pm_b under the key $PK \in \mathcal{CK}$. Also, the two *find* clauses guarantee the input messages can not be queried to the encryption oracle in advance.

Table 4. Challenge phase

Let testPENC =
  OT3($pm_0 : cleartext, pm_1 : cleartext$):=
  find $u_{PE_0} \leq q_{PE}$ **suchthat defined**$(PK_3[u_{PE_0}], pm_3[u_{PE_0}])$ &&
    $(PK = PK_3[u_{PE_0}])$ && $(pm_0 = pm_3[u_{PE_0}])$ **then end else**
  find $u_{PE_1} \leq q_{PE}$ **suchthat defined**$(PK_3[u_{PE_1}], pm_3[u_{PE_1}])$ &&
    $(PK = PK_3[u_{PE_1}])$ && $(pm_1 = pm_3[u_{PE_1}])$ **then end else**
  get keystruct$(= PK, = asymmetric, = true, pks_1, = obfuscation)$ **in**
  let $pm = $ if b then pm_1 else pm_0 **in**
  $pk_1 \leftarrow pkgen(pks_1); pr_1 \xleftarrow{R} pseed;$
  return$(\mathcal{PE}(pm, pk_1, pr_1))$.

Modelling the Final Phase. The final phase of our formalization is captured by secrecy property and correspondence property. We model the statement 1 in the final phase as *one-session secrecy* of b. A process Q preserves the *one-session secrecy* of b when, with overwhelming probability, the adversary interacting with Q cannot distinguish any element of the array b from an uniformly-distributed random number by a single test query. Hence, if our processes preserve the one-session secret of b, then with overwhelming probability, the adversary can not distinguish a test query that outputs b from one that outputs a random boolean value (*true* or *false*). Then naturally, the adversary can not distinguish which message has been selected.

We model the statements 2 & 3 & 4 in the final phase as *correspondence* assertions, which are properties of the form "if some events have been executed, then some other events have been executed" or "if some events have been executed, then some formula holds". We define an event *forge* that would be executed after a forgery happens and prove that *forge* has not been executed.

4.3   Results

We use CryptoVerif to prove the secret and correspondence properties for the cryptographic support commands in the computation model. Before we show the results, we present the cryptographic assumptions in our proof.

Modelling the Cryptographic Assumptions. The symmetric encryption scheme is assumed to be indistinguishable under chosen plaintext attacks (IND-CPA) and satisfies ciphertext integrity (INT-CTXT). These two properties guarantee indistinguishability under adaptive chosen ciphertext attacks(IND-CCA2), as shown in [1]. The asymmetric encryption scheme is also assumed to be IND-CCA2 secure. The MAC and signature scheme are both assumed to be strongly unforgeable under chosen message attacks (SUF-CMA). The key-wrapping scheme implements an Encrypt-then-MAC scheme. The encryption scheme is IND-CPA secure and the MAC scheme is SUF-CMA secure. As show in [1], this composite encryption scheme is IND-CCA2 secure. For these assumption, we use the definitions built in CryptoVerif library except for a slight modification in the definitions of IND-CPA and INT-CTXT. As an example, we show the definition of IND-CPA as follows.

> **foreach** $i' \leq n'$ **do** $r \xleftarrow{R} keyseed;$
>   **foreach** $i \leq n$ **do** $Oenc(x : bitstring) := r' \xleftarrow{R} seed;$ **return**$(enc(x, kgen(r), r'))$
> $\approx$
> **foreach** $i' \leq n'$ **do** $r \xleftarrow{R} keyseed;$
>   **foreach** $i \leq n$ **do** $Oenc(x : bitstring) := r' \xleftarrow{R} seed;$ **return**$(enc'(Z_T, kgen'(r), r'))$

In this definition, Z_T is a const of the same length as the plaintext, consisting only of zeros. Hence it denotes a situation that one can not distinguish the ciphertext of an arbitrary message x from that of a constant Z_T. Our modification is embodied in Z_T. The original definition in [3] is a function $Z : bitstring \rightarrow bitstring$. But the authors also claim that they can prove that $Z(x)$ does not depend on x when x is of a fixed-length type. We assume the symmetric encryption scheme is a block cipher such that the length of the plaintext is fixed. Therefore, the replacement of function Z by const Z_T is valid.

Mechanized Proof. The security properties presented in the final phase can be mechanically proved using CryptoVerif. The validity of the result depends on the soundness of CryptoVerif.

The security result for the cryptographic support commands in TPM 2.0 can be formalized as the following theorem.

Theorem 1. *The cryptographic support commands defined in Sect. 2 are secure, under the assumptions of a symmetric encryption scheme against adaptive chosen-ciphertext attack, a public-key encryption scheme against adaptive chosen-ciphertext attack, a strong existentially unforgeable message-authentication code and a strong existentially unforgeable signature scheme.*

CryptoVerif can then automatically prove the theorem by querying the following properties:

> **query secret1** b
> **query event** $forge ==> false$

The proof done by CryptoVerif consists of applying cryptographic transformations for the security assumptions, with some simplifying processes and other syntactic transformations between two of them. As a consequence, all queries are proved in the final game generated by CryptoVerif. We refers the readers to get the input of CryptoVerif in [17] and execute it by oneself.

5 Conclusion

In this paper, we use an unusual, peculiar but interesting way to automatically prove the cryptographic support commands in TPM 2.0. These commands includes key creations, encryption, signature, etc. We model these commands with a security policy expressed in the notion of modern cryptography. Then we express the security policy using a probabilistic polynomial-time process calculus. We prove that these commands satisfy this security policy with the assistance of automated tool CryptoVerif who works in the computational model.

A possible extension of this work lies in modelling a more complex control flow and handling a situation of state transition. This can lead to a more precise proof.

Acknowledgments. The research presented in this paper is supported by the National Grand Fundamental Research 973 Program of China under Grant No. 2013CB338003 and the National Natural Science Foundation of China under Grant Nos. 61402455, 61602455. We also thank the anonymous reviewers.

References

1. Bellare, M., Namprempre, C.: Authenticated encryption: relations among notions and analysis of the generic composition paradigm. In: Okamoto, T. (ed.) ASIACRYPT 2000. LNCS, vol. 1976, pp. 531–545. Springer, Heidelberg (2000). doi:10.1007/3-540-44448-3_41
2. Blanchet, B.: Computationally sound mechanized proofs of correspondence assertions. In: 20th IEEE Computer Security Foundations Symposium (CSF 2007), pp. 97–111. IEEE, Venice, July 2007
3. Blanchet, B.: A computationally sound mechanized prover for security protocols. IEEE Trans. Dependable Secur. Comput. **5**(4), 193–207 (2008)
4. Blanchet, B., Pointcheval, D.: Automated security proofs with sequences of games. In: Dwork, C. (ed.) CRYPTO 2006. LNCS, vol. 4117, pp. 537–554. Springer, Heidelberg (2006). doi:10.1007/11818175_32
5. Cachin, C., Chandran, N.: A secure cryptographic token interface. In: 22nd IEEE Computer Security Foundations Symposium, CSF 2009, pp. 141–153. IEEE (2009)
6. Chu, X., Feng, D.: On the provable security of TPM2. 0 cryptography APIs. Int. J. Embed. Syst. **7**(3–4), 230–243 (2015)
7. Cortier, V., Steel, G.: A generic security API for symmetric key management on cryptographic devices. Inf. Comput. **238**, 208–232 (2014)
8. Daubignard, M., Lubicz, D., Steel, G.: A secure key management interface with asymmetric cryptography. In: Abadi, M., Kremer, S. (eds.) POST 2014. LNCS, vol. 8414, pp. 63–82. Springer, Heidelberg (2014). doi:10.1007/978-3-642-54792-8_4
9. Delaune, S., Kremer, S., Steel, G.: Formal security analysis of PKCS# 11 and proprietary extensions. J. Comput. Secur. **18**(6), 1211–1245 (2010)
10. ISO/IEC 11889:2015: Information Technology - Trusted Platform Module Library - Part 1 & Part 2 & Part 3 & Part 4
11. Künnemann, R.: Automated backward analysis of PKCS#11 v2.20. In: Focardi, R., Myers, A. (eds.) POST 2015. LNCS, vol. 9036, pp. 219–238. Springer, Heidelberg (2015). doi:10.1007/978-3-662-46666-7_12
12. Scerri, G., Stanley-Oakes, R.: Analysis of key wrapping APIs: generic policies, computational security. In: 29nd IEEE Computer Security Foundations Symposium, CSF 2016. IEEE (2016)
13. Shao, J., Feng, D., Qin, Y.: Type-based analysis of protected storage in the TPM. In: Qing, S., Zhou, J., Liu, D. (eds.) ICICS 2013. LNCS, vol. 8233, pp. 135–150. Springer, Heidelberg (2013). doi:10.1007/978-3-319-02726-5_11

14. Shao, J., Qin, Y., Feng, D., Wang, W.: Formal analysis of enhanced authorization in the TPM 2.0. In: Proceedings of 10th ACM Symposium on Information, Computer and Communications Security (ASIACCS 2015), pp. 273–284. ACM (2015)
15. Trusted Computing Group: Trusted Platform Module Library Specification, Family "2.0", Level 00, Revision 01.16. http://www.trustedcomputinggroup.org/resources/tpm_library_specification
16. Wang, W., Qin, Y., Feng, D.: Automated proof for authorization protocols of TPM 2.0 in computational model. In: Huang, X., Zhou, J. (eds.) ISPEC 2014. LNCS, vol. 8434, pp. 144–158. Springer, Heidelberg (2014). doi:10.1007/978-3-319-06320-1_12
17. Wang, W.: CryptoVerif Input for Cryptographic Support Commands in TPM 2.0. https://github.com/WangWeijin/TPM-2.0-Cryptographic-Support-Commands
18. Zhang, Q., Zhao, S., Qin, Y., Feng, D.: Formal analysis of TPM2. 0 key management APIs. Chin. Sci. Bull. **59**(32), 4210–4224 (2014)

Network Security

How to Meet Big Data When Private Set Intersection Realizes Constant Communication Complexity

Sumit Kumar Debnath$^{(\boxtimes)}$ and Ratna Dutta

Department of Mathematics, Indian Institute of Technology Kharagpur,
Kharagpur 721302, India
sd.iitkgp@gmail.com, ratna@maths.iitkgp.ernet.in

Abstract. This paper presents the *first* PSI protocol that achieves constant ($O(1)$) communication complexity with linear computation overhead and is fast even for the case of large input sets. The scheme is proven to be provably secure in the standard model against semi-honest parties. We combine *somewhere statistically binding (SSB) hash function* with *indistinguishability obfuscation (iO)* and *Bloom filter* to construct our PSI protocol.

Keywords: PSI · SSB hash · iO · Bloom filter

1 Introduction

Electronic information is increasingly often shared among unreliable entities. In this context, one interesting problem involves two parties that secretly want to determine intersection of their respective private data sets while none of them wish to disclose the whole set to other. One can adopt Private Set Intersection (PSI) protocol to address this problem preserving the associated security and privacy issues. It is a two-party cryptographic protocol where each party engages with their private sets. On completion of the protocol either only one of the participants learns the intersection and other learns nothing, yielding one-way PSI or both of them learn the intersection, yielding mutual PSI (mPSI). PSI has emerged a great attention in the recent research community due to its numerous applications in real-life such as privately comparing equal-size low-entropy vectors, collaborative botnet detection, testing of fully sequenced human genomes, affiliation-hiding authentication, social networks, location-based services, privacy preserving data mining, social networks, online gaming etc.

Our Contribution: Our goal is to construct a PSI whose communication cost is optimal while the computation cost is comparable with the existing schemes.

In this paper, we design a new PSI protocol based on *Bloom filter* [2] that is significantly more efficient than all the existing PSI protocols. We adopt a novel two-party computation technique and make use of *somewhere statistically binding (SSB) hash function* [11,13] along with *indistinguishability obfuscation*

© Springer International Publishing AG 2016
K.-Y. Lam et al. (Eds.): ICICS 2016, LNCS 9977, pp. 445–454, 2016.
DOI: 10.1007/978-3-319-50011-9_34

(iO) [1,7]. Starting point of our construction is the approach of [13] of secure function evaluation (SFE) for "multi-decryption".

In our protocol, the client B sends SSB hash value of its private input set to the server A who in turn transmits to B an SSB hash key, obfuscated version of a hard-coded circuit and a Bloom filter. The use of SSB hash reduces the communication complexity of our protocol to constant ($O(1)$) which is due to only three bit-strings of length m (size of a Bloom filter), $p(\kappa)|C|$ (size of an obfuscated circuit) and $w\lfloor \log_2 n \rfloor$ (size of an element of $\mathbb{Z}_{n^w}$), where $p(\kappa)$ is a polynomial in security parameter κ, w is a positive integer, n is the product of two large primes and $\lfloor n \rfloor$ stands for the largest integer less than or equal n. On the other hand, the computation overhead of our protocol is $O(v + L)$ which depends on an SSB hash key computation, a circuit obfuscation, v many Pseudorandom function (PRF) evaluations by the server A and L many circuit evaluation by the client B. Our protocol is secure against semi-honest adversaries in the standard model. For simplicity, we employ the SSB hash [13] based on the Damgård-Jurik cryptosystem [4] secure under the Decisional Composite Residuosity (DCR) assumption. However, any SSB hash can be integrated to construct our PSI protocol.

Constructing PSI for big data sets is a challenging task while efficiency and scalability need to be preserved. Our PSI can easily be adopted to solve this big data issue. To the best of our knowledge, [5,6,16–18] are the most efficient PSI protocols, among which only [5,17] solve the big data issue. All of these protocols attain linear computation complexity while none of them achieve constant communication complexity. On a more positive note, our PSI is the *first* to achieve *constant* communication complexity.

2   Preliminaries

Throughout the paper, the notations κ, $a \leftarrow A$, $x \hookleftarrow X$ and $\{\mathcal{X}_t\}_{t \in \mathcal{N}} \stackrel{c}{\equiv} \{\mathcal{Y}_t\}_{t \in \mathcal{N}}$ are respectively used to represent "security parameter", "a is output of the procedure A", "variable x is chosen uniformly at random from set X" and "the distribution ensemble $\{\mathcal{X}_t\}_{t \in \mathcal{N}}$ is computationally indistinguishable from the distribution ensemble $\{\mathcal{Y}_t\}_{t \in \mathcal{N}}$". Formally, $\{\mathcal{X}_t\}_{t \in \mathcal{N}} \stackrel{c}{\equiv} \{\mathcal{Y}_t\}_{t \in \mathcal{N}}$ means for all probabilistic polynomial time (PPT) distinguisher $\mathcal{Z}$, there exists a negligible function $\epsilon(t)$ such that $|Prob_{x \leftarrow \mathcal{X}_t}[\mathcal{Z}(x) = 1] - Prob_{x \leftarrow \mathcal{Y}_t}[\mathcal{Z}(x) = 1]| \leq \epsilon(t)$. A function $\epsilon : \mathbb{N} \to \mathbb{R}$ is said to be negligible function of κ if for each constant $c > 0$, we have $\epsilon(\kappa) = o(\kappa^{-c})$ for all sufficiently large κ.

Definition 1. Pseudorandom Function [10]: *A random instance $f_k(\cdot)$ is said to be Pseudorandom Function (PRF) for a randomly chosen key k, if the value of the function cannot be distinguished from a random function $\hat{f} : D \to E$ by any PPT distinguisher $\mathcal{Z}$ i.e., $|Prob[\mathcal{Z}^{f_k}(1^\kappa) = 1] - Prob[\mathcal{Z}^{\hat{f}}(1^\kappa) = 1]|$ is negligible function of κ.*

A PRF $f_k(\cdot)$ is an efficiently computable function i.e., one can compute $f_k(x)$ using a PPT algorithm for any given $x \in D$. For example, the PRF of [12]:

$f_k(x) = g^{1/(k+x)}$ if $gcd(k+x, n)$ is 1, 1 otherwise. The pseudorandom function is secure under the Decisional Q-Diffie-Hellman Inversion (DHI) assumption [12].

2.1   Damgård-Jurik Cryptosystem [4]

The Damgård-Jurik cryptosystem DJ is a generalization of the Paillier cryptosystem [14] and consists of algorithms (KGen, Enc, Dec) which work as follows:

- DJ.KGen(1^κ) $\rightarrow$ (pk, sk): On input 1^κ, a user does the following:
  - selects two large primes p, q independently of each other;
  - sets $n = pq$ and $\gamma = lcm(p - 1, q - 1)$;
  - chooses an element $g \in \mathbb{Z}^*_{n^{w+1}}$ for some $w \in \mathbb{N}$ such that $g = (1 + n)^j x$ mod n^{w+1} for a known j relatively prime to n and $x \in \widetilde{G}$, where $\mathbb{Z}^*_{n^{w+1}} = G \times \widetilde{G}$, G being a cyclic group of order n^w and $\widetilde{G}$ is isomorphic to $\mathbb{Z}^*_n$;
  - computes d using the Chinese Remainder Theorem satisfying that d mod $n \in \mathbb{Z}^*_n$ and $d = 0$ mod γ;
  - sets the public key pk $= (n, g, w)$ and the secret key sk $= d$;
  - publishes pk and keeps sk secret to itself.
- DJ.Enc(pk, m) $\rightarrow$ (c): Using the public key pk of a decryptor, an Encryptor encrypts a message $m \in \mathbb{Z}_{n^w}$ by selecting $r \leftarrowtail \mathbb{Z}^*_{n^{w+1}}$ and computing ciphertext $c = g^m r^{n^w}$ mod n^{w+1}.
- DJ.Dec(sk, c) $\rightarrow$ (m): On receiving the ciphertext c from the encryptor, the decryptor uses its decryption key sk $= d$ to compute c^d mod n^{w+1}. The decryptor then applies recursive version of the Paillier decryption mechanism [4] to obtain $(j \cdot m \cdot d)$ mod n^w and $(j \cdot d)$ mod n^w respectively from $a = c^d = (1 + n)^{(j \cdot m \cdot d)}$ mod n^{w+1} and $a = g^d = (1 + n)^{(j \cdot d)} x^d = (1 + n)^{(j \cdot d)}$ mod n^{w+1}. As $(j \cdot d)$ and $(j \cdot m \cdot d)$ are known to the decryptor, it can compute $m = (j \cdot m \cdot d)(j \cdot d)^{-1}$ mod n^w.

The scheme is additively homomorphic as there exists an operation $\oplus$ over $\mathbb{Z}_{n^{w+1}}$ DJ.Enc(pk, m_1; r_1) $\oplus$ DJ.Enc(pk, m_2; r_2) = DJ.Enc(pk, $m_1 + m_2$; r_3) for randomness $r_3 = r_1 r_2$, where $+$ is over $\mathbb{Z}_{n^w}$ and $\mathbb{Z}_{n^{w+1}}$ respectively. We can define homomorphic subtraction $\ominus$ over $\mathbb{Z}_{n^{w+1}}$ as DJ.Enc$_{pk}(m_1; r_1)$ $\ominus$ DJ.Enc$_{pk}(m_2; r_2)$ = DJ.Enc$_{pk}(m_1 - m_2; r_4)$ for randomness $r_4 = \frac{r_1}{r_2}$, where the operations $-$ is over $\mathbb{Z}_{n^w}$. Furthermore, by performing repeated $\oplus$ operation, we can implement an operation $\otimes$ over $\mathbb{Z}_{n^{w+1}}$ as DJ.Enc$_{pk}(m_1; r_1)$ $\otimes$ $m_2 = \oplus^{m_2}$(DJ.Enc$_{pk}(m_1; r_1)$) = DJ.Enc$_{pk}(m_1 \cdot m_2; r_5)$ for randomness $r_5 = r_1^{m_2}$, where $\cdot$ is over $\mathbb{Z}_{n^w}$ and $\mathbb{Z}_{n^{w+1}}$ respectively. The semantic security of the cryptosystem DJ holds under the DCR [14] assumption defined below:

Definition 2. Decisional Composite Residuosity (DCR) Assumption [14]: *On input 1^κ, let RGen be an algorithm that generates an RSA modulus $n = pq$, where p and q are distinct large primes. The DCR assumption states that given an RSA modulus n (without its factorization) and an integer z, it is computationally hard to decide whether z is an n-th residue modulo n^2, i.e., whether there exists $y \in \mathbb{Z}^*_{n^2}$ such that $z \equiv y^n \pmod{n^2}$.*

2.2 SSB Hash [11,13]

A somewhat statistically binding (SSB) hash SSBHash consists of PPT algorithms (Gen, $\mathcal{H}$, Open, Verify) along with a finite block alphabet $\Sigma = \{0,1\}^{l_{\mathsf{blk}}}$, output size l_{hash} and opening size l_{opn}, where $l_{\mathsf{blk}}(\kappa), l_{\mathsf{hash}}(\kappa), l_{\mathsf{opn}}(\kappa)$ are fixed polynomials in the security parameter κ. An SSB hash satisfies the following three properties – Correctness, Index Hiding and Somewhere Statistically Binding. For more details see [11,13]. We describe below the DCR based SSB hash of [13] which uses Damgård-Jurik cryptosystem as described in Sect. 2.1 and considers $\Sigma = \mathbb{Z}_{n^w}$ i.e., $l_{\mathsf{blk}} = \lfloor w \log_2 n \rfloor$, output domain as $\mathbb{Z}_{n^w}$ i.e., $l_{\mathsf{hash}} = \lfloor w \log_2 n \rfloor$ and opening domain as $\times^{\alpha}(\mathbb{Z}_{n^w}) = \mathbb{Z}_{n^w} \times \ldots \times \mathbb{Z}_{n^w}$ (α times) i.e., $l_{\mathsf{opn}} = \alpha \lfloor w \log_2 n \rfloor$

- SSBHash.Gen$(1^{\kappa}, 1^{l_{\mathsf{blk}}}, L, i) \to (hk)$: Without any loss of generality, we assume that $L = 2^{\alpha}$ is an integer with $L \leq 2^{\kappa}$. A setup authority runs the key generation algorithm for Damgård-Jurik cryptosystem DJ on input 1^{κ} to receive $(\mathsf{pk} = (n, g, w), \mathsf{sk} = d) \leftarrow$ DJ.KGen(1^{κ}). Let $(b_{\alpha}, \ldots, b_1)$ be the binary representation of the index $i \in \{0, \ldots, L-1\}$. For $l = 1, \ldots, \alpha$, the setup authority computes $g^{b_l} \gamma_l^{n^w} = c_l = $ DJ.Enc$(\mathsf{pk}, b_l; \gamma_l)$, $gR_l^{n^w} = 1_{\mathsf{ch}_l} = $ DJ.Enc$(\mathsf{pk}, 1; R_l)$ and sets $\mathsf{hk} = (\mathsf{pk}, h, 1_{\mathsf{ch}_1}, \ldots, 1_{\mathsf{ch}_{\alpha}}, c_1, \ldots, c_{\alpha})$ as public SSB hash key, where $h : \mathbb{Z}_{n^{w+1}}^{*} \to \mathbb{Z}_{n^w}$ is a collision resistant hash function.
- SSBHash.$\mathcal{H}(\mathsf{hk}, s) \to (z = H_{\mathsf{hk}}(s))$: Let $s = (s[0], \ldots, s[L-1]) \in \Sigma^L$, where $\Sigma = \mathbb{Z}_{n^w}$. Let T be a binary tree of height α with L leaves. A user considers the leaves as being at level 0 and the root of the tree at level α. The user inductively and deterministically associates a value ct_v at each vertex $v \in T$ in bottom-up fashion as follows:
    - If $v \in T$ is the j-th leaf node (at level 0), $j \in \{0, \ldots, L-1\}$, then the user associates v the value $\mathsf{ct}_v = s[j] \in \mathbb{Z}_{n^w}$.
    - If $v \in T$ is a non-leaf node at level $l \in \{1, \ldots, \alpha\}$ with children v_0, v_1 having associated values $\mathsf{ct}_0, \mathsf{ct}_1$ respectively then the user associates v the value $\mathsf{ct}_v = h(c_v^{*})$, where $c_v^{*} = [\mathsf{ct}_1 \otimes c_l] \oplus [\mathsf{ct}_0 \otimes (1_{\mathsf{ch}_l} \ominus c_l)] \in \mathbb{Z}_{n^w}$, $c_l, 1_{\mathsf{ch}_l}$ being the ciphertexts and h being the hash function extracted from $\mathsf{hk} = (\mathsf{pk}, h, 1_{\mathsf{ch}_1}, \ldots, 1_{\mathsf{ch}_{\alpha}}, c_1, \ldots, c_{\alpha})$ and $\otimes, \oplus, \ominus$ are operations as described in the Sect. 2.1. Note that c_v^{*} is the encryption of ct_{b_l}. The associated value at the root of T is the final output $z = H_{\mathsf{hk}}(s) \in \mathbb{Z}_{n^w}$.
- SSBHash.Open$(\mathsf{hk}, s, j) \to (\pi)$: The user outputs ct_v values associated to siblings v of the nodes along the path form the root to the j-th leaf in T. In other words, if PathNode(j) denotes the set of nodes on the path from the root to the j-th leaf in T and HangNode(j) is the set of sibling nodes of all $v \in$ PathNode(j), then $\pi = \{\mathsf{ct}_v | v \in$ HangNode$(j)\}$.
- SSBHash.Verify$(\mathsf{hk}, z, j, u, \pi) \to (\mathsf{accept}, \mathsf{reject})$: A verifier can recompute the associated values of all the nodes in the tree T that lie on the path from the root to the j-th leaf by utilizing the value u as associated to the j-th leaf node together with the values in π as the associated values of all the sibling nodes along the path. The verifier checks whether the recomputed value at the root is indeed z. If it is z then the verifier outputs accept; otherwise, outputs reject.

2.3 Bloom Filter [2]

Bloom filter (BF) is a data structure that represents a set $X = \{x_1, \ldots, x_v\}$ of v elements by an array of m bits and uses k independent hash functions $H_{\mathsf{Bloom}} = \{h_0, \ldots, h_{k-1}\}$ with $h_i : \{0,1\}^* \to \{0, \ldots, m-1\}$ for $i = 0, \ldots, k-1$ to insert elements or check the presence of an element in that array. Let $\mathsf{BF}_X \in \{0,1\}^m$ represent a Bloom filter for the set X and $\mathsf{BF}_X[i]$ denotes its i-th bit, $i = 0, \ldots, m-1$. We describe below three operations that can be performed using Bloom filter:

- *Initialization:* Set 0 to all the bits of an m-bit array, which is an empty Bloom filter with no elements in it.
- *Add(x):* To add an element $x \in X \subseteq \{0,1\}^*$ into a Bloom filter, x is hashed with the k hash functions in $H_{\mathsf{Bloom}} = \{h_0, \ldots, h_{k-1}\}$ to get k indices $h_0(x), \ldots, h_{k-1}(x)$. Set 1 to the bit position of the Bloom filter having indices $h_0(x), \ldots, h_{k-1}(x)$. Repeat the process for each $x \in X$ to get $\mathsf{BF}_X \in \{0,1\}^m$ – the Bloom filter for the set X.
- *Check(x̂):* Given BF_X, to check whether an element $\hat{x}$ belongs to X without knowing X, $\hat{x}$ is hashed with the k hash functions in $H_{\mathsf{Bloom}} = \{h_0, \ldots, h_{k-1}\}$ to get k indices $h_0(\hat{x}), \ldots, h_{k-1}(\hat{x})$. Now if atleast one of $\mathsf{BF}_X[h_0(\hat{x})], \ldots, \mathsf{BF}_X[h_{k-1}(\hat{x})]$ is 0, then $\hat{x}$ is not in X, otherwise $\hat{x}$ is *probably* in X.

Bloom filter allows *false positive* whereby an element that has not been inserted in the filter can mistakenly pass the set membership test. This happens when an element $\hat{x}$ does not belong to X but $\mathsf{BF}_X[h_i(\hat{x})] = 1$ for all $i = 0, \ldots, k-1$. On the contrary, Bloom filter never yields a false negative i.e., an element that has been inserted in the filter will always pass the test. This is because if $\hat{x}$ belongs to X then each of $\mathsf{BF}_X[h_0(\hat{x})], \ldots, \mathsf{BF}_X[h_{k-1}(\hat{x})]$ is 1. Given the number v of elements to be added and a desired maximum false positive rate $\frac{1}{2^k}$, the optimal size m of the Bloom filter is $m = \frac{vk}{\ln 2}$.

2.4 Indistinguishability Obfuscation [1,7]

Definition 3. Indistinguishability Obfuscation (iO): *An indistinguishability obfuscator $\mathcal{O}$ for a circuit class $\mathcal{C}_\kappa$ is a PPT uniform algorithm satisfying the following requirements:*

- *(Correctness): For any circuit $C \in \mathcal{C}_\kappa$, if we compute $\overline{C} \leftarrow \mathcal{O}(1^\kappa, C)$ then $\overline{C}(x) = C(x)$ for all inputs x i.e., $Prob[\overline{C} \leftarrow \mathcal{O}(1^\kappa, C) : \overline{C}(x) = C(x)] = 1$ for all inputs x.*
- *(Indistinguishability): For any κ and any two circuits $C_0, C_1 \in \mathcal{C}_\kappa$, if $C_0(x) = C_1(x)$ for all inputs x then the circuits $\mathcal{O}(1^\kappa, C_0)$ and $\mathcal{O}(1^\kappa, C_1)$ are indistinguishable i.e., for all PPT adversaries $\mathcal{Z}$, $\big|Prob[\mathcal{Z}(\mathcal{O}(1^\kappa, C_0)) = 1] - Prob[\mathcal{Z}(\mathcal{O}(1^\kappa, C_1)) = 1]\big| \leq \epsilon(\kappa)$, where $\epsilon(\kappa)$ is negligible function of κ.*

We consider only polynomial-size circuits i.e., the circuit class C_κ consists of circuits of size at most κ. This circuit class is denoted by P/poly and the first candidate iO for this circuit class was introduced by Garg et al. [7]. Their construction is secure in generic matrix model. Following this, a single instance-independent assumption based iO for P/poly were proposed by [8,15].

3 Protocol

Protocol Requirements: The protocol computes the intersection of the server A's private input set $Y = \{y_1, \ldots, y_v\}$ and the client B's private input set $X = \{x_0, \ldots, x_{L-1}\}$. Without any loss of generality we may assume that $X, Y \subseteq \mathbb{Z}_{n^w}$. If not, we can choose a collision resistant hash function ha : $\{0,1\}^* \to \mathbb{Z}_{n^w}$ to make the elements of X, Y as members of $\mathbb{Z}_{n^w}$. Auxiliary input includes the size L of B's input set, the security parameter κ, the Bloom filter parameters $(m, H_{\mathsf{Bloom}} = \{h_0, \ldots, h_{k-1}\})$. Without any loss of generality we can assume that $L = 2^\alpha$ for some integer $\alpha \leq \kappa$. If not, we can add 0's as the members of the set X to make its cardinality of the form 2^α. We integrate Bloom filter presented in Sect. 2.3, indistinguishability obfuscation (iO) scheme $\mathcal{O}$ described in Sect. 2.4 together with an SSB hash function SSBHash with alphabet $\Sigma = \mathbb{Z}_{n^w}$ i.e., $l_{\mathsf{blk}} = \lfloor w \log_2 n \rfloor$, output domain $\mathbb{Z}_{n^w}$ i.e., $l_{\mathsf{hash}} = \lfloor w \log_2 n \rfloor$ and opening domain $\times^\alpha(\mathbb{Z}_{n^w})$ i.e., $l_{\mathsf{opn}} = \alpha \lfloor w \log_2 n \rfloor$, where $n = pq$ is the product of two large primes p and q, and w is a positive integer. We require a circuit $C = C[\mathsf{hk}, z, \mathsf{ke}]$ as defined in Fig. 1. We also assume that C includes some polynomial-size padding to make it sufficiently large. Furthermore, we define an augmented circuit $C^{\mathsf{aug}} = C^{\mathsf{aug}}[\mathsf{hk}, z, \mathsf{ke}, \bar{k}, i^*]$ as in Fig. 2 which will be used in Sect. 3.1 for the security proof of our scheme. We need the padding in C to match its size with C^{aug}.

Construction: The protocol completes in two phases: off-line phase and online phase. In the off-line phase, the server A generates a SSB hash key hk and makes hk public. On the other hand, online phase consists of three algorithms: PSI.Request, PSI.Response and PSI.Complete. The client B runs PSI.Request algorithm to generate a SSB hash value of its input set X with the SSB hash key hk and sends it to A who in turn runs PSI.Response algorithm to generate an obfuscated circuit $\overline{C}$, a Bloom filter $BF_{\overline{Y}}$ and sends these to B. The client B then runs the algorithm PSI.Complete to get the intersection of X and Y.

Constraints: Hash key hk, hash value z, PRF key ke.
Input: $i \in \{0, \ldots, L-1\}, x \in \mathbb{Z}_{n^w}, \pi \in \times^\alpha(\mathbb{Z}_{n^w})$.
Output: 0 or PRF $f_{\mathsf{ke}}(x)$.
1. Check whether SSBHash.Verify($\mathsf{hk}, z, i, x, \pi$) is accept or reject. If reject, then output 0.
2. Otherwise, output $f_{\mathsf{ke}}(x)$.

Fig. 1. Description of circuit $C[\mathsf{hk}, z, \mathsf{ke}](i, x, \pi)$

Constraints: Old values (hash key hk, hash value z, PRF key ke), New values (PRF
key $\bar{k}, i^* \in \{0, ..., L-1\}$)
Input: $i \in \{0, ..., L-1\}, x \in \mathbb{Z}_{n^w}, \pi \in \times^\alpha(\mathbb{Z}_{n^w})$.
Output: 0 or PRF $f_{ke}(x)$ or PRF $f_{\bar{k}}(x)$.
1. Check whether SSBHash.Verify(hk, z, i, x, π) is accept or reject. If reject, then output
0.
2. Otherwise, if $i \geq i^*$, then output $f_{ke}(x)$, else if $i < i^*$ output $f_{\bar{k}}(x)$.

Fig. 2. Description of circuit $C^{\text{aug}}[\text{hk}, z, \text{ke}, \bar{k}, i^*](i, x, \pi)$

A high level description of our PSI protocol is presented in Fig. 3. We now
describe below the off-line and online phases of our protocol.
Off-line Phase: On input 1^κ, the server A does the following:

(i) Runs the algorithm SSBHash.Gen on input $1^\kappa, 1^{l_{\text{blk}}}, L = 2^\alpha, 0$ to generate
   a SSB hash key hk $\leftarrow$ SSBHash.Gen($1^\kappa, 1^{l_{\text{blk}}}, L, 0$), where $l_{\text{blk}} = \lfloor w \log_2 n \rfloor$,
   where hk $= (\text{pk}, h, 1_{\text{ch}_1}, \ldots, 1_{\text{ch}_\alpha}, c_1, \ldots, c_\alpha)$, pk $= (n, g, w)$ $h : \mathbb{Z}^*_{n^{w+1}} \rightarrow$
   $\mathbb{Z}_{n^w}$ is a collision resistant hash function, $1_{\text{ch}_l} = \text{DJ.Enc}(\text{pk}, 1; R_l)$ and $c_l =$
   $\text{DJ.Enc}(\text{pk}, 0; \gamma_l)$.
(ii) Makes hk public.

Online Phase: It consists of the following three algorithms:

- PSI.Request(hk) $\rightarrow z$: The client B proceeds as follows:
  (i) Sets $s[i] = x_i \in \Sigma = \mathbb{Z}_{n^w}$, for $i = 0, .., L-1$, where $X = \{x_0, \ldots, x_{L-1}\}$
     $\subseteq \mathbb{Z}_{n^w}$ is B's private input set.
  (ii) Computes $z = H_{\text{hk}}(s) \leftarrow$ SSBHash.$\mathcal{H}$(hk, s). Note that $z \in \mathbb{Z}_{n^w}$.
  (iii) Finally, sends z to A.
- PSI.Response(z) $\rightarrow (\overline{C}, \text{BF}_{\overline{Y}})$: The server A, on receiving the request z from
  B, does the following:
  (i) Chooses a PRF key ke $\leftarrow \mathbb{Z}^*_n$ for PRF $f_{ke}(x) = g^{1/(ke+x)}$ if $gcd(\text{ke} + x, n)$
     is 1, 1 otherwise, where $x \in \{0,1\}^Q$, ke $\in \mathbb{Z}^*_n$ and $Q = \lfloor w \log_2 n \rfloor$.
  (ii) Designs a circuit as described in Fig. 1.
  (iii) Constructs an obfuscated circuit $\overline{C} \leftarrow \mathcal{O}(1^\kappa, C)$ of C.
  (iv) Generates a Bloom filter $\text{BF}_{\overline{Y}}$ of the set $\overline{Y} = \{f_{ke}(y_1), \ldots, f_{ke}(y_v)\}$, where
     $f_{ke}(y_j) = g^{1/(ke+y_j)}$ for $j = 1, \ldots, v$ and $Y = \{y_1, \ldots, y_v\} \subseteq \mathbb{Z}_{n^w}$ is A's
     private input set.
  (v) Sends the obfuscated circuit $\overline{C}$ together with $\text{BF}_{\overline{Y}}$ to B.
- PSI.Complete($\overline{C}, \text{BF}_{\overline{Y}}$) $\rightarrow (\overline{X} = X \cap Y)$: On receiving $(\overline{C}, \text{BF}_{\overline{Y}})$ from A, the
  client B starts with an empty set $\overline{X}$ and does the following
  (i) For each $i = 0, \ldots, L-1$
     – generates opening $\pi_i = \text{SSBHash.Open}(\text{hk}, s, i) \in \times^\alpha(\mathbb{Z}_{n^w})$ using
       the already computed values ct_v's during the calculation of $z \leftarrow$
       SSBHash.$\mathcal{H}$(hk, s) and computes PRF values $f_{ke}(x_i) \leftarrow \overline{C}(i, x_i, \pi_i)$.
       Note that s, x_i are known to B.

Common input: $\mathsf{hk} = (\mathsf{pk}, h, 1_{\mathsf{ch}_1}, ..., 1_{\mathsf{ch}_\alpha}, c_1, ..., c_\alpha)$
Auxiliary input: $L = 2^\alpha, \kappa, m, H_{\mathsf{Bloom}} = \{h_0, ..., h_{k-1}\}$

A's private input: B's private input:
$Y = \{y_1, ..., y_w\}$ $X = \{x_0, ..., x_{L-1}\}$

$\quad$ $z = H_{\mathsf{hk}}(s) \leftarrow \mathsf{PSI.Request(hk)}$,
$\quad$ where $s = (s[0], ..., s[L-1])$,
$\quad$ $s[i] = x_i$, for $i = 0, ..., L-1$

$\qquad\qquad\qquad\qquad \xleftarrow{\quad z \quad}$

$(\overline{C}, \mathsf{BF}_{\overline{Y}}) \leftarrow \mathsf{PSI.Response}(z)$,
where $\overline{Y} = \{f_{\mathsf{ke}}(y_1), ..., f_{\mathsf{ke}}(y_v)\}$,
$\mathsf{ke} \twoheadleftarrow \mathbb{Z}_n^*, \overline{C} \leftarrow \mathcal{O}(1^\kappa, C)$,
$C = C[\mathsf{hk}, z, \mathsf{ke}](i, x, \pi)$

$\qquad\qquad\qquad\qquad \xrightarrow{\quad \overline{C}, \mathsf{BF}_{\overline{Y}} \quad}$

$\quad$ output $\overline{X} = X \cap Y \leftarrow \mathsf{PSI.Complete}(\overline{C}, \mathsf{BF}_{\overline{Y}})$,
$\quad$ where $\overline{X} = \{x_i \in X \,|\, f_{\mathsf{ke}}(x_i) \in \mathsf{BF}_{\overline{Y}}\}$
$\quad$ with $f_{\mathsf{ke}}(x_i) \leftarrow \overline{C}(i, x_i, \pi_i)$,
$\quad$ $\pi_i = \mathsf{SSBHash.Open}(\mathsf{hk}, s, i)$, for $i = 0, ..., L-1$

Fig. 3. Communication flow of our PSI

- checks whether $f_{\mathsf{ke}}(x_i)$ is in the set $\overline{Y}$ corresponding to the Bloom filter $\mathsf{BF}_{\overline{Y}}$. If yes, then x_i is included in $\overline{X}$.
(ii) Outputs the final $\overline{X}$ as the intersection of the sets X and Y.

Correctness: The correctness of our protocol follows from the following fact in the PSI.Complete phase executed by B:
$f_{\mathsf{ke}}(x_i)$ passes the check step of $\mathsf{BF}_{\overline{Y}} \Leftrightarrow f_{\mathsf{ke}}(x_i) \in \overline{Y}$ except with negligible probability $\frac{1}{2^k} \Leftrightarrow$ there exists $y_j \in Y$ such that $f_{\mathsf{ke}}(x_i) = f_{\mathsf{ke}}(y_j) \Leftrightarrow x_i = y_j$ as $f_{\mathsf{ke}}(\cdot)$ is a one-to-one $\Leftrightarrow x_i \in X \cap Y \Leftrightarrow \overline{X} = X \cap Y$ (by the construction of $\overline{X}$).

Complexity: In our construction, size of the public parameter hk is $(2\alpha + 1)\lfloor w \log_2 n \rfloor + \log_2 n + |h|$ bit and 2α exponentiations are required to generate hk. The communication complexity includes three bit-strings of length m, $\lfloor w \log_2 n \rfloor$ and $m + poly(\kappa)(|C|)$, where $|h| =$ length of the hash function $h : \mathbb{Z}_n^{w+1} \to \mathbb{Z}_n^w$ and $m = \frac{kv}{\ln 2}$, $|C| =$ length of the circuit $C = C[\mathsf{hk}, z, \mathsf{ke}](i, x, \pi)$. The computation complexity of our PSI is displayed in Table 1.

Table 1. Computation complexity of our PSI protocol

		Exp	Inv	H_{BF}	H_{SSB}	EC	FHE$_{\mathsf{Enc}}$	FHE$_{\mathsf{Dec}}$	FHE$_{\mathsf{Eval}}$
A	PSI.Response	v	v	kv		$2\eta(2M+5)^2 + 4(2M+5)$			
B	PSI.Request	$3(L-1)$	$L-1$		$L-1$				
B	PSI.Complete		kL				$2L$	L	$2L$

$\alpha = \log_2 L$, $M = 2\eta + 5$, $\eta =$ length of oblivious matrix branching program, $\eta \le 4^d$, $d =$ depth of the circuit C, Exp= number of exponentiations, Inv= number of inversions, $H_{\mathsf{BF}} =$ number of hash operations for Bloom filter, $H_{\mathsf{SSB}} =$ number of hash operations for SSB hash

3.1 Security

Theorem 1. *If H is an SSB hash based on* DJ *encryption, $\mathcal{O}$ is an iO scheme and the associated PRF $f_{\mathsf{ke}}(\cdot)$ is secure then the protocol presented in Sect. 3 between a server A and a client B is a secure computation protocol in the semi-honest adversarial model* [5,9] *except with negligible probability $\frac{1}{2^k}$.*

Proof. Due to limited space, proof will appear in the full version.

4   Conclusion

In this work, we introduce the idea of constructing PSI utilizing *SSB hash*, *Bloom filter* and *iO*. Compared to the existing PSI schemes, our PSI is the most efficient PSI scheme. More significantly, it is the *first* to achieve *constant* communication complexity with linear computation cost. Our protocol works fast even for big data sets. Security of our scheme is analyzed in the semi-honest setting without any random oracles.

References

1. Barak, B., Goldreich, O., Impagliazzo, R., Rudich, S., Sahai, A., Vadhan, S., Yang, K.: On the (im)possibility of obfuscating programs. In: Kilian, J. (ed.) CRYPTO 2001. LNCS, vol. 2139, pp. 1–18. Springer, Heidelberg (2001). doi:10.1007/3-540-44647-8_1
2. Bloom, B.H.: Space/time trade-offs in hash coding with allowable errors. Commun. ACM **13**(7), 422–426 (1970)
3. Brakerski, Z., Gentry, C., Vaikuntanathan, V.: (Leveled) fully homomorphic encryption without bootstrapping. In: Proceedings of 3rd Innovations in Theoretical Computer Science Conference, pp. 309–325. ACM (2012)
4. Damgård, I., Jurik, M.: A generalisation, a simpli.cation and some applications of Paillier's probabilistic public-key system. In: Kim, K. (ed.) PKC 2001. LNCS, vol. 1992, pp. 119–136. Springer, Heidelberg (2001). doi:10.1007/3-540-44586-2_9
5. Dong, C., Chen, L., Wen, Z.: When private set intersection meets big data: an efficient and scalable protocol. In: Proceedings of 2013 ACM SIGSAC Conference on Computer & Communications Security, pp. 789–800. ACM (2013)
6. Freedman, M.J., Hazay, C., Nissim, K., Pinkas, B.: Efficient set intersection with simulation-based security. J. Cryptol. **29**(1), 115–155 (2016)
7. Garg, S., Gentry, C., Halevi, S., Raykova, M., Sahai, A., Waters, B.: Candidate indistinguishability obfuscation and functional encryption for all circuits. In: 2013 IEEE 54th Annual Symposium on Foundations of Computer Science (FOCS), pp. 40–49. IEEE (2013)
8. Gentry, C., Lewko, A.B., Sahai, A., Waters, B.: Indistinguishability obfuscation from the multilinear subgroup elimination assumption. In: 2015 IEEE 56th Annual Symposium on Foundations of Computer Science (FOCS), pp. 151–170. IEEE (2015)
9. Goldreich, O.: Foundations of Cryptography: Volume 2, Basic Applications, vol. 2. Cambridge University Press, Cambridge (2009)

10. Goldreich, O., Goldwasser, S., Micali, S.: How to construct random functions. J. ACM (JACM) **33**(4), 792–807 (1986)
11. Hubacek, P., Wichs, D.: On the communication complexity of secure function evaluation with long output. In: Proceedings of 2015 Conference on Innovations in Theoretical Computer Science, pp. 163–172. ACM (2015)
12. Jarecki, S., Liu, X.: Efficient oblivious pseudorandom function with applications to adaptive OT and secure computation of set intersection. In: Reingold, O. (ed.) TCC 2009. LNCS, vol. 5444, pp. 577–594. Springer, Heidelberg (2009). doi:10.1007/978-3-642-00457-5_34
13. Okamoto, T., Pietrzak, K., Waters, B., Wichs, D.: New realizations of somewhere statistically binding hashing and positional accumulators. In: Iwata, T., Cheon, J.H. (eds.) ASIACRYPT 2015. LNCS, vol. 9452, pp. 121–145. Springer, Heidelberg (2015). doi:10.1007/978-3-662-48797-6_6
14. Paillier, P.: Public-key cryptosystems based on composite degree residuosity classes. In: Stern, J. (ed.) EUROCRYPT 1999. LNCS, vol. 1592, pp. 223–238. Springer, Heidelberg (1999). doi:10.1007/3-540-48910-X_16
15. Pass, R., Seth, K., Telang, S.: Indistinguishability obfuscation from semantically-secure multilinear encodings. In: Garay, J.A., Gennaro, R. (eds.) CRYPTO 2014. LNCS, vol. 8616, pp. 500–517. Springer, Heidelberg (2014). doi:10.1007/978-3-662-44371-2_28
16. Pinkas, B., Schneider, T., Segev, G., Zohner, M.: Phasing: private set intersection using permutation-based hashing. In: 24th USENIX Security Symposium (USENIX Security 2015), pp. 515–530 (2015)
17. Pinkas, B., Schneider, T., Zohner, M.: Faster private set intersection based on OT extension. In: USENIX Security, vol. 14, pp. 797–812 (2014)
18. Shi, R.-H., Mu, Y., Zhong, H., Cui, J., Zhang, S.: An efficient quantum scheme for private set intersection. Quantum Inf. Process. **15**(1), 363–371 (2016)

Novel MITM Attacks on Security Protocols in SDN: A Feasibility Study

Xin Wang[1,2,3], Neng Gao[1,2], Lingchen Zhang[1,2(✉)], Zongbin Liu[1,2],
and Lei Wang[1,2]

[1] State Key Laboratory of Information Security,
Institute of Information Engineering, Chinese Academy of Sciences,
Beijing 100093, China
{wangxin,gaoneng,zhanglingchen,liuzongbin,wanglei}@iie.ac.cn
[2] Data Assurance and Communication Security Research Center,
Chinese Academy of Sciences, Beijing 100093, China
[3] University of Chinese Academy of Sciences, Beijing 100049, China

Abstract. Software-Defined Networking (SDN) is a new paradigm that
offers services and applications great power to manage network. Based on
the consideration that the entire network visibility is the foundation of
SDN, many attacks emerge in poisoning the network visibility, which lead
to severe damage. Meanwhile, many defense approaches are proposed to
patch the controller. It is noticed that powerful adversaries can bypass
existing approaches to poison topology information and attack security
protocols. In this paper, we present a method that the adversary can
attack security protocols under existing approaches (*e.g.* TopoGuard,
SPHINX). We also investigate a number of security protocols that may
be compromised by our MITM attacks and propose an approach to detect
the existence of the adversary. Our evaluation shows that the defense
solution can effectively detect the fake link in normal environment. We
hope our research can attract more attention on SDN security.

Keywords: SDN · Security protocols · MITM

1 Introduction

Software-Defined Networking (SDN) changes the traditional network architecture by separating the control plane of switching equipment from the data plane.
Nowadays, SDN, particularly its popular realization OpenFlow, has been increasingly employed in academic environments and real-world production networks.
Compared with traditional network architecture, SDN implements a unified controller that can support holistic network visibility and flexible programmability.
Network applications can make global decisions based on flow conditions provided by the controller. Once the topology information provided by SDN controller is falsified, all operations based on network topology are incorrect.

The fundamental of SDN is the correct topology information. Most security approaches which primarily concentrate on network/rule authorization,

© Springer International Publishing AG 2016
K.-Y. Lam et al. (Eds.): ICICS 2016, LNCS 9977, pp. 455–465, 2016.
DOI: 10.1007/978-3-319-50011-9_35

conflict resolution or network resource consumption/scalability will be meaningless. Recently, in order to overcome topology attacks, Hong *et al.* proposed TopoGuard [6], which is the first method to study the network topology visibility exploitation and fix security omissions to detect attacks on topology information. Dhawan *et al.* proposed SPHINX [4]. They also found several attacks on SDN controllers which violate network topology and data plane forwarding. Although these schemes can defend against most of topology visibility attack, they are vulnerable to complicated attacks constructed by the adversary.

In this paper, we analyze the drawbacks in network topology management of the mainstream OpenFlow networks and propose novel MITM (Man-In-the-Middle) attacks on many security protocols. Besides, we also analyze the existing mainstream patches [4,14] and figure out some new attacks on network visibility. If an adversary host which links to two different SDN switches relays LLDP packets from one switch to another simultaneously, SDN controller will take this internal link as a normal link according to the existing SDN link discovery method. Compared with the traditional network, it is difficult for SDN controller to find this middle man. According to the original intention of SDN design, OpenFlow controller does not handle the application layer protocols. If these two conditions are satisfied, the adversary can breach most application layer security protocols in SDN by careful design. In this paper, we propose solutions for fake link detection by analyzing the transfer time of LLDP to defend against this MITM attack. Our evaluation shows that it is possible to detect the fake link and prevent such severe MITM attacks.

In short, our paper makes the following contributions:

- The security analysis is performed on TopoGuard and SPHINX which defend against Network Topology Poisoning Attacks and new MITM attacks on security protocols in SDN architecture are figured out.
- Security protocols that can be hijacked by our attacks are found out and possible approaches to defend against these MITM attacks are also proposed.
- Experiments are implemented to validate the proposed solution.

2   Background

2.1   Software Defined Networking

Software Defined Networking is a new paradigm that decouples control plane of network device from its data plane and implements all control plane as a unified software platform, which is called the SDN controller. OpenFlow is a popular realization. The SDN controller can guarantee the topology visibility of whole network and make the best routing decision according to the topology information. Besides, we can easily configure security policies in centralized controller.

2.2   Attacks on Link Discovery Service

Different from legacy network, topology management is unique in SDN networks. SDN controller provides such visibility to upper service/apps. Once this visibility is falsified, upper services will be influenced. In topology management, we focus on link discovery service. Link discovery service is used to find switch-to-switch link in SDN networks, which is an active process. By means of link discovery service, SDN provides controller with secure network topology.

Attacks on internal link discovery are presented due to the lack of integrity detection of LLDP packet in OpenFlow controller. There are two main types of attack on link discovery: fake LLDP injection attack and LLDP relay attack. Due to the open source feature of SDN controller, the adversary can obtain the syntax of LLDP packet. Then he can generate new LLDP packet or modify the content of received LLDP packet (e.g. DPID of switch or the port number field) and forward this packet to the linked switch. Then topo information is polluted. In addition to the fake LLDP injection attack, the adversary can also fabricate internal links in a relay fashion. When receiving LLDP packet from one target switch, the adversary relays it to another target switch without any modification. Then the adversary constructs a fake topology view to the OpenFlow controller that there is an internal link between these two target switches. This relay attack is the basis of launching MITM attack.

2.3 Mainstream Patches

Some methods have been proposed to solve attacks on link discovery service with TopoGuard [6] and SPHINX [4] as representatives. In order to defend against fake LLDP injection, TopoGuard adds a controller-signed TLV into the LLDP packet and checks the signature when the LLDP packets are received. In order to defend against LLDP relay attack, TopoGuard marks the switch ports as SWITCH and HOST according to the types of received packet. If LLDP packet is received from switch port, it will be assigned SWITCH. If host-traffic packet is detected, it will be assigned HOST. Once the port has been marked, this port is suspicious if the traffic received from this port does not match its label. SPHINX maintains flow graphs, which are the graph theoretic representation of traffic flow. In the graph, edges indicate flow metadata and nodes represent the switches. Flow graphs provide a clean mechanism that aids detection of diverse constraint violations for network topology. Once new packet violates flow graphs, SPHINX will raise alerts. In addition, SPHINX also checks the port metadata to ensure that only a single neighbor is permitted per active port at a switch. Besides, links in SPHINX should be bidirectional in flow graphs. However, when adversaries mute all host-generated traffic and relay LLDP packets, these schemes won't raise an alert.

3 Man-In-The-Middle Attack on Security Protocols

3.1 Threat Model

With the extension of internal network scope, the benefits obtained from direct internal attacks in the network increases. Since our goal is to establish fake internal link and launch MITM attack within SDNs, our threat model exclusively focuses on scenarios where the adversary initiates attacks within the SDN. Thus, we model SDNs as a closed system. We consider an enterprise SDN setup with no traffic across OpenFlow and non-OpenFlow network. We assume a trusted controller and trusted switches, but we do not trust the end hosts. We also assume SDN applications are trusted. In addition, we assume the adversary can establish simple network with the aid of legacy routers and switches.

3.2   Man-In-The-Middle Attack

In this paper, we will introduce a new MITM attack that is difficult to defend in the mainstream SDN architecture. Our attack is based on the fact that there are no effective means to defend against LLDP relay attack if the adversary mutes its host-generated traffic and only relays LLDP packets. In order to establish middle man in the link successfully, we discuss two ways, *i.e.* by physical links and by a tunnel. An intuitive relay method is to set up physical links (*e.g.* cable or wireless) between two switches using middle adversary shown in Fig. 1. In order to increase the scope of this attack, two adversaries can link switch 1 and switch 3 separately and then exchange LLDP packets using another legacy net. This approach may require adversaries to build up a small network. In order to circumvent the detection of protection schemes, the adversary needs to mute all host-generated traffic when relaying LLDP packets. Another way is to make a tunnel by utilizing third-party host. As shown in Fig. 1, compromised host 1 transfers the received LLDP packet to host 2, then host 2 relays it to compromised server. After receiving this packet, the server then transfers it to switch 3. Then controller thought switch 1 connects to switch 3. This method is easy to defend in existing patches because the types of packets in this switch port are different.

After the establishment of fake internal link, the adversary can take MITM. We use the attack on Https as an example. When the compromised user accesses the service of compromised server without protection of https, the middle man can get the user's network information directly. When communication parties use Https, the middle man can still achieve the login information without being detected by existing patches, which is our main contribution. In our experiment,

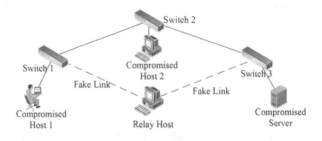

Fig. 1. Attack scenario

we test one way SSL authentication. TopoGuard is chosen as the OpenFlow controller. We deploy a linear network topology, as shown in Fig. 1, where we have a compromised host connecting two ingress switches in the network. When the compromised user accesses the compromised server, the server will redirect the access to https. The redirection traffic will pass through the adversary but won't be changed. After that the compromised host will send SSL request to the server. When the middle adversary receives this request, he will modify the payload using his parameters and send this packet to the server using the compromised host's packet header. Because the packet header doesn't change, the traffic will not be transmitted to the controller. Then the server begins to transmit the certificate to the compromised host. The adversary relays this packet to the host and receives the response from this host at this time. After receiving the response, the adversary discards this packet and generates the adversary's response packet with the compromised host's address. Then the adversary sends the modified https response packet to the server. At this step there are still no PACKET_IN packets. Then the server and the adversary carry out the key exchange and establish the connection between them. In this procedure, the adversary acts as the role of the client and establishes https connection with the server. After the establishment, the adversary will transmitted the information of server to the client with the normal http packets. From the perspective of the client, he receives what he wants if he does not notice what he reviews has changed from https to http. In this case all useful information from the compromised host are obtained by the adversary, and the adversary even can change the content the server sends. In the whole procedure OpenFlow controller doesn't recognize the existence of the adversary. TopoGuard could not find the mismatch of the switch port type of the adversary. Because OpenFlow controller almost deals with layer 4 and lower protocols, it can't recognize the difference between http and https. The whole attack process is similar with SSL strip. In addition, the attack pattern is almost the same when the adversary launches SSLSniff [2] (which attack SSL using forged certificates) except that the adversary needs to forge and replace the certificate of the server. The drawback of SSLSniff is that the client browser will require certificate verification and this will raise the alarm.

Our main contribution is to propose a method that compromises most security protocols using the inherent loopholes of link discovery service in SDN. As to https, if the compromised user pays more attention on the browser address bar and identifies the difference, this attack will fail. But for those users who lack security awareness, it is unpractical for them to notice the difference. In addition, another prerequisite for the attack's success is that the service provider doesn't use two-way authentication. In order to improve access speed, most commercial web sites in China use one-way authentication, including taobao.com, jd.com, baidu.com. Different from SSLSniff, our attack doesn't change the certificate of server. Because the middle man in SDN is difficult to avoid and our attack doesn't change the certificate in SSL procedure, our attack scheme is universal.

3.3 Influenced Security Protocols

Besides the attack on Https, we also investigate attacks on other protocols by the means of fake internal link. We mainly focus on application layer protocols. We test many protocols and use the method similar to https attack. In practical application, legal users are always identified by password. By using Https attack mentioned above, we have already got all information about the compromised host and can impersonate him using the password. But we still explore security protocols that can be hijacked. Our test results are shown in Table 1. Many security protocols use certificate to guarantee the legitimacy of public key. If the middle man fails to falsify server's certificate, we directly use client's password to login because most login process is protected by https. Our results consider the basic situation. The No stands for impossible in any situation using our scheme.

Table 1. Influenced security protocols

Security protocol	Possible to break?
Https	Yes
IPSec	No
PGP	Yes
VPN	Yes
S/MIME	Yes
SSH	Yes

3.4 Countermeasures

There are two conditions for MITM attacks. First, SDN controller doesn't handle application protocols. Only when the switch's buffer is overflow or the switch is set, the controller can get whole packet instead of packet header. Second, the prerequisite of the MITM attacks is the existence of that middle man. If we can take solutions to break one of these two conditions, the attack can't be successful.

Full Packet Inspection. The naive way is to set the switch to upload the entire packet to the controller. However, the communication time between the controller and the switch will sharply increase under this case, thereby reducing the communication efficiency of the whole network. In addition, the existing switch rule only matches layer 4, layer 3 and layer 2 packets, it is still useless when the adversary launches the above MITM attacks.

Middleware Inspection. From user's point of view, our attack is the same as that in legacy network. It is practical to transfer the solution in legacy network to SDN. Because our mentioned attack will change https to http, IDS (Intrusion Detection System) will be useful. In current SDN design, IDS is deployed as a middle box, and it needs OpenFlow controller to transfer packets to both the destination and IDS itself, just as written in [13]. IDS and other defensive measures put additional burden on the controller, and they are hard to deploy ([13]). Shin *et al.* [15] also proposed a new way to make IDS as an OpenFlow application, but it brought efficiency loss and needed time to prove its usability.

Fake Link Inspection. In order to defend against MITM attacks, the direct method is to find fake link. From the opinion of OpenFlow controller, it is hard to distinguish the difference between the real link and the fake link. But the approach of establishing the fake link provides the possibility. In the procedure of fake link establishment, the adversary needs to relay LLDP packet from one switch to another. Compared with the normal LLDP transmission procedure, the adversary needs to add two times forwarding process of network interface card. This will increase the transmission time. In particular, the transmission time is longer when two hosts conspire to transfer LLDP. If we can distinguish the different latency of link discovery procedure, we will find the fake link.

In order to find the link latency, we can insert timestamp in TLV of LLDP packet. By means of the newest Floodlight version 1.2 which can calculate the LLDP latency, we can directly get the time. Besides, we can also insert timestamp in echo_request. When we receive the echo_reply, we can get the echo_latency by decreasing the timestamp using the current time. Floodlight version 1.2 calculates the LLDP_latency time using the similar method as the echo latency did. When we get the LLDP_latency and echo_latency, we can get the transmission time in the link through LLDP_latency minus echo_latency. Then we can compare the transmission time of different link. In the normal link, the transmission time is basically equal. If the transmission time is too bigger than others, it is questionable. Then we can label this link as questionable and not save this link. Then we need resend LLDP packet to the switch in this link and calculate the transmission time again. If the transmission time is still too longer than other links, we can conclude that this link is fake. Then we can put this link to fake link store and set the survive time. In the whole survive time, we will not resend LLDP packet if we find this fake link again.

This countermeasure is credible in most cases. It may fail only if a link is in paralysis due to congestion. But SDN controller without our countermeasure will evade the paralyzed link because most packets will be discarded if the paralyzed link is selected. Thus our judgement would not affect the data transmission results and the potential false positives of the countermeasure is negligible. If the congestion is relieved, the countermeasure can judge correctly again.

4   Evaluation

4.1   Experimental Setup

In order to test the effectiveness of MITM attack, we implement simple testbed. Our testbed is shown in Fig. 1 (where the controller host does not show up).

The controller is TopoGuard in one of these servers. The connections among them are illustrated in Fig. 1. All of our servers are Lenovo Thinkcenter with Intel I5 CPUs and 12 GB of RAM running 64 bit Ubuntu Linux V13.11. The adversary server has two Rtl8139PCI NICs. Our OpenFlow switches are NET-GRARWR3800 with 100M bandwidth which run OpenWRT firmware with an OpenFlow extension.

4.2   Implementation

In order to implement the adversary host, we use netfilter [1] in Linux to transfer the packet and to realize MITM attack. Netfilter is a subsystem of Linux and provides a set of management mechanism of hook function. We use netfilter to transfer the packet from one NIC (Network Interface Card) to another. We also prohibit the response to external requests. Besides, we change the procedure of SSLStrip [10] so that we can follow the procedure of our MITM attack.

In order to defend against this MITM attack, we use the way of fake link inspection mentioned above. In Floodlight 1.2, we can directly get the LLPD_latency and echo_latency. We only need to change LinkDiscoveryManager in Floodlight to resend LLDP packet and determine whether the link is fake. We can rely on the existing solutions to solve our problem.

4.3   Effectiveness

A successful attack on Https will be shown in this subsection.

We made a one-way SSL verification website in compromised server 10.0.0.3 and visited this website from the compromised host. We can get the page with address of "https://10.0.0.3". Then we connected relay host to switch 1 and switch 3 respectively. We wrote a script that sended the received LLDP packets to another port in relay host repeatedly. Then we modified SSL-strip [10] from github to follow the processing order as mentioned in Sect. 3. Then we visited this website in the compromised host again. We can get the same page with address of "http://10.0.0.3". The only difference of web browsing is the protocol.

From the experiment result, we can conclude that the compromised user didn't recognize the difference if he ignored the difference in browser address bar. We can assure that our attack scheme can bypass the protection of TopoGuard.

4.4   Performance

In this subsection, we use our fake link inspection scheme to test the transmission time of the link in Fig. 1. In the test, a different background flow is also utilized to simulate realistic environment and the background flow exists in every link. We can observe the results in Table 2. The unit of time in the table is millisecond.

The fake link (s1<->s3) can be easily distinguished from the results. We can clearly detect the fake link by the proposed approach, and the MITM attack can not be successful if we turn down this link.

Table 2. LLDP transmission time (ms)

Background velocity (b/s)	s1<->s2 (ms)	s2<->s3 (ms)	s1<->s3 (ms)
1 M	0.766	0.639	5.345
5 M	0.591	0.370	6.341
10 M	0.406	0.723	10.154
50 M	0.544	0.371	25.178

5 Discussion

The reason for the existence of topology pollution is due to the lack of verification in SDN architecture. Topology management has never been included in OpenFlow Specification, but most of existing OpenFlow controllers and switch vendors follow a certain convention for handling topology management. This may be a root cause for explaining all controllers expose the similar vulnerabilities. With SDN bringing new security challenges, we should not be superstitious in its design. In order to systematically investigate the potential verification loss, designing a new security fuzzer for SDN will be helpful, which is our future work.

Our attack on the data plane is easy to succeed in existing LAN (*e.g.* campus network, the company's internal network). But it has shortcomings. Due to the fact that the host must connect to two different switches, the MITM attack can only launch in small area. This will reduce the damage of the attack even the adversaries conspire to commit crime. Our attack scheme pays more attention to the LAN area. If our host stands nearby the gateway switch, we believe this attack will have a greater threat.

6 Related Work

Many security schemes have been proposed to enhance the security of SDN. OF-RHM [5] proposes OpenFlow Random Host Mutation to dynamically mutate IP addresses of hosts inside an LAN (Local Area Network). POFMTD [9] proposes POF Random Protocol Mutation to dynamically mutate protocols in the communication process. Avant-Guard [12] shows a new attack (which is called data-to-control plane saturation attack) against SDN networks and provides solutions to prevent such attacks. Our attack is ascribed to the deficiency of verification. There are many verification approaches used to check network invariants. Veri-Flow [3] provides a set of efficient algorithms to check rule modification events in real time. Header Space Analysis (HSA) [8] leverages static analysis to detect forwarding and configurations errors. NetPlumber [7] introduces a real time policy checking tool using Header Space Analysis. SE-Floodlight [11] proposes security constraint enforcement, role-based authorization, an authentication service and a security audit service to solve rule conflict and multiple applications conflict. All these schemes pay little attention on the formation of topology information. Their schemes can not solve the attacks on topology information.

Several works have noticed the attack on topology information. [6] is the first method to point out the Host Location Hijacking Attack and Link Fabrication Attack, which seriously challenge the core advantage of SDN. Concurrent with [4,6] unifies detection of attacks on network topology using flow graphs. Based on these methods, we proposes new attacks bypassing their defensive measures.

7   Conclusion

In this paper, we propose new SDN-specific MITM attacks in LAN which can bypass existing defense (*e.g.* TopoGuard, SPHINX). We demonstrate that the adversary can easily launch MITM attack on security protocols to get host privacy by poisoning the network topology information. The solutions to mitigate the harm of this kind of attack are also proposed. Besides, we investigate the security protocols which will be broken in our MITM attack. With the publication of this paper, we hope that our work will attract more attention to SDN security and contribute to the perfection of SDN specification.

Acknowledgments. This work was supported by National 863 Program of China under award No. 2013CB338001.

References

1. netfilter. http://www.netfilter.org//
2. SSLSniff. https://moxie.org/software/sslsniff/
3. Khurshid, A., Zhou, W., Caesar, M., Godfrey, P.B.: VeriFlow: verifying network-wide invariants in real time, vol. 42, pp. 467–472. ACM, New York, September 2012. http://doi.acm.org/10.1145/2377677.2377766
4. Dhawan, M., Poddar, R., Mahajan, K., Mann, V.: SPHINX: detecting security attacks in software-defined networks. In: NDSS (2015)
5. Jafarian, J.H., Al-Shaer, E., Duan, Q.: OpenFlow random host mutation: transparent moving target defense using software defined networking. In: Proceedings of the First Workshop on Hot Topics in Software Defined Networks (2012)
6. Hong, S., Xu, L., Wang, H., Gu, G.: Poisoning network visibility in software-defined nerworks: new attacks and countermeasures. In: NDSS 2015 (2015)
7. Kazemian, P., Chang, M., Zeng, H.: Real time nework policy checking using header space analysis. In: NSDI 2013 (2013)
8. Kazemian, P., Varghese, G., McKeown, N.: Header space analysis: static checking for nerworks. In: NSDI 2012 (2012)
9. Ma, D., Xu, Z., Lin, D.: A moving target defense approach based on POF to thwart blind DDoS attack (2014)
10. moxie0: sslstrip. https://github.com/moxie0/sslstrip
11. Porras, P.A., Cheung, S., Fong, M.W., Skinner, K., Yegneswaran, V.: Securing the software-defined network control layer. In: Proceedings of the 2015 Network and Distributed System Security Symposium (NDSS), San Diego, California (2015)
12. Shin, S., Yegneswaran, V., Porras, P., Gu, G.: AVANT-GUARD: scalable and vigilant switch flow management in software-defined networks. In: CCS 2013 (2013)

13. Shin, S., Wang, H., Gu, G.: A first step towards network security virtualization: from concept to prototype. IEEE Trans. Inf. Forensics Secur. **10**, 2236–2249 (2015)
14. Hong, S., Xu, L., Wang, H., Gu, G.: Poisoning network visibility in software-defined networks: new attacks and countermeasures. In: NDSS (2015)
15. Yoon, C., Park, T., Lee, S., Kang, H., Shin, S., Zhang, Z.: Enabling security functions with SDN: a feasibility study. Comput. Netw. **85**, 19–35 (2015)

A Practical Scheme for Data Secure Transport in VoIP Conferencing

Dali Zhu[1], Renjun Zhang[1,2], Xiaozhuo Gu[1], and Haitao Zhu[1(✉)]

[1] Institute of Information Engineering, Chinese Academy of Sciences, Beijing, China
{zhudali,zhangrenjun,guxiaozhuo,zhuhaitao}@iie.ac.cn
[2] University of Chinese Academy of Sciences, Beijing, China

Abstract. In the Multi-party VoIP conferencing system, it is important to provide properties of non-repudiation, unforgeable, and privacy. Previous work usually achieve these goals by using digital signature, TLS, IPsec, or other cryptographic tools. However, many approaches either compromise performance or lack of formal security proof, or both. In this work, we construct a practical Multi-party VoIP conferencing scheme based on the Boneh-Canetti-Halevi-Katz construction. Our work focus on the data secure transport stage, (i.e., we assume that the group session key is already distributed in the key distribution stage.). In comparison with previous work, our scheme gives a new paradigm for achieving properties of non-repudiation, unforgeable, and privacy simultaneously. The new paradigm avoids digital signature that have been shown time-consuming. On the other hand, our scheme is provable security. We prove the non-repudiation property in a formal way, and give proof sketches of unforgeable property and privacy property.

Keywords: VoIP applications · Boneh-Canetti-Halevi-Katz scheme · Public-key encryption

1 Introduction

Voice over IP (VoIP) technologies are widely adopted due to their flexibility and low cost. For a typical VoIP implementation, voice data is transformed into digital data, then encoded to data packets and sent to the receiver through IP networks. The receiver decrypts the data packets and recovers the voice data. Because data packets are delivered and exposed to the unsecure public internet, so security is an important consideration [12]. In the real applications, there are numerous threats and vulnerabilities present in VoIP protocols and products [6,7].

Multi-party VoIP conferencing system is an important application of VoIP. In the typical Multi-party VoIP conferencing system, there is one media server and many clients (see Fig. 1). In this work, we suppose the media server plays the role of Conference Control Manager. The entire system is divided into two stages: key distribution and voice data transport. Our work is only focus on the data secure transport stage (i.e., we assume that the group session key is

© Springer International Publishing AG 2016
K.-Y. Lam et al. (Eds.): ICICS 2016, LNCS 9977, pp. 466–475, 2016.
DOI: 10.1007/978-3-319-50011-9_36

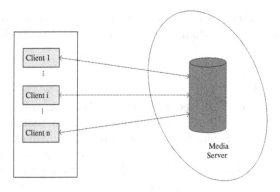

Fig. 1. An abstraction model of the typical Multi-party VoIP conferencing system

already distributed in the key distribution phase.). The media server is usually assumed to be honest, but we can not ensure that all clients are honest. Consequently, when communication is started, several security problems should be considered: non-repudiation, unforgeable, privacy, forward-secure, backward-secure, collusion-resistant, etc.

In this paper, we mainly study the problem of non-repudiation, unforgeable, and privacy in voice data secure transport stage. Specially, we study the following problem.

The Problem. Suppose the media server and clients share the same group session key. Consider the following scenario: a client p_i encrypts the voice data by using group session key and sends the ciphertext to the media server. But p_i does not admit the fact later. This event is called *repudiation*. On the other hand, adversaries can intercept the encrypted voice data, and send fake ciphertexts to the media server. This event is called *forgery*.

There are two widely accepted methods to issue repudiation and forgery problem: digital signature and Message Authentication Code (MAC). Digital signature is a common solution to the repudiation and forgery problem. MAC is usually used to solve the forgery problem in symmetric setting. But the computing overhead of digital signature is large, roughly 2–3 orders of magnitude less efficient than MAC [5]. Though MAC is more efficient, it does not provide the non-repudiation property, and it limited in the private-key setting. How to design an efficient Multi-party VoIP conferencing system with properties of non-repudiation, unforgeable and privacy is still a difficult problem.

Our Contribution. In this work, we propose a practical solution to the above problem. Briefly, we construct a new framework of Multi-party VoIP conferencing scheme with properties of non-repudiation, unforgeable, and privacy. Our construction is based on Boneh-Canetti-Halevi-Katz (BCHK) scheme [2]. Compared with previous work, our scheme avoids using digital signature. And our result is provable security. We prove the non-repudiation property in a formal way, and give proof sketches of the unforgeable property and privacy property. Though the paradigm is easy to instantiate, we still view our work as a feasibility result.

1.1 Related Work

In security, a survey of VoIP security research had been present in [6,7]. Wu et al. [12] proposed a VoIP secure encryption solution that has properties of privacy and integrity, but without a security proof. Kuntze et al. [8] presented a scheme to achieve non-repudiation for VoIP based on the interval chaining signatures technique. Kuntze et al.'s result can extends to the decentralized multi-party conversations. Though the scheme in [8] is efficient, the security analysis is not rigorous, and only against some particular attacks.

Wang and Liu [10] proposed a scheme to protect privacy for an end-to-end VoIP. In their construction, they applied the Elliptic-Curve Diffie-Hellman algorithm for key negotiation. However, their work only concentrate on the key negotiation phase. In data transport stage, they only use the popular AES algorithm to encrypt/decrypt voice packets. Their work also lack of identity authentication mechanisms, and lack of a rigorous security proof. The line of research is continued in [14,16], who proposed an authenticated key agreement protocol based on Elliptic-Curve Cryptography. But the work in [14,16] suffered from same problems with wang et al.'s construction [10]. In other practical systems, TLS, IPsec, SRTP were utilized to enhance the security [1,9,11], but their work still focus on performance, such as packet loss, etc.

Boneh, Canetti, Halevi and Katz proposed an efficient public-key encryption cryptosystem secure against adaptive chosen-ciphertext attacks (CCA) based on Identity Based Encryption scheme (IBE) [2–4]. While we analyse the security proof of BCHK scheme, we find out the encapsulation scheme in [2] (a weak variant of commitment, in the rest of the paper, we do not distinguish these two concepts) can guarantee properties of integrity and non-repudiation simultaneously. This excellent feature convinces us that the encapsulation scheme can replace MAC and digital signature in practical systems. Boneh et al. also give an instantiation of the encapsulation scheme. Motivated by Boneh et al.'s work, we construct a Multi-party VoIP conferencing scheme.

Organizations. The rest of the paper is organized as follows. In Sect. 2 we review some standard definitions related to our construction. Section 3 presents the security model. In Sect. 4, we give our construction for data secure transport. We present security analysis in Sect. 5.

2 Preliminaries

2.1 Notation

The notation $\{0,1\}^k$ denotes the set of binary strings of length n. If S is a finite set, we use $x \leftarrow S$ to denote sampling an element x uniformly from a probability distribution S. We use $[n]$ to denote the set $\{1, \ldots, n\}$.

2.2   Commitment Schemes

We recall a definition of commitment scheme, and a weak variant of commitment in [2].

Definition 1. *A commitment scheme is a tuple of three probability polynomial time algorithms (K, Com, Vrfy) with the property that:*

- *K takes as input the security parameter 1^λ, generates a public commitment key ck.*
- *Com takes as input the commitment key ck, a message m, and a random coins r, outputs a commitment c.*
- *Vrfy takes as input the public commitment key ck, an opening op, and a message m. If the commitment c is valid, then output 1, else output 0.*

A commitment scheme must be *hiding* and *binding*. Hiding requires that the commitment reveals no information about message. Binding requires that it is infeasible to open a honestly-generated commitment in two different ways. Boneh et al. [2] proposed the "encapsulation" scheme which is a weak variant of commitment. Details of the definitions are given below. For simplicity, we use the same symbol.

Definition 2. *An encapsulation scheme $\Pi = (\text{Init}, \mathcal{S}, \mathcal{R})$ consists of three probability polynomial time algorithms, where*

- *Init given security parameter 1^λ, outputs the public commitment key pub.*
- *$\mathcal{S}$ given security parameter 1^λ and a string pub, outputs (r, com, dec) where $r \in \{0,1\}^\lambda$, com is the commitment string and dec is the decommitment string.*
- *$\mathcal{R}$ given (pub, com, dec), outputs $r \in \{0,1\}^\lambda \cup \{\bot\}$, where $\bot$ is a special symbol to indicate decapsulation fails.*

The encapsulation scheme also should be binding and hiding, but it only needs to satisfy *computational hiding* and *computational binding*. Specially, the computational hiding and computational binding are defined as follows.

Definition 3 (Computational hiding). *We say the encapsulation scheme is computational hiding if for all probability polynomial time adversary $\mathcal{A}$ we have*

$$| \Pr[pub \leftarrow \text{Init}(1^\lambda); b \leftarrow \{0,1\}; r_0 \leftarrow \{0,1\}^\lambda; (r_1, com, dec) \leftarrow \mathcal{S}(1^\lambda, pub) :$$
$$\mathcal{A}(1^\lambda, pub, com, r_b) = b] - 1/2|$$

is negligible.

Definition 4 (Computational binding). *We say the encapsulation scheme is computational binding if for all probability polynomial time adversary $\mathcal{A}$ we have*

$$\Pr[pub \leftarrow \text{Init}(1^\lambda); (r, com, dec) \leftarrow \mathcal{S}(1^\lambda, pub); dec' \leftarrow \mathcal{A}(1^\lambda, pub, com, dec) :$$
$$\mathcal{R}(pub, com, dec') \notin \{\bot, r\}]$$

is negligible.

2.3 Boneh-Canetti-Halevi-Katz Scheme

The Boneh-Canetti-Halevi-Katz scheme [2] is a methodology to build chosen-ciphertext secure public key encryption schemes from any CPA-secure identity-based encryption schemes. It consists of three probability polynomial time algorithms.

Key Generation: Given security parameter 1^λ, run $(PK, msk) \leftarrow \text{Setup}(1^\lambda)$, where PK is the public key, and msk is the master secret key; Run $Pub \leftarrow \text{Init}(1^\lambda)$ where pub is a string. Let $pk = (PK, pub)$, and $sk = msk$.

Encryption:

- The sender obtains (r, com, dec) by running $\mathcal{S}(1^\lambda, pub)$, where r is the encapsulated random value, com is the commitment string that plays the role of the *identity*, and dec is the decommitment string.
- Taking as input the plaintext $m|dec$, the sender computes $C \leftarrow \mathcal{E}_{PK}(com, m|dec)$. Then the sender computes a message authentication code $tag \leftarrow \text{Mac}_r(C)$, where r is the MAC key. The final ciphertext is $\langle com, C, tag \rangle$.

Decryption: On inputs the ciphertext $\langle com, C, tag \rangle$, the receiver derives the secret key SK_{com}, then decrypt the ciphertext C by using SK_{com} and obtains $m|dec$. The receiver then recovers r by running $\mathcal{R}(pub, com, dec)$. If $r \neq \perp$ and the tag is valid, the receiver outputs m. Otherwise, the receiver outputs $\perp$.

3 The Security Model

We consider the security model with two games respectively. Game 1 is the non-repudiation game that associates with binding property of encapsulation scheme. Game 2 is the unforgeable game that relates to unforgeable property of MAC.

Game 1: Non-repudiation Game [2]

Setup: The challenger takes as input the security parameter 1^λ and generates $pub \leftarrow \text{Init}(1^\lambda)$.

Challenge: The challenger run $(r, com, dec) \leftarrow \mathcal{S}(1^\lambda, pub)$ on inputs 1^λ and pub. Then the challenger sends $(1^\lambda, pub, com, dec)$ to adversary $\mathcal{A}$.

Decision: Upon receiving $(1^\lambda, pub, com, dec)$, $\mathcal{A}$ outputs dec'. If $\mathcal{R}(pub, com, dec') \notin \{r, \perp\}$, $\mathcal{A}$ wins the game.

We say the scheme is non-repudiation if for any polynomial time adversary $\mathcal{A}$, the probability of winning the game is negligible.

Game 2: Unforgeable Game

Setup: The challenger takes as input the security 1^λ and generates a random key k. An adversary $\mathcal{A}$ is given 1^λ.

Challenge: The adversary $\mathcal{A}$ is allowed to query an oracle $\mathrm{Mac}_k(\cdot)$ that inputs a message m and outputs a tag $t \leftarrow \mathrm{Mac}_k(m)$. Let $\mathcal{Q} = \{(t_i, m_i)_{i \in [n]}\}$ denote the set of all queries and responses between $\mathcal{A}$ and $\mathrm{Mac}_k(\cdot)$.

Forge: The adversary $\mathcal{A}$ outputs a pair (m, t). If $\mathrm{Vrfy}_k(m, t) = 1$ and $m \notin \mathcal{Q}$, the adversary $\mathcal{A}$ wins the game.

We say the scheme is unforgeable if for any polynomial adversary $\mathcal{A}$ the successful probability is negligible.

4 Construction for Data Secure Transport Scheme

In this section, we present our construction for the data secure transport stage. We first give a sketch of the idea, then present the details of the construction.

4.1 Sketch of the Idea

The sender first generates a random MAC key r, then use the encapsulation scheme to encapsulate r. This yields the commitment string *com* and the decommitment string *dec*. Then the sender encrypts *com*, *dec*, *m* together by using a group session key, and computes a tag on the ciphertext. After that, the sender sends the ciphertext and tag (c, t) to the receiver. According to the binding property, the receiver does not open to another r'. Upon receiving (c, t), the media server first decrypts c, then recovers the MAC key r. After that, the media server verifies the validity of t. If t is valid, the receiver recovers m. The media sever also needs to transmits the *processed* message (For simplicity, we omit the audio mixing process) to the remaining clients.

4.2 The Construction

Suppose there is one media server and n clients. The Data Secure Transport Scheme consists of the following five algorithms:

- **Key Generation:**

On inputs the security parameter 1^λ and outputs a string *pub*.

- **Encryption by the i'th client:**

The client p_i computes

$$(r_i, com_i, dec_i) \leftarrow \mathcal{S}(1^\lambda, pub)$$

where the random string r_i is the MAC key, com_i is the commitment string, and dec_i is the decommitment string. Next p_i encrypts $m_i|com_i|dec_i$ with respect to the group session key GK, thus p_i computes

$$C_i \leftarrow \text{Enc}_{GK}(m_i|com_i|dec_i)$$

Then p_i computes a MAC for the ciphertext C_i by using r_i

$$\text{tag}_i \leftarrow \text{Mac}_{r_i}(C_i)$$

Finally, p_i sends the ciphertext $\langle C_i, \text{tag}_i \rangle$ to the media server.

– Decryption by the media server:

Upon receiving $\langle C_i, \text{tag}_i \rangle$, the media server decrypts the ciphertext as

$$m_i|com_i|dec_i \leftarrow \text{Dec}_{GK}(C_i)$$

Next, the media server runs decommitting process to output the MAC key r_i

$$r_i \leftarrow \mathcal{R}(pub, com_i, dec_i)$$

If $r_i \neq \perp$ and $\text{Vrfy}_{r_i}(C_i, \text{tag}_i) = 1$, the receiver outputs m_i. Otherwise, it rejects the ciphertext and outputs $\perp$.

– Encryption by the media server:

Suppose m_i changes into m_i' after the audio mixing procedure. We write pub_s for the public string that generates by the media server. The media server computes $(r_{s_j}, com_{s_j}, dec_{s_j}) \leftarrow \mathcal{S}(1^\lambda, pub_s)$, where $j \in [n]$, $j \neq i$ and $r_{s_j} \in \{0,1\}^k$. Then encrypts $C_{s_j} \leftarrow \text{Enc}_{GK}(m_i'|com_{s_j}|dec_{s_j})$. After that the media server computes a tag on C_{s_j} which denoted as $\text{tag}_{s_j} \leftarrow \text{Mac}_{r_{s_j}}(C_j)$. Finally, the media server sends $\langle C_{s_j}, \text{tag}_{s_j} \rangle$ to the j'th client p_j.

– Decryption by the j'th client member p_j:

Upon receiving the ciphertext $\langle C_{s_j}, \text{tag}_{s_j} \rangle$, p_j decrypts the ciphertext as

$$m_i'|com_{s_j}|dec_{s_j} \leftarrow \text{Dec}_{GK}(C_{s_j})$$

Next, p_j runs the decommitting process $r_{s_j} \leftarrow \mathcal{R}(pub, com_{s_j}, dec_{s_j})$ and outputs the MAC key r_{s_j}. If $r_{s_j} \neq \perp$ and $\text{Vrfy}_{r_{s_j}}(C_{s_j}, \text{tag}_{s_j}) = 1$, p_j outputs m_i'. Otherwise, p_j outputs $\perp$.

It is not hard to verify that the above scheme is correct. We will give a proof about the security in next section.

Differences Between Our Scheme and BCHK Shceme. We point out the main difference between our scheme and BCHK scheme. First, we use group session key to replace master public key and master secret key in BCHK scheme. Second, in BCHK scheme the commitment *com* is the "identity". In our scheme, we do not utilize the identity-based encryption scheme, the commitment *com* does not represent the sender identity, and we combine *com* into the plaintext.

5   Security Analysis

We begin by proving the non-repudiation property. Then we will prove the unforgeable property. Note that the following two theorems is implicit in the security proof of BCHK scheme. Finally we will give a proof sketch about the privacy property.

5.1   Non-repudiation

The proof is loosely based on Theorem 2 in [2]. The method of proof is called *reduction*, almost the only sort of proof in cryptography, which converts any efficient adversary $\mathcal{A}$ that attacks the scheme into an efficient algorithm $\mathcal{A}'$ that solves the hard problem [5]. The proof of Theorem 1 also refers to a similar proof in [13]. The style of proof refers to [15].

Theorem 1. *If the binding property of the encapsulation scheme holds, then the above construction is non-repudiation.*

Proof. We prove this theorem by contradiction. Suppose the scheme is not non-repudiation, then we can construct an adversary $\mathcal{B}$ that breaks the binding property of encapsulation scheme. Define $\mathcal{B}$ as follows:

Setup: $\mathcal{B}$ receives $(1^\lambda, pub, com^*, dec^*)$ from its challenger, where com^* is the commitment of r^*. Then $\mathcal{B}$ generates a symmetric key $GK' \leftarrow \{0,1\}^n$. $\mathcal{B}$ sends 1^λ and pub to adversary $\mathcal{A}$. $\mathcal{B}$ sets an empty table T.

Encryption Query: When $\mathcal{A}$ makes an encryption query for message m, $\mathcal{B}$ answers it as follows:

1. Takes as input $(1^\lambda, pub)$, outputs (r', com, dec) where $r' \in \{0,1\}^n$.
2. Computes $C \leftarrow \text{Enc}_{GK'}(m|com|dec)$.
3. Computes $tag \leftarrow \text{MAC}_{r'}(C)$, then returns $\langle C, tag \rangle$ to $\mathcal{A}$.

Challenge: The adversary $\mathcal{A}$ outputs a pair of messages m_0, m_1 of the same length, and sends (m_0, m_1) to $\mathcal{B}$. $\mathcal{B}$ chooses a random bit b from $\{0,1\}$, and computes $C^* \leftarrow \text{Enc}_{GK'}(m_b|com^*|dec^*)$. Then a MAC $tag^* \leftarrow \text{Mac}_{r^*}(C^*)$ is computed. $\mathcal{B}$ sends $\langle C^*, tag^* \rangle$ to adversary $\mathcal{A}$ as the challenge ciphertext.

Decryption Query: If $\langle C, tag \rangle$ is a response to the previous encryption query for a message m, returns m. Else, after receiving the ciphertext $\langle C_i, tag_i \rangle$, $\mathcal{B}$ decrypts C_i and obtains $(m_i|com_i|dec_i)$. Then $\mathcal{B}$ checks whether $com_i = com^*$ and $dec_i = dec^*$. If yes, $\mathcal{B}$ stores $\langle C_i, tag_i \rangle$ in the table T and no longer decrypts it. Otherwise, $\mathcal{B}$ run $r_i \leftarrow \mathcal{R}(pub, com_i, dec_i)$, and checks whether tag_i is valid. If yes, outputs m_i. Otherwise, outputs $\perp$.

  $\mathcal{B}$ simulates perfectly. If $\mathcal{A}$ wins the games, then $\mathcal{B}$ wins. But according to the binding property of encapsulation scheme, $\mathcal{B}$ can not learn a value dec' with the property that $\mathcal{R}(pub, com^*, dec') \notin \{\perp, r^*\}$. Thus, the successful probability of $\mathcal{B}$ is negligible. Therefore, the adversary $\mathcal{A}$ does not exist.

5.2   Unforgeable

The proof of Theorem 2 is similar in spirit to the security proof of BCHK scheme, so we only give a sketch.

Theorem 2. *If the hiding property of the encapsulation scheme holds and the message authentication code is secure, then the above scheme is unforgeable.*

Proof. The MAC key r is hidden according to the hiding property of encapsulation scheme, so the adversary can not obtain the real MAC key. In order to make a forgery, the adversary may chooses a random key r'. But the security of the MAC implies that the successful probability of the adversary is negligible.

5.3   Privacy

Though we mainly emphasize the non-repudiation property and unforgeable property, the privacy property is necessary. We also give a proof sketch here. Because in the interactive procedure, the MAC key r, the commitment string *com*, and the decommitment string *dec* are encrypted by using the group session key. From the security of symmetric encryption scheme, any adversary who is outside the group can not obtain any useful information. This shows that the privacy property holds.

Acknowledgment. The authors would like to thank the reviewers for their useful feedback. This research is supported by the "Strategic Priority Program" of Chinese Academy of Sciences, Grant No. Y2W0012306, and the National Natural Science Foundation of China (Grant No. 61602475).

References

1. Barbieri, R., Bruschi, D., Rosti, E.: Voice over IPsec: analysis and solutions. In: 18th Annual Computer Security Applications Conference (ACSAC 2002), Las Vegas, NV, USA, 9–13 December 2002, pp. 261–270 (2002)
2. Boneh, D., Canetti, R., Halevi, S., Katz, J.: Chosen-ciphertext security from identity-based encryption. SIAM J. Comput. **36**(5), 1301–1328 (2007)
3. Boneh, D., Katz, J.: Improved efficiency for CCA-secure cryptosystems built using identity-based encryption. In: Menezes, A. (ed.) CT-RSA 2005. LNCS, vol. 3376, pp. 87–103. Springer, Heidelberg (2005). doi:10.1007/978-3-540-30574-3_8
4. Canetti, R., Halevi, S., Katz, J.: Chosen-ciphertext security from identity-based encryption. In: Cachin, C., Camenisch, J.L. (eds.) EUROCRYPT 2004. LNCS, vol. 3027, pp. 207–222. Springer, Heidelberg (2004). doi:10.1007/978-3-540-24676-3_13
5. Katz, J., Lindell, Y.: Introduction to Modern Cryptography. Chapman & Hall/CRC Cryptography and Network Security Series. Chapman & Hall/CRC, Boca Raton (2007)
6. Keromytis, A.D.: A comprehensive survey of voice over IP security research. IEEE Commun. Surv. Tutor. **14**(2), 514–537 (2012)
7. Keromytis, A.D.: A survey of voice over IP security research. In: Prakash, A., Sen Gupta, I. (eds.) ICISS 2009. LNCS, vol. 5905, pp. 1–17. Springer, Heidelberg (2009). doi:10.1007/978-3-642-10772-6_1

8. Kuntze, N., Schmidt, A.U., Hett, C.: Non-repudiation in internet telephony. In: Venter, H., Eloff, M., Labuschagne, L., Eloff, J., Solms, R. (eds.) SEC 2007. IIFIP, vol. 232, pp. 361–372. Springer, Heidelberg (2007). doi:10.1007/978-0-387-72367-9_31

9. Salsano, S., Veltri, L., Papalilo, D.: SIP security issues: the SIP authentication procedure and its processing load. IEEE Netw. **16**(6), 38–44 (2002)

10. Wang, C., Liu, Y.: A dependable privacy protection for end-to-end VoIP via Elliptic-Curve Diffie-Hellman and dynamic key changes. J. Netw. Comput. Appl. **34**(5), 1545–1556 (2011)

11. Wang, X., Zhang, R., Yang, X., Jiang, X., Wijesekera, D.: Voice pharming attack and the trust of VoIP. In: 4th International ICST Conference on Security and Privacy in Communication Networks, SECURECOMM 2008, Istanbul, Turkey, 22–25 September 2008, p. 24 (2008)

12. Wu, C.-Y., Wu, K.-P., Shih, J., Lee, H.-M.: VoIPS: VoIP secure encryption VoIP solution. In: Chang, R.-S., Kim, T., Peng, S.-L. (eds.) SUComS 2011. CCIS, vol. 223, pp. 84–93. Springer, Heidelberg (2011). doi:10.1007/978-3-642-23948-9_11

13. Xue, R.: Theory of Public Key Encryption (The Chinese Version). Science Press, Beijing (2016)

14. Zhang, L., Tang, S., Zhu, S.: An energy efficient authenticated key agreement protocol for SIP-based green VoIP networks. J. Netw. Comput. Appl. **59**, 126–133 (2016)

15. Zhang, R.: Tweaking TBE/IBE to PKE transforms with chameleon hash functions. In: Katz, J., Yung, M. (eds.) ACNS 2007. LNCS, vol. 4521, pp. 323–339. Springer, Heidelberg (2007). doi:10.1007/978-3-540-72738-5_21

16. Zhu, S., Yang, F., Zhang, L., Tang, S., Li, J.: ECC-based authenticated key agreement protocol with privacy protection for VoIP communications. In: 2013 IEEE International Conference on Green Computing and Communications (GreenCom) and IEEE Internet of Things (iThings) and IEEE Cyber, Physical and Social Computing (CPSCom), Beijing, China, 20–23 August 2013, pp. 2114–2118 (2013)

Author Index

Printed in the United States
By Bookmasters